Issues and Agents in International
Political Economy

International Organization **Readers**

Issues and Agents in International Political Economy, 1999

Theory and Structure in International Political Economy, 1999

ISSUES AND AGENTS IN INTERNATIONAL POLITICAL ECONOMY

An *International Organization* Reader

edited by
Benjamin J. Cohen and Charles Lipson

The MIT Press

Cambridge, Massachusetts and London, England

The contents of this book were first published in *International Organization* (ISSN 0162-2889), a publication of The MIT Press under the sponsorship of the IO Foundation. Except as otherwise noted, copyright for each article is owned jointly by the IO Foundation and of the Massachusetts Institute of Technology.

Beth V. Yarbrough and Robert M. Yarbrough, "Cooperation in the Liberalization of International Trade: After Hegemony, What?" IO 41 (1) (winter 1987); Klaus Stegemann, "Policy Rivalry Among Industrial States: What Can We Learn from Models of Strategic Trade Policy?" IO 43 (1) (winter 1989); Judith Goldstein, "International Law and Domestic Institutions," IO 50 (4) (autumn 1996); Stephen J. Kobrin, "Testing the Bargaining Hypothesis in the Manufacturing Sector in Developing Countries," IO 41 (4) (autumn 1987); Helen V. Milner and David B. Yoffie, "Between Free Trade and Protectionism: Strategic Trade Policy and a Theory of Corporate Trade Demands," IO 43 (2) (spring 1989); Louis W. Pauly and Simon Reich, "Enduring MNC Differences Despite Globalization," IO 51 (1) (winter 1997); Jeffry A. Frieden, "Invested Interests: The Politics of National Economic Policies in a World of Global Finance," IO 45 (4) (autumn 1991); Michael C. Webb, "International Economic Structures, Government Interests, and International Coordination of Macroeconomic Adjustment Policies," IO 45 (3) (summer 1991); Stephan Haggard and Sylvia Maxfield, "The Political Economy of Financial Internationalization in the Developing World," IO 50 (1) (winter 1996); Mark W. Zacher, "Trade Gaps, Analytical Gaps: Regime Analysis and International Commodity Trade Regulation," IO 41 (2) (spring 1987); Oran R. Young, "The Politics of International Regime Formation: Managing Natural Resources and the Environment," IO 43 (3) (summer 1989); Brian Hanson, "What Happened to Fortress Europe? External Trade Policy and Liberalization in the European Union," IO 52 (1) (winter 1998).

Library of Congress Cataloging-in-Publication Data

Issues and agents in international political economy / edited by
  Benjamin J. Cohen and Charles Lipson.
    p.   cm.—(*International organization* reader)
  Includes bibliographical references.
  ISBN 0-262-03267-8 (hc : alk. paper).—ISBN 0-262-53160-7 (pbk. : alk. paper)
  1. International trade. 2. International business enterprises. 3. International finance.
4. International economic relations. I. Cohen, Benjamin J. II. Lipson, Charles. III. Series:
International Organization readers.
HF1379.I847   1999
382—dc21   98-50262
                                                                             CIP

Contents

Contributors

Volume Editors

Benjamin J. Cohen is Louis G. Lancaster Professor of International Political Economy at the University of California, Santa Barbara.

Charles Lipson is Associate Professor of Political Science and Co-Director of the Program on International Politics, Economics, and Security at the University of Chicago, Chicago, Illinois.

Contributors

Jeffry A. Frieden is Professor of Government at Harvard University, Cambridge, Massachusetts.

Judith Goldstein is Professor of Political Science at Stanford University, Stanford, California.

Stephan Haggard is Professor in the Graduate School of International Relations and Pacific Studies at the University of California, San Diego, and Director of the University of California's Institute on Global Conflict and Cooperation.

Brian Hanson is a doctoral candidate in the Department of Political Science, MIT, Cambridge, Massachusetts.

Stephen J. Kobrin is William Wurster Professor of Multinational Management at the Wharton School and Director of the Joseph H. Lauder Institute of Management and International Affairs at the University of Pennsylvania, Philadelphia, Pennsylvania.

Sylvia Maxfield is a Visiting Scholar at the Harvard Institute for International Development, Cambridge, Massachusetts.

Helen V. Milner is Professor of Political Science at Columbia University, New York, New York.

Louis W. Pauly is Professor of Political Science and Director, Centre for International Studies, University of Toronto, Canada.

Simon Reich is Professor of Political Science at the Graduate School of Public and International Affairs and Department of Political Science at the University of Pittsburgh, Pittsburgh, Pennsylvania.

Klaus Stegemann is Professor of Economics, Department of Economics, Queen's University at Kingston, Kingston, Ontario.

Michael C. Webb is Associate Professor of Political Science at the University of Victoria, Victoria, B.C.

Beth V. Yarbrough is Professor of Economics at Amherst College, Amherst, Massachusetts.

Robert M. Yarbrough is Visiting Professor of Economics at Amherst College, Amherst, Massachusetts.

David B. Yoffie is Max and Doris Starr Professor of International Business Administration at Harvard Business School, Boston, Massachusetts.

Oran R. Young is Professor at the Institute of Arctic Studies at Dartmouth College, Hanover, New Hampshire.

Mark W. Zacher is Professor of Political Science and Research Director of the Institute of International Relations at the University of British Columbia, Vancouver, B.C.

Abstracts

Cooperation in the Liberalization of International Trade: After Hegemony, What? (1987)
by Beth V. Yarbrough and Robert M. Yarbrough

Given the potential of international trade to be mutually beneficial and the existence of transaction and adjustment costs, nations engage in a variety of forms of trade liberalization (e.g., unilateral, multilateral, minilateral). The extent of transaction-specific investment and the viability of hegemonic cooperation are determinants of the scope for opportunistic protectionism and, therefore, determinants of the form of successful liberalization. Trade-specific assets imply a vulnerability to opportunistic protectionism, imparting a Prisoner's Dilemma payoff structure to trade liberalization. The hypothesis of hegemonic stability implies that the presence of a hegemonic state is both necessary and sufficient for a liberal trading system; the hypothesis of hegemonic cooperation, on the other hand, implies that the presence of a hegemon is one possible way of breaking the Prisoner's Dilemma in the presence of substantial transaction-specific investment for trade. We use trade-specific assets and hegemonic cooperation to explain the historical variation in the forms of trade liberalization: unilateral by 19th-century Britain, multilateral by the postwar United States, and minilateral more recently.

Policy Rivalry Among Industrial States: What Can We Learn from Models of Strategic Trade Policy? (1989)
by Klaus Stegemann

The economic theory of international trade has changed dramatically over the last decade by admitting into its mainstream a body of literature that focuses on the implications of monopolistic and oligopolistic elements in international markets. By applying the tools of the "new" industrial organization in an international context, two new classes of models have emerged: models of intra-industry trade and models of strategic trade policy. The policy implications of models of strategic trade policy were quite disturbing for the economics profession, since these models demonstrated that the classical harmony between national and cosmopolitan welfare maximization does not exist if one assumes opportunities for strategic manipulation of oligopolistic international industries. This article reviews two prominent models of strategic trade policy—the Brander-Spencer model and the Krugman model—and relates them to more familiar earlier concepts, such as Stackelberg's asymmetrical duopoly solution and the venerable infant-industry argument for government intervention. The primary purpose of this article, however, is to provide a synopsis of the large literature addressing the question of whether models of strategic trade policy can give guidance for government policy.

International Law and Domestic Institutions: Reconciling North American "Unfair" Trade Laws (1996)
by Judith Goldstein

While scholars have written much about the role played by international institutions in cooperative behavior among nations, they have not examined the domestic political motives that may lie behind nations' decisions to join such organizations. Two-level games analysis provides a framework for studying domestic politics not as a constraint upon nations that enter into international agreements but as a catalyst for nations to center into agreements. The dispute settlement procedures of the North American Free Trade Agreement and its predecessor, the Canada-U.S. Free Trade Agreement, offer an empirical illustration of this point.

Testing the Bargaining Hypothesis in the Manufacturing Sector in Developing Countries (1987)
by Stephen J. Kobrin

The bargaining power model of HC-MNC (host country-multinational corporation) interaction conceives of economic nationalism in terms of rational self-interest and assumes both inherent conflict and convergent objectives. In extractive industries, there is strong evidence that outcomes are a function of relative bargaining power and that as power shifts to developing HCs over time, the bargain obsolesces. A cross-national study of the bargaining model, using data from 563 subsidiaries of U.S. manufacturing firms in forty-nine developing countries, indicates that while the bargaining framework is an accurate model of MNC-host country relationships, manufacturing is not characterized by the inherent, structurally based, and secular obsolescence that is found in the natural resource industries. Shifts in bargaining power to HCs may take place when technology is mature and global integration limited. In industries characterized by changing technologies and the spread of global integration, the bargain will obsolesce very slowly and the relative power of MNCs may even increase over time.

Between Free Trade and Protectionism: Strategic Trade Policy and a Theory of Corporate Trade Demands (1989)
by Helen V. Milner and David B. Yoffie

Conventional theories of the political economy of trade argue that industries in import-competing businesses favor protectionism, while multinational firms and export-dependent corporations advocate unconditional free trade. However, many multinational industries have recently advocated "strategic" trade policies: that is, they are willing to support free trade at home only if foreign markets are opened or foreign governments reduce subsidies to their firms. If demands for strategic trade policy were adopted by the United States, they could represent a threat to the General Agreement on Tariffs and Trade (GATT) and the multilateral trading system. This article seeks to explain the emergence of these new corporate trade demands and thereby broaden theories of the political economy of trade. The article begins with the widely supported position that multinational and export-oriented firms prefer unconditional free trade. Building on concepts from theories of industrial organization and international trade, the article then hypothesizes that rising economies of scale and steep learning curves will necessitate that these firms have access to global markets via exports. If growing dependence on world markets is combined with foreign government subsidies or protection, the trade preferences of firms will shift from unconditional free trade to demands that openness at home be contingent on openness overseas. The manner in which firm demands then get translated into industry demands will vary with the industry's structure. If the industry consists of firms with symmetric strategies, it will seek strategic trade policy; but if the industry is highly segmented, it will turn toward protectionism. The article concludes with a preliminary test of these hypotheses in four brief studies of the politics of trade in the semiconductor, commercial aircraft, telecommunications equipment, and machine tool industries.

National Structures and Multinational Corporate Behavior: Enduring Differences in the Age of Globalization (1997)
by Louis W. Pauly and Simon Reich

Liberal and critical theorists alike claim that the world political economy is becoming globalized. If they are right, leading corporations should gradually be losing their national characters and converging in their fundamental operations and strategies. In fact, recent evidence shows little blurring or convergence at the cores of multinational corporations based in Germany, Japan, and the United States. They continue to diverge fairly systematically in their internal governance and long-term financing structures, in their approaches to research and development as well as in the location of basic research facilities, and in their overseas investment and intrafirm trading strategies. Durable national institutions and distinctive ideological traditions still seem to shape crucial corporate decisions. In short, the foundations of leading corporate markets are not converging, and markets in this sense are not replacing political leadership and the necessity for negotiated adjustments among states.

Invested Interests: The Politics of National Economic Policies in a World of Global Finance (1991)
by Jeffry A. Frieden

Capital moves more rapidly across national borders now than it has in at least fifty years and perhaps in history. This article examines the effects of capital mobility on different groups in national societies and on the politics of economic policymaking. It begins by emphasizing that while financial markets are highly integrated within the developed world, many investments are still quite specific with respect to firm, sector, or location. It then argues that contemporary levels of international capital mobility have a differential impact on socioeconomic groups. Over the long run, increased capital mobility tends to favor owners of capital over other groups. In the shorter run, owners and workers in specific sectors in capital-exporting countries bear much of the burden of adjusting to increased capital mobility. These patterns can be expected to lead to political divisions about whether or not to encourage or increase international capital market integration. The article then demonstrates that capital mobility also affects the politics of other economic policies. Most centrally, it shifts debate toward the exchange rate as an intermediate or ultimate policy instrument. In this context, it tends to pit groups that favor exchange rate stability against groups that are more concerned about national monetary policy autonomy and therefore less concerned about exchange rate stability. Similarly, it tends to drive a wedge between groups that favor an appreciated exchange rate and groups that favor a depreciated one. These divisions have important implications for such economic policies as European monetary and currency union, the dollar-yen exchange rate, and international macroeconomic policy coordination.

International Economic Structures, Government Interests, and International Coordination of Macroeconomic Adjustment Policies (1991)
by Michael C. Webb

Analysts have commonly argued that there has been a decline in international coordination of the kinds of policies that governments can use to manage the international payments imbalances that emerge when different governments pursue different macroeconomic policies. The decline typically has been attributed to a posited decline in American hegemony. In contrast, this article argues that international coordination of macroeconomic adjustment policies (trade and capital controls, exchange rate policies, balance-of-payments financing, and monetary and fiscal policies) was at least as extensive for much of the 1980s as it had been in the 1960s. There was, however, a shift away from coordination of balance-of-payments financing and other policies that have limited direct consequences for domestic economic and political conditions and a concurrent shift toward coordination of monetary and fiscal policies that are critically important for domestic politics and economics. This change is best explained as a consequence of changes in the structure of the international economy. Most important, international capital market integration encouraged governments to coordinate monetary and fiscal policies because balance-of-payments financing and exchange rate coordination alone are insufficient to manage the enormous payments imbalances that emerge when capital is able to flow internationally in search of higher interest rates and appreciating currencies.

The Political Economy of Financial Internationalization in the Developing World (1996)
by Stephan Haggard and Sylvia Maxfield

In the last decade a growing number of developing countries have opened their financial systems by liberalizing capital flows and the rules governing the international operations of financial intermediaries. One explanation of this rush toward greater financial internationalization is that increasing interdependence generates domestic and foreign political pressures for capital account liberalization. While we find evidence for that hypothesis, we find that the proximate cause in developing countries more frequently is found in balance of payments crises. Politicians perceive that financial openness in the face of crisis can increase capital inflows by indicating to foreign investors that they will be able to liquidate their investments and by signaling government intentions to maintain fiscal and monetary discipline. The argument is explored through case studies of Chile, Indonesia, Mexico, and South Korea.

Trade Gaps, Analytical Gaps: Regime Analysis and International Commodity Trade Regulation (1987)
by Mark W. Zacher

Studies of international regimes have sought to describe international collaborative arrangements in more systematic terms than in the past, and to analyze their development in terms of major schools of international relations theory. This article refines the commonly used definition of regimes and elucidates the major hypotheses of one theoretical school, structural realism. The strength and nature of the international commodity trade regime are systematically described, and their development is analyzed in terms of the major hypotheses of structural realism. In large part, these hypotheses are supported by the analysis of what is a relatively weak international regime.

The Politics of International Regime Formation: Managing Natural Resources and the Environment (1989)
by Oran R. Young

Why do actors in international society succeed in forming institutional arrangements or regimes to cope with some transboundary problems but fail to do so in connection with other, seemingly similar, problems? This article employs a threefold strategy to make progress toward answering this question. The first section prepares the ground by identifying and critiquing the principal models embedded in the existing literature on regime formation, and the second section articulates an alternative model, called institutional bargaining. The third section employs this alternative model to derive some hypotheses about the determinants of success in institutional bargaining and uses these hypotheses, in a preliminary way, to illuminate the process of regime formation in international society. To lend empirical content to the argument, the article focuses throughout on problems relating to natural resources and the environment.

What Happened to Fortress Europe?: External Trade Policy Liberalization in the European Union (1998)
by Brian T. Hanson

In an era when many fear the breakdown of the global trading order through the emergence of relatively closed regional trading blocs, assessing the efforts of European integration on external European Union trade is particularly important. Surprisingly, despite a severe recession accompanied by record levels of unemployment, a history of increasing protection under similar economic circumstances, and alarming predictions about "fortress Europe," external trade policy in the region has liberalized in recent years. Prominent trade policy explanations emphasizing changing interest group demands or changing ideas of policymakers are inadequate to account for this significant change in trade policy. Instead, much of this liberalization can be best understood as an unforeseen consequence of the Single European Act. Completing the single market undermined the effectiveness of national trade measures and made it difficult to enact new trade barriers, thus producing a liberal bias in European policy.

Preface

Benjamin J. Cohen and Charles Lipson

"*I*nternational society," *Robert Gilpin wrote in a seminal article in* International Organization *in 1971, "is increasingly rent between its economic and its political organization. On the one hand, powerful economic and technical forces are creating a highly integrated transnational economy, blurring the traditional significance of national boundaries. On the other hand, the nation-state continues to command men's loyalties and to be the basic unit of political decision."[1] Gilpin's astute observation appeared as part of a special issue of* International Organization *devoted to the then novel topic of "Transnational Relations and World Politics," edited by Joseph Nye and Robert Keohane.[2] A principal purpose of the issue—summarized so well by Gilpin—was to highlight the dynamic and reciprocal interaction of economics and politics in international affairs, which had only rarely been addressed in an integrated way in the past. With that pioneering publication, it may fairly be said, the modern field of international political economy was born. Decades later, scholars still wrestle with the implications of the inherent tension between an increasingly globalized world economy and a still potent nation-state system.*

The study of international political economy may be conducted at either of two levels: fundamental theory and structure or concrete issues and actors. International Organization *has been at the forefront of intellectual development at both levels, producing much of the literature that has successfully stimulated and shaped thinking by specialists in the field. A companion to this volume,* Theory and Structure in International Political Economy, *reproduces key contributions at the former level. This volume provides a sample of influential articles focusing more narrowly on specific issues and actors in international political economy.*

The volume is divided into four sections organized by issue area: trade, multinational firms and globalization, money and finance, and emerging issues. Section I addresses trade, traditionally considered the very core of the field of international political economy. Exchanges of goods and services were the earliest form of economic integration between states; even today, broad specialization of production within a global division of labor remains the foundation of each nation's ongoing

---

1. Gilpin 1971.
2. Nye and Keohane 1971.

participation in the world economy. Problems of trade policy and management of the trading system deservedly continue to attract a great deal of attention from scholars.

The multinational firm, perhaps the single most influential class of private actors in international political economy, is the topic of Section II. Through the vehicle of direct foreign investment, multinationals create production and financial networks that transcend frontiers as never before in history. The result is a newer and more intense form of integration that many have come to view as more or less synonymous with the popular term globalization. Scholars are only beginning to appreciate the full extent of the impact of multinational firms on domestic and world politics.

Section III addresses issues of money and finance in both advanced industrial societies and newly developing economies. Questions here involve the interaction of monetary sovereignty and balance-of-payments relations among states as well as the role that financial markets and capital mobility play in shaping contemporary policy and politics.

Section IV is reserved for specialized or emerging issues in the world economy, such as commodity trade, management of the international environment, and economic regionalism.

Central to all these issue areas is the question of actor behavior: What explains how and why critical agents act as they do? Actors may be either public or private— politicians or political institutions (including regional and multilateral institutions) on the one hand, individuals or societal organizations (including, most importantly, multinational firms) on the other. Likewise, behavior may be unilateral or collective, cooperative or conflictual, static or changing. In a diverse and highly uncertain world, seeking to comprehend the sources and inspiration of actor behavior— what motivates individual agents and what determines how they respond to specific characteristics of their environment—is manifestly valuable. The core challenge for scholarship is twofold: How is behavior best analyzed, and can actions be predicted?

Answers vary, of course, depending in part on the intellectual perspectives of particular scholars. Differences persist between champions of either parsimony or descriptive accuracy—between those who would deliberately exclude much detail for the sake of analytical tractability and those who would sacrifice a degree of formal rigor for the sake of factual completeness. Spare structural models, for all their value in isolating key variables and relationships, are criticized for oversimplifying the messy complexities of reality. More layered multivariate approaches, in contrast, for all their empirical richness, are faulted for losing sight of the forest for the trees. Little room exists for a satisfactory compromise between the demands of analytical economy and empirical verisimilitude. Regrettably, therefore, we are still far from anything that might be described as a general, unified theory of behavior in international political economy.

Nonetheless, much insight has been accumulated as a result of successive efforts such as those collected in this volume. The roots of governmental policy, for example, are now understood to be far more tangled than typically assumed for analytical purposes by early realist or neorealist theory. The black box of the state has been opened wide, albeit at some sacrifice to parsimony, to take account of a myriad of significant influences on policymakers—political as well as economic, external as well as internal, cognitive as well as material. Political influences may derive from the self-interested pursuit of gain by societal actors or politicians, the laws and institutions of government, or the broader geostrategic and diplomatic environment in which all states must operate. Economic influences may reflect transactions costs, market structures, or technological developments at both the domestic and international levels. Cognitive influences may be rooted in enduring aspects of culture or emerge more spontaneously as a result of self-conscious learning and adaptation. Likewise, motivations of private agents are now understood to encompass far more than the single-minded preoccupation with material welfare emphasized by conventional economic theory. Individuals and firms may also pursue multiple objectives and may even appear to behave irrationally at times. Clearly, all actors act strategically within limits set by existing institutions and the prevailing distribution of relevant capabilities and information.

Answers also vary depending on the specific issue at hand. Trade debates, for example, typically tend to involve a wider range of actors both at home and abroad—to be more "politicized," in short—than questions of monetary or exchange-rate policy. Emerging issues such as environmental management, in contrast, are more likely to reflect the influence of ideas and learning than older, more established policy challenges. Economic considerations may dominate at the level of preference formation; political considerations, in the context of policy implementation or international negotiations. Domestic factors may dominate explanations of behavior by individual states; international variables may dominate when it comes to understanding collective action or intergovernmental cooperation. The sources and inspiration of actor behavior, obviously, are many and diverse. But even a high degree of diversity does not preclude a gradual accumulation of knowledge and understanding, as the essays in this volume convincingly demonstrate.

References

Gilpin, Robert. 1971. The Politics of Transnational Economic Relations. *International Organization* 25 (3):48–69.

Nye, Joseph S., Jr., and Robert O. Keohane, eds. 1971. Transnational Relations and World Politics. *International Organization* 25 (3). Special issue.

I.
Trade

Trade is the cornerstone of the global economy—the most fundamental link between national economic systems. Few states have ever deliberately promoted self-sufficiency (autarky) as a national policy goal; fewer still have even come close to attaining absolute economic independence. The material costs of a country providing all of its needs from its own resources are simply too daunting to bear; the gains to be derived from less costly imports, paid for with the proceeds of export sales, are too attractive to ignore. Governments may jealously guard their political sovereignty. But they also appreciate the undoubted benefits of exchange based on some degree of specialization within a global division of labor. The case for open markets is understood by all.

Why, then, is free trade so difficult to organize and defend? Herein lies one of the central puzzles for students of international political economy. Without question, barriers to trade have been greatly reduced in the years since World War II. There is also no question that trade itself has rapidly grown—even more rapidly, in fact, than world output in general, thus greatly increasing the degree of interdependence between individual national economies. Yet significant elements of mercantilism continue to lurk in the policies of nearly every sovereign government, despite the manifest advantages of trade. Numerous and complex barriers still limit the movement of goods and services across state frontiers, and new protectionist restrictions remain an ever-present threat. The process of market liberalization, whether regional or multilateral, is slow, laborious, and often stalled. The management of the collective system is repeatedly endangered by acts of unilateralism at the national level. Clearly, a dissonance exists between the economics and the politics of trade that calls out for systematic analysis and explanation.

In response, International Organization has provided an important venue over the years for advancing relevant theory and understanding. The domestic sources of foreign trade policy were explored by Helen V. Milner, Judith Goldstein, Joanne Gowa, David A. Lake, John A. C. Conybeare, and Paul Midford.[1] The complexities of trade negotiations were examined by Robert D. Tollison and Thomas D. Willett, John

---

1. See Milner 1987; Goldstein 1988 and 1989; Gowa 1988; Lake 1988; Conybeare 1991; and Midford 1993.

S. Odell, R. Harrison Wagner, and Robert L. Paarlberg.[2] The role of power in trade relations was examined by Timothy J. McKeown, Scott C. James and David A. Lake, and Edward D. Mansfield.[3] Links between trade and security issues were analyzed by Kal J. Holsti and Stefanie Ann Lenway.[4] A complementary pair of review essays was provided by Benjamin J. Cohen and J. David Richardson.[5]

One of the most fundamental issues in global trade is how to preserve the benefits of market liberalization. In the absence of formal mechanisms at the international level to enforce compliance with negotiated commitments, we can never escape the risk that states may at some time or other be tempted to renege on existing bargains—to resort to what Beth Yarbrough and Robert Yarbrough (Chapter 1) call "opportunistic protectionism." The question, then, is what can be done to minimize the danger of noncompliance. Liberalization, the Yarbroughs observe, may take any of several forms, including unilateral, multilateral, or minilateral. Which of these forms will be most successful in preserving interstate commitments depends on the scope available for opportunistic behavior. And what determines the scope for opportunism? The answer, contend the Yarbroughs, using a transactions-cost framework of analysis, will depend on both the extent of investment in transaction-specific assets for trade and the viability of hegemonic cooperation. The more investment there is in trade-specific assets, the greater the country's vulnerability to opportunistic protection by others, hence the greater the need for a hegemonic power able and willing to preserve multilateral cooperation. When little trade-specific investment exists, unilateral liberalization is correspondingly more viable. When no obvious hegemon exists, successful cooperation may be feasible only on a minilateral basis enforced through issue linkage, hostages, and repeated play.

Klaus Stegemann (Chapter 2), too, recognizes the risk of opportunistic protectionism but is more interested in motivation: why, despite the myriad benefits of open markets, governments might nonetheless prefer interventionism to laissez faire. Some trade theorists once suggested that activist policy might be justified by the so-called new international economics that first emerged in the economics literature in the early 1980s. Traditional trade models were built on the assumption of perfect competition, leaving little room for trade policy to improve a nation's economic welfare. So-called strategic trade models, in contrast, accept the possibility of imperfect competition, incorporating such features as product differentiation, scale economies, and barriers to entry. In such models, a country's comparative advantage is not fixed but rather may be shaped by state policy: gains from trade may be enhanced by increasing a country's share of the excess profits or positive externalities associated with oligopolistic competition. Does this mean that protectionism is vindicated after all? Not necessarily, replies Stegemann, who stresses the hazards of using abstract theory as a guide to practical policy. As most trade theorists have now come to recognize, the conditions needed to make strategic trade initiatives successful are strict and not

2. See Tollison and Willett 1979; Odell 1980; Wagner 1988; and Paarlberg 1997.
3. See McKeown 1983; James and Lake 1989; and Mansfield 1992.
4. See Holsti 1986; and Lenway 1988.
5. See Cohen 1990; and Richardson 1990.

always realistic. Caution is therefore called for in sorting out situations where government intervention might or might not turn out to be in a nation's interest.

Judith Goldstein (Chapter 3) takes the opposite tack. If the temptation to intervene is so great, why do states ever commit to cooperative trade agreements? Her analysis takes us directly into the realm of domestic politics in the formulation of foreign economic policy. Most theorists stress the constraints imposed by domestic politics on international bargains. Diverse societal groups lobby to prevent potentially damaging concessions, hamstringing government negotiators. Goldstein, in contrast, emphasizes the catalytic role that domestic politics may play—in particular, the way that various actors may see in international agreements not a threat but rather an opportunity to further their own interests. This important insight sheds new light on the interaction between internal and international factors in international political economy and opens fresh possibilities for explaining state behavior.

References

Cohen, Benjamin J. 1990. The Political Economy of International Trade. *International Organization* 44 (2):261–82.

Conybeare, John A. C. 1991. Voting for Protection: An Electoral Model of Tariff Policy. *International Organization* 45 (1):57–82.

Goldstein, Judith. 1988. Ideas, Institutions, and American Trade Policy. *International Organization* 42 (1):151–78.

———. 1989. The Impact of Ideas on Trade Policy: The Origins of U.S. Agricultural and Manufacturing Policies. *International Organization* 43 (1):31–72.

Gowa, Joanne. 1988. Public Goods and Political Institutions: Trade and Monetary Policy Processes in the United States. *International Organization* 42 (1):15–32.

Holsti, Kal J. 1986. Politics in Command: Foreign Trade as National Security Policy. *International Organization* 40 (3):643–71.

James, Scott C., and David A. Lake. 1989. The Second Face of Hegemony: Britain's Repeal of the Corn Laws and the American Walker Tariff of 1846. *International Organization* 43 (1):1–30.

Lake, David A. 1988. The State and American Trade Strategy in the Pre-Hegemonic Era. *International Organization* 42 (1):33–58.

Lenway, Stefanie Ann. 1988. Between War and Commerce: Economic Sanctions as a Tool of Statecraft. *International Organization* 42 (2):397–426.

Mansfield, Edward D. 1992. The Concentration of Capabilities and International Trade. *International Organization* 46 (3):731–64.

McKeown, Timothy J. 1983. Hegemonic Stability Theory and 19th-Century Tariff Levels in Europe. *International Organization* 37 (1):73–91.

Midford, Paul. 1993. International Trade and Domestic Politics: Improving on Rogowski's Model of Political Alignments. *International Organization* 47 (4):535–64.

Milner, Helen V. 1987. Resisting the Protectionist Temptation: Industry and the Making of Trade Policy in France and the United States During the 1970s. *International Organization* 41 (4):639–65.

Odell, John S. 1980. Latin American Trade Negotiations with the United States. *International Organization* 34 (2):207–28.

Paarlberg, Robert L. 1997. Agricultural Policy Reform and the Uruguay Round: Synergistic Linkage in a Two-Level Game? *International Organization* 51 (3):413–44.

Richardson, J. David. 1990. The Political Economy of Strategic Trade Policy. *International Organization* 44 (1):107–36.

Tollison, Robert D., and Thomas D. Willett. 1979. An Economic Theory of Mutually Advantageous Issue Linkages in International Negotiations. *International Organization* 33 (4):325–50.

Wagner, R. Harrison. 1988. Economic Interdependence, Bargaining Power, and Political Influence. *International Organization* 42 (3):461–84.

Cooperation in the liberalization of international trade: after hegemony, what?
Beth V. Yarbrough and Robert M. Yarbrough

> *Nations dwell in perpetual anarchy, for no central authority imposes limits on the pursuits of sovereign interests. . . . Because as states, they cannot cede ultimate control over their conduct to an supranational sovereign, they cannot guarantee that they will adhere to their promises. The possibility of a breach of promise can impede cooperation even when cooperation would leave all better off. Yet, at other times, states do realize common goals through cooperation under anarchy.*
>
> K. A. Oye, *Cooperation under Anarchy,* p. 1.

Contracts are agreements that are legally enforceable by the state. Each nation's contract law specifies the conditions under which nonperformance under a contract may be met with state enforcement and the punishments that may be imposed (e.g., monetary damages or specific performance). The enforcement institutions embodied in a state's contract law are obviously valuable in facilitating transactions, economic and otherwise. The transactions facilitated by contracts are mutually beneficial to the parties involved since the contractual relationship must, by definition, be voluntary.[1] Despite the mutuality of benefits under a contract, breach is sometimes advantageous to a party; and the complex institution of contract law is designed to prevent and compensate for breach. Were it not for the enforcement and

This article draws on portions of a manuscript read at the National Bureau of Economic Research Conference on the Political Economy of Trade Policy, MIT Endicott House, Dedham, Massachusetts, 10–11 January 1986. We appreciate comments by the participants at the conference and by the members of the editorial board of *International Organization*. Financial support from the NBER and a Trustee-Faculty Fellowship from the Trustees of Amherst College is gratefully acknowledged.

1. For example, contractual promises extracted through duress, fraud, or undue influence may be exempt from enforcement.

International Organization 41, 1, Winter 1987, pp. 1–26

remedy available in contract law, many potentially mutually beneficial transactions would not be undertaken.

It can be argued that it is the absence of this enforcement mechanism of
the state which makes international economic relations more insecure and
more obviously discordant than economic relations confined within a single
nation. The relationship of states to international law is quite different from
the relationship of citizens to the law of a single state: "A higher propensity
to deny the rule of law . . . and to resort to coercion is a characteristic
distinguishing international from domestic politics. . . . Organs of state are,
international lawyers remind us, immune from international law."[2] The
same concept of sovereignty (i.e., authority over citizens with no recourse to
higher law) which contributes to domestic stability and order also contributes to international "anarchy," for states have little recourse to higher law
in their dealings with one another.[3]

Prognosticators of the future of international trade appear to split into two
groups according to their perception of this international anarchy.[4] One
group, concerned with the rise of pressures for protectionism and aware of
the lack of an efficacious worldwide policy-making and enforcement structure, foresees at best the stagnation of trade liberalization and at worst the
return to protectionism at levels reminiscent of the 1930s. Of particular
concern to a subset of this group is the decline in the willingness and/or
ability of the United States to perform a leadership or hegemonic role in the
world trading system.[5] Proposed solutions range from the creation of a single
worldwide government to more modest proposals for supranational institutions to handle certain issues of worldwide concern, including international
trade policy. The current outlook from this perspective is rather pessimistic:
the mechanisms that it sees as prerequisites for cooperation do not appear to
be forthcoming, despite recognition of the mutual gains from cooperation. A
second group, on the other hand, also aware of increased protectionist pressures and decreased leadership potential by the United States, foresees
either persistence of the liberalizing force from the period of U.S. hegemony

2. J. A. C. Conybeare, "International Organization and the Theory of Property Rights,"
International Organization 34 (Summer 1980), pp. 325–26.

3. J. Stoessinger, "The Anatomy of the Nation-State and the Nature of Power," in M. Smith,
R. Little, and M. Shackleton, eds., *Perspectives on World Politics* (London: Croom Helm,
1981), p. 26.

4. The members of the two groups discussed here accept to a greater or lesser extent the
desirability of a liberal international trading system. A third group could be added, including
many Marxist analysts, who do not accept the basic premise of mutual gains from liberal world
trade.

5. A variety of perspectives can be found in R. Gilpin, *U.S. Power and the Multinational
Corporation* (New York: Basic, 1975); C. P. Kindleberger, *The World in Depression* (Berkeley:
University of California Press, 1973), and "Dominance and Leadership in the International
Economy," *International Studies Quarterly* 25 (June 1981), pp. 242–54; R. Keohane, "The
Theory of Hegemonic Stability and Changes in International Economic Regimes," in O. R.
Holsti, R. M. Siverson, and A. L. George, eds., *Change in the International System* (Boulder:
Westview, 1980); S. D. Krasner, "State Power and the Structure of International Trade,"
World Politics 38 (April 1976), pp. 317–43; and D. Snidal, "The Limits of Hegemonic Stability
Theory," *International Organization* 39 (Autumn 1985), pp. 579–614.

or evolution of viable alternative institutions to maintain the openness of the world trading system.[6] For this group, international anarchy is more apparent than real, a misnomer for subtle patterns of cooperation which are poorly understood.

Informed by the second tradition, this article asks: Given the potential of liberal international trade to be mutually beneficial for all participants, what types of institutional arrangements can facilitate liberalization (i.e., cooperation) under different conditions in the world economy? We focus less on *whether* or *when* trade liberalization will occur,[7] or *where*—that is, in which industries,[8] than on *how* and *in what form* trade liberalization will occur.[9] Liberalization can be unilateral, multilateral, or minilateral[10] and can be accompanied by varying degrees of bargaining, threats, harmony, discord, and explicit coordination. Why has trade liberalization historically taken different forms? To answer this question, we construct a theory to connect the various forms of observed liberalization with the economic and political environments in which they occur. The framework we adopt emphasizes the role of transaction costs[11] and the resulting hazards of opportunism in determining the forms of successful trade liberalization.[12] Rather than prescribing

6. See Conybeare, "International Organization"; R. Keohane, *After Hegemony: Cooperation and Discord in the World Political Economy* (Princeton: Princeton University Press, 1984); S. Strange, "Protectionism and World Politics," *International Organization* 39 (Spring 1985), pp. 233–60; and B. V. Yarbrough and R. M. Yarbrough, "Free Trade, Hegemony, and the Theory of Agency," *Kyklos* 38, fasc. 3 (1985), pp. 348–64, "Reciprocity, Bilateralism, and Economic 'Hostages': Self-Enforcing Agreements in International Trade," *International Studies Quarterly* 30 (March 1986), pp. 7–21, and "Opportunism and Governance in International Trade: After Hegemony, What?" (Paper read at the National Bureau of Economic Research Conference on the Political Economy of Trade Policy, MIT Endicott House, Dedham, Mass., 10–11 January 1986).

7. These questions are the focus of the traditional hegemonic stability literature as well as of business-cycle theories of trade policy.

8. This question is emphasized in political economy, public choice, and pressure-group theories of trade policy.

9. The other questions mentioned can also be addressed using the framework developed in this article. However, we chose to limit our focus to the single question of the various possible forms of international trade liberalization. Understanding the historical variation in the structure of international trade liberalization is essential to progress toward a general structural or systemwide theory of trade policy. Some theories that have been suggested (e.g., hegemonic stability) may be able to explain this historical variation; others (e.g., business-cycle theories or domestic pressure-group theories) seem by their nature less likely to be able to address this question, although they certainly play a role in the actual determination of trade policy.

10. J. D. Richardson has suggested the term *minilateralism* for agreements among small numbers of like-minded participants; see, for example, his "Trade-Policy Implications of 'Strategic' Economic Models" (Paper read at the NBER Conference on the Political Economy of Trade Policy, MIT Endicott House, Dedham, Mass. (10–11 January 1986).

11. Transaction costs include information, negotiation, contracting, and inspection or enforcement costs. See R. Coase, "The Problem of Social Cost," *Journal of Law and Economics* 3 (October 1960), pp. 1–44.

12. This general approach to problems has come to be known by various names, including transaction-costs economics and the economics of organization. See O. E. Williamson, *The Economic Institutions of Capitalism* (New York: Free, 1985); B. V. Yarbrough and R. M. Yarbrough, "Institutions for the Governance of Opportunism in International Trade," *Journal of Law, Economics, and Organization* (forthcoming).

trade policies, we highlight the potential costs of prohibiting some trade practices, the complete role of which in facilitating cooperation may yet be imperfectly understood.[13]

We view the extent of transaction-specific investment and the viability of hegemonic cooperation as determinants of the scope of opportunistic protectionism and, therefore, as determinants of the *form* of successful liberalization. When there is little investment in transaction-specific assets for trade, then opportunistic protectionism is unlikely and unilateral liberalization is viable, regardless of whether or not the world economy is dominated by a hegemonic country. Arguably, such a situation characterized the position of 19th-century Britain, which did indeed pursue unilateral liberalization. When substantial investment in trade-related transaction-specific assets does occur, then trade liberalization takes on characteristics of a Prisoner's Dilemma and unilateral liberalization is not viable. Under the Prisoner's Dilemma, cooperation or liberalization can still emerge. A hegemonic country can facilitate cooperation, for example, the United States' support of the multilateral GATT (General Agreements on Tariffs and Trade) system following World War II. Or, in the absence of a hegemon, minilateral cooperation can arise through the use of issue linkage, hostages, and repeated play. This last case, minilateral cooperation, can be argued to approximate the situation of recent years.

1. Transaction costs, adjustment costs, and opportunism: the need for cooperation

Traditional economic trade theory provides a powerful demonstration of the potential gains from international specialization and trade according to comparative advantage. Given a few basic assumptions,[14] unrestricted international trade maximizes total world income and welfare from a fixed quantity of available resources and technology. Even if one or more of these assumptions are violated, restrictions on international trade are generally a second-best remedy. By ignoring transaction and adjustment costs associated with international trade liberalization, this traditional view posits trade as a situation of near-perfect harmony (excepting the nationalistic "optimal" tariff), a positive-sum game with little role for strategy, negotiation, or disagreement. Implicit in the near-perfect harmony of the orthodox economic view of trade is the absence of a role for cooperation in Keohane's sense of the word.[15]

13. For a similar caution in a business-regulation context, see B. Klein, "Transaction Cost Determinants of 'Unfair' Contractual Relations," *American Economic Review* 70 (1980), pp. 356–62.

14. The primary assumptions include competitive output and factor markets, the absence of external effects in production or consumption, and the absence of economies of scale.

15. Keohane, *After Hegemony*, especially pp. 51–55.

Each country, acting in its individual self-interest, chooses unilaterally to liberalize trade; and total world income is maximized as an (unintended) result.

We maintain the traditional assumption that unrestricted international trade maximizes total world income by facilitating specialization according to comparative advantage.[16] By contributing to a more efficient use of the world's resources, liberalization by any country (e.g., elimination of a tariff or loosening of a quantitative restriction) contributes to the gains from trade. Despite this positive effect of a country's liberalization on the total gains from trade, a more liberal policy may impose a number of costs on an individual country, especially interindustry resource dislocations and (undesired) redistributions of domestic income.

These costs, typically referred to as "adjustment costs," constitute an effective barrier to liberalization only in the presence of substantial transaction costs. With zero transaction costs, "winners" from liberalization could compensate "losers" without cost; tax-subsidy schemes could effect any desired sectoral realignments; the future benefits of improved resource allocation could be borrowed against to cover current adjustment costs; and the barrier to liberalization which adjustment costs represent would disappear. Even the optimal tariff argument for a welfare-enhancing tariff by a large country relies on transaction costs insofar as the harm that such a tariff imposes on trading partners exceeds the benefit to the tariff-raising country. With no transaction costs, the trading partners could pay the large country to forgo the tariff, and world welfare would rise. Therefore, it is transaction costs that turn adjustment costs into a potent source of discord.

The explicit consideration of transaction and adjustment costs introduces two bases of protectionism or of failure to liberalize trade. The first, well-known source is the internal distributional effect of liberalization. By blocking costless compensation of losers (e.g., owners of resources employed in import-competing sectors)[17] by gainers (e.g., domestic consumers and owners of resources in export-oriented sectors), transaction costs may bring about an outcome in which domestic interest groups are able to effect governmental trade policies that do not maximize national, much less world, welfare. A larger-scale reflection of the same phenomenon is the "free-riding" problem where small states pursue protectionist policies in the belief that those policies do not significantly influence the openness of the world trading system. In each case, self-interest on the part of each individual

---

16. Factors such as monopoly power, economies of scale, and externalities in production and consumption are ignored or, alternatively, are assumed to be dealt with using policies other than restrictions on trade.

17. The division of gainers and losers refers to the short run. In the long run, the owners of resources used intensively in production of the country's goods of comparative advantage gain from liberalization, while the owners of resources used intensively in production of the country's goods of comparative disadvantage lose according to the Stolper-Samuelson Theorem.

interest group causes a less than socially optimal amount of liberalization. This problem has been widely studied in both its domestic and international versions. Proposed solutions range from domestic trade adjustment assistance programs to special efforts to convince small (particularly developing) countries of the advantages to all of trade liberalization.

A second source of protectionism as a result of transaction costs is more subtle and less studied. Not only may a country choose policies that are less liberal than the socially optimal policies, but a country may renege on negotiated commitments to liberalization. A trade liberalization agreement consists merely of policy commitments by the signatory countries. One country, by choosing to ignore or cheat on its commitment to liberalization while other countries abide by theirs, may gain by avoiding resource reallocation costs, redistributions of domestic income, or other adjustment costs. Such a policy (protection in violation of a negotiated commitment to liberalization) can be referred to as "opportunistic protectionism." By definition, opportunism is possible only in the presence of transaction costs; otherwise agreements could be designed and enforced without cost in such a way as to make opportunistic violations impossible. So transaction costs not only block efforts to deal with the intracountry distributional impact of liberalization; they also introduce the potential hazard of opportunistic violations of commitments to liberalization.

A transaction that would be mutually beneficial if all parties abided by their commitments may not be mutually beneficial if one or more parties reneges. When opportunistic nonperformance in a transaction is a hazard, then obtaining the mutual benefits from the transaction requires designing a governance structure to control nonperformance. In everyday economic transactions, these governance structures include such common arrangements as collateral to prevent opportunistic nonrepayment of loans, the use of brand names to convey information about quality, better business bureaus to provide information about the reliability of firms, automobile "lemon" laws to protect car buyers from opportunistic dealers, and product guarantees or free samples to compensate for or prevent dissatisfaction with a product's quality. By making transactions more secure, each of these arrangements facilitates mutually beneficial transactions that otherwise might not be undertaken.[18] Each of the arrangements is an example of cooperation; and the cooperation is needed because the possibility of opportunism introduces an element of conflict among the commonality of interests.

The same problem arises in international trade liberalization. After arriving at a mutual agreement to liberalize trade policies, one country may find it advantageous to renege on its commitments. Other parties to the agreement

---

18. This is a functional view of institutions, holding that the existence of institutions can be understood through the functions that those institutions serve. For a discussion in terms of international issues, see Keohane, *After Hegemony*, especially chaps. 5 and 6.

may be harmed if such opportunism occurs. Under these circumstances, a need for cooperation replaces harmony. But the orthodox neoclassical framework has little to say about the possible mechanisms for cooperative organization and governance of international trading relations because the neoclassical viewpoint is basically apolitical and ahistorical. Such a theory cannot adequately address the particular forms that trade agreements have historically taken (e.g., unilateral by 19th-century Britain, multilateral by the postwar United States, or minilateral recently). These "organizational" distinctions in the form of cooperation are assumed away in neoclassical theory, where international trade occurs in an idealized, harmonious world of zero transaction costs.

When a country behaves opportunistically by imposing protection proscribed under a trade agreement, the total gains from trade are reduced. So long as liberalization involves adjustment costs and cheating cannot be easily detected and traced to the guilty country, incentives exist to behave opportunistically. That liberalization does indeed impose adjustment costs on a country hardly needs documentation. The anarchic nature of international economic relations prevents effective detection and punishment of opportunistic states; even if detection were easy (which we shall argue is not the case), punishment would be problematic.

At first glance, the problem of detecting opportunistic violations of trade agreements may appear trivial. After all, governments and international organizations collect mountains of trade statistics; tariff lists are publicly available; and it is possible to trace goods through customs. However, several factors make this observation misleading. First, there is no uniform international consensus about whether or not a trade agreement automatically becomes domestic law in signatory countries. In most cases, international agreements have no direct effects but must be converted into domestic law and enforced domestically.[19] The U.S. Congress, for example, has periodically altered the domestic status of agreements reached through GATT negotiations.[20] This additional step introduces the opportunity for individual states to alter the terms of an agreement through definitional changes as well as by stating explicit reservations to specific terms. The result of this process can be a signed agreement embodying substantial differences among the signatory parties over the behaviors that are or are not acceptable under the (now multiple) terms. Detecting violations under such conditions is not a trivial problem.

Second, trade agreements, like domestic contracts, are not intended to be binding under all circumstances. It is a well-established principle of contract

19. S. Piccioto, "Political Economy and International Law," in S. Strange, ed., *Paths to International Political Economy* (London: Allen & Unwin, 1984), p. 172.

20. R. E. Baldwin, "The Changing Nature of U.S. Trade Policy since World War II," in Baldwin and A. O. Krueger, eds., *The Structure and Evolution of Recent U.S. Trade Policy* (Chicago: University of Chicago Press, 1984), pp. 5–27.

law that situations arise in which, as a result of unforeseen changes in circumstance, it is impossible or in no one's interest to honor the contract.[21] Failure to perform in such situations (e.g., if an entertainer dies prior to a contractually scheduled concert or if a transportation strike makes timely delivery of promised goods impossible) is termed *discharge* rather than *breach*. But parties may disagree over whether performing is in fact impossible (in which case discharge may be permitted) or whether one party is opportunistically making such a claim in order to breach the contract without punishment. A country that had promised to permit unrestricted access for imports of an agricultural product might, for example, claim to have discovered a dangerous chemical, pesticide, or disease in the product and close its market to imports. In a rather colorful episode during the spring of 1985 (a period of depressed prices for most agricultural products in the United States), three northern states halted imports of hogs from Canada, claiming that the hogs had been treated with the unapproved antibiotic chloramphenicol. Canadian producers denied use of the antibiotic, calling the states' action (opportunistic) protectionism. U.S. producers had, in fact, been pressing for relief from the effects of Canadian exports. Detecting whether or not a country is acting opportunistically or in good faith in such circumstances may be difficult, costly, or even impossible. Japan often explicitly uses the doctrine of *rebus sic stantibus* (so long as principal circumstances remain unchanged) in its commercial treaties.[22] This doctrine, as its name suggests, permits agreements to be broken should unexpected changes make honoring the commitments undesirable. The use of this "escape clause" is not popular with Japan's trading partners for obvious reasons; and the status of the clause vis-à-vis international law is murky.

A third factor hampering the detection of opportunistic protection under trade agreements is more obvious: the inability to define precisely the behaviors that are or are not permissible. A brief list of recent trade disputes should suffice to illustrate this point. The United States and the EC (European Community) have a long-standing argument over which "domestic" policies constitute subsidies to exports and are therefore proscribed under the GATT. Are controlled natural gas prices in the United States a subsidy to exported goods that use gas as an input? What about export credits at low interest rates? At what levels do interest rates become "artificially low"? Is government subsidized or insured research and development an export subsidy for the commercial products that result? Within the EC itself, the use of different exchange rates to finance different activities, particularly agricultural trade at so-called "green rates," has been a source of disagreement because an artificial exchange rate can have essentially the same impact as

21. See, for example, A. T. Kronman, "Mistake, Disclosure, Information, and the Law of Contracts," *Journal of Legal Studies* 7 (January 1978), pp. 1–34.
22. T. B. Millar, ed., *Current International Treaties* (New York: New York University Press, 1984), p. 2.

an export subsidy. In trade between the developed and developing countries, transshipment under quantitative restrictions (i.e., clandestine rerouting through unrestricted third countries) provides a classic case of an opportunistic violation that may be exceedingly difficult to detect or prove. For example, Britain has claimed that Japan circumvented its voluntary restraint on automobile exports to Britain by shipping from Australia.[23] Even after an opportunistic violation of an agreement *is* established to have occurred, the problem of forcing termination of the practice or of imposing punishment in the fact of national sovereignty still exists. The problems of detection and enforcement make opportunism a real threat to cooperation.

The goal of opportunistic protectionism is not generally to halt trade. Rather, a threat is made to halt trade in order to force a renegotiation leading to more favorable terms for the opportunistic country (in the same sense that the goal of blackmail is not to reveal the secret but to transfer resources from the victim to the blackmailer). Of course, the threat may be successful or unsuccessful depending upon the opportunistic country's ability to judge the scope of its power. Italy in 1887 imposed a new tariff averaging 60 percent which abrogated treaties with Austria-Hungary, Switzerland, Spain, and France. Renegotiation with more favorable terms for Italy rather than a radical reduction in trade was presumably the goal since speedy renegotiations did occur with Austria-Hungary, Switzerland, and Spain. With France, however, Italy apparently miscalculated. Efforts at renegotiation were unsuccessful; and a decade-long trade war of retaliation and counterretaliation ensued. Interestingly, Italy did not abrogate its existing treaty with (more powerful) Germany at the same time.[24]

Recognition of the problem of opportunism in international trade relations has important implications for the expected structure of international trade agreements. In considering any agreement, each party must evaluate not only the effect on the country as a whole and the domestic distributional consequences should the agreement be reached and honored, but the likelihood and impact of opportunism as well. As a result, the form of cooperation should reflect the extent of the threat of breach.

In analyzing different forms of trade liberalization, it is possible to combine what have been viewed as two major competing theories of international trade policy: hegemonic cooperation and surplus capacity, each a key element in defining the politico-economic environment within which trade relations take place. It has been argued elsewhere that a synthesis of the two perspectives may prove more useful than either taken in isolation.[25] The

23. P. F. Cowhey and E. Long, "Testing Theories of Regime Change: Hegemonic Decline or Surplus Capacity?" *International Organization* 37 (Spring 1983), p. 178.

24. J. A. C. Conybeare, "Trade Wars: A Comparative Study of Anglo-Hanse, Franco-Italian, and Hawley-Smoot Conflicts," in K. A. Oye, ed., *Cooperation under Anarchy* (Princeton: Princeton University Press, 1986), p. 159.

25. Cowhey and Long, "Testing Theories."

hazard of opportunism under an international trade agreement depends, first, upon the extent of assets that are specific to international trade (a consideration closely related to the existence of surplus capacity) and, second, upon whether or not the agreement is reached in a hegemonic or nonhegemonic environment (as in the hegemonic cooperation hypothesis).

2. Transaction-specificity and surplus capacity: the bars in the Prisoner's Dilemma

The crux of the Prisoner's Dilemma game typically used to describe international trade problems lies in one aspect of the payoff structure: a defection harms a cooperating party more than it does a defecting party. It is this vulnerability to opportunism, or cost of naiveté, which renders defection the dominant strategy regardless of the other player's strategy. This issue arises within the context of international trade as the question of whether or not a country that is cooperating by complying with a liberalization agreement is made worse off by a trading partner's opportunistic protectionism than had the countries never agreed to cooperate in liberalization. The answer to this question, and therefore the extent to which the Prisoner's Dilemma accurately characterizes the situation, depends upon the extent of transaction-specific investment in trade.

By definition, transaction-specific investment is undertaken to be used in specific transactions; and the value of such assets in alternative uses is low.[26] Transaction-specificity is related to but usefully distinguished from what are usually referred to as "specialized" assets. The distinction has important implications for the vulnerability to opportunism. A few examples will illustrate the relationship between transaction-specificity and the hazard of opportunistic protectionism. Consider the Soviet-European gas pipeline. European technology helped build the pipeline in exchange for the promise of Soviet natural gas exports. Once completed, the pipeline is susceptible to Soviet opportunism since, if the Soviets reduce the amount of gas they are willing to export to Europe (i.e., by placing a quota on exports), the pipeline loses part of its value to the Europeans. The lack of good alternative uses for the pipeline (a transaction-specific asset) from the point of view of the Europeans implies that they could be forced to settle for less than the promised amount of natural gas. If European technology and personnel are required on a continuing basis to maintain the pipeline, then the hazard of European opportunism may also exist. It may be possible for Europeans to demand more than the agreed-upon quantity of natural gas exports in exchange for continued maintenance of the asset. The hazard of opportunism is not a

---

26. Williamson, *Economic Institutions*. Transaction-specific investment can occur in any durable asset, including human skills. The term *capital* is used to denote durability.

result of a traditional monopoly nor of the specialized purpose of the pipeline (to carry natural gas) but, rather, of the pipeline's specificity to one particular transaction, namely, Soviet-European trade in gas. The European countries do not have a monopoly in the supply of pipeline technology, nor the Soviets in the supply of natural gas. Prior to the construction of the pipeline, a number of possible buyers and sellers existed. However, once the transaction-specific investment in the pipeline is undertaken, the Soviets and Europeans find themselves in a bilateral monopoly. The Soviets cannot use the pipeline to provide non-European buyers with natural gas; and the Europeans cannot use the pipeline to obtain gas from non-Soviet suppliers. As a result of a breakdown of the unique relationship, the value of the asset depreciates.

A different example of transaction-specific assets is presented by the refusal (for political or security reasons) of the United States to provide replacement parts for military equipment sold to a number of countries. The assets are specific in the sense that continued trade with the United States is necessary to retain their usefulness. The United States then has the option of exploiting its position by charging high prices for replacement parts or by providing the parts only in exchange for some concession. Of course, the United States may also refuse to provide the parts on any terms, using its power in the transaction to keep the equipment out of commission. The purchasers of that equipment could have bought similar non-U.S. equipment and the U.S. firms could have sold their equipment elsewhere; the initial relationship was not a monopoly. But once the U.S. equipment is purchased, then a monopoly results. As a third example, the U.S. computer industry made a substantial transaction-specific investment in its development of computer hardware and software capable of using Japanese kanji characters. The market for such a capability outside of Japan is quite limited, making Japan's ability to close its market to the technology a substantial threat. Japan, on the other hand, has invested in the capital equipment and skills necessary to produce automobiles meeting the safety and pollution standards set by the United States. A complete closure of the U.S. automobile market to Japan could impose losses up to the value of those trade-specific assets. In each case, by threatening to withdraw from the relationship, one country can extract from the other an amount up to the difference between the value of the current transaction and the best available alternative. The alternative involves a loss of at least part of the asset's value since the asset is specific to a transaction between two particular parties. The lack of an alternative use with approximately equal value is the source of the potential for opportunism in each case. A transaction-specific asset renders the trading relationship irreversible (or reversible only at a cost equal to the value of the specific asset).

International trade tends to give rise to transaction-specific investment by altering the pattern of production and investment in the participating economies. Transaction-specific assets can take a number of forms; but for present purposes the most important are "dedicated assets," which are specialized to a particular relationship the loss of which would result in significant excess capacity and associated losses.[27] Dedicated assets are common in international trade. The process of specialization according to comparative advantage involves investing in increased productive capacity designed to service export markets. In the absence of transaction and adjustment costs and specific assets, these structural effects of liberalization do not block cooperation; if two states agree to liberalize trade and one country invests in capacity for servicing the other's market, that investment can be easily dismantled or redirected in the event that the agreement breaks down. But once transaction-specific assets are introduced, one party can "hold up" the other for an amount equal to the excess of the value of the current trading relationship over the value of the best alternative. The greater is the potential return from such opportunism, the stronger the safeguards (i.e., the assurances against opportunism) that will be required in order for countries to enter into liberalization agreements.

As noted earlier, the primary form of transaction-specific investment in international trade consists of dedicated assets, or productive capacity designed for trade so that the loss of markets results in losses through surplus capacity. Susan Strange and others have put forward the existence of surplus capacity as an explanation for increased pressures for protectionism and decreased momentum in trade liberalization.[28] They argue that when productive capacity in an industry substantially exceeds the level of demand at remunerative prices for a sustained period (i.e., not merely at a stage of the business cycle), then antiliberalization pressure rises. Surplus capacity is argued to have increased recently as a result of a rise in the capital intensity of production in many sectors, a rise in the number of industrialized or industrializing countries competing in world markets, and an accelerated pattern of change in the demands for manufactured products owing to shocks such as changes in petroleum prices.[29]

Surplus capacity is similar to the presence of dedicated assets in that both imply a loss of asset value owing to a loss of markets. The existing literature on surplus capacity emphasizes the tendency of industries that find themselves in a situation of surplus capacity to exert pressure for governmental assistance in the form of trade barriers. Because we are interested primarily in the perceived hazard of opportunism and its effect on the form of trade

27. Williamson, *Economic Institutions*, especially pp. 194–95.
28. S. Strange, "The Management of Surplus Capacity: or, How Does Theory Stand up to Protectionism 1970s Style?" *International Organization* 33 (Summer 1979), pp. 303–34; S. Strange and R. Tooze, eds., *The International Politics of Surplus Capacity* (London: Butterworth, 1980); L. Tsoukalis and A. da Silva Ferreira, "Management of Industrial Surplus Capacity in the European Community," *International Organization* 34 (Summer 1980), pp. 355–76; Cowhey and Long, "Testing Theories."
29. Cowhey and Long, "Testing Theories," p. 163.

liberalization, our focus is somewhat different. The possibility of losing markets which would result in surplus capacity becomes important since the possibility itself (whether or not it actually materializes) lessens willingness to enter into trade-liberalizing agreements.

The existence of dedicated assets and potential surplus capacity results in a Prisoner's Dilemma payoff structure since a country that agrees to liberalize trade and undertakes associated specific investment stands to lose the value of that investment should its partners impose opportunistic protectionism, leaving the country worse off than had the agreement never been reached. When transaction-specific assets result in a Prisoner's Dilemma, then the success of trade liberalization depends upon an institutional arrangement for breaking the dilemma. One possibility is suggested by a theory of hegemonic cooperation.

3. Hegemonic stability versus hegemonic cooperation

A hegemon is a state that is dominant in its leadership in the world economy.[30] Among other attributes of leadership, such a country is willing and able to act as an arbitrator in disputes and to support international cooperative institutions such as the GATT but is not omnipotent or able to impose its leadership without regard to the positions of other countries. If it is to lead, the hegemon must do so on terms that convince other states to follow or defer to its leadership. The precise role of the hegemon has been viewed by various writers as the provision of international stability, international security, rules of behavior, stability of expectations, and enforcement of rules.

The most common version of the hegemonic stability hypothesis views trade liberalization as a public good that must be provided by a hegemonic country. Nonhegemonic countries are free-riders that have inadequate incentives to contribute to the maintenance of a liberal trading system. The main source of disagreement among analysts in the hegemonic-stability tradition concerns the extent of benevolence or exploitation on the part of the hegemon. In the view of some, the hegemon is benevolent, overcoming the tendency of other countries to free-ride by carrying the burden of system-maintenance on its own shoulders with little or no reward for its efforts. For others, the hegemon is exploitative and coercive, forcing other countries into openness that serves primarily if not exclusively the interests of the hegemon itself.[31]

The traditional version of the hegemonic stability hypothesis predicts that

---

30. For more extensive discussion of the concept of hegemony, see the works mentioned in nn. 5 and 6.

31. This line of reasoning, if carried further, leads to the Marxist view of hegemony as represented in the work of Stephen Hymer, e.g., "The Efficiency (Contradictions) of Multinational Corporations," *American Economic Review* 60 (1970), pp. 441–48.

the presence of a hegemonic country is both necessary and sufficient for an open trading system and, further, that the hegemon is instrumental in bringing about that system. Full historical support for the hypothesis would find Britain and the United States, during their respective periods of hegemony, actively and successfully promoting a cooperative, open trading system and would also find movements away from such a cooperative, open system at all other times. The actual empirical evidence is mixed.[32] Although the periods of hegemony were relatively open by historical standards, Britain did not pursue worldwide liberalization very actively; and nonhegemonic periods have not been uniformly characterized by a lack of cooperation or openness.

The view of hegemonic cooperation taken here involves a related but slightly different role for the hegemon in trade liberalization.[33] This alternative view avoids several theoretical criticisms of the hegemonic stability hypothesis[34] and appears to be consistent with the (admittedly limited and sometimes ambiguous) empirical evidence. We focus on two issues that Keohane suggests have been inadequately addressed by the literature on hegemonic stability: the incentives facing the hegemon and the incentives facing other countries to defer or defect.[35] The hypothesis of hegemonic cooperation also helps resolve the scientific problem of evaluating a theory that applies to only two cases (Britain and the United States). By attempting to say something about the particular form that trade liberalization would take under different conditions, this perspective puts forth additional potentially refutable implications for evaluation.

To avoid reneging on liberalization agreements and to avoid the costs of the associated protectionism, the rewards to individual countries for participating in the world trading system must discourage such opportunism. As noted above, problems of both detection and enforcement arise. The gains to a country from opportunistic protectionism come at the expense of the country's trading partners; and hegemonic cooperation focuses on the hegemon's role as provider of a reward structure intended to discourage beggar-thy-neighbor opportunism.

Two aspects of the hegemon's role facilitate cooperation. Ex ante, an acceptable allocation among countries of the costs and benefits of liberalization must be achieved if an agreement is to be reached. This negotiation stage aligns the incentives of the participating countries and forms the "car-

32. See, for example, T. J. McKeown, "Hegemonic Stability Theory and 19th-Century Tariff Levels in Europe," *International Organization* 37 (Winter 1983), pp. 73–91; Cowhey and Long, "Testing Theories"; Keohane, *After Hegemony*; Snidal, "Limits."

33. For a detailed explanation, see Yarbrough and Yarbrough, "Free Trade, Hegemony." The terminology *hegemonic cooperation* is from Keohane, *After Hegemony*, p. 55.

34. See J. A. C. Conybeare, "Public Goods, Prisoners' Dilemmas and the International Political Economy," *International Studies Quarterly* 28 (1984), pp. 5–22.

35. Keohane, *After Hegemony*, p. 39.

rot'' aspect of the hegemon's role. Ex post, the hegemon must be willing and able to monitor countries for compliance with their commitments and to apply agreed-upon punishments in the case of opportunism. This monitoring stage forms the ''stick'' of the enforcement mechanism. Under a system of hegemonic cooperation, the ''stick'' should be applied rarely since an effective hegemon can persuade other countries to follow rather than relying on force. This is consistent with John Gannett's observation in a military context that the actual use of force is evidence of the breakdown of power, of impotence rather than strength.[36]

The reward to each country for compliance under hegemonic cooperation must be sufficient to compensate it for forgoing opportunistic protectionism; that is, the reward must at least cover the adjustment costs that the country incurs as a result of its compliance with liberalization. The hegemon must absorb these costs and pay each country an additional side-payment to ensure compliance. The larger the side-payments, the stronger are the incentives provided (but the higher the costs to the hegemon). The size of the side-payments is determined through bargaining between the hegemon and other countries. The constraints on that bargaining are that the side-payments must be positive and that the residual from the gains from trade (which is the reward to the hegemon for its efforts) must be positive. The threat to each country is that, should it act opportunistically, then the hegemon will alter its trade policy in such a way as to punish defection. The enforcement power of the hegemon depends on its ability to influence a large share of world trade through its own policies, including retaliation and control of access to its market. It has been estimated, for example, that protectionism by the United States can immediately and directly affect one-half of the world's trade.[37] The hegemon's trade policy is therefore a response to the policies of other countries; and a hegemon would not necessarily be expected to pursue pure free trade.

It will be in the hegemon's interest to act as a cooperative mechanism so long as opportunistic protection in the absence of the hegemon's enforcement reduces the total gains from trade sufficiently to make the residual the hegemon's most favored outcome. The hegemon shares the gains from openness with other countries to achieve their cooperation; but net gains remain for the hegemon. Should this cease to be the case, then the hegemon ceases to perform its role in the world trading system.[38]

The argument over whether the hegemon is benevolent or exploitative

36. J. Gannett, "The Role of Military Power," in Smith et al., *Perspectives*, p. 71.

37. A. I. MacBean and P. N. Snowden, *International Institutions in Trade and Finance* (London: Allen & Unwin, 1981), p. 79.

38. For a more detailed examination of the incentives facing the hegemon in its bargaining with other countries, see B. V. Yarbrough and R. M. Yarbrough, "Side-payments and Holdouts in a Principal-Agent Model" (Working paper, Department of Economics, Amherst College, 1985).

becomes more subtle in this view. Hegemonic cooperation is mutually beneficial to all participants; however, there is no reason to expect the gains to be distributed evenly. The hegemon is breaking the Prisoner's Dilemma that results from the inability of various countries to make binding precommitments to avoid opportunistic protectionism. Consider the classic Prisoner's Dilemma with two alleged criminals each facing a sentence of thirty days in jail if both confess, twenty days in jail if neither confesses, or ten days (for the confessor) and forty days (for the nonconfessor) in jail if only one confesses. Assume also that each individual values a day in jail at one dollar, that is, each would be willing to pay one dollar to reduce the time spent in jail by one day. Then the two together would be willing to pay up to twenty dollars for some sort of institution that would allow them to cooperate. They might, for example, each pay a five-dollar bribe to the police officer to interrogate them in the same room at the same time. If their pleas could be entered simultaneously and in one another's presence, then the incentive to defect would be eliminated. Each prisoner would be better off by five dollars; and the police officer would be better off by the amount of the bribe ($10), ignoring any societal costs of releasing the individuals as well as the risk that the officer might be discovered accepting the bribe and fired. Cooperation is valued by the prisoners; and the police officer is able to facilitate the cooperation by changing the rules of the game.[39] Is the officer self-interested, altruistic, benevolent, or exploitative? Each term has an element of truth; the important point is that all have been made better off. Similarly, a hegemon able to alter the nature of the Prisoner's Dilemma facing participants in the international trading system can establish an environment for mutually beneficial cooperation.

The theory of hegemonic cooperation in the presence of transaction costs views a hegemon as facilitating cooperation in a Prisoner's Dilemma situation. However, the extent to which the Prisoner's Dilemma accurately characterizes payoffs in international trade and, therefore, the role of a hegemon, depends upon the character of investment undertaken for trade-related purposes. This causes the implications of hegemonic cooperation to differ somewhat from those of the traditional hegemonic stability hypothesis. The hypothesis of hegemonic stability implies that the presence of a hegemonic state is *both necessary and sufficient* for a liberal trading system. The hypothesis of hegemonic cooperation, on the other hand, implies that the presence of a hegemon is *one possible way* of breaking a Prisoner's Dilemma in trade policy, a dilemma that exists *only* in the presence of substantial transaction-specific investment for trade. Before turning to a brief examination of the history of trade liberalization, a word of comparison is in order

39. See E. D. Elliott, B. A. Ackerman, and J. C. Millian, "Toward a Theory of Statutory Evolution: The Federalization of Environmental Law," *Journal of Law, Economics, and Organization* 1 (Fall 1985), p. 325.

between our analysis of transaction-specificity and opportunism in international trade and Albert Hirschman's well-known argument that the potential to stop trade is an important source of national power.[40]

4. Opportunistic protection versus national-power trade policy

Hirschman examined the pursuit of national power as a goal of international trade policy, a goal that implied the importance to each state of gains relative to those of other states. The primary tool of such a power policy, according to Hirschman, was fostering a monopoly position in one's exports (implying a vulnerability of one's trading partners to trade stoppages) and avoiding a monopoly position in one's import suppliers (implying a lack of vulnerability to stoppages). The ability to monopolize trade in certain products was viewed as largely technologically determined, with market size also an important consideration.

There are three major differences between our analysis and that of Hirschman. First and foremost, the assumed purpose of international trade differs. Hirschman explored the possibility of a power-oriented policy in international trade which could imply steps inconsistent with a wealth- or income-maximizing policy. We do not wish to argue here over the pros and cons of the wealth-maximization goal versus the power goal. Nonetheless, the distinction is important to a comparison of our argument with that of Hirschman. According to our perspective, international trade liberalization increases total world income, implying that in a world of zero transaction costs all countries could agree to eliminate trade barriers. But, of course, transaction costs are positive, which introduces the hazard of opportunistic protectionism. When such opportunism occurs, the "victimized" country may be worse off than had no liberalization agreement been reached. This will be true if the country invested in substantial transaction-specific assets for trade which provide the partner country with the basis for a hold-up.

The problem is, therefore, a Prisoner's Dilemma: neither country can credibly promise ex ante not to behave opportunistically; and this barrier can prevent a mutually beneficial transaction (i.e., trade liberalization) from occurring. The goal, then, is to arrive at some sort of institutional arrangement to facilitate credible commitments to compliance, thereby removing the block to completion of the mutually beneficial transaction. The vulnerability to opportunism is inherently associated with the desired activity (liberalization), and the goal is to *break* the link. Hirschman's perspective is quite different. The goal of the power policy is to *foster* vulnerability to

---

40. A. O. Hirschman, *National Power and the Structure of Foreign Trade* (Berkeley: University of California Press, 1945).

opportunism in order to act opportunistically. In fact, the trade involved in such a power policy might not be beneficial but might serve merely to create a dependency that could then be exploited. If the goal of trade is solely to foster exploitable dependency, then the trade presumably imposes costs on the opportunistic country during the "set-up" period; and the expected power gains during subsequent periods would have to offset these costs. This limitation may be important since any power gains are inherently short-lived since they are based on the victim's inability to find alternative sources of trade, a condition that does not usually last forever.

This point suggests the second distinction between our argument and that of Hirschman. The deliberate fostering of dependence which can then be exploited seems to require an asymmetry of information about the relationship between the parties. Either the intended victim must be for some reason so desperate to trade with the opportunistic country that the potential danger is ignored; or the intended victim must be unaware of the danger being plotted. The framework we develop, on the other hand, does not reply on this asymmetry of information. Both parties are assumed to be aware of any potential opportunism that might result from a particular trade agreement. The point is that when the potential for opportunism exists and is known ex ante, the agreement will take a form that can secure against the opportunism. In a mutually beneficial transaction, both parties have an incentive to arrive at some arrangement that will facilitate the agreement, just as lenders and borrowers have an incentive to arrive at an arrangement (e.g., collateral) to prevent the risk of opportunistic nonrepayment that could otherwise prevent a mutually beneficial loan from being made.

A third, more subtle difference is in the assumed source of asset specificity. For Hirschman, a country wants to be a monopolist in its export markets and a competitor in its import markets; and these market structures are largely determined by technology along with the relative sizes of markets. Transaction-specific investment is a much broader category than technologically based monopoly. As noted earlier in the example of the gas pipeline, transaction-specific investment can transform *any* relationship into a bilateral monopoly. Because the transaction-specific investment transforms a previously competitive situation into a monopoly subject to opportunism, the importance of these issues is much larger than it would appear based on the few technological monopolies of strategic minerals, unique patents, and such.

5. The politico-economic environment and the form of international cooperation

When the hazard of opportunistic protectionism is high, and a Prisoner's Dilemma results, there are incentives for parties to an international trade agreement to renege on the agreement's commitments. To the extent that parties to a potential agreement are aware of the scope for ex post opportunism, that awareness will be reflected in the form of the agreement. This can happen in three ways. First, if it is obvious to all parties that no agreement could be enforced in the face of the incentives for opportunistic protectionism, then no agreement may be reached despite the existence of mutual gains from trade. This outcome is the trade analogy to the school of arms-control thought which holds that meaningful arms control is impossible, despite the mutual gains from arms control, because no agreement can be mutually verifiable and enforceable. The dilemma defeats the prisoners; and cooperation does not emerge. The second possible outcome is that efforts may be channeled into negotiation of naive agreements that ignore the possibility of opportunism. Such agreements will be difficult to reach and short-lived, so the implications of this second possibility are not unlike those of the first: gains from trade are eventually lost because of bargaining problems that transaction costs and opportunism pose. The arms-control analogy would be a simple mutual promise to eliminate weapons with no monitoring or enforcement mechanism. An example of this behavior in international trade is provided by the Anglo-Hanse trade wars (1300–1700). The two sides repeatedly negotiated agreements to provide for relatively free trade; but the agreements repeatedly broke down, starting successive rounds of the trade wars.[41] The third possibility is to use an understanding of the incentives for opportunism to construct enforceable agreements. This is a costly process; but in a world of transaction costs and opportunism, the choice is not between protectionism and ideal trade agreements enforced without costs. Similarly, the arms-control choice is not between an uncontrolled arms race and a costlessly enforced ideal arms-control agreement. Rather, the relevant choice is between forgoing the benefits of trade (or arms control) and designing effective governance structures to facilitate trade (or arms-control) agreements. This link between the degree of hazard of opportunistic protectionism and the benefits to particular institutional arrangements implies that we may expect different forms of international trade liberalization to be successful under various conditions. Historically, the major forms of trade liberalization have been unilateral, multilateral, and minilateral; we shall now examine each briefly.

6. Unilateralism: 19th-century Britain

We expect unilateral trade liberalization only from countries facing little or no threat of opportunism; for example, whenever the country had little investment in trade-specific assets that could be held up by an opportunistic

---

41. Conybeare, "Trade Wars," especially pages 152–58.

trading partner. The most commonly cited historical example of extensive unilateral trade liberalization is the case of mid-19th-century Britain.[42] Although Britain was (at least by most definitions) a hegemonic power, its hegemony alone cannot explain the unilateral policy since the later hegemon, the United States, did not pursue unilateral liberalization.

Further, Timothy McKeown has argued that the actions of 19th-century Britain provide evidence against the traditional version of hegemonic stability theory.[43] That theory, according to McKeown, predicts that Britain would conduct an active, persuasive policy for lowering tariffs, use its bargaining strength in other areas to coerce other nations into lowering tariffs, and be successful in these efforts. The empirical evidence suggests that none of these predictions held and that both France and the Zollverein, the other major industrialized areas of the period, followed liberal policies despite a general lack of pressure to do so from Britain. In addition, Britain maintained a number of restrictive measures dictated by domestic interests. The smaller powers maintained their trade barriers in the face of substantial reductions by Britain, France, and the Zollverein. All of these observations are consistent with the view of hegemonic cooperation which sees a crucial role for the hegemon in systemwide liberalization only in the presence of transaction-specific investment that turns international trade liberalization into a Prisoner's Dilemma. This condition was not met during the period of British hegemony; and we predict that Britain would follow a unilateral trade policy: liberal but maintaining barriers demanded by domestic interest groups and not pressuring for systemwide liberalization.

Unilateral liberalization was feasible for Britain because of its industrial strength, high rate of capacity utilization, and need for raw material and export markets. Purchasers of manufactured goods from Britain faced limited alternative suppliers, while in most cases export markets and raw material sources were highly substitutable. Britain would have been vulnerable, of course, to a simultaneous stoppage of trade by a sizable group of its trading partners, but such a group was unlikely to form since defection from the group and continued trade with Britain would have been beneficial for each country. Those British investments that were highly vulnerable to opportunism were protected through the links of empire. Surplus capacity was not a problem for Britain; and the industrializing British labor force was becoming relatively mobile for the time.[44] Most smaller countries maintained trade barriers; but Britain liberalized unilaterally, capturing gains from trade

---

42. See J. T. Cuddington and R. I. McKinnon, "Free Trade versus Protectionism: A Perspective," in *Tariffs, Quotas and Trade: The Politics of Protectionism* (San Francisco: Institute for Contemporary Studies, 1979). The bilateral Cobden-Chevalier treaty was an exception to the basic unilateralism of Britain's trade policy, but noneconomic considerations were prominent in the negotiation of the treaty.
43. McKeown, "Hegemonic Stability."
44. Cuddington and McKinnon, "Free Trade," p. 12.

and incurring low bargaining and enforcement costs. Britain was a hegemon as defined by most measures of status relative to other countries, but hegemony cannot be the explanation for the unilateral form of its trade liberalization.

7. Multilateralism: postwar America and the early GATT years

By the end of World War II, transportation and communication costs had declined precipitously from their levels during the period of British hegemony a century earlier. Manufacturing technology had made large-scale production efficient; and the number of industrialized economies had expanded substantially, although several were in ruins from the war. Another major change in the nature of trade was a move away from intersectoral trade (e.g., the exchange of agricultural products for manufactured goods) to intra-industry or even intrafirm trade in manufactures. Much of this trade, by its nature, gives rise to trade-specific assets and to a vulnerability to opportunism. This runs counter to the common argument that dependence on imported food is the ultimate vulnerability. Food, however, is not transaction-specific; if one food supplier halts trade, a large number of alternative suppliers are typically available. Of course, if all suppliers halted trade simultaneously, then the problem would be much more serious; but such concerted action has been rare historically (and for good economic reasons). On the other hand, a manufacturing industry that imports a unique component for use in its manufacturing process may be unable to locate an alternative supplier quickly. Or the producer of a unique component may be unable to sell the product should the original buyer threaten to end the relationship. Therefore, the rise of trade in manufactures and especially of intra-industry trade is associated with an increase in trade-specific assets. Firms can protect these assets from opportunism through internalization in the form of intracorporate trade. However, this still leaves a vulnerability to governmental trade policies. Trade-specific assets imply a vulnerability to opportunistic protectionism, imparting a Prisoners' Dilemma payoff structure to the trade-liberalization game. Hegemonic cooperation implies that in the presence of substantial trade-specific assets, a hegemonic country can facilitate cooperation and liberalization by breaking the Prisoners' Dilemma in which individual countries find themselves.

The GATT framework supported by U.S. hegemony appears to fit the model of hegemonic cooperation well. The GATT consists of a set of continuously negotiated rules for trade policies and a set of arbitration or dispute-settlement procedures for members. The goal of the GATT framework is an open, cooperative trading system; but the emphasis has always been on negotiation and arbitration rather than on "free trade" as a dogmatic ideology. GATT contracting parties never committed themselves to follow free trade; protectionist policies to aid domestic industries were always permitted on a number of grounds. In turn, the framework provides for punishment of protectionism (primarily in the form of withdrawn concessions or countervailing duties), but only protectionism that violates specific GATT commitments.

Hegemonic cooperation based upon U.S. leadership implies that the United States should have actively provided "carrots" to other countries to ensure their support for liberalization under the GATT. In fact, the United States not only initiated and "marketed" the entire GATT system but in exchange for support continued to tolerate a number of practices that it would have liked to see terminated. These included preference systems such as that between Britain and the Commonwealth countries, the use of quotas for balance-of-payments problems, and the continuation of both tariffs and quotas by LDCs for "development" reasons. Each of these practices clearly violated the central GATT norm of nondiscriminatory liberalization. The United States also permitted continued discrimination against its own exports during the early years of the GATT by not demanding reciprocity in liberalization from either Europe or the developing countries. At the same time, the United States provided substantial aid for the reconstruction of Europe, primarily in the form of grants rather than loans. Each of these items represents a "carrot," or a concession made by the United States to achieve the support of other countries. Developing countries continue to be generally excused from demands for reciprocity within the GATT framework, a side-payment that was (and is) clearly necessary to bring about even lukewarm support for the system.

The enforcement or "stick" role of U.S. trade policies was also clear during the early postwar years. The United States never threatened to retaliate against all protectionism on the part of its trading partners; and it rarely claimed seriously to follow free trade policies itself. As noted above, continued discrimination in a number of forms against U.S. exports was tolerated in the early years of the GATT. The United States also excluded several sectors from liberalization (most notably, agriculture and later textiles) for its own domestic reasons. U.S. policy was designed to promote an open trading system, especially in manufactures; and retaliation was reserved for protectionism in violation of commitments within the GATT. The same principles of nondiscriminatory liberalization which formed the norms of GATT liberalization also applied for the most part to punishment under the GATT.[45]

The United States pushed other countries toward liberalization, though only at a mutually acceptable pace. For example, the U.S. battle to gain entry for Japan into the GATT was a long one. The battle was finally won

45. See Yarbrough and Yarbrough, "Reciprocity, Bilateralism," p. 12.

gradually over a number of years. First, Japan was allowed to send an observer to the GATT. Next, after a four-year push by the United States, Japan was admitted as a signatory country, but other countries were allowed to continue to discriminate against Japan in their trade policies. Finally, over the next four years, the discriminatory trade practices were gradually dropped.

The success of the GATT in its early years was crucially dependent upon U.S. hegemony in the world trading system. The enforcement powers of the GATT or any other body against a sovereign state are, in a legal sense, almost nonexistent. In the absence of strong legal enforcement, a strong arbitrator is necessary to ensure cooperation. The arbitration that successful multilateral agreements contain is unlikely in the absence of a hegemon to act as an enforcer and supporter of international institutions such as the GATT.

8. Minilateralism: cooperation in the 1980s

When international trade involves large-scale trade-specific assets, the international trade liberalization game takes on a Prisoner's Dilemma payoff structure. A hegemonic country can alter the rules of the game to facilitate cooperation, which is to the advantage of all. When the world trading system is not dominated by a hegemonic country, then cooperation requires alternative institutional arrangements to break the Prisoner's Dilemma. Each party compares the discounted present value of the expected benefits from cooperation against the discounted present value of the expected benefits from opportunism; and cooperation occurs only when its expected benefits outweigh those of opportunism.

Liberalization agreements among small groups of countries (i.e., bilateralism or minilateralism as opposed to multilateralism) are more likely to be successful under such circumstances for two reasons. First, the benefits and costs of liberalization must be carefully allocated among participating countries to arrive at a mutually acceptable agreement. Such allocations become more difficult as the number of parties rises, so small groups enjoy an advantage at the bargaining or negotiation stage. Second, an agreement once reached must somehow be enforced; and overcoming the difficulties of detecting opportunism requires effort. Monitoring within a small group is less costly and more effective than monitoring within a large group, so small groups also enjoy an advantage over larger ones at the enforcement stage. Multilateralism, nondiscrimination, and most-favored-nation status were the most important norms within the GATT during the early years when cooperation was based upon U.S. hegemony. More recently, the outstanding examples of successful trade liberalization have been bilateral or minilateral. Automobile trade between the United States and Canada has been relatively free for the last twenty years even though the industry worldwide has been subject to a growing web involving almost every conceivable form of trade barrier. In current negotiations, the United States and Canada are seeking to extend the liberalization beyond the automobile industry to a free-trade pact eliminating all barriers to trade. Israel has completed bilateral free-trade pacts with both the EC and the United States. The agreement between Israel and the United States (although obviously supported by a special political relationship) has generated particular interest as a model for future liberalization because of its successful handling of several previously troublesome areas of trade. Even within the GATT itself, with its strong organizational commitment to multilateralism, agreements among small groups (at least in comparison with the ninety contracting parties) have become more common. Most of the progress made in sticky areas at the Tokyo Round (e.g., the codes on subsidies, government procurement, and other nontariff barriers) occurred in a minilateral framework. Those successes earned some temporary and grudging support for a less than completely multilateral approach even from those who believe that the hope for long-term liberalization continues to lie in multilateralism.[46]

Beyond the use of minilateralism to alleviate bargaining and monitoring problems, the main tools for promoting cooperation under a Prisoner's Dilemma with no hegemon include issue linkage, the use of self-enforcing agreements or the threat of cancellation for noncompliance, and the provision and taking of economic "hostages."[47] Examples of each can easily be found in recent international trade relations.

Issue linkage has a long and interesting history in international trade negotiations. Linkage can occur in two forms. The first and most obvious is linkage of several goods on which trade is to be liberalized in a single agreement. One stage of the U.S.-Israeli free-trade pact, for example, covers aluminum, gold jewelry, radio-navigational equipment, refrigerators, cut roses, and tomatoes. These are goods that proved to be especially sensitive in the negotiations and are included in the final stage of the pact to take effect (in 1995). A second, more extensive means of linkage is the formation of long-standing groups such as customs unions within which a range of decisions are made collectively. Linkages can be forged not only across issue-areas at a point in time but across time as well. By creating an iterated game situation, such groups make a contribution toward cooperation along the lines Robert Axelrod suggests.[48]

Continuity is important for two reasons. First, the essence of the transaction-specificity of assets is that it places a premium on continuity of

---

46. For example, R. Vernon, "International Trade Policy in the 1980s," *International Studies Quarterly* 26 (December 1982), pp. 504–5.

47. O. E. Williamson, "Credible Commitments: Using Hostages to Support Exchange," *American Economic Review* 73 (1983), pp. 519–40.

48. R. Axelrod, *The Evolution of Cooperation* (New York: Basic, 1984).

trading relationships. Otherwise, the value of the assets is lost since they are, by definition, less valuable in alternative relationships. Second, because of the possibility of continuity, intertemporal linkages become incentives for cooperation. Ironically, these two roles imply that continuity is both an inhibitor and a facilitator of cooperation. The need for continuity (or its mirror image, the vulnerability to opportunistic protectionism) that arises in the presence of transaction-specific assets is the source of the Prisoner's Dilemma payoff structure that blocks cooperation. But continuity in the sense of ability to make future cooperation contingent on current cooperation can prevent opportunism.

Agreements that explicitly use future benefits from a relationship as a carrot for current cooperation are called "self-enforcing agreements."[49] Cancellation is the only possible punishment for opportunistic violations in a self-enforcing agreement; so if a party behaves opportunistically, then the other party automatically terminates the agreement. As a principle of self-help, self-enforcing agreements are used in areas where effective third-party enforcement is lacking; and international trade is obviously one such area. The need for self-enforcing agreements automatically to impose punishment on an opportunistic party provides a nonprotectionist argument for reciprocity. The increased emphasis in recent years on reciprocity has been interpreted as a move toward a less open trading system. It has been argued that the meaning of the term *reciprocity* has been changed from a positive concept involving mutual liberalization to a negative concept involving threats and retaliation similar to "tit-for-tat." Even threats to withdraw from future cooperation may induce cooperation, however, in an international system where agreements need strong elements of self-enforcement.[50]

Voluntary provision of a hostage or bond by a party to a trade agreement serves two purposes. First, the hostage raises the cost of opportunism by the value (to the provider) of the hostage. Second, the willingness to provide a hostage signals to the recipient the provider's intention not to behave opportunistically. During the 15th-century trade wars between England and the Hanseatic League, English merchants in Prussia were required to post direct bonds against the levying of British taxes on traders from the League. Unfortunately for the prospects for cooperation, the use of the hostages violated a cardinal rule: punishment was not reliably directed at those responsible for opportunism. Retaliation was sanctioned against any citizen of the other side, so the true enforcement power of the hostages was lost.[51] In a more modern context, some forms of technical trade standards such as

---

49. For development of the general theory of self-enforcing agreements, see L. Telser, "A Theory of Self-enforcing Agreements," *Journal of Business* 27 (1980), pp. 27–44; for international applications, see Yarbrough and Yarbrough, "Reciprocity, Bilateralism."

50. J. L. Goldstein and S. D. Krasner, "Unfair Trade Practices: The Case for a Differential Response," *American Economic Review* 74 (1984), pp. 282–87; Axelrod, *Evolution.*

51. Conybeare, "Trade Wars," pp. 153–57.

safety, pollution, and health regulations may serve as a form of hostage taking. Exporting countries must invest in the (transaction-specific) assets necessary to meet the standards; and a loss of the market means losing the value of the assets.

Conclusion

Given the potential of international trade to be mutually beneficial and the existence of transaction costs and associated enforcement problems, a variety of forms of trade liberalization agreements should be expected. In particular, the alternative to unilateral liberalization or to multilateral non-discriminatory liberalization is not necessarily protectionism. We have focused on the politico-economic environment (hegemonic or nonhegemonic) and on the extent of transaction-specific investment as the determinants of the scope for opportunism and, therefore, as the determinants of the form of successful trade agreements.

When investment is generic or footloose, the discipline of the marketplace provides an adequate governance structure for trade; and unilateral liberalization is viable as in the case of 19th-century Britain. When investment is transaction-specific, the discipline of the marketplace must be bolstered or replaced. A hegemonic country may act as an arbitrator and supporter of international institutions, thereby facilitating multilateral liberalization conducted at least cost under institutions such as the GATT during the period of U.S. hegemony. In a nonhegemonic politico-economic environment, agreements must become more self-contained. Minilateral, reciprocal agreements embodying binding precommitments to compliance are most likely to be successful under such circumstances; and such agreements have, in fact, become prevalent during the decline of U.S. hegemony.

Policy rivalry among industrial states: what can we learn from models of strategic trade policy?
Klaus Stegemann

The new international economics

The theory of international trade has changed drastically over the last decade by admitting into its mainstream a body of literature that focuses on the implications of monopolistic elements in international markets. Until the mid-1970s, trade theory had hardly been touched by the "monopolistic competition revolution."[1] Trade models were built on the assumption of perfect competition, thus ruling out product differentiation, scale economies, and barriers to entry. Furthermore, the mainstream models of international trade were entirely static, explaining trade flows on the basis of fixed factor endowments, given tastes, given products, and given technology. These models thus made no allowance for the possibility that a country's comparative advantage could change as a function of private economic activity or might even be shaped by government policy. Mainstream theories left little scope for trade policy to improve a nation's welfare. Only one case was generally conceded: the possibility that a "large" country by restricting free trade could exploit monopoly or monopsony power in international markets, if such power was not exploited by competing domestic exporters or importers, respectively; and even this single exception, the so-called "optimum tariff," was shown long ago to be potentially self-defeating if the trading partner to

I thank Jonas Fisher, Katrien Kesteloot, Stephen Krasner, Denis Paquin, Martin Prachowny, and an anonymous referee for helpful comments on earlier versions of this paper. A German translation has been published in Manfred E. Streit, ed., *Wirtschaftspolitik zwischen ökonomischer und politischer Rationalität: Festschrift für Herbert Giersch* (Wiesbaden: Gabler, 1988), pp. 3–25.

1. In this regard, little has changed in the ten years following Harry Johnson's comprehensive survey. Harry G. Johnson, "International Trade Theory and Monopolistic Competition Theory," in R. E. Kuenne, ed., *Monopolistic Competition Theory: Studies in Impact: Essays in Honor of E. H. Chamberlin* (New York: Wiley, 1967), pp. 203–18.

International Organization 41, 1, Winter 1989, pp. 73–100

be exploited took retaliatory measures.[2] Theories suggesting that countries should nurture a competitive advantage of certain industries through temporary protection remained essentially outside the mainstream in a special branch labeled "development economics" and were discounted for not being "rigorous" enough.[3]

This state of affairs changed dramatically in the early 1980s, when the "new international economics" burst on the scene.[4] Avinash Dixit did not exaggerate when summing up the apparent implications of the new wisdom for trade policy:

> Recent research contains support for almost all the vocal and popular views on trade policy that only a few years ago struggled against the economists' conventional wisdom of free trade. Now the mercantilist arguments for restricting imports and promoting exports are being justified on grounds of "profit shifting." The fears that other governments could capture permanent advantage in industry after industry by giving each a small initial impetus down the learning curve now emerge as results of impeccable formal models. The claim that one's own government should be aggressive in the pursuit of such policies because other governments do the same is no longer dismissed as a non sequitur.[5]

The term "strategic trade policy" was adopted to characterize one branch of the new thinking that has received the greatest attention in the economists'

2. Harry G. Johnson, "Optimum Tariffs and Retaliation," *Review of Economic Studies* 21 (1953–1954), pp. 142–53.

3. Albert O. Hirschman, *Essays in Trespassing: Economics to Politics and Beyond* (Cambridge: Cambridge University Press, 1981), pp. 1–24; Gerald M. Meier, *Leading Issues in Economic Development,* 4th ed. (New York and Oxford: Oxford University Press, 1984), pp. 111–47; Anne O. Krueger, "Trade Policies in Developing Countries," in R. W. Jones, ed., *International Trade: Surveys of Theory and Policy* (selections from the *Handbook of International Economics*) (Amsterdam: North-Holland, 1986), pp. 131–81. As Krugman candidly admits, "Lack of formalization essentially barred alternatives to comparative advantage, however plausible, from the mainstream of international economics." Paul R. Krugman, "New Theories of Trade Among Industrial Countries," *American Economic Review* 73 (May 1983), p. 343. While mainstream economics reluctantly tolerated the "infant-industry" argument for intervention, it was not accepted as a "first-best" argument for interfering with free trade, as discussed in a subsequent section of this article.

4. The original contributions, which appeared in the late 1970s and early 1980s, mostly in the form of journal articles, are too numerous to cite. An early synopsis was attempted by Krugman, "New Theories of Trade," pp. 343–47; and Gene M. Grossman and J. David Richardson, *Strategic Trade Policy: A Survey of Issues and Early Analysis,* Special Papers in International Economics, no. 15 (Princeton: International Finance Section, 1985). Several conference volumes include contributions from the principal proponents of the new international economics as well as pertinent references: Henryk Kierzkowski, ed., *Monopolistic Competition and International Trade* (Oxford: Clarendon Press, 1984); and Paul R. Krugman, ed., *Strategic Trade Policy and the New International Economics* (Cambridge, Mass.: MIT Press, 1986). See also the text by Elhanan Helpman and Paul R. Krugman, *Market Structure and Foreign Trade* (Cambridge, Mass.: MIT Press, 1985); and essays edited by David Greenaway and P. K. M. Tharakan, *Imperfect Competition and International Trade: The Policy Aspects of Intra-Industry Trade* (Brighton: Wheatsheaf Books, 1986).

5. Avinash K. Dixit, "Trade Policy: An Agenda for Research," in Krugman, *Strategic Trade Policy,* p. 283.

debate on the policy implications of new trade models. The attribute "strategic" indicates that these models incorporate international interdependence of policy actions in an oligopolistic environment. Thus, each government takes into account some response by foreign firms or governments in calculating its best course of action. In this article, two specific models of strategic trade policy will be examined more closely. One is by James Brander and Barbara Spencer, who have made several pioneering contributions to the literature on this subject.[6] Indeed, "Brander-Spencer profit shifting" has become almost a synonym for strategic trade policy. The other model is by Paul Krugman, who has shown how a country might gain by protecting its home market if this enables a domestic industry to move down the "learning curve" more rapidly relative to foreign rivals.[7] The overriding issue, to be discussed in later sections, is whether these models and others like them might justify a reorientation of trade policy. First, however, it will be useful to explain briefly what caused the new theories to emerge in the early 1980s.

As others have pointed out,[8] the new thinking on international trade was a response of the economics profession (mostly in North America) to three related challenges: new evidence that could not be explained with existing models, the availability of new analytical tools, and new (more urgent) demands for government intervention. The new evidence was first observed in Europe when the Common Market removed restrictions on trade in industrial products between member countries. Two phenomena, in particular, posed a challenge to the received theories of international trade. One was the observation that intra-industry specialization was much more important than inter-industry specialization in the Common Market.[9] Thus, member countries essentially retained the same industries as they might have without European integration, and rapidly growing trade consisted largely of an exchange of differentiated industrial products. Which country makes which products within any manufacturing industry and how successful a country is in comparison with other countries cannot be explained exclusively on the basis of differences in natural ability or factor proportions. Variables such as entrepreneurial initiative, investment in human capital, research and

6. See the following articles by James A. Brander and Barbara J. Spencer: "Tariffs and the Extraction of Foreign Monopoly Rents and Potential Entry," *Canadian Journal of Economics* 14 (August 1981), pp. 371–89; "Tariff Protection and Imperfect Competition," in Kierzkowski, *Monopolistic Competition and International Trade,* pp. 194–206; "Trade Warfare: Tariffs and Cartels," *Journal of International Economics* 16 (May 1984), pp. 227–42; "Export Subsidies and International Market Share Rivalry," *Journal of International Economics* 18 (February 1985), pp. 83–100; and "International R&D Rivalry and Industrial Strategy," *Review of Economic Studies* 50 (October 1983), pp. 707–22.

7. Paul R. Krugman, "Import Protection as Export Promotion: International Competition in the Presence of Oligopoly and Economies of Scale," in Kierzkowski, *Monopolistic Competition and International Trade,* pp. 180–93.

8. Krugman, "New Theories of Trade," pp. 343–47; and J. David Richardson, "The New Political Economy of Trade Policy," in Krugman, *Strategic Trade Policy,* pp. 257–82.

9. Bela Balassa, "Tariff Reductions and Trade in Manufactures Among the Industrial Countries," *American Economic Review* 56 (June 1966), pp. 466–73.

development, product design, economies of scale, and learning by doing were recognized to be crucial for the explanation of intra-industry trade. The other principal observation posing a challenge to received theories of international trade was the acknowledgment that fierce international rivalry was an important characteristic of many manufactured goods industries, especially those industries that would be called "growth industries" or "high tech" or "leading edge" industries.

The fact that the structure of such industries was oligopolistic and that firms might employ oligopolistic strategies in an international context was not as disturbing as the realization that countries (governments) might adopt strategic policy postures to improve the competitive position of their national industries. Again, this phenomenon first came to attention in Europe.[10] The creation of the Common Market in the early 1960s made national (and regional) governments especially conscious of new opportunities for growth and of rivalry among jurisdictions for the realization of these opportunities. Thus, governments in deploying what we now call "industrial policies" recognized that they were competing with other governments in the Common Market and that one government's policy choice could affect the decisions of another or the decisions of firms in another jurisdiction. For Europe as a whole, there also existed an awareness of rivalry with the United States, though the so-called "technology gap" and the direct investment challenge were not usually perceived to originate directly from U.S. government policy.[11] The notion of international policy rivalry became commonplace on both sides of the Atlantic when Japan, in less than a decade, matured from a lagging to a leading industrial nation. The speed and success of Japan's conversion seemed to require a new explanation. By some, the explanation was found in the legendary Japanese Ministry of International Trade and Industry (MITI), which was believed to have engineered the rapid change in Japan's comparative advantage.[12]

The emergence of new evidence alone could not have redirected mainstream theorizing on international trade if new analytical tools had not become available. In the main, the "new" international economics was developed by applying the tools of the "new" industrial organization in an international context.[13] From these endeavors emerged two classes of models

10. Klaus Stegemann, *Wettbewerb und Harmonisierung im Gemeinsamen Markt* (Cologne: Carl Heymanns, 1966), especially pp. 89–107 dealing with "growth competition" among industrial states.

11. M. V. Posner, "International Trade and Technical Change," *Oxford Economic Papers*, n. s. 13 (October 1961), pp. 323–41; Charles P. Kindleberger, *Foreign Trade and the National Economy* (New Haven, Conn.: Yale University Press, 1962), pp. 84–98.

12. Chalmers A. Johnson, *MITI and the Japanese Miracle: The Growth of Industrial Policy, 1925–1975* (Stanford, Calif.: Stanford University Press, 1982).

13. Alexis Jacquemin, *The New Industrial Organization: Market Forces and Strategic Behaviour* (Cambridge, Mass.: MIT Press, 1987). The subject of this article is discussed in the final chapter of Jacquemin's book, pp. 168–82. See also Paul R. Krugman, "Industrial Organization and International Trade," in R. Schmalensee and R. Willig, eds., *Handbook of Industrial Organization* (Amsterdam: North-Holland, forthcoming).

that have made a significant impact on the discussion of trade policy: models of intra-industry trade and models of strategic trade policy. Intra-industry trade models explain why similar industrial countries trade so much with each other and why so much of their trade consists of an exchange of similar products. The typical assumptions of these models correspond to Edward Chamberlin's model of monopolistic competition: a large number of producers (free entry), differentiated products, and increasing returns to scale for each product or variant.[14] The implications of the new models of intra-industry trade for economic policy are not seriously controversial because the implications tend to complement the policy recommendations derived from traditional trade models. Gains from trade are enhanced in the case of intra-industry trade because of greater utilization of scale economies (rationalization effect), greater product variety, and increased competition among suppliers of similar goods. Furthermore, potential objections to trade liberalization, such as adverse effects on the domestic income distribution and adjustment costs, tend to be weaker in the case of intra-industry trade.[15]

Models designed to explain intra-industry trade, with few exceptions,[16] imply that the production of traded goods is not associated with rents or external effects that might be captured by any of the participating countries. Thus, it does not matter for a country whether its industry specializes in the production of, say, electric toothbrushes, microwave ovens, or mainframe computers. This is the critical point on which the other class of new models differs. Indeed, for models of strategic trade policy, everything hinges on the assumption that increasing the domestic production of some tradable good or service means increasing a country's share in potential monopoly rents or external benefits associated with this activity. Thus "profit shifting" is the name of the game. The various models of strategic trade policy then show how government intervention could result in a national gain (usually at the expense of other countries) and what would be the optimum form of intervention for this purpose. The authors of these models typically use the theory of strategic games to model the policy behavior of a small number of countries acting as agents in support of domestic producers in an international oligopolistic industry. In the following two sections of this article,

14. A comprehensive survey of models of intra-industry trade can be found in David Greenaway and Chris Milner, *The Economics of Intra-Industry Trade* (Oxford: Basil Blackwell, 1986), pp. 7–55. It should be noted that Chamberlin used the term "monopolistic competition" to cover both his "large group case" and his "small group case." Edward H. Chamberlin, *The Theory of Monopolistic Competition* (Cambridge, Mass.: Harvard University Press, 1933). Current usage in economics reserves the term monopolistic competition for the large group case, whereas Chamberlin's small group case is called "oligopoly." As will become apparent below, models of strategic trade policy always assume the small group case, indeed usually the smallest group possible, duopoly. But oligopolistic structures have also been used to model intra-industry trade.

15. David Greenaway and P. K. M. Tharakan, "Imperfect Competition, Adjustment Policy, and Commercial Policy," in Greenaway and Tharakan, *Imperfect Competition and International Trade*, pp. 11–19.

16. James A. Brander, "Intra-Industry Trade in Identical Commodities," *Journal of International Economics* 11 (January 1981), pp. 1–14.

two representative models of strategic trade policy will be described in some detail.

The policy implications of models of strategic trade policy—taken at face value—were indeed disturbing. Suddenly, mainstream economists, using the latest tools of the trade, appeared to justify an "activist" trade policy or an "activist" industrial policy; suddenly, modes of intervention that had always been denounced by mainstream economists as "protectionist" or "mercantilist" policies were shown to enhance national welfare (rather than merely serving the interests of particular domestic groups at the expense of others). It is unlikely that the new wisdom would have attracted much attention had there not been a shift in the political mood in the United States towards greater protectionism.[17] The response of the economics profession was, of course, predominantly traditional. Thus, it would be pointed out that the (then) strong dollar was the primary cause of the declining international competitiveness of formerly leading U.S. industries, or that social trends (such as the power of organized labor and increased government regulation) had reduced the adaptability of the U.S. economy and that these trends ought to be reversed. Yet the mood was ripe for unorthodox thinking.

A crucial perceptual factor supporting intense protectionist sentiments in the United States is the feeling that American industries have fallen behind in international competition, not because of lack of effort or ability but because other countries are using "unfair" means to propel their own industries. This "collective nursing of grievance"[18] may reflect the trauma of a nation accustomed to being "number one" in most international contests that matter for the national image. In any event, as a result of this grievance, Americans became more interested in scrutinizing the economic policies of their trading partners, especially Japan. Popular writings on the "Japanese challenge"[19] painted a picture of the U.S. economy becoming the castaway residual of other countries' sectoral planning. To defend its economic prosperity, the United States would have to join the game, would have to implement its own industrial policy, or would at least have to deter other countries from taking advantage of American naiveté and openness.

Not surprisingly, the new models of strategic trade policy were embraced warmly by those who favored a more activist industrial policy but had lacked

17. The reasons for this shift have been summarized admirably in J. David Richardson, "The New Political Economy of Trade Policy," pp. 259–70. As shown in detail by Destler, the capacity of U.S. institutions to resist protectionist pressures had been eroding for many years prior to the early 1980s, when protectionist forces appeared to gain the upper hand. I. M. Destler, *American Trade Politics: System Under Stress* (Washington, D.C.: Institute for International Economics, and New York: Twentieth Century Fund, 1986), chaps. 3–8. For a qualifying view, see Judith L. Goldstein, "The Political Economy of Trade: Institutions of Protection," *American Political Science Review* 80 (March 1986), pp. 161–84.

18. Richardson, "The New Political Economy of Trade Policy," p. 266.

19. Michael Borrus, *Responses to the Japanese Challenge in High Technology: Innovation, Maturity, and the U.S.–Japanese Competition in Micro-electronics* (Berkeley, Calif.: Berkeley Roundtable on the International Economy, 1983).

formal models to support their recommendations.[20] But the new theories seemed to be welcomed also by a significant segment of the traditionally anti-interventionist economics profession.[21] At last in good conscience, economists could recommend (tolerate) popular modes of government intervention because it had been demonstrated in formal models that, in situations of strategic international rivalry, intervention could serve to enhance national welfare. The most dramatic break with past doctrine, however, was the apparent implication of the new models that trade policy should be used as an instrument of industrial policy.[22] Models of strategic trade policy seemed to destroy the near-consensus shared by all economists that trade policy typically is not an efficient way of intervening.

As will be shown below, a more sober assessment is beginning to take hold. Indeed, the authors of the theories of strategic trade policy are anxious to put some distance between themselves and those who recommend an activist trade policy or industrial policy.[23] It is now recognized that the new theories are incomplete or are at least insufficiently developed to serve as a basis for policy advice. Models of strategic trade policy merely demonstrate the possibility that a government, under certain assumptions, can improve national welfare by "shifting profits" from foreign to domestic producers. A theoretical possibility does not necessarily imply that such a policy could be implemented successfully under real-world conditions. However, it seems

20. Krugman, *Strategic Trade Policy,* pp. 18–19; and Michael Borrus, Laura D'Andrea Tyson, and John Zysman, "Creating Advantage: How Government Policies Shape International Trade in the Semiconductor Industry," in Krugman, *Strategic Trade Policy,* pp. 92–94.

21. Richard G. Harris, *Trade, Industrial Policy and International Competition* (Toronto: University of Toronto Press, 1985).

22. Definitions of "industrial policy" vary. For the purpose of this article, Brander's suggested definition is most appropriate: "Industrial policy should be thought of as involving some form of industry-, firm-, or project-specific policy (targeting), and arising from a coordinated government plan to influence industrial structure in particular, well-defined ways (coordination)." James A. Brander, "Shaping Comparative Advantage: Trade Policy, Industrial Policy, and Economic Performance," in R. G. Lipsey and W. Dobson, eds., *Shaping Comparative Advantage,* Policy Study no. 2 (Toronto: C. D. Howe Institute, 1987), p. 29. Having surveyed the writings of principal proponents of a coordinated industrial policy for the United States (ibid., pp. 28–42), Brander found to his surprise that "the industrial policy advocates reviewed here all claim to oppose protection and to support an open trading system" (ibid., p. 52). Yet this seems to be a matter of semantics. Targeting of traded products or of "strategic" sectors, in competition with other industrial states, almost inevitably (and deliberately) affects international trade. Thus, the borderline between trade policy and other instruments of industrial policy becomes blurred if one considers targeting of specific goods or industries in a strategic international context. Indeed, proponents of a common industrial policy for the European Community have insisted on treating internal-market policies and external-trade policies as integral parts of a unified strategy aimed at helping European advanced-technology sectors to become competitive with their American and Japanese rivals. Joan Pearce and John Sutton with Roy Batchelor, *Protection and Industrial Policy in Europe* (London: Routledge & Kegan Paul for the Royal Institute of International Affairs, 1986), pp. 4–9 and chaps. 4–6 and 11.

23. Brander, "Shaping Comparative Advantage," pp. 27–28 and 39–41; Paul R. Krugman, "Strategic Sectors and International Competition," in R. M. Stern, ed., *U.S. Trade Policies in a Changing World Economy* (Cambridge, Mass.: MIT Press, 1987), p. 207; and Paul R. Krugman, "Is Free Trade Passé?" *Economic Perspectives* 1 (Fall 1987), pp. 138–43.

clear also that the economics profession cannot simply return to its previous policy posture, even if the current models of strategic trade policy have been found wanting as blueprints for policy action. This point will be argued in the concluding section.

One final introductory remark seems in order: All models of strategic trade policy are based on the assumption that it is the objective of any government's economic policy measures to enhance the welfare of its own jurisdiction. Thus, for a nation-state, the government's objective is to enhance national welfare, duly taking account of all relevant repercussions. It should be understood that this assumption is by no means novel or restricted to models of strategic trade policy. Indeed, as Eli Heckscher has pointed out, the objective of national welfare maximization was common to mercantilists and classical free traders; the free trade doctrine was cosmopolitan only in its consequences:

> From the point of view of economic policy . . . the most important aspect to note is that it was out of concern for the interests of their own country that free trade theorists demanded free exchange with other countries. Had it been otherwise their views would obviously not have had much prospect of success in any country, and certainly not in England.[24]

Maximization of national welfare is also assumed to be the government's objective in most neoclassical contributions to the normative theory of trade.[25] Therefore, one should not conclude that the new theories of strategic trade policy can be characterized as "nationalistic" or "mercantilist" because their authors have assumed a different policy objective. They have not. The point of models of strategic trade policy is that the classical harmony between national and cosmopolitan welfare maximization may disappear if one assumes opportunities for strategic manipulation of international oligopolistic industries. In other words, the authors of the new theories have demonstrated that a country could enhance national welfare at the expense of other countries' welfare in a range of circumstances not previously considered by traditional trade theory, which conceded an international policy conflict only for the optimum tariff case. However, the term "mercantilist" occasionally is used in this article as a convenient way of expressing the sentiment that has been associated with this term since Adam Smith, namely, that a certain policy is judged to be shortsighted or futile from a national welfare per-

24. Eli F. Heckscher, *Mercantilism*, vol. 2, translated by M. Shapiro, revised edition edited by E. F. Soderlund (London: Allen & Unwin, 1955), pp. 13–14. See also Lionel Robbins, *The Theory of Economic Policy in English Classical Political Economy* (London: Macmillan, 1952), pp. 9–11.

25. Corden's comprehensive review of the post–World War II literature on the subject clearly bears out the statement in the text: W. M. Corden, "The Normative Theory of International Trade," in Jones, *International Trade*, pp. 63–130. See also W. M. Corden, *Trade Policy and Economic Welfare* (Oxford: Clarendon Press, 1974), especially pp. 2–5.

spective because of factors not considered (or suppressed) by the proponents of the policy.

Profit shifting between countries: an application of Stackelberg's duopoly solution

Models of strategic trade policy attempt to formalize the popular notion that a government can enhance national welfare by promoting domestic development of industries that create substantial factor rents or external benefits. The models pioneered by James Brander and Barbara Spencer focus on strategies that might shift monopoly profits from a foreign to a domestic producer. Monopoly profits are assumed to occur for an international industry because entry to the industry is restricted. The idea of profit shifting can be explained most easily with reference to a 1985 version of the Brander-Spencer model,[26] which corresponds closely to Heinrich von Stackelberg's "asymmetrical" duopoly solution.[27]

Brander and Spencer assume an industry consisting of two firms making a homogeneous product. The two firms are located in two different countries and serve a common export market in a third country. In fact, Brander and Spencer assume initially that all sales and profits are made in the third country. This assumption enables them to equate an increase in a national producer's profit (minus subsidies) with an increase in national welfare. The problem of profit shifting, then, is how intervention by the government of one of the producing countries can increase the profit that its domestic producer extracts from the duopolists' common export market.[28]

Each firm in the Brander-Spencer model is assumed to use output as its action parameter (choice variable). Both are assumed to behave like Cournot duopolists; that is, each chooses its rate of deliveries to the common export market on the assumption that the other producer's rate of deliveries is given. In the absence of government intervention, the equilibrium in the Brander-Spencer model thus corresponds to the Cournot (Nash) solution. But as Stackelberg discovered over fifty years ago, a sophisticated duopolist who anticipates the other firm's Cournot adjustment to his own changes in output can do better than a Cournot duopolist. Each supplier can increase its profit by occupying an "independent supply position" (now called

26. Brander and Spencer, "Export Subsidies."

27. Heinrich von Stackelberg, *Grundlagen der theoretischen Volkswirtschaftslehre*, 2d ed. (Tübingen: J. C. B. Mohr, 1951), pp. 206–18; and Stackelberg, *The Theory of the Market Economy*, trans. Alan T. Peacock (London: W. Hodge, 1952), pp. 190–204. I am referring to Stackelberg's textbook, in the German and English versions, because the textbook is most accessible. Stackelberg first published his duopoly solution in various places in 1932–34, including *Marktform und Gleichgewicht* (Vienna: J. Springer, 1934), pp. 16–24.

28. Potential effects of intervention on the welfare of consumers in the two producing countries are integrated into the model at later stages. Brander and Spencer, "Export Subsidies," pp. 90–91 and 94–95.

"Stackelberg leader" position) if its rival is content to take a Cournot duopolist's "dependent supply position" (now called "Stackelberg follower" position).[29] Brander and Spencer use exactly this idea for their basic model of international profit shifting, except that they cast the government of one of the producing countries in the role of a rule maker that manipulates its national firm to act as if it were the Stackelberg leader. Thus, while both firms behave like Cournot duopolists all of the time, one government is assumed to grant an export subsidy (which in this case is equivalent to a production subsidy) to induce its national champion to produce the volume that corresponds to the Stackelberg leader position, whereas the other government is assumed to remain inactive. The outcome is, of course, the same as for Stackelberg's asymmetrical duopoly: the total volume of sales is increased by the intervention and per-unit profit falls, but because the follower "makes room for the leader," the leading country's share of the market increases sufficiently to increase its total profit; meanwhile, the follower's profit is reduced because the follower sells a lower volume than it would without the intervention and receives less per unit.

As acknowledged by Brander and Spencer, an "important assumption" of their model is "that the government understands the structure of the industry and is able to set a credible subsidy on exports in advance of the quantity decision by firms."[30] Indeed, the assumption that a government can make a credible commitment to maintaining a leadership position while a firm cannot do so is the only reason that Brander and Spencer need (can justify) government intervention in their model. Even without intervention, each duopolist would have an incentive to occupy the position of a Stackelberg leader if its rival would be content to act as a follower. But moving from a Cournot equilibrium to a leadership position is not considered a "credible choice" for either firm acting on its own, because the other duopolist cannot be expected to reduce its output. In the absence of government intervention, the two firms are assumed to be on an equal footing. Each knows that an expansion of output by either duopolist cannot be profitable if the other is determined not to retreat. An export subsidy for one firm changes the situation. Expansion of the subsidized firm's output is now regarded as a "credible choice" by its rival because an expansion would be privately profitable even if the rival would not reduce its output. "In essence, the government's prior action in setting a subsidy changes the domestic firm's set of credible actions."[31] This statement by Brander and Spencer

---

29. Stackelberg, *Grundlagen*, pp. 210–11; and *Theory of the Market Economy*, pp. 194–95. While Alan Peacock's translation used the literal equivalent of "Unabhängigkeitsangebot" and "Abhängigkeitsangebot," the now common terms "leader" and "follower" were adopted very early to describe Stackelberg's duopoly in English. Wassily Leontief, "Stackelberg on Monopolistic Competition," *Journal of Political Economy* 44 (August 1936), pp. 555–56.

30. Brander and Spencer, "Export Subsidies," p. 85.

31. Ibid., p. 89. See also James A. Brander, "Rationales for Strategic Trade and Industrial Policy," in Krugman, *Strategic Trade Policy*, pp. 28–29.

implies that the acting government, in the view of the foreign firm, is "credibly committed" to its intervention; thus, the foreign firm must believe that subsidization would continue even in the event that the attempted profit shifting failed because the foreign firm refused to retreat. Brander and Spencer suggest that government intervention is credible in this sense because governments have an incentive, known to all agents, to maintain a "reputation" for credibility.[32]

The subsidy, by lowering the firm's marginal cost, has the effect of shifting outward the subsidized firm's reaction curve.[33] With both duopolists moving along their reaction curves, a new Cournot equilibrium is attained at an increased level of output for the subsidized firm and at a reduced level for its foreign rival. To be optimal from a national point of view, the rate of subsidization must be such that it moves the Cournot equilibrium to a position that is equivalent to the asymmetrical Stackelberg solution that would be attained if the domestic duopolist were able to act as a leader in the absence of subsidization. However, the type of intervention is not crucial, as long as the government is credibly committed. An intervention causing an equivalent irreversible capacity decision might actually be more credible than an export subsidy.[34] Gene Grossman and J. David Richardson have pointed out that the intervention must be visible and transparent to be credible to the foreign rival.[35] Hidden subsidies would not serve the purpose of strategic trade policy as modeled by Brander and Spencer. Yet hidden subsidies might serve the same purpose if they induced domestic producers to make an appropriate irreversible commitment that is visible and credible to foreign rivals.

Brander and Spencer are, of course, aware that it is not sufficient to simply show that one producing country has a unilateral incentive to capture a larger share of a profitable export market: "Surely the two producing nations face similar incentives and there also may be some response by the importing nation."[36] They thus proceed to examine the case of a Cournot (Nash) equilibrium in subsidies in which each exporting country is assumed to choose its best subsidy level, taking the subsidy level of the other country as given. Not surprisingly, Brander and Spencer arrive at the conclusion that the "noncooperative solution is jointly suboptimal for the producing

32. Brander and Spencer, "Export Subsidies," p. 84. Jacquemin suggests that government intervention has credibility "based on its reputation and/or resources or because of the expected inertia of policies, once adopted." Jacquemin, *The New Industrial Organization,* p. 172.

33. The passage in the text refers to a well-known graph that has been used since Stackelberg to illustrate his oligopoly solution and related ones. For details, consult any intermediate microeconomics text or an industrial organization text, such as Roger Clarke, *Industrial Economics* (Oxford: Basil Blackwell, 1985), pp. 45–47.

34. Avinash K. Dixit, "The Role of Investment in Entry Deterrence," *Economic Journal* 90 (March 1980), pp. 95–106; and "How Should the United States Respond to Other Countries' Trade Policies?" in Stern, *U.S. Trade Policies in a Changing World Economy,* pp. 245–82.

35. Grossman and Richardson, *Strategic Trade Policy: Survey of Issues,* p. 11.

36. Brander and Spencer, "Export Subsidies," p. 94.

countries,"[37] which means that the total profit extracted from the export market is less than it would be with a cooperative solution. The jointly optimal policy would be for both producing countries to impose a tax on exports to the third country, thereby shifting the duopolists' reaction curves inward. The optimal set of tax rates would be such that the duopolists are induced to move from the Cournot solution to the lower export levels of a profit-maximizing cartel. Brander and Spencer assume that the producing countries are "unable to make binding agreements of this sort."[38]

In sum, the Brander-Spencer model of strategic trade policy comprises all three cases that Stackelberg added to the Cournot solution: Stackelberg's asymmetrical duopoly; the case of both duopolists trying to be leaders simultaneously (Bowley's duopoly); and the case of joint monopolization.[39] Each case can be brought about in the model by government intervention that changes the "set of credible actions" for one or both producers. Brander and Spencer emphasize the asymmetrical case because they wish to demonstrate why a government might have an incentive to subsidize sales to a profitable export market. But do they have a policy conclusion? While the first case suggests an aggressive policy, the second counsels retaliation (which might lead to mutually agreed policy abstention), and the third comes closest to orthodox theory in recommending agreed export restrictions to exploit jointly held market power. Brander admits that the policy implications of the profit-shifting model are not very robust to changes in assumptions, but he believes that the basic point is more general than the specific model: "This point is that government action can alter the strategic game played by foreign and domestic firms. In profitable markets domestic firms are made better off if foreign firms can be induced to contract (or to expand more slowly than they otherwise would)."[40] Thus, it seems useful to broaden the argument somewhat by reviewing briefly one other prominent model of strategic trade policy before asking questions about the practical policy implications of the new theories.

Racing down the learning curve: a strategic infant-industry argument

Paul Krugman has designed a model that adds a strategic dimension to the familiar infant-industry argument for government intervention.[41] Historically and in popular view, the infant-industry problem has always been perceived as a problem of international rivalry, particularly policy rivalry between old

37. Ibid., p. 95.
38. Ibid., p. 96.
39. Stackelberg, *Theory of the Market Economy*, pp. 194–95.
40. Brander, "Rationales for Strategic Trade," p. 30.
41. Krugman, "Import Protection as Export Promotion."

industrial countries and aspiring ones. Alexander Hamilton, whose 1791 "Report on the Subject of Manufactures" presented the reasons why he and many of his contemporaries believed that temporary protection was required to help fledgling American manufacturing industries become established, included the suggestion that conspiracies of foreign producers, possibly with the support of a foreign government, might have attempted to discourage the development of manufacturing in the United States. Indeed, the following passage describes very succinctly the interaction of moves and counter-moves typical of strategic policy postures and even includes the notion of credibility provided by state intervention:

> Combinations by those engaged in a particular branch of business in one country, to frustrate the first efforts to introduce it into another, by temporary sacrifices, recompensed perhaps by extraordinary indemnifications of the government of such country, are believed to have existed, and are not to be regarded as destitute of probability. The existence or assurance of aid from the government of the country, in which the business is to be introduced, may be essential to fortify adventurers against the dread of such combinations, to defeat their effects, if formed and to prevent their being formed, by demonstrating that they must in the end prove fruitless.[42]

But as presented in contemporary trade texts until the early 1980s, the infant-industry argument had been purged of its strategic dimension; that is, the theoretical argument for intervention did not depend on recognized policy rivalry or on anticipated reactions by foreign rival firms.[43]

The thrust of the textbook argument has been that the case for supporting infant industries, if valid at all, is based on the existence of "domestic distortions" in the intervening country.[44] Three types of relevant distortions are commonly mentioned in the literature: imperfections in the capital market that make it impossible (or too expensive) for potentially profitable new industries to get started; external benefits of learning by doing that occur

---

42. Alexander Hamilton, "Report on the Subject of Manufactures" (1791), in H. C. Syrett, ed., *The Papers of Alexander Hamilton*, vol. 10 (New York and London: Columbia University Press, 1966), pp. 268–69. The suggestion that other states had to use temporary protection for their manufacturing industries to overcome British retardation strategies was spelled out in greater detail by Friedrich List, *The National System of Political Economy*, trans. S. S. Lloyd (London: Longmans, Green, 1885). See especially pp. 86–87 (the case of Prussia), 94–103 (the United States), and 388–402 (the German Zollverein).

43. See, for example, Richard E. Caves and Ronald W. Jones, *World Trade and Payments* (Boston: Little, Brown, 1973), pp. 260–61 and 556–57; Miltiades Chacholiades, *International Trade Theory and Policy* (New York: McGraw-Hill, 1978), pp. 525–30; and Wilfred J. Ethier, *Modern International Economics* (New York: W. W. Norton, 1983), pp. 200–202. An exception is Richardson, who in his 1980 textbook offered an "old-fashioned" strategic interpretation of the infant-industry argument. J. David Richardson, *Understanding International Economics: Theory and Practice* (Boston and Toronto: Little, Brown, 1980), pp. 291–94.

44. Corden, "Normative Theory of International Trade," pp. 91–92. For a more extensive review of the literature on infant-industry arguments and "pseudo-infant-industry arguments," see Corden, *Trade Policy and Economic Welfare*, pp. 248–79.

when pioneering firms cannot retain the workers they train during the start-up phase; and external benefits of learning by doing that result from knowledge diffusion, which again may be particularly significant during the infancy stage of an industry. For each type of distortion, the optimum form of intervention is a domestic intervention, such as loan guarantees, training assistance, or subsidies for research and development, respectively. Temporary protection of the home market would be an unnecessarily costly form of intervention, since the problem that policymakers are trying to correct is not a "trade distortion."[45] Foreign firms or foreign governments have no parts to play in the traditional textbook exposition.[46] The acting country is a small country that takes world market prices as given. An intervention enabling an infant industry to slide down its learning curve gradually expands the country's production possibility frontier. National welfare increases because the country is able to do more with given resources. But there are no rents to be shifted between countries, and no responses are expected from foreign firms or governments. Being an extension of the traditional trade model, the traditional infant-industry argument assumes a perfectly competitive world market, with numerous foreign firms that have finished learning, and a domestic industry that requires temporary assistance to catch up.

Krugman[47] radically redirected the focus of the analysis by making unorthodox assumptions that imply that there is an opportunity for a country to achieve a different kind of welfare gain through the strategic deployment of import restrictions. His analysis depends on two basic ingredients: international oligopoly and economies of scale. Regarding oligopoly, Krugman assumes two firms, one domestic and one foreign. Each firm produces a single product that it sells in several segmented markets, for example, domestic and foreign markets. The products of the two firms are close substitutes, but they need not be perfect substitutes. Like Brander and Spencer, Krugman assumes that both firms at all times act as Cournot duopolists. The result is "a multi-market Cournot model."[48] Regarding his second basic ingredient, Krugman distinguishes three different forms of scale economies leading to as many versions of his general model. It is only in the third version, when Krugman introduces economies of learning by doing, that his analysis comes close to the familiar infant-industry argument, although the conclusion is the same in each version: by giving its domestic producer a privileged position in the home market, a country gives it an advantage in scale of production over a foreign rival; this scale advantage translates into lower marginal costs and higher market share even in unprotected markets.[49]

45. Corden, "Normative Theory of International Trade," p. 92.
46. For a typical example, see Chacholiades, *International Trade Theory and Policy,* pp. 528–30.
47. Krugman, "Import Protection as Export Promotion."
48. Ibid., p. 182.
49. Ibid., p. 181.

When one government excludes the foreign producer from a market previously open to it, the intervention causes opposite effects on the marginal cost of the two rivals. The domestic producer will sell more in its market from which the foreign rival has been excluded, and thus, the domestic firm's marginal cost will fall; the foreign firm's marginal cost will rise as it produces less when excluded from the protected market.[50] But the effects do not end here, because both firms are induced by opposite changes in their marginal cost to adjust sales also in unprotected markets. The domestic firm will expand its output further, while the foreign firm will retreat some more. These adjustments again have opposite effects on each firm's marginal cost, and the process continues until a new multimarket Cournot equilibrium is reached. The essential feature of the model thus is the circular causation from output to marginal cost to output; and it is this circularity that "makes import protection an export promotion device."[51] Krugman does not provide a national welfare analysis for his model of strategic trade policy. Yet it is clearly implied in his argument that additional exports are profitable for the domestic producer; thus, export prices must exceed marginal cost, and the expansion of exports must result in a higher absolute profit from foreign sales. It is, therefore, conceivable that the country's welfare gain due to additional profits on exports and lower costs of output sold domestically exceeds the loss of consumers' surplus caused by protection of the home market.

At this point, it must be obvious that Krugman's strategy is simply Brander-Spencer profit shifting by other means. Indeed, Krugman employs the same formal apparatus as Brander and Spencer, except for his assumptions concerning scale economies and market segmentation. His Figure 11.5 clearly illustrates this connection: home market protection moves out the domestic duopolist's reaction curve in the unprotected market, but it also shifts in the foreign duopolist's reaction curve.[52] The result is a new Cournot equilibrium in which the domestic firm gains a greater market share in the export market for two reasons: its reduced marginal cost has made expansion attractive, and the foreign rival is willing to retreat. By symmetry, the foreign firm has two reasons to retreat: its rival's credible expansion and its own higher marginal cost. As in the Brander-Spencer model, the strategic rationale of government intervention is that the intervention induces a profitable expansion of export sales when it would not be credible for any duopolist to attempt such an expansion on its own. Krugman does not determine the optimal level of intervention that would correspond to attaining the Stackelberg

---

50. For simplicity, Krugman assumes that home market protection takes the form of total exclusion of the foreign rival, thereby allowing the domestic producer to move from a Cournot duopoly equilibrium to a monopoly position. A nonprohibitive tariff or quota would have the same result, in principle, because the duopolists would move to a new Cournot equilibrium entailing a lower rate of sales for the foreign firm and a higher rate for the domestic firm in the protected market.

51. Krugman, "Import Protection as Export Promotion," p. 185.

52. Ibid., p. 186. See also footnote 33 above.

leadership position in the Brander-Spencer model, nor does he deal with the case of two (or more) countries facing similar incentives, let alone cases in which countries of different size are involved.[53]

Racing down the learning curve in the Krugman model motivates government intervention only because of its strategic effect. The domestic firm extracts a higher profit from an export market because a foreign rival makes room for the government-supported firm. While Krugman in one version of his model assumes "dynamic" returns to scale that are also required for the traditional infant-industry argument, he does not depend on external benefits of learning by doing, or any other domestic distortion, to motivate government intervention. Yet much of the nonformal discussion of strategic trade policy, and of the "technology race" in particular, has emphasized external benefits of generating knowledge as the reason for protecting or promoting certain strategic sectors. Indeed, in a recent paper, Krugman has discounted the profit-shifting motive for strategic trade policy and has suggested that "the best bet for finding strategic sectors may be to focus on external benefits."[54] But he then proceeds to show why only a subset of knowledge-generating industries might justify intervention to establish a domestic presence in those industries. Krugman distinguishes three types of knowledge: knowledge that can be internalized by firms, knowledge that spreads beyond firms but not beyond national boundaries, and knowledge that once generated becomes available internationally.[55] In the first case, there is no external benefit and no reason for intervention. In the third case, externalities occur, but there is no reason for any country to be concerned about maintaining domestic activities to generate this type of knowledge if it is available internationally. Only the "middle ground" of geographically limited diffusion of knowledge might motivate intervention to secure this type of externality for the domestic economy in competition with other countries.[56]

Models designed to demonstrate that countries can gain by promoting domestic development of strategic sectors that create substantial external benefits could use essentially the same structure as models of international profit shifting. But the case for intervention can be made more compelling by the inclusion of "first-mover advantages" that might enable a country to preempt foreign rivals or to attract a larger share of rents for domestic factors of production.[57] The general point is that trade patterns and potential gains

53. Making the appropriate assumptions, one can show that home market protection might force the foreign rival to go out of business or not to enter the industry in the first place. Thus, home market protection would establish an international monopoly position for the domestic firm. See Jacquemin, *New Industrial Organization,* pp. 172–74.

54. Krugman, "Strategic Sectors and International Competition," p. 221.

55. Ibid., p. 222.

56. Helpman and Krugman, *Market Structure and Foreign Trade,* pp. 45–66.

57. "First-mover advantages" are defined by O. E. Williamson, *Markets and Hierarchies* (New York: Free Press, 1975), p. 34. "The basic phenomenon is this: Winners of initial contracts acquire, in learning-by-doing fashion, non-trivial information advantages over nonwinners." Other first-mover advantages include occupying the best locations, hiring the most suitable

from trade are more sensitive to policy intervention if one removes the orthodox assumptions of constant returns to scale and perfect competition. As Brander states, "Particularly with dynamic increasing returns, current policy can have important permanent effects on trade because temporary learning advantages can lead to long-term comparative advantage."[58] By the same token, potential first-mover advantages could be a reason for several countries to become caught in technology races that cause overinvestment and losses to all.

Do models of strategic trade policy provide guidance for government action?

There can be no doubt that the theory of international trade has been revitalized dramatically by at last receiving (accepting) an infusion of ideas from models that formerly were used almost exclusively for the field of domestic industrial organization. The revitalization has manifested itself as a rich yield of theoretical and empirical research.[59] By design, this research came much closer than the traditional international economics to dealing with problems that concern individual firms, industries, interest groups, and policymakers in the real world. Moreover, as economists undertook to focus on questions that had previously been excluded by the assumption of perfect competition, there appeared to develop a new consensus concerning the strategic potential of activist trade policy or activist industrial policy.

Traditionally, the question whether policymakers ought to be concerned with the promotion of certain strategic sectors that constitute valuable stakes in international competition could be viewed as a sort of litmus test for distinguishing between trained economists and lay commentators. Whereas for an economist trained in traditional trade theory there exists no reason to favor the domestic development of particular sectors over all other sectors, "to non-economists (and a few defrocked economists) it seems obvious that some sectors are more desirable than others."[60] This dichotomy became

---

internationally mobile talent, securing the first patents, setting industry standards, and so forth. Trade-related aspects of first-mover advantages are reviewed by Harris, *Trade, Industrial Policy and International Competition,* pp. 86–92. I am not aware of formal models of strategic trade policy that have incorporated this concept, except for Kala Krishna, "High Tech Trade Policy," Discussion Paper no. 1300 (Cambridge, Mass.: Harvard Institute of Economic Research, 1987), who recently developed a trade model demonstrating the advantage for first movers of determining industry standards. See also R. C. Rao and David P. Rutenberg, "Preempting an Alert Rival: Strategic Timing of the First Plant by Analysis of Sophisticated Rivalry," *Bell Journal of Economics* 10 (Autumn 1979), pp. 412–28.

58. Brander, "Shaping Comparative Advantage," p. 12. See also Paul R. Krugman, "The Narrow Moving Band, the Dutch Disease, and the Competitive Consequences of Mrs. Thatcher," *Journal of Development Economics* 27 (October 1987), pp. 41–55.

59. Richard E. Caves, "International Trade and Industrial Organization: Problems, Solved and Unsolved," *European Economic Review* 28 (August 1985), pp. 377–95.

60. Krugman, "Strategic Sectors and International Competition," p. 208.

much less distinct with the advent of the new international economics. Indeed, visitors to the Cambridge, Massachusetts, area in 1984 might have believed they were witnessing a doctrinal revolution: the Young Turks of the profession had joined popular "defrocked" economists in attacking the old wisdom, "strategic" appeared to be synonymous with "divine," and the salvation of the American economy seemed to depend on the acceptance of the new gospel. Only three years later, all signs point towards restoration. The heretics are recanting, and the economics profession is again closing ranks against any kind of protectionist ideas. Why did the attempted revolution go by so quickly? A combination of reasons seems to have been responsible: the realization that the apparent policy implications of models of strategic trade policy are highly sensitive to changes in the special assumptions of these models; the difficulty of identifying real-world situations in which the special assumptions apply; the recognition that the costs of implementing strategic trade policies might easily exceed the benefits, even if appropriate "target" industries could be identified; and the apprehension that economic theory was becoming a supplier of intellectual ammunition for powerful forces that favor protection of particular sectors for the "wrong" reasons.

By now there exists a substantial literature discussing the intrinsic shortcomings of models of strategic trade policy. On a purely theoretical level, the general message is that the new clothes, though elegantly tailored, tend to be rather fragile. Jonathan Eaton and Gene Grossman have made this point by providing a synopsis of models of strategic trade or strategic industrial policy for a variety of assumptions about market structure and firm behavior.[61] Under the Brander and Spencer assumptions,[62] an export subsidy should be used to shift oligopolistic profits towards the domestic firm; yet the optimal intervention changes to an export tax if one substitutes Bertrand conjectural variations for Cournot behavior.[63] Indeed, any type of government intervention becomes welfare-reducing if one assumes that the home firm's conjectures are "consistent" in the sense that its beliefs about the foreign firm's response to its own actions are borne out exactly by the foreign firm's actual response; a domestic duopolist needs no prompting to assume the position of a Stackelberg leader if it correctly anticipates its foreign rival to act as a follower in the absence of intervention. As Stackelberg recognized early on, the asymmetrical solution could be an equilibrium if one of the duopolists is "manifestly stronger" than the other.[64] Government interven-

---

61. Jonathan Eaton and Gene M. Grossman, "Optimal Trade and Industrial Policy Under Oligopoly," *Quarterly Journal of Economics* 101 (May 1986), pp. 383–406.

62. Brander and Spencer, "Export Subsidies."

63. Eaton and Grossman, "Optimal Trade and Industrial Policy Under Oligopoly," pp. 391–93. J. Bertrand, in an 1883 critique of Cournot's duopoly model, demonstrated that the equilibrium outcome was altered drastically if one assumed that each duopolist conjectured that its rival's price (rather than output) would not change in response to its own actions. See Clarke, *Industrial Economics*, p. 44.

64. Stackelberg, *Theory of the Market Economy*, p. 194.

tion is not indicated either if the foreign rival proves unwilling to make room for the domestic firm's expansion in spite of state support. Thus, even if the structure of the most simplified Brander-Spencer model is assumed, the conjectural element of the oligopolistic relationship makes it practically impossible to extract a reliable policy prescription. According to Grossman and Richardson, "The case for active trade policy in an imperfectly competitive environment rests crucially on the behavior of oligopolistic firms. One might even say it rests uneasily, since the behavior in question has to do with intrinsically subjective conjectures."[65]

Policy prescriptions derived from Brander-Spencer type models also tend to be highly sensitive to the values of certain parameters, such as the number of firms assumed to exist in the acting country. If the number is greater than one, there arises a conflict between the profit-shifting motive for intervention and the traditional terms-of-trade motive which would require an export tax to utilize the country's market power in the export market. The Brander-Spencer prescription of an export subsidy holds only if the number of domestic firms is "not too large."[66] Furthermore, export subsidies or other measures promoting home production are likely to cause the number of firms to increase. Such policy-induced entry can raise the industry's average cost and can cause all benefits of profit shifting (plus subsidies) to be dissipated.[67] It should also be recalled that the Brander-Spencer prescription for profit shifting was derived under the simplifying assumption that the good in question is not consumed in the acting country. When domestic consumption is introduced into these models, two additional motives for intervention appear which may again lead to different policy prescriptions.[68] The prevalence of several conflicting motives for intervention in itself represents an obstacle to implementing strategic trade policies, because the government has to balance the different motives and would have to use more than one policy tool to achieve an optimal outcome. Further compensating interventions would be required if the strategic intervention has undesired effects on the domestic distribution of income. Finally, critics of models of strategic trade policy have pointed out that a policy designed to shift profits from foreign to domestic producers can increase national welfare only to the extent that the affected domestic producers are domestically owned.[69] This condition is becoming more questionable every day as we witness the spread of multinational firms, international joint ventures, and partnerships, particularly in industries that are typically considered targets for strategic intervention.

65. Grossman and Richardson, *Strategic Trade Policy: Survey of Issues,* p. 14.

66. Eaton and Grossman, "Optimal Trade and Industrial Policy Under Oligopoly," p. 397.

67. Ignatius Horstmann and James R. Markusen, "Up the Average Cost Curve: Inefficient Entry and the New Protectionism," *Journal of International Economics* 20 (May 1986), pp. 225–47.

68. Eaton and Grossman, "Optimal Trade and Industrial Policy Under Oligopoly," pp. 399–403.

69. Krugman, "Strategic Sectors and International Competition," p. 219; and Beth V. Yarbrough and Robert M. Yarbrough, *The World Economy: Trade and Finance* (Chicago: Dryden Press, 1988), p. 254.

The authors of models of strategic trade policy have had a difficult time trying to identify real-world industries to which their policy prescriptions might apply. Barbara Spencer has suggested seven broad characteristics of industries for which "targeting" by trade policy (or equivalent industrial policy) is "most likely to lead to a national benefit."[70] While consistent with the models from which they have been derived, her criteria are still too ambiguous to serve as a guide for practical policy. Take, for example, Spencer's first two requirements: (1) for an export subsidy to improve domestic welfare, the target industry "must be expected to earn additional returns (expressed in profits or greater returns to workers) sufficient to exceed the total cost of the subsidy"; and (2) subsidization of the domestic industry "should lead foreign rival firms to cut back capacity plans and output."[71]

The first requirement implies barriers to entry "both to make subsidization initially beneficial and to preserve the gain in profits for a reasonable length of time."[72] But as Grossman and others have pointed out, the Brander-Spencer argument applies only to truly "natural" oligopolies where the opportunities for entry are limited at all stages of development.[73] If entry (including policy-induced entry) increases competition at later stages, profits will be dissipated, as discussed above. Similarly, if lack of natural entry barriers allowed vigorous competition at earlier stages of industry development, seemingly abnormal profits of successful firms might be only normal profits if one took account of those who tried but did not succeed. In other words, so-called "excess profits" of firms that are protected by entry barriers, such as patent rights, goodwill, or economies of scale, may in fact represent a risk premium required to reward risky large-scale investments that firms had to make to obtain those very patents, the goodwill, or economies of scale. If entry barriers are insignificant at the early stages of development, returns adjusted for risk will tend to be normal over the lifetime of the investment. If the government has a policy of targeting successful firms in Brander-Spencer-Krugman fashion, the prospect of subsidization will attract more investment at the early stages than would be attracted without the policy. As Grossman has pointed out, "This creates a distortion of resource allocation akin to that ascribed to export subsidies in a fully competitive world, because the appropriate long-run view of the industry would indicate that the excess profits to be captured by one country or the other by means of strategic policy are nonexistent."[74]

When presenting her second requirement for successful targeting, Spencer shifts the emphasis towards policies that "preempt the foreign competition"

---

70. Barbara J. Spencer, "What Should Trade Policy Target?" in Krugman, *Strategic Trade Policy*, p. 69.

71. Ibid., pp. 71 and 73, respectively.

72. Ibid., p. 71.

73. Gene M. Grossman, "Strategic Export Promotion: A Critique," in Krugman, *Strategic Trade Policy*, pp. 57–58; and Dixit, "Trade Policy: Agenda for Research," pp. 292–93.

74. Grossman, "Strategic Export Promotion: A Critique," pp. 57–58.

because she believes that preempting policies are less likely to be affected by ambiguity concerning conjectural variations discussed above:

> Government policies that increase domestic capacity are likely to serve as signals to foreign governments and firms that domestic output will be higher so that the return on investment to foreign firms will be lower. Such policies are likely to be most effective in reducing foreign capacity if they occur relatively early in the product cycle before plans for foreign capacity have been finalized. . . . Although they are not necessary, large and inflexible capital requirements are likely to increase the chances of this type of behavior.[75]

But a preempting strategy is even more vulnerable to the Grossman critique if entry barriers are insignificant at the early stages of development. A policy supporting all applicants could not capture any excess profits and, indeed, would result in a waste of the nation's resources. A more selective preempting policy, on the other hand, would have to contend with problems generally discussed under the heading of "picking winners."[76] How would the government know which firms are likely to be the most successful innovators? How could it justify preemptive selective support at a scale large enough to matter for a strategic posture? How would inevitable mistakes be corrected in a political process that is even more averse to admitting failure than the decision-making process of large corporations?

The problems of picking winners become more complicated if several potential target industries compete for the services of an essential factor of production for which supply is not perfectly elastic over the relevant period. The original profit-shifting models ignored this aspect because, in the established tradition of partial equilibrium analysis, they focused on one oligopolistic industry in an otherwise perfectly competitive economy. Dixit and Grossman have explored the implications of assuming several oligopolistic industries that are linked by a common resource in fixed supply, namely, "scientists."[77] Not surprisingly, Dixit and Grossman find that the case for Brander-Spencer-Krugman type policies is weakened fatally in their scenario. An attempt to shift profits by inducing one domestic producer to expand output necessarily results in reducing the rents captured by others that must contract. But only differential subsidy rates affect allocation: "If a general subsidy is applied, the real beneficiaries are the scientists whose wages

---

75. Spencer, "What Should Trade Policy Target?" pp. 72–73.

76. Harris, *Trade, Industrial Policy and International Competition,* pp. 111–44; Donald G. McFetridge, "The Economics of Industrial Policy," in D. G. McFetridge, ed., *Canadian Industrial Policy in Action* (Toronto: University of Toronto Press, 1985), pp. 17–31; and Manfred E. Streit, "Industrial Policies for Technological Change: The Case of West Germany," in C. T. Saunders, ed., *Industrial Policies and Structural Change* (London: Macmillan, 1987), pp. 129–42.

77. Avinash K. Dixit and Gene M. Grossman, "Targeted Export Promotion with Several Oligopolistic Industries," *Journal of International Economics* 21 (November 1986), pp. 233–49.

rise."[78] Dixit and Grossman also demonstrate that even under the assumptions of the simplest model, policymakers would have to apply some subtle reasoning and would require practically unavailable information to select those industries that will create above-average rents in relation to their requirements of the fixed factor at the margin. In the absence of reliable discriminating information, there is no case for intervention: "When industries are indistinguishable as candidates for targeting, and when all draw on a common, inelastically supplied resource, there is no benefit from selecting any one of them for promotion (unless the profit-shifting effects are increasing in output, in which case any one industry should be chosen for targeting)."[79]

Spencer names one example for government targeting of an industry that "broadly fits" the criteria developed in her paper: the European Airbus consortium.[80] This example has been used by several other authors.[81] The wide-body commercial jet aircraft industry is an oligopolistic industry on a worldwide scale. Airbus has managed to capture a substantial share of this market at the expense of previously dominant U.S. producers. There can be little doubt that government subsidization has allowed Airbus to win a larger share than an unsupported European aircraft industry might have obtained. As Spencer states, "Indeed it is rather unlikely that an unsupported private European firm would have entered the market at all."[82] Industry analysts suggest that the market can probably accommodate only two firms to produce the next generation of wide-body jets at a profit. Boeing is likely to be one of the winners; the other contenders are McDonnell-Douglas, Lockheed, and Airbus. Brander explains that "subsidization of the European entrant gives that firm an edge [and] if those subsidies persuade McDonnell-Douglas and Lockheed not to try to enter the market, then the subsidies will have the [strategic] effect described in this paper."[83] Yet achieving a strategic effect is no guarantee that the interventions required to make Airbus a successful contender will produce results that enhance the national welfare of the countries bearing the costs of supporting the European consortium.[84]

78. Ibid., p. 238.
79. Ibid., p. 241.
80. Spencer, "What Should Trade Policy Target?" p. 84.
81. Paul R. Krugman, "The U.S. Response to Foreign Industrial Targeting," *Brookings Papers on Economic Activity* 15, no. 1, 1984, p. 83; Avinash K. Dixit and Albert S. Kyle, "The Use of Protection and Subsidies for Entry Promotion and Deterrence," *American Economic Review* 75 (March 1985), p. 139; Harris, *Trade, Industrial Policy and International Competition,* p. 30; Brander, "Rationales for Strategic Trade," p. 31; William H. Branson and Alvin K. Klevorick, "Strategic Behavior and Trade Policy," in Krugman, *Strategic Trade Policy,* pp. 244–46; Pearce and Sutton, *Protection and Industrial Policy in Europe,* pp. 149–51; and Jacquemin, *New Industrial Organization,* p. 176.
82. Spencer, "What Should Trade Policy Target?" p. 84.
83. Brander, "Rationales for Strategic Trade," p. 31.
84. See the harsh critique of West German involvement in the Airbus program contained in the latest annual report of the German government's council of economic advisors: Sachverständigenrat, *Vorrang für die Wachstumspolitik* (Stuttgart and Mainz: Kohlhammer, 1987). Governments are surely capable of selecting spectacular losers. There is a literature on examples

If the intervention is motivated by external benefits, as discussed in the context of the infant-industry argument above, other policies could be more efficient, or there might be no practical policy for which the long-term benefits exceed the costs of intervention. Moreover, the large firms involved must be expected to play their own games against each other and against various governments concerned.[85] It should also be recognized that the example of Airbus points to additional theoretical and practical problems because each strategic intervention is just one move in a repeated game for this industry.[86] Finally, a strategic policy in support of any individual industry cannot, in practice, be kept separate from policies concerning other industries. Thus, the United States has linked European support for Airbus to other contentious issues, such as grain exports.[87]

William Branson and Alvin Klevorick report on a research project sponsored by the National Bureau of Economic Research (NBER) which brought together academic economists and staff of the U.S. Trade Representative (USTR) for the purpose of assessing the applicability of analytical concepts of strategic trade policy to major problem areas on the agenda of the USTR.[88] The sectors discussed were semiconductors, large commercial jet aircraft, telecommunications equipment, automobiles, and steel. With the possible exception of jet aircraft, the study found little scope for strategic use of trade policy tools. Indeed, "a recurrent question was whether a particular product or particular industry was appropriately on the trade policy agenda."[89] Domestic policy changes were judged to be more suitable for dealing with the perceived problems of most of the named sectors, and the strategic aspects of the suggested domestic policies did not seem to be important. Other authors, who have traditionally taken an orthodox view on matters of trade policy, also reacted with great caution or have denied the practical relevance of models of strategic trade policy.[90]

---

of unsuccessful targeting in spite of strategic effect, such as the Concorde supersonic jet and fast breeder reactors: Pearce and Sutton, *Protection and Industrial Policy in Europe;* Herbert Kitschelt, "Four Theories of Public Policy Making and Fast Breeder Reactor Development," *International Organization* 40 (Winter 1986), pp. 65–104; and Henning Klodt, *Wettlauf um die Zukunft: Technologiepolitik im internationalen Vergleich* (Tübingen: J. C. B. Mohr, 1987).

85. Krugman, "U.S. Response to Foreign Industrial Targeting," p. 103.

86. Branson and Klevorick, "Strategic Behavior and Trade Policy," p. 245; and Dixit and Kyle, "Use of Protection and Subsidies," p. 151.

87. *Globe and Mail,* Toronto, 29 January 1987.

88. Branson and Klevorick, "Strategic Behavior and Trade Policy."

89. Ibid., p. 252.

90. William R. Cline, "U.S. Trade and Industrial Policy: The Experience of Textiles, Steel, and Automobiles," in Krugman, *Strategic Trade Policy,* pp. 211–39; John Whalley, "Brander's 'Shaping Comparative Advantage': Remarks," in Lipsey and Dobson, *Shaping Comparative Advantage,* pp. 83–89; Richard G. Lipsey, "Report on the Workshop," in Lipsey and Dobson, *Shaping Comparative Advantage,* pp. 109–53; and Alan V. Deardorff and Robert M. Stern, "Current Issues in Trade Policy: An Overview," in Stern, *U.S. Trade Policies in a Changing World Economy,* pp. 15–68.

Where does the economics profession go from here?

The new thinking on trade policy was embraced enthusiastically by authors who favor a more activist trade policy or industrial policy for the United States. In fact, some authors—such as Michael Borrus, Laura Tyson, and John Zysman—thought they had known the answer all along: "The mounting evidence in our work on the semiconductor industry led us to accept these results as empirical realities even before they had been derived as formal possibilities in the new trade theory literature."[91] The warm response by policy activists and industry lobbyists created a potentially embarrassing disequilibrium situation for the economics profession: here were the shining new theories that could not serve (and generally were not intended to serve) as a practical guide to a new policy, yet the immediate effect of these theories was to lend new ideological support to mercantilist interventionism. This disequilibrium situation caused a strong reaction in the form of additional theoretical work (reported in the previous section) which demonstrated the limitations of the pioneering efforts but also pushed trade theory further into previously uncharted territory. As a result, trade theorists are able to discuss new questions in a more orderly fashion and with greater confidence. The profession's new analytical confidence strongly supports the conclusion that strategic trade policy of the Brander-Spencer-Krugman type is fraught with too many problems to be tried in practice; or if it is tried, strategic trade policy is unlikely to enhance a nation's welfare. This is not, however, the end of the matter. The economics profession still has to face the fact that in the real world of international trade policy there are strategic issues. The incidence of potentially strategic issues appears to have increased, or these issues have become more complex, because of increased international interdependence and more diversified government intervention at the microeconomic level. What is perhaps equally important, most non-economists tend to perceive many more matters of trade and industrial policy as being "strategic" in the sense that foreigners are trying to gain something at our expense or that we ought to try to get something at their expense. Economists have to meet this challenge if they wish to retain a useful role in the formation of their country's trade policy and in the development of more harmonious international economic relations.

As has been mentioned at several points in this article, economic models of strategic trade policy emerged in reaction to the debate on industrial policy in the United States. A major characteristic of that debate in the United States and elsewhere is the perception that trade policy and domestic policies

---

91. Borrus, Tyson, and Zysman, "Creating Advantage," p. 92; and David A. Lake, "The State and American Trade Strategy in the Pre-Hegemonic Era," *International Organization* 42 (Winter 1988), p. 33. Lake approvingly refers to the recent economic literature on strategic trade policy for his historical analysis of U.S. trade policy during the period 1887–1939, but he does not make use of economic models.

for the development of specific sectors are inextricably linked to each other. This linkage is a direct challenge to the economics profession's "domestic distortions approach" that has dominated the normative theory of international trade in the post–World War II period.[92] The aim of the trade theorists who developed the domestic distortions approach was to focus attention on the fact that there is a domestic distortion at the root of most problems that policymakers might try to solve by interfering with free international trade. Protection for economically weak groups, for example, can be traced back to a perceived distortion in the domestic distribution of income; protection of new industries might be intended to deal with problems caused by domestic capital market imperfections or external benefits of domestic production, as mentioned above in the context of the traditional infant-industry argument. In each case, the optimal policy is not a trade intervention but a domestic intervention that either removes the distortion or compensates for the distortion by intervening as closely as possible to its origin. Of course, the optimal policy would be to abstain from intervening if the costs to society of the best possible policy option exceed its potential benefits. Trade interventions, if they can be justified at all, are "second-best" ways of dealing with domestic distortions; a trade intervention causes what Corden has called "by-product distortions" that are wasteful if a less costly domestic intervention can correct the distortion.[93] The normative impact of the domestic distortions approach thus was to downgrade the role of trade policy and to create a near-consensus in the economics profession that trade ought to be insulated from domestic policy pressures. This approach was reasonably in tune with international developments when the industrialized economies were growing strongly, industries suffering severe adjustment problems were the exception, and trade liberalization within the General Agreement on Trade and Tariffs (GATT) and on a regional basis was perceived to take care of the principal strategic problem, the dismantling of exorbitant trade barriers built up during the period between the two World Wars. However, when growth slowed and when sectoral adjustment pressures mounted and the "new protectionism" sprung up in spite of GATT and the teachings of the economics profession, it became apparent that the domestic distortions approach had never really been accepted by policymakers and non-economist contributors to the trade policy debate.[94]

92. Corden, "Normative Theory of International Trade," p. 86.
93. Ibid., p. 88. For an exposition in detail, see Klaus Stegemann, "The Efficiency Rationale of Anti-Dumping Policy and Other Measures of Contingency Protection," in J. Quinn and P. Slayton, eds., *Non-Tariff Barriers After the Tokyo Round* (Montreal: Institute for Research on Public Policy, 1982), pp. 21–69.
94. Economists in response have developed a whole new subdiscipline—public choice theory—attempting to explain why what in their view is sound advice based on economic theory often is ignored or is followed by perverse policy implementation. The following examples are pertinent in the context of trade policy: Ronald Findlay and Stanislaw Wellisz, "Endogenous Tariffs, the Political Economy of Trade Restrictions, and Welfare," in J. N. Bhagwati, ed., *Import Competition and Response* (Chicago: University of Chicago Press, 1982), pp. 223–34;

A major shortcoming of the domestic distortions approach, one that is most relevant in the present context, has been its (implicit) assumption that other countries would not react to a country's domestic policies designed to correct domestic distortions. This assumption is implied in the so-called "small country" assumption. In the case of a small country, even if its domestic policies cause its exports to increase or its imports to decline, these effects are insignificant for all trading partners and, thus, they have no reason to react. However, in the real world, the number of relevant trading partners tends to be small for industries in which governments intervene most heavily, and domestic distortions, such as excess capacity with rigid input and output prices, tend to prevail in several industrial countries simultaneously. Therefore, industries such as steel and shipbuilding become "sensitive sectors" in an international context. If a major producing country, or a group of countries in the case of the European Community, intervenes to correct a domestic distortion, producers in competing countries are likely to feel injured and will use the foreign intervention as an argument for demanding government assistance. Similarly, domestic policies designed to support the development of "strategic sectors" (almost by definition) are undertaken simultaneously in a small number of countries trying to promote the same industries or technologies. Thus, the domestic measures of one country turn into a matter of concern for its trading partners. Reactions by other countries would not necessarily invalidate the domestic distortions approach if the affected countries all adopted domestic policies to correct their own domestic distortions. However, it has turned out to be more common for countries to react by imposing trade restrictions.[95]

In sum, the evidence around us—increasing international economic interdependence, rekindled protectionism, and the increase in policy actions with real or perceived strategic intent—will continually force the economics profession to address the issues that authors of models of strategic trade policy have tried to address. Yet the principal tasks are not new. One task is to sort out situations in which government intervention can be justified

---

Wolfgang Mayer, "Endogeneous Tariff Formation," *American Economic Review* 74 (December 1984), pp. 970–85; and Robert E. Baldwin, *The Political Economy of U.S. Import Policy* (Cambridge, Mass.: MIT Press, 1985). See also the survey by Bruno S. Frey, "The Public Choice View of International Political Economy," *International Organization* 38 (Winter 1984), pp. 199–223.

95. This problem has been made more severe by easy access to the anti-dumping and countervailing duty mechanisms of the United States, the European Community, Canada, and Australia. These mechanisms are practically automatic in the sense that, almost without exception, producers are entitled to protection against imports that are subsidized or sold below full cost if these imports are found to cause private material injury. The process does not include any consideration of the costs of intervention or a consideration of policy alternatives. Richard Dale, *Anti-Dumping Law in a Liberal Trade Order* (New York: St. Martin's Press, 1980); Klaus Stegemann, "Anti-Dumping Policy and the Consumer," *Journal of World Trade Law* 19 (September–October 1985), pp. 466–84; Destler, *American Trade Politics: System Under Stress,* chap. 6; and Deardorff and Stern, "Current Issues in Trade Policy," pp. 24–28.

as being in the national interest and situations in which it cannot. The other principal task is to find solutions to "prisoner's dilemma" problems at the international level. These problems result when individual countries are able (or are perceived to be able) to undertake actions that increase national welfare at the expense of others, but if other countries do the same or retaliate, all are likely to lose.

For the first task, it will be essential to demonstrate that not all issues perceived to be strategic are truly strategic; and for those issues that are strategic, it will be essential to investigate whether feasible forms of government intervention (or responding to foreign interventions) would, indeed, increase national welfare. Economists will thus retain their traditional role of throwing cold water on mercantilist ideas. They will continue to resist the popular presumption that a policy typically enhances national welfare if it raises the market share of domestic producers at the expense of foreign producers. Economists will continue to lay bare the group interests that are served by a particular policy at the expense of other groups in society. They will continue to require that any intervention be justified by a specific distortion in the market and by achievable benefits that exceed the costs of intervention. Economists will also continue to resist the popular presumption that the policies of other countries typically have an adverse effect on the welfare of their own country.[96] Yet it must be recognized that the notion of the state having the responsibility to "shape" the comparative advantages of its industry in competition with other states is politically powerful. As has been noted in previous sections, formal economic models still cannot take account of the technological linkages and dynamic effects that are stressed by policy activists; besides, no theorist could ever hope to refute the possibility that a country might gain by engaging in a policy of targeting particular sectors or products. As Brander has suggested, economists could make a more useful contribution on this issue by carefully analyzing prominent cases of past policies, domestic and foreign. The record might well serve to dampen the enthusiasm of policy activists.[97]

The second principal task, solving international prisoner's dilemma problems, will be easier if economists succeed with the first, because prisoner's dilemma situations are less likely to arise with less interventionism and a sharpened understanding of truly strategic problems. The debate on models of strategic trade policy has compelled trade theorists to give more attention to prisoner's dilemma situations in a world of oligopolistic competition among industrial states. This may well turn out to be the most constructive contribution of that debate. Under the assumptions of traditional trade theory, prisoner's dilemma problems were bound to receive little attention; the op-

96. Krugman, "U.S. Response to Foreign Industrial Targeting"; and Dixit, "How Should the United States Respond?"
97. Brander, "Shaping Comparative Advantage," pp. 47–51. See also Lipsey, "Report on the Workshop," pp. 138–48; and the references cited in footnote 84 above.

timum tariff case was the only case of international policy conflict considered. Therefore, economists have analyzed international prisoner's dilemma problems infrequently and mainly in the context of tariff protection.[98] It will be much more difficult to find theoretical and practical solutions for the more complex situations arising with multidimensional nontariff interventionism.[99] For both tasks, the economics profession will have to borrow from the experience of related disciplines, and economists will have to pay more attention to institutional details affecting practical policy choices.[100] Furthermore, it will be necessary to recognize differences in size and interests of major and minor players that affect their roles in international economic rivalry and cooperation.[101]

98. Johnson, "Optimum Tariffs and Retaliation"; Wolfgang Mayer, "Theoretical Considerations on Negotiated Tariff Adjustments," *Oxford Economic Papers* 33 (March 1981), pp. 135–53; Marie Thursby and Richard Jensen, "A Conjectural Variation Approach to Strategic Tariff Equilibria," *Journal of International Economics* 14 (February 1983), pp. 145–61; and John Whalley, *Trade Liberalization Among Major World Trading Areas* (Cambridge, Mass.: MIT Press, 1985).

99. Richardson, "New Political Economy of Trade Policy"; and Dixit, "How Should the United States Respond?"

100. A combination of economics and political science has been used successfully in research on U.S. trade policy, such as in Baldwin, *Political Economy of U.S. Import Policy;* and Destler, *American Trade Politics: System Under Stress.* Computer simulation work of the "prisoner's dilemma" by Robert Axelrod, a political scientist, has greatly stimulated the discussion of international economic policies by economists. Robert Axelrod, *The Evolution of Cooperation* (New York: Basic Books, 1984). This work is favorably reviewed by several of the authors cited above, including Brander, "Rationales for Strategic Trade and Industrial Policy," pp. 39–43; Richardson, "New Political Economy of Trade Policy," pp. 270–74; Brander, "Shaping Comparative Advantage," pp. 23–27; Deardorff and Stern, "Current Issues in Trade Policy," pp. 55–56; and Dixit, "How Should the United States Respond?" pp. 278–79. For an early adaptation of Axelrod's work to trade policy, see Judith L. Goldstein and Stephen D. Krasner, "Unfair Trade Practices: The Case for a Differentiated Response," *American Economic Review* 74 (May 1984), pp. 282–87.

101. An innovative approach to this problem that combines the theory of "hegemonic stability" and the concept of "transactions cost economics" has been proposed by Beth V. Yarbrough and Robert M. Yarbrough, "Cooperation in the Liberalization of International Trade: After Hegemony, What?" *International Organization* 41 (Winter 1987), pp. 1–26. See also Susan Strange, "The Persistent Myth of Lost Hegemony," *International Organization* 41 (Autumn 1987), pp. 551–74. John A. C. Conybeare, *Trade Wars: The Theory and Practice of International Commercial Rivalry* (New York: Columbia University Press, 1987) very much focuses on the relative size of players in his explanation of trade wars. Conybeare's study is highly recommended because it adds methodological and historical perspectives to the debate on economic models of strategic trade policy.

International law and domestic institutions: reconciling North American "unfair" trade laws
Judith Goldstein

Whereas much has been written about how international institutions may facilitate cooperative behavior among nations, less attention has been paid to such institutions' domestic political purposes. This essay focuses on the purposes international organizations serve for policymakers at home. It concentrates on the less studied side of two-level games analysis, thereby developing a domestic logic for membership in international institutions.[1] Instead of envisioning domestic politics as a constraint upon those nations that enter into international agreements, signing an agreement is suggested to be a strategy whereby domestic actors further their own interests. Here, the answer to a commonly asked question of why nations would agree to specific rules of international conduct is that these rules present a solution to a domestic problem.

The empirical portion of this article centers on the dispute-settlement procedures that appear in the North American Free Trade Agreement (NAFTA) but date initially to the 1988 Canadian–U.S. Free Trade Agreement (FTA). In this initial treaty Canada and the United States agreed to establish rotating binational boards to hear appeals on particular trade matters. The resultant autonomy these boards displayed is theoretically counterintuitive, given the relative power of the two nations and the boards' limited mandate. The boards not only ruled repeatedly in a pro-Canadian manner but also significantly changed the way the U.S. bureaucracy responded to petitions for protection against Canadian products, even in the absence of a change in

Special thanks go to Patrick Desouza for his help in this project. A number of people made excellent comments on earlier drafts, including John Ferejohn, Brian Gaines, Geoff Garrett, Joanne Gowa, Lloyd Gruber, Robert Keohane, John Odell, Alan Rugman, Anne-Marie Slaughter, and the *International Organization* referees. Dan Drezner provided much appreciated research assistance. I thank the Hewlett Foundation for financial assistance.

1. On two-level games, see Putnam 1988. For empirical studies on the relationship between international economic cooperation and domestic trade politics, see Keohane and Nye 1977; Winham 1986; Odell 1985; and Evan, Jacobson, and Putnam 1995.

International Organization 50, 4, Autumn 1996, pp. 541–64
© 1996 by The IO Foundation and the Massachusetts Institute of Technology

domestic law. (As of this writing, only two trade panels have been organized under NAFTA rules. The logic here applies as well to these cases.) Below I argue that the explanation for anomalous U.S. behavior resides in the structural relationship between the President and Congress and in presidential interests in international oversight of his own bureaucracy.

This inquiry is organized around two general questions stemming from the empirical case study. First, how did a weak international institution with no sanctioning power lead to a significant change in the behavior of the U.S. bureaucracy, even without a change in domestic law? Second, assuming rational behavior, why would the United States bind itself to an international agreement in which the distribution of gains went to the weaker party? After a brief review of the history of the FTA, I examine each of these questions in turn.

FTA and administered protection

Canada and the United States have long been each other's best trading partner. In 1991, trade between the two countries reached $176 billion, $91 billion in exports from Canada and $85 billion in exports from the United States. The relative importance of this trade, however, is not symmetric. The United States accounts for almost 80 percent of all Canadian exports, while Canada buys only 25 percent of total U.S. exports. By one estimate, the bilateral trading relationship is fifteen times as important to Canada as it is to the United States.[2]

Given the magnitude of this dyadic relationship, the conclusion of the FTA in 1989 was no surprise. The agreement eliminated all tariffs on bilateral trade over ten years, opened up government contracts to competitive bidding, and barred many border restraints on bilateral energy trade. Most innovative, however, was the creation of a dispute-settlement procedure regarding the adjudication of domestic trade law in each country. For the first time, each nation agreed to international arbitration of trade disputes.

In large part, Canada originally envisioned the FTA as a mechanism to reform aspects of existing U.S. trade law. The origins of this idea can be traced to the Macdonald Report. The Macdonald commission, formally named the Royal Commission on the Economic Union and Development Prospects for Canada, was assembled in late November 1982 by Liberal Prime Minister Pierre Elliott Trudeau. Its chair, Donald Macdonald, was charged with devising an agenda for economic and regional policy in Canada. The commission conducted hearings, commissioned reports, and received written and oral testimony on Canada's economic future. The final report covered a wide breadth of issues from electoral reform to labor relations. But of all issues

2. Cameron 1988, 15.

covered, that of trade with the United States gained the most attention. The report recommended an agreement with the United States so as to both extricate Canada from the threat of U.S. protectionism and create an incentive for Canadian industries to be more competitive. In Macdonald's words:

> Although the U.S. is already our largest trading partner . . . we cannot count on continued growth. Tariff barriers between the two countries have been sharply reduced. . . . [But] a greater threat to us are non-tariff barriers against Canadian goods. Existing U.S. trade legislation already allows U.S. companies to harass their foreign competition constantly. The provisions include countervailing duties against subsidized imports, anti-dumping duties, emergency relief from seriously injurious imports, retaliations against "unfair" trade practices and reliefs from imports deemed prejudicial to U.S. national security. . . . Only by negotiating a free trade deal with the U.S. can we assure our future as a trading nation.[3]

Even before the release of the final commission's report in September 1985, Conservative Prime Minister Brian Mulroney initiated discussions with President Reagan on bilateral trade issues. The first meeting between the two, the Shamrock Summit, took place in Quebec City in March 1985. The goal of that engagement was "to establish a climate of greater predictability and confidence for Canadians and Americans alike to plan, invest, grow and compete more effectively with one another and in the global market."[4] As a result, both sides commissioned reports, to be completed within six months, on how to eliminate existing trade barriers and resolve bilateral trade disputes.

In 1985, public support in Canada for a formal trade agreement was widespread. In May, Canada's Conference of Western Premiers called for bilateral negotiations to liberalize trade over the next ten years. In August, premiers of the ten provinces met at their regular Premiers' Conference, and nine of the ten endorsed the notion of an agreement. In September, the Macdonald Report was issued along with seventy-two volumes of research studies. When Mulroney opened Parliament and announced that he would approach the United States to begin negotiations on a free trade accord, he was echoing the sentiment of the majority of Canadian leaders.

Long a defender of free trade, President Reagan announced his intention to conclude a trade agreement under fast-track procedures on 10 December. (Fast-track authority delimits congressional involvement to a veto within sixty days of a President's announcement that he will conclude an agreement and is a promise to bring the treaty's implementation legislation to a vote under a closed rule.) Of all the items of concern to the agreement negotiators, the reconciliation of Canadian and U.S. unfair trade laws was the most difficult.

3. Ibid.
4. Declaration by the Prime Minister of Canada and the President of the United States regarding trade in goods and services, Quebec, 18 March 1985. Cited in Schott 1988.

Although a senior and experienced negotiator, Simon Reisman found his U.S. counterpart, Peter Murphy, both uninterested and unwilling to put U.S. trade law on the agenda.[5]

The continuing problems posed by unilateral U.S. protectionism were apparent to Canadian negotiators from the start. FTA discussions began in May 1986 on the eve of the announcement of raised duties on wood shakes and shingles. The duties were partially a response to pressure mounted by the Senate Finance Committee, whose 10 to 10 vote on fast-track authority indicated organized resistance to a treaty. This was followed two months later by Congress's agreement to subsidies for U.S. wheat farmers on a proposed sale to the People's Republic of China and the Soviet Union—two of Canada's largest customers. Then in October, the U.S. Commerce Department ordered a 15 percent tariff hike on Canadian lumber to compensate for low Canadian stumpage fees. As the U.S. Commerce Department noted in defending its assessment of still another countervailing duty, this one against Canadian exporters of groundfish, U.S. actions were not oriented toward undercutting efforts at achieving an agreement but toward creating a "level playing field" in the American market.[6]

Eighteen months after negotiations began, the two sides came to an agreement.[7] In the preceding months, Canadian frustration had been great, leading Reisman to break off the talks shortly before the October 1987 deadline—only ninety days before the expiration of U.S. fast-track authority. A final agreement was concluded only after the intercession of U.S. Secretary of State James Baker and Special Trade Representative Clayton Yeutter. In terms of redress from unfair trade laws, the FTA provided Canada with some protections against tariffs in cases in which it was the tertiary supplier. Only if imports from Canada were substantial and constituted a serious threat to domestic producers would Canada be affected by a decision rendered against the primary exporter. The two countries also agreed to consult before imposition of emergency trade remedies and to allow either side to ask a new bilateral trade commission to resolve disputes over the interpretation of the agreement.

More unusual in the agreement was the provision of binational panels to decide whether an administrative decision in an antidumping (AD) or countervailing duty (CVD) case was in accordance with domestic law. These panels would replace judicial review in each of the home countries, with the costs of such a review not paid by the petitioning producer but by the home government. On the troublesome definition of unfair trade in U.S. law, Canada merely obtained a promise that the United States would enter into negotiations over the next five to seven years.

5. On the negotiation process, see Doern and Tomlin 1991; and Hart 1994.
6. Cameron, Clarkson, and Watkins 1988, 47.
7. U.S.—Canada FTA 1988 (hereafter cited as FTA).

The universal postmortem on the agreement was that Canada did not obtain her key objective. In fact, commentators suggested that instead of obtaining guaranteed access through a change in U.S. trade laws, the FTA legitimated U.S. use of unfair trade laws. In practice, this did not occur. As shown below, the boards used their power to remand cases to undercut trade sanctions and in the process created new interpretations of U.S. law that significantly influenced the disposition of unfair trade petitions by the U.S. bureaucracy.

Internationalizing domestic law

Background

In Chapter 19 of the FTA, the parties agreed that either could request the creation of a binational panel to review the decisions of the administrative agencies that had ruled on either an AD or CVD case. The panels replaced national judicial review. In the United States, the panel had jurisdiction over determinations by both the Commerce Department and the International Trade Commission (ITC). In the absence of the FTA, the decisions of both bodies could be reviewed by the Court of International Trade (CIT), by the U.S. Court of Appeals for the Federal Circuit, and eventually by the U.S. Supreme Court. By contrast, the Canadian Import Tribunal was the primary administrative decision maker in Canada. In the absence of the FTA, the tribunal's decisions could be reviewed by the Deputy Minister of the Department of National Revenue. The final orders of the Import Tribunal were appealable to the Federal Court of Appeals; redetermination by the Deputy Minister could be appealed to the Tariff Board and subsequently to the Federal Court of Appeals on a question of law only.

Under the procedures specified in the FTA, either government had discretion to ask for review upon its own initiative but it was required to ask for a review requested by a private party entitled to seek domestic judicial review of a final determination by an administrative body.[8] Decisions made by the binational panel were binding upon both governments.[9] (This "binding" authority was especially important to the Canadian government, which believed that only a binding dispute resolution procedure combined with a restitution remedy would ensure its access to the U.S. market and counter superior U.S. bargaining power.)[10] In addition, the agreement provided that "[n]either Party shall provide in its domestic legislation for an appeal from a panel decision to its domestic courts."[11] Coupled with the requirement that "domestic procedures for judicial review may not be commenced until the time

8. Ibid., art. 1904, par. 5.
9. Ibid., art. 1904, par. 9.
10. Graham, 1988.
11. FTA, art. 1904, par. 11. Canon 1991, 690–91, discusses the U.S. domestic process in the light of this provision.

for requesting a panel . . . has expired," the agreement created a strong incentive for petitioners to use the FTA procedures and not domestic courts.

The check to possible abuse of panel authority was the "extraordinary challenge procedure" that was available if a party felt that a member of a panel was guilty of gross misconduct, bias, or conflict of interest and that such conduct materially affected the panel's decision and threatened the integrity of the review process.[12] However, the threshold criteria for invoking the extraordinary challenge procedure were made very demanding and, therefore, reinforced the authority of the panels.

In making its decision, a binational panel was to use the general legal principle that a "court of the importing Party otherwise would apply to a review of a determination of the competent investigating authority."[13] At least in the United States, under current administrative process jurisprudence, this general legal principle had, in the past, led to considerable deference to the initial determination of the administrative agency, producing no real check on administrative decisions. U.S. negotiators did not direct the panels to develop a jurisprudence of their own, suggesting an acceptance of this standing principle. Rather, by statute the panel was given the right either to uphold a final determination by an administrative body or remand it to the administrative authority for a policy response not inconsistent with the decision.

Panels contained five members, two appointed by each government.[14] Governments could veto up to four candidates but were to agree on the fifth.[15] If the governments could not agree on the fifth member, the four appointed panelists were to choose the fifth. If they also could not agree, the fifth member was to be picked by lot from the roster of candidates, now purged of names that were peremptorily challenged.[16] The original rosters from which panelists were selected comprised fifty eligible individuals, picked in equal numbers by both sides.[17] The majority were assumed to be lawyers, including the chair.[18] Government officials, except judges, were not eligible.[19] For the purpose of appeals, an Extraordinary Challenge Committee could be impaneled by the same basic procedure. Rather than five panelists, the committee would consist of three members chosen from a roster of ten judges.[20]

Even though the domestic judicial route was not foreclosed, the agreement biased the incentives of petitioners toward international arbitration in a number of ways. Even beyond the benefit of having national representation, petitioners were guaranteed that a decision would be made by a panel in no

12. FTA. art. 1904, pars. 13 and 14.
13. Ibid., par. 3.
14. Ibid., annex 1901.2, par. 2.
15. Ibid.
16. Ibid., par. 3.
17. Ibid., par. 1.
18. Ibid., par. 2.
19. Ibid., par. 1.
20. Ibid., annex 1904.13, par. 1.

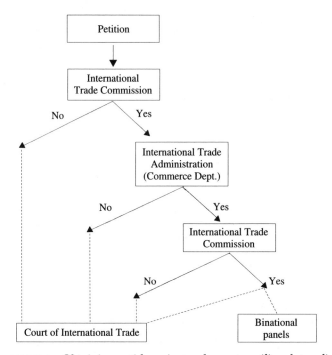

FIGURE 1. *Obtaining antidumping and countervailing duty relief*

more than 315 days; the average time through the courts was two and a half times that long. As important, the cost of an appeal—the most expensive part of the unfair trade process—was significantly reduced under FTA procedures.

The logic of a veto player

With passage of the treaty, binational judicial review replaced domestic courts as the "veto player," or the last mover in the administration of unfair trade law. In that the preferences of panels were more pro–free trade than were the preferences of the courts, the outcomes of petitions for protection moved in the preferred direction of the panel. The panels moved U.S. policy in a liberal direction through their power to remand cases and by instructing agencies on what adjudication procedures the FTA boards would and would not accept. Previous to the FTA, CIT rulings had defended the autonomy of the two U.S. agencies that decided unfair trade cases, the U.S. International Trade Administration (ITA) in the Department of Commerce and the International Trade Commission (ITC).

Figure 1 details the procedures for gaining unfair trade relief in the United States before and after passage of the FTA. As illustrated, the petition process moves from the ITC for a preliminary determination on the value of the case to

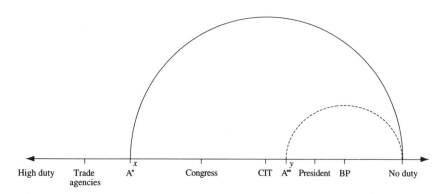

FIGURE 2. *Probable arrangement of political actors' preferences in setting unfair trade policy, where CIT = Court of International Trade and BP = binational Canada–U.S. Free Trade Agreement panels*

the Commerce Department for a decision on whether or not there has been dumping or subsidization of the product in question and if so, finally back to the ITC for an evaluation of whether or not a U.S. industry has been hurt because of these foreign practices. As Figure 1 suggests, appeal is possible after each agency decision. U.S. industry can ask the court to remand a negative decision to the agency, a U.S. producer can ask for an increase in a final duty, or a foreign producer can appeal a final positive decision. It is this last group that is affected by binational arbitration. Instead of appealing to the U.S. CIT, the treaty provides the option of a binational review board.

The importance of the procedural change for the United States is displayed in Figure 2. Figure 2 suggests a probable arrangement of preferences for the political actors involved in setting unfair trade policy. Given these preferences, we can then determine what would be the outcome of a trade petition under the scenarios of domestic judicial review and international review. Individual bureaucrats, congressional leaders, and Presidents will vary in their preference for free trade. However, we can deduce the general ordering of preferences from their structural characteristics. Those with the most to gain from the AD or CVD duty will be the petitioning group. Their ideal point would be at the protectionist end of the continuum. Moving to the right of the figure, we assume that trade agencies will be closest to the proprotection groups; although Congress has formal oversight duties, logic suggests that it will drift toward and/or become captured by special interests. Although not separated for this purpose, the Commence Department would logically be more affected by special interests than would the ITC, given the proscription against a partisan majority on the ITC. The assumption that Congress will favor protection more than the President derives from the asymmetry between the organization of consumer and producer groups. Congressional representatives, because of the size of their constituencies, are more likely to support producer groups that are hurt by imports. Presidents, with a national constituency, have far more opportunities to trade amongst constituents and thereby act in the "national interest." The CIT falls between Congress and the President, since they share authority to name judges. (Congress confirms CIT judges, but their appointments are for life, giving the court more freedom than the ITC, whose commissioners—also confirmed by Congress—hold a fixed term.) I assume that, on average, binational panel members are closest to the free trade side, since half are Canadians. (Similarly, for Canadian cases, I assume that panel members for the United States will be biased toward the U.S. side. This assumption derives from the political nature of the selection process. Lists of members are vetted through Congress. Therefore individuals on the lists should approximate congressional preferences and not what would be expected from a purely professional board.)[21]

The administrative arrangement in the pre-FTA world predicts an outcome circumscribed, first, by the preferences of the CIT and, second, by those of Congress. Thus, the bureaucracy is constrained by the court to choose a policy that is within the win set of the CIT but as close to its ideal point as possible. (The win set is the set of outcomes the CIT prefers to the reversion point. The reversion point is the outcome in the absence of a change in government policy.) The courts are indifferent between the reversion point, which in this case is no additional duty, and point A^*. The outcome is x—the optimal proposal point for the U.S. bureaucracy. At point x and all points to the right, the agency can be confident that the court will not overturn its decision. (In the absence of the court, agency outcomes would be at the agency's ideal point. In theory, if an agency's decisions drifted too far from Congress's preferences, it would be "reined in" through congressional budget and appointment powers. The CIT is also a medium for congressional oversight over the bureaucracy, moving policy closer to that preferred by Congress. To do that, however, the court must be on the free trade side of Congress. This may help explain why Congress changed the structure of the Customs Court, from an Article 1 [of the U.S. Constitution] to an Article 3 court, which gave the President agenda control on choosing judges.)[22]

Now consider the administrative arrangement if decisions can be taken to a binational panel. The inclusion of representatives of Canada can be assumed to move the preferences of the new "veto player" in the direction of the reversion point. If the veto player moves toward openness, the optimal proposal point moves to the right. That point is now given by y—the new optimal proposal point. If the bureaucracy makes a decision that is to the left of this point, the court will intervene. Thus after some initial period in which the boards

21. On congressional oversight of the ITC, see Goldstein and Lenway 1989.
22. Goldstein 1995.

establish a reputation, we would expect that the bureaucracy will make more pro–free trade decisions in cases that the binational boards could potentially veto. Point y is closer to the President's but farther from Congress's preferred policy, a point to which I will return below.

Empirical consequences

This theoretical logic is borne out by a change in behavior of the bureaucracy and a resultant shift in U.S. policy. In the years preceding the agreement, the aggregate number of U.S.-imposed unfair trade sanctions on imports had increased dramatically. The increase in interest in unfair trade remedies mirrored a more general rise in the number of U.S. petitions filed with both the ITC and the Commerce Department against foreign products. Although the percentage of unfair trade rulings that awarded protection was not significantly different from the analogous proportion of other trade cases—such as the "escape clause" cases—the number of petitions for unfair trade relief dwarfed that of petitions filed under other trade statutes. (The escape clause, or Article 19, of the General Agreement on Tariffs and Trade allows countries to be excused from trade reduction agreements in cases in which the decline in protection has led to significant harm to a U.S. industry. The ITC has jurisdiction over these petitions, though the President can overturn its rulings.) Thus, for example, since 1958 about 150 escape-clause rulings have been handed down, of which less than 25 percent have gained both ITC and presidential approval. In the same period, more than 1,000 AD and almost 400 CVD cases were heard. Of these, some protection for the U.S. producer was awarded in about 20 percent of the AD and 60 percent of the CVD cases.[23]

Although Canada represents a small number of these cases, petitions against Canadian exporters have become more frequent. In part, the increase is due to the transparency of trade subsidies in Canada; the rise is also attributable to the state of the Canadian economy in the 1980s, which forced exporters to cut profit margins, thereby becoming liable for selling products below U.S. cost-of-production standards. Table 1 gives the number of cases and the outcomes leveled against Canadian products in the years preceding and since passage of the FTA. As predicted, the probability of a positive AD or CVD order against a Canadian product declined with passage of the FTA.

We can obtain a second measure of the effect of the FTA on U.S. behavior by examining the share of unfair trade orders against Canada as a proportion of Canadian imports to the United States. To do this, we calculate the number of AD orders issued against Canada in any given year and compare it to the proportion of Canadian imports. (By this measure, if a country's imports comprised 30 percent of the total imported into the United States, and AD orders were issued against 30 percent of that country's imports, the ratio would

---

23. Goldstein 1993.

TABLE 1. *Completed trade cases involving Canadian products*

	Type					
	Countervailing duty			Antidumping duty		
Year	Affirmative	Negative	% Affirmative	Affirmative	Negative	% Affirmative
1964–73	0	0	NA	6	0	100%
1974–79	4	2	67%	2	0	100%
1980–88	15	9	63%	10	6	63%
1989–93	2	4	33%	2	6	25%

equal 1.00.) In 1987, before the FTA, the Canadian ratio of AD orders to its share of U.S. imports was 0.83. By the close of 1990, that number had been reduced to 0.33.[24] This reduction in unfair trade duties occurred only in Canadian trade. Comparatively, European Community dumping orders increased in this period, going from 0.90 to 1.05. U.S. dumping orders against imports from Japan similarly increased, moving from 1.88 in 1987 to 1.40 by the end of 1990.[25]

The explanation for this shift resides with the rulings of the binational panels. Table 2 provides a list of completed cases; seven additional cases were terminated by joint agreement of the parties. Since the first panel in 1989, the decision rendered by the U.S. bureaucracy was fully upheld only five times, representing findings in 33 percent of the completed cases. In one case, the panel increased the duty; in the others, duties were reduced. In most of the cases (67 percent), the panel sent the judgment back to the agency for reanalysis. Of those cases that were remanded, the board remained dissatisfied with the bureaucracy's response to its criticism in 66 percent of cases and once again returned the case. Cases bounced from the agency to the panel up to three times, with a total of eighteen remands in this period.[26] Although panels under both the FTA and NAFTA may not change U.S. law, the readoption of interpretations made by previous panels suggests that new case law may be developing. For example, the FTA panel on softwood lumber publicly adopted the rule used by panel members in a previous steel rail case, stating that, "while this Panel is not bound by previous binational panel decisions, it may be guided by such decisions."[27]

24. Anderson 1993, 103.
25. Ibid.
26. GAO 1995.
27. Ibid., 83.

TABLE 2. *Canada–U.S. Free Trade Agreement binational panel reviews, 1989–95*

Product	Type[a]	Value ($ million)	Remands
Red raspberries	AD	8	2
Paving equipment	AD	NA	0
Paving equipment	AD	NA	0
Fresh, chilled, frozen pork	CVD	356	2
Steel rail	CVD	7	1
Steel rail	AD	7	0
Steel rail	CVD/AD*	7	0
Fresh, chilled, frozen pork	CVD/AD*	356	2
Paving equipment	AD	NA	3
Live swine	CVD	75	2
Live swine	CVD	75	2
Softwood lumber	CVD	2,873	2
Magnesium	CVD	53	1
Magnesium	AD	53	0
Magnesium	CVD/AD*	53	1

[a]AD = antidumping duty; CVD = countervailing duty; * = injury determination.
Source. U.S. GAO 1995.

In sum, as is illustrated below, the FTA boards created a reputation, through repeated remands, for being suspicious of the manner in which the U.S. bureaucracy handled unfair trade cases. They did this through a series of initial decisions in which they specified procedures for the bureaucracy to follow. The bureaucracy had the choice of accepting the panels' orders or readjudicating the case. After repeated remands, often of the same case, the bureaucracy sent forward fewer cases. The result is the reduction in positive rulings against Canadian products noted in Table 1.

A comparison of bureaucratic oversight before and after passage of the FTA also demonstrates the importance of the panels. Although the authority of the binational review board is formally the same as that granted to the previous oversight group (the CIT), the behavioral records of the two judicial agents differ in the suggested direction. In the 1980s, the CIT either remanded AD and CVD cases to the bureaucracy or overturned a decision an average of 22 percent of the time compared with the 67 percent rate of panels under the FTA. When one considers that 47 percent of CIT decisions in this period involved American producer claims that the U.S. bureaucracy had either not given or given too little protection, this difference is even more pronounced. If we look only at Canadian products in the 1980s, the CIT wrote fifty-six opinions on twenty-three AD and CVD cases.[28] Of these fifty-six opinions, eighteen, or 32 percent, either remanded the case to the bureaucracy or overturned an earlier ruling—slightly more than the overall CIT average. Ten of the twenty-three cases concerned U.S. corporate complaints of underprotection. If we look just at the cases brought by Canadian corporations in protest of a final AD or CVD ruling, the CIT intervened so as to change substantially an order in only four cases. Thus, the CIT affirmed the decision of the bureaucracy in 69 percent of cases, far exceeding the 33 percent rate for the panels. If we look at CIT activity for all countries during the same period for which we report FTA data, we find a remand rate for the U.S. court of 33 percent, compared with a 67 percent remand rate for the binational courts.

The data suggest that Canadian products faced fewer trade sanctions after passage of the FTA. This occurred not only because FTA boards ruled more often in favor of Canadian exporters than had the CIT, thereby undercutting a duty determination, but also because the incidence of positive determinations by the U.S. bureaucracy declined. The assumption that this latter change in behavior is related to the creation of the FTA boards is supported by an absence of either a change in U.S. behavior on unfair trade cases against other countries or a significant change in either Canadian behavior or economic circumstance.

Creating precedent

The mechanism by which this change in oversight forum affected a change in behavior was the interpretation of U.S. law by binational judges. The detailed explanations by binational board members for their decisions created new guidelines for the U.S. bureaucracy of what procedures would and would not be accepted upon judicial review. Below I review three cases, respectively concerning red raspberries, paving equipment, and pork products, to illustrate the process of bureaucratic learning through repeated remands by binational boards.

The first binational panel was invoked by Canadian exporters of red raspberries to challenge a determination by the U.S. Department of Commerce's ITA that they were dumping.[29] The ITA had its choice of standards by which to compare Canadian pricing. Instead of using standard measures such as home-market price or third-country sales, the ITA calculated a comparison price by using a constructed value. The panel ordered the ITA to provide a reasonable justification on remand. The Commerce Department offered a variety of justifications. On 2 April 1990, the panel found the explanations not sufficient and instructed the Commerce Department on remand to use

28. For the data reported on the CIT, see Goldstein 1995.
29. *Red raspberries from Canada,* USA-89-1904-01 (Ottawa and Washington, D.C.: Binational Secretariat).

home-market sales to calculate prices. The Commerce Department filed an amended determination on 2 May 1990 eliminating duties on the exporters.

The U.S. bureaucracy did not respond as sanguinely to other cases.[30] In a case on paving equipment, a panel reviewed an ITA complaint accusing a Canadian company of selling its goods at less than fair value. The ITA had determined in favor of the Canadian party. But when the U.S. competitor served the Canadians notice that it intended to ask for review in the U.S. CIT, the Canadian party filed for binational panel review to move adjudication to a more neutral forum. Immediately thereafter, on 8 May, the U.S. government filed a complaint with the binational panel. As it turned out, the panel selected was the same one that had ruled against the Canadians in the first paving equipment case by affirming a Commerce Department determination as to the scope of its decision.[31] The panel in the first paving case was made up of three Americans and two Canadians. Still, the Canadians felt that the case would receive a fairer hearing, despite the composition of the panel.

The Canadian judgment proved prescient, but when the panel ruled favorably for the Canadian party, the U.S. party requested an extraordinary challenge to the decision in a letter to the U.S. Trade Representative (USTR). This was the first time that such a challenge was invoked. The USTR, however, did not see grounds for pursuing the extraordinary challenge, granting additional credence to the authority of the panel procedures.

Panels faced a different challenge in the series of cases concerning the Canadian export of pork products to the United States. In these cases, the difficulty was not the feeling of private parties that the choice of forum was determinative of outcome. Rather, in these situations, the resistance of bureaucracies themselves to outside authority was at stake. Canadian pork producers had requested a binational panel to challenge the formula that the U.S. Commerce Department was using to place a CVD on their product.[32] The Canadians alleged that the Commerce Department used a conversion factor that placed on producers a variety of subsidies given to other parts of the industry. The panel was composed of three Americans and two Canadians.

The panel affirmed some of the Commerce Department's determinations but remanded most of the determinations to the agency as not in accord with the law. Although the Commerce Department initially resisted, it applied the conversion factor suggested by the panel, reducing the duty from eight cents to three cents per kilo.

But when the Canadian pork producers asked the binational panel to review an ITC finding that there was a threat of material injury to U.S. producers, bureaucratic resistance increased. The panel was composed, in this case, of

30. *Replacement parts for self-propelled bituminous paving equipment from Canada,* USA-89-1904-02 (Ottawa and Washington, D.C.: Binational Secretariat).

31. Ibid.

32. *Fresh, chilled, or frozen pork from Canada,* USA-89-1904-06 (Ottawa and Washington, D.C.: Binational Secretariat).

three Canadians and two Americans. On 24 August 1990, the panel found that the ITC's CVD determination used questionable statistics, producing erroneous assessments. The panel then remanded the administrative determination to the ITC. In response, on 23 October 1990, the ITC reported its findings, maintaining its finding of material injury by reason of subsidized imports.

On 22 January 1991, the panel once again remanded the case to the ITC, explicitly holding that its findings were not supported by substantial evidence and that there was no evidence of causation. Finally, in line with the panel's views, on 12 February 1991, the ITC held that the U.S. pork industry was not materially injured. Of great importance is the ITC's opinion following the second remand order. The ITC stated that it changed its determination only because of the panel's decision, even though the commission believed that the second remand order violated the spirit of the FTA. The commission expressly noted that the panel's conclusions were "counter intuitive, counter factual, and illogical, but legally binding."[33] In this case, the U.S. government did appeal the panel order, asking for an Extraordinary Challenge Committee. That committee, however, unanimously dismissed the request, affirming the panel's decision.[34] Grudging adherence by the ITC and affirmation by the Extraordinary Challenge Committee strengthened the institutional status of the dispute-resolution mechanisms.

In summary, the FTA and later NAFTA have created a dispute-settlement mechanism that can and has fundamentally altered the behavior of the U.S. bureaucracy. This occurred because binational boards—with more liberal preferences—became the last mover in unfair trade cases, a position previously held by the courts. This enabled importers, frustrated by a decision by the U.S. trade bureaucracy, to choose to petition to a forum in which they had a higher chance of getting their preferred outcome. Binational boards institutionalized their preferences by stipulating acceptable procedures with each remand. The result is that the ITA and the ITC have become more risk-averse in dealing with Canadian and now Mexican cases, choosing to follow the methods prescribed by the binational boards, not procedures used in cases filed against other countries. The outcome is what Canada and Mexico had hoped for: greater relief from U.S. unfair trade law.

Binding itself to international arbitration

The prediction that U.S. behavior would move in the direction of more openness is supported by the data on Canadian cases. The Canadians wanted the FTA as a means to change U.S. unfair trade protection. The outcome was

33. U.S. International Trade Commission, *Fresh, chilled, or frozen pork from Canada,* 2d remand determination, inv. no. 701-TA-298, 12 February 1991. Secretariat case no. USA 1904-89-11.

34. *Fresh, chilled, or frozen pork from Canada,* ECC-91-1904-01USA (Ottawa and Washington, D.C.: Binational Secretariat).

just such a change in behavior, even though the statutes themselves were not changed. Canadian negotiators were not able to abrogate U.S. law, but in a majority of cases, the review process led to lowered duties through either partial or full remands to the ITA and/or the ITC. In addition, the structure of and the jurisdiction afforded to binational panels have led to a partial reinterpretation of U.S.-levied AD and CVD. Although either a revision in U.S. law or national treatment for Canadian products would have been a superior solution from the perspective of Canadian exporters, the treaty did shift U.S. policy in their preferred direction.

What explains this outcome, given that conventional models of international politics would predict that the United States would dominate in any international bargaining situation? Although economists would argue that the virtue of lowered barriers to trade is a sufficient explanation for such a policy, few political analysts would suggest that U.S. behavior was motivated by such an interest. If the key interest of negotiators was an agreement establishing low prices for U.S. consumers and producers, there would have been little contest with Canadians. Low prices through an open regional market were the centerpiece of Canada's vision for the FTA. Negotiations, however, stalled on just this point. The United States would not guarantee access to Canadian products as if they were "made in America."

Similarly, the suggestion that the United States capitulated on the issue of binational panels because it was outmaneuvered at the bargaining table leaves much unexplained. If Canada was able to manipulate the closing days of negotiations, why did she not obtain her preferred outcome, exceptions for Canadian products from U.S. trade law? Instead, the agreement included the U.S. idea of arbitration panels covering only AD and CVD law.

The explanation offered here is rooted in the political relationship between the President and the trade bureaucracy. While the President has the ability to either veto or set the amount of protections to be granted to a U.S. producer under most trade statutes, such authority is absent in the area of CVDs and ADs. This lack of authority partially explains the vast increase in such cases relative to other forms of protection in the years preceding the FTA. Where Presidents have regularly overturned, for reasons of national interest, recommendations to close the U.S. market, they have found themselves unable to countervail against a decision of the bureaucracy under CVD and AD law.

The proposal for a binational dispute-settlement procedure was included in the FTA because it was a logical solution to multiple problems. Given Canadian intransigence on obtaining some relief from U.S. trade law, this concession allowed Canadian trade representatives to return to Ottawa with a politically acceptable deal. The individual supporting the idea of binational judicial review was an important member of the U.S. House Ways and Means Committee, who could help carry the legislation through Congress. Most important, the solution solved a key problem facing the executive in making trade policy: controlling a bureaucracy with protectionist preferences. The

President's foreign economic policy goals frequently had been frustrated by the power of an autonomous trade bureaucracy. Both the FTA and NAFTA reduced that autonomy and were therefore preferred by the President even though it reduced the ability of the United States to retaliate to unfair trade competition abroad.

U.S. trade laws

A review of U.S. trade policy shows two dimensions on which U.S. trade laws vary: the intent of the exporter and presidential autonomy. Escape-clause relief is an example of a law that protects U.S. producers who are unable to compete with "fairly" traded imports; Section 301, Section 337, AD, and CVD laws are examples of statutes that protect U.S. producers from competition from "unfairly" traded goods. The second dimension of difference is administrative—in all but AD and CVD cases, the executive can either dismiss a case or fundamentally change the amount of relief granted by the bureaucracy on grounds of the national interest. For many reasons, from foreign policy to domestic efficiency concerns, Presidents want control over the placement of a tariff on foreign goods. Given the structure of U.S. trade law, Presidents do not have this control for AD and CVD cases. Marked by the period in which these laws were first written, these laws give Presidents little latitude or control over this aspect of trade policy.[35]

The impetus for legislating the United States' first AD law was Section 5 of the Federal Trade Commission Act of 1914, which stated "unfair methods of competition are declared unlawful." In 1919, the U.S. Tariff Commission submitted a report to the House Ways and Means Committee suggesting that current law did not protect domestic manufacturers from foreign unfair trade practices. The report recommended that "some official body moving along lines sanctioned by Congress in the Federal Trade Commission Act, may reasonably be specifically instructed to deal with dumping as a manifestation of unfair competitive methods"[36]; AD legislation, in its modern form, appeared two years later, in 1921.

The intent of AD laws is to counter international price discrimination. Unlike other laws that stop price discrimination, AD legislation targets competition and injury to individual competitors, not to competition itself. Under 1947 General Agreement on Tariffs and Trade rules, dumping is defined as the introduction of products of one country into the market of another at "less than normal value of the products." "Less than normal value" is either a price that is less than the comparable price of a like product destined for consumption in the exporting country or, in the absence of such a domestic price, the highest comparable price for a like product in a third country or the

---

35. On the historical origins of trade policy, see Goldstein 1993.
36. U.S. Tariff Commission 1919.

cost of production of the product in the country of origin (plus selling costs and profits).[37]

While dumping involves corporations, CVDs apply to practices of governments. Through state "subsidization" of home producers, nation-states attempt to increase their share of world trade. Because long-term dumping often reflects such a state policy, the two laws work together. Both counteract what are considered illegitimate forms of international trade.

If a nation directly or indirectly gives a bounty or a grant—that is, a subsidy—to one of its domestic producers, U.S. law stipulates that an additional duty equal to the net amount of the subsidy will be levied on that product when it is imported into the United States. Current CVD legislation appeared in the Tariff Act of 1930, but similar mandates against such foreign practices were promulgated in both 1909 and 1913. In 1909, CVDs were part of the maximum and minimum arrangements. These stipulated two tariff schedules, with the higher applied to nations using undue discrimination against the United States with "tariff rates or provisions, trade or other regulations, charges, exactions in any other manner" or on export bounty or duty. In 1913, the U.S. Secretary of the Treasury was authorized "to impose additional duties equal to the amount of any grant or bounty on exportation given by any foreign country."

The procedures by which an industry obtains either an AD or a CVD are virtually the same (see Figure 1). In CVD cases before 1979, the law neither delineated how the investigation should be conducted nor described the appropriate criteria to consider. Rather, upon completion of the investigation, the Secretary of the Treasury would decide whether to impose the duty and assign an appropriate "equalizing" amount. After the United States agreed to the International Subsidy Codes in 1979, expanded criteria including a material injury test to be determined by the ITC were added.

AD criteria always have been more defined. The major component in the procedure is the determination of whether sales were at less than fair value. Although often charged with being inconsistent and highly discretionary, when compared with CVD law, the criteria for such a determination are considerably more detailed. If a positive ruling is made, the case goes to the ITC to determine whether domestic "injury" resulted from the dumping. Until 1979, the ITC had wide discretion in its determinations. No hearing was necessary, even if requested by the petitioners. Such discretion was modified after the Tokyo Round, when the United States agreed to follow the General Agreement on Tariffs and Trade's AD codes.

Overall, AD and CVD legislation reveals a far clearer censure of foreign trade than does a law such as the escape clause. The arguments that low prices combat inflation, provide consumers with cheap goods, or are a healthy part of trade hold no weight when the goods are foreign. The result is that the

---

37. Jackson 1979a, 3.

standards for aid receipt in both AD and CVD cases are much lower than those stipulated for other trade remedies. As U.S. producers met increasing competition in their home market, this lower standard made these laws a popular means for obtaining government aid against foreign imports. And as industry increasingly relied on these statutes, Presidents found themselves unable to stop industries from acquiring "administered protection" and unable to muster a majority in Congress to change these laws.

The FTA and U.S. presidential autonomy

The existence of variation in presidential authority over product-specific protection helps to explain why the FTA and NAFTA set up two quite separate methods to deal with trade disputes. Where the President has control over the final adjudication of a trade law, disputes are settled in a more political setting. But in the areas in which the executive does not have discretionary authority— CVD and AD cases—the United States agreed to binding international dispute-resolution panels.

The settlement process of most trade disputes—including problems with trade remedies as diverse as under the escape clause, Section 301, and Section 337 (patent violations)—is detailed in Article 18 of the FTA (Article 20 of NAFTA). Where Chapter 19 created the binational panels that had "binding" authority over a narrow set of issues, Chapter 18 created a formal institution, the Canada–United States Trade Commission composed of representatives of both governments, that had high visibility but limited powers. Disputes not settled by the commission in thirty days could be referred to arbitration. On the request of either party, however, the commission could use an alternative procedure, that is, to convene a panel of experts to make recommendations. Countries, however, could ignore the panel's findings. Unlike Chapter 19 procedures, Chapter 18 is a traditional dispute-settlement mechanism characterized by state-to-state bargaining.

Under the FTA, far fewer Chapter 18 than Chapter 19 cases were investigated. Canada initiated only one case; the United States initiated four. Of these, only the first two involved real disputes; the other three involved the clarification of regulations. And consistent with a relative power interpretation of the agreement, the three cases in which there was a final ruling all favored the United States.

Although a complete explanation of the genesis of the variation between these two dispute-settlement mechanisms would entail delving into the history of the negotiations themselves, it is clear, *ex post,* that in Section 19 the President obtained an institutional arrangement and policy closer to his preferred position than was the status quo. Section 18 procedures—in which the President retains full control over outcomes—would have been even more preferred, but binding arbitration was still superior to having a bureaucracy make decisions unfettered by presidential foreign policy concerns. According to this logic, binding arbitration is one more way in which the executive office has succeeded in reining in Congress, the U.S. bureaucracy, and import-competing interest groups. Thus, the President's acquiescence to an independent international organization moved U.S. policy in a free trade direction without decreasing his domestic authority.

Where presidential support for the treaty is logical, congressional endorsement is more difficult to explain. Although the President plays a key role in trade policymaking, presidential power remains circumscribed by Congress. Congressional agreement is necessary for any change in trade law and on all trade treaties. Congressional oversight includes budget setting and appointment powers to the multitude of agencies and courts, domestic and international, that set trade policy. Although Congress usually acquiesces to presidential leadership, the reduction in the powers of the Treasury Department in 1979, repeated disputes over appointments of ITC commissioners, and increasing interest group pressure on congressional representatives to obtain product-specific protection are reminders to the executive that his independence could be easily constrained.[38]

More than the President, Congress has felt an increase in social pressures that have resulted from the growing U.S. trade imbalance. To some extent, Congress shields itself from group pressures by delegating trade powers to the President and granting the President the autonomy to deny protection if not in the national interest. Inadvertently however, by making unilateral trade protectionism more difficult to attain, Congress encouraged relief under unfair trade laws. Because AD and CVD decisions remain out of the President's direct jurisdiction, rational industries increasingly petitioned for trade relief under these statutes. The increased salience of unfair trade relief then made it politically infeasible for Congress to liberalize these trade laws. Rather, congressional action since the 1970s has been the opposite: legislation has led to eased standards and greater autonomy for the bureaucracy.[39]

In that congressional and presidential preferences may not be the same on the issue of free trade, congressional agreement to a treaty with binational arbitration may be explained by a procedural rule. The FTA was sent to Congress under an agreed-upon closed rule or "fast-track" authority, thereby foreclosing a congressional veto of one aspect but not the total negotiated agreement; Congress had to vote for the FTA in its entirety. When viewed as a whole, the FTA was crafted to please a majority of the members of Congress. The United States received considerable access to the Canadian market, both in trade and foreign direct investment. The FTA contained specific and elaborate provisions for large industries such as automobile manufacturing. Thus, bundled together within the agreement were both access to the Canadian market, something business groups supported, and binding arbitration. And

38. On the U.S. Congress and trade policy, see Pastor 1980.
39. Goldstein 1993.

even the arbitration procedures gave Congress some statutory control. In principle, Congress retained control over the pool of U.S. panelists.

An explanation, however, that relies on fast-track procedures and bundling as explanations for congressional behavior still begs the question. Why would Congress grant, *ex ante,* fast-track authority knowing that this dilemma would arise? The simplest response may be that congressional preferences are less protectionist than is assumed, given the structure of the institution. Certainly Congress does not speak with one voice. The parties differ in their commitment to the U.S. trade liberalization program as do the chambers. Congress recognizes that trade, a policy that renders specific benefits and diffuse costs, is prone to collective action problems and suboptimal outcomes. Both parties remain committed to a general policy of trade openness, and most senior members of the trade subcommittees are more free trade–oriented than is the majority. The idea of the binational panels came from a congressman who has repeatedly defended a policy of liberal trade. Overall, the historical record on Congress and trade shows a pattern of rabble-rousing that draws attention to constituent problems but rarely leads to item-specific protectionism, as was the custom a hundred years ago.

"True" congressional preferences on the FTA and on trade in general may be more liberal than those deduced from the structure of the institution.[40] Congressional members were involved in all aspects of the negotiation process of the FTA. The binational panel proposal—named after its author, Sam Gibbons, chair of the House Trade Subcommittee—was defended in testimony both because it was necessary to gain Canadian consent and because it expanded the role of judicial review in the trade-making process.[41]

In sum, Congress may not only defend policies that benefit constituents but as well support rules such as fast-track, binational judicial review or an executive veto as a convenient shield from powerful interest groups. Although the House Ways and Means Committee retains oversight control over who is eligible to sit on the binational boards, the committee failed to intervene under the FTA. Ways and Means has been somewhat more active in the expansion of the list under NAFTA, but even so, congressional consent to NAFTA is good evidence that Congress was not interested in curtailing the panel process, even given the activist decisions of many of the boards.

Conclusions: the internationalization of law

We can now return to the issues raised at the start of this article. Two key insights, about international institutions in general and the power of interna-

---

40. For empirical support for the existence of a freer-trade Congress, see Pastor 1980. See also Destler, Odell, and Elliott 1987.
41. U.S. House 1988, 87 and 99. See also Doern and Tomlin 1994, 186–88.

tional law in particular, may be derived from this study. First, international institutions can and do directly constrain domestic policy. This can occur even when a nation's laws do not change and the international body is powerless to sanction. In the case of the FTA and NAFTA, the incentives of the domestic bureaucracy were affected by an oversight agency that had the authority only to remand. In that the panels resolved individual disputes by offering general guidelines for how cases should be handled, they created a new and shared understanding of how the United States should administer its own domestic law. This observation confirms what are often normative arguments on the benefits of international law made by members of the legal community.[42] However, the causal story here is neither a belief in the need to observe common rules and norms nor a fear that cheating will undermine cooperation. Rather, U.S. agreement to constrain its behavior was a function of the interests of powerful domestic actors.[43]

Second, and as important, the degree of asymmetry in the benefits of a specific international agreement cannot be assessed merely by looking at the relative aggregate power of national signatories.[44] As well, a number of domestic factors—institutional structures in particular—will influence the form and the ultimate authority of international agreements. The variation between Chapters 18 and 19 of the Canadian–U.S. agreement makes sense in the context of the power and interests of the U.S. President. This is not to say that national power is unimportant, but that the form and extent of U.S. agreements may be directed as much at domestic concerns as by considerations of the more aggregate national interest.

International institutions facilitate cooperative behavior among nations. As well, they may serve a number of specific political purposes for policymakers at home. In this case, the President delegated control to an independent international organization because it was consistent with his long-standing interest in constraining opponents of trade liberalization. In this sense, the FTA became an international solution to a domestic problem. It was an arrangement that blocked the ability of losers to erode support for an agreement supported by a majority coalition, demonstrating what institutionalists have repeatedly argued: institutional arrangements do not have neutral distributional consequences. Nations that are constrained by domestic institutions may not only have an international bargaining edge but, as well, international bargains can be a means of empowering particular domestic actors.

42. See, among others, Lowenfeld 1994; Hudec 1987; and Jackson 1979a.
43. For the neoliberal argument suggesting that dispute settlement is a functional response to problems of enforcement, see Keohane 1984. For rules as a response to problems of incomplete contracting, see Milgrom and Roberts 1992.
44. For an analysis of the distribution of gains using aggregate power, see Krasner 1993.

References

Anderson, Keith B. 1993. Antidumping laws in the United States. *Journal of World Trade* 27(2): 99–117.

Barton, John, and Barry Carte. 1993. International law and institutions for a new age. *Georgetown Law Journal* 81:535–62.

Cameron, David. 1988. The Canada–United States Free Trade Agreement, Department of Political Science, Yale University, New Haven, Conn. Unpublished.

Cameron, Duncan, Stephen Clarkson, and Mel Watkins. 1988. Market access, in *The free trade deal,* edited by Duncan Cameron. Toronto:Lorimer.

Cannon, James, Jr. 1991. Binational panel dispute settlement under Article 1904 of the United States–Canada Free Trade Agreement: A procedural comparison with the United States Court of International Trade. *Law and Policy in International Business* 22:689–719.

Destler, I. M., John Odell, with Kimberly Ann Elliott. 1987. *Anti-protectionism: Changing forces in United States trade politics.* Washington, D.C.: Institute for International Economics.

Doern, G. Bruce, and Brian Tomlin. 1991. *Faith and fear.* Toronto: Stoddart.

Evans, Peter, Harold Jacobson, and Robert Plutnam, eds. 1995. *Double-edged diplomacy.* Berkeley: University of California Press.

Goldstein, Judith. 1993. *Ideas, interests, and American trade policy.* Ithaca, N.Y.: Cornell University Press.

———. 1995. Judicial review and American trade policy, Stanford University, Stanford, Calif. Unpublished.

Goldstein, Judith, and Stephanie Lenway. 1989. Interests or institutions: An inquiry into congressional–ITC relations. *International Studies Quarterly* 33:303–27.

Graham, William. 1988. The role of the Commission in the Canada–U.S. Free Trade Agreement: A Canadian perspective, in *United States/Canada Free Trade Agreement: The economic and legal implications.* Washington, D.C.: American Bar Association.

Hart, Michael A. 1994. *Decision at midnight.* Vancouver: University of British Columbia.

Hudec, Robert. 1987. Dispute resolution under a North American free trade area: The importance of domestic legal setting. *Canada–U.S. Law Journal* 12:329–36.

Jackson, John. 1979a. Governmental disputes in international trade relations: A proposal in the context of GATT. *Journal of World Trade Law* 13:1–21.

———. 1979b. Introduction: Perspectives on antidumping law and policy. In *Antidumping law: Policy and implementation,* vol. 1 of *Michigan yearbook of international legal studies.* Ann Arbor: University of Michigan Press.

Keohane, Robert. 1984. *After hegemony.* Princeton, N.J.: Princeton University Press.

Keohane, Robert, and Joseph Nye. 1977. *Power and interdependence: World politics in transition.* Boston: Little Brown.

Krasner, Stephen. 1993. Global communications and national power: Life on the Pareto frontier. *World Politics* 45:336–66.

Lowenfeld, Andreas. 1994. Remedies along with rights: Institutional reform in the new GATT. *American Journal of International Law* 88:477–88.

Milgrom, Paul, and John Roberts. 1992. *Economics, organization, and management.* Englewood Cliffs, N.J.: Prentice-Hall.

Odell, John. 1985. The outcomes of international trade conflicts: The U.S. and South Korea, 1960–1981. *International Studies Quarterly* 29:263–86.

Pastor, Robert. 1980. *Congress and the politics of U.S. foreign economic policy.* Berkeley: University of California Press.

Putnam, Robert. 1988. Diplomacy and domestic politics: The logic of two-level games. *International Organization* 42:427–60.

Schott, Jeffrey J. 1988. The Free Trade Agreement: A U.S. assessment. In *The Canada–United States Free Trade Agreement: The global impact,* edited by Jeffrey Schott and Murray Smith. Washington, D.C.: Institute for International Economics.

United States–Canada Free Trade Implementation Act of 1988 (FTA). U.S. Public Law 100-449, 28 September 1988.

U.S. General Accounting Office. 1995. *U.S.–Canada Free Trade Agreement: Factors contributing to controversy in appeals of trade remedy cases to binational panels.* Briefing report to congressional requesters. Doc. no. GGD-95-175BR, June.

U.S. House. 1988. Committee on Judiciary. Subcommittee on Courts. *Hearings on the U.S.–Canada Free Trade Agreement.* 102d Cong., 2d session, April 18.

U.S. Tariff Commission. 1919. *Information concerning dumping and unfair foreign competition in the U.S. and Canada's antidumping law.* Washington, D.C.: Government Printing Office.

Winham, Gilbert. 1986. *International trade and the Tokyo Round negotiation.* Princeton, N.J.: Princeton University Press.

II.
Multinational Firms and Globalization

O ne of the central features of the modern world economy is the accelerating spread of business enterprise across political frontiers, carried by a rising tide of direct foreign investment. National markets once linked mainly by conventional arm's-length trade are now increasingly and intimately entwined by flows of capital, technology, and managerial expertise. Production and financial structures that were once framed mainly by sovereign states are now increasingly defined by the cross-border activities of private firms.

Two implications seem to follow. One is that the world economy is rapidly becoming globalized, as pressures grow for ever deeper convergence between national economic systems and behavior. The other is that domestic and international politics are being rapidly transformed by the emergence of a powerful new class of societal actors—multinational enterprises. Both implications are controversial and have generated a good deal of discussion among scholars.

One of the earliest contributions to this discussion was a seminal special issue of International Organization on "Transnational Relations and World Politics," edited by Joseph Nye and Robert Keohane, which included some of the very first systematic analyses ever published of the then new role of multinational firms in the global economy.[1] A decade later the subject was revisited in the pages of International Organization by Raymond Vernon, who is widely acknowledged to have pioneered the study of the politics of multinational enterprise.[2] Subsequently, many scholars have debated the role played by politics—and, in particular, the power of the United States—in creating the environment in which multinationals have been able to flourish. (For more on these issues, see the companion to this volume, Theory and Structure in International Political Economy.) Other specialists, focusing on consequences rather than causes, have addressed implications for policy at both the national and international levels. The bargaining relationship between multinationals and governments, for example, was examined by Dennis J. Encarnation and Louis T. Wells and Barbara Jenkins.[3] Problems of regulation were evaluated by Kathryn Sik-

1. Nye and Keohane 1971.
2. Vernon 1981.
3. See Encarnation and Wells 1985; and Jenkins 1986.

kink, Simon Reich, Susan Sell, and C. S. Eliot Kang.[4] The increasingly complex interaction of state and corporate decision making was explored by Jonathan B. Tucker, Vicki L. Golich, and Kenneth A. Rodman.[5] Broader implications for the traditional territorial state and national identity were debated by Ethan B. Kapstein and John G. Ruggie.[6]

Multinational firms come in all shapes and sizes, of course, and engage in a wide range of business, from extracting natural resources and assembling parts to providing the most sophisticated manufacturing and financial services. Banking enterprises, by convention, are typically analyzed separately and will be taken up in the next section of this volume. Here we concentrate on the emerging role of nonfinancial enterprises in the politics of the world economy today.

The rise of multinational firms has added to the complexity of politics in both host and home countries—the states where direct investment takes place as well as those where enterprises originate. In economically developing host countries, it was once thought, the relationship between multinationals and government typically took the form of an "obsolescing bargain." Initial negotiations on terms of prospective investments were expected to favor multinationals, which possess considerable advantages vis-à-vis poor and often isolated developing nations. But once capital was "sunk," it became effectively hostage to the policies of the host government. The resulting shift of relative power could thus be assumed to lead eventually to a renegotiation of terms less favorable to corporate interests. As Stephen J. Kobrin (Chapter 4) points out, however, the obsolescing–bargain model is really applicable mainly to cases involving natural-resource industries, which now account for a diminishing proportion of total direct investment. In the rapidly growing manufacturing sector, Kobrin shows, the story is much more complicated. Obsolescence is possible in such cases, too. But extensive empirical evidence suggests that it is by no means inevitable. Depending on circumstances, changes in bargaining power may be almost completely out of the control of host governments. Corporate negotiating leverage could even increase rather than decrease over time.

In home countries, too, multinationals have become powerful political actors, changing the equation of forces on a wide range of policy issues. Most evident is their influence on the politics of foreign trade policy, as Helen Milner and David Yoffie (Chapter 5) demonstrate in a penetrating analysis of corporate trade preferences. Traditionally, debate over trade policy was viewed as a simple, dichotomous contest between protectionism and free trade. Industries lobbied either for trade restrictions or unconditional liberalization. More recently, however, many multinational firms have begun to advocate a third type of policy—a "strategic" trade policy based on the principle of specific reciprocity—supporting lower barriers at home only when reciprocated by a comparable opening of key markets abroad. Milner and

4. See Sikkink 1986; Reich 1989; Sell 1995; and Kang 1997.
5. See Tucker 1991; Golich 1992; and Rodman 1995.
6. Kapstein and Ruggie 1993.

Yoffie attribute the emergence of industry-wide strategic trade demands to three critical variables: changes in industry economics (including, in particular, economies of scale and cumulative learning effects), foreign government policy intervention, and variations in industry structure. Their analysis emphasizes how much more complex policy formulation has become in an era of accelerating globalization.

Of particular importance in this context is the underlying nature of the multinational firm itself. As national economic systems grow ever closer, are corporations, too, shedding their distinctive characteristics to become more alike in their fundamental strategies and operations? That is the crucial question addressed by Louis Pauly and Simon Reich (Chapter 6). For most theorists, the answer appears self-evident: the logic of integrating markets is bound to drive corporations to define their interests increasingly in a global context, leading to deep structural convergence in terms of both organization and behavior. According to Pauly and Reich, however, little empirical evidence exists to support such a proposition. On the contrary, detailed study of multinational firms based in the United States, Germany, and Japan shows just the opposite. Firms continue to diverge systematically along a variety of dimensions, including internal governance and long-term financing structures, approaches to research and development, and overseas investment and intrafirm trading strategies. Institutional and ideological legacies of distinctive national histories continue to shape core corporate preferences. This inertia, in turn, suggests that domestic politics and the substance of state policies may well resist prolonged convergence as well. The world economy may be rapidly globalizing, but continuing to refine our understanding of the behavior of diverse multinational firms as well as governments remains essential.

References

Encarnation, Dennis J., and Louis T. Wells, Jr. 1985. Sovereignty En Garde: Negotiating with Foreign Investors. *International Organization* 39 (1):47–78.

Golich, Vicki L. 1992. From Competition to Collaboration: The Challenge of Commercial-class Aircraft Manufacturing. *International Organization* 46 (4):899–934.

Jenkins, Barbara. 1986. Reexamining the "Obsolescing Bargain" : A Case Study of Canada's National Energy Program. *International Organization* 40 (1):139–66.

Kang, C. S. Eliot. 1997. U.S. Politics and Greater Regulation of Inward Foreign Direct Investment. *International Organization* 51 (2):301–33.

Kapstein, Ethan B., and John G. Ruggie. Territoriality and Who Is "Us"? *International Organization* 47 (3):501–506.

Nye, Joseph S., Jr., and Robert O. Keohane, eds. 1971. Transnational Relations and World Politics. *International Organization* 25 (3). Special issue.

Reich, Simon. 1989. Roads to Follow: Regulating Direct Foreign Investment. *International Organization* 43 (4):543–84.

Rodman, Kenneth A. 1995. Sanctions at Bay? Hegemonic Decline, Multinational Corporations, and U.S. Economic Sanctions Since the Pipeline Case. *International Organization* 49 (1):105–37.

Sell, Susan. 1995. Intellectual Property Protection and Antitrust Policy in the Developing World: Crisis, Coercion, and Choice. *International Organization* 49 (2):315–50.

Sikkink, Kathryn. 1986. Codes of Conduct for Transnational Corporations: The Case of the WHO/ UNICEF Code. *International Organization* 40 (4):815–40.

Tucker, Jonathan B. 1991. Partners and Rivals: A Model of International Collaboration in Advanced Technology. *International Organization* 45 (1):83–120.

Vernon, Raymond. 1981. Sovereignty at Bay: Ten Years After. *International Organization* 35 (3):517–29.

Testing the bargaining hypothesis in the manufacturing sector in developing countries
Stephen J. Kobrin

Introduction

Relationships between developing host countries and multinational corporations are characterized by antipathy and mutuality of interest.[1] When conflict and compatibility coexist, a range of mutually satisfactory agreements (that is, each party's perceived benefit/cost ratio is positive) are possible. The actual distribution of benefits depends on the terms of the agreement which are, in turn, a function of the relative bargaining power of the host country (HC) and multinational corporation (MNC).

The bargaining power model of HC-MNC interaction, which conceives of economic nationalism in terms of rational self-interest,[2] assumes both inherent conflict between foreign investors and developing countries and ". . . a foundation of convergent interests."[3] Observers disagree about the relative balance of convergent and divergent interests, the nature of the bargaining process, the determinants of outcomes, and the implications of the model for states and the interstate system. However, the bargaining model is accepted by a wide range of scholars, including mainstream economists, such as

An earlier version of this paper was presented at the annual meeting of the American Political Science Association in Washington, D.C., on 28 August 1986.

I would like to thank Bill Greene and Robert Kurdle for help with the statistics and Ben Gomes-Casseres, Joseph Grieco, Briance Mascarenhas, Tom Murtha, Theodore Moran, José de la Torre, and Lou Wells for comments.

1. In his study of foreign enterprise in developing countries, Isaiah Frank concludes that, ". . . it is fair to state that in much of the developing world, relations between transnational corporations and host countries have been marked by considerable tension." Frank, *Foreign Enterprise in Developing Countries* (Baltimore: Johns Hopkins University Press, 1980), p. 25.

2. Theodore H. Moran, "Multinational Corporations and the Developing Countries: An Analytical Overview" in Theodore H. Moran, ed., *Multinational Corporations: The Political Economy of Foreign Direct Investment* (Lexington, Mass.: Lexington, 1985), pp. 3–24.

3. Douglas C. Bennett and Kenneth E. Sharpe, "The World Automobile Industry and Its Implications" in Richard S. Newfarmer, ed., *Profits, Progress, and Poverty* (Notre Dame: University of Notre Dame Press, 1985), p. 22.

International Organization 41, 4, Autumn 1987, pp. 609–38

Charles Kindleberger and Raymond Vernon, and dependency theorists, such as Peter Evans. In its general terms, it is *the* currently accepted paradigm of HC-MNC relations in international political-economy.

Much of the bargaining literature focuses on vertically integrated, extractive investments characterized by risk, sunk costs, government learning, and oligopolistic rivalry.[4] In the natural resource industries, there is strong evidence that: 1) outcomes are a function of relative bargaining power (the model applies); and 2) from the point of view of the MNC, the bargain obsolesces over time as power shifts to developing HCs.

There have been relatively few attempts to apply the obsolescing bargain model to manufacturing investment. Manufacturing is more heterogenous than natural resources and both the modes of HC-MNC interaction and the determinants of relative bargaining power are more complex. Although the basic assumptions of the bargaining model appear valid in this context, authors question its implications, especially the systematic shift of power to host countries. The issue is important as manufacturing investment is a keystone of industrialization in many countries.

This article reports a cross-national study of the bargaining model using data from 563 subsidiaries of U.S. manufacturing firms in forty-nine developing countries. My objective is to compliment the case study literature with a broad empirical test that forces explicit conceptualization and operationalization. Given the constraints imposed by a static test of a dynamic phenomenon, my immediate goals are limited to testing the applicability of the bargaining model to the manufacturing sector and identifying the determinants of change in the distribution of power.

I first review the development of the bargaining paradigm in the literature and then discuss its application to the manufacturing sector. Next, I summarize empirical studies, operationalize the concept, present the methodology. After an analysis of research results, I finally apply the findings to draw some conclusions about the probability of obsolescence.

The obsolescing bargain

Kindleberger, noting the arguments against foreign direct investment arising from the "peasant, the populist, the mercantilist, or the nationalist which each of us harbors in his breast,"[5] models HC-MNC interaction as a bilateral monopoly. As the interests of host countries and foreign investors are likely to diverge, the two parties become antagonists and governments seek to

---

4. Richard S. Newfarmer, "International Industrial Organization and Development: A Survey," in Newfarmer, *Profits, Progress and Poverty*, p. 17.

5. Charles P. Kindleberger, *Six Lectures on Direct Investment* (New Haven, Conn.: Yale University Press, 1969), p. 145.

renegotiate the initial concession agreement when the initial advantages of MNCs erode.

"Most instances of direct investment in less developed countries are akin to bilateral monopoly, where the reserve prices of the two parties are far apart, and there is no determinate solution such as the competitive price." Relying primarily on petroleum sector examples, he concludes, ". . . in the bilateral monopoly, non-zero sum game represented by direct investment in the less developed country, there has been a steady shift in the advantages from the side of company to that of the country."[6]

Kindleberger articulates the essential components of the bargaining model: divergent interests; some degree of mutuality (the possibility of joint or non-zero sum gains); differences resolved through a bargaining process with outcomes a function of relative power; and changes in relative power over time. As a number of critics have noted, however, the bilateral monopoly model is static and assumes power is a function of the demand of each party for resources that the other possesses. It does not deal with uncertainty or politics—especially host country politics—or distinguish between potential power and its implementation.[7]

Vernon emphasizes the dynamics of the process and the role of uncertainty. He also bases his observations primarily—although not entirely—on trends in natural resource industries where MNCs possess considerable advantages relative to the very poor and often isolated developing host countries and the initial "bargains" reflect this marked asymmetry of power as well as the high risk of extractive ventures.[8]

Vernon concludes, however, that "almost from the moment that the signatures have dried on the document, powerful forces go to work that quickly render the agreements obsolete in the eyes of the government."[9] Once invested, fixed capital becomes "sunk," a hostage and a source of host country bargaining strength. The high risk associated with exploration and development diminishes when production begins. Technology, once arcane and proprietary, matures over time and becomes available on the open market. Through development and transfers from foreign direct investment the

6. Kindleberger, *Six Lectures,* pp. 149, 150.
7. Douglas C. Bennett and Kenneth E. Sharpe, "Agenda Setting and Bargaining Power: The Mexican State vs. Transnational Automobile Companies," *World Politics* 32 (October 1979), pp. 57–89; Moran, "Multinational Corporations and the Developing Countries"; Newfarmer, "International Industrial Organization"; and George Philip, "The Limitations of Bargaining Theory: A Case Study of the International Petroleum Company in Peru," *World Development* 4 (March 1976), pp. 231–39.
8. C. Fred Bergsten, Thomas Horst, and Theodore H. Moran, *American Multinationals and American Interests* (Washington, D.C.: Brookings Institution, 1978) and Raymond Vernon, *Sovereignty at Bay: The Multinational Spread of U.S. Enterprise* (New York: Basic Books, 1971).
9. Raymond Vernon, "The Obsolescing Bargain: A Key Factor in Political Risk," in Mark B. Winchester, ed., *The International Essays for Business Decision Makers,* vol. 5 (Houston: Center for International Business, 1980).

host country gains technological and managerial skills that reduce the value of those possessed by the foreigner.[10] In Theodore Moran's words, the host country "moves up a learning curve that leads from monitoring industry behavior to replicating complicated corporate functions."[11]

Vernon's model assumes both conflict and mutuality of interest, includes an initial agreement reached as a result of an often unequal (and sometimes implicit) bargaining process, and then posits a virtually *inevitable* shift in bargaining power to the host country which ultimately results in renegotiation. "In short, the foreign enterprise whose successful establishment had rested on some superior capability or knowledge lost its security of position as time eroded the initial advantage."[12]

Although there are exceptions,[13] the obsolescence of the bargain in the raw materials context is a function of inherent changes over time: it is endogenous. Bergsten, Horst, and Moran conclude the shift in power is cumulative, irreversible, and accelerating: "The obsolescing bargain constitutes a fundamental structural change in natural resource industries."[14]

To summarize, there is considerable agreement that the bargaining model applies to the extractive sector. Its components include: 1) a conflict of host country and MNC objectives;[15] 2) the possibility of joint or shared gains;[16] 3) bargaining over the actual distribution of joint gains;[17] and 4) at least in the

10. For detailed applications of the obsolescing bargain in the petroleum and copper industries, see Stephen J. Kobrin, "Diffusion as an Explanation of Oil Nationalization," *Journal of Conflict Resolution* 29 (March 1985), pp. 3–32 and Theodore H. Moran, *Multinational Corporations and the Politics of Dependence: Copper in Chile* (Princeton, N.J.: Princeton University Press, 1974).

11. Moran, *Multinational Corporations and the Politics of Dependence*, p. 164.

12. Vernon, *Sovereignty at Bay*, p. 27.

13. In the petroleum industry, for example, the development of offshore production in deep and difficult areas and the need for tertiary recovery have markedly increased the technological intensity of production and, in these circumstances, the MNCs have regained at least some bargaining power. Vernon argues that the proposition is complex, and when the technology of the industry grew more intensive or the optimum scale level expanded, the firms' initial advantages were restored. See Vernon, *Sovereignty at Bay*, p. 27.

14. Bergsten, Horst, and Moran, *American Multinationals*, pp. 143 and 322.

15. The conflict between the parties reflects differences over distribution of the joint gains from the investment (over taxation, pricing of state-supplied inputs, wage levels, and the like) and differences in objectives that render desired individual gains incompatible. The objectives of a private, profit-oriented firm and a more diffuse nation-state are likely to conflict, which is exacerbated since the former is a global actor concerned with returns to the system as a whole, while the latter is essentially local, concerned (at least ultimately) with impacts within its territory. "The problem is to redirect the global rationality of the multinational when it conflicts with the necessities of local accumulation: the State must continually coerce or cajole the multinationals into undertaking roles that they would otherwise abdicate." Peter B. Evans, *Dependent Development: The Alliance of Multinational, State, and Local Capital in Brazil* (Princeton, N.J.: Princeton University Press), p. 44.

16. Both firms and governments see net benefits from the participation of multinationals. See Bennett and Sharpe, "The World Automobile Industry."

17. The outcome of the bargaining process is determined by a great deal more than relative capabilities. A number of authors have noted that constraints, including the domestic political process, intervene between potential and actual power. See Bennett and Sharpe, "Agenda

case of the natural resource industries, a shift in relative power over time to the HCs.

Although the erosion of MNC bargaining power (at least over the longer run) is well established as the null hypothesis for extractive industries, the issue is far from settled for manufacturing firms. I now turn to application of the bargaining model to the manufacturing sector.

The manufacturing sector

Significant differences between extractive and manufacturing investment affect application of the model. While the variation between sub-sectors makes generalization difficult, most manufacturing investments do not entail the degree of risk, the national salience, or the large sunk costs typical in the extractive sector. Furthermore, inter- and intra-industry competition may well be more intense.

More important are differences in technology, global integration, MNC flexibility, and the impact of domestic politics. In many manufacturing industries, technology is more intense and dynamic than in natural resources. The pace and complexity of research and development may be beyond the capability (and geographic reach) of the host government. Bergsten, Horst, and Moran[18] argue that where technology is complex, rapidly changing, and closely held, the shift in bargaining power to developing countries proceeds least rapidly.

Manufacturing firms, particularly those with diversified product lines, have a good deal more flexibility and control than extractive investors; if bargaining power erodes, they may be able to exercise considerable choice in their response to host country demands. They can move to a new activity such as export, begin more complex manufacturing, add more value locally, manufacture new products, or incorporate additional technology to counter government requests.[19]

Although we find global integration in both extractive and manufacturing sectors, the process and its effects on HCs differ significantly. In the natural resources, the need for large capital expenditures under very uncertain conditions motivated extension of control over all stages of production through vertical integration.[20] International integration was an artifact of the geo-

Setting''; Dennis Encarnation and Louis T. Wells, Jr., ''Competitive Strategies in Global Industries: A View From The Host Country,'' Paper presented at the Harvard Business School's 75th Anniversary Colloquium on Global Industries, Boston, Mass., 1984; and Phillip, ''The Limitations of Bargaining Theory.''

18. Bergsten, Horst, and Moran, ''American Multinationals.''

19. Bennett and Sharpe, ''The World Automobile Industry,'' and Vernon, ''The Obsolescing Bargain.''

20. Neil H. Jacoby, *Multinational Oil* (New York: Macmillan, 1974).

graphical separation of reserves and major markets. As recent events in petroleum have demonstrated, it is not inherent.[21]

In certain manufacturing sectors—autos, electronics, and computers are excellent examples—the optimum scale of production or technological intensity has expanded to the point where multi-market or transnational competition is required for survival; most national markets are simply too small to support efficient manufacturing or generate even minimally competitive research and development budgets. International integration or global competition is an inherent requisite of efficient production.

The impact of domestic politics, which can limit the ability of host countries to mobilize potential sources of power, may also differ across sectors. As Moran[22] and others have demonstrated, a broad range of diverse interest groups often unite behind the government in conflict with natural resource investors exacerbating the erosion of bargaining power. That is less likely to be true in manufacturing, where investments are typically much smaller, less salient, and more thoroughly integrated into the local economy. After entry, as the firm becomes entrenched, its network of relationships with labor, suppliers, distributors, and customers may actually enhance its bargaining power over time.[23]

Case studies

While the case study literature is limited, there is no evidence of an unambiguous shift in bargaining power to HCs manufacturing. In fact, case studies of automobiles and pharmaceuticals indicate that bargaining power is not eroding. Douglas Bennett and Kenneth Sharpe conclude that the balance of power in a manufacturing industry such as automobiles may shift towards transnational firms over time, and Gary Gereffi finds that, as the MNC's source of power is often beyond the reach of the host country, and as it is likely to forge alliances with local groups, the firm's bargaining power may be weakest at the moment of entry and stronger thereafter.[24]

A counter example is provided by Joseph Grieco's[25] intensive case study of IBM's divestment in India as he finds technological changes enhanced rather than diminished the host country's bargaining power. (He argues that this case is not typical.) In summarizing a number of case studies, Gereffi and Richard Newfarmer conclude that, ". . . the growth of foreign invest-

21. Kobrin, "Diffusion as an Explanation."

22. Moran, *Multinational Corporations and the Politics of Dependence*.

23. Bennett and Sharpe, "Agenda Setting."

24. For automobiles, see Bennett and Sharpe, "Agenda Setting," and "The World Automobile Industry." For pharmaceuticals, see Gary Gereffi, "Drug Firms and Dependency in Mexico: The Case of the Steroid Hormone Industry," *International Organization* 32 (Winter 1978), pp. 237–86 and "The Global Pharmaceutical Industry and Its Impact in Latin America," in Newfarmer, *Profits, Progress, and Poverty*, pp. 259–98.

25. Joseph Grieco, "Between Dependency and Autonomy: India's Experience with the International Computer Industry," *International Organization* 36 (Summer 1982), pps. 609–632.

ment in manufacturing does not appear to have shifted bargaining power in favor of host governments."[26]

The available case studies are limited to a single sector in a single country. They do appear to confirm that the first three elements of the bargaining model—conflict, compatibility, and resolution through bargaining—apply to manufacturing. While the evidence is mixed, there is reason to suspect that the fourth—obsolescence—may not. I now turn to a brief review of statistical studies of the obsolescing bargain hypotheses in the manufacturing sector.

Statistical studies

Four statistical tests of the bargaining model have been reported in the international business literature. N. Fagre and Louis Wells test the hypothesis on a Latin American sample of the Harvard Business School's U.S. Multinational Data, using foreign ownership as the dependent variable.[27] Multiple regressions are significant, but their explanatory power is weak (R-squared of 12–14 percent). Coefficients for technological and advertising intensity, intra-system transfers (integration), and product diversity are significant. The results are consistent with a bargaining model, but the absence of any measure of host country capabilities means that industry structure rather than relative bargaining power is modeled.

Thomas Poynter studied "government intervention" in 104 subsidiaries of MNCs in Tanzania, Zambia, Indonesia, and Kenya during the early 1970s.[28] The dependent variable—the measure of intervention—is subsidiary managers' ex-post perception of changes in the structure and characteristics of their firm. Intra-system sourcing, subsidiary exports, employment of local nationals, firm size, strategic importance, and subsidiary contact with elites or the government were found significant at *.10* or better on a univariate basis. The tests show some relationship between firm characteristics and "intervention," but again, the lack of host country variables makes it impossible to draw any conclusions about relative bargaining power.

26. Gary Gereffi and Richard S. Newfarmer, "International Oligopoly and Uneven Development: Some Lessons From Industrial Case Studies" in Newfarmer, *Profits, Progress, and Poverty*, p. 387.

27. Although they argue that an ideal dependent variable would be some measure of the outcome of all HC-MNC negotiations, that data is not available and they use foreign ownership instead. As firm or state preferences may vary, raw ownership may not represent actual bargaining outcomes; they attempt two adjustments to reflect corporate and country objectives. To try to correct for company objectives, they subtracted the average for all a firm's subsidiaries in Europe (where ownership is generally unrestricted), and to adjust for country objectives they used the average ownership for all U.S. subsidiaries in that country. N. Fagre and Louis T. Wells, Jr., "Bargaining Power of Multinationals and Host Governments," *Journal of International Business Studies* 13 (Fall 1982), pp. 19–24.

28. Thomas A Poynter, "Government Intervention in Less Developed Countries: The Experience of Multinational Corporations," *Journal of International Business Studies* 13 (Spring/Summer 1982), pp. 9–25.

Donald Lecraw tests the bargaining hypothesis on data from 153 subsidiaries of multinationals in six industries in Thailand, Malaysia, Singapore, Indonesia, and the Philippines, using ownership to measure bargaining outcomes.[29] He includes one host country characteristic among his dependent variables, "attractiveness," measured subjectively through interviews. Measures of technological leadership, advertising intensity, subsidiary exports, MNC size, MNC-subsidiary integration, host country attractiveness, competition, and time are significant in the multiple regression with an R-squared of 63 percent. While Lecraw's results are certainly consistent with a bargaining framework, all but one of the independent variables reflect firm or industry characteristics.

Benjamin Gomes-Casseres tests the bargaining hypotheses as part of a much larger cross-national study of MNC ownership strategies (in both industrialized and developing countries) using the Harvard MNC data base. He develops a model of the propensity to joint venture in countries where ownership is not restricted (industrialized and developing), predicts the probability of a joint venture in restricted countries, and uses the residual as the dependent variable in analyses of bargaining power. While his study is too complex to summarize here, he includes measures of both industry and project structure, and host country characteristics. Although he does not attempt to draw inferences about obsolescence, he concludes that the bargaining framework applies and that "countries with large, growing, high-income markets were often able to insist on joint ventures, especially in marketing intensive industries."[30]

Both the case and statistical studies are consistent with the bargaining hypothesis: outcomes in the manufacturing sector are a function of relative bargaining power. Any conclusions about obsolescence, however, must be drawn from the case studies alone, and there the evidence is mixed. I now turn to operationalization of the obsolescing bargain concept.

Operationalization

In the bilateral monopoly formulation of the model, relative bargaining power is a function of the demand of each party for resources supplied by

---

29. Lecraw uses both raw ownership and an adjustment reflecting MNC and host country objectives. He takes the highest level of ownership for a given MNC in any country as its objective, and the lowest level of ownership for any MNC in a given country as the country's objective, and calculates bargaining success as:

$$(\text{actual--HC objective})/(\text{MNC objective--actual}).$$

Donald J. Lecraw, "Bargaining Power, Ownership, and Profitability of Transnational Corporations in Developing Countries," *Journal of International Business Studies* 15 (Spring/Summer 1984), pp. 27–43.

30. Benjamin Gomes-Casseres, "Multinational Ownership Strategies," DBA thesis, Harvard Business School, Boston, 1985, p. 345.

the other; the outcome is analogous to a price determined through negotiation in an imperfect market. As many authors have noted, however, such political factors as differences in the will to bargain or constraints that may prevent the actualization of potential power are ignored.

The difference between potential and actual power is important. As Robert Keohane and Joseph Nye note,[31] there is rarely a one-to-one relationship between control over resources and impacts on outcomes: ". . . power resources are not automatically translated into effective power over outcomes. Translation occurs by way of a political bargaining process in which skill, commitment, and coherence can . . . belie predictions based on the distribution of power resources."

Klaus Knorr argues that coercive power is generated in apparent exchange transactions if an actor: 1) has a substantial degree of monopoly power; 2) superior market knowledge and is able to exploit the other's ignorance; 3) demand that is inordinately intense and inelastic; or 4) access to coercive power derived from "military, economic, or some other power base."[32]

In the case of MNC-HC bargaining, actual power is a function of: 1) resources controlled by one party and demanded by the other; 2) constraints that prevent potential power from being implemented; and 3) the ability of either party to limit the behavior of the other directly (economic or political coercion). The first and second points encompass Knorr's first three conditions and the third point encompasses the last.

Power arising from the *relative demand for resources* flows from differences in capabilities, including the availability of substitutes. It is a function of firm-specific assets or ownership advantages[33] and imperfect markets that allow the firm to contain the advantages; host country capabilities that allow it to substitute for the firm's resources; and host country resources that are demanded by the firm, and the firm's ability to substitute for those resources.

Two types of *constraints* exist. First, politics may limit the ability of a host country (or MNC) to exploit power resulting from relative demand for resources. As neither host countries nor their governments are coherent or monolithic actors, various societal groups and government agencies will have different objectives relative to foreign investment, and the domestic political process may affect the translation of potential power into control over outcomes.[34] A business firm is also a political organization that is made

31. Robert O. Keohane and Joseph S. Nye, *Power and Interdependence: World Politics in Transition* (Boston: Little, Brown, 1975), p. 225.
32. Klaus Knorr, *The Power of Nations* (New York: Basic Books, 1975), p. 8.
33. John H. Dunning, "Explaining Changing Patterns of International Production: In Support of the Eclectic Theory," *Oxford Bulletin of Economic and Statistics* 41 (November 1980), pp. 269–95.
34. See Dennis Encarnation and Louis T. Wells, Jr., "Sovereignty en Garde: Negotiating With Foreign Investors," *International Organization* 39 (Winter 1985), pp. 47–78; Stephen E.

up of coalitions competing for power, and intra-firm conflict over objectives may constrain its ability to fully exploit its potential power.[35]

Second, structural characteristics of the MNC or HC may affect relative demand for resources or limit resource-based bargaining power. In globally integrated industries, for example, interdependence may constrain the bargaining power of host countries.[36] If efficient manufacture requires global rationalization, then subsidiaries are dependent on the larger system for inputs—including both material and technology—and for the disposal of outputs. The automony or freedom of action of any given country is limited since its output has value only in combination with that from other units in the system. Interdependence constrains autonomy.

Constraints also limit the ability of the MNC to translate control over resources into control over outcomes. The amount of competition in an industry, for example, affects the availability of substitutes, and thus relative demand for resources.

The MNC or HC may be able to prevent outcomes desired by the other party through *coercive power,* which is exogenous to the transaction. The most obvious example is formal colonial relationships that inhibit the freedom of host countries. The threat of home country military or political intervention is another form of potential coercion—for example, the U.S. government's restriction of Agency for International Development payments to Peru was an attempt to influence the dispute between that country and Exxon's (then Esso's) subsidiary.[37]

The line between resources and constraints is diffuse and its location may be situationally specific. Relative bargaining power is a function of: 1) relative demand for resources; 2) constraints on the implementation of potential power; and 3) negotiating skills:

$$RES_{MNC}, RES_{HC}, CONST_{MNC}, CONST_{HC}, NEGOT$$

Guisinger, "A Comparative Study of Country Policies," in Stephen E. Guisinger and Assocs., *Investment Incentives and Performance Requirements* (New York: Praeger, 1985), pp. 1–55; Barbara Jenkins, "Reexamining the Obsolescing Bargain," *International Organization* 40 (Winter 1986), pp. 139–65; and Philip, "The Limitiations of Bargaining Theory." Gereffi and Bennett and Sharpe demonstrate the constraints on state power exercised by the web of alliances built by MNCs in the pharmaceutical and automobile industries. See Gary Gereffi, "The Renegotiation of Dependency the Limits of State Autonomy in Mexico," in Moran, *Multinational Corporations and the Developing Countries,* pp. 83–106, and Bennett and Sharpe, "The World Automobile Industry."

35. See Jeffrey Pfeffer, *Organizations and Organization Theory* (Boston: Pitman, 1982).

36. While one could view access to a globally integrated production network as a resource possessed by the MNC and demanded by the host for the promise of increased efficiency, it is also a constraint on host country bargaining power.

37. See Jessica Pernitz Einhorn, *Expropriation Politics* (Lexington, Mass.: D. C. Heath, 1974). Knorr specifically refers to Western businesses dealing with authorities and landowners in developing countries. The literature of dependence is based on an assumption of constraints imposed on the autonomy of Third World actors as a result of the penetration of investment from the industrialized countries: "The Power of Nations," p. 16.

where RES_{MNC} and RES_{HC} are resources controlled by each party and demanded by the other, $CONST_{MNC}$ and $CONST_{HC}$ are constraints imposed on the MNC and HC respectively that affect the translation of potential bargaining power into control over outcomes, and NEGOT reflects relative negotiating ability. While the actual form of the equation will be dealt with later, I should note that the resource itself is not the source of power, but rather, the demand for it by the other party; it is relative power that is of interest.

Determinants of bargaining power

I do not attempt to model the entire process or to capture all the nuances of the interaction between a firm and a host country over time. As I shall discuss in detail later, my objective is a broad test, across as many industries and host countries as is possible, of the applicability of the bargaining model to the manufacturing sector.

To that end, I deal only with power resources and structural constraints as determinants of bargaining outcomes: I do not include constraints arising from domestic politics, coercion, or negotiating ability, which would require longitudinal case studies. Although the model presented is an admittedly incomplete representation of the bargaining process, I shall argue that it is sufficient to draw unbiased inferences. I return to this subject when discussing research method.

MNC power resources

The sources of MNC resource-based bargaining power can be derived from the theory of the MNC or foreign direct investment. Foreign investors possess advantages or firm-specific assets (for example, technology or capital), which market imperfections allow the firm to contain. The combination of firm-specific advantages and market imperfections results in a MNC preference for ordering economic transactions through internal administrative hierarchies (that is, vertical or horizontal integration), rather than the external market and provides the economic power to do so.[38] The firm-specific advantages discussed most frequently in the literature include: technology, managerial skills, capital, and access to markets.

Developing countries seek foreign direct investment to access the *technology* of MNCs. Technological complexity, intensity, and rate of change all

---

38. See Peter Buckley and Mark Casson, *The Future of the Multinational Enterprise* (New York: Holmes & Meier, 1976); Dunning, "Explaining Changing Patterns"; Alan Rugman, *Inside the Multinationals* (New York: Columbia University Press, 1981); and David J. Teece, "The Multinational Enterprise: Market Failure and Market Power Considerations," *Sloan Management Review* 23 (Spring 1981), pp. 3–17.

correlate positively with bargaining power.[39] Similarly, the *managerial complexity* of the enterprise is a source of bargaining power.[40]

MNC bargaining power is not a simple function of the intensity of technology or complexity of management, but of each *relative* to host country capabilities. The administrative capability of the government and its specific industry knowledge,[41] as well as the technological and managerial capabilities of local nationals, must be taken into account. Furthermore, changes in international markets for technology can affect relative bargaining power by allowing HCs to purchase capabilities that they lack.[42]

The role of *capital* is ambiguous. The size of the required investment, relative to the resources of the HC, can be a source of MNC power.[43] However, large amounts of capital, once sunk, are relatively immobile (assuming asset specificity) and may have "hostage value," increasing the bargaining power of the host country. Whether capital intensity serves as a MNC power resource or constraint depends on capital/labor ratios, the importance of internal versus external markets, and other factors affecting the potential mobility of the investment.[44]

Access to markets or export potential is a MNC power resource. The ability to export may arise from technical or managerial capabilities that allow production of a competitive product or from the MNC's global network, which may provide informational or logistical advantages.

Advertising intensity and product differentiation play a major role in the theory of foreign direct investment and a number of authors argue that they serve as a source of bargaining power for the MNC.[45] Advertising intensity and brand loyalty serve as a barrier to entry and a source of monopolistic advantage. While advertising for differentiated products increases preferences for internalization rather than market-oriented links, and while it undoubtedly provides advantages over less skilled local firms, it is far from

39. Bergsten, Horst, and Moran, *American Multinationals;* Encarnation and Wells, "Competitive Strategies"; Fagre and Wells, "Bargaining Power"; Lecraw, "Bargaining Power"; Theodore H. Moran, "Multinational Corporations and Dependency: A Dialogue for Dependentistas and Non-dependentistas," *International Organization* 32 (Winter 1977), pp. 79–100; Charles Oman, *New Forms of International Investment in Developing Countries* (Paris: OECD, 1984); Vernon, *Sovereignty at Bay;* Raymond Vernon, "Sovereignty at Bay Ten Years After," *International Organization* 35 (Summer 1981), pp. 517–30.

40. Poynter, "Government Intervention," and Vernon, *Sovereignty at Bay.*

41. Moran, *Multinational Corporations and the Politics of Dependence.*

42. Moran, *Multinational Corporations and the Politics of Dependence;* Oman, *New Forms;* Vernon, "The Obsolescing Bargain."

43. Bennett and Sharpe, "The World Automobile"; Gomes-Casseres, "Multinational Ownership Strategies"; Lecraw, "Bargaining Power"; and Poynter, "Government Intervention."

44. See, Bergsten, Horst, and Moran, "American Multinationals"; Encarnation and Wells, "Competitive Strategies"; Guissenger, "A Comparative Study"; Moran, "Multinational Corporations and Dependency"; and Oman, "New Forms."

45. Encarnation and Wells, "Sovereignty en Garde"; Newfarmer, "International Industrial Organization"; and Phillip Shepherd, "Transnational Corporation and the International Cigarette Industry," in Newfarmer, *Profits, Progress, and Poverty,* pp. 63–112.

clear why it should provide a source of power relative to the host government. One argument is that the creation of popular demand for differentiated products means that a host government risks alienating constituents if it moves against the MNC.

Finally, *employment* may be a resource provided by an MNC and demanded by the host country. The intensity of demand will be a function of economic conditions in the HC.

MNC constraints

The MNC faces constraints on exercising resource-based power. The degree of *competition in the industry* affects the ability of the host country to turn to alternative sources of supply.[46] Thus, the MNC's bargaining power is greater to the extent that the industry is more concentrated and that it is a dominant firm. The MNC is also constrained to the extent the HC government is an important *distributor or customer,* either directly or through state-owned firms.[47]

Host country power resources

The major HC power resource is access to the domestic market, and its value is a function of its size (population or income), its rate of growth (as an indication of future potential), and its development in terms of income per capita.[48] While control of natural resources is less important in manufacturing than in the extractive sector, it is still a source of potential bargaining power. The availability of inexpensive and productive labor, can be important in manufacturing.[49] Last, if the HC government offers incentives, or is a financier or supplier of materials, it can enhance bargaining power.

Host country constraints

Constraints limit the ability of the HC to implement potential power arising from control of resources. They include the degree of global integration in the industry which has been discussed already[50] and the degree of compe-

46. Oman, "New Forms"; Moran, "Multinational Corporations and Dependency"; Newfarmer, "International Industrial Organization."

47. Encarnation and Wells, "Sovereignty en Garde," and Evans, "Dependent Development."

48. Bennett and Sharpe, "Agenda Setting"; Frank, *Foreign Enterprise;* Guissenger, "A Comparative Study"; Oman, *New Forms;* and Vernon, *Sovereignty at Bay.*

49. Evans, *Dependent Development.*

50. Bennett and Sharpe, "Agenda Setting"; Fernando Coronil and Julie Skurski, "Reproducing Dependency: Auto Industry Policy and Petrodollar Circulation in Venezuela," *International Organization* 36 (Winter 1982), pp. 61–94; Evans, *Dependent Development;* Fagre and Wells, "Bargaining Power"; Lecraw, "Bargaining Power"; and Poynter, "Government Intervention."

tition among countries for the investment. As Guissenger notes,[51] competition is likely to be greatest for "exports platforms" that are labor rather than capital intensive, and that are designed to serve external markets, and thus are mobile; competition will be lowest for investments designed to serve the domestic market.

Balance-of-payments difficulties or severe external debt problems may increase a HC's demand for FDI, or limit its freedom of action because of conditions imposed by international financial organizations or commercial banks. Similarly, dependence of the economy on foreign direct investment may constrain an HC, either because of the control current investors exercise or the fear of repelling future investors. Last, political instability or uncertainty may decrease the attractiveness of a market to investors and constrain a host country's bargaining power.

The bargaining outcome

Multinationals and host countries bargain over a wide range of issues, including local ownership, exports, value added locally, investment size, incentives, tax rates and exemptions, employment of local nationals, and location of research and development facilities. A valid measure of the bargaining outcome requires an aggregate of outcomes across issue-areas *relative to MNC and HC objectives*. For the MNC, the relative bargaining outcome is the sum across issue-areas of the MNC objective, minus the actual outcome, divided by the MNC objective, less the HC objective:

$$BOUT = ((MNCOBJ - ACTOUT)/(MNCOBJ - HCOBJ)_i)$$

There are two major problems with operationalization of the bargaining outcome on a macro, cross-national basis: the only issue-area for which outcomes can be estimated across a significant number of cases is ownership;[52] and MNC and HC objectives are not observable directly.

Local ownership is only one of a number of issues that are the subject of HC-MNC bargaining, and its relative importance depends on specific circumstances. In some cases, local production requirements, exports, employment, technology transferred, or local research and development facilities may be more important to the host country and the MNC than who owns the equity. Furthermore, bargaining involves trade-offs: MNCs may provide other benefits to the HC, such as technology or exports, to retain 100 percent of the subsidiary. In two recent cases in Mexico, for example,

---

51. Guissenger, "A Comparative Study." See also Oman, *New Forms*.
52. Ownership is used as the dependent variable in three of the four existing cross-national studies of bargaining power: Gomes-Casseres, "Multinational Ownership Strategies"; Fagre and Wells, "Bargaining Power"; and Lecraw, "Bargaining Power." Poynter used a subjective estimate of intervention in "Government Intervention."

IBM and Ford were able to negotiate exceptions to the statutory limit of 49 percent foreign ownership (they both obtained 100 percent) in return for technology and exports.[53]

Thus, using foreign ownership as an indication of the bargaining outcome: 1) focuses on only one of a number of the issues on the table, and 2) may misrepresent the outcome in cases where other resources, such as technology or exports, are traded for a wholly owned subsidiary. The second possibility is the most serious, as it implies that foreign ownership may not be a comparable proxy for bargaining outcomes across cases.

However, it is clear that local ownership requirements are widespread and that governments and investors consider the issue important. While policymakers have tended towards pragmatic application, a large number of developing countries in all regions of the world either require national ownership of at least some investments at entry or require a phased divestment of existing ventures over time.[54] Paul Beamish, summarizing a number of empirical studies, found that government pressure in developing countries was the dominant motivation for joint ventures.[55] Gomes-Casseres reports interviews with several major MNCs who said that the only motivation for many of their joint ventures abroad was host government pressure.[56]

There is no doubt that MNCs consider ownership to be important. Given market imperfections, firm-specific assets, such as technology or the ability to promote differentiated products, can often be exploited more efficiently through internalization with unambiguous control. Isaiah Frank[57] concludes that, although a substantial minority of MNCs are willing to accept some local equity participation, few transnationals prefer local partners. Furthermore, integrated global operations may require control from the center that is uninhibited by the conflicting objectives of a joint-venture partner, whether public or private.[58]

Although ownership is only one of a number of issues on the table, it is important to both host countries and MNCs, and the parties often have

53. See "Ford's Better Idea South of the Border," *Business Week,* 9 January 1984, p. 43; and "IBM Concessions to Mexico," *New York Times,* 25 July 1985.

54. United Nations Centre on Transnational Corporations (UNCTC), *Transnational Corporations in World Development: Third Survey* (London: Graham & Trotman, 1985).

55. In the LDCs, 57% of respondents indicated that government suasion was a motivation and only 38% said that skill acquisition was important. Beamish found that, in contrast, the dominant reason for entering a joint venture in the developed countries (64% of respondents) was a need for the partner's skills, and only 17% reported government suasion as a determinant. See Paul W. Beamish, "The Characteristics of Joint Ventures in Developed and Developing Countries," *Columbia Journal of World Business* 20 (Fall 1985), pp. 13–20. In their study of the auto industry in Mexico, Bennett and Sharpe noted that, despite the conclusions drawn from the economics of industrial organization, government feels that the nationality of the owner does make a difference in the firm's behavior and thus its performance. See "Agenda Setting," note on p. 66.

56. Gomes-Casseres, "Multinational Ownership Strategies."

57. Frank, "Foreign Enterprise," p. 145.

58. Bergsten, Horst, and Moran, *American Multinationals,* and Oman, *New Forms.*

divergent interests. Ownership is the only measure of bargaining outcomes that is consistent with a broad cross-national and cross-industry test of the model. The pertinent question—which I shall discuss later—is the limits that use of ownership as the dependent variable places on the validity and generalizability of conclusions drawn from this study.

Observed bargaining outcomes are not true reflections of bargaining power, as they do not consider either MNC or host country objectives. Host countries vary in terms of political-economic ideology (for example, Singapore versus Mexico), policy choice for exerting control over foreign investors, and effectiveness of application. MNCs' objectives also vary, both as a function of underlying structural conditions and as a result of managerial choice.

All else equal, a firm's propensity to joint venture is a function of the returns to internalization as a means of exploiting its firm-specific advantage. To the extent that unambiguous control over the deployment of an asset generates greater returns, the firm will prefer to prevent or minimize outside involvement. Thus, the same factors that—at least in part—determine the MNC's bargaining power also determine its preferences for wholly owned operations. A dominant firm in a technologically intensive industry will prefer to exploit this asset internally and have the bargaining power to do so.

Intra-industry preferences also differ due to managerial choice or experience: considerable variance, for example, exists within the auto industry and among tire firms.[59] There is also evidence of systematic preference differences by nationality, with American firms less inclined to accept joint ventures than European or Japanese.[60] Given that variance in MNC objectives can result from factors related to both industry structure and managerial choice, it is difficult to determine whether differences in observed ownership stem from differences in preferences or bargaining power. I shall return to the question of estimating unobserved preferences.

Research method

The obsolescing bargain is a longitudinal phenomenon that involves transfer and learning as a result of interaction between a firm (or an industry) and a given host government over time. However, my objective is a broad test of the applicability of the bargaining hypothesis to the manufacturing sector across as many industries in as many developing countries as possible. That rules out case studies or time-series analysis, forces reliance on aggregate cross-national data, and implies a sacrifice of depth for breadth.

Testing a longitudinal phenomenon cross-sectionally requires an assump-

59. See Bennett and Sharpe, ''Agenda Setting,'' and Peter J. West, ''International Expansion and Concentration of the Tire Industry and Implications for Latin America,'' in Newfarmer, *Profits, Progress, and Poverty.*
60. Frank, ''Foreign Enterprise.''

tion that the points on the cross-section, in this study country-firm intersections, represent successive historical points in some typical case. Thus, the subsidiary-country observations in this study can be taken as representing a continuum of points, with varying differences in HC and MC bargaining power that could be achieved in a single case over time. While the assumption is obviously imperfect, it underlies a relatively large number of cross-sectional studies of development and modernization.[61]

The sample

Given evidence of significant differences in preference for joint-ventures by nationality of investor, the population is restricted to U.S. manufacturing firms in developing countries. Furthermore, the study is limited to large, international firms (roughly Fortune 500, with at least 20 percent of sales abroad), which account for the vast majority of foreign direct investment.[62]

Public sources were used to identify subsidiaries, determine the percent owned by the parent, and the products produced.[63] One hundred thirty-nine firms that appeared to manufacture in non-European developing countries were sent an exhibit summarizing the public-source information and asked to confirm or correct the data.

Seventy-five of the 128 firms actually manufacturing in developing countries (58.6 percent) responded,[64] providing usable data on 563 subsidiaries in 49 countries. Respondents were compared to the population by industrial sector and percent of sales generated abroad; standard chi-squared tests reveal a very low probability that the two distributions are not identical. (Appendix 1 details the distribution of subsidiaries by country.)

61. See, Irma Adelman and Cynthia Taft Morris, *Society, Politics, and Economic Development* (Baltimore: Johns Hopkins University Press, 1967).

62. For example, in 1975, 180 U.S. manufacturing multinationals accounted for 71% of sales of U.S. direct investors abroad. Joan P. Curhan, William H. Davidson, and Rajan Suri, *Tracing the Multinationals: A Sourcebook on U.S.-Based Enterprises* (Cambridge, Mass.: Ballinger, 1977). Given the very large number of smaller firms, including them would increase the size of a representative sample beyond the capabilities of this article. Limiting the sample of U.S.-based firms controls for national differences in the propensity to share ownership. While this limits generalization, it only introduces bias if one can argue that there are systematic differences in bargaining power attributed to nationality. I cannot.

63. I used the Conference Board's *Key Company Directory* (New York 1983) to select 203 firms that are equivalent in size to the Fortune 500 and have at least 20% of their sales generated abroad. Firms in extractive sectors (petroleum or mining), conglomerates that could not be classified by industry, and those in sectors that tend to be heavily export based (e.g., aircraft) were eliminated, leaving 162 firms. The review of public sources identified 139 with manufacturing subsidiaries in developing countries. See *International Directory of Corporate Affiliations: Who Owns Whom? 1984/85*, (Willmette, Ill.: National Register, 1984); *Moody's Industrial Manual* (New York: Moody's Investors Services, 1984); John Stopford, John H. Dunning, and Klaus Haberlich, *World Directory of Multinational Enterprises*, vols. 1 and 2 (New York: Facts on File, 1980).

64. Eleven of the firms contacted in the mailed survey indicated that they no longer manufactured in developing countries. They were removed from the relevant population.

The independent variables

The independent variables (power resources and constraints) are operationalized at three levels of analysis: the individual subsidiary (for example, products produced and ownership); the country (GNP); and the industry (R&D intensity). Estimating subsidiary characteristics from industry level data is necessary to obtain a broad cross-national sample but implies a loss of accuracy that affects variance explained in the dependent variable.

Using *Forbes Annual Report on American Industry*,[65] parent firms and subsidiaries are categorized into fourteen industrial sectors based on their primary product (see appendix 2). Table 1 details the specification of MNC and HC power resources.

The dependent variable

An accurate and valid estimate of the bargaining outcome requires an adjustment to raw foreign ownership to reflect MNC and HC objectives.[66] As many of the same factors determine both joint venture propensity and bargaining power, differences in MNC objectives that are a function of industry characteristics are taken into account. However, variation resulting from individual firm strategy or managerial preference and from differences in host country ideology, policy choice, or application are not.

While other researchers have attempted to estimate objectives from the distribution of ownership across countries and firms, that is not feasible in this study.[67] More important, the validity of these estimates is questionable, as goals are situationally specific: the MNC's objectives are a partial function of country characteristics, and HC objectives certainly vary by industry.[68]

I use two variables to attempt to control for differences in objectives: host

65. Forbes Annual Report on American Industry, 1986, included in *Forbes,* 13 January 1986, p. 4.

66. Raw parent ownership of subsidiary of 60% has very different implications as a measure of bargaining outcome if: 1) the MNC's objective is 100% and the HC's is 50%, or 2) the MNC's is 66% and the HC's 40%.

67. Lecraw estimated MNC objectives from the highest ownership level for the firm in any country and the HC objective from the lowest ownership level for any firm in that country. However, the sample included only six industries in five countries; Lecraw, "Bargaining Power." In this article, there are a number of firms with too few subsidiaries and countries with too few investors to apply that technique.

68. As noted already, MNCs in industrialized host countries are more likely to rank the prospective partners' skills as an important motivation for entering the joint venture than those in developing host countries. Thus, MNC preferences are likely to vary depending on country characteristics and taking the highest observed ownership level as proxy for true preferences will be misleading.

TABLE 1. *Specification and sources for the independent variables*

MNC POWER RESOURCES
1. Technology. R&D Parent research and development spending as a percent of sales.[a]
2. Parent size. SALES 1983 world wide sales.[b]
3. Subsidiary size. SUBSIZE Assets per affiliate by subsidiary industry.[a]
4. Employment. EMP Employees per affiliate by subsidiary industry.[a]
5. Export potential. EXP Percent of affiliate sales exported by industry of subsidiary.[a]

MNC CONSTRAINTS
1. Concentration. CONC Percent of sales of world's 20 largest firms in parent industry accounted for by 3 largest.[c]

HC POWER RESOURCES
1. Size-population. POP 1982.[d]
2. Size-Gross Domestic Product. GDP 1982 GDP.[e]
3. Growth. GRW Average annual growth, GDP 1975–81.[d]
4. Per capita income. CAP/GDP 1982.[f]
5. Technological/managerial capacity. HM Harbison/Meyers index: second- and third-level school enrollment ratios 1984.[g]

HC CONSTRAINTS
1. Global integration. PINTEG Percent of total parent exports sold to affiliates, by industry of parent.[a]
2. Foreign direct investment. FDI Stock of FDI 1978.[h]
3. DEBT. Service payments on external debt as a percentage of exports of goods and services, 12/31/83.[i]
4. Political risk. RISK Frost and Sullivan World Political Risk Forecast rating for country 10/1/85. Letter rating transposed to numerical scale.
5. Internationalization. OS Percent of parent's sales overseas.[b]
6. Restrictions. REST Host country ownership restrictions coded as no restrictions, restrictions on new investment, restrictions on existing investment.[h]

Source.
a. Bureau of Economic Analysis, *U.S. Direct Investment Abroad: 1982 Benchmark Survey* (Washington, D.C.: Department of Commerce, 1985).
b. The Conference Board, *The Key Company Directory* (New York: Conference Board, 1983).
c. John H. Dunning and R. Pearce, *The World's Largest Industrial Enterprises: 1962–1983* (New York: St. Martin's, 1985).
d. United Nations, *33rd Statistical Yearbook 1982* (New York: United Nations, 1985).
e. International Monetary Fund, *International Financial Statistics Supplement on Output Statistics* (Washington, D.C.: International Monetary Fund, 1984).
f. United Nations, *National Accounts Statistics 1982: Analysis of Main Aggregates* (New York: United Nations, 1985).
g. United Nations Educational and Scientific Organization, *UNESCO Statistical Yearbook 1984* (Paris: UNESCO, 1984).
h. United Nations Center on Transnational Corporations, *Transnational Corporations in World Development: Third Survey* (London: Graham & Trotman, 1985).
i. World Bank, *World Bank Annual Report* (Washington, D.C.: World Bank, 1985).

TABLE 2. *Distribution of parent ownership percentage*

Percent owned	*Percent of firms*
	(N = 563)
20–29	2.1
30–39	3.8
40–49	12.2
50–59	8.0
60–69	4.5
70–79	4.0
80–89	3.2
90–99	3.2
100	59.0
	100.0
Summary	
Minority J-V (20–49%)	18.1
50–50	5.2
Majority J-V (51–89%)	14.5
Wholly owned (90–100%)	62.2
	100.0

countries categorized by nominal ownership policy (REST), and the internationalization of the firm in terms of the percent of its sales generated abroad (OS). Host countries are classified as those having no ownership restrictions, those requiring at least some local ownership for all new investment, and those attempting to require (partial) divestment of existing investment.[69]

There is considerable evidence that internationalization is an important determinant of firm strategy. More international firms are more likely to have centrally integrated strategies that increase the costs of joint ventures. Assuming that internationalization and experience correlate, the value of the potential partner's contribution will be reduced.[70]

As we can see in Table 2, the majority (62.2 percent) of the subsidiaries in the sample are wholly owned (90 percent or more). Majority joint ventures account for 14.5 percent, "50-50" shares 5.2 percent, and minority joint ventures 18.1 percent. Two points should be noted. First, almost two-thirds of the subsidiaries of a representative sample of large, international U.S.-based manufacturing firms were still wholly owned in 1986. Second, the distribution is truncated, as 59 percent of the cases lie at the upper limit (100 percent).

69. UNCTC, "Transnational Corporations."

70. Gomes-Casseres, "Multinational Ownership"; John Fayerweather, *International Business Strategy and Administration*, 2d ed. (Cambridge, Mass.: Ballinger, 1982); and Richard D. Robinson, *International Business Management*, 2d ed. (Hinsdale, Ill.: Dryden, 1978).

Tests

My objectives are to assess the applicability of the bargaining model to manufacturing investors in developing countries and to draw inferences about factors affecting shifts in bargaining power. As this requires simultaneously evaluating the effects of a number of independent variables on the dependent variable, a multiple regression model is appropriate. Given the distribution of ownership already reported, however, Ordinary Least Squares is not. The dependent variable is constrained and truncated: it can only vary from 20 to 100, and 59 percent of the observations fall at the upper bound (100 percent). This conflicts with the linearity assumption of OLS, and its use may produce seriously biased estimates of coefficients.[71]

A number of limited dependent variable regression models have been developed, the most familiar of which is Tobit. A Tobit model is used to evaluate relationships, with upper truncation and a limit of 100 explicitly specified.[72] There are several factors that may limit the amount of variance[73] that can be explained. First, a longitudinal phenomenon is evaluated cross-sectionally. Second, ownership is only one of a number of bargaining issues, and its relative importance is case-specific. Third, observed ownership is not the bargaining outcome, and controls for MNC and HC objectives are imperfect. Fourth, the variance to be explained is limited, since well over half the cases are found at the upper bound.

The primary question is whether the estimates of coefficients are biased significantly. That, in turn, is a function of whether any important explanatory variables have been omitted and are contained in the error term. In this case, the primary omissions are intra-state or intra-firm political constraints on implementation of resource-based power and relative negotiating skills. My assumption is that their distribution is random, or at least not sufficiently systematic to significantly bias the coefficients.

While evaluation of the applicability of the overall bargaining framework requires only analysis of the significance and signs of the coefficients, evaluation of the dynamics of the process is considerably more problematic be-

71. Takeshi Amemiya, "Tobit Models: A Survey," *Journal of Econometrics* 24 (1984), pp. 3–61; William H. Greene, "LIMDEP," mimeo, New York University, Graduate School of Business Administration, 1984; G. S. Maddala, *Econometrics* (New York: McGraw-Hill, 1977).

72. The specific model used is contained in the LIMDEP package developed by William Greene of New York University. It uses the Davidon/Fletcher/Powell algorithm to obtain maximum likelihood estimates. Green's example of forecasting demand for a sports stadium of fixed capacity that is sold out a significant proportion of the time is directly analogous. Tobit (originally Tobit's probit, but no longer limited to binary dependent variables) is a non-linear regression model that uses the maximum likelihood technique to estimate parameters and explicitly accounts for the limited range of the dependent variable. See Greene, "LIMDEP," pp. 136–137 and Maddala, *Econometrics*.

73. While the overall significance of the equation is evaluated through a test of the likelihood ratio and the algorithm provides estimates of coefficients and their significance, it does not produce an estimate of variance explained.

TABLE 3. *Variables significant at .05 or better (univariate basis)*

MNC resources	HC constraints
SALES	PINTEG
RD	FDI
ADV	FDI / GDP
MNC constraints	controls
CONC	OS
	REST
HC resources	
POP	
HM	

cause the values of the coefficients must be used to estimate the relative importance of specific MNC and power resources and constraints. If the regression is not completely specified and the error term is not random, the estimates of the coefficients may be biased.

The applicability of the bargaining model is tested by observing the relationship between power resources and constraints and observed foreign parent ownership. MNC power resources and HC constraints should be positively related to ownership; HC power resources and MNC constraints should be negatively related. If coefficients are significant and the signs as predicted, the hypothesis that the bargaining model applies to the manufacturing sector cannot be rejected.

A formal test of the hypothesis that bargaining power systematically shifts to HCs over time is beyond the capabilities of this study. However, inferences can be drawn from the data which inform a more extended discussion of obsolescence in the conclusions.

Results

Two additional independent variables were created from existing data. Relative bargaining power implies that MNC technological intensity is evaluated relative to HC capabilities. One means to capture this relationship is simply to include both RD and HM (the index of educational enrollment levels) in the multivariate equation. Another is to create a comparative variable directly—in this case, HM/RD, a measure of HC capabilities relative to industry technology (RELHM). Similarly, FDI can be normalized for the size of the host economy either by including GDP in the equation or by creating a term FDI/GDP.

Given the distributional properties of ownership, evaluating univariate relationships with potential explanator variables is problematic. However, Table 3 lists those that are significant at the .05 level, using ordinary Pearson correlation. Subsidiary size, employment, export potential, per capita in-

TABLE 4. *Tobit results*

(N = 554)
Log-likelihood = − 1389.0
Unrestricted slopes log-likelihood = − 1447.7

Chi-squared = 121.4		df = 8		
			Significance = .000	
Variable	Coefficient	Standardized coefficient	T ratio	Sig. level
Constant	14.186		.887	.375
RD	.755	.836	4.597	.000
ADV	25.041	.461	3.892	.000
GDP	− .052	− .218	− 1.720	.086
RELHM	− 20.341	− .358	− 2.679	.007
PINTEG	.308	.256	2.191	.028
LFDI	8.070	.622	4.176	.000
OS	.710	.335	3.256	.001
REST	− 28.254	.508	− 3.827	.000

come, GDP growth, the debt service ratio, and political risk all are *not* significantly related to ownership levels, either on a univariate basis or in subsequent multivariate analysis. Given problems of operationalization and testing at this aggregate level, this certainly *does not* prove that those variables are not determinants of bargaining power. There is clear case evidence, for example, that export potential is an important bargaining resource for MNCs.

A number of authors suggest industry competitiveness (CONC) as an important constraint on MNC bargaining power. While CONC is significant on a univariate basis, its effect on ownership disappears when technology and global integration are included: the partial correlation coefficient of CONC, controlling for RD and PINTEG, is not significant. Concentration levels are a function of other industry characteristics, such as technological intensity or scale requirements, that create barriers to entry and oligopolistic conditions in the first place. Thus, while an HC may have more bargaining power in a competitive industry, the degree of competitiveness itself is likely to be a function of underlying factors that directly affect relative bargaining power.

The multivariate Tobit regression is reported in Table 4. The overall equation is highly significant: the likelihood ratio is 60.7 and chi-squared 121.4. Two variables not significant on a univariate basis are included: GDP and relative capabilities (RELHM). GDP is used to control for FDI and is marginally significant (.086) in itself. The index of human resource capabilities (HM) is not significant when the other terms are added, but RELHM is highly significant.[74]

74. While population is significant in a multivariate equation, it is a redundant measure of

Two MNC power resources, technology and advertising intensity (RD and ADV), are included but, as discussed already, the constraint on MNC power (competition) appears to have an intervening rather than a direct effect. Two HC power resources, market size and relative capabilities (GDP and RELHM), are included as are two constraints on HC bargaining power, global integration and FDI (PINTEG and FDI).[75] Last, the two control variables, MNC internationalization and HC restrictions (OS and REST), are both significant. With the exception of GDP, all the coefficients are significant at .03 or better.

Regression results are consistent with a bargaining model. MNC ownership is a function of variables posited as sources of MNC and HC power and constraints on the HC. The signs are as predicted: coefficients of MNC power resources and HC constraints positive and HC power resources (GDP and RELHM) negative. REST (coded 1 for countries with explicit ownership restrictions) is negative and the percent of the firm's sales generated overseas (OS) is positively related to ownership, indicating a preference for wholly owned subsidiaries among the more international firms.

The significance of relative capabilities (RELHM) further confirms the bargaining model; host country technical and managerial capabilities—as indicated by educational achievement—*relative* to industry technological intensity is a determinant of ownership. At the least, one cannot reject the hypothesis that the level of parent ownership of manufacturing subsidiaries of MNCs is determined by relative bargaining power.

As already discussed, direct examination of whether the bargain obsolesces falls outside the limits of this study, given the static framework and industry level aggregation. Although in theory the current foreign ownership level of each of the subsidiaries should reflect relative bargaining power, in practice a government's ability to renegotiate previous arrangements has limits. In a number of countries, such as Mexico, existing investment was "grandfathered" when restrictions on foreign ownership were legislated.[76] Historical factors, which are not captured in the cross-section, may well be relevant.[77]

---

country size once GDP is included and the latter has the advantage of serving as a control for FDI. FDI/GDP is also significant, but redundant. MNC sales is not significant in the Tobit regression.

75. As FDI distribution is highly skewed upwards, it was transformed logarithmically.

76. See Gereffi, "The Global Pharmaceutical Industry." As food processing and consumer products firms have been international for quite some time, it is reasonable to assume that, in many instances, their subsidiaries existed prior to the ownership restrictions. Whiting explicitly notes that most food processing firms were in Mexico before the 1973 Foreign Investment Law that restricted foreign ownership in most instances to 49%. Van R. Whiting, Jr., "Transnational Enterprise in the Food Processing Industry," in Newfarmer, *Profits, Progress*, p. 365.

77. Eighty-two of the observations are in Brazil and 107 in Mexico. Thus, the two countries account for one-third of all observations and the question of sample bias must be dealt with. First, it should be noted that the unit of analysis is the country–industry intersection, not the country alone. Second, there is no theoretical reason to assume Mexico or Brazil are outliers.

The statistical analysis can be used to ascertain the relative importance of determinants of bargaining power. I shall proceed by first using the results to isolate the important determinants of relative bargaining power and then discuss their probable impact on obsolescence in the conclusions.

The standardized coefficients, which may be compared directly, are reported in Table 4. MNC power resources and constraints on HC bargaining power dominate the equation. Technological intensity (RD) has the strongest effect on ownership by far with a standardized coefficient of .84. That is almost twice the value of host country capabilities relative to industry technology (RELHM) and almost four times as large as the index of market size (GDP). The coefficient of the other MNC resource, advertising intensity (.46), is also larger than that of the HC resources.

The second most important term in the equation is the level of FDI (.62), which acts as a constraint on HC autonomy. That could result from either the political power to established investors—the patterns of alliances discussed in the literature—or from dependence of future investment. While its effect is weaker, global integration of the firm (PINTEG: .26) also acts as a constraint on bargaining power.

Conclusions

What can we infer about potential shifts in bargaining power in manufacturing industries over time? From the MNC's viewpoint, obsolescence follows a decline in the relative importance of MNC resources or HC constraints, or an increase in the importance of HC power resources or MNC constraints. The significance of RELHM means that obsolescence cannot be ruled out. Even though technology dominates the equation, if the level of host country technological and managerial capacity relative to industry technological intensity increases, HC bargaining power will also increase.

Similarly, while there are obviously structural limits on market growth (regardless of income levels per head, Costa Rica can never become a large market), increases in market size should improve HC bargaining power. However, the effect of market size is very weak: GDP is only marginally significant and its standardized coefficient (.22) is the smallest in the equation.[78]

To check for the possibility of bias, dummy variables for Mexico and Brazil were added to the Tobit regression. Although both are significant, with two exceptions the coefficients for the other variables are unchanged. The standardized coefficient of REST is slightly reduced and that of GDP increased. The change in GDP, however, is confounded by the high correlation between each of the dummies and GDP. I conclude that the results and findings are unchanged when the two country dummies are added.

78. Gomes-Casseres found stronger support for market size as a determinant of host country bargaining power. Gomes-Casseres, ''Multinational Ownership.''

The results indicate that obsolescence is possible and that shifts in bargaining power to HCs are most likely in relatively low technology industries that are not integrated globally. In fact, a separate analysis of food and consumer products subsidiaries, which are characterized by low levels of technology and global integration, supports that conclusion. An HC power resource, market size, dominates the regression equation and a cross-tabulation of ownership by level of host country restriction (REST) reveals a dramatic and significant difference in mean levels of foreign ownership in countries that explicitly attempt to renegotiate existing agreements.[79]

In many of the most important industries that are characterized by innovative and intensive technology or global integration, however, changes in bargaining power may be almost completely out of the developing host countries' control. Obsolescence depends on the rate of technological development and the degree of global integration, and there may be little that the HC can do to affect either.

The intensity of technology is increasing in most international industries. When R&D expenditures as a percentage of sales in a sample of 239 large firms in 17 industries are compared for 1977 and 1982, all of the industries but one show an increase in technological intensity over the period, with the average increase 22 percent.[80]

Shifts in relative bargaining power depend on whether the rate of technological and managerial development in the host country is greater than the rate of innovation in the industry. Aside from a small number of developing countries (such as those characterized as newly industrialized), that appears to be unlikely. Furthermore, as the vast majority of this sort of research and development—and virtually all undertaken by MCNs[81]—is located in the industrialized home countries, the technological developments are likely to be beyond the reach or control of developing host countries.

Although the effect of global integration[82] is relatively weak, it has enor-

79. Multivariate analysis on the advertising intensive sub-sample indicates that country size (POP) is the most important HC power resource while the amount of FDI is a significant constraint. Host country capabilities (HM or RELHM) are not significant, nor are other HC resources or constraints. As virtually all of this sort of FDI is market-driven, the relationship with market size is not surprising. A cross-tabulation of ownership (categorized as wholly owned, majority joint venture, and minority joint venture) and a three-way categorization of host country restrictions on ownership reveal significant differences in ownership of existing investments. In contrast to the other two categories, where about 77% of subsidiaries are wholly owned, only a minority of advertising intensive subsidiaries are wholly owned (28%), while 40% are majority joint ventures and 32% minority.

80. John H. Dunning and R. Pearce, *The World's Largest Industrial Enterprises: 1962–1983* (New York: St. Martin's 1985), p. 166.

81. The 1982 Benchmark Study reports R&D expenditures of $260 million by or for subsidiaries in LDCs and $37,590 million by and for parents in the U.S. Bureau of Economic Analysis, *U.S. Direct Investment Abroad: the 1982 Benchmark Survey* (Washington, D.C.: Department of Commerce, 1985).

82. PINTEG and R&D are correlated (r = .55), and part of the reason for the relative weakness of the coefficient of the former is the dominance of R&D. That is, the reason industries, such as computers and electronics, are integrated globally is their R&D intensity.

mous significance for future shifts in bargaining power. If MNC bargaining power is based on technology, or even levels of FDI in the country, HC can take steps to improve its position. It can develop local resources through educational efforts, implement initiatives to gain industry specific expertise, or facilitate domestic investment to lessen dependence on FDI.

Global integration, however, reflects underlying changes in industry structure that require a transnational scope of operation. While some trade-offs may be possible at the margin by accepting more expensive automobiles or computers or slightly obsolete technology, the HC's freedom of action is limited. If an industry is inherently transnational, or if industry economics require global integration, the bargaining power of any single host country (developed as well as developing) will be constrained.

Thus, Dennis Encarnation and Louis Wells conclude: "As the penalties of withdrawing the domestic market from global competition have become clearer, a number of countries have moved toward more open borders."[83] Similarly, Bennett and Sharpe argue that with global integration of sourcing and production, even the automotive MNC's home countries may not have the full complement of facilities within their borders to manufacture a complete vehicle. They conclude: "This global integration of production will have significant, probably painful, implications for the major producing countries."[84]

Global integration is a complex phenomenon that includes "real" flows of raw material, components, and final products as well as flows of technology, capital, and management between the units of the MNC. While it is an admittedly imperfect measure, we can obtain some indication of trends by comparing the percentage of total subsidiary sales to other affiliates in the 1977 and 1982 Benchmark Surveys of Foreign Direct Investment.[85] Although trends overall are mixed, the five industry groups that are relatively highly integrated (over 25 percent of sales to affiliates)—autos, chemicals, computers, electronics, and scientific instruments—show increases over the five-year period. The average increase is 13 percent.

Conclusions about obsolescence are speculative and only partially based on empirical results. But it does appear that although potential shifts in bargaining power to the HC cannot be ruled out, manufacturing is not characterized by the inherent, structurally based, and secular obsolescence that is found in the natural resource-based industries.

In industries where technology is mature or widely available and global integration limited, shifts in bargaining power to HCs will result from in-

83. Encarnation and Wells, "Competitive Strategies," p. 45.
84. Bennett and Sharpe, "The World Automobile Industry," p. 204.
85. Temporal comparisons of the measure of integration used in this study (the percentage of parent exports going to affiliates) are confounded by trends in total U.S. exports. For the 1977 data, see Bureau of Economic Analysis, *U.S. Direct Investment Abroad 1977* (Washington, D.C.: Department of Commerce, 1981).

creases in local capabilities, expansion of the domestic market, and the increased ability of the HC government to make and implement policy, which is a function of a number of factors that have only been partially discussed. In other industries, characterized by changing technologies and the spread of global integration, the bargain will obsolesce slowly, if at all, and the relative power of MNCs may even increase over time.

In summary, a bargaining framework based on relative demand for resources and constraints on the implementation of power is an accurate model of MNC--host country relationships in a wide range of sectors. However, in contrast to the resource-based industries, obsolescence does not appear to be structurally inherent in manufacturing. Given the importance of manufacturing investment to MNCs and the developing countries, we must increase our understanding of the process and the determinants of relative bargaining power. That will require a good deal of further research, especially a broadening of the very limited base of intensive case studies.

APPENDIX 1. *Subsidiaries by country*

Country	Number of subsidiaries
Argentina	30
Bolivia	2
Brazil	82
Chile	10
Colombia	25
Costa Rica	5
Dominican Republic	4
Ecuador	9
El Salvador	1
Guatemala	8
Honduras	1
Jamaica	3
Mexico	107
Nicaragua	1
Panama	4
Peru	8
Uruguay	6
Venezuela	45
China	3
Hong Kong	3
India	18
Indonesia	15
Korea	15
Malaysia	20
Pakistan	8
Philippines	29
Singapore	19
Sri Lanka	2
Taiwan	19
Thailand	13
Egypt	4
Iran	1
Kuwait	1
Lebanon	1
Morocco	5
Tunisia	2
Turkey	2
Saudi Arabia	8
Sudan	2
Ghana	2
Ivory Coast	1
Kenya	7
Liberia	1
Malawi	1
Nigeria	5
Senegal	1
Zaire	2
Zambia	1
Zimbabwe	1

APPENDIX 2. *Parent industry classification*

Industry	Percent of firms
(N = 563)	
Apparel	0.0
Automotive	16.5
Chemical	14.5
Computer	1.8
Construction/building materials	1.4
Pharmaceuticals	10.8
Electrical equipment	5.3
Electronics	4.4
Food processing	21.1
Household products	10.1
Industrial machinery	3.0
Medical equipment	1.2
Paper and packaging	9.6
	100.0

Between free trade and protectionism: strategic trade policy and a theory of corporate trade demands
Helen V. Milner and David B. Yoffie

Ever since Adam Smith and David Ricardo challenged the intellectual foundations of mercantilism, theories of commercial policy have debated the merits of free trade versus protectionism. Since free trade was shown to be superior in terms of efficiency, scholars have long puzzled over why governments would ever choose protectionism. Part of the answer to this debate was usually found by looking at the interests of firms.

Examination of firms' demands has a long tradition in the political economy of international trade. In the extensive literature on the preferred trade policies of firms and corporate influence on setting trade policy,[1] studies have pointed to two findings. First, manufacturing firms in the postwar period have tended to seek either protection or free trade; the choices of firms have been dichotomous. Second, import-competing firms with no foreign operations have tended to battle for protection, while multinational firms and export-dependent corporations tended to prefer lower trade barriers.

One problem with these approaches is that corporate trade demands no longer fit into the traditional free trade versus protectionism dichotomy. Increasing numbers of multinational firms that historically supported uni-

An earlier version of this article was presented at the annual meeting of the American Political Science Association, August 1987, Washington, D.C. We are grateful for financial support from the Harvard Business School Division of Research, for the research assistance of John Coleman, and for the helpful comments from participants of the CFIA seminar at Harvard, PIPES seminar at the University of Chicago, IPE seminar at UCLA, and RIIC seminar at Columbia. In particular, we thank Jagdish Bhagwati, Richard Caves, David Collis, John Conybeare, Stephan Haggard, Robert Keohane, Stephen Krasner, Richard Nelson, David Richardson, Gene Salorio, Kamal Shehadi, Lou Wells, and two anonymous reviewers.

1. See E. E. Schattschneider, *Politics, Pressures, and the Tariff* (Englewood Cliffs, N.J.: Prentice-Hall, 1935); Raymond Bauer, Ithiel de Sola Pool, and Lewis Dexter, *American Business and Public Policy* (Chicago: Aldine, 1972); Timothy McKeown, "Firms and Tariff Regime Change: Explaining the Demand for Protection," *World Politics* 36 (January 1984), pp. 215–33; and R. Baldwin, *The Political Economy of U.S. Import Policy* (Cambridge, Mass.: MIT Press, 1986).

International Organization 43, 2, Spring 1989, pp. 239–72

laterally opening their home market have publicly advocated a third type of policy—a "strategic" trade policy of demanding trade barriers for the home market if foreign markets are protected. Indeed, recent political events show the growing prevalence of such behavior. For instance, the U.S. semiconductor industry has pressed the American government to threaten Japan with closure of the domestic markets unless Japanese firms buy more American microchips. U.S. commercial aircraft manufacturers have also pursued a similar strategy against their European rival, Airbus. Since these new strategic demands appeal to American governmental norms of fairness in international trade,[2] they could have a greater impact on policy in the late 1980s and 1990s than traditional pleas for protection. Moreover, if these strategic demands, which resemble requests for specific reciprocity, were adopted by the U.S. government, the United States could undermine the current General Agreement on Tariffs and Trade (GATT) regime, which is based on diffuse reciprocity in the form of unconditional most-favored-nation status.[3]

These new strategic demands by firms are not easily comprehensible within traditional models of the political economy of trade. Most studies of corporate trade demands have ignored the possibility of strategic trade policy as an option for firms. Specific reciprocity has usually been studied in the context of political strategies pursued by governments to appease certain domestic groups.[4] In addition, traditional approaches, which look at variables such as the capital and labor intensity of an industry and its position in the product or business cycle, tend to assume that demands for free trade and protectionism are *unconditional*. Yet the willingness of firms to support free trade or protectionism may be contingent upon the behavior of their foreign rivals and their governments. The central purpose of this article is to broaden the theory of corporate trade preferences by explaining why and under what conditions firms will demand contingent rather than noncontingent policies.

We begin by arguing that trade positions of firms can only be studied by enriching the dependent variable to include strategic demands as well as the standard poles of protectionism and free trade. We suggest that new variables must also be considered when predicting which industries are likely to act strategically on international trade. We explain the emergence of industry-wide strategic trade demands with three variables: changes in industry economics, foreign government policy intervention, and variations in industry structure. We show that as industries require greater economies of scale or

2. V. Aggarwal, R. Keohane, and D. Yoffie, "The Dynamics of Negotiated Protectionism," *American Political Science Review* 81 (June 1987), pp. 345–66.

3. Robert Keohane, "Reciprocity in International Relations," *International Organization* 40 (Winter 1986), pp. 1–28.

4. See John Evans, *The Kennedy Round in American Trade Policy: The Twilight of GATT?* (Cambridge, Mass.: Harvard University Press, 1971), chap. 2; and Keohane, "Reciprocity in International Relations."

become subject to significant cumulative learning effects, they become more dependent on access to foreign markets. If that access to world markets is impeded by foreign government protection or subsidies, domestic firms realize that their preferred policies will depend upon the choices of their foreign rivals. They will see themselves in a strategic situation in which the ability of "one participant to gain [its] ends is dependent to an important degree on the choices or decisions that the other participant will make."[5] This interdependence will lead firms that formerly advocated unconditional free trade to demand that free trade at home be contingent on reciprocal access to foreign markets.

Finally, we suggest that the degree of industry segmentation critically affects the speed, intensity, and substance of a given industry's trade response. When firms in an industry follow similar competitive strategies, changes in economics are likely to be widely recognized and translated relatively quickly into strategic trade demands. However, when competition is highly fragmented into numerous "strategic groups,"[6] the industry as a whole will react more slowly to external threats. If a slow industry-wide response is coupled with a rapid deterioration in competitive position, the industry is more likely to turn toward protectionism rather than strategic trade policy.

Theories of corporate trade preferences

Most theories on the political economy of trade have focused on the demand for protection rather than on the more general problem of illuminating the range of corporate trade demands. Many of these theories of protection posit that for a given set of industries, protectionist policies at home are preferable to other trade solutions. They state that firms will seek to maximize their profits via domestic trade barriers if they face comparative disadvantage, if they believe they can capture excessive rents through tariffs, and so forth.[7]

Helen Milner, John Odell and I. M. Destler, and others have recently

5. T. Schelling, *The Strategy of Conflict* (Cambridge, Mass.: Harvard University Press, 1960), pp. 9–10.

6. Michael Porter, "The Structure Within Industries and Companies' Performance," *Review of Economics and Statistics* 61 (May 1979), pp. 214–27.

7. There is a very large theoretical and empirical literature on the subject of which domestic groups seek protection. See, for example, W. Stolper and P. Samuelson, "Protection and Real Wages," *Review of Economic Studies* 9 (November 1941), pp. 58–73; and A. Krueger, "Political Economy of the Rent-Seeking Society," *American Economic Review* 64 (June 1974), pp. 291–303. For empirical tests of similar theories, see, for example, Richard Caves, *Multinational Enterprise and Economic Analysis* (Cambridge: Cambridge University Press, 1976); Baldwin, *Political Economy of U.S. Import Policy;* J. Pincus, *Pressure Groups and Politics in Antebellum Tariffs* (New York: Columbia University Press, 1977); E. Ray, "Determinants of Tariff and Nontariff Trade Restrictions in the U.S.," *Journal of Political Economy* 81 (February 1981), pp. 105–21; and R. Lavergne, *The Political Economy of U.S. Tariffs* (Toronto: Academic Press, 1983).

expanded these arguments by explaining why certain firms prefer free trade.[8] According to their line of reasoning, exporters and multinational firms, especially those with extensive global intra-firm trade flows in the manufacturing sector, will be committed to free trade and opposed to protectionism at home. Since barriers to trade impose higher costs on their business, these firms see free trade as a profit-maximizing strategy. Protectionism imposes costs on these companies by restricting access to low-cost imported inputs, disrupting intra-firm trade flows, and reducing their relative competitiveness vis-à-vis domestically oriented rivals. Protectionism at home could also increase the probability of retaliation against fixed foreign assets or exports. As Milner[9] demonstrated empirically, a number of American manufacturing industries that faced serious foreign competition in the domestic market resisted the temptation to ask for protection. In each case, these industries were dominated by multinational firms that did not want to risk retaliation or jeopardize their significant global intra-firm trade flows.

A gap in the literature exists, however, in that none of these theories has specifically addressed what happened to the preferences of internationally oriented manufacturing industries that were faced with a combination of competitive pressure and foreign protectionism. Underlying most theoretical analyses was an assumption that multinational firms would retain an unconditional commitment to free trade. This was a reasonable assumption because capital was mobile for multinational manufacturing firms, which meant that they could either invest in a local market and circumvent trade barriers or invest in other low-wage countries to reduce their costs.[10] It has never been a surprise that firms in the agricultural sector would demand specific reciprocity, because most farmers lacked mobility when confronted with trade barriers. But there was no reason to expect foreign protectionism to alter the trade preferences of manufacturing firms, since direct investment was an option that did not hurt their international competitive position.[11]

8. Helen Milner, "Resisting the Protectionist Temptation," Ph.D. diss., Harvard University, 1986; John Odell and I. M. Destler, *The Politics of Anti-Protection* (Washington, D.C.: Institute for International Economics, 1987); and T. Pugel and I. Walter, "U.S. Corporate Interests and the Political Economy of U.S. Trade Policy," *Review of Economics and Statistics* 67 (August 1985), pp. 465–73.

9. Helen Milner, *Resisting Protectionism: Global Industries and the Politics of International Trade* (Princeton, N.J.: Princeton University Press, 1988).

10. In addition to direct investment in the competitors' market and investing in other low-wage countries, a third strategy was to license technology and earn a royalty on the firm's fixed research and development investment. As long as multinational firms could earn a substantial return with any of these three strategies, one should expect them to remain committed to free trade.

11. The key variable in this analysis is mobility of factors of production. In the absence of mobility, such as in most agricultural production, it is not surprising that foreign protectionism would produce domestic demands for retaliation or reciprocity. However, in industries in which key factors (such as capital) are mobile and multinational firms have unique products that could not be easily replicated by domestic producers, foreign trade barriers could even be the preferred option. Since protectionism increases local prices, a multinational firm might be able to earn excessive returns behind tariff or quota barriers.

The color television industry in the 1970s is a case in point. Japan's market for televisions was closed to American investment and American products while Japanese firms started to grab market share in the United States. Consistent with traditional expectations, domestic firms (such as Zenith) lobbied for protection, while multinational firms (such as RCA) retained their commitment to free trade, earned royalties from Japanese firms by licensing technology, and simply moved production offshore to improve their cost position.[12] Just as British policymakers assumed in the 1840s that Britain would be better off with free trade at home even if other countries continued to be protectionist,[13] scholars have recently assumed that the profit-maximizing strategy of most multinational firms was free trade at home and that the strategy was independent of actions by foreign rivals and their governments.

Our puzzle was that strategic trade demands were being voiced by exactly the same type of firms that historically were committed to unconditional free trade: the internationally oriented manufacturers. No available theory could explain why some firms, but not others, would develop such strategic trade demands. How, then, can we understand the emergence of these strategic trade demands that make free trade at home contingent on free trade abroad?

A theory of strategic trade demands

Recent economic theories of international trade shed light on the changes in trade demands. Relaxing many of the strict assumptions of neoclassical economics, these new theories of strategic trade policy focus on trade under imperfect competition. While the literature on this subject is diverse, one of its central conclusions is that free trade is not always optimal and that protectionism—policies that restrict imports or promote exports—can increase national income by raising the profitability of firms in certain imperfect markets.[14] As one economist argues: "As a consequence [of imperfect competition], it is possible for firms to earn profits above the rate of return earned

12. David B. Yoffie, "Zenith and the Color Television Fight," Harvard Business School Case no. 9-383-070, rev. April 1986.

13. Arthur Stein, "The Hegemon's Dilemma," *International Organization* 38 (Spring 1984), pp. 355–86; and Keohane, "Reciprocity in International Relations."

14. See J. Brander and B. Spencer, "Tariffs and the Extraction of Foreign Monopoly Rents Under Potential Entry," *Canadian Journal of Economics* 14 (August 1981), pp. 371–89; A. Dixit, "International Trade Policies for Oligopolistic Industries," *Economic Journal* 94 (Supplement 1984), pp. 1–16; B. Spencer and J. Brander, "International R&D Rivalry and Industrial Strategy," *Review of Economic Studies* 50 (October 1983), pp. 707–22; A. Auquier and R. Caves, "Monopolistic Export Industries, Trade, Taxes, and Optimal Competition Policy," *Economic Journal* 89 (September 1979), pp. 559–81; J. Eaton and G. Grossman, "Optimal Trade and Industrial Policy Under Oligopoly," *Quarterly Journal of Economics* 101 (May 1986), pp. 383–406; D. DeMeza, "Commercial Policy Toward Multinational Monopolies," *Oxford Economic Papers* 31 (July 1979), pp. 334–37; and Paul Krugman, *Strategic Trade Policy and the New International Economics* (Cambridge, Mass.: MIT Press, 1986).

in purely competitive industries. Trade policy then emerges as a national attempt to obtain as large a share of these international profits as possible."[15] Although the new economic models are not very robust, conclusions derived from their use have spawned a deluge of research about why protection might help certain industries and thus improve national welfare.

These theories provide a starting point for understanding why corporate demands will become strategic, because they identify three key market imperfections that potentially can be exploited by government policy: (1) large economies of scale, (2) steep learning curves, and (3) sizable research and development (R&D) requirements.[16] From the point of view of firms, the first two conditions are most important because they create the possibility of receiving increased rents. If an industry's production of goods and services has very large economies of scale or significant learning effects, then access to foreign markets and the behavior of foreign firms and governments directly affect the profitability of the domestic industry.[17] Under these conditions, corporate profitability at home becomes interdependent with the actions of other countries.

The logic of this interdependence is that large economies of scale involve higher fixed costs and greater risks for firms. The ability to realize a return on the large initial investment necessitates a growing sales volume. If market share at home is not large enough for all domestic firms to realize the minimum scale necessary to break even, then access to foreign markets via exports becomes critical. Similarly, if the effects of learning (for example, reduced costs of production over time due to greater experience and knowledge of the manufacturing process) are important, the first firm or national industry to build a large sales base will have lower costs that cannot be profitably replicated by competitors. Since one or more of these economic changes can cause barriers to entry to rise over time, foreign protectionism or subsidies could give foreign competitors "first-mover advantages," cost advantages that later entrants could not match.[18] In an industry in which the U.S. market is open and a large foreign market is closed, foreign competitors would be able to achieve more efficient scale as a result of increased volume

15. J. Brander, "Rationales for Strategic Trade and Industrial Policy," in Krugman, *Strategic Trade Policy,* p. 25.

16. Krugman, *Strategic Trade Policy,* chaps. 2 and 4.

17. The third condition, rising R&D requirements, also creates market imperfections. However, these imperfections are not internal to the firm, like scale and learning; rather, they are "external economies" that are typically captured by other parties—not the individual firm—through "spillover" effects. Hence, while strategic trade policy for an industry with high R&D requirements can be used to increase a *nation's* welfare, there is no reason to believe that high R&D requirements will change the incentives for individual *firms* to demand strategic trade policy.

18. This assumes that market size is limited and that no technological innovation would make existing products or processes obsolete. See Pankaj Ghemawat, "Sustainable Advantage," *Harvard Business Review* 64 (September–October 1986), pp. 53–58.

in domestic and overseas sales, while domestic competitors would be squeezed into a portion of the domestic market. And once firms in the industry fall behind, they would be unable to recover profitably.

Under these two economic conditions—large economies of scale and steep learning curves—access to foreign markets and control over the home market would become a firm's top priorities. Firms that were formerly unconditional free traders would have to recalculate their positions on international trade if their industry undergoes these economic changes *and* foreign governments adopt trade or industrial policies that could give foreign competitors first-mover advantages. In the absence of foreign government intervention, internationally oriented firms are likely to continue to support unconditional free trade, since the benefits of strategic trade policy would be small relative to the risk of retaliation. Ceteris paribus, the same would be true if a foreign government fails to create a competitive edge for its firms. Assuming a foreign government has no reputation for successful intervention, internationally oriented industries would not want to incur the potential costs associated with strategic trade policy.[19] But if a foreign government has been successful in creating competitive advantages abroad—for example, increasing its firms' market shares in the United States and reducing U.S. firms' profits—then we should expect even the staunchest supporters of unconditional liberalization to make free trade at home contingent on freer trade abroad. In other words, strategic trade demands would become apparent.

In the absence of these key economic changes, multinational manufacturers would not have strong incentives for strategic trade policy. Without large economies of scale and steep learning curves, a multinational firm facing foreign trade barriers could adjust to increased international competition through conventional direct investment strategies: it could either invest directly in the protectionist country (like automobile firms did in Europe in the 1950s and 1960s) or move offshore to reduce labor costs (like RCA did in the 1970s). With changes in scale and learning, however, direct access via exports to foreign markets is critical. As many economic studies have shown, the building of new plants abroad may be inefficient if there are significant changes in economies of scale or learning effects in production. Direct foreign investment will limit domestic production volumes, and for-

19. Ceteris paribus refers here to the reputation of the foreign government for successfully intervening in its domestic industries. For decades, governments around the world have intervened in their economies. However, most of these interventions, especially by Latin American and European countries, have failed. Numerous factors, including poor government policies and inept management, have produced these failures. Hence, multinational firms that face large economies of scale or steep learning curves would not want to fight half the governments in the world just because those governments were intervening in their own industries. In the absence of some competitive loss, the costs would outweigh any benefits. On the other hand, if a foreign government had a reputation for successful industrial intervention, firms might seek strategic trade policy preemptively, even before their competitive positions suffered.

eign operations may not reach an efficient scale of operations.[20] Large-scale exporting from a domestic base will be the best option.

Hence, the combination of these market imperfections and successful foreign government intervention should lead internationally oriented firms to view unconditional domestic free trade as the worst possible outcome. With the loss of export markets due to foreign protection and the undesirability of investing around the barriers because of learning and scale effects, these firms will increasingly lose sales to their foreign rivals. Similar to the trade position of agricultural exporters, who also do not have the option of investing abroad when faced with foreign protection, internationally oriented firms with large economies of scale or steep learning curves will resort to strategic trade demands in order to pry foreign markets open.

Changing industry economics combined with successful foreign government subsidies or protection should alter the trade demands of individual firms within the industry. However, the speed with which the industry itself acts is also critical. Strategic trade policy is only useful to an industry *before* foreign firms gain long-term sustainable advantages. Once foreign firms achieve first-mover advantages, access of domestic firms to the foreign market would no longer be of interest, since they would be uncompetitive and therefore unable to sell even if the foreign market were open. Thus, if domestic firms fall inexorably behind, their only choices are to exit or to advocate unconditional protectionism.

A simple profit-maximizing model of the firm in perfect competition would assume that all firms are identical and that if collective goods problems could be overcome, all firms would quickly and unanimously advocate a common political position. However, assuming that all firms are identical is invalid in industries characterized by imperfect competition.[21] Firms may have different competitive positions, which means that even an industry with a small number of firms may not have a unified position on trade.

Take two hypothetical examples: one is a three-firm, highly segmented industry that is facing intense import pressure from Korea and Taiwan in one market segment; the other is a fifty-firm commodity industry in which all firms are essentially identical in size and product line, 100 percent of the production is domestic, and all firms compete directly against lower-cost imports. For the sake of clarity, let's say that the three-firm industry produces footwear and consists of one purely domestic footwear firm that competes head-on against Far Eastern producers, one maker of cowboy boots with no foreign competition, and one full-line multinational manufacturer that

20. Caves, *Multinational Enterprise and Economic Analysis,* pp. 43–44. Caves also discusses in this book the alternative approach of technology licensing. However, like direct investment, simply earning royalties would not be attractive in industries that have large economies of scale or significant learning effects.

21. R. E. Caves and M. E. Porter, "From Entry Barriers to Mobility Barriers: Conjectural Decisions and Contrived Deterrence to New Competition," *Quarterly Journal of Economics* 91 (May 1977), pp. 241–61.

sources and distributes a significant percentage of its shoes from the Far East.[22] A priori, one might expect very different trade responses from these two industries. The three-firm industry would start with highly divergent trade interests, while the fifty-firm industry would have strong, immediate incentives to cooperate for protection. As a result, the three-firm industry would probably take longer to reach an industry-wide trade consensus.

Our hypothesis is that the speed and intensity of corporate demands for strategic trade action will be similarly affected by the structure of competition within an industry, especially the level of industry segmentation into strategic groups. A strategic group, as defined by Michael Porter, consists of one or more firms following "similar strategies": "Such a group could consist of a single firm or could encompass all the firms in an industry. Firms within a strategic group resemble one another closely and, therefore, are likely to respond in the same way to disturbances, to recognize their mutual dependence quite closely, and to be able to anticipate each other's reaction quite accurately."[23] If the majority of firms in an industry have relatively similar competitive strategies, they are more likely to respond in a consistent way politically to a change in industry economics and foreign government intervention. The more homogeneous the competitive strategies pursued by firms in the industry—that is, the fewer distinctive strategic groups there are— the greater the likelihood that all firms will identify the threat posed by foreign government intervention and respond similarly to that threat by adopting strategic trade demands.

However, if there are a number of distinctive strategic groups, as in the footwear example described above, then a more complicated pattern should emerge. In highly segmented industries, some firms may be unaffected in the short term by a foreign competitive threat.[24] They may not perceive the foreign threat in a similar way to other firms, or they may not respond to that threat similarly. Indeed, the more distinctive the strategic groups, the less likely a common industry response will develop. Some firms may favor strategic trade policy, while other firms favor outright protectionism and still others advocate free trade. This will necessitate bargaining among the firms and perhaps the making of side-payments to various firms in order to reach

22. While this footwear example is hypothetical, it has some similarities to the actual structure of the American footwear industry. See David B. Yoffie, *Power and Protectionism: Strategies of the Newly Industrializing Countries* (New York: Columbia University Press, 1983), chap. 5. Although there are over 200 American shoe companies, footwear is a highly segmented industry. In *Resisting Protectionism,* Milner also describes how these types of differences within the American footwear industry impeded the creation of a unified trade position.

23. Porter, "The Structure Within Industries," p. 215.

24. Strategic groups have been defined by economists in various ways. The dimensions of strategic groups could range from marketing strategies to dimensions that are only important for international trade (such as global versus domestic production strategies) or for specific product segments. Our analysis of strategic groups focuses only on dimensions of industries that are related to the firms' positions in international trade and competition. For an operational definition, see footnote 26.

a unified position. In highly segmented industries, this process of consensus-building will be costly and time-consuming. It will mean that the development of an industry-wide response to foreign government intervention is slower than when the industry is less fragmented.

If the industry response is slow in these fragmented industries and foreign government intervention leads to a rapid deterioration in net income and market share, then the domestic industry will lose its first-mover advantages and become increasingly uncompetitive. Under these conditions in imperfect markets, strategic trade policy will have little value. Access to foreign markets will no longer solve the industry's problems. If the competitiveness of the industry declines rapidly, only unconditional protection at home will allow its firms to survive. Therefore, rapid losses in industries with large numbers of strategic groups are likely to produce demands for trade barriers, no matter what policies are pursued abroad.

If, on the other hand, there is a slow deterioration in the industry's market position (characterized by lower profits rather than acute losses and by only marginal declines in market share), then there is a greater probability that the industry will have time to bargain its way toward strategic trade policy. As long as most firms in the industry have a substantial domestic market share and continue to be competitive internationally, they will realize that access to foreign markets remains crucial to their future survival. Strategic government action will still be appealing to them.

This argument about corporate demands is presented in Figure 1. Multinational and export-oriented industries start as unconditional demanders of free trade. As the economics of the industry change and foreign governments intervene, the conditions are created for a change in corporate responses to foreign competition. If a foreign government has no reputation for successful intervention and fails to create a competitive edge for its firms, then internationally oriented industries are likely to remain free traders.[25] But if the industry loses some competitiveness (loses domestic market share and profitability), then two possibilities arise. In an industry in which few strategic groups exist and firms follow similar strategies, there should be a quick turn toward strategic trade policy. In an industry that is highly segmented and has distinctive strategic groups, the speed of industry-wide decline will condition the response. If there is rapid deterioration, firms are likely to favor unconditional protection of the home market. If, on the other hand, there is slow deterioration, firms are likely to see advantages of demanding strategic trade policy.

Case studies

To examine this argument, we studied four industries that had a history of supporting free trade: the semiconductor, commercial aircraft, telecom-

---

25. For a discussion of reputation, see footnote 19.

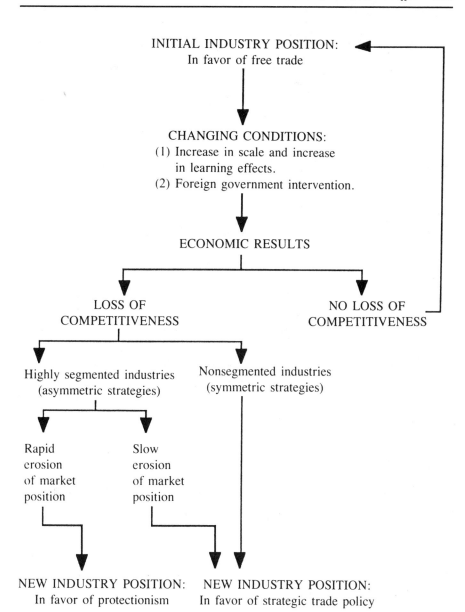

FIGURE 1. *Effects of changing market conditions and government policy on corporate trade demands*

TABLE 1. *Operating indicators for industry samples (as percentage of sales)*

	1975	1976	1977	1978	1979	1980	1981	1982	1983	1984	1985	1986
Semiconductors												
Capital expenditures	6.0	9.0	11.0	14.0	13.0	15.0	18.0	15.0	14.0	21.0	17.0	n.a.
Operating profits	−3.6	10.0	10.6	12.0	13.2	15.5	7.0	3.1	10.1	16.1	−4.2	n.a.
Foreign sales	27.9	29.0	30.4	32.2	32.7	34.9	30.4	30.7	31.7	37.4	37.5	n.a.
Commercial aircraft												
Capital expenditures	2.2	2.0	2.4	4.2	5.4	5.1	4.0	3.4	1.5	2.1	2.3	3.7
Operating profits	6.7	9.4	10.4	7.4	6.6	5.4	2.0	−0.8	0.5	1.0	4.5	3.9
Foreign sales	49.9	59.0	55.8	38.1	45.3	52.8	55.3	39.1	39.7	30.9	37.3	38.1
Machine tools												
Capital expenditures	2.7	3.8	2.9	3.8	4.5	5.3	5.3	4.7	4.1	7.3	3.3	3.0
Operating profits	8.9	9.3	10.1	14.5	16.7	17.1	16.7	11.9	−1.7	0.6	−0.3	−0.1
Foreign sales	35.1	30.6	28.4	29.1	26.6	28.6	24.4	21.2	26.8	16.4	17.0	23.3
Telecommunications equipment												
Capital expenditures	4.2	3.2	3.8	4.2	4.2	5.4	5.3	5.9	7.3	15.2	10.1	8.4
Operating profits	4.8	6.9	12.4	12.3	12.2	12.0	11.3	9.7	4.1	9.7	8.1	7.7
Exports 3661[a]	4.2	4.4	3.6	4.9	4.6	5.0	5.4	7.0	6.7	6.1	5.2	4.7
Exports 3662[b]	9.2	10.7	10.0	9.9	9.6	8.5	8.6	7.9	7.4	6.9	6.4	6.1

[a]Exports 3661 = telephone and telegraph apparatus.
[b]Exports 3662 = radio and television communications equipment.

Sources. For semiconductors, Semiconductor Industry Association (SIA), *Performance of the Semiconductor Industry, 1975 to 1985: Sales, Employment, Capacity, Productivity, and Investment* (Cupertino, Calif.: SIA, 1986), which provides information for over fifty semiconductor firms, including both discrete and integrated circuit producers. For commercial aircraft, Annual Reports and 10-K Reports (filed with Securities and Exchange Commission) of Boeing and McDonnell Douglas, various years. For machine tools, Annual Reports and 10-K Reports of Cincinnati Milacron, Cross and Trekker, Giddings and Lewis, Gleason Works, and Monarch Machine Tool Company, various years; and National Machine Tool Builders' Association (NMTBA), *Economic Handbook of the Machine Tool Industry, 1982–83* (Washington, D.C.: NMTBA, 1984), p. 255. For telecommunications equipment, Annual Reports and 10-K Reports of InteCom, Mitel, Northern Telecom (switching equipment), Rolm Corp., and Western Electric (commercial equipment; name changed to AT&T Technologies in 1983), various years.

munications equipment, and machine tool industries. Since all of the major firms in these industries had significant multinational production, extensive global intra-firm trade, or high levels of exports (see Table 1), the industries would, according to conventional theory, be expected to continue to support free trade, even in times of high import penetration. The case studies would be expected to show no variation on the dependent variable; they should all be free traders. But evidence of their behavior in the mid-1980s is contrary to these predictions. Three of these industries made strategic trade demands on the U.S. government, while the fourth advocated outright protection. We were puzzled by the fact that these particular cases no longer seemed to fit existing models. The cases are used to uncover why firms' demands changed from free trade to strategic trade or protectionism.

Our research strategy involved examining the initial trade demands of these four industries and following their trade positions over time. We interpreted a shift in demands by researching their congressional testimonies, public statements, filings with the International Trade Commission (ITC), and interviews. Interpretation problems could exist in examining publicly stated interests, since demands for protectionism could simply be couched in strategic terms. Therefore, we took two steps to guard against this. First, we defined an industry's demand as strategic only if the industry communicated to the government that its strategy was conditional—that is, the industry indicated that it wanted to close the home market only if the foreign market was not (further) opened. Second, we discounted communicated demands unless we found evidence that firms made efforts to gain access to foreign markets—for example, the firms had high international marketing expenditures or important foreign assembly or sales operations.

Next we traced any shift in demands to shifts in the economics of the industry.[26] We then looked at the degree of openness of the foreign markets and at the evidence of foreign government intervention. Evidence of successful protection or export subsidies abroad was presumably the proximate catalyst for changes in corporate demands. Without evidence of this intervention, the firms' requests for aid were more likely to be disguised appeals for unconditional protection. Finally, we should note that the cases discussed below only represent a partial test: the sample is small because there are few real-world examples, to date, of demands for strategic trade policy; and

---

26. Measures for these variables come from the literature on industrial organization. For economies of scale, we use minimum efficient scale when possible; otherwise, we use capital expenditure as a percentage of total sales. For learning effects, we use declining average production costs per unit over time. Changes in any one variable alone would increase market imperfections and thereby predispose firms to become more strategic about trade; simultaneous changes in both variables would greatly intensify the demand for strategic trade policy.

For indicators of strategic groups, we have not used conventional concentration ratios, since we do not believe they adequately capture the concept of strategic groups. We define strategic groups in terms of the key structural variables of each industry, which can range from different end uses to different manufacturing strategies. See Caves and Porter, "From Entry Barriers to Mobility Barriers"; and Porter, "The Structure Within Industries."

the relationship between the empirical work and the model was iterative. We continued to refine the model as we learned more about our cases.

The semiconductor industry

The modern semiconductor industry began in 1959 with the invention of the integrated circuit (IC). Initially, the industry had relatively low entry costs, moderate economies of scale but significant learning effects (costs fell as much as 30 to 40 percent with every doubling in volume), and relatively long product cycles. To capitalize on these features, most firms employed global strategies from the beginning. Even the smallest semiconductor companies had international sales offices with exports that averaged about 20 percent of production.[27] In addition, the majority of firms had extensive overseas assembly operations.[28]

Through the mid-1970s, semiconductor producers predictably favored unconditional free trade. American semiconductor firms, working through various associations, supported U.S. government efforts at general trade liberalization during the Tokyo Round negotiations and strongly advocated the reduction of all U.S. tariffs on semiconductors. Although tariff reductions on semiconductors were linked in U.S. government negotiations with reciprocal reductions by Japan, some of the largest semiconductor firms were in favor of tariff liberalization through the early 1980s, even in the absence of Japanese concessions.[29]

In the mid-1970s, several changes occurred in the economics and technology of the industry. First, product innovation slowed and competition became more intense. Second, the industry moved from large-scale integration (LSI) of chips to very large scale integration (VLSI). A result of this change was that microelectronics became much more capital-intensive. Estimates for building a world-class production facility varied, but most analysts concurred that the cost had risen ten- to twenty-fold from 1975 to 1985. Capital expenditures increased from under 10 percent of revenue to almost 20 percent over the same period. Every step in the production process became more capital-intensive, expensive, and intricate.

Another related change was that it became difficult for any firm in the industry to be large and successful without producing high-volume memory chips. High-volume products were considered essential because they acted as "technology drivers": skills learned in manufacturing a high-volume prod-

27. Milner, "Resisting the Protectionist Temptation," p. 347.
28. J. Grunwald and K. Flamm, *The Global Factory: Foreign Assembly in International Trade* (Washington, D.C.: The Brookings Institute, 1985).
29. The chief executive officer of one of the largest merchant semiconductor firms reported in an interview that elimination of tariffs allowed his firm to cut the positions of twenty-one full-time bookkeepers who were responsible for reporting to the U.S. Customs Department on the firm's imports from its overseas assembly operations. He noted that getting tariff cuts from Japan was much less important than his firm's ability to import freely.

uct could be transferred to complicated, higher value-added devices and help "drive" the firm down a very steep learning curve. The production of dynamic random access memory (DRAM) chips—a 1971 American invention—fulfilled this role for the industry. All major firms wanted a "technology driver" such as this to stimulate improvements in quality, reliability, performance, and yield. Yield, or the percentage of usable chips on a wafer, tended to be low for new semiconductors (say 10 percent) but would rise rapidly as volume cumulated. These learning effects were a major determinant of cost and thus were of critical competitive importance in these products.[30]

A third major change was that in the late 1970s and early 1980s, Japan emerged as both a large player and an enormous market for semiconductors. A decade earlier, Japanese firms were largely confined to the licensing of American products and production of ICs that suited Japan's consumer electronics companies. Concerned about dependence on consumer electronics, Japan's Ministry of International Trade and Industry (MITI) began a four-year VLSI program from 1976 to 1979 in order to make Japan an equal in advanced information technology. The most important elements of the program included government provision or coordination of collective goods such as R&D funds, technical education, production and product targets, price controls, and restrictions on access to the domestic market. In capital and R&D expenditures, Japan began outpacing the United States.[31]

The VLSI program was a great success. By the end of 1979, the Japanese held 43 percent of the U.S. market for 16K DRAMs; in 1981, they supplied about 70 percent of the 64K DRAMs in the U.S. market; and in 1984 and 1985, they pre-empted American entry into 256K DRAMs and gathered 90 percent of the market. Japanese dominance of the DRAM and other commodity chip markets had a uniform effect on the major players in the American industry. While smaller firms continued to thrive on the production of one or two specialized types of chips, the largest merchant manufacturers lost enormous sums of money in commodity chips, forcing the majority to stop making DRAMs. Of the largest American semiconductor merchants, only Texas Instruments, which had DRAM production in Japan, remained in the market by late 1985. Japanese efforts to drive their manufacturing processes down the learning curve, combined with a recession in user industries, led to price cuts on commodity chips ranging from 75 to 90 percent in less than 12 months.

Since all large American semiconductor firms believed they needed a "technology driver," the industry as a whole became increasingly disturbed by its inability to penetrate Japan's market. Japan's success in the electronics

30. David B. Yoffie, "The Global Semiconductor Industry," Harvard Business School Case no. 9-388-052, 1987.

31. Dan Okimoto, T. Sugano, and F. Weinstein, eds., *Competitive Edge: The Semiconductor Industry in the U.S. and Japan* (Stanford, Calif.: Stanford University Press, 1985).

industry had made it the world's second largest market for semiconductors (35 percent) in 1985, only slightly behind the United States (38 percent).[32] In the meantime, Japan's share of the U.S. market grew to almost 17 percent by 1985, while the American share of Japan's semiconductor sales had hovered around 10 percent for almost a decade, despite expanded marketing expenditures by American firms.[33]

Rising imports, alone, might have led to any number of trade responses from the semiconductor industry. When imports started to rise in the mid-1970s, the industry remained in favor of free trade, and U.S. firms simply adjusted by moving offshore to reduce labor costs. U.S. semiconductor firms had not anticipated Japanese government success, because Japan's reputation for promoting industry was only in its nascent stages. In addition, U.S. managers were confident that they could "out-innovate" Japan.[34] If the semiconductor industry had been a traditional industry, without huge economies of scale, the mounting Japanese threat could have been met with either additional investment overseas or a turn toward protectionism. In the mid-1980s, however, the industry decided to advocate strategic trade policy. Protectionism was still seen as undesirable, but the combination of huge scale and continued Japanese protection led most large firms to perceive direct access to the Japanese market as necessary for survival. Since all of the large U.S. chip firms followed a similar strategy of relying on "technology drivers," it was also likely that the industry would respond quickly to the Japanese threat.

In June 1985, the Semiconductor Industry Association (SIA) filed a petition under Section 301 of the 1974 Trade Act, charging Japan with unfair trade practices and asking the U.S. government to retaliate against Japanese firms unless there was substantial improvement in the U.S. share of Japan's market. According to the petition, the Japanese market remained closed while Japanese companies were selling products below cost at predatory prices for the sole purpose of building market share.[35]

Not only did the SIA file this trade suit, but individual firms also filed suits later in 1985, charging Japan with dumping erasable programmable read-only memory (EPROM) chips on the U.S. market.[36] Intel, Advanced Micro Devices (AMD), and National Semiconductor—all firms dependent upon exports with extensive overseas operations—were responsible for the EPROM suit. One of the objectives of this suit was to add bargaining power to the

32. Instat, Inc., "Information Company for the Electronics Industry," mimeograph, Semiconductor Industry Conference, New York, 4 June 1987. By 1987, the Japanese market had reached 49 percent of the world market, compared to 39 percent for the United States.

33. Semiconductor Industry Association (SIA), "Japanese Market Barriers in Microelectronics," memorandum in support of a petition pursuant to Section 301 of the Trade Act of 1974 as Amended, 14 June 1985.

34. Yoffie, "The Global Semiconductor Industry."

35. SIA, "Japanese Market Barriers."

36. In 1984, a small semiconductor manufacturer, Micron Technology, also filed a dumping suit against Japanese producers of 64K DRAMs. This suit, however, was not widely supported.

Section 301 negotiations. The firms also stated that if dumping did not stop and the Japanese market was not liberalized, they would ask the government to impose antidumping duties on EPROMs or even request a separate quota.[37]

The SIA's two primary objectives in filing the Section 301 petition were to ensure a U.S. market share of at least 20 percent in Japan by the early 1990s and to stop Japanese dumping of memory products in the United States and third country markets. The SIA made it clear that unconditional closure of the U.S. market was not its goal; rather, it wanted the government to threaten the use of sanctions against Japan for dumping and unfair trade practices in order to force the opening of the Japanese market.[38]

In July 1986, the U.S. government negotiated an agreement with Japan that mirrored the industry's demands. When it appeared that Japan was not honoring the agreement, the SIA requested that the U.S. government retaliate to force compliance. But once again, the request was for strategic action rather than unconditional protectionism. Despite continued losses and severe industry distress, the SIA requested sanctions on products that used semiconductors rather than on the chips themselves. In April 1987, the U.S. government imposed 100 percent tariffs on $300 million worth of Japanese consumer and office goods. Approximately $165 million of sanctions remained in force at the end of 1988 because of the lack of progress in opening Japan's market.

The commercial aircraft industry

The politics and economics of the commercial aircraft industry share similarities as well as differences with those of the semiconductor industry. Production of semiconductors was an emerging technology with many players; however, the commercial aircraft business was relatively mature and highly concentrated, with only four significant players worldwide in the mid-1970s. Three were American firms: Boeing, McDonnell Douglas, and Lockheed (the latter exited the business by the end of the decade). And one was European: Airbus Industrie. The commonalities were that both industries faced steep learning curves and huge capital requirements, making global strategies, large export volumes, and some overseas operations a necessity. The United States also dominated the international market for both products through the mid-1970s.

Perhaps the most notable feature of the commercial aircraft industry was that it could take five years to get a plane from the drawing board to final production, and there was no guarantee of market success. There had never been a case in which advance orders guaranteed the firm would break even when it began production. As a result, the introduction of a new airplane

---

37. J. Coleman and D. Yoffie, "The Semiconductor Industry Association and the Trade Dispute with Japan," Harvard Business School Case no. 0-387-205, 1987.
38. Interviews with SIA officials, April 1987, Washington, D.C.

was often a decision that risked the company's entire future. Furthermore, through 1980, no firm had broken even before 300 planes were sold. Since 1952, no European jetliner had ever reached that level, and only six U.S. planes had attained that goal.[39]

Almost equally important to achieving sales volume was getting a first order by new customers. Each commercial aircraft remained in service for an average of twenty-two years. Since customers would have to train their engineers and maintenance personnel for particular planes, there were significant economies to sticking with one aircraft type. Therefore, once an airline bought a plane, it usually stayed with the same brand for a decade or more.

The competition for first orders in the aircraft industry was always intense, but through the mid-1970s, companies competed within distinctive strategic groups. Boeing and others designed aircraft to meet very specific needs regarding range and seating capacity. There were enormous differences between a plane that would serve a "long haul" versus a "short haul" and low-density versus high-density routes.[40] As can be seen in Figure 2, there was strong competition between Boeing and McDonnell Douglas for the mid-range, 100- to 150-passenger planes; but Airbus had a distinctive position in the short-to-medium range, 250-passenger planes, and Boeing had the top end of the market to itself.[41]

According to our argument, the American aircraft industry should have been an unconditional supporter of free trade in the 1970s. Since Boeing and McDonnell Douglas were profitable and export-dependent and had extensive overseas connections, both could be expected to oppose any closure of the American market. Although McDonnell Douglas rarely testified before Congress on trade issues, Boeing emphasized at congressional hearings during the 1970s that it opposed import restrictions "or any other constraints to free trade."[42] While Boeing remained concerned with Airbus, it did not seek trade remedies but merely continued its traditional policy of asking for R&D assistance, tax credits, and greater availability of Export-Import Bank export financing.

Between the late 1970s and the mid-1980s, two important changes occurred in the economics and politics of the commercial aircraft industry. First, the

39. M. Salter, "Turbulent Skies: Airbus vs. Boeing," Harvard Business School Case no. 0-386-193, 1987.

40. Laurence Phillips, "Air Carrier Activity at Major Hub Airports and Changing Interline Practices in the United States' Airlines Industries," *Transportation Research* 21A (May 1987), pp. 215–21.

41. We have excluded Lockheed from this discussion for two reasons. First, Lockheed did not compete directly with Airbus in the 1970s; its major competitor was McDonnell Douglas. Second, scandals, bribes, and bankruptcy of Lockheed's core business meant that Lockheed's position on trade policy was relatively unimportant for the commercial aircraft industry.

42. Testimony of Robert Bateman (Washington representative, Boeing Co.), in U.S. Congress, Senate Committee on Commerce, *Hearings Before the Subcommittee on Foreign Commerce and Tourism*, 92d Cong., 2d sess., 1972, p. 350.

cost of launching a new design for large aircraft in the 1980s rose to $5 billion, which was greater than McDonnell Douglas's net worth.[43] Analysts also concluded that minimum efficient scale had increased. Competitive pressure on prices required companies to sell a minimum of 400 planes to break even, with the versions planned for the early 1990s expected to need 600 planes. Given the small size of the market for any particular model, the higher break-even figure meant that if two companies tried to produce a plane for the same category, at least one company would lose money—and probably both would.[44]

Second, deregulation of American airlines and liberalization in European airline routes altered the economics of aircraft manufacturing. Airline routes changed dramatically, leading to demands for smaller planes that offered a wider range.[45] All manufacturers rushed to produce the same type of aircraft, which altered the structure of competition. The once highly segmented aircraft industry became much less fragmented, as all firms invaded each other's territory (see Figure 3). Airbus, in particular, became an aggressive competitor during this period. Founded in 1970 by the French and West German governments, Airbus Industrie developed into a consortium of nine European nations who heavily subsidized R&D, provided export financing, and helped in other parts of the manufacturing process. Although Airbus allegedly never made a profit or recovered any of its R&D expenses, the government-subsidized manufacturer raised its share of the world commercial aircraft market from 3 percent in the early 1970s to 30 percent in 1979. By the mid-1980s, Airbus was successfully attacking McDonnell Douglas and Boeing head-on.[46]

Under these conditions, our argument is that this industry should move from an unconditional free trade position toward strategic trade policy. However, the extreme segmentation of the aircraft industry through the early 1980s suggests a slower response than that of the semiconductor industry. If the aircraft industry had not been characterized by such large economies of scale and steep learning curves, in all likelihood its response would have been different. In the absence of global scale requirements, for instance, American firms might have asked for simple closure of the U.S. market. Alternatively, European intervention might have provoked greater foreign

43. Testimony of James Worsham (vice president, McDonnell Douglas), in U.S. Congress, House Committee on Energy and Commerce, *Hearings Before the Subcommittee on Commerce, Consumer Protection, and Competitiveness,* 23 June 1987, unpublished draft.

44. "Aircraft Industry Survey," *The Economist,* 1 June 1985; and Howard Banks, "Airbus Comes of Age," *Forbes,* 23 February 1987, pp. 36–37.

45. Rex Toh and Richard Higgins, "The Impact of Hub and Spoke Network Centralization and Route Monopoly on Domestic Airline Profitability," *Transportation Journal* 24 (Summer 1985), pp. 16–27.

46. Airbus's share of the world market was approximately 17 percent between 1980 and 1985. See U.S. Department of Commerce, *U.S. Industrial Outlook, 1987* (Washington, D.C.: GPO, 1987), pp. 34–37. However, Airbus reportedly grabbed 44 percent of all new orders during the first quarter of 1987, according to the *Dow Jones News Service,* 7 May 1987.

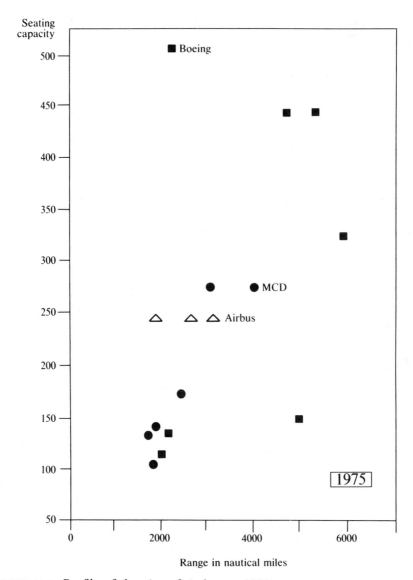

FIGURE 2. *Profile of the aircraft industry, 1975*

Note. MCD = McDonnell Douglas. Figure excludes the Lockheed L1011, which has approximately 250 seats and a range of 5000 nautical miles.
Source. Adapted from R. Moriarty, ''The Airframe Industry (M),'' Harvard Business School Case no. 9-582-013, 1982.

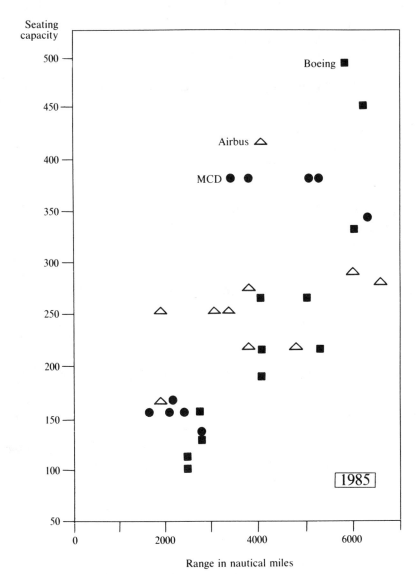

FIGURE 3. *Profile of the aircraft industry, 1985*

Note. MCD = McDonnell Douglas. Profile is from data up to June 1985.
Source. Calculated from data in *The Economist*, 1 June 1985, p. 9.

investment in Europe and elsewhere. In effect, U.S. aircraft manufacturers would have had other, less costly options to deal with European competition if they had not faced large scale and learning effects. A strategic trade response was most likely once these other options were eliminated.

The actual evolution of trade preferences by the commercial aircraft manufacturers followed our expectations. By the late 1970s, U.S. firms increasingly complained about Airbus. At first, the focus was on European export subsidies. Since export subsidies were another form of protectionism that could be used to build market share and drive a competitor down the learning curve, both Boeing and McDonnell Douglas called for a halt to the "predatory export financing war."[47] By the 1980s, Boeing, in particular, made stronger and more complicated demands. Boeing pointed to political interference on Airbus's behalf by its national backers—for example, the promise of landing rights in Paris and promises of a nuclear power plant in Iran in exchange for purchases from Airbus. The charges against Airbus included its willingness to undersell at all costs and its use of political pressure to buy from Airbus.[48] Although Boeing was regarded in the industry as the low-cost producer, Boeing representatives said that they could not profitably sell planes at the Airbus price.

Boeing did not support unilateral closure of the American market. "We have no desire or intent to see Airbus excluded from the U.S. market," Boeing's chief executive officer asserted. Yet following the start of formal U.S.–European negotiations in the GATT meetings in 1987, Boeing officials said they would consider the talks successful only if Europe would eliminate all subsidies, stop political pressure in aircraft sales, and force Airbus to establish prices that would recoup all costs. Failing such an agreement, Boeing threatened to file a Section 301 petition as well as antidumping and countervailing duty suits against Airbus, noting that "under any one of these laws, the U.S. government could negotiate with Airbus to limit the quantity of exports, eliminate subsidies, impose taxes, or reach some other solutions."[49]

In the meantime, McDonnell Douglas intensified its lobbying effort (with some support from Boeing), asking the U.S. government to force Airbus to withdraw plans for a new plane, the A340.[50] When President Reagan put

47. Testimony of Jack Pierce (treasurer, Boeing Co.), in U.S. Congress, Senate Committee on Commerce, *Hearings Before the Subcommittee on Export-Import Bank Extension*, 97th Congress, 2d sess., 1978, p. 551; and testimony of James McMillan (vice president, McDonnell Douglas), in U.S. Congress, Senate Committee on Commerce, *Export Policy, Part 4, Banking, Housing and Urban Affairs: Hearings Before the Subcommittee on International Finance and Commerce*, 97th Congress, 2d sess., 1978.

48. Testimony of T. A. Wilson (chairman, Boeing Co.), in U.S. Congress, House Committee on Ways and Means, *Competitive Conditions in the U.S. Civil Aircraft Industry and Forest Products Industry: Hearings Before the Subcommittee on Trade*, 98th Congress, 2d sess., 1984, pp. 3–5.

49. Testimony of O. M. Roetman (vice president, Boeing Co.), in *Hearings*, 23 June 1987.

50. Paul Lewis, "Airbus Group Acts to Mollify U.S.," *The New York Times*, 24 December 1985.

Europe's support for Airbus on a list of unfair trade practices to be investigated in the autumn of 1985, it was assumed that McDonnell Douglas was the primary instigator.[51] Initially, McDonnell Douglas had attempted a joint venture with Airbus which would have avoided fierce competition between the MD-11 and the A340. When that failed, the company stepped up its charges against the European manufacturer, claiming it was subsidizing deals and stealing customers.[52] In early 1987, American negotiators threatened to curb European aircraft exports under Section 301 of the U.S. trade law.[53] Although McDonnell Douglas did not publicly urge such action, it did emphasize in a congressional hearing that "should the July [1987] GATT discussions fail, then action by the U.S. government to level the competitive playing field will be necessary."[54]

The continued profitability of the two American aircraft firms deterred the industry from making its demands for strategic trade policy as quickly and as strongly as those voiced by the semiconductor industry. Nonetheless, the aircraft industry's trade preferences in the 1980s moved closer to a position of strategic trade policy than to one of unconditional free trade or protectionism. Our argument implies further that continued Airbus success across the board should push the industry toward more unified, tougher strategic trade policy demands.

The telecommunications equipment industry

The economics of the telecommunications equipment industry were unlike those of the semiconductor and commercial aircraft industries before the 1970s. Up to the late 1960s, AT&T had a near monopoly over telecommunications equipment, since it "required that only equipment provided by them [AT&T] could be attached to the telephone lines provided by them."[55] This monopoly position was not due to inherent characteristics of the equipment market; barriers to entry were low for making equipment. Rather, AT&T's legal monopoly over telephone services provided it with a virtual monopoly over telecommunications equipment.[56]

The U.S. telecommunications equipment industry did not face foreign competition until 1968, when the U.S. courts stripped AT&T of its equipment monopoly and made import competition possible.[57] Imports, however, made only marginal gains over the next decade, reaching only 4 percent of the

51. "America Turns Up Heat on Airbus," *The Economist,* 5 July 1986, p. 62.
52. "Airbus Soars on American Anger," *Sunday Times,* 8 February 1987.
53. *The Economist,* 5 July 1986; and Salter, "Turbulent Skies."
54. Testimony of James Worsham, in *Hearings,* 23 June 1987.
55. Gerald Brock, *The Telecommunications Industry: Dynamics of Market Structure* (Cambridge, Mass.: Harvard University Press, 1981), p. 235.
56. Ibid., pp. 235–36.
57. See the Carterphone decision, in U.S. Congress, Senate Committee on Finance, *The Telecommunications Trade Act of 1984: Hearings Before the Committee on Finance,* 98th Congress, 2d sess., 1984, pp. 1–3.

consumption. But by 1983, imports had surged, capturing 11 percent of the U.S. market.[58] Moreover, in customer premises equipment, which included telephones and private branch exchanges (PBXs), imports rose to 19 percent.[59]

As the U.S. market opened up in the 1970s, foreign firms moved into the United States, and American firms moved abroad. Exports rose from 3 percent to 7 percent of domestic production over the decade.[60] The combination of growing exports and stronger international ties led the U.S. telecommunications equipment industry to favor free trade. While not heavily involved in international trade issues before 1979, the industry advocated lower trade barriers through multilateral negotiations.[61] It had a positive trade balance, and its growing export dependence outweighed concerns over import penetration.

In the late 1970s and early 1980s, the structure of the industry began to change. First, U.S. firms increasingly adopted global strategies. International operations became more salient as American companies, including AT&T, realized that foreign sales were important for their future profitability. International marketing efforts also increased as American firms entered into joint ventures with foreign companies.[62] By the mid-1980s, most U.S. firms had become substantial international actors who viewed foreign markets as crucial to their success.

Second, deregulation of the U.S. market affected the telecommunications equipment industry. While initiated in 1968, the most significant deregulation came in 1982 with the decision to divest AT&T of its operating companies. This opened the U.S. market unilaterally to foreign competition. The United States was the first large country in the world to take such a bold step. And once the American telephone operating companies were freed from AT&T, they began switching from domestic equipment suppliers to less costly foreign sources.[63]

Almost all other major telecommunications markets were either controlled by a state-owned firm or heavily subsidized and protected. Most foreign telephone agencies that regulated these markets also had strong regulations to buy domestic goods. Foreign producers having access to the U.S. market,

58. U.S. International Trade Commission (USITC), *Changes in the U.S. Telecommunications Industry and the Impact on U.S. Telecommunications Trade*, no. 1542 (Washington, D.C.: USITC, 1984), p. 19.

59. Ibid., p. 22.

60. Ibid., p. 19.

61. U.S. Congress, Senate Committee on Finance, *Private Advisory Committee Reports on the Tokyo Round of the Multilateral Trade Negotiations*, 96th Congress, 1st sess., 1979; and USTIC, no. 1542, pp. 8–9.

62. J. Paul, ed., *High Technology, International Trade and Competition: Robotics, Computers, Telecommunications, and Semiconductors* (Park Ridge, N.J.: Noyes Press, 1984), p. 115; and *Standard and Poor's Industry Survey: Telecommunications* (New York: Standard & Poor, August 1986), p. 34.

63. *The Washington Post*, 20 May 1984, pp. G1 and G11; and *The New York Times*, 1 June 1984, pp. D1 and D33.

in combination with foreign markets remaining closed, eroded the ability of U.S. firms to compete globally. Japan's world market share in telecommunications equipment rose from 2.7 to 4 percent between 1983 and 1984, while the U.S. share remained stable at about 6.3 percent.[64]

Third, U.S. deregulation intensified competition based on price. Cost competitiveness, which was increasingly linked to the use of electronics and computer technologies, suddenly became a driving force. The need for lower costs and the introduction in the 1980s of new technologies, such as digital switching and fiber optics, raised the importance of scale and learning effects.[65] As Table 1 shows, capital expenditures increased dramatically in the 1980s. All major U.S. manufacturers now faced significant pressure to expand sales: a larger market share would mean in turn lower prices, greater sales, more revenues for R&D, more innovation, and, thus, a more competitive position in the future. Furthermore, virtually every U.S. telecommunications equipment company began to see this race as international. No longer could any firm survive by producing just for the U.S. market.[66]

The combination of changing economics and successful foreign government protection and intervention should lead to the emergence of strategic trade policy demands by U.S. firms, if our argument is correct. The speed with which these demands arise, however, should be influenced by the degree of fragmentation within the domestic industry. Although telecommunications equipment manufacturers were segmented into four distinct product groups, the American industry was actually dominated by a few major firms that had similar strategies in their equipment businesses. AT&T was the giant, controlling at least 20 percent of each market segment; but ITT, GTE, and Rolm (an IBM subsidiary) had secondary positions in most product areas. All of these players, in addition to many smaller specialty firms, such as Motorola in the mobile telecommunications area, perceived the need to compete for global scale economies. Even though their product offerings varied, virtually all of the American firms sought foreign sales and felt similar exclusion from foreign markets.[67]

Indeed, changes in the economics of the telecommunications equipment industry, combined with continued closure of foreign markets, had a profound and rapid political effect on U.S. producers. As early as the late 1970s,

64. *National Journal* 17 (16 March 1985), p. 590.

65. W. Adams, ed., *The Structure of American Industry,* 6th ed. (New York: Macmillan, 1982), pp. 307–14; and Organization for Economic Cooperation and Development (OECD), *Telecommunications* (Paris: OECD, 1983), p. 15.

66. J. Aronson and P. Cowhey, *When Countries Talk: Global Telecommunications for the 1980s* (New York: Ballinger, 1988), pp. 16–18.

67. The industry structure was complicated by its multinationality. Several foreign-owned firms, including Northern Telecom (Canadian), Mitel (Canadian), Siemens (German), and NEC (Japanese), had American manufacturing operations. Northern Telecom, in particular, was a large player in the United States and was occasionally considered an American company in international trade negotiations. For the purposes of this article, however, we are considering the "industry" to be U.S.–owned companies.

industry-wide trade preferences began shifting. During the Tokyo Round when negotiations to open government procurement to foreign companies started, the U.S. telecommunications equipment manufacturers wanted other governments to open telecommunications procurement to foreign competition. According to one study, it was the U.S. industry that "provided the initial impetus to negotiate the [government procurement] code."[68] In particular, the U.S. firms pushed to include Japan in this code, largely because the United States ran a telecommunications equipment trade surplus with most countries other than Japan.[69] When negotiations within GATT over the code broke down, the industry pushed for a bilateral agreement which held that if the Japanese telecommunications monopoly, Nippon Telephone and Telegraph (NTT), continued to discriminate against American goods, Japanese firms would be barred from U.S. government procurement contracts.[70] This was the first explicit industry demand for reciprocity.

In the 1980s, demands for reciprocal access by the American manufacturers became increasingly forceful. As early as 1981, Motorola, a highly multinational firm, started to file antidumping and countervailing duty petitions and to vocally advocate retaliation against Japan in the absence of market liberalization.[71] While Motorola was initially alone among telecommunications manufacturers in speaking out, the majority of larger U.S. firms had adopted similar strategic trade preferences by the mid-1980s. Most firms in the industry felt cheated by the NTT agreement, which produced few sales of American goods. The industry complained bitterly of the "asymmetry" in U.S.–Japanese trade relations, with the U.S. market being open and the Japanese one closed. From their closed, subsidized domestic market, the Japanese could reap economies of scale that gave them competitive advantages abroad.[72] This concern was exacerbated after the dismantling of AT&T's monopoly. As one industry spokesman stated, "By opening our markets and creating economies of scale for our foreign competition, we can expect that they will be more competitive in markets in which we both

68. S. Lenway, *The Politics of U.S. International Trade* (Boston: Pitman, 1985), p. 174.

69. Lenway (ibid., pp. 179–80) describes a split in preferences among U.S. firms, claiming some wanted greater access and some closure of the U.S. market. Timothy Curran, on the other hand, suggested that it was the U.S. Trade Representative, not the industry, that pushed for the negotiations with NTT. He implied that U.S. firms wanted closure of the U.S. market. But this is odd, given that the U.S. firms visited Japan to discuss the NTT case before and during the actual negotiations. See Timothy Curran, "Politics and High Technology: The NTT Case," in I. M. Destler and Hideo Sato, eds., *Coping with U.S.–Japanese Conflicts* (Lexington, Mass.: Lexington Books, 1982); and U.S. Congress, House Committee on Ways and Means, *Trade with Japan: Hearings Before the Committee on Ways and Means*, 97th Congress, 2d sess., 1980, pp. 151–61.

70. Lenway, *Politics of U.S. International Trade*, p. 186.

71. David B. Yoffie, "Motorola and Japan," Harvard Business School Case no. 9-383-070, 1983.

72. International Trade Administration (ITA), *The Telecommunications Industry* (Springfield, Va.: Department of Commerce, 1983), pp. 12–13 and 31; and Paul, *High Technology*, pp. 120–25.

compete.''[73] At this point, American companies realized that leaving the U.S. market open while others were closed was the worst choice, since it would make them uncompetitive in the future and worse off than if all markets were closed.

Their mounting concerns led equipment manufacturers to pressure Congress for legislation that would open foreign markets. Every year after 1982, a new telecommunications trade bill was introduced and debated in Congress. While differing slightly, all aimed to create, as the industry demanded, "an international free trade environment."[74] The bills authorized the President to negotiate trade barrier reductions in telecommunications over a certain period and if after that time no progress was made, to close the U.S. market. Through these bills, the industry sought "reciprocal access," which it believed would be forthcoming only if the U.S. negotiators had some "leverage." The industry saw the legislation as "market opening" and felt the United States had to "use access to our market as leverage to secure market opening concessions from [abroad].''[75] Since U.S. firms were actively seeking foreign sales, these demands would not appear to be disguised appeals for protectionism. For instance, AT&T, GTE, and Rolm all expanded their sales operations in Japan in the mid-1980s in an effort to penetrate that market.[76]

Closure of the U.S. market was not the industry's primary demand; indeed, the firms felt that such closure would be "self-defeating." But, having learned from other industries, the U.S. telecommunications equipment manufacturers realized that "if we don't get our act together, and fast, the Japanese are going to do to us in [segments of telecommunications] what they have already done in autos.''[77] Between 1980 and 1983, then, the U.S. firms had moved from an unconditional free trade position toward a strong strategic trade policy.[78] If the industry had not needed access to foreign markets to reach an efficient scale of operations, import competition in the United States would have brought a different response. It is likely that the U.S. industry, being largely domestic in orientation, would have sought unconditional protection. But the new economics of the industry made strategic trade demands its best option.

73. Testimony of J. McDonnell (telecommunications group spokesman for the Electronics Industry Association), in U.S. Congress, *Telecommunications Trade Act of 1984: Hearings,* p. 38.

74. Testimony of E. W. Weeks (spokesman for AT&T), ibid., pp. 35–37.

75. U.S. Congress, Senate Committee on Finance, *Export of U.S. Telecommunications Products: Hearings Before the Committee on Finance,* 99th Congress, 1st sess., 1985, pp. 57–67.

76. *Business Week,* 17 June 1985, p. 112a.

77. *Business Week,* 21 May 1984, pp. 179–81.

78. Early in 1981, IBM and ITT both objected to reciprocity legislation; but by 1983, neither openly opposed it. In fact, only two firms, both foreign-owned—Northern Telecom and NEC—testified against the reciprocity legislation. See U.S. Congress, *Telecommunications Trade Act of 1984: Hearings,* pp. 81–109; and U.S. Congress, *Export of U.S. Telecommunications Products: Hearings,* pp. 230–38.

The machine tool industry

In the 1960s, the U.S. machine tool industry was a "craft" industry.[79] It had a large number of small firms that each produced a few, particular machine tools. It was highly segmented and had limited economies of scale; virtually every product segment was unique, and there was little competition among segments. But U.S. producers as a group were global leaders, possessing the most advanced technology and almost a third of all world production in the mid 1960s.[80] The American machine tool builders were also substantial international players, exporting one-fifth of their production and having some overseas operations by the early 1970s.[81] American builders could therefore be expected to promote freer trade.

Throughout much of the 1970s, the U.S. producers did endorse trade liberalization. Despite rapidly rising import competition and other economic difficulties, the American firms supported a liberal international trading system. They approved of the tariff reductions negotiated in the GATT Tokyo Round, and they pressed the U.S. government to relax its export restrictions on Communist countries.[82] Indeed, during the late 1970s, the U.S. machine tool industry's top priority was to promote exports. Despite increased foreign competition at home, U.S. machine tool companies increased exports as well as offshore production. Protectionist sentiment was not evident until the end of the decade.

In the late 1970s, the economics of the industry changed to some extent owing to the advent of numerical control (NC) and computer numerical control (CNC) machine tools, which depended on electronics and computer technology. First, it required larger capital investments to retool and automate factories.[83] Second, it added new "learning curve" effects associated with high-technology electronics.[84] Finally, it reduced the industry's segmentation at the low end of the market by making the characteristics of standard and specialized tools converge.[85] While important within the industry, these changes still left the toolmakers in a fragmented, small-scale industry compared to our other cases.

These changes prompted some reorganization of production by American manufacturers. While the Japanese consolidated their industry in the early

79. B. Carlsson, "Firm Strategies in the Machine Tool Industry in the U.S. and Sweden," unpublished working paper, October 1984; and D. Collis, "The Machine Tool Industry," Harvard Business School Case no. 9-387-087, 1986.

80. Collis, "The Machine Tool Industry," p. 21.

81. National Machine Tool Builders' Association (NMTBA), *Economic Handbook of the Machine Tool Industry* (Washington, D.C.: NMTBA, various years).

82. Milner, "Resisting the Protectionist Temptation," pp. 320–42.

83. D. Collis, "The Machine Tool Industry and Industrial Policy, 1955–82," Harvard Business School Business History Seminar, February 1987, pp. 10–21; and E. Sciberras and B. Payne, *Machine Tool Industry: Technical Change and International Competitiveness* (Essex: Longman, 1985), chap. 8.

84. Collis, "The Machine Tool Industry" (1986).

85. Sciberras and Payne, *Machine Tool Industry*, pp. 153–55.

1970s and began exporting low-cost, standardized NC machine tools in the mid-1970s, structural changes in the American industry started in the early 1980s. At that time, a new wave of mergers occurred, and this reduced the industry's fragmentation and increased its capital base. American firms also started manufacturing NC tools.[86] Most of the large U.S. firms, however, concentrated on the production of specialized, advanced tools for which price competition was limited. The smaller firms that produced standardized NC tools were overwhelmed by Japanese imports, which captured 80 percent of the U.S. market in these tools by the mid-1980s.[87] First-mover advantages thus swung to the Japanese.

Japanese competitiveness in machine tools had been promoted by government programs. Beginning in the 1950s, the Japanese government began subsidizing and protecting the industry in order to create strong domestic firms. Provision of capital at low costs, control of imports and technology, and use of an "administrative guidance cartel" marked this early program. In the early 1970s, a new policy, which attempted to promote the development of standardized NC tools, was devised. This policy involved the creation of a single firm to develop NC units for industry, provision of a broad R&D subsidy, and continued protection of the standardized NC segment.[88] The policy was very successful, and Japanese firms gained increasing control over the U.S. and world market.[89] This successful government intervention in Japan and elsewhere was perceived to be a serious threat to the U.S. industry. As one U.S. toolmaker expressed, "The threat that imports pose to domestic industry is especially ominous because the substantial competitive advantages that imports enjoy are attributable in large part to direct [foreign] government subsidization or the efforts of governmental coordination of machine tool production."[90]

In terms of our argument, this case provides mixed evidence. While the American firms had experienced some changes in their economics (like those in our other cases), the changes for the machine tool firms were of lesser magnitude. But Japanese government intervention had successfully occurred. Thus, some of the preconditions we identify for the emergence of

86. Collis, "The Machine Tool Industry" (1986), pp. 13–18.

87. Sciberras and Payne, *Machine Tool Industry;* and G. Guenther, *Machine Tools: Imports and the U.S. Industry, Economy, and Defense Industrial Base* (Washington, D.C.: Congressional Research Service, July 1986).

88. Collis, "The Machine Tool Industry" (1986), pp. 8–11.

89. Imports into the United States rose from 10 percent of consumption in 1973 to 25 percent in the early 1980s, with the Japanese share rising to about 45 percent of all of these imports. See NMTBA, *Economic Handbook,* p. 126. The Japanese controlled about 70 percent of all U.S. imports of NC lathes and machining centers by 1985. See *Asian Wall Street Journal,* 15 September 1986, p. 4. Moreover, the Japanese share of world exports of machine tools grew from 3.5 percent in 1970 to 15 percent in 1983, while the U.S. share fell from 11.7 to 4.8 percent over the same period. See Collis, "The Machine Tool Industry" (1986), p. 22.

90. Testimony of R. Blakeman (spokesman for NMTBA and Iowa Precision Industries), in U.S. Congress, Joint Economic Committee, *Machine Tool Industry and the Defense Industrial Base: Hearings Before the Joint Economic Committee,* 99th Congress, 1st sess., 1985.

strategic trade demands were apparent. If the economics had changed more dramatically or if Japan had had a strong reputation for successfully promoting these types of industries, we might have expected the U.S. machine tool industry to give up its free trade stance and start pursuing strategic trade policy in the mid-1970s. But by the time machine tool manufacturers agreed on a trade policy in the 1980s, they proposed unconditional protectionism. Although the industry considered filing an antidumping suit in the late 1970s, it remained quiet until 1982, when one firm, Houdaille, launched a suit against the Japanese. Documenting extensive Japanese government intervention in the industry, Houdaille tried to halt Japanese imports by using a little-known section of the U.S. tax code. Houdaille's request was subsequently denied, but the entire industry petitioned in 1983 for import quotas under the national security provision (Section 232) of U.S. trade law. After years of executive indecision and congressional pressure, President Reagan decided in 1986 to negotiate export restraints with Japan, West Germany, Taiwan, and Switzerland. Although the industry wanted imports held to 17.5 percent of the market, these agreements left them at 1981 levels, or about 24 percent.[91]

Thus, the U.S. machine tool industry's preference by the mid-1980s was for protection. While complaining bitterly of foreign government assistance, the industry did not seek to link import quotas to reductions in this assistance, nor did it complain about access to foreign markets. Since the industry had lost its competitive advantage in low-end NC tools, access to foreign markets was not a concern; and in the specialized NC tools, competitors' markets were fairly open.[92]

Why, given rising import competition and extensive Japanese government policy initiatives in the machine tool industry, did the American industry not seek strategic trade policies? Three factors influenced its preference for protection. First, as mentioned above, changes in the economics of the machine tool industry were not as pronounced as those of the other sectors we studied. Scale and learning had become more important, but relative to other industrial sectors, the machine tool sector remained largely small-scale and "craft-like."[93] As Table 1 illustrates, measures of scale economies often ranked below those of the other industries examined and below the average for a larger sample of American industries. Hence, the advantages of strategic trade policy to deal with the Japanese threat were less important for most American machine tool manufacturers.

Second, the American machine tool industry was highly segmented, with

91. R. Gutfleish, "Why Protection? U.S. Corporate and State Responses to a Changing World Economy," Ph.D. diss., University of California at Berkeley, 1987, chap. 7.

92. U.S. Congress, *Machine Tool Industry: Hearings;* and U.S. Congress, House Committee on Ways and Means, *U.S.–Japan Trade Relations: Hearings Before the Committee on Ways and Means,* 98th Congress, 1st sess., 1983.

93. Carlsson, "Firm Strategies," p. 17; and Sciberras and Payne, *Machine Tool Industry,* p. 93.

little similarity in strategies or interdependence among firms. When the Japanese began to invade the low end of the American machine tool market in 1976, it was not universally perceived as a threat. Average profits remained high between 1976 and 1982, in part because of a boom in consumption and in part because the largest U.S. firms concentrated on high-technology, specialized tools, which were initially unaffected by the import invasion. The smaller U.S. firms who competed directly against Japanese imports recognized the threat, but many were forced out of business before they could establish an industry-wide consensus.[94] Thus, despite rapidly rising imports, the extreme fragmentation of the industry slowed its response. It took almost six years before the industry was able to create a unified position on trade. And by that time, many U.S. machine tool companies could not compete at home or abroad.

Finally, the industry's international exposure was no longer as significant by the 1980s. Exports dropped and multinational operations were scaled back.[95] This reduced the industry's resistance to trade barriers, since the costs of protection were lower. As one industry spokesman noted, retaliation was no longer a concern, since the U.S. builders did not export to Japan or West Germany in any quantity.[96] The loss of export markets, combined with rising import competition and only minimal advantages of scale, made unconditional protection of the U.S. market a more preferred strategy than the use of strategic trade demands. The machine tool case provides interesting evidence on the behavior of internationally oriented firms in the presence of moderate economies of scale and learning effects. When faced with the loss of international competitiveness and new foreign competition at home, these firms will be less concerned with access to foreign markets and thus more likely to seek unconditional protection at home. The case then provides interesting counterfactual speculation on what our other industries might have demanded if they had not had very sizable economies of scale, steep learning curves, and important international operations.

Conclusions

As industries have become increasingly global and government intervention more pervasive, corporate trade demands have moved away from the stan-

94. Collis, "The Machine Tool Industry" (1986), p. 14.
95. Sciberras and Payne, *Machine Tool Industry,* p. 49.
96. In 1981, one-third of all U.S. machine tool exports went to three countries: Mexico, Canada, and the United Kingdom. The industry was not asking for restrictions on imports from any of these countries. Moreover, Japan and West Germany—two of the countries affected by U.S. export restraints—took less than 10 percent of all U.S. machine tool exports. See USITC, *Foreign Industrial Targeting,* no. 1517 (Washington, D.C.: USITC, 1984), p. 223 and Table B-25; and testimony of Jack Latona (spokesman for Houdaille Industries), in *Machine Tool Industry: Hearings,* p. 144.

dard poles of free trade and protectionism toward a more complex response, which we have called strategic trade policy. Using a combination of political and economic variables, we have tried to explain this phenomenon and thereby supplement traditional models of corporate trade preferences.

We also conducted empirical research and found evidence of strategic trade demands in three cases: the semiconductor, commercial aircraft, and telecommunications equipment industries. Each of these originally favored unconditional free trade. Yet as the economics of the industries changed, so did their trade demands. Between the mid-1970s and the mid-1980s, all three industries exhibited large and increasing economies of scale as well as steep learning curves. In addition, foreign government intervention had successfully created competitive advantages for foreign firms. The combination of import penetration and foreign government intervention led American firms to believe that they would be at a competitive loss if foreign governments did not stop protecting their markets and subsidizing their firms. Furthermore, American firms in these industries had relatively similar corporate strategies, which led to early industry-wide recognition of the competitive threat. For these industries, free trade at home in combination with protection abroad was viewed as the worst possible outcome.

There were also some important differences among our cases. The timing and intensity of demands for strategic trade policy varied. The semiconductor industry responded the most quickly and with the greatest intensity, followed by telecommunications equipment and then commercial aircraft. The semiconductor industry was the only one to file government petitions, formally asking for retaliation in the absence of foreign market openness. According to our argument, we should have expected this result for two reasons: corporate business strategies were the most similar in the semiconductor industry because of the need for a "technology driver"; and the industry suffered the greatest losses in profitability and share. The telecommunications equipment industry, which pushed annually for reciprocity legislation, could be expected to follow closely behind the semiconductor industry because foreign government intervention in telecommunications was the most obvious and extensive and because the major *American* telecommunications equipment firms had relatively similar competitive strategies. The commercial aircraft industry was the slowest because it started out as the most highly segmented of the three industries. Over the last decade, however, Airbus has slowly eaten into America's market share, while McDonnell Douglas's and Boeing's interests have grown closer. If American aircraft or telecommunications equipment manufacturers suffer increased losses in their market shares or profits, we would anticipate more intense demands for strategic trade policies, similar to those of semiconductor manufacturers.

The machine tool industry did not respond to foreign competition by turning to strategic trade policy. This was also understandable in light of our argument. While the economics of the machine tool industry did change toward greater scale and learning intensity, these changes were much less significant than for the other industries. In addition, because of its extensive segmentation and dissimilar firm strategies, the industry was very slow to respond to foreign competition. Large firms moved into high-technology segments, avoiding near term competition from the Japanese, while many small firms were forced out of business. By the time the whole industry felt threatened in the early 1980s, it had already lost its competitive edge and was reducing its international operations. Its interest in reducing foreign subsidies or opening foreign markets was gone, and noncontingent protection of the U.S. market was the only hope for its survival. Although this is a negative case of strategic trade policy, it remains consistent with the model.

There are at least three important implications that flow from this discussion of corporate trade demands. First, technological change and the globalization of competition will lead an increasing number of industries to experience economic changes analogous to those we have found in the semiconductor, aircraft, and telecommunications equipment industries.[97] Furthermore, foreign government intervention in these sectors in Japan, Europe, and the newly industrializing countries has also been rising.[98] Therefore, if we are right, increasing demands for strategic trade policy will appear across a broader spectrum of U.S. industries.

Second, the impact of these demands on the state are more likely to be acted upon than previous demands for unconditional protectionism. In the postwar period, the executive branch of the U.S. government has resisted calls for trade barriers unless industries have been able to demonstrate severe economic distress or unfair competitive practices abroad.[99] Strategic trade policy demands, in contrast, are likely to have greater political appeal. Most strategic trade demands will come from high-technology industries, which government trade officials are more apt to favor.[100] Moreover, the demands are for a ''level playing field''; they appeal to the norm of rectifying unfair trade practices, a norm embedded in U.S. trade law. Corroborating evidence of this assertion can be seen in our cases. The semiconductor industry received unprecedented government attention, including the first sanctions against Japan in manufacturing trade in the postwar period. In addition, U.S. government trade negotiations with Japan and Europe have focused heavily on telecommunications equipment and commercial aircraft, despite the lack of formal petitions from either industry. The U.S. government thus has been very responsive to the demands of these sectors.

97. Michael Porter, ed., *Competition in Global Industries* (Boston: Harvard Business School Press, 1986), chap. 1.

98. Bruce Scott and George Lodge, eds., *U.S. Competitiveness in the World Economy* (Boston: Harvard Business School Press, 1985), chap. 1.

99. Baldwin, *Political Economy of U.S. Import Policy;* and Aggarwal, Keohane, and Yoffie, ''Dynamics of Negotiated Protectionism.''

100. David B. Yoffie, ''Protecting World Markets,'' in Tom McCraw, ed., *America Versus Japan: A Comparative Study in Business Government Relations* (Boston: Harvard Business School Press, 1986).

Third, if the U.S. government does turn increasingly toward strategic trade policy, then we may see significant changes in the international trading system. We would expect a global movement away from unconditional most-favored-nation status and toward specific reciprocity and greater bilateralism. To date, the United States has participated in this trend only in an ad hoc fashion. If the United States begins to promote strategic trade policy broadly, new norms in international trade could be established de facto. These norms would be a further move away from those of GATT, since they would promote a trading system based on bilateral and sectoral arrangements involving strict reciprocity. Whether this new system would promote stability or efficiency is highly debatable.

National structures and multinational corporate behavior: enduring differences in the age of globalization
Louis W. Pauly and Simon Reich

Liberal and critical theorists alike claim that the world political economy is becoming globalized. If they are right, leading corporations should gradually be losing their national characters and converging in their fundamental strategies and operations. Multinational corporations (MNCs) should be the harbingers of deep global integration. In fact, recent evidence shows little blurring or convergence at the cores of firms based in Germany, Japan, or the United States.

In contrast to expectations now common both inside and outside academia regarding the imminent emergence of a truly global economy, this article shows that MNCs continue to diverge fairly systematically in their internal governance and long-term financing structures, in their approaches to research and development (R&D) as well as in the location of core R&D facilities, and in their overseas investment and intrafirm trading strategies. Durable national institutions and distinctive ideological traditions still seem to shape and channel crucial corporate decisions. Across the leading states of the three regions now commonly referred to

Much of the empirical material presented here originated in two reports commissioned by the Office of Technology Assessment: U.S. Congress 1993 and 1994. The authors were members of the original project team. William Keller led the team, and Paul Doremus was principally responsible for the research and development chapters and much of the statistical compilation upon which we rely in this article. Further empirical analysis related to the theme of this article can be found in the original reports as well as in the book, tentatively entitled *Multinationals and the Limits of Globalization,* which the four of us are now completing. For support that facilitated this article, Simon Reich thanks the Sloan Foundation and the International Affairs Fellowship Program of the Council on Foreign Relations. Louis Pauly is grateful for a sabbatical leave grant from the University of Toronto and a research grant from the Social Sciences and Humanities Research Council of Canada. Yoshiko Koda, Viktoria Murphy, and Arik Preis provided excellent research assistance. We are also indebted to many business executives, government officials, and scholars who commented, often critically, on various versions of the original Office of Technology Assessment reports as well as on the earlier drafts of this article, which were presented at the 1995 annual meetings of the International Studies Association and the American Political Science Association and at various university workshops. Special efforts were made by Alfred Chandler, Jonathan Crystal, Benjamin J. Cohen, Michael Donnelly, Kenneth Freeman, Lawrence Friedman, Robert Gilpin, William Greider, Peter Katzenstein, Stephen Krasner, Theodore Lowi, Michael Mastanduno, Helen Milner, John Odell, Alan Rugman, Richard Samuels, Harley Shaiken, Ulrike Schaede, Susan Strange, Raymond Vernon, and four anonymous reviewers, none of whom is responsible for the final result.

International Organization 51, 1, Winter 1997, pp. 1–30

as the "Triad," the foundations of corporate markets are not converging. Markets in this sense are not replacing political leadership and the necessity for negotiated adjustments among states.

Analytical context

The MNC—as empirical reality or as metaphor for the technological, financial, and managerial sinews of convergence in the contemporary world economy—is central to a number of contemporary research programs in the fields of international relations and international political economy. One strand of that research involves specifying the forces fundamentally driving corporate behavior and reshaping the relationship between that behavior and government policy.

Relying on the assumption that, at base, the logic of globally integrating markets ultimately drives corporate behavior, two important bodies of theory on the political implications of MNCs are now evolving. Although much more highly nuanced than their forebears in the 1960s and 1970s, recent studies within the liberal tradition suggest that increasingly mobile capital and the necessary responsiveness of firms to cross-national technological and financial incentives are beginning to constrain even leading industrial states and their societies in broadly comparable ways.[1] In complementary fashion, recent work in a more critical tradition explores the socioeconomic phenomenon of "globalization" and generally supports the idea that a noose, woven in substantial part by the intensifying operations of MNCs, is tightening around the neck of traditional forms of national political organization.[2] Only a small leap of imagination, a leap constantly made these days in scholarly circles, is necessary to draw central themes of these research programs together in the following terms.

Important industrial sectors currently are in ferment. Multinational firms at the center of those sectors are defining their interests ever more clearly in a global context. As they pursue those interests, they themselves become more alike through their interaction in increasingly integrated markets. Across a widening range of industries, transnational or global forces are reshaping basic corporate structures.[3] This is placing similar pressures on distinctive national institutions and policies. Consequent adaptations in those institutions and policies may not necessarily be "liberal" in the classic sense of the term; they may, to the contrary, rationalize cartels and other antiliberal agglomerations of power. Nevertheless, deep structural convergence at the level of the firm is profoundly changing the political economy of the world. In light of the history of economic nationalism, liberals imply, this transformation is probably not a bad thing, but its associated costs should be better understood. In light of the history of capitalism, their critical interlocutors respond,

1. Milner and Keohane 1996, chap. 1. Compatible arguments are made in Milner 1988; Rogowski 1989; Frieden 1991; Goodman and Pauly 1993; and Andrews 1994.

2. See Group of Lisbon 1995, 68–77; Carnoy, Castells, and Cohen 1993, 4–5; Castells 1991; Barnet and Cavanagh 1994; and Gill 1995.

3. Cerny 1995, 621.

this transformation may indeed be a bad thing for a substantial portion of the world's population, but it is, in any case, inevitable.

This article cuts into the middle of this stylized synthesis and explores the counterintuitive proposition that leading MNCs are *not* converging toward common patterns of behavior at their cores. In positive and more specific terms that lend themselves to comparative empirical testing, the proposition may be restated as follows: the institutional and ideological legacies of distinctive national histories continue significantly to shape the core operations of multinational firms based in Germany, Japan, and the United States. If basic insights behind current liberal and critical research programs are plausible, empirically oriented analysts should be able to cast serious doubt on such a proposition by finding fairly unambiguous evidence of basic structural and strategic convergence inside multinational firms themselves.

Using a different terminology in his magisterial *Scale and Scope,* Alfred Chandler sketched the rise before the 1940s of three fundamentally different kinds of industrial enterprise in Britain, Germany, and the United States.[4] In his conclusion, he asked whether such national patterns endure. Our research was motivated by the desire to contribute to an answer and to raise new theoretical and policy questions concerning its implications. We acknowledge at the outset that tracing the causal arrow— between the legacies of distinctive national histories, the core structures of firms, important firm strategies, and specific governmental policies responding to or seeking to affect corporate behavior—is not a simple matter. The empirical analysis of this article concentrates on the first three items and on the linkages among them.[5] This analysis convinces us that those linkages remain very strong.

A related but theoretically distinct body of thought has a long pedigree in the realist literature on MNCs. Some twenty years ago, to cite the most prominent and influential example, Robert Gilpin related the global spread of American firms after 1945 to the security interests and international political dominance of the United States.[6] *U.S. Power and the Multinational Corporation* represented a response to research that came to the fore in American academic circles from the 1960s onward, some of which left the impression of an impending split between corporations and the states that originally chartered them.[7] In the aftermath of oil, currency, and debt crises in later years, analysis of state–firm relations became more refined as states apparently returned to center stage.[8]

In Europe, meanwhile, a substantial body of research developed both on diverse host country reactions to multinational corporate expansion as well as on distinctions between American and British MNCs and their emerging Continental counterparts.[9]

---

4. Chandler 1990. Also see Chandler 1962, 1964, and 1977.
5. For an analysis of broad national structural variations that, unlike the present analysis, focuses on national and corporate competitiveness, see Porter 1990.
6. Gilpin 1975. Also see Hymer 1976 (based on a Ph.D. dissertation from 1960).
7. See Ball 1967; Cooper 1968; Morse 1970; Vernon 1971; Keohane and Nye 1972; and Wilkins 1974.
8. See Vernon 1977; Keohane and Nye 1977; Bergsten, Horst, and Moran 1978; Kudrle 1985; Robinson 1983; Ostry 1990; Dunning 1992a and 1992b; and Moran 1993.
9. See Dunning 1958; Servan-Schreiber 1967; Reddaway 1968; Turner 1970; Franko 1976; Stopford and Turner 1985; Hertner and Jones 1986; and van Tulder and Junne 1988.

Influenced by such work, research also commenced on the evolution of MNCs in Japan as well as in parts of the developing world.[10] In the 1990s, the revival of the European Community's single-market program stimulated new research in Europe. Although they noted behavioral discrepancies between European firms, these studies began to speculate about the emergence of new regional (as opposed to national or "Anglo-Saxon") corporate identities.[11] At the same time, U.S. scholars were again debating the question of whether the era of the global corporation, prematurely heralded in the 1960s, had finally arrived.[12]

The world had indeed changed a great deal since Gilpin's 1975 book first appeared.[13] Systemic power had become more diffuse, and national economies had become much more open. At the same time, intrafirm trade was accelerating and cross-border direct and portfolio investments were mushrooming. In certain industrial sectors, such as pharmaceuticals, semiconductors, and telecommunications, cross-border mergers and acquisitions, strategic alliances, and trumpeted international redeployments of corporate resources suggested a qualitative change in the nature of multinational corporate behavior. Careful comparative business studies suggested that receding national divergences might still be important in industries characterized by "regulated competition."[14] In many industrial sectors, however, the global corporation seemed a caricature no more.[15]

Argument

This article takes a different position. Certainly firms must continuously adapt to dynamic markets in order to survive, and certainly that adaptation must now take place in a world where short-term capital is highly mobile and where certain technologies are changing quite rapidly. But we argue that the underlying nationality of the firm remains the vitally important determinant of the nature of its adaptation. That nationality is not necessarily given by the location of corporate headquarters or the addresses of principal shareholders, although it usually still is. More fundamentally, it is given by historical experience and the institutional and ideological legacies of that experience, both of which constitute the essential structures of states. Because of them, we hypothesize, there remain systematic and important national differences in the operations of MNCs—in their internal governance and long-term financing, in their R&D activities, and in their intertwined investment and trading strategies.

We chose these operations for analysis because they provide a window on the very core of the MNC. They shed light on how MNCs are ultimately controlled and on the nature of their basic funding; where they locate and how they maintain the critical

---

10. See Tsurumi 1983; Campbell and Burton 1994; Wells 1983; and Lall et al. 1983.
11. See Franko 1991; and Jones and Schröter 1993.
12. Associated debate came prominently into public view, for example, in Reich 1990 and Tyson 1991.
13. For his own later reflections, see Gilpin 1987, chap. 6; and 1994.
14. Yoffie 1993.
15. The rising prominence of firms as political actors is highlighted by Stopford and Strange 1991; and Eden and Potter 1993.

mass of their R&D operations; and how they manage the linkage between trade and investment as their international expansions proceed.

Obviously, this is an ambitious agenda, especially within the confines of a short article. We nevertheless consider it important to take this initial step, especially in the context of the larger debates currently under way in the field of international political economy. With regard to the ultimate political implications of multinational firms, empirical research has tended to focus on the more obvious aspects of their behavior: where they place production facilities, how they market their products, and how they use and deepen short-term financial markets. Although the technical barriers to cross-disciplinary and broadly comparative analysis are daunting, scholars of politics must probe more deeply.

In the end, our analysis supports the view that national structures remain decisive. For scholars interested in the broader implications of corporate behavior, they do not just "matter." In analytical terms, they retain their priority with respect to other factors currently reshaping the world of the modern corporation.[16] The evidence we marshal below to test this argument strongly suggests that the domestic structures within which a firm initially develops leave a permanent imprint on its strategic behavior.[17]

To assess the extent to which we are really dealing with lagging indicators or something more fundamental, we adopt a theoretical stance more subtle than orthodox realism. Stephen Krasner recently captured some of this subtlety. When states are understood as institutional structures or polities, Krasner suggested, then the basic institutional structures of MNCs may be influenced or even determined by the characteristics of states. "In this perspective, institutional structures, not actors, are the units of analysis."[18]

Our approach has much in common with this understanding, but we go two steps further. First, the institutions worth emphasizing in such a conceptualization should be seen as embodying durable ideologies that link states and firms in distinctive ways. Second, those institutions and ideologies may be viewed as dynamic, but they change much more slowly than the firm-level operations rooted within them. Although corporate activity is not simply a product of internal organizational logic, the dominant causal arrow in such an analysis runs from slowly changing national structures through corporate structures and strategies to the actual behavior of firms in the marketplace.[19]

---

16. Our argument and evidence are not incompatible with a constructivist theoretical agenda, but they do challenge scholars probing the connection between global economic transformation and political identity to make clearer distinctions among states. See Ruggie 1993.

17. Adapting a term from electromagnetics, economists label such a process of marking "hysteresis," by which they typically imply a lagging effect after a causal force has been removed. See Krugman 1986; and Grossman and Richardson 1985. Business analysts refer in the same way and with the same implication to "corporate inertia" and "path dependence." Yoffie 1993, 17. Our argument and evidence raise strong doubts about the inevitable erosion of the effects of history.

18. Krasner 1996. Also see Sally 1994.

19. Philip Wellons's study of international banking provides an example of the plausible outcome of such causal reasoning. In one of the most "global" of industries, Wellons shows how banks from different home states do not behave alike in the face of similar opportunities and challenges. See Wellons 1987. Also see Wellons 1986; Biersteker 1987; Murtha and Lenway 1994; and Kapstein 1994.

In essence, we modify what the theoretical literature of international political economy labels the domestic structures approach. The ideological dimension was not usually stressed in early theoretical work along these lines. We are not referring here, however, to what the older literature on MNCs called "economic nationalism," a concept that is too general to be of much analytical use. Adapting Emanuel Adler's terms, we see ideologies as providing broad orienting frameworks or belief systems that, when combined with national institutions, define "collective understandings" of roles, beliefs, expectations, and purposes. Richard Samuels, whose use of the term "technonationalism" we adapt below in the Japanese case, provides an exemplary model of how ideology and institutions can be mutually constitutive and mutually reinforcing.[20] Although such an approach can accommodate the fact that the core strategies and structures of corporations can and do change, it sees such developments as constrained by permissive changes in underlying institutional and ideological structures. The novelty of our analysis is to link such institutional and ideological structures not to governmental policy outcomes but to the most fundamental behavior of MNCs in a broadly comparative context. Where much related literature examines the influence of domestic structures on public-sector actors and policies, we probe their influence on the largest private-sector actors, actors that theorists of the internationalization/globalization phenomenon now commonly depict as increasingly autonomous.

Our empirical analysis deliberately focuses on leading MNCs from leading states. Firms from small home markets, often viewed as harbingers of a truly global economy, have long had to demonstrate high levels of external adaptability. There is nothing new in Swiss companies compensating for a small home market by expanding externally. Among the ranks of the world's largest public firms, however, the number of prominent firms from small home markets remains quite small. In terms of market valuation in 1995, Germany, Japan, and the United States accounted for seventy-five of the world's top one hundred firms. Britain accounted for eleven, but no other country accounted for more than five.[21] Moreover, although some of our evidence draws on the larger industrial base of the European Union, we view the German base as distinctive enough and regionally dominant enough to be the central analog to the American and Japanese cases. Of Europe's top one hundred firms, twenty-seven are German. They account for the largest share of European industrial production and sales, and, across key technology-intensive sectors, German firms hold a much larger—and rising—share of world production than firms based in any other European country.[22]

---

20. See, respectively, Katzenstein 1977; Adler 1987, 17; and Samuels 1994, 33–78. Other work in this tradition includes Krasner 1978; Zysman 1983; Gourevitch 1986; Hall 1986; Samuels 1987; Katzenstein 1984; Krauss and Reich 1992; Steinmo, Thelen, and Longstreth 1992; Hart 1992; Garrett and Lange 1995; Katzenstein 1996; and Markovits and Reich forthcoming.

21. *Wall Street Journal*, 2 October 1995, p. R32.

22. See Commission of the European Communities 1993, 27; and OECD 1994. Grieco 1990 employs a similar logic.

TABLE 1. *National differences that condition corporate structures and strategies*

	United States	*Germany*	*Japan*
Political institutions	Liberal democracy; divided government; highly organized interest groups	Social democracy; weak bureaucracy; corporatist organizational legacy	Developmental democracy; strong bureaucracy; "reciprocal consent" between state and firms
Economic institutions	Decentralized, open markets; unconcentrated, fluid capital markets; antitrust tradition	Organized markets; tiers of firms; bank-centered capital markets; universal banks; certain cartelized markets	Guided, bifurcated, difficult-to-penetrate markets; bank-centered capital markets; tight business networks/cartels in declining industries
Dominant economic ideology	Free enterprise liberalism	Social partnership	Technonationalism

In Table 1 we summarize the kinds of domestic structures in the United States, Germany, and Japan that we first suspected might exert a significant shaping influence on corporate behavior. Each of the structures is clearly an ideal type and can be unpacked. Indeed, a great deal of comparative research and contentious debate is devoted to just such a task.[23] As it reminds us, hard and fast demarcation lines are difficult to draw in the real world. Nevertheless, a critical mass of that research now associates these labels with recognizably different and relatively enduring patterns of economic and political organization. It also provides a basis for the central inference guiding our own more limited study. The weight of the evidence presented below strongly suggests that the putative relationship between such domestic structures and core aspects of multinational corporate behavior is not spurious.

It would obviously be simpleminded, however, to argue that one explanation captures the essential reality for all firms all of the time. The chemical industry, for example, is clearly subject to high transportation costs and particular hazards, which cannot help but influence some aspects of the behavior of all chemical companies regardless of nationality. Nevertheless, in basic corporate structures and strategies across a range of industrial sectors, striking differences of an aggregate nature remain. Market-led explanations, whether emphasizing the determinative force of product maturities, sectoral idiosyncrasies, or broad technological changes, are ultimately unsatisfying. The enduring institutional and ideological foundations within which leading firms remain most deeply embedded offer more plausible explanations.

23. See, for example, Berger and Dore 1996.

Empirical evidence

To examine our central proposition we collected and analyzed a wide range of empirical evidence, including aggregate and sectoral statistical data, case studies, relevant secondary literature, and information culled from an series of confidential interviews undertaken between 1992 and 1994 with senior executives from MNCs in Europe, Japan, and the United States. The following is a summary of our findings.

Corporate governance and financing

U.S. corporate managers are highly constrained by dynamic and deep capital markets; their Japanese counterparts are effectively bound by complex but reliable networks of domestic relationships; and the managers of German MNCs retain a relatively high degree of operational independence. The circumstances of individual firms vary, but across the board such differences reflect the fact that corporations continue to govern themselves quite differently across the three home countries.[24] Those differences persist and are reflected in the varying priorities German, Japanese, and American MNCs assign to the maximization of shareholder value, to the autonomy of their managers, and to the stabilization of employer–employee relations.

The term "corporate governance" refers broadly to the rules and norms that guide the internal relationships among various "stakeholders" in a business enterprise, including owners, directors, managers, creditors, suppliers, employees, and customers. For comparative purposes, our emphasis here is on the central relationships between the managers of a corporation and the owners of voting shares. Those relationships are intermediated by boards of directors and focused on respective rights and obligations that are either specified in law or legitimated by long-standing custom and practice.[25] They are the products of unique national histories. Since MNCs span a number of legal jurisdictions, their governance often seems more complicated than it is for local firms. The core internal structures of almost all MNCs are nevertheless still clearly associated with prevailing norms in the jurisdiction within which their head offices are located. It is here that we observe the most direct influence of deeper institutions and ideologies.

Patterns of shareholding provide a starting point for understanding key differences. In the early 1990s, nearly 90 percent of the voting shares of publicly listed corporations in the United States were held by individual households, pension funds, and mutual funds. In Japan, that number was closer to 30 percent and in Germany closer to 15 percent. Conversely, banks held less than 1 percent of publicly listed shares in the United States but nearly 10 percent in Germany and 25 percent in Japan.

---

24. For accessible overviews of the issue, see Fukao 1995; and U.S. General Accounting Office 1993.

25. Inspired by Williamson 1988, much of the current and relevant analytical literature refers to the owners as "principals" and the managers as "agents."

At the same time, nonfinancial firms held a negligible number of such shares in the United States but 25 percent in Japan and nearly 40 percent in Germany.[26]

The dispersion and mobility of shareholders in the United States help to fixate the managers of American corporations on short-term financial performance, a fixation that may ultimately bolster competitive strengths by forcing rapid adjustments.[27] Over the long run, however, such imperatives can complicate life for firms that face direct competition in their home markets from rivals capable of longer-term planning because of their higher degree of insulation from capital market pressures. A few U.S. MNCs sometimes demonstrate similar capabilities but always within clear limits. The Ford Motor Company and Motorola—both of which have long-term shareholders with significant stakes derived from their original founders—are two examples of such American companies. German and Japanese MNCs, however, continue to demonstrate a general capacity in this regard. As Jay Lorsch and Elizabeth McIver put it, "In contrast to the United States' primary focus on shareholder value, these other countries' corporations are seen as durable national assets that serve a broad base of constituents. Quality products, market share, and employment are just as legitimate as goals as return on shareholder investment. While some US top managers and directors prefer this perspective themselves, they are swimming against the dominant national tide."[28]

More subtle differences in the character of relationships between banks and corporations also persist. In the United States, banks provide MNCs mainly with secondary financing, cash management, selective advisory work, and various other finance-related services. The historical trend, moreover, has been for corporations to reduce their reliance on commercial bank financing and to fund their long-term investments from retained earnings or directly from the capital markets.

Conversely, in Germany and Japan and across leading industrial sectors, banks perform a steering function. This function has evolved considerably as national industrial development has proceeded but nevertheless remains important. Before the financial bubble of the 1980s finally burst, commentators on Japan frequently argued that the centrality of banks was breaking down and that the long-term financing operations of Japanese MNCs were converging toward the American norm. Despite considerable weakness in bank balance sheets, such a proposition looks less plausible today. In Germany, it looks even less plausible.

In the United States, the ratio of bank loans to corporate financial liabilities, a rough measure of the relative importance of banks in the financing of corporations, fell into the 25–35 percent range from the early 1980s through the early 1990s. In both Germany and Japan, the comparable ratio stayed consistently in the 60–70 percent range. The numbers for bank deposits as a proportion of corporate financial

---

26. Data are from Deutsche Bundesbank, Tokyo Stock Exchange, ProShare, and Federal Reserve Board, cited in Kester 1993.
27. Roe 1994.
28. Lorsch and McIver 1992. Also see Lorsch and McIver 1989.

assets show similar levels of divergence.[29] But such broad comparisons can oversimplify differences in deeper corporate structures.

Throughout the postwar period and in various high-technology sectors, most notably in electronics and transportation systems, Japanese MNCs became famous for pursuing aggressive strategies keyed to market share, not return on investment. Even recently, for example, the U.S. market share of Japanese auto manufacturers barely budged from 1993 (22.8 percent) through 1995 (22.4 percent), despite remarkable shifts in the relative value of the yen.[30] Probing the factors that continue to sustain this capacity has itself become something of a growth industry. Numerous studies have highlighted the linkage between such strategies and corporate governance and financing structures back home. Those structures appear to facilitate the sharing of information and the management of business and financial risks across allied firms in a manner that varies considerably from the American norm. Michael Porter encapsulated the distinction by labeling the Japanese system "patient capital," although it is unclear whether corporate owners or consumers constitute the more patient party. The distinction, however, is more complicated than the label implies.[31]

In Japanese MNCs, institutional cross-shareholding caps a complex system of corporate control. Large volumes of minority equity claims commonly are spread among lenders, customers, suppliers, and affiliates, and even small holdings can signify an important relationship. Despite some recent flux associated with an enormously wrenching economic restructuring, our research unearthed no evidence that such arrangements are now changing in a fundamental way. Indeed, in the course of an extensive series of interviews with senior corporate executives in Japan, we were repeatedly told that the reverse is true. A number of our interlocutors suggested, for example, that much of the widely reported turbulence experienced in the Japanese corporate equity market in the early 1990s reflected the exceptional efforts of some shareholders, mainly troubled financial institutions, to increase dividend flows at a time when the routine capital gains of the past could no longer be assured.[32] Certainly, as Table 2 shows, within the largest Japanese corporate networks changes in cross-shareholding arrangements over the past decade have been marginal.

Many of the executives we interviewed believed that successfully charting their way through the difficult 1990s depended on maintaining the essential structure of their equity bases and, more important, of the relationships thereby signified. Moreover, the prospect of punishment for breaches in network solidarity clearly exists. Bankers as well as their corporate clients explained to us repeatedly that all members of industrial groups understood that any firm contemplating appreciable sales of shares in related banks or companies would elicit immediate retaliation. The

---

29. IMF 1992, 3.

30. *New York Times,* 2 February 1996, C6.

31. Porter et al. 1992. See also Orru, Hamilton, and Suzuki 1989; Prowse 1992; Kester 1992; Pauly 1994; Johnson, Tyson, and Zysman 1989; Gerlach 1992; Aoki and Patrick 1994; Tilton 1996; and Uriu 1996.

32. Confidential interviews, Japan, 20 September–2 October 1993. Also see Lichtenberg and Pushner 1992.

TABLE 2. *Average cross-shareholdings within major Japanese corporate networks, in percentages*[a]

	Mitsui	Mitsubishi	Sumitomo	Fuyo	Sanwa	DKB
1980	17.62	29.26	26.74	16.26	16.78	14.12
1985	17.87	25.18	25.01	15.79	16.84	13.33
1988	17.09	26.87	24.42	15.29	16.38	12.24
1991	16.58	26.37	24.67	15.62	16.67	12.16
1992	16.58	26.33	24.65	15.62	16.72	12.19
1993	16.77	26.11	24.45	14.90	16.41	11.92

[a]Average of the ratios of stocks in one member company owned by other companies within the group. These are the largest of the networks of affiliated companies characteristic of the Japanese industrial economy. Commonly referred to as *keiretsu,* they are more accurately called *kigyō shūdan,* or enterprise groups. These six groups cross a diversity of markets, and each has a trading company and/or major commercial bank at its center. The banks are now Sakura Bank (after the merger of Mitsui Bank and Taiyo Kobe Bank), Mitsubishi Bank of Tokyo, Sumitomo Bank, Fuji Bank, Sanwa Bank, and Dai Ichi Kangyo Bank.
Source. Kigyō Keiretsu Sōran 1987, 1990, 1993, and 1994. Tokyo: Toyo Keizai Shinposha.

consequent sense of responsibility for collectively managing difficult processes of restructuring within tight traditional constraints is palpable.[33]

Within Japan's leading industrial groups, furthermore, and especially during periods of crisis, managers continue to be constrained effectively and directly by their bankers and by the firms to which they supply key components. Affiliates are crucial, and arm's-length relationships still are not the norm. Hopelessly weak affiliates tend to be quickly and quietly liquidated or merged. Even apparently informal supplier ties can be decisive in such instances.

Obvious parallels exist in the case of Germany, although observers have often overemphasized the coordinating role of banks in the German industrial system. Especially in elite German MNCs, however, and most evidently during crises, the lead bank remains critically important. Although economists continue to debate the implications of this phenomenon and to underline the declining role of banks in small and medium-sized German firms, the evidence supporting its endurance in the largest and most outwardly oriented German firms remains convincing.[34]

The supervisory boards of German MNCs reinforce the functions of banks both directly and indirectly.[35] Bankers hold nearly 10 percent of the seats on the supervisory boards of the one hundred largest industrial corporations in Germany. By contrast, insurance companies hold approximately 2 percent of the seats; trade

33. Also see Lincoln, Gerlach, and Takahashi 1992.
34. See Edwards and Fischer 1994; and Baums 1994.
35. See Wever and Allen 1993; Ziegler, Bender, and Biehler 1985; and Coleman 1994.

unions, 12 percent; employees, 36 percent; other industries, 25 percent; individual investors, 10 percent; and governmental agencies, 5 percent.[36] In the largest German corporations, however, the lead bank also provides the board chairman. Since three banks dominate the corporate financing market, this means that many supervisory boards are interlocked. Underpinning such linkages are cross-shareholding arrangements, albeit to a lesser extent than in Japan. The bankers' role is further enhanced by peculiarities of Germany's proxy voting system, which in the case of MNCs often leaves banks effectively in control of over 50 percent of voting shares.

Our interviews provided no support for the increasingly common view that the power of banks in corporate Germany is broken. Similarly, despite talk about bold American moves toward German-style universal banking, long-standing sensitivities concerning financial concentration, a now-institutionalized decentralization and "vesting" of particularistic interests in the financial sector, and attendant difficulties in designing new risk-management techniques militate against deep-seated change in the U.S. system. For different reasons, we noted a similar reticence inside Japanese MNCs on the subject of fundamental change in patterns of corporate financing.

Prominent analysts commonly herald the dawn of a "Darwinian" global contest among competing corporate systems. As Franklin Edwards and Robert Eisenbeis put it, "Legal and institutional impediments that fail this test will cease to exist."[37] In such a context, it is ironic that we did not find evidence for, or credible expectations of, substantive convergence in core structures of corporate governance and basic financing across Germany, Japan, and the United States.

Research and development

The world's leading MNCs remain firmly rooted in distinctive national systems of innovation. Science and high technology–oriented American MNCs are somewhat more willing than others to invest in overseas R&D facilities, but on an annual basis such spending still represents less than 15 percent of their total R&D budgets. With an emphasis on the commercialization of production in technology-intensive sectors, Japanese firms conduct remarkably little R&D abroad, even in the United States where they have a very large production and sales presence. Mainly in certain sectors and in line with their own process-oriented traditions, German MNCs have made significant R&D commitments in the United States but limited investments elsewhere outside of Germany. Across the board, the vast majority of corporate R&D spending abroad is employed in efforts to customize products for local markets or to gather knowledge for transfer back home.

R&D sows the seeds for corporate futures. How much, how consistently, and where such activity takes place are therefore all vital questions, both for individual corporations and for the economies within which they operate. To move beyond the simplified portrait painted by aggregate statistics, our analysis differentiated between

---

36. Based on data from the Federal Association of German Banks in Schneider Lenné 1994, 303.
37. Edwards and Eisenbeis 1992.

basic activities and product customization facilities. Our findings indicate that convergence of a sort is taking place—but not the kind liberal analysts might anticipate. Leading firms from Germany, Japan, and the United States behave comparably in that they tend to maintain their basic R&D operations at home. Those operations comprise important building blocks for national systems of innovation that, though not completely autonomous or unchanging, do remain remarkably distinctive.[38] Significant variances are also reflected in overall corporate spending patterns, in the nature of R&D facilities abroad, and in the willingness to transfer key technologies outside the home base.

Differences in corporate R&D strategies have existed across the leading industrial states for many years. Japanese business spending on R&D as a percentage of gross domestic product (GDP), for example, rose rapidly throughout the 1980s and eclipsed that of the United States in 1989 before peaking in 1990 at 2.2 percent. Comparable U.S. spending fell consistently after peaking in 1985 at 2.1 percent, increased temporarily in 1991, and then resumed its pattern of decline. German firms, for their part, reduced their R&D spending precipitously in the late 1980s and early 1990s. At 1.7 percent of GDP in 1993, their spending was well below the levels registered by their Japanese and U.S. competitors.[39]

Beneath such statistics, other national patterns remained distinctive. In contrast to their U.S. counterparts, for example, Japanese chief executive officers typically note that when their firms are under duress, real cuts in R&D spending (as opposed to trimming back growth rates) are a last resort.[40] They view only the avoidance of cuts in permanent employment as more important than maintaining R&D budgets. This is reflected in relevant data. Before their widely noted troubles at the start of the 1990s, Japanese firms had increased their R&D spending by an average of 8 percent per year for an entire decade. Comparable figures for British, French, German, and U.S. firms were 1.6, 4.6, 3.9, and 3.9 percent, respectively.[41]

Sustained national differences are also reflected in patterns of corporate R&D spending abroad. Even though an absolute increase in R&D spending by foreign MNCs in the United States occurred during the last decade, an increase that appeared to be partly related to acquisitions in such R&D-intensive sectors as chemicals, U.S. firms remained more likely than their competitors to conduct R&D abroad. Even in their case, however, the scale of expansion from a low base was modest. In 1982, R&D spending by majority-owned foreign affiliates of U.S. manufacturers accounted for 8.7 percent of total corporate R&D budgets. One decade later, that amount increased only to 12.7 percent, despite a 43.2 percent expansion in total corporate R&D budgets. In addition, the manufacturing R&D intensity—that is, R&D spending as a percentage of total sales—is much higher for American MNCs in their home-based operations than it is in their foreign subsidiaries. In the early 1990s,

---

38. See Nelson 1993; Lundvall 1992; and Mowery 1994.
39. OECD (DSTI) 1994–95.
40. Confidential interviews with senior executives of Japanese MNCs, 20 September–2 October 1993, Japan.
41. U.S. Congress 1994, 62.

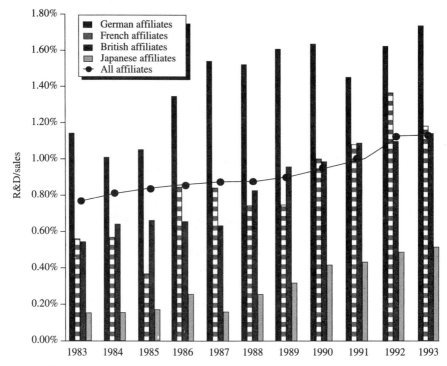

FIGURE 1. *Research and development (R&D) intensity of foreign affiliates in the United States, 1983–93*

Source. U.S. Department of Commerce, Bureau of Economic Analysis, *Foreign Direct Investment in the United States* (Washington, D.C.: Department of Commerce, annual surveys).

U.S. manufacturers reported an average R&D intensity of 2.1 percent at home, while their foreign subsidiaries registered 0.8 percent.[42]

Figure 1 graphs the ratio of R&D spending to sales for foreign firms in the United States. As the figure shows, R&D intensity has not changed dramatically over the past decade, and national patterns are consistent. German affiliates in particular were much more likely to conduct R&D in the United States than were their Japanese counterparts. In part, foreign R&D intensity in the United States correlates with the sectoral location of incoming foreign direct investment. German firms, and European firms more generally, have tended to invest proportionately more in manufacturing facilities in such sectors as pharmaceuticals. Japanese firms, as discussed below, have focused on wholesaling operations.

All things considered, the behavior of Japanese firms in the United States differs strikingly from their European counterparts. Figure 2 graphs the R&D intensity of

---

42. U.S. Congress 1994, 7.

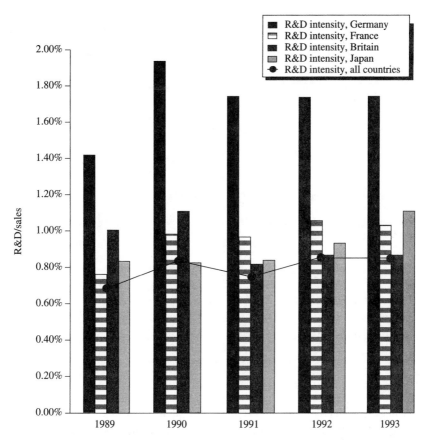

FIGURE 2. *Research and development (R&D) intensity of U.S. affiliates in foreign markets, 1989–93*

Sources. U.S. Department of Commerce, Bureau of Economic Analysis, *U.S. Direct Investment Abroad* (Washington, D.C.: Department of Commerce, annual surveys); and U.S. Department of Commerce, Bureau of Economic Analysis, *Survey of Current Business,* August 1987–August 1995.

U.S. affiliates in foreign markets. Looking at the two figures, German firms in the United States most closely replicate the R&D patterns of U.S.-based firms in Germany. In this regard, the data suggest a notable reciprocal interaction between U.S. and German MNCs. Conversely, the lower R&D intensity of Japanese MNCs in the United States and its incommensurability with the behavior of U.S. MNCs in Japan suggest a notable lack of reciprocal interaction.

In general, Japanese firms are the most reluctant to shift R&D activities abroad. While they formed by the early 1990s the largest national group of foreign investors in the United States (based on historical cost values), their U.S. operations had by far the lowest R&D intensities. Although historical cost analysis skews the comparison

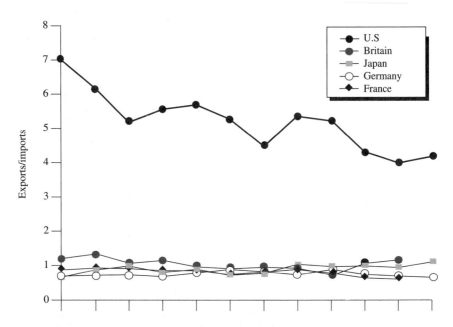

FIGURE 3. *Ratio of technology exports to imports for selected countries, 1982–93*

Source. Organization for Economic Cooperation and Development, *Main Science and Technology Indicators,* Economic Analysis and Statistics Division Database, no. 1 (1994) and no. 1 (1995).

by inflating the value of the relatively new investment of Japanese firms and deflating the value of older European investment, the fact that the overwhelming proportion of all inward flows of foreign direct investment into the United States occurred after 1980 tends to limit this effect. The outcome, in any event, is also reflected in aggregate data for R&D spending by manufacturing firms in the United States, which show Canadian affiliates in 1992 accounting for 19 percent, German affiliates for 16 percent (a comparable level to Swiss and British affiliates), and Japanese affiliates for 10 percent, despite their much larger market presence.[43]

Finally, MNCs based outside the United States also demonstrate a distinct tendency to limit the export of their core technological competencies. In the United States, conversely, technology exports are five times the level of technology imports. As Figure 3 shows, Germany, Japan, and other industrial economies have long maintained a ratio of less than 1 to 1. MNCs provide the channel for much of the flow of technology abroad, mainly from parents to affiliates. In comparative terms, the aggregate data suggest that U.S. MNCs are much more active in this regard than their counterparts in other countries.

43. Calculated based on data in U.S. Department of Commerce 1994, table H-4.

Investment and intrafirm trade

The foreign direct investment strategies of U.S. MNCs are broadly based on and reflective of the expectation of competitive inward flows. Moreover, those strategies incorporate a relatively high willingness to outsource key parts of production processes. American MNCs, in other words, rely much less than their rivals on intrafirm and intra-affiliate trading (hereafter referred to as IFT) strategies. The investment strategies of Japanese MNCs, by way of contrast, exhibit both a strong outward orientation from a home base that is secure from external challenge and a heavy reliance on intrafirm trade. German MNCs also exhibit an outward orientation in their investment strategies. That orientation is more selective than that of Japanese MNCs and reflects a narrower industrial base. Like Japanese corporations, however, German firms rely quite heavily on IFT. In short, the external investment operations of German and Japanese firms tend to enhance the prospects for overall exports from their home bases, while comparable American operations tend to substitute for U.S. exports.

Despite occasional fluctuations, the United States has long been the favored destination for new foreign direct investment inflows. In terms of outward flows, Japanese firms led all others during the latter years of the 1980s, but U.S. firms regained the leading position in 1991.[44] Aggregate comparison, however, fails to capture the markedly diverse corporate strategies that underpinned those flows.

Foreign investments undertaken by U.S. firms tend to be "trade-displacing." Their Japanese and, to a lesser but increasing extent, their German analogs tend to be "trade-creating."[45] In short, new overseas plants built by Japanese and increasingly by German MNCs tend to create conduits for increasing trade flows, specifically imports from their own home bases and affiliated networks.[46] For this reason, analysts have convincingly argued that such investment should be understood as "strategic."[47]

The hypothesis that Japanese and, to a lesser extent, German firms employ such a strategic approach is highly contentious, but aggregate statistical evidence continues to render it plausible. Across all of its manufacturing industries, for example, intrafirm exports as a percentage of total Japanese exports remained at about 40 percent from the late 1980s through the early 1990s.[48] The issue can be examined more rigorously, however, by comparing the direct investment behavior of foreign affiliates in the United States with that of U.S.-based multinationals abroad. The reliability of direct comparisons of IFT on a national basis is, however, severely limited by the lack of comparability of national databases and the complete absence of other statistical data sources.

44. Data from OECD 1994.
45. The question of whether high-technology intrafirm trade will decrease as firms become more deeply embedded in advanced host economies is contentious. See Vernon 1966, 190–207; Dunning 1977; Wells 1972; Helleiner 1981; and U.S. Congress 1994, 144–48.
46. See Kojima 1978; and Gilpin 1989.
47. Encarnation 1992. Also see Lincoln 1990; and Encarnation and Mason 1990.
48. See MITI 1989, tables 1-19 to 1-24; and MITI 1991, tables 1-22 to 1-27.

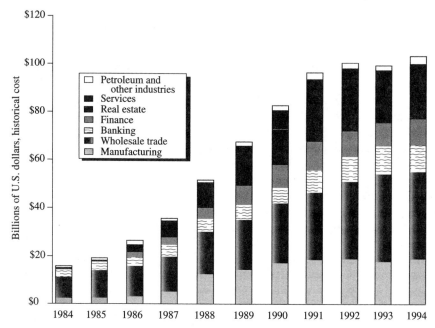

FIGURE 4. *Japan's direct investment position in the United States, by sector, 1984–94*

Source. U.S. Department of Commerce, Bureau of Economic Analysis, *Survey of Current Business,* August 1987–August 1995.

We can avoid this difficulty by focusing on meaningful bilateral comparisons within the same data set, such as the behavior of foreign affiliates in the United States compared with that of U.S.-based MNCs abroad. In 1992, Japanese firms as a group became for the first time the largest foreign investors in the United States. As Figure 4 shows, in a largely unrestricted environment the biggest proportion of this investment went into wholesaling facilities and distribution outlets. This stands in sharp contrast to the investment position of American MNCs in Japan, which is shown in Figure 5. U.S. MNC investment was heavily weighted toward manufacturing facilities.

Moreover, as a percentage of total foreign direct investment in the United States, Japanese investment in wholesaling operations in the United States rose from 41 percent of total incoming foreign direct investment in 1985 to 50 percent in 1993.[49] Many have argued that this emphasis on wholesaling operations reflects the relative youth of Japanese investments in the U.S. market by the standards of European firms and that over time it will fall to European levels; but the disparity is enormous. As a percentage of total foreign direct investment in the United States, the wholesaling operations of German firms fell from 15 percent in 1985 to 10.5 percent in 1993,

49. U.S. Congress 1994, 118.

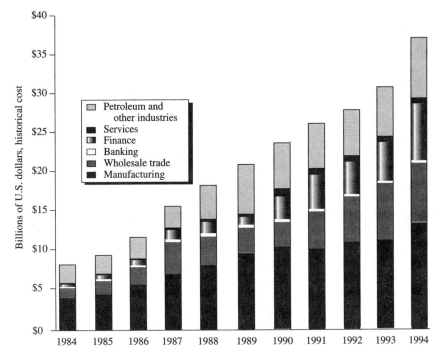

FIGURE 5. *U.S. direct investment position in Japan, by sector, 1987–94*

Source. U.S. Department of Commerce, Bureau of Economic Analysis, *Survey of Current Business,* August 1987–August 1996.

while comparable figures for British firms were 13.9 and 9.9 percent, and for French firms 1.5 and 2.7 percent, respectively.

The intrafirm trading operations of Japanese firms in the United States also continued to grow during the 1990s in relative terms. By the end of the 1980s, for example, IFT imports in the U.S. automobile sector accounted for an estimated 40–50 percent of all imports. Between 1988 and 1990, the value of intrafirm imports by Japanese auto affiliates in the United States tripled to $4 billion. This represented an increase from 75 to 95 percent of total intrafirm imports in this sector.[50] Japanese auto executives expected this level to drop as their suppliers moved their own operations to the United States, although this drop was likely to be due to the replacement of direct IFT imports with indirect imports through traditional affiliated networks.[51] In 1993, affiliated companies accounted for 43 percent of all suppliers to Japanese auto transplants in the United States.[52]

50. OECD 1993, 20.
51. Confidential interviews with senior executives of Japanese MNCs, 20 September–2 October 1993, Japan.
52. U.S. Congress 1994, 147.

TABLE 3. *Foreign content of intermediate goods purchased by foreign affiliates in the United States, by sector and country, 1990 and 1991*

	All countries		France		Germany		Japan		Great Britain	
	1990	*1991*	*1990*	*1991*	*1990*	*1991*	*1990*	*1991*	*1990*	*1991*
All industries	19.4	19.6	12.1	10.7	21.6	19.9	30.2	31.7	9.6	9.2
All manufacturing	16.7	17.3	17.3	16.2	21.4	20.9	28.4	28.0	9.4	10.0
Chemicals and allied products	12.1	13.2	9.6	9.5	18.4	18.5	5.1	7.2	11.6	13.2
Primary and fabricated metals	14.0	14.1	7.3	6.9	20.0	21.4	6.6	5.9	7.2	7.3
Nonelectrical machinery	31.0	30.4	NAª	20.3	25.9	25.5	48.5	45.3	12.9	9.5
Electric and electronic equipment	30.7	28.6	NA	37.5	43.7	39.2	41.4	38.1	11.3	14.3
Motor vehicles and equipment	40.4	45.1	NA	NA	NA	NA	49.3	52.8	NA	NA
Wholesale trade	32.3	33.9	11.6	12.1	39.9	39.6	34.6	38.3	15.3	12.2

ªNA = data unavailable (suppressed to avoid disclosure of individual companies' data).
Source. Adapted from U.S. Department of Commerce, Bureau of Economic Analysis, *Survey of Current Business,* October 1993, 64, table 10.

Is such a pattern confined to the automobile industry? Alternatively, is it a product of anomalies in statistical databases? Examining variations in the foreign content of intermediate goods purchased by foreign affiliates in the United States across differing sectors addresses such questions and, as Table 3 shows, indicates that indeed a pattern does exist. In this respect, not only Japanese but also German affiliates differ markedly from other major investors in the United States.[53]

While the Japanese behavior generates considerable, if not always publicly expressed, antipathy among American corporate executives, the German behavior does not. The reason seems to be that the bilateral U.S.–German relationship is widely perceived to be more or less balanced in key industries.

Together with starkly divergent patterns of reliance on IFT by Japanese and German firms, such data suggest the importance not of investment maturity or governmental policies on the receiving end, but of purposive corporate strategies. As for the quite exceptional nature of the Japanese data, the overall emphasis of Japanese affiliates in the United States on IFT and wholesaling may help to explain

53. Confidential interviews with senior executives and government officials in Germany and the United States, 1–12 November 1993 and February–April 1994, respectively.

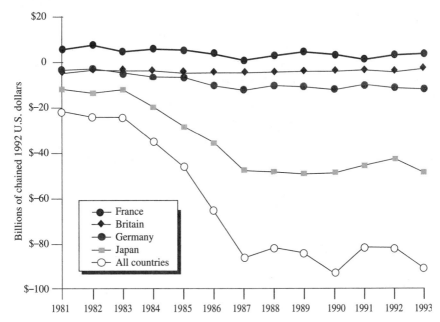

FIGURE 6. *Merchandise trade balance of foreign affiliates in the United States, by nationality of ownership, 1981–93*

Sources. U.S. Department of Commerce, Bureau of Economic Analysis, *Foreign Direct Investment in the United States,* table G-7/H-7 (Washington, D.C.: Department of Commerce, annual surveys); and U.S. Department of Commerce, Bureau of Economic Analysis, *Survey of Current Business,* October 1993.

the fact that they are alone among foreign investors in Europe and the United States in their strong preference for establishing new firms rather than acquiring existing ones.[54]

Some observers expected Japanese affiliates in the United States to begin reexporting from their new manufacturing facilities as they matured, but experience has confounded that expectation. The percentage of exports from Japanese affiliates as a proportion of their total sales actually fell—from over 12 percent in the early 1980s to approximately 6 percent in 1988 before rising marginally from that level in the early 1990s. Over the same period, IFT as a percentage of the value of all Japanese exports to the United States across all industries rose from 20 percent to over 50 percent.[55] Again, as Figure 6 displays, this pattern contrasts markedly with the collective behavior of MNCs from other major industrial countries in the United States, with the partial exception of those from Germany.

54. Yamawaki 1994, table 3-3, 97.
55. MITI 1989, tables 1-19 to 1-24; MITI 1991, table 1-11 and 1-22 to 1-27; and MITI 1993, table 2-16.

More broadly, since much of the aggregate flow of world imports and exports now occurs through intrafirm and affiliated networks, IFT constitutes a much higher proportion of bilateral flows between the United States and Japan than between the United States and Europe. Between 1983 and 1992, IFT accounted for an average of 70 percent of all U.S.-Japanese merchandise trade each year, compared with 43 percent of U.S.–European trade. Furthermore, over that same period and regardless of the direction of flow, Japanese MNCs accounted for fully 93 percent of IFT between Japan and the United States. In the end, the evidence suggests that IFT accounts for an overwhelming percentage of all U.S. imports from Japan and that Japanese firms control almost all of it. In contrast, and notwithstanding the fact that German firms tend to behave more like Japanese firms when it comes to intrafirm and affiliated trade, U.S.–European IFT is much more balanced in the aggregate.[56]

Counterpressures are widely reported to be building on both Japanese and German firms that will reduce their ability to use overseas operations as conduits for exports from their own facilities or from long-standing networks of suppliers in their home bases. Fluctuating currencies and domestic labor costs frequently are mentioned in this regard. Although anecdotes abound, we found little hard evidence of fundamental shifts in the overseas investment and trading strategies of American, German, and Japanese MNCs.

Conclusion

This article examined evidence on the question of structural and strategic convergence at the cores of leading MNCs across the Triad. In contrast to liberal or critical theories, which lead to credible expectations that the fundamental structures and strategies of multinational firms are converging in meaningful ways, we sketched remarkably enduring divergence across Germany, Japan, and the United States in patterns of internal governance and long-term financing. We also identified a tendency for MNCs based in those countries to maintain an overwhelming share of their R&D spending at home, and we noted stark national differences in willingness to export new technology from the home base. Finally, we found divergence along national lines in the strategic linkages firms construct between their overseas investments and their intrafirm and intra-affiliate trading activities: Japanese and, to a lesser extent, German firms lie on one end of the spectrum and American (and British) firms on the other. Table 4 briefly summarizes the most important patterns in the evidence.

Set out in this schematic fashion, none of these patterns will come as a surprise to students of comparative business history. But their endurance into the 1990s does raise important questions for students of international political economy in light of contemporary debates on the causes and consequences of deepening cross-national economic integration. Our analysis supports the view that recognizable and patterned

56. U.S. Congress 1994, 136–37.

TABLE 4. *Multinational corporate structures and strategies*

	United States	Germany	Japan
Direct investment	Extensive inward and outward	Selective/outward orientation	Extensive outward; limited competition from inward
Intrafirm trade	Moderate	Higher	Very high
Research and development	Fluctuating; diversified; innovation oriented	Narrow base/process, diffusion orientation	High, steady growth; high-technology and process orientation
Corporate governance	Short-term shareholding; managers highly constrained by capital markets; risk-seeking, financial-centered strategies	Managerial autonomy except during crises; no takeover risk; conservative, long-term strategies	Stable shareholders; network-constrained managers; takeover risk only within network/aggressive market share–centered strategies
Corporate financing	Diversified, global funding; highly price sensitive	Concentrated, regional funding; limited price sensitivity	Concentrated, national funding; low price sensitivity

differences persist in the behavior of leading MNCs. The precise nature of those differences in turn suggests that we not rule out as an explanation what is popularly termed corporate "nationality." Even when other possible influences on corporate behavior (for example, governmental policy on incoming foreign direct investment) provide identical background conditions, striking differences appear—most commonly along national lines.[57] In sum, the correlation between these patterns of corporate behavior and the domestic structures outlined earlier in this article is not likely to be spurious.[58]

Recall our orienting proposition on the link between basic domestic structures in the home base and core aspects of firm behavior. The evidence surveyed suggests a logical chain that begins deep in the idiosyncratic national histories that lie behind durable domestic institutions and ideologies and extends directly to structures of corporate governance and long-term corporate financing. Those structures in turn appear plausibly linked to continuing diversity in the corporate foundations of national innovation systems and in the varying linkages between foreign direct investment and IFT strategies.

Of course, the evidence only supports the claim of a causal link; it does not prove it. The evidence, however, comes from an examination of the three leading home states of contemporary MNCs and of a range of key industrial sectors. Additionally, we have examined core aspects of firm behavior in a comparative light. We conclude

57. For analysis of how domestic institutions influence and channel firm demands in the face of incoming foreign direct investment, see Crystal 1995.
58. Keller et al. forthcoming.

that a modified domestic structures approach provides a better fit for the patterns identified in the data than do alternative approaches, which draw their understanding of multinational corporate behavior from the relevant liberal, critical, or realist literatures sketched above. Neither liberal nor critical alternatives lead one to expect the persistent divergence found at the firm level. A straightforward realist alternative would miss important variations in the degree of that divergence and, with its traditional emphasis on central policymaking authorities, could easily lead to a misunderstanding of what that divergence means.

Consider several counterarguments. On the basis of the evidence, the contention that the particular mores evident in Japanese corporate technology development programs are becoming disconnected from the stabilizing influence of cross-held corporate equity bases and broader networks of managerial accountability in Japan seems implausible. Equally implausible is the argument that the investment behavior of German firms is becoming unhinged from the security provided by dominant banks back home. Finally, we consider it unlikely that the slightly more global behavior exhibited by U.S. firms in both their R&D and investment strategies is not related to deliberate efforts to compensate for the peculiarities of their highly dynamic and periodically unstable financial foundations.

In sum, we surmise that the behavior we have surveyed divides into three distinctive syndromes. Moreover, because the general lines of demarcation may credibly be labeled "national," the proposition that those syndromes are durably nested in broader domestic institutional and ideological structures cannot easily be dismissed. Such a conceptualization, we believe, is more precise and more useful in focusing further research than the much more amorphous concept of culture, which has been cited in recent work on the putative emergence of three increasingly integrated regional blocs.[59] At a time when many observers emphasize the importance of cross-border strategic alliances, regional business networks, and stock offerings on foreign exchanges—all suggestive of a blurring of corporate nationalities—our findings underline, for example, the durability of German financial control systems, the historical drive behind Japanese technology development through tight corporate networks, and the very different time horizons that lie behind American, German, and Japanese corporate planning. The gulf between nationally diverse domestic structures may narrow in the future, but we cannot count on leading MNCs to drive such a process.

Pending further research, our own answer to Chandler's question—whether differences like those sketched in *Scale and Scope* endure—must be in the affirmative. We have found little evidence to support the opposite view, namely, that such core patterns are inevitably eroding as a fully integrated global system of industrial enterprise and innovation emerges.

The implications of our analysis are diverse, but four deserve to be highlighted here. First, since multinational firms are key actors in the development and diffusion of new technologies, their national rootedness appears to remain a vital determinant

---

59. For example, see Rugman 1993.

of where future innovation takes place.[60] In this regard, the main danger for political and economic theorists is not underestimating the impact of technological change but extrapolating the future on the basis of atypical industrial sectors or anodyne exceptions drawn from the experiences of a few large firms from small states, where the size of home markets and the limitations of local resources have long required externally oriented strategies.

Second, the globalization template upon which much current theoretical and policy debate rests remains quite weak. German, Japanese, and U.S. corporations insert themselves into the home markets of their rivals, albeit with varying degrees of success. They then appear to adapt themselves at the margins but not much at the core. To the extent that fundamental differences in corporate structure and strategy create sanctuary markets or other difficult-to-surmount advantages, pressures will likely build from within corporations themselves for countervailing governmental responses. In Germany and Japan, for example, we consistently heard corporate decision makers heap derision on the idea that key technologies could ever be left to develop in markets organized around straightforward "laissez-faire" principles. Our evidence suggests further that the increasingly common idea, that mobile corporations are "arbitraging" diverse national structures and forcing deep structural convergence across diverse societies, is chimerical. Convergence may be apparent at the level of popular culture and perhaps not coincidentally in the sales reports and marketing campaigns of MNCs; but below the surface, where the roots of leading MNCs remain lodged, our research suggests durable sources of resistance. It also suggests the need for deeper analysis of the foundations of such apparently global markets as the oft-cited capital markets that link the interests of multinational intermediaries and their corporate clients.[61]

Third, and following on this latter point, our analysis is relevant to the growing debate over whether markets or, more precisely, huge sprawling commercial hierarchies are replacing states as allocators of public values. Our evidence does not speak directly to this debate, but it does imply that for leading societies any such shift is primarily an internal matter. To put the matter bluntly, power, as distinct from legitimate authority, may indeed be shifting within those societies, but it is not obviously shifting away from them and into the boardrooms of supranational business enterprises. Some of those societies may be structurally better equipped than others to deal with the consequences of internal power shifts. But none need to accept the now-conventional corporate line that such shifts are inevitable global phenomena. If certain domestic structures in leading societies are evolving in such a way as to render constraining corporate power more difficult, they should be adjusted internally. The situation would seem quite different, however, for societies not in possession of a large, diversified, and rooted industrial base. From their point of view, power may indeed be shifting in the direction of a few leading states and increasingly concentrated commercial hierarchies embedded in those states. Such

---

60. See David 1985; Krugman 1991; and Schwartz 1994.
61. See Cohen 1996; and Pauly forthcoming.

perceptions may help explain the apparently increasing efforts of many smaller states to negotiate adjustments and seek redress through multilateral institutions.

Finally, our reading of analytical literatures relevant to the contemporary study of multinational corporate behavior, together with our own initial empirical examination, leads us to conclude that further comparative elaboration and testing of a domestic structures approach to international theory at the level of the firm is worthwhile. At the center of important analytical and policy debates related to the themes of this article is the seminal work of American and British scholars, studying American and British firms, writing for American and British audiences, and exporting conclusions packaged as deductive theories to the rest of the world. The actual experiences of firms based in Germany and Japan, not to mention other industrialized and industrializing countries, are worthy of much deeper study as we try to understand the causes and consequences of multinational corporate behavior.

References

Adler, Emanuel. 1987. *The power of ideology.* Berkeley: University of California Press.

Andrews, David. 1994. Capital mobility and state autonomy. *International Studies Quarterly* 38:193–218.

Aoki, Masahiko, and Hugh Patrick, eds. 1994. *The Japanese main bank system.* New York: Oxford University Press.

Ball, George. 1967. Cosmocorp: The importance of being stateless. *Columbia Journal of World Business* 2(November–December): 25–30.

Barnet, Richard J., and John Cavanagh. 1994. *Global dreams: Imperial corporations and the new world order.* New York: Simon and Schuster.

Baums, Theodor. 1994. The German banking system and its impact on corporate finance and governance. In *The Japanese main bank system,* edited by Masahiko Aoki and Hugh Patrick. New York: Oxford University Press.

Berger, Suzanne, and Ronald Dore, eds. 1996. *National diversity and global capitalism.* Ithaca, N.Y.: Cornell University Press.

Bergsten, C. Fred, Thomas Horst, and Theodore Moran. 1978. *American multinationals and American interests.* Washington, D.C.: Brookings Institution.

Biersteker, Thomas J. 1987. *Multinationals, the state, and control of the Nigerian economy.* Princeton, N.J.: Princeton University Press.

Campbell, Nigel, and Fred Burton, eds. 1994. *Japanese multinationals.* London: Routledge.

Carnoy, Martin, Manuel Castells, and Steven Cohen. 1993. *The new global economy in the informational age.* University Park: Pennsylvania State University Press.

Castells, Manuel. 1991. *The informational city.* Cambridge, Mass.: Basil Blackwell.

Cerny, Philip G. 1995. Globalization and the changing logic of collective action. *International Organization* 49:595–625.

Chandler, Alfred D., Jr. 1962. *Strategy and structure.* Cambridge, Mass.: MIT Press.

———. 1964. *Giant enterprise.* New York: Harcourt Brace and World.

———. 1977. *The visible hand.* Cambridge, Mass.: Harvard University Press.

———. 1990. *Scale and scope.* Cambridge, Mass.: Belknap Press.

Cohen, Benjamin J. 1996. Phoenix risen: The resurrection of global finance. *World Politics* 48:268–96.

Coleman, William D. 1994. Banking, interest intermediation, and political power. *European Journal of Political Research* 26:31–58.

Commission of the European Communities. 1993. *Panorama of EC industry.* Luxembourg: Office of Official Publications of the European Communities.

Cooper, Richard. 1968. *The economics of interdependence.* New York: McGraw Hill.

Crystal, Jonathan. 1995. After protectionism: Political conflict over incoming foreign direct investment. Paper presented at the 91st annual meeting of the American Political Science Association, 31 August–3 September, Chicago.

David, Paul. 1985. Clio and the economics of QWERTY. *American Economic Review* 75:332–37.

Dunning, John H. 1958. *American investment in British manufacturing.* London: Allen and Unwin.

———. 1977. Trade, location of economic activity, and MNEs. In *The international allocation of economic activity,* edited by Bertil Ohlin, Per-Ove Hesselborn, and Per Magnus Wijkman. London: Macmillan.

———. 1992a. *Multinational enterprises and the global economy.* Reading, Mass.: Addison-Wesley.

———. 1992b. The global economy, domestic governance, strategies and transnational corporations. *Transnational Corporations* 1(3): 7–45.

Eden, Lorraine, and Evan Potter, eds. 1993. *Multinationals in the global political economy.* New York: St. Martin's.

Edwards, Franklin R., and Robert A. Eisenbeis. 1992. Financial institutions and corporate time horizons: An international perspective. Unpublished background paper for Porter 1992.

Edwards, Jeremy, and Klaus Fischer. 1994. *Banks, finance, and investment in Germany.* Cambridge: Cambridge University Press.

Encarnation, Dennis. 1992. *Rivals beyond trade.* Ithaca, N.Y.: Cornell University Press.

Encarnation, Dennis, and Mark Mason. 1990. Neither MITI nor America: The political economy of capital liberalization in Japan. *International Organization* 44:25–54.

Franko, Lawrence G. 1976. *The European multinational.* London: Harper and Row.

———. 1991. Global corporate competition. *Business Horizons,* November–December, 14–22.

Frieden, Jeffry. 1991. Invested interests: The politics of national economic policies in a world of global finance. *International Organization* 45:425–51.

Fukao, Mitsuhiro. 1995. *Financial integration, corporate governance, and the performance of multinational companies.* Washington, D.C.: Brookings Institution.

Garrett, Geoffrey, and Peter Lange. 1995. Internationalization, institutions, and political change. *International Organization* 49:627–55.

Gerlach, Michael. 1992. *Alliance capitalism.* Berkeley: University of California Press.

Gill, Stephen. 1995. Globalisation, market civilisation and disciplinary neo-liberalism. *Millennium* 24:399–423.

Gilpin, Robert. 1975. *U.S. power and the multinational corporation.* New York: Basic Books.

———. 1987. *The political economy of international relations.* Princeton, N.J.: Princeton University Press.

———. 1989. Where does Japan fit in? *Millennium* 18:329–42.

———. 1994. No one loves a political realist. Princeton University. Unpublished.

Goodman, John B., and Louis W. Pauly. 1993. The obsolescence of capital controls? Economic management in an age of global markets. *World Politics* 46:50–82.

Gourevitch, Peter. 1986. *Politics in hard times.* Ithaca, N.Y.: Cornell University Press.

Grieco, Joseph S. 1990. *Cooperation among nations.* Ithaca, N.Y.: Cornell University Press.

Grossman, G. M., and J. D. Richardson. 1985. *Strategic trade policy.* Papers in International Finance 15, International Finance Section, Department of Economics, Princeton University, Princeton, N.J.

Group of Lisbon. 1995. *Limits to competition.* Cambridge, Mass.: MIT Press.

Hall, Peter. 1986. *Governing the economy.* Oxford: Oxford University Press.

Hart, Jeffrey A. 1992. *Rival capitalists.* Ithaca, N.Y.: Cornell University Press.

Helleiner, Gerald K. 1981. *Intra-firm trade and the developing countries.* New York: St. Martin's.

Hertner, Peter, and Geoffrey Jones, eds. 1986. *Multinationals: Theory and history.* Aldershot, England: Edward Elgar.

Hymer, Stephen. 1976. *The international operations of national firms.* Cambridge, Mass.: MIT Press.

International Monetary Fund (IMF). 1992. *International capital markets: Developments, prospects, and policy issues.* Washington, D.C.: IMF.

Johnson, Chalmers, Laura D'Andrea Tyson, and John Zysman, eds. 1989. *Politics and productivity.* New York: Ballinger.

Jones, Geoffrey, and Harm G. Schröter, eds. 1993. *The rise of multinationals in continental Europe.* Aldershot, England: Edward Elgar.

Kapstein, Ethan. 1994. *Governing the global economy.* Cambridge, Mass.: Harvard University Press.

Katzenstein, Peter J., ed. 1977. *Between power and plenty.* Madison: University of Wisconsin Press.

————. 1984. *Small states in world markets.* Ithaca, N.Y.: Cornell University Press.

————. 1996. *The culture of national security.* Ithaca, N.Y.: Cornell University Press.

Keller, William W., Louis W. Pauly, Simon Reich, and Paul N. Doremus. Forthcoming. *Multinationals and the limits of globalization.* Princeton, N.J.: Princeton University Press.

Keohane, Robert O., and Joseph Nye, eds. 1972. *Transnational relations and world politics.* Cambridge, Mass.: Harvard University Press.

Keohane, Robert, and Joseph Nye. 1977. *Power and interdependence.* Boston: Little, Brown.

Kester, Carl. 1992. Industrial groups as systems of corporate governance. *Oxford Review of Economic Policy* 8(3): 24–44.

Kojima, Kiyoshi. 1978. *Direct foreign investment: A Japanese model of multinational business operations.* London: Croom Helm.

Krasner, Stephen. 1978. *Defending the national interest.* Princeton, N.J.: Princeton University Press.

————. 1996. Power politics, institutions, and transnational relations. In *Bringing transnational relations back in,* edited by Thomas Risse-Kappen. Cambridge: Cambridge University Press.

Krauss, Ellis S., and Simon Reich. 1992. Ideologies, interests, and the American executive: Toward a theory of foreign competition and manufacturing trade policy. *International Organization* 46:857–97.

Krugman, Paul, ed. 1986. *Strategic trade policy and the new international economics.* Cambridge, Mass.: MIT Press.

Krugman, Paul. 1991. *Geography and trade.* Cambridge, Mass.: MIT Press.

Kudrle, Robert T. 1985. The several faces of the multinational corporation. In *An international political economy,* edited by W. Ladd Hollist and F. Lamond Tullis. Boulder, Colo.: Westview.

Lall, Sanjaya, et al. 1983. *The new multinationals: The spread of third world enterprises.* New York: John Wiley and Sons.

Lichtenberg, Frank, and George Pushner. 1992. Ownership structure and corporate performance in Japan. NBER working paper no. 4092, National Bureau of Economic Research, Cambridge, Mass.

Lincoln, Edward. 1990. *Japan's unequal trade.* Washington, D.C.: Brookings Institution.

Lincoln, James, Michael Gerlach, and Peggy Takahashi. 1992. *Keiretsu* networks in the Japanese economy. *American Sociological Review* 57:561–85.

Lorsch, Jay, and Elizabeth McIver. 1989. *Pawns or potentates: The reality of America's corporate boards.* Boston: Harvard Business School Press.

————. 1992. Corporate governance and investment time horizons. Council on Competitiveness, Washington, D.C. Unpublished.

Lundvall, Bengt-Åke. 1992. *National systems of innovation.* New York: St. Martin's.

Markovits, Andrei S., and Simon Reich. Forthcoming. *The German predicament: Memory and power in the new Europe.* Ithaca, N.Y.: Cornell University Press.

Mason, Mark, and Dennis Encarnation, eds. 1994. *Does ownership matter? Japanese multinationals in Europe.* Oxford: Clarendon.

Milner, Helen. 1988. *Resisting protectionism.* Princeton, N.J.: Princeton University Press.

Milner, Helen, and Robert Keohane, eds. 1996. *Internationalization and domestic politics.* Cambridge: Cambridge University Press.

Ministry of International Trade and Industry (MITI). Industrial Policy Bureau, International Business Affairs Division. Various years. *Kaigai Toshi Tokei Soran* (Statistics of overseas investment). Tokyo: MITI.

Moran, Theodore, ed. 1993. *Governments and transnational corporations.* London: Routledge.

Morse, Edward. 1970. The transformation of foreign policies. *World Politics* 22:371–92.

Mowery, David C. 1994. *Science and technology policy in interdependent economies.* Boston: Kluwer.

Murtha, Thomas P., and Stefanie Ann Lenway. 1994. Country capabilities and the strategic state. *Strategic Management Journal* 15:113–29.

Nelson, Richard, ed. 1993. *National innovation systems: A comparative analysis*. New York: Oxford University Press.

Organization for Economic Cooperation and Development (OECD). 1994. *Review of foreign direct investment*. Paris: OECD.

———. Directorate for Science, Technology, and Industry (DSTI). 1993. *Globalisation of industrial activities: Sector case study of globalization in the automobile industry*. Paris: OECD.

———. DSTI. 1994–95. *Main science and technology indicators*. Paris: OECD.

Orru, Marco, Gary G. Hamilton, and Mariko Suzuki. 1989. *Patterns of inter-firm control in Japanese business*. Papers in East Asian Business and Development, no. 7. Davis: Institute of Governmental Affairs, University of California.

Ostry, Sylvia. 1990. *Governments and corporations in a shrinking world*. New York: Council on Foreign Relations Press.

Pauly, Louis W. 1994. National financial structures, capital mobility, and international economic rules. *Policy Sciences* 27:343–63.

———. Forthcoming. *Who elected the bankers? Surveillance and control in the world economy*. Ithaca, N.Y.: Cornell University Press.

Porter, Michael. 1990. *The competitive advantage of nations*. New York: Free Press.

Porter, Michael, et al. 1992. *Capital choices: A report to the Council on Competitiveness*. Washington, D.C.: Council on Competitiveness.

Prowse, Stephen D. 1992. The structure of corporate ownership in Japan. *Journal of Finance* 47:1121–40.

Reddaway, W. B., et al. 1968. *U.K. investment overseas*. Vols. 1 and 2. Cambridge: Cambridge University Press.

Reich, Robert B. 1990. Who is us? *Harvard Business Review* 68(January–February): 53–64.

Robinson, John. 1983. *Multinationals and political control*. New York: St. Martin's.

Roe, Mark J. 1994. *Strong managers, weak owners: The political roots of American corporate finance*. Princeton, N.J.: Princeton University Press.

Rogowski, Ronald. 1989. *Commerce and coalitions*. Princeton, N.J.: Princeton University Press.

Ruggie, John Gerard. 1993. Territoriality and beyond: Problematizing modernity in international relations. *International Organization* 47:139–74.

Rugman, Alan. 1993. Drawing the border for a multinational enterprise and a nation-state. In *Multinationals in the global political economy*, edited by Lorraine Eden and Evan Potter. New York: St. Martin's.

Sally, Razeen. 1994. Multinational enterprises, political economy and institutional theory. *Review of International Political Economy* 1(spring): 161–92.

Samuels, Richard. 1987. *The business of the Japanese state*. Ithaca, N.Y.: Cornell University Press.

———. 1994. *"Rich nation, strong army": National security and the technological transformation of Japan*. Ithaca, N.Y.: Cornell University Press.

Schneider Lenné, Ellen. 1994. The role of German capital markets. In *Capital markets and global governance*, edited by Nicholas Dimsdale and Martha Prevezer. Oxford: Clarendon.

Schwartz, Herman. 1994. *States versus markets*. New York: St. Martin's.

Servan-Schreiber, J. J. 1967. *Le défi Americain* (The American challenge). Paris: Denoël.

Steinmo, Sven, Kathleen Thelen, and Frank Longstreth. 1992. *Structuring politics*. Cambridge: Cambridge University Press.

Stopford, John, and Susan Strange. 1991. *Rival states, rival firms*. Cambridge: Cambridge University Press.

Stopford John, and Louis Turner. 1985. *Britain and the multinationals*. New York: John Wiley and Sons.

Tilton, Mark. 1996. *Restrained trade: Cartels in Japan's basic materials industries*. Ithaca, N.Y.: Cornell University Press.

Tsurumi, Yoshi. 1983. *Multinational management: Business strategy and government policy*. Cambridge, Mass.: Ballinger.

Turner, Louis. 1970. *Invisible empires: Multinational companies and the modern world.* London: Hamish Hamilton.

Tyson, Laura D'Andrea. 1991. They are not us. *American Prospect* (winter): 37–49.

Uriu, Robert M. 1996. *Troubled industries: Confronting economic change in Japan.* Ithaca, N.Y.: Cornell University Press.

U.S. Congress. Office of Technology Assessment. 1993. *Multinationals and the national interest: Playing by different rules.* Document no. OTA-ITE-569. Washington, D.C.: Government Printing Office.

———. 1994. *Multinationals and the U.S. technology base.* Document no. OTA-ITE-612. Washington, D.C.: Government Printing Office.

U.S. Department of Commerce. Bureau of Economic Analysis (BEA). 1994. *Foreign direct investment in the United States.* Washington, D.C.: Department of Commerce.

U.S. General Accounting Office. 1993. *Competitiveness issues: The business environment in the United States, Japan, and Germany.* Document no. GAO/GGD-93-124, August.

van Tulder, Rob, and Gerd Junne. 1988. *European multinationals in core technologies.* New York: Wiley.

Vernon, Raymond. 1966. International investment and international trade in the product cycle. *Quarterly Journal of Economics* 80:190–207.

———. 1971. *Sovereignty at bay.* New York: Basic Books.

———. 1977. *Storm over the multinationals.* Cambridge, Mass.: Harvard University Press.

Wellons, Philip. 1986. International debt: The behavior of banks in a politicized environment. In *The politics of international debt,* edited by Miles Kahler. Ithaca, N.Y.: Cornell University Press.

———. 1987. *Passing the buck: Banks, governments and third world debt.* Boston: Harvard Business School Press.

Wells, Louis T., ed. 1972. *The product life cycle and international trade.* Cambridge, Mass.: Harvard University Press.

———. 1983. *Third world multinationals.* Cambridge, Mass.: MIT Press.

Wever, Kirsten, and Christopher S. Allen. 1993. The financial system and corporate governance in Germany. *Journal of Public Policy* 13:183–202.

Wilkins, Mira. 1974. *The maturing of multinational enterprise: American business abroad from 1914 to 1970.* Cambridge, Mass.: Harvard University Press.

Williamson, Oliver. 1988. Corporate finance and corporate governance. *Journal of Finance* 43:567–91.

Yamawaki, Hideki. 1994. Entry patterns of Japanese multinationals in U.S. and European manufacturing. In *Does ownership matter? Japanese multinationals in Europe,* edited by Mark Mason and Dennis Encarnation. Oxford: Clarendon.

Yoffie, David, ed. 1993. *Beyond free trade: Firms, governments, and global competition.* Boston: Harvard Business School Press.

Ziegler, Rolf, Donald Bender, and Herman Biehler. 1985. Industry and banking in the German corporate network. In *Networks of corporate power,* edited by Fruns N. Stokman, Rolf Ziegler, and John Scott. Cambridge: Polity.

Zysman, John. 1983. *Governments, markets, and growth.* Ithaca, N.Y.: Cornell University Press.

III.
Money and Finance

Money and finance are integral to the operation of markets, domestic or international. By money we mean anything that serves as a generalized medium of exchange, unit of account, and store of value. By finance we mean the institutional structure that serves to mobilize savings and provide credit to borrowers. Without money, there can only be the inconvenience of primitive and inefficient barter. Money facilitates multilateral exchange, promoting specialization in output and an increasingly efficient division of labor. Without finance, there can only be a limited amount of growth of productive capacity and income. A financial structure facilitates investment, promoting economic development and a rising standard of living.

Money and finance are also intensely political, raising profound questions of both distribution and governance. Money, after all, is command over resources: a means to exercise dominion over factors of production (land, labor, capital) as well as to purchase goods and services for final use. Those with money have power—or at least some kinds of power. Those with access to finance are privileged, those without go wanting. What could be more political? Money is also notoriously unstable, as any student of financial history well knows. Money by itself does not produce wealth. But if money is not managed effectively to avoid price instability or debt crises, the processes by which production is organized and income generated can be seriously impeded.

Monetary governance is difficult enough within any single state. But in relations among states, matters become even more complicated because of the long-standing convention of national monetary sovereignty based on separate and distinct national currencies. Economically, monetary sovereignty means that currencies that are legal tender in one place are not likely to be directly usable elsewhere. From this stems a need for mechanisms and arrangements, such as the foreign-exchange and other international markets, to facilitate currency trades and other transactions between national financial systems. Politically, monetary sovereignty means that each state has its own balance of payments, exchange rate, and policy priorities. From this stems a need for mechanisms and arrangements, for such matters as currency values and access to finance, to minimize frictions and, if possible, to facilitate cooperation *between governments. The international political economy of money and finance is found in these twin economic and political imperatives.*

In this area, as in the fields of trade and investment, International Organization *has provided an important venue for advancing theory, especially since the postwar revival of global financial markets and consequent increase of capital mobility in the 1960s and 1970s. Implications of the interplay of states and markets for the governance of monetary relations were analyzed by John S. Odell, Benjamin J. Cohen, and Joanne Gowa.[1] Issues related to international borrowing and debt were addressed by Jeffry A. Frieden, Charles Lipson, Miles Kahler, Albert Fishlow, and Benjamin J. Cohen.[2] The evolving roles of multilateral financial organizations were examined by William Ascher, Richard E. Feinberg, and Graham Bird.[3] Regulatory questions were highlighted by James P. Hawley and Ethan B. Kapstein.[4] An important review essay was recently contributed by David M. Andrews and Thomas D. Willett.[5]*

Following in this same tradition, Michael Webb (Chapter 7) takes up the critical issue of monetary cooperation among states. Webb questions the common view that by the early 1990s policy coordination had significantly declined. Rather, he argues, it is the form of cooperation that has changed. Earlier in the postwar period, coordination consisted largely of "external" measures designed to manage payments imbalances caused by incompatible national macroeconomic policies (such as balance-of-payments financing and exchange-rate coordination). Today, in contrast, cooperation encompasses the direct coordination of national monetary and fiscal policies themselves—policies that had previously been considered strictly "internal." What accounts for this shift in the form of cooperation? The explanation, Webb continues, is found in the massive increase of capital mobility that has occurred in recent decades. This is a development that in his view must be regarded as a fundamental transformation in the structure of the international monetary system. Controversially, Webb contends that financial-market integration has made it virtually impossible for governments to pursue significantly divergent macroeconomic policies.

Jeffry Frieden, in a germinal article published in 1991 (Chapter 8), takes a different tack, formally disaggregating the state to explore the domestic rather than interstate implications of a heightened degree of international capital mobility. Of specific concern to Frieden are the distributional consequences of monetary relations and how these may be expected to influence policy preferences and political debate. Key socioeconomic groups, he demonstrates, are systematically and differentially affected by an integration of national capital markets; and these diverse impacts, in turn, are likely to lead to fundamental political divisions over a range of public policy issues, from the regulation of financial activity to the management of exchange

1. See Odell 1979; Cohen 1982; and Gowa 1984.
2. See Frieden 1981; Lipson 1981; Kahler 1985; Fishlow 1985 and 1986; and Cohen 1985.
3. See Ascher 1983; Feinberg 1988; and Bird 1996.
4. See Hawley 1984; and Kapstein 1989 and 1992.
5. Andrews and Willett 1997.

rates. Frieden's article has sparked considerable scholarly interest in the effect of external monetary relations on internal politics and policymaking.

An especially insightful example of this emerging interest is provided by Stephan Haggard and Sylvia Maxfield's study of financial liberalization in the developing world (Chapter 9). Haggard and Maxfield ask why a growing number of developing countries have voluntarily opened their financial systems to internationally mobile capital despite the risks involved and over the objections of sectoral interests favored by capital controls. The authors answer this question by stressing two kinds of international pressure that have constrained government choices with respect to external financial policy. One pressure is the growing role of foreign trade in most developing economies, which has increased the political voice and influence of foreign investors as well as of domestic actors with foreign commercial ties. The other, paradoxically, is found in balance-of-payments crises, which have forced political authorities to court the good will of foreign investors in order to discourage a liquidation of their investments or to encourage an inflow of needed funds. This type of analysis helps to fill in some of the key links in the chain from capital mobility to national economic policy.

References

Andrews, David M., and Thomas D. Willett. 1997. Financial Interdependence and the State: International Monetary Relations at Century's End. *International Organization* 51 (3):479–511.

Ascher, William. 1983. New Development Approaches to the Adaptability of International Agencies: The Case of the World Bank. *International Organization* 37 (3):415–40.

Bird, Graham. 1996. The International Monetary Fund and Developing Countries: A Review of the Evidence and Policy Options. *International Organization* 50 (3):477–512.

Cohen, Benjamin J. 1982. Balance-of-Payments Financing: Evolution of a Regime. *International Organization* 36 (2):457–78.

———. 1985. International Debt and Linkage Strategies: Some Foreign-Policy Implications for the United States. *International Organization* 39 (4):699–728.

Feinberg, Richard E. 1988. The Changing Relationship Between the World Bank and the International Monetary Fund. *International Organization* 42 (3):545–60.

Fishlow, Albert. 1985. Lessons from the Past: Capital Markets During the 19th Century and the Interwar Period. *International Organization* 39 (3):383–439.

———. 1986. The East European Debt Crisis in the Latin American Mirror. *International Organization* 40 (2):567–75.

Frieden, Jeffry A. 1981. Third World Indebted Industrialization: International Finance and State Capitalism in Mexico, Brazil, Algeria, and South Korea. *International Organization* 35 (3):407–31.

Gowa, Joanne. 1984. Hegemons, IOs, and Markets: The Case of the Substitution Account. *International Organization* 38 (4):661–83.

Hawley, James P. 1984. Protecting Capital from Itself: U.S. Attempts to Regulate the Eurocurrency System. *International Organization* 38 (1):131–66.

Kahler, Miles. 1985. Politics and International Debt: Explaining the Crisis. *International Organization* 39 (3):357–82.

Kapstein, Ethan B. 1989. Resolving the Regulator's Dilemma: International Coordination of Banking Regulations. *International Organization* 43 (2):323–47.

————. 1992. Between Power and Purpose: Central Bankers and the Politics of Regulatory Convergence. *International Organization* 46 (1):265–87.

Lipson, Charles. 1981. The International Organization of Third World Debt. *International Organization* 35 (4):603–32.

Odell, John S. 1979. The U.S. and the Emergence of Flexible Exchange Rates: An Analysis of Foreign Policy Change. *International Organization* 33 (1):57–82.

Invested interests: the politics of national economic policies in a world of global finance

Jeffry A. Frieden

A striking characteristic of the contemporary international economy is the great mobility of capital across national borders. Technological innovations, economic trends, and government policies have brought international investment to extremely high levels. Many business executives, politicians, and observers believe that capital now moves so freely that the financial markets of industrialized countries are essentially subsets of one global market. This is widely regarded as a fundamental change in the international economy—something new or at least not seen since the classic gold standard. It is also widely believed to have generated such prominent developments as European Community (EC) movement toward a single currency, harmonization of taxes across national borders, and international convergence of macroeconomic policies.

Economists have devoted a great deal of time and energy to analyzing the economic implications of the movement of capital across national borders. Other social scientists have also analyzed the political implications of international investment. The studies of this latter group have tended to focus on one or another subset of the issue, such as multinational corporations in developed and developing countries, foreign borrowing by developing nations, and the politics of international banking.[1] Despite the quantity and quality of work on

I am grateful to the Social Science Research Council, the German Marshall Fund, the UCLA Academic Senate Committee on Research, and the UCLA International Studies and Overseas Programs for their financial support. I also thank Benjamin J. Cohen, Barry Eichengreen, Judith Goldstein, Joanne Gowa, Robert Keohane, Stephen Krasner, David Lake, Edward Leamer, Timothy McKeown, Louis Pauly, Frances Rosenbluth, John Ruggie, and Michael Wallerstein for their helpful comments and suggestions.
1. For prominent examples from each of these issue-areas, see Helen V. Milner, *Resisting Protectionism: Global Industries and the Politics of International Trade* (Princeton, N.J.: Princeton University Press, 1988); Peter Evans, *Dependent Development: The Alliance of Multinational, State, and Local Capital in Brazil* (Princeton, N.J.: Princeton University Press, 1979); David G. Becker et al., *Postimperialism: International Capitalism and Development in the Late Twentieth Century* (Boulder, Colo.: Lynne Rienner, 1987); Robert Kaufman and Barbara Stallings, eds., *Debt and*

specific aspects of the politics of cross-border investment, this literature remains disjointed and short on general analytic principles.

This article proposes a framework for analyzing the politics of international capital mobility. It focuses on the distributional implications of cross-border capital movements and on the distributional implications of various economic policies in light of the high degree of international capital mobility.

The first section describes just how mobile capital is today and discusses the implications of existing levels of financial integration for national economic policy autonomy. It argues that while financial capital is extremely mobile across borders, other types of investment (especially in equities and sector-specific capital) are far less mobile. In this context, foreseeable levels of international capital mobility restrict but do not eliminate the possibility for national economic policies. Sectoral policies remain feasible, as do policies whose goals directly or indirectly involve the exchange rate.

The second section of the article examines the policy preferences of various socioeconomic groups toward financial integration. It emphasizes the differential effects of the increase in capital mobility and focuses on questions concerning which actors are better (or worse) off after financial integration than before and how the various actors can be expected to respond politically to this change in the economic environment. The conclusion here is twofold. Over the long run, international financial integration tends to favor capital over labor, especially in developed countries. But in the shorter run, which is more relevant to politics and policies, the issue is more complex: in the developed world, financial integration favors capitalists with mobile or diversified assets and disfavors those with assets tied to specific locations and activities such as manufacturing or farming.

The third section of the article explores what high levels of financial integration imply for the policy preferences of economic interest groups in regard to such other issues as macroeconomic policy and the exchange rate. The section takes a high level of capital mobility as given, to see how various interest groups are expected to behave in this environment. It argues that international capital mobility tends to remake political coalitions by way of its impact on the effects of national policies. The political division between producers of tradable goods and producers of nontradable goods and services is likely to become more important, as are distinctions between internationally diversified and undiversified investors. All of these factors have significant implications for the analysis of politics and economic policy in the advanced industrialized nations.

Development in Latin America (Boulder, Colo.: Westview Press, 1989); Benjamin J. Cohen, *In Whose Interest? International Banking and American Foreign Policy* (New Haven, Conn.: Yale University Press, 1987); and Charles Lipson, *Standing Guard: Protecting Foreign Capital in the Nineteenth and Twentieth Centuries* (Berkeley: University of California Press, 1985). The bodies of literature, of course, are far too large to cite or discuss here.

The relationship between international capital mobility and national policies is a prominent example of the much-discussed impact of external conditions on domestic politics.[2] Elucidating this specific relationship thus also serves the broader purpose of clarifying the domestic effects of international trends. The article, then, both develops an integrated approach to the politics of international capital movements and addresses more general conceptual issues about the interaction of the domestic and international political economies. In so doing, it presents a summary and empirical illustrations not only of the direct impact of international capital mobility on the effectiveness of national economic policy but also of the distributional effects of capital mobility on the social groups whose demands themselves affect national economic policy.

Capital mobility and national economic policies

It would be foolish to inquire about the effects of integrated international capital markets on interest group competition over national economic policy if such policy could not be implemented in a financially integrated world or if contemporary international capital markets were not in fact highly integrated. The initial question therefore concerns the degree to which national economic policy autonomy is compromised by existing levels of international capital mobility.

The events of the 1970s and the 1980s have led many to conclude that capital mobility severely limits or contravenes national policy. Between 1978 and 1982, for example, private financial inflows swamped Chile's conservative policies even as private financial outflows thwarted Mexico's free-spending policies. In mid-1981, the economic expansion attempted by the new French Socialist government rapidly confronted a large capital outflow and a run on the franc, leading to a reversal of the policies soon after their adoption.[3] Parallel stories about government efforts hampered by capital and currency movements could be told about many other developing and developed countries in the past two decades. Some observers have drawn dire conclusions, such as that of John Freeman, who observed that in the context of the globalization of finance "the nation state has become at best immobilized and at worst obsolete."[4]

2. The two quintessential works on this subject are Peter Gourevitch's *Politics in Hard Times: Comparative Responses to International Economic Crises* (Ithaca, N.Y.: Cornell University Press, 1986) and Ronald Rogowski's *Commerce and Coalitions: How Trade Affects Domestic Political Alignments* (Princeton, N.J.: Princeton University Press, 1989).

3. Jeffrey Sachs and Charles Wyplosz, "The Economic Consequences of President Mitterand," *Economic Policy* 2 (April 1986), pp. 262–322.

4. See John Freeman, "Banking on Democracy? International Finance and the Possibilities for Popular Sovereignty," mimeograph, University of Minnesota, 1990. From a politically different quarter, former Citibank chief executive officer Walter Wriston has said similar things about the impact of financial internationalization—but approvingly: "It's a new world and the concept of sovereignty is going to change. . . . The idea of fifteenth-century international law is gone. It hasn't laid down yet, but it's dead. It's like the three-mile limit in a world of Inter-Continental Ballistic

The first step in evaluating the effects of contemporary levels of international capital mobility is to get a clear picture of where the levels stand in relation to the past. Long-term capital movements across borders were relatively limited for the first twenty-five years after World War II and took place primarily in the form of direct investment. Today, long-term international investment flows are extraordinarily large, and direct investment has been dwarfed by other, more arms-length, forms of cross-border capital movements.

According to one source, net international bond and bank lending was $440 billion in 1989, up from $180 billion just five years earlier. Capital outflows from the thirteen leading industrialized countries averaged $444 billion in 1989, with almost two-thirds of the amount consisting of portfolio investment, in contrast to $52 billion in the late 1970s, with two-thirds consisting of foreign direct investment. Capital outflows were equivalent to 15 percent of world merchandise trade in 1989, in contrast to 7 percent in the late 1970s.[5] According to another source, the outstanding stock of international bank and bond lending was $3.6 trillion in 1989, equivalent to 25 percent of the aggregate gross national product (GNP) of the industrialized countries, in contrast to under $200 billion and 5 percent of aggregate GNP in 1973.[6]

Recent changes in regulations and technology have made it possible for money to travel across borders almost instantly, giving rise to massive short-term international financial transactions. In April 1989, foreign exchange trading in the world's financial centers averaged about $650 billion *a day,* equivalent to nearly $500 million a minute and to forty times the amount of world trade a day. Markets for short-term international financial instruments are comparably large, although exact figures are not available.[7]

Impressive as these numbers are, they do not amount to full international capital mobility. In fact, economic studies have consistently shown that borders and currencies are still substantial barriers to investment flows.[8] Although

---

Missiles." Wriston is cited in my *Banking on the World: The Politics of American International Finance* (New York: Harper & Row, 1987), p. 115. See also Walter Wriston, *Risk and Other Four-Letter Words* (New York: Harper & Row, 1986).

5. Bank for International Settlements (BIS), *Sixtieth Annual Report* (BIS: Basle, 1990), pp. 63, 82, and 125.

6. See Morris Goldstein, Donald Mathieson, and Timothy Lane, "Determinants and Systemic Consequences of International Capital Flows," in *Determinants and Systemic Consequences of International Capital Flows* (Washington, D.C.: International Monetary Fund, 1991), p. 5. This assumes a low level of international bond lending in 1973, which is almost certainly the case. Exact figures are not available.

7. See BIS, *Sixtieth Annual Report,* pp. 208–9. See also pp. 146–52, which offer data regarding some short-term instruments and indicate that open positions in interest rate futures and options totaled about $1.6 trillion at the end of 1989.

8. The early classic work was M. Feldstein and C. Horioka's "Domestic Savings and International Capital Flows," *Economic Journal* 90 (June 1980), pp. 314–29. For more on the issue and debates over it, see Ralph Bryant, *International Financial Intermediation* (Washington, D.C.: Brookings Institution, 1987), pp. 82–86. For a recent test, see Tamim Bayoumi, "Saving-Investment Correlations: Immobile Capital, Government Policy, or Endogenous Behavior?" *IMF Staff Papers* 37 (June 1990), pp. 360–87.

these barriers have been and are still being reduced, there are a number of reasons why international investment is by no means yet a seamless web. First, movement of capital across borders still involves country and currency risks. Investors must take into account the possibility that assets in one country may be riskier than those in another country and that movements in exchange rates may affect the return on their investments. Of course, both of these problems are addressed by adjustments to asset prices and returns and by forward markets, but they imply that capital movements among industrialized countries are more difficult than capital movements within them.[9]

Second, while some forms of capital do move quite easily across borders, others remain more geographically specific. Most assertions of full international capital mobility refer to international transfers of financial assets, especially bonds and bank claims. Equity markets appear to be far less integrated,[10] and other forms of capital still less so. In most interpretations, this is because many forms of capital, such as technological and managerial knowledge, skills, and networks, are specific to their current use and cannot easily be transferred from place to place.[11] Although detailed analyses do not exist, most observers would probably agree that financial capital is most mobile across borders, followed by equities and then by firm- or sector-specific capital assets.[12]

The greater international mobility of financial assets, the more modest international mobility of other assets, and the continued importance of unexpected exchange rate movements must all be taken into account in assessments of national policy autonomy in the contemporary international economy. The appraisal can be divided into policy targeted at well-defined segments of the economy (industries, sectors, and regions) and policy of macroeconomic import. The baseline is the assertion that asset markets are

9. The most careful assessment of the Feldstein-Horioka findings, updated through the late 1980s, emphasizes the great increase in capital mobility and the continued importance of currency premiums. See Jeffrey A. Frankel, "Quantifying International Capital Mobility in the 1980s," in Douglas Bernheim and John Shoven, eds., *National Saving and Economic Performance* (Chicago: University of Chicago Press, 1991), pp. 227–60.

10. For rough evidence on intranational and international stock price differentials, see Barry Eichengreen, "Is Europe an Optimum Currency Area?" mimeograph, University of California at Berkeley, 1990, pp. 6–9. The differentials may have to do with nontransferable advantages accruing to national owners, such as greater access to information or to monitoring and enforcement mechanisms.

11. The modern theory of foreign direct investment is based on the proposition that multinational firms exist precisely because they facilitate (but do not make costless) the international transmission of such specific assets. The classic statement by Caves is still probably the most appropriate here. See Richard E. Caves, "International Corporations: The Industrial Economics of Foreign Investment," *Economica* 38 (February 1971), pp. 1–27.

12. This is a conclusion made by Frankel in "Quantifying International Capital Mobility in the 1980s." One indication of the high degree to which markets for financial assets are integrated is the virtual disappearance of significant spreads between domestic and offshore interest rates in most currency instruments of members of the Organization for Economic Cooperation and Development (OECD). Regarding this subject, see Goldstein, Mathieson, and Lane, "Determinants and Systemic Consequences of International Capital Flows," pp. 7–11.

internationally linked to varying degrees: financial markets are closely linked, equity markets are less connected, and markets for firm- and sector-specific capital are quite nationally segmented. In other words, among industrialized countries, financial capital flows freely but other assets flow relatively less freely or very little.

Inasmuch as capital is specific to location, increased financial integration has only limited effects on policies targeted at particular industries. Whether or not a sector-specific policy is effective depends greatly on how easily firms can enter the sector. Financial markets can affect the ease of entry by extending funds to new firms. The easier it is for new firms to enter the sector, the more quickly the benefits of the policy to preexisting firms will dissipate and thus the less effective the policy will be. This is a general feature of sector-specific policies and holds as long as financial capital is mobile domestically; it would be true even if capital were not mobile internationally.

Where cross-border financial flows reduce entry barriers to a favored sector, they contravene sector-specific policy. International capital mobility may have increased the ability of foreign producers to respond to trade protection by locating in the protected market; inasmuch as the purpose of protection was to support locally owned firms, this objective may be frustrated. The proliferation of Japanese-owned automobile factories in the United States in response to automobile import controls may have been made easier by the integration of financial markets and may have reduced some of the benefits of the controls to shareholders and employees of American-owned automobile manufacturers.[13]

All in all, however, increased financial capital mobility probably has little effect on most sector-specific policies. Supporters of such policies can generally design them to avoid their frustration by financial flows, domestic or international. Financial capital mobility, within or across borders, is not likely to affect the impact of cash transfers to farmers on their incomes. Nor can financial flows significantly impede government health and safety standards. Financial integration may make it more difficult to design some sector-specific policies to avoid undesirable side effects (namely, benefits accruing to untargeted firms), but it rarely makes them unsustainable.

On the other hand, integration of financial markets has significant effects on the effectiveness and the differential distributional impact of national macro-economic policies. To get a handle on the issue, it is useful to start with what

13. Although I am unaware of any studies of this phenomenon, arguments to this effect are frequently heard among American competitors of the Japanese transplants, often in the context of complaints over the Japanese firms' access to low-cost Japanese funds. There are reasons to doubt the accuracy of the argument, however. First, most foreign direct investment is funded in the host country. Second, if Japanese firms have privileged access to Japanese finance, then financial markets are not fully integrated. The result might be due to preferential ties among Japanese financial and nonfinancial firms, which would constitute a "natural" barrier to financial capital mobility. Further study in this regard is required. A related issue is the effect of foreign-owned branch plants on political lineups in the host country. For anecdotal evidence that Japanese investment in the United States has created or reinforced domestic interest groups that favor freer trade, see "Influx of Foreign Capital Mutes Debate on Trade," *The New York Times,* 8 February 1987, p. I13.

might be called the Mundell-Fleming conditions, taken from the most influential approach to payments balance developed in the early 1960s.[14] These conditions include the possibility that financial assets may be fully mobile across borders. (In what follows, I use "capital mobility" to mean the mobility of financial capital, as does the literature in question.)

Simply put, the Mundell-Fleming approach indicates that a country can have at most two of the following three conditions: a fixed exchange rate, monetary policy autonomy, and capital mobility. Without capital mobility, national authorities can adopt and sustain a monetary policy that differs from the policies of the rest of the world and can hold their exchange rate constant; however, with mobile capital, the attempt will be contravened by financial flows. Assume the authorities want an expansionary monetary policy. Without capital mobility, a fall in interest rates will lead to a rise in demand, and the economy will be stimulated (we ignore longer-term effects on the payments balance). With capital mobility, reduced domestic interest rates will lead to an outflow of capital in search of higher interest rates abroad, and long before monetary policy has a real effect, interest rates will be bid back up to world levels.[15]

The reason for the result is straightforward: if capital is fully mobile across borders, interest rates are constrained to be the same in all countries and national monetary policy can have no effect on national interest rates. However, to go back to the original conditions, if capital mobility is given (or imposed), monetary policy can be effective if the value of the currency is allowed to vary. Monetary policy operates, in other words, via exchange rates rather than via interest rates as in a typical closed-economy model. With capital mobility, monetary expansion greater than that in the rest of the world causes a financial outflow in which investors sell the currency; the result is currency depreciation. Depreciation in most cases stimulates the economy as prices of foreign goods rise relative to prices of domestically produced goods, thereby increasing local and foreign demand for locally produced goods.[16]

A parallel story can be told about fiscal policy. If capital is not mobile and the exchange rate is fixed, expansionary fiscal policy raises national interest rates as the government finances increased spending by floating more bonds. The

14. See the following works of Robert A. Mundell: "The Appropriate Use of Monetary and Fiscal Policy Under Fixed Exchange Rates," *IMF Staff Papers* 9 (March 1962), pp. 70–77; "Capital Mobility and Stabilization Policy Under Fixed and Flexible Exchange Rates," *Canadian Journal of Economics and Political Science* 29 (November 1963), pp. 475–85; and "A Reply: Capital Mobility and Size," *Canadian Journal of Economics and Political Science* 30 (August 1964), pp. 421–31. The basic model can be found in any good textbook discussion of open-economy macroeconomics; a useful survey is W. M. Corden's *Inflation, Exchange Rates, and the World Economy,* 3d ed. (Chicago: University of Chicago Press, 1986).

15. The argument presented here is in simplified form. Variation in monetary autonomy is actually along a continuum, not dichotomous: the choice is not starkly between full monetary independence and none at all; it is instead among different degrees of autonomy.

16. This ignores the potential contravening effects of the depreciation on national income; that is, it assumes that substitution effects dominate income effects or that expenditure switching dominates expenditure reduction.

resultant "crowding out" of private investment dampens the expansion. However, if capital moves freely across borders, bonds floated to finance increased government spending are bought by international investors, and there is no effect on interest rates, which are set globally.[17] Relaxing the fixed exchange rate constraint has different effects with fiscal policy than with monetary policy. If the exchange rate varies, as foreigners buy more government bonds the resultant capital inflow causes a currency appreciation that tends to reduce domestic demand for domestically produced goods and thus to dampen the fiscal expansion.[18]

The general point is that in a world of fully mobile capital, national policy cannot affect the national interest rate;[19] it can, however, affect the exchange rate. The above discussion of open-economy macroeconomics is meant simply to highlight this result.

It may seem unimportant that the world has changed from one in which national macroeconomic policy operated primarily via interest rates to one in which policy operates primarily via exchange rates, but several points to defend the significance of this observation can be made. First, the distributional effects of interest rate changes are different from those of exchange rate changes. If monetary expansion in a stylized world before capital mobility (BCM) meant lower interest rates, then monetary expansion in a stylized world after capital mobility (ACM) means depreciation. To take one distributional example, lower interest rates are good for the residential construction industry, while depreciation is bad for it inasmuch as it tends to switch domestic demand away from nontradable goods and services. By the same token, manufacturers might have been more sympathetic to a tight money stance in the past, when the principal effect of this stance was to raise interest rates, than they are now, when the principal effect is a currency appreciation that tends to increase import penetration. This means that policy preferences of economic interest groups, and therefore political coalitions, are likely to differ between the BCM and ACM worlds. I later return to this point and discuss it in detail.

Second, although by definition there is an international component to exchange rate changes, there is not necessarily an international component to

17. The point is not that foreigners buy all the government bonds but, rather, that the increased domestic demand for credit is met by an increased supply of credit as capital flows in, with the result that the price of credit remains unchanged. This of course assumes that the deficit country is not large enough to affect world interest rates, which may not always be the case. It also assumes that the government does not engage in monetary policies that accommodate the fiscal expansion.

18. For a good survey and evaluation, see Michael M. Hutchison and Charles A. Pigott, "Real and Financial Linkages in the Macroeconomic Response to Budget Deficits: An Empirical Investigation," in Sven Arndt and J. David Richardson, eds., *Real-Financial Linkages Among Open Economies* (Cambridge, Mass.: MIT Press, 1987), pp. 139–66.

19. More accurately, it does not affect the *covered* interest rate—that is, the interest rate minus (or plus) the market's expectation of currency movements. Obviously, if investors expect a currency to fall, they demand a higher interest rate for securities denominated in it, and vice versa. Covered interest parity appears to have held well from the mid-1970s onward among almost all major currencies.

interest rate changes. If monetary expansion simply reduces national interest rates, chances are that most foreigners will be indifferent. If, however, it leads to currency depreciation in the expansionary country, foreigners are likely to be concerned about their resultant loss of competitiveness.[20]

Third, the focus on how macroeconomic policy takes effect through the exchange rate helps clarify some observed anomalies of the ACM world. If an American administration in the BCM world had pursued fiscal expansion and monetary stringency, the result might well have been that the policies canceled each other out: tight money would have reinforced the "crowding out" effects of the fiscal expansion. As it was, however, in the ACM world, the Reagan-Volcker fiscal expansion and monetary stringency of the early 1980s had a markedly different impact. Fiscal policy was largely financed by foreign borrowing, which reduced or eliminated the effects of crowding out and contributed to appreciation of the dollar. At the same time, tight money reinforced the rise of the dollar by strengthening the international investment attractiveness of dollar-denominated securities. The result was striking both on macroeconomic grounds, as the dollar soared and the United States became a major net debtor to the rest of the world, and on distributional grounds, as the dollar appreciation devastated U.S. producers of tradable goods (manufacturing and agriculture) and favored producers of nontradable goods and services (real estate, health care, leisure activities, and education).

To summarize this section, financial capital moves across the borders of developed countries with great ease, while other asset markets are less integrated and some capital remains quite fixed. In this context, while global financial integration may reduce the efficacy of some sector-specific policies, it does not impede most of them. And while international financial integration does not make national macroeconomic policy obsolete, it does shift the effect of macroeconomic policy from the interest rate to the exchange rate. These features of the ACM world are expected to have a significant impact on the interests of various domestic economic interest groups. I return to ACM interest group competition over economic policy after first looking at the expected effects of the shift from BCM to ACM itself.

The distributional effects of capital mobility

The distinction I draw here is nuanced but important. On the one hand, I am interested in how economic agents are expected to act in a world characterized by capital mobility: What sorts of policies will be pursued by what sorts of groups and coalitions? On the other hand, I am interested in how the shift from

---

20. For an illuminating discussion of cross-border effects, see Michael Mussa, "Macroeconomic Interdependence and the Exchange Rate Regime," in Rudiger Dornbusch and Jacob Frenkel, eds., *International Economic Policy: Theory and Evidence* (Baltimore, Md.: Johns Hopkins University Press, 1979), pp. 160–204.

a pre-1970 world of limited capital mobility to a post-1980 world of relatively high capital mobility affected the interests and influence of economic agents: Who gained and who lost as we went from capital immobility to capital mobility? And what are the political implications of these gains and losses? In other words, in one context I analyze the dynamics of the ACM world; in another context, I compare conditions in the BCM world with those in the ACM world.

The first set of questions addressed in this section pertains to the overall impact of international financial integration on major economic interest groups in advanced industrialized societies. Once again, I have recourse to rudimentary tools of economic analysis. There are, however, several different (albeit potentially complementary) approaches that contend for attention. Many analyses focus implicitly or explicitly on the portfolio choice approach or on an application of the Heckscher-Ohlin model of international trade. While these give interesting insights, I believe that they are not directly relevant to our political and policy questions. After reviewing them, then, I summarize and discuss the "specific-factors" model, which I believe is best suited to assessing the distributional effects of increased capital mobility and to determining the impact of these distributional effects on lobbying for policy.

Perhaps the most common and simplest possible cut into the problem is to look at increased capital mobility from the standpoint of investors facing portfolio decisions, whom it must help. It can hardly be bad for capitalists to have more investment options than before, which is what capital mobility gives them. By the same token, increasing the options of capital presumably reduces those of labor by making it less costly for capital to move rather than accede to labor demands.

This surmise captures important effects of increased financial integration. The wider menu of investments open to asset-holders increases their influence on governments, labor, and others. The 1980s may have indeed seen a secular shift in response to increased capital mobility, in which governments all over the world were forced to provide more attractive conditions for capitalists. Such conditions include everything from lower wealth and capital gains taxes to relaxed regulation of financial activities and labor relations. In a world in which financial capital moves freely across borders, it is difficult for one country to insist on stiff capital taxation when other countries are removing or reducing it. Inasmuch as this effect holds, increased financial integration implies an across-the-board, lasting increase in the social and political power of capital.[21]

---

21. American tax reform in 1986, for example, was followed by widespread OECD movement toward the new American corporate tax rates. By 1989, direct corporate tax rates in the principal EC member countries were all in the 35 to 42 percent range. See Price Waterhouse, *Tax: Strategic Corporate Tax Planning* (London: Mercury Books, 1989). Across industries, there is evidence that such footloose sectors as finance face lower effective tax rates. In the United States in 1983, for example, while twenty-four nonfinancial industries paid an average effective federal income tax rate of 17.5 percent, the three financial sectors (insurance, investment, and financial services companies) paid an average of 8.5 percent. See "New Threat to Smokestack America," *The New York Times*, 26 May 1985, p. 3:1.

But this picture is incomplete, for it ignores the dynamic effects of aggregate portfolio choices on asset-holders. The ability of capital to move freely across borders can in fact be bad for capitalists in a given country or good for labor in it. The result depends on the country's underlying endowment of capital and other resources, and this leads some to believe that the Heckscher-Ohlin approach is the appropriate analytic tool.

According to the Heckscher-Ohlin trade model, the effects of goods movements on returns to factors will vary according to whether the factors are locally scarce or abundant. Perhaps the best-known extension is the Stolper-Samuelson theorem, which posits that protection (that is, decreased trade) benefits the locally scarce factor: protection is good for labor in a labor-poor country and is good for capital in a capital-poor country. The intuition is straightforward. With trade, demand for the product in which the country has a comparative advantage will rise, and this comparative advantage is a function of how well endowed the country is with various factors. A labor-rich country tends to export products that use labor intensively; the more the country trades, the more labor is used, and the more wages rise. Trade and factor movements are substitutes: exporting labor and labor-intensive products have the same effect, as do exporting capital and capital-intensive products.

In the Heckscher-Ohlin view, then, increased capital mobility (like increased world trade) benefits capital where it is abundant and hurts capital where it is scarce. Capital flows out of capital-rich countries, raising the return to local capital, and flows toward capital-poor countries, lowering the return to local capital. The effect is analogous to that examined by Ronald Rogowski, who assessed periods in which there was an exogenous increase or decrease in world trade to explore the Heckscher-Ohlin effects on national politics.[22]

To illustrate the above points, we can compare two countries with opposite sets of endowments. In the BCM world, the first country is rich in capital and poor in labor, so its local interest rates are relatively low and its local wages relatively high. In the ACM world, capital is free to move to countries in which the rate of return is higher; the local interest rates rise to the world level, and local wages fall. In this case, the result favors capital and disfavors labor, but this is purely a function of the beginning endowments—which are characteristic of most developed countries. Now take the opposite case. In the BCM world, the second country is poor in capital and rich in labor, so its local interest rates are relatively high and its local wages relatively low. In the ACM world, capital will flow in, reducing the local interest rates and tending to raise wages. In this case, since the local rate of return on capital is constrained to fall to the (lower) world level, local capitalists are harmed while local workers benefit.

This may capture some of what has happened as capital mobility has advanced. Capitalists in the developed world (in countries relatively rich in capital) have probably benefited from international capital mobility. It might be argued that the developing countries' access to international financial

---

22. Rogowski, *Commerce and Coalitions.*

markets tended to strengthen labor (perhaps by increasing investment in labor-intensive activities), but this seems far from clear-cut.

In fact, while the Heckscher-Ohlin approach may be useful in predicting long-term economic trends, it is probably not a very good way to analyze the distributional effects of international factor movements, for several reasons. First, it is extremely sensitive to the number of factors involved. The predictions are straightforward with two factors, but they become ambiguous at best with more than two. Second, it assumes that capital, labor, and other factors can move costlessly from one activity to another within a country, even if they are internationally immobile. This is certainly untrue, since an automobile factory cannot costlessly be converted into a brewery, nor can a seamstress costlessly become an aerospace engineer. Although factors of production may move from one use to another over the long run, they cannot do so in the short and medium run, which is the time frame more relevant to political analysis. And, third, empirical evidence suggests that political behavior, especially with regard to economic policy, is less commonly factoral (laborers as a class, capitalists as a class) than sectoral (the steel industry, the dairy farming industry).[23]

As useful as the Heckscher-Ohlin approach may be for long-term economic analysis, it is more appropriate to investigate the political economy of international trade and capital movements with an approach which assumes that at least some factors of production are specific to a particular use for at least the short run. In this "specific-factors" model, changes in the relative prices of goods have their principal effect on the sector-specific producers of the goods, rather than on a whole class of factor-owners. Thus, an increase in milk prices is good for dairy farmers rather than landowners as a whole; a decline in clothing prices is bad for owners and workers in the garment industry rather than for capitalists or workers as a class.[24]

23. The classic statement is Stephen Magee's "Three Simple Tests of the Stolper-Samuelson Theorem," in Peter Oppenheimer, ed., *Issues in International Economics* (London: Oriel, 1980), pp. 138–53. In *Commerce and Coalitions,* pp. 16–20, Rogowski addresses these objections and more; needless to say, I am unconvinced by his treatment. Benjamin J. Cohen has pointed out to me that this simple transfer of the Heckscher-Ohlin approach from trade to capital movements ignores the inherent differences between the two realms and especially the importance of expectations in determining asset prices (and therefore capital movements). This may be another reason to avoid a straightforward application of the approach to capital movements.

24. The seminal modern statement is Ronald W. Jones's "A Three-Factor Model in Theory, Trade, and History," in Jagdish Bhagwati et al., eds., *Trade, Balance of Payments, and Growth* (Amsterdam: North-Holland, 1971), pp. 3–21. Two other important articles, which essentially argue for combining specific factors in the short run with the Heckscher-Ohlin approach in the long run, are Wolfgang Mayer's "Short-Run and Long-Run Equilibrium for a Small Open Economy," *Journal of Political Economy* 82 (September 1974), pp. 955–68, and Michael Mussa's "Tariffs and the Distribution of Income: The Importance of Factor Specificity, Substitutability, and Intensity in the Short and Long Run," *Journal of Political Economy* 82 (November 1974), pp. 1191–1204. Based on these two articles, the approach is sometimes known as the Mayer-Mussa framework. For a useful summary and geometric representation of the short-term and long-term adjustment processes, along with a critique of the Heckscher-Ohlin assumption of intersectoral capital mobility, see J. Peter Neary, "Short-Run Capital Specificity and the Pure Theory of International Trade," *The Economic Journal* 88 (September 1978), pp. 488–510.

In the specific-factors approach, which I regard as most useful to the task at hand, the economy is organized into activities (or sectors) to which factors are specific, along with factors that can move freely from activity to activity. The classic setup is an economy in which capital is specific either to the production of clothing or to the production of housing, while labor is an input for both sectors and can move freely from the garment industry to the construction industry. The result, as mentioned above, is that changes in the prices of goods have their principal effects on the specific factors, with collateral (and generally ambiguous) effects on the mobile factor. In the above example, an increase in the relative price of clothing, perhaps due to a tariff, is good for capital in the garment industry and bad for capital in the housing industry; its effect on labor depends on the mix of clothing and housing that workers consume. If, however, the supply (thus, the price) of the mobile factor changes, the interests of the specific factors are opposed to those of the mobile factor. In the above example, if the supply of labor shrinks and wages rise, this is unambiguously good for workers and bad for capital in the garment and construction industries, since the price of their labor input rises.[25]

The application of the specific-factors approach to our problem is straight-forward. I clarify again that with capital mobility I mean the mobility of financial capital rather than sector-specific capital. A secular increase in international capital mobility implies movement of financial assets from capital-rich to capital-poor countries (from low to high interest rates) and therefore an increase in the supply of finance to countries poor in capital and a reduction in the supply of finance to countries rich in capital. Specific factors in capital-poor countries do well, since they can now borrow at lower interest rates; specific factors in capital-rich countries do badly, since they must now pay higher interest rates; and owners of liquid financial assets in capital-rich countries do well, while those in capital-poor countries do badly.

I should note that the distinction made here between capital-rich and capital-poor countries may be somewhat misleading, or at least incomplete. Capital flows in response to differences in rates of return, and interest rates can vary for reasons other than underlying endowments of capital. The United States was a net capital importer in the 1980s not because it had suddenly become capital-poor but, rather, because national savings were insufficient to finance domestic investment; foreign savings were especially needed to help fund the government budget deficit. By the same token, many developing countries became net capital exporters during the 1980s, as they lost access to overseas finance and had to service their existing debts. Countries can import

---

25. In a slight variation on the usual specific-factors or Ricardo-Viner model, the one presented here implies that there are both mobile and specific forms of both labor and capital. The effect of relative price movements and changes in endowments thus depends in part on the potential substitutability of the forms of factors or the factors themselves—for example, substitutability of mobile for specific labor or of mobile labor for mobile capital. For our purposes, it is sufficient to stop with the simpler version. Adding complexity to the model does not fundamentally change the analytic points; it only changes the details of their empirical application.

or export capital for reasons that have little to do with their endowments, especially over the short and medium run. Nonetheless and over the longer run, developed countries tend to be net capital exporters, while developing countries tend to be net capital importers. The point is simply that actual applications require attention to specific national circumstances.

In any case, I believe that the specific-factors model has three important features which make it useful for the analysis of the political economy of international finance. First, it emphasizes the political relevance of short-term fluctuations in the returns to different sorts of economic activity, rather than longer-term changes in the conditions of workers or capitalists as a class. Second, it assumes that most people and investments are "caught" in their current activity to one degree or another. To be sure, some are more caught than others, but there is no recourse to the highly unrealistic assumption common in other models that, for example, automobile workers faced with import penetration will have no trouble finding jobs at the same wage in another industry. Third, it recognizes that some factors may be mobile, while others are specific. For example, it is consonant with the specific-factors approach to assume that unskilled labor is quite mobile among industries, while skilled labor is industry-specific, or to assume that financial capital is mobile among industries, while physical capital is industry-specific. This feature allows for variations in the degree to which people or investments are "stuck" in one place. These three interrelated emphases—on the political significance of the short run, on the relative specificity of most people and investments to their current activity, and on the possibility that some factors are more mobile than others—seem both realistic and analytically useful.

For those unfamiliar with the method, it may be helpful to identify it as a sectoral approach to political economy as opposed to a class-based approach.[26] In the class-based approach, differences among workers are less important than differences between workers and capitalists; the same is held to be true of capitalists and landowners. Politics is competition among these classes, not within them. In the sectoral approach, steelworkers have cross-cutting interests. On the one hand, they are workers, and their interests in the long run are similar to those of other workers. On the other hand, they produce steel, and their interests in the short run are similar to those of managers and shareholders in the steel industry. Politics, in this view, is primarily competition among various sectors of the economy, although long-term class interests sometimes play a role.

The specific-factors or sectoral view of the world tells us a great deal about the distributional implications of capital mobility. As indicated above, as we

---

26. I refer here to those Marxist (and non-Marxist) views that assume labor-capital contradictions to be the principal axis of political conflict. Many other Marxists focus on intraclass differences or blocs; for a good example of relevance to the issue at hand, see Stephen R. Gill and David Law, "Global Hegemony and the Structural Power of Capital," *International Studies Quarterly* 33 (December 1989), pp. 475–99.

move from a BCM to an ACM world, financial capital leaves areas where rates of return are lower and enters areas where they are higher. Interest rates go up in capital-exporting regions and down in capital-importing regions; interest rate variations affect not only owners of financial assets but also borrowers, for whom they are a cost of production. In comparison with the BCM world, in the ACM world things are better for owners of financial assets in capital-exporting countries and for owners of sector-specific assets (capital, skills, and land) in capital-importing countries, and vice versa.

We can also introduce another important set of economic actors: internationally diversified (multinational) corporations. In the specific-factors view of the world, a crucial dimension of variation is the mobility or specificity of an asset, be it an investment, skill, or plot of land. In many ways, the dimension of diversification parallels that of specificity. An investor who holds an asset that can easily be moved from use to use is in a parallel position to an investor whose asset portfolio includes a large number of different economic activities. The most vulnerable position is to hold an asset that is completely specific to one industry; it is analogously vulnerable to have an asset portfolio that includes firms in only one industry.[27] In this sense, firms with operations that are diversified with respect to activity and location can be regarded as less specific and more mobile than firms whose operations are "stuck" in one activity and one place. The preferences of multinational corporations, with operations in many countries facing different conditions, thus parallel the preferences of investors with more mobile assets and diverge from those of nationally and sectorally specific corporations.[28]

A simple "map" of sectoral interests can thus be drawn in line with the specific-factors approach. On this map, increased capital mobility is generally good for financial asset-holders in the developed world and bad for those in the developing world; it is good for multinational corporations; and it is bad for (nonmultinational) specific factors in the developed world and good for those in the developing world.[29]

---

27. The point is not that portfolio diversification is the same as asset mobility but, rather, that the policy implications are parallel. A more sophisticated but somewhat more controversial version of this argument might focus on multinational corporations as combinations of intangible assets within a vertically integrated firm; the relevant literature is surveyed by Martin Perry in "Vertical Integration: Determinants and Effects," in R. Schmalensee and R. D. Willig, eds., *Handbook of Industrial Organization,* vol. 1 (Amsterdam: North-Holland, 1989), pp. 183–255. Inasmuch as such assets can more easily be moved within multinational corporations, this does in fact make the assets of these corporations more geographically mobile than those of other firms in similar industries. See, for example, Daniel M. Shapiro, "Entry, Exit, and the Theory of the Multinational Corporation," in Charles P. Kindleberger and David B. Audretsch, eds., *The Multinational Corporation in the 1980s* (Cambridge, Mass.: MIT Press, 1983), pp. 103–22.

28. For an application of similar ideas to the cases of U.S. and French trade policies in the 1920s and the 1970s, see Milner, *Resisting Protectionism.*

29. It is worth emphasizing again that these conclusions abstract from many specifics that may indeed override them. For example, in the early 1980s, financial asset-holders in many Latin American countries benefited strongly from capital mobility. In the context of political instability and strong and unsustainable currency appreciations, they were able to get their money out of

A few examples indicate the plausibility of this sectoral map. The opening of global financial markets to the less developed countries (LDCs) was good for industries in the Third World, which were suddenly able to borrow at reduced rates of interest. Industrial production in the LDCs grew rapidly as foreign finance flowed in, benefiting owners and managers (and usually workers) in these industries.[30] By the same token, overseas lending from developed countries almost certainly raised the cost of capital to industries at home, contributing to the problems of industrial sectors in Western Europe and North America. More generally, the increased financial integration of the advanced industrialized countries strengthened competitive pressures on specific industries and contributed to the industrial restructuring taking place in them.[31]

In line with the approach, the interests of two groups—the owners and managers of financial assets and the multinational corporations—are opposed to those of the specific factors, so that financial and multinational interests in the developed countries are expected to diverge from the interests of specific nationally based industrial sectors. This would appear a fair generalization from the experience of the 1970s and 1980s. The principal beneficiaries of the broad economic trends of the last two decades have been internationally oriented firms and the financial services industries; the principal losers have been nationally based industrial firms.[32]

These conclusions about the distributional effects of increased financial integration can be turned around to predict expected patterns of political support and opposition to policies that will increase international capital mobility. Perhaps the most obvious policies in this regard concern the removal of barriers to capital movements across borders, but they also include efforts to strengthen organizations that police international financial markets, especially the International Monetary Fund (IMF).

In the developed world, I expect support for increased financial integration from owners and managers of financial assets and from multinational firms with

---

Latin America and to overseas bank accounts. On the process, see Donald Lessard and John Williamson, eds., *Capital Flight and Third World Debt* (Washington, D.C.: Institute for International Economics, 1987). Clearly, other characteristics of these political economies outweighed the tendencies discussed here.

30. For a more detailed argument to this effect, see Jeffry A. Frieden, "Third World Indebted Industrialization: State Capitalism and International Finance in Mexico, Brazil, Algeria, and South Korea," *International Organization* 35 (Summer 1981), pp. 407–31. The degree to which workers and others benefited from the capital inflow would depend, in this framework, on how specific their assets were.

31. For an elaboration of this argument, see Frieden, *Banking on the World*, especially pp. 196–246.

32. Much of this discussion abstracts to an extent from the effects of specific policy episodes, such as those involving the United States in the 1980s. I return to this problem in the following section of the article. My discussion here also does not take into account such significant national variations as different rates of productivity growth on the part of domestically based firms.

internationally diversified investments.[33] I expect opposition to increased financial integration from specific industries, especially those tied to a particular national market. It is my opinion that this accurately, albeit in the broadest terms, describes patterns of political activity on these issues. In the United States, support for financial deregulation, including deregulation of international financial relations, has come primarily from the country's financial centers and its internationally oriented nonfinancial corporations; domestic manufacturing and farm groups have been ambivalent or hostile.[34] By the same token, support for American backing of the IMF has been strongest in these sectors, while again opposition to government commitments to the international financial order have been concentrated in the industrial and agricultural heartlands.[35]

Europe's leading financial and multinational firms have been the stronghold of support for breaking down remaining barriers to EC financial and monetary integration.[36] Although systematic evidence is not available, indications are that the strongest backers of financial deregulation are in the EC's leading financial centers.[37] The chief Japanese promoters of international financial deregulation have been, again, financial and multinational firms. In Japan, the issue is complex, with major battles within the financial community over the contours

33. This must be qualified on the basis of the institutional and industrial structure of the various sectors. For example, in cases in which the domestic financial services industry or subsections of it are local cartels, financial integration may serve to undermine the cartel. Such nuances are of course important, but so broad a sweep as in this article cannot do them justice.

34. See David Dollar and Jeffry Frieden, "The Political Economy of Financial Deregulation in the United States and Japan," in Giacomo Luciani, ed., *Structural Change in the American Financial System* (Rome: Fondazione Olivetti, 1990), pp. 72–102. Again, this generalization ignores specific national policy episodes, such as that involving American capital imports in the 1980s. In my own defense, however, I can note that those involved in political debates over the regulation of international financial flows to and from the United States do appear to have longer-term considerations in mind.

35. For details on the 1983 IMF quota increase debate, see Frieden, *Banking on the World,* pp. 179–90.

36. Again, as mentioned above, this should be qualified with careful attention to national institutional differences. In such countries as Spain and Italy, the national banking system tended to function as a protected cartel, so that the removal of capital controls and financial regulations may have harmed segments of the financial community. The issue is not clear-cut; banks might support the removal of capital controls but oppose the entry of foreign banks, and the stronger local banks might welcome deregulation if this would allow them to begin building relations with banks abroad. This is, of course, a topic on which further research must be done.

37. See Benjamin J. Cohen, "European Financial Integration and National Banking Interests," in Pier Carlo Padoan and Paolo Guerrieri, eds., *The Political Economy of European Integration* (London: Harvester Wheatsheaf, 1989), pp. 145–70. For an interesting perspective on the implications of financial deregulation, see the following works of Vittorio Grilli: "Financial Markets and 1992," *Brookings Papers on Economic Activity,* no. 2, 1989, pp. 301–24; and "Europe 1992: Issues and Prospects for the Financial Markets," *Economic Policy* 9 (October 1989), pp. 388–421. Regarding the important issue of the U.S. response to European and Japanese policies, see Thomas Bayard and Kimberly Ann Elliot, "Reciprocity in Financial Services: The Schumer Amendment and the Second Banking Directive," mimeograph, 1990.

of the regulatory changes. Nonetheless, the general patterns appear consonant with the approach set forth here.[38]

To summarize this section, the distributional effects of increased cross-border capital mobility can be striking. In a general and long-term sense, it may be that international financial integration increases the influence of capital by making it easier for owners of financial assets to take them abroad in response to national policies they do not like. The more immediate results in the developed world have been to drive a wedge between two camps, the first consisting of the financial sector, owners of financial assets, and integrated multinational firms, all of which have gained with financial integration, and the second consisting of firms specific to a particular industry and location, all of which have been harmed by the generally increased competition for scarce loanable funds. The clear prediction is for conflict between these "integrationist" forces and "anti-integrationist" forces. But political debate has not been and will not be restricted to policies directly concerned with increasing or retarding international capital mobility, and it is to the distributional and political implications of financial integration itself for these other debates that we now turn.

The distributional effects of economic policies in a financially integrated world

While the political divisions likely to emerge over the desired degree of international financial integration are important, the general increase in international capital mobility is also likely to change interest group activity on a wide range of other economic policy problems. Global financial integration has already shifted much political activity directly or indirectly toward the exchange rate in ways that imply new socioeconomic and political divisions. It raises problems of international policy cooperation that may be too new to analyze in detail. And, in some ways, financial integration may have an impact on the strength of sectoral lobbying. This section surveys these expected effects. Again, the problem here is not to do with the level of financial integration itself; I take as given a high level of international capital mobility in order to see how this level affects political behavior and policy in other realms.

38. Two excellent studies are Louis W. Pauly's *Opening Financial Markets: Banking Politics on the Pacific Rim* (Ithaca, N.Y.: Cornell University Press, 1988) and Frances McCall Rosenbluth's *Financial Politics in Contemporary Japan* (Ithaca, N.Y.: Cornell University Press, 1989). In Japan, as in some European nations, members of the banking community were reluctant to see international competition threaten their domestic cartel, but the rapid globalization of financial markets appears to have led them to regard deregulation as the better of two evils. For a more detailed elaboration of this argument, see Dollar and Frieden, "The Political Economy of Financial Deregulation in the United States and Japan." For an argument that is complementary in many ways to the one presented here, see John Goodman and Louis Pauly, "The New Politics of International Capital Mobility," mimeograph, Harvard University Business School and University of Toronto, 1990.

One preliminary observation has to do with the potential effects of increased international capital mobility on the intensity of sectoral interests of owners of capital. The starting point is that the more specific the asset is to its current use—that is, the more substantial is the cost attached to moving the asset from its current use to its best alternative use—the more incentive the owner of the asset will have to lobby for supportive government policies.[39] Agents in a sector to which exit and entry are costless have little or no incentive to spend time, energy, and money to get government support, since this support will be dissipated by new entrants into the sector.

To pick up from the previous discussion of the effects of financial capital mobility on sectoral policies, inasmuch as global financial integration makes it easier for investors to get into or out of a particular sector, it reduces the incentive for sectoral lobbying. Although there is little evidence that this effect has been large, it is theoretically plausible. An integrated worldwide financial market of enormous size, compared with many segmented national markets, might indeed allow for the development of instruments and mechanisms that would facilitate the redeployment of capital from one use to another. These could include broader and deeper futures markets and insurance schemes, better information to potential borrowers and lenders, and more readily available venture finance.[40]

If indeed international financial integration does reduce barriers to entry and exit of investors to and from specific economic activities, it could reduce the sectoral orientation of lobbying by investors.[41] If financial integration makes it easier for firms to exit and enter many different sectors, their attachment to a particular sector may be reduced. Inasmuch as this takes place, we might

39. There are a number of ways of thinking about this. In one, the result obtains because difficulty of exit from a sector constitutes a barrier to entry to it: the knowledge that investment in the sector contains an important irreversible component will reduce the likelihood of new investors entering in response to relative price changes that may not be permanent. In this sense, barriers to exit *are* barriers to entry; since entry barriers increase the effectiveness of sector-specific policies in aiding existing agents in the sector, they increase the returns to political lobbying.

40. Possibilities such as these tend to imply imperfect competition—increasing returns and learning-by-doing—in the financial sector, which is almost certainly the case. For a representative theoretical approach along these lines, see Stephen D. Williamson, "Increasing Returns to Scale in Financial Intermediation and the Non-Neutrality of Government Policy," *Review of Economic Studies* 53 (October 1986), pp. 863–75.

41. This is just a restatement of the general notion that the capital markets and political lobbying are in some sense substitutes (albeit imperfect ones). This idea sounds absurd to most political scientists, but perform the following thought experiment: if import-competing automobile manufacturers could sell all of their equipment to the Japanese at a price that would allow them to make a market profit, their incentive to engage in costly and time-consuming lobbying for protection would be much lower. Or, alternatively, if autoworkers could in some way sell their skills and their seniority to Japanese autoworkers for an amount equal to what they might have hoped to earn with these skills and seniority, their incentive to lobby would be lower. The fact that markets for these assets are incomplete or nonexistent simply serves to point out that the politicization of the issue is expected. While there are not markets for these assets, there are good markets for other assets—and we expect owners of such assets to be less politically active.

expect more political action by owners of capital as a class and less participation of capitalists in sectoral lobbying.

However, as argued above, even if this trend exists, it is embryonic and its impact has yet to be felt: the sector specificity of capital has not been measurably reduced by international financial integration. The most prominent effect of increased capital mobility is not on the level of sectoral lobbying but, rather, on the character of sectoral lobbying and the policy preferences arising when the sectors are thrown together in pursuit of government support.

The impact of capital mobility on the expected political lineup over macroeconomic policy is in fact striking. Two interrelated dimensions of policy choice are especially important: the degree of exchange rate flexibility and the level of the exchange rate itself. With regard to the first dimension, the Mundell-Fleming conditions serve as a point of reference.[42] Recall that, with capital mobility, a country faces something of a trade-off between exchange rate stability and monetary policy autonomy: the more the country's exchange rate is held constant, the less its monetary policy can deviate from that of the rest of the world. While some actors will favor a low degree of exchange rate flexibility (a fixed rate such as the gold standard) despite the loss of monetary policy autonomy, others will be willing to accept a high degree of exchange rate flexibility (freely floating rates) in exchange for policymaking autonomy. With regard to the second dimension, which is the preferred level of the exchange rate itself, some fixing of exchange rates is assumed. While some actors will prefer a high (more appreciated) exchange rate, others will prefer a low (more depreciated) exchange rate. The two dimensions and the expected policy preferences of socioeconomic actors along them are presented in Figure 1 and discussed in detail below. We should keep in mind that the figure provides only rough approximations; variation is, of course, along a continuum rather than dichotomous.

The first dimension involves the desired degree of exchange rate flexibility, which can be presented most starkly as whether the rate should be fixed or flexible. Fixing the rate in a world of mobile capital implies forgoing national monetary policy autonomy in favor of greater certainty about the value of the currency; in other words, it gives priority to a stable exchange rate over the ability of national policy to affect domestic prices. This is especially attractive to two groups of actors whose economic activities directly involve international trade and payments and who therefore are highly sensitive to currency fluctuations. International traders and investors and the producers of export-oriented tradable goods tend to suffer from exchange market volatility, since it

---

42. Some complications may result from this melding of the Mundell-Fleming and specific-factors models. The Mundell-Fleming model generally assumes some unutilized resources and some wage stickiness, while the specific-factors model does not. The contradiction may be relevant for the analysis of effects on national welfare, but it does not appear to matter much for the short- and medium-term distributional effects, which are the focus here. For a discussion, see Corden, *Inflation, Exchange Rates, and the World Economy*, pp. 22–34.

Preferred degree of exchange rate flexibility
and national monetary policy autonomy

		High	Low
Preferred level of the exchange rate	*Low*	Import-competing producers of tradable goods for the domestic market	Export-oriented producers of tradable goods
	High	Producers of nontradable goods and services	International traders and investors

FIGURE 1. *Synopsis of the policy preferences of various socioeconomic actors in a world of mobile capital*

makes their business riskier.[43] By the same token, these actors are relatively unconcerned about domestic macroeconomic conditions, since they can respond to depressed local demand by shifting their business to other countries.

In contrast, two other groups of actors tend to be highly concerned about domestic macroeconomic conditions and thus favor the national monetary policy autonomy made possible by a flexible exchange rate. The first of these groups consists of producers of nontradable goods and services. Since their business does not involve the use of foreign exchange and since currency volatility has only indirect effects at best on them, they tend to have no clear preference for stable exchange rates.[44] The second group consists of producers of import-competing tradable goods for the domestic market, who tend to be relatively indifferent about exchange rate volatility (which may even reduce import pressure inasmuch as it makes importing riskier) and primarily concerned about policymaking autonomy.

The preferences of the various groups are relevant, most prominently, to policy debates about stabilizing exchange rates. Based on the above arguments,

43. There are exceptions: producers of tradable goods in which competition is not primarily on price (and is instead, for example, on quality) will be less sensitive to exchange rate movements.
44. Inasmuch as a devaluation changes the price of tradable goods relative to that of nontradable goods, it affects producers in the nontradables sector. However, such price volatility affects all national nontradables producers more or less equally and is therefore far less significant to them than it is to tradables producers, who see their output change in price relative to that of their competitors.

we can expect multinational firms, international investors more generally, and internationally oriented producers of tradable goods to be more sympathetic to currency stability, while we can expect producers in the nontradables sector and producers of import-competing tradable goods to be most interested in national monetary policy autonomy.

In policy debates about the level of the exchange rate, which is the second dimension noted in Figure 1, we can expect the interests of various economic sectors to track the relative price changes involved in depreciation or appreciation of the currency. From a differential distributional standpoint, the lower (more depreciated) the exchange rate, the higher is the price of tradable goods relative to nontradable goods. This, of course, tends to help producers of tradable goods—whose output prices rise more than the prices of the nontradable inputs they use—and to hurt producers of nontradable goods. Producers in the tradables sector therefore favor a weaker currency that makes their products more competitive in home and foreign markets. In contrast, producers in the nontradables sector generally benefit from currency appreciation, which raises the domestic relative price of their products and lowers the domestic relative price of tradable goods.[45] Similarly, international traders and investors, who are interested in purchasing assets overseas, favor a strong currency.[46]

---

45. For those unfamiliar with the approach, the real exchange rate can be expressed as the relationship between the price of nontradable goods and that of tradable goods. By assumption, the price of tradables is set on world markets and cannot be changed (in foreign currency terms) by national policy. In other words, the foreign currency price of tradables is an anchor around which domestic prices move. Depreciation makes tradables relatively more expensive in domestic currency terms, while nontradables become relatively cheaper. Appreciation has the opposite effects. In the real world, these effects can be offset, for example by characteristics of product markets, but there is little doubt that the general pattern holds. When the dollar was strong, the dollar prices of television sets and clothing were low, while the price of housing soared. As the dollar fell, the dollar price of hard goods rose, while the price of housing stagnated or declined. Despite some controversy about the approach, it is close enough to consensual to warrant its use.

One important consideration to keep in mind is the extent to which the relative price effect (say of an appreciation on raising demand for nontradable goods) may be counteracted by the macroeconomic effect (say of reduced aggregate demand more generally); this is, so to speak, the contest between the income and substitution effects or between expenditure reduction and expenditure switching. For a useful survey and application to the LDCs, see Sebastian Edwards, *Real Exchange Rates, Devaluation and Adjustment* (Cambridge, Mass.: MIT Press, 1989). For more technical essays, see John Bilson and Richard Marston, eds., *Exchange Rate Theory and Practice* (Chicago: University of Chicago Press, 1984). Another point to keep in mind is that the nontradable goods and services sector includes those who operate behind prohibitive barriers to trade (especially quotas).

46. Of course, from the standpoint of an overseas investor, the desire for a strong home currency to allow greater purchases of overseas assets is balanced by the desire to maximize home currency earnings from these assets, which demands a weak home currency. The best possible scenario, as usual, is to buy cheap and sell dear—that is, to buy foreign currency when the home currency is strong and sell it when the home currency is weak. There are a number of defensible theoretical reasons why international investors might favor strong home currencies; it is probably enough to note here that empirically they tend to do so. On the relationship between foreign direct investment and the exchange rate, see Steven W. Kohlhagen, "Exchange Rate Changes, Profitability, and Direct Foreign Investment," *Southern Economic Journal* 44 (July 1977), pp. 43–52.

Preliminary evidence seems to bear out these expectations both on the dimension of exchange rate flexibility and on that of the level of the exchange rate itself.[47] Perhaps the arena in which the choice between monetary policy autonomy and currency stability has been posed most directly is in the development of the exchange rate mechanism of the European Monetary System (EMS) and the subsequent movement toward a single EC currency.[48]

The above discussion has systematic predictions about private-sector attitudes toward the exchange rate mechanism (ERM) of the EMS.[49] I expect the ERM to be most favorable for, and to evince the most enthusiasm from, firms in the financial sector, major exporters, and diversified multinational corporations with major investments or customers in the EC. Evidence is scanty, but some can be presented. One study of potential British winners and losers from Britain's affiliation with the ERM essentially tracks my expectations. Internationally oriented manufacturing and finance and related services were expected to do well, while the domestically oriented manufacturing and services sectors were expected to be weaker.[50] Of Britain's twelve corporate members in the Association for Monetary Union in Europe, a private-sector lobbying organiza-

47. Practically the only systematic empirical study on these issues in recent years is I. M. Destler and C. Randall Henning's *Dollar Politics: Exchange Rate Policymaking in the United States* (Washington, D.C.: Institute for International Economics, 1989), which appears to bear out some of these observations. The issue is somewhat clouded by the difficulty, which Destler and Henning recognize, of separating debates over the level of the exchange rate from debates over its volatility; in the early 1980s in the United States, the former tended to dominate the latter. The authors note that international financial institutions benefit from exchange market volatility, which can make their trading desks extremely profitable. However, they should—and many do—weigh this benefit against the cost of international business foregone because of uncertainty about currency values. At least some portion of the international business of American money-center banks is due to the widespread belief in the reliability of the dollar and the American macroeconomic environment more generally.

48. The literature on the EMS is now enormous, and almost all of it is purely economic in content. For an excellent survey along these lines, see Francesco Giavazzi and Alberto Giovannini, *Limiting Exchange Rate Flexibility: The European Monetary System* (Cambridge, Mass.: MIT Press, 1989). For a good study that discusses many of the domestic and international political aspects of the EMS, see Peter Ludlow, *The Making of the European Monetary System* (London: Butterworth, 1982); unfortunately, events have moved far beyond what Ludlow described in 1982.

49. I avoid three issues that are more closely associated with a single currency per se: the potential welfare costs of reduced seignorage opportunities, the welfare gains associated with reduced transactions costs, and the potentially differential impact of these reduced transactions costs on various economic agents. I focus entirely on the more immediate issue of the differential effects of fixed but adjustable exchange rates within the EMS. For a discussion of some of these other issues, see Barry Eichengreen, "One Money for Europe?" *Economic Policy* 5 (April 1990), pp. 118–87.

50. See S. G. Warburg Securities, *Into the ERM: The Outlook for the UK Economy and Equity Market,* London, August 1990. A summary table is on p. 31, but more useful sectoral summaries are on pp. 32–52. The projections are complicated a bit (for our purposes) by the study's conflation of greater exchange rate stability with a firmer pound sterling, both of which it expects to ensue but which may operate in slightly different directions distributionally, as I discuss below. The study also notes that while 45 percent of profits from firms in the *Financial Times* stock exchange index are from overseas activities (exports and profits of foreign affiliates), only 13 percent come from the EC and 17 percent from North America. This may help explain some of the British reluctance to tie sterling to the ERM, especially at a time when the European currencies were appreciating strongly against the dollar.

tion for rapid currency union, eight are from firms in the financial and related services sectors, two are from diversified multinational corporations, and two are major exporters.[51] In the absence of systematic empirical work, few serious assessments can be made, but the patterns are suggestive.[52]

The second dimension, the level of the exchange rate, is a familiar topic of debate in many countries, especially those for which international trade is very important and those which have a history of exchange rate volatility (characteristics that apply primarily to developing and small developed countries). Political conflict over the exchange rate has become important in larger nations as well. One striking example is the United States, where between 1981 and 1986 much of the political activity that might otherwise have taken the form of pressure for trade protection instead focused on trying to get the authorities or other actors to force the dollar to depreciate relative to the currencies of the country's major trading partners.[53] The evidence, especially from the United States in the 1980s, appears consonant with the expectations presented above.[54]

These varying exchange rate preferences in turn affect preferences toward different macroeconomic policies. With capital mobility, an expansionary monetary policy leads to depreciation of the currency, while an expansionary fiscal policy leads to appreciation. Producers of tradable goods should thus prefer monetary expansion, and producers of nontradable goods and services should prefer fiscal expansion. This will especially be the case if the fiscal expansion takes the form of a direct or indirect increase in spending on nontradable goods, which is quite likely where government spending is involved (defense, infrastructure, and social spending are generally nontradable). This may help explain the peculiar pattern of U.S. economic policy during the Reagan years. With the administration's principal bases of support in the defense community, in real estate and related sectors, and in the international investors group, pressures were for increased spending on nontradables. The resultant appreciation might have been countered by monetary expansion, as was in fact demanded by the tradable goods producers hurt by the import surge, but the nontradables constituencies wanted it reinforced by tight money, not dissipated. In other words, the mix of loose fiscal and tight monetary policies may have been less a mistake, as most economists and observers

---

51. The twelve corporate members are Barclays, British Aerospace, British American Tobacco, British Petroleum, Citibank, Ernst and Young, Goldman Sachs, Imperial Chemical Industries, Midland Montagu, Salomon International, Shearson Brothers, and S. G. Warburg. The Association of Corporate Treasurers is also a member.

52. For an evaluation of many of these developments, see Jeffrey Frankel, "The Making of Exchange Rate Policy in the 1980s," mimeograph, University of California at Berkeley, 1990. Again, the political economy component of Frankel's discussion focuses, as did most of the debates, on the level of the exchange rate rather than on its volatility.

53. In *Dollar Politics,* pp. 17–80, Destler and Henning provide an excellent interpretive survey of the course of dollar politics and policies over the 1980s.

54. For descriptions of the interplay of the various interest groups, see Destler and Henning, *Dollar Politics;* Frankel, "The Making of Exchange Rate Policy in the 1980s"; and C. Randall Henning, "International Monetary Policymaking Within the Countries of the Group of Five," mimeograph, 1990.

concluded at the time, than it was a reflection of the dominance of political pressures from nontradable goods producers and other supporters of a strong dollar over tradable goods producers who wanted a weaker dollar.

Another issue that has gained in importance in a world of great capital mobility is international policy coordination. Because financial integration can make it difficult for national authorities to pursue macroeconomic policies that differ from those of their financial "neighbors," it may make sense to coordinate such policies. This would, for example, avoid competitive currency depreciations, in which a country pursuing an expansionary monetary policy and thus currency depreciation against its trading partners finds itself foiled as its partners match the monetary expansion and depreciation, leaving the currencies' relative levels unchanged. Alternatively, countries trying to prevent their currencies from depreciating might unnecessarily bid up interest rates in a competitive attempt to avoid a capital outflow. The obvious solution to such problems is for the relevant policymakers to cooperate in targeting exchange rates and other macroeconomic indicators.[55]

There are many potential problems with international macroeconomic policy coordination. Some believe that such government intervention is less desirable than letting the markets take their course; others believe that the difficulties of coordination are nearly insurmountable.[56] Among the coordination problems is that slight divergences in views among national policymakers may make welfare-improving cooperation extremely difficult.[57] It is indeed likely that the domestic political underpinnings of the potential cooperating governments will differ, leading to different preferences or interpretations about the gains from cooperation and how they might best be achieved.

In this light, once again the differential domestic distributional effects of such policy coordination are relevant. Not surprisingly, I expect those whose economic activities are most sensitive to foreign financial and exchange market conditions to be most favorable to the sacrifice of national policy autonomy implied by policy coordination. International investors, traders, and the like are apt to be well disposed, while those in the nontradables sector—whose businesses may be harmed by the sacrifice of autonomy with little or no corresponding benefit from coordination—are prone to be opposed. A related set of issues has to do with the coordination of other national policies, such as

---

55. One influential and controversial proposal was offered by John Williamson and Marcus Miller in *Targets and Indicators: A Blueprint for the International Coordination of Economic Policy* (Washington, D.C.: Institute for International Economics, 1987).

56. For some representative surveys of this rapidly growing literature, see Martin Feldstein, ed., *International Policy Coordination* (Chicago: University of Chicago Press, 1988); and Jeffrey Frankel, *Obstacles to International Macroeconomic Policy Coordination,* Princeton Studies in International Finance no. 64 (Princeton, N.J.: Department of Economics, International Finance Section, 1988).

57. For a demonstration of this point, see Jeffrey Frankel and Katharine Rockett, "International Macroeconomic Policy Coordination When Policy-Makers Do Not Agree on the True Model," *American Economic Review* 78 (June 1988), pp. 318–40. The argument is controversial; among other things, it assumes that policymakers try to maximize national welfare, ignores the potential costs of not cooperating (or not appearing to cooperate), and makes it difficult to explain circumstances in which coordination has apparently been achieved.

taxation.[58] On this subject, there is so little analytic work and indeed so little experience in the real world that coordination is mostly speculation. However, both the trends within the EC and the discussions among other developed countries indicate that it will likely be a topic of great importance in the 1990s.

These observations have to do with the interests in play, not necessarily with the outcome of political conflict among them. Political and policy outcomes will of course depend on how intense preferences are, how concentrated and organized the various interests are, and how political and other social institutions influence their interaction. How successful the various interest groups will be at obtaining their objectives will vary from case to case and from country to country. Nonetheless, a clear understanding of the economic interests involved is a crucial starting point for analysis.

This section can be summarized quite simply. Financial integration has implications for the distributional effects—and therefore the politics—of national policies. Over the long run, access to broader and deeper financial markets may tend to reduce the sectoral specificity of capital and thereby dampen some sectoral demands—but this gradual process is unlikely ever to *eliminate* such demands. The more immediate implication is that political lineups over macroeconomic policies are likely to change quite significantly.

A trade-off between national macroeconomic policy autonomy and exchange rate stability has developed, with international investors and traders more willing to give up autonomy for stability and with the nontradables and domestically oriented sectors more interested in autonomy than in fluctuations in the exchange rate. Conflict has intensified not only over the flexibility but also over the level of the exchange rate. While support for monetary expansion and depreciation has tended to come from producers of tradable goods, support for monetary contraction and appreciation has come from international investors and producers of nontradable goods and services. At the same time, the coordination of national macroeconomic policies has become an important political problem at both the international and the domestic level. Not surprisingly, those for whom overseas economic conditions are more relevant (international investors and traders and producers of tradable goods) will favor more coordinated policies—and thus a surrender of more national policy autonomy—than will those for whom domestic conditions are determinant.

Conclusions

Without repeating the points made in the article, I can emphasize a few conclusions. Hampered as national governments may be or appear to be in the

---

58. See, for example, Alberto Giovannini, "National Tax Systems Versus the European Capital Market," *Economic Policy* 9 (October 1989), pp. 346–86.

face of an internationally integrated financial system, they continue to have weapons in their policy arsenal. These weapons may not be as sharp or numerous as before, but they exist. Many sectoral policies can be effective, as can macroeconomic policies if policymakers allow the exchange rate to vary.

However, the distributional implications of international capital mobility are striking. In the long run, owners of capital have probably gained relative to other groups. In the shorter run, owners and workers in specific sectors in the developed world face serious costs in adjusting to increased capital mobility.

International capital mobility also changes the pattern of lobbying over national policies. It may, over the long run, dampen some sectoral demands from owners of capital. More specifically, and in the shorter run, it tends to shift debate toward the exchange rate as an intermediate or ultimate policy instrument, thereby driving a wedge between those more sensitive and those less sensitive to exchange rate fluctuations and between those who favor currency appreciation and those who favor depreciation. To some extent, this tracks a division of the economy between producers of tradable goods on the one hand and international investors and producers of nontradable goods and services on the other.

This article sets forth a series of propositions that can be brought to bear on a wide variety of problems having to do with the politics of the international movement of capital. Such problems, it is safe to project, will be of great analytic and policy importance in years to come. The possibility for the empirical evaluation of the approach presented here and for further theoretical and empirical elaboration is clear. As we approach 1992 and as parallel developments evolve elsewhere in the world, the opportunity for and necessity of such work will be enormous, and a better understanding of what is at stake will be of great importance.

International economic structures, government interests, and international coordination of macroeconomic adjustment policies
Michael C. Webb

One of the most dramatic changes in the structure of the international economy in recent decades has been the rapid growth of international capital markets. This article examines the impact of international capital market integration on patterns of international coordination in a key area of interest to governments: macroeconomic adjustment policies. These are policies that governments can use to reconcile national macroeconomic objectives with international market pressures; they include trade and capital controls, exchange rate policies, balance-of-payments financing, and monetary and fiscal policies.

The article focuses on changes in patterns of coordination of these types of policy between the 1960s and the 1980s. It identifies a shift away from coordination of balance-of-payments financing and other policies intended to *manage* international payments imbalances caused by incompatible national macroeconomic policies and a concurrent shift toward coordination of monetary and fiscal policies themselves. This change, it argues, was a consequence of the tremendous increase in capital mobility that occurred between the mid-1960s and the early 1980s. If national economies are insulated from one another by weak market linkages and government controls, as they were in the late 1950s and the 1960s, the international payments imbalances generated by unilateral fiscal and monetary policymaking are small enough to be managed without sacrificing macroeconomic policymaking autonomy itself. But if capital is internationally mobile, as it was by the late 1970s, the payments imbalances that emerge when different countries pursue different macroeconomic policies

Earlier versions of this article were presented at the 1990 annual meetings of the Canadian Political Science Association in Victoria, B.C., and the American Political Science Association in San Francisco. I am grateful to the Social Sciences and Humanities Research Council of Canada, the Eisenhower World Affairs Institute, and the MacArthur Foundation for funding of the research. I also thank Steve Krasner, Judy Goldstein, Mark Zacher, Jan Thomson, Jeffry Frieden, Geoffrey Garrett, Alexander George, Michael Hawes, Keisuke Iida, and the reviewers of *International Organization* for their criticisms and suggestions.

International Organization 45, 3, Summer 1991, pp. 309–42

are too large to be ignored or managed; governments can reduce payments imbalances and stabilize their external economic positions only by coordinating their monetary and fiscal policies.

On both empirical and theoretical grounds, this argument contrasts with the conventional international political economy view of the evolution of international monetary relations[1] over the past three decades. Most analysts argue that monetary relations in the 1950s and 1960s were characterized by more extensive international policy coordination than they were in the 1970s and 1980s and that the reduced coordination made international economic conditions much less stable in the more recent decades. The key factor, from their perspective, was the change from a system of fixed exchange rates in the 1960s to a system of flexible exchange rates in the 1970s and 1980s. This change, they assert, lessened the constraints on national macroeconomic policymaking autonomy. Furthermore, in explaining the posited decline in policy coordination and the greater economic instability of the 1970s and 1980s, many contributors to the literature point to declining American hegemony. This argument can be found in realist, liberal institutionalist, and neo-Marxist analyses of international economic policy coordination.[2]

The analysis of the record of international coordination of macroeconomic adjustment policy undertaken in this article suggests that coordination was at least as extensive in the late 1970s and the 1980s as it was in the late 1950s and the 1960s[3] but that the types of policy subject to coordination did change. International coordination in the 1960s focused on balance-of-payments financing and exchange rate coordination—policies that are inherently international. Coordination of monetary and fiscal policies was negligible; policymaking was unilateral. Governments maintained fixed exchange rates in the 1960s

---

1. The subject area on which this article focuses is often labeled international monetary relations; the term "international macroeconomic adjustment policies" is preferable because it captures the wide range of nonmonetary policies that can also be used to reconcile national macroeconomic objectives with international market constraints.

2. For examples of realist analyses, see Robert Gilpin, *U.S. Power and the Multinational Corporation: The Political Economy of Foreign Direct Investment* (New York: Basic Books, 1975); and Stephen D. Krasner, "State Power and the Structure of International Trade," *World Politics* 28 (April 1976), pp. 317–43. For a critique and prominent examples of liberal institutionalist analyses, see Joseph M. Grieco, "Anarchy and the Limits of Cooperation: A Realist Critique of the Newest Liberal Institutionalism," *International Organization* 42 (Summer 1988), pp. 485–507; Charles P. Kindleberger, "Dominance and Leadership in the International Economy: Exploitation, Public Goods, and Free Rides," *International Studies Quarterly* 25 (June 1981), pp. 242–54; and Robert O. Keohane, *After Hegemony: Cooperation and Discord in the World Political Economy* (Princeton, N.J.: Princeton University Press, 1984). Kindleberger argued that American hegemony was a *substitute* for international coordination. Keohane argued that American hegemony *facilitated* coordination, although coordination was also possible when the distribution of international power was oligarchic. For examples of neo-Marxist analyses, see Robert W. Cox, *Power, Production, and World Order: Social Forces in the Making of History* (New York: Columbia University Press, 1987); and Fred L. Block, *The Origins of International Economic Disorder: A Study of United States International Monetary Policy from World War II to the Present* (Berkeley: University of California Press, 1977).

3. Throughout the article, these periods are labeled "the 1980s" and "the 1960s," respectively.

because low capital mobility and limited trade flows (in contrast to the 1980s) meant that these rates could be maintained without seriously constraining national macroeconomic policymaking autonomy. The fixed exchange rate system was abandoned in the early 1970s, when increasing capital mobility made it impossible for governments to stabilize exchange rates without subordinating monetary policy to that end.[4] Thereafter, coordination efforts began to focus on monetary and fiscal policies—policies that had traditionally been considered "internal."

Although international economic instability was much greater in the 1980s than in the 1960s, this was less a consequence of the posited erosion of American hegemony that it was of the increasing international integration of capital markets. As capital became more mobile, international economic policy coordination had to become more extensive simply to maintain the level of stability achieved in the 1960s. On the one hand, coordination efforts in the 1980s faced substantial obstacles and as a result were insufficient to maintain or improve the level of economic stability. On the other hand, there was no decline in the overall level of coordination of macroeconomic adjustment policies. The only change was the above-mentioned shift in the types of policy coordinated at the international level. Theories of declining American hegemony do not explain why the types of policy subject to coordination might change, nor are the findings based on these theories consistent with the observed overall pattern of international coordination. While it is not the purpose of this article to reformulate hegemonic stability theories, the concluding section will suggest some possible reasons for the inconsistencies.

The remainder of this article is divided into three sections. The first section describes how the structure of the international economy affects the strategies available to governments in their efforts to deal with international imbalances and argues that changes in structural conditions result in changes in the advantages and disadvantages of pursuing given types of policy. The second section examines the record of policy coordination in the 1960s and 1980s. The analysis shows that the model developed in the earlier section does help explain patterns of international coordination. But it also reveals the limits of the economic-structural argument by identifying other factors (especially domestic political variables) that consistently affect how states react to the incentives generated by the international environment in different periods. The final section summarizes the findings and discusses some of their broader implications for the study of the international political economy.

Throughout the article, "international coordination" is defined as a process involving both negotiation and mutual policy adjustment on the part of various

---

4. Thus, the shift from fixed to flexible exchange rates can be explained by the argument of this article; it is not an exogenous variable. For a detailed discussion of the issue, see Michael C. Webb, "International Coordination of Macroeconomic Adjustment Policies, 1945–1989," Ph.D. diss., Stanford University, Stanford, Calif., 1990, chaps. 7 and 8.

governments.[5] In determining whether policies were coordinated, this definition directs us to look for evidence that national policies were different as a result of an international agreement (either formal or informal) than they would have otherwise been.

The usage of the term "structure" in this article differs from that found in the mainstream international relations theory. Neorealist theory defines the international structure in terms of political anarchy (the absence of an authority to resolve disputes among sovereign states) and the distribution of power among states.[6] The argument of this article points to the inadequacy of the neorealist definition.[7] The distribution of power alone cannot explain patterns of macroeconomic policy coordination, an area central to the concerns of governments; we also need to look at characteristics of the international economy that persist over time and systematically influence how governments relate to each other. As described in detail below, all of the governments included within the scope of this study (namely, the governments of advanced capitalist countries) responded in a similar, though not identical, fashion to changes in international capital mobility. According to Kenneth Waltz, if different states act similarly in response to similar phenomena, we are justified in thinking that there may be some kind of structural effect at work.[8]

Other factors also justify considering international capital mobility as a structural element. The current structure of the international economic system (characterized by openness to trade and capital flows) was created in part by the actions of the units, as individual states took decisions that permitted open international capital markets to emerge.[9] Specifically, capital market integra-

5. This definition closely resembles Keohane's definition of cooperation in *After Hegemony*, pp. 51–52. I have used the term "coordination" because "cooperation" is often used more broadly in the literature on international monetary relations to include information sharing, international consultations, and other processes that do not involve negotiated policy adjustments. The definition presented here differs from Wallich's frequently cited definition of coordination as "a significant modification of national policies in recognition of international economic interdependence." See Henry C. Wallich, "Institutional Cooperation in the World Economy," in Jacob A. Frenkel and Michael L. Mussa, eds., *The World Economic System: Performance and Prospects* (Doyer, Mass.: Auburn House Publishing, 1984), p. 85. Wallich's definition is inappropriate for the purposes of this article because it does not distinguish independent policymaking that takes international factors into account from internationally negotiated adjustments to national policy. As Wallich's article makes clear, his definition also includes a normative bias, favoring (and labeling as coordination) policies that accept the desirability and legitimacy of making national policy conform to international market pressures. This would exclude, for example, mutual policy adjustments by governments seeking to prevent market forces from undermining their abilities to achieve their objectives.

6. See Kenneth N. Waltz, *Theory of International Politics* (Reading, Mass.: Addison-Wesley Publishing Company, 1979).

7. For a more fundamental challenge, see John Gerard Ruggie, "Continuity and Transformation in the World Polity: Toward a Neorealist Synthesis," *World Politics* 35 (January 1983), pp. 261–85.

8. Waltz, *Theory of International Politics*, pp. 69–73.

9. For a theoretical discussion of the meaning of structure and its relationship to the actions of individual units, see Alexander E. Wendt, "The Agent-Structure Problem in International

tion was an unintended consequence of state decisions to liberalize trade in a technological environment that made large-scale, short-term capital flows economically possible. Logically, therefore, governments could change the structure of the international economic system to eliminate the constraint that international capital mobility imposes on national macroeconomic policymaking autonomy. However, it would be both difficult and costly for any individual government, including that of the United States, to reverse the process. Short of a severe depression (which is made less likely by the policy coordination that capital market integration has encouraged) or large-scale international conflict, governments of the advanced capitalist countries are unlikely to block international capital mobility. This mobility has persisted over time, even through the worst world recession since the 1930s, and is likely to continue to persist. We are therefore justified in considering it an element of the international economic structure and studying the effects of this structure on the policies of individual governments.

Economic structures and incentives for international policy coordination

The purpose of an economic-structural approach to the international politics of macroeconomic adjustment is to help us understand some key incentives that governments face when choosing among alternative patterns of international coordination of macroeconomic adjustment policies.[10] We can begin with the simple assumption that the primary objective of macroeconomic policy in all countries is to achieve favorable macroeconomic conditions. In practice, governments want to achieve some combination of low inflation, low unemployment, and economic growth. Governments seek favorable economic conditions because severe economic problems hurt their reelection prospects and at worst could bring a return to the political and social instability experienced in the 1920s and 1930s.

The pursuit of favorable domestic economic conditions can lead different governments to choose different macroeconomic policies. Domestic political circumstances vary greatly, and this influences the policy choice. For example, conservative governments may put greater emphasis on keeping interest rates high to prevent inflation or maintain the value of capital, while left-wing

---

Relations Theory," *International Organization* 41 (Summer 1987), pp. 335–70. In this article, I focus more on the impact of structure on the units or agents (governments, in this case) than on the impact of government actions on the structure.

10. This kind of approach makes certain standard assumptions about the ability of governments to recognize and respond rationally to structural stimuli. As discussed in a subsequent section of this article, these assumptions often are not met in practice. Nevertheless, governments do appear to respond to the incentives identified in this section often enough to make this a good starting point for understanding patterns of international coordination.

governments may put a higher priority on maintaining full employment. In addition, economic problems also vary across countries at any one point in time, encouraging different countries to address different problems and thereby pursue different policies.

When different countries pursue different macroeconomic policies, it is likely that external payments imbalances, exchange rate movements, or both will result. A number of different types of policy could be used to reconcile national macroeconomic objectives with international constraints imposed by the resulting payments imbalances or exchange rate movements.[11] In this article, these will be labeled "international macroeconomic adjustment policies." Three categories of policy are relevant:

(1) *External policies.* Governments could seek to eliminate payments imbalances by manipulating trade and capital controls. Deficit countries might restrict imports and capital outflows; surplus countries might encourage imports and restrict capital inflows. Alternatively, governments could adjust exchange rates; deficit countries might devalue, while surplus countries might revalue.

(2) *Symptom management policies.* Governments might try to manage payments imbalances by financing them (using national reserves, international borrowing, or both) and by intervening in foreign exchange markets to manage the international market flows that are symptomatic of different macroeconomic policies in different countries.

(3) *Internal policies.* Governments could adjust monetary and fiscal policies to eliminate the imbalances between savings, investment, and consumption that generate trade imbalances and to eliminate the cross-national interest rate differentials that generate speculative international capital flows.

This article develops an informal model to help explain how governments choose among alternative patterns of coordination of these types of policy. If governments always adjusted internal policies to eliminate external imbalances (as some liberal economists prescribe), there would be no interest in international policy coordination. But the kinds of monetary and fiscal policies required to eliminate external imbalances often conflict with the domestic political pressures that cause governments to pursue disequilibrating policies in the first place. Because of these domestic political pressures, deficit and surplus countries alike often want to avoid or postpone internal adjustment.

Attempts to avoid or postpone internal adjustment typically raise issues of international policy coordination. Governments may want to persuade foreign governments to adjust their policies to help manage or eliminate the international imbalance. In particular, deficit countries favor international policy coordination that sees surplus countries reflating their economies, revaluing

---

11. The schema presented here is based on Cooper's categorization and is commonly employed in the literature. See Richard N. Cooper, *The Economics of Interdependence: Economic Policy in the Atlantic Community* (New York: McGraw-Hill, 1968), chap. 1.

their currencies, expanding their imports, and helping the debtor countries finance their deficits. Similarly, governments may favor international agreements to limit others' use of external strategies of adjustment. In particular, surplus countries favor international coordination to deter deficit countries from restricting imports and sharply devaluing their currencies[12] and to encourage deficit countries to rely on the internal strategy of deflation. Surplus countries may be willing to provide international financing to persuade deficit countries to limit their resort to external strategies of adjustment and make it easier for them to deflate by giving them time to do so gradually.

All countries do not face the same incentives for policy coordination. Certain structural asymmetries in the degree of interest in macroeconomic adjustment policy coordination are likely to affect the pattern of coordination. First, it is generally more difficult for deficit countries to prevent deficits from having a deflationary impact than it is for surplus countries to insulate their economies from the potential inflationary consequences of external surpluses.[13] This means that deficit countries typically have a stronger interest in international coordination to spread the burden of adjustment to others, matched with a lesser ability to bargain for changes in foreign government policies. An exception is deficit countries with large domestic markets (especially the United States), since they could use the threat of restricting market access as a powerful lever in bargaining with surplus countries. Second, larger and less trade-dependent countries are typically able to sustain macroeconomic payments imbalances and to tolerate international instability more easily than are smaller and more trade-dependent countries. The fact that the former are under less pressure to adjust policies to eliminate international imbalances gives them an advantage in international bargaining.[14]

Interest in international coordination of macroeconomic adjustment policies can exist whenever countries are not completely autarkic. But which types of policy will be adjusted to eliminate disequilibria and which types will be subject to international coordination depend critically on the structure of the international economy. Two aspects of the international economic structure are important: the degree of international integration of markets for goods and

---

12. Although surplus countries would generally be opposed to drastic devaluation by deficit countries, they might well favor moderate changes, especially if these were an alternative to trade restrictions. In any case, surplus countries would prefer that decisions about deficit country exchange rate changes be coordinated internationally to give them the opportunity to protect their interests.

13. Deficit countries would typically run out of foreign exchange reserves before surplus countries exhausted their ability to accumulate reserves and "sterilize" their impact on the domestic money supply. Sterilized intervention involves making sales of government securities (or purchases, in the case of deficit countries) in the domestic market to offset the impact that changes in foreign exchange reserves would otherwise have on the total supply of reserves in the banking system.

14. These arguments about international economic asymmetries as sources of bargaining power are inspired by Hirschman and others. See Albert O. Hirschman, *National Power and the Structure of Foreign Trade* (Berkeley: University of California Press, 1945).

services and the degree of international capital market integration. In practice, the two may be more or less closely linked, but for purposes of explication, they will be considered separately in what follows.

Differences between countries in the expansiveness of macroeconomic policy spill over into trade balances. Expansionary policies stimulate demand at home, which tends to stimulate imports and depress exports. Higher imports and lower exports worsen the trade balance. The reverse process occurs in countries that pursue relatively restrictive macroeconomic policies.

For both deficit and surplus countries, the magnitude of trade imbalances increases as international trade increases relative to the size of the national economy. Thus, as international trade becomes more important, countries face larger international payments imbalances as a consequence of divergent macroeconomic policy choices, and each government's interest in international policy coordination to reduce its burden of adjustment increases. Nevertheless, if economies are linked only by trade,[15] the international payments imbalances that result when different countries pursue different macroeconomic policies will be relatively small and slow to emerge—relative, that is, to the imbalances generated by short-term capital flows.

Thus, when national economies are linked only by trade, governments can deal with their payments imbalances by pursuing moderate adjustments to external policies or turning to symptom management policies. When trade flows are low, few industries in either deficit or surplus countries would be hurt, so the likelihood of a protectionist response to deficits is higher.[16] But when trade flows are moderate or high, numerous domestic industries in both surplus and deficit countries are likely to oppose an intensification of trade restrictions by deficit countries[17] and will instead encourage their governments to search for alternative ways to deal with the payments imbalance.

One alternative would be to manipulate exchange rates, allowing them either to depreciate and thereby eliminate deficits or to appreciate and eliminate surpluses. If governments preferred to maintain fixed exchange rates, international macroeconomic imbalances could be managed by surplus countries

---

15. Economies may be linked by long-term investment as well, but this investment is not highly sensitive to short-term macroeconomic policy differentials.

16. In the 1940s and 1950s, the leading surplus country, the United States, financed West European and Japanese payments deficits in the hope that this would encourage trade liberalization in the future and help governments in these countries resist threats from the Soviet Union and domestic communists. At the time, U.S. exports to Western Europe and Japan were not critical for the highly insulated American economy.

17. Some domestic industries in deficit countries would always favor protection, but the argument here is that as the importance of trade increases, there will be more industries which oppose restrictions that would interfere with their international operations. See, for example, Helen V. Milner, *Resisting Protectionism: Global Industries and the Politics of International Trade* (Princeton, N.J.: Princeton University Press, 1988); and Stephen D. Krasner, "United States Commercial and Monetary Policy: Unravelling the Paradox of External Strength and Internal Weakness," in Peter J. Katzenstein, ed., *Between Power and Plenty: Foreign Economic Policies of Advanced Industrial States* (Madison: University of Wisconsin Press, 1978), pp. 51–87.

TABLE 1. *The G-7 countries: trade (exports plus imports) of goods and services, expressed as a percentage of national GDP, 1955–89*

	1955	1960	1965	1970	1975	1980	1985	1989
Britain	48	43	39	45	54	52	57	52
Canada	39	35	38	43	47	54	54	50
France	27	27	25	31	37	45	47	43[a]
Germany	37	36	36	40	47	57	66	62
Italy	23	27	28	32	42	44	44	37[a]
Japan	24	21	20	21	26	31	29	27
United States	9	10	9	12	17	25	20	25

[a]Data are for 1988.
Sources. For 1955 data, Organization for Economic Cooperation and Development (OECD), *National Accounts Statistics, 1952–1981,* vol. 1 (Paris: OECD, 1983). For 1960–75 data, OECD, *National Accounts Statistics, 1960–1988,* vol. 1 (Paris: OECD, 1990). For 1980–89 data, OECD, *Quarterly National Accounts,* no. 1, 1990.

lending money to deficit countries. This option would appeal to deficit countries seeking to avoid drastic deflation or trade protectionism and might appeal to surplus countries seeking to avoid reflation or the loss of access to the markets of deficit countries.

However, the appeal of this form of symptom management is crucially dependent on the sums involved. If payments deficits are relatively small, as they are when economies are linked internationally only by trade, surplus countries may well be willing to finance them, even if deficit countries show little sign of implementing more fundamental adjustments.[18] This can give governments considerable freedom to pursue independently chosen macroeconomic policies in the face of trade deficits or surpluses.

The degree of international integration of national markets for goods and services can be roughly measured by the share of imports and exports relative to the size of the national economy, or gross domestic product (GDP).[19] Table 1 presents this data for the seven leading advanced capitalist countries since the

18. Surplus countries lent money year after year to Britain and the United States in the mid-1960s. For a detailed discussion of why creditor countries and institutions that lent money to Britain did not insist on fundamental reforms to eliminate Britain's balance-of-payments weakness, see Susan Strange, *Sterling and British Policy: A Political Study of an International Currency in Decline* (London: Oxford University Press, 1971), pp. 289–95.

19. The ideal measure would be the sensitivity of imports and exports to macroeconomic policy changes, but reliable data on this are not available for the countries and time periods in question. The volume of imports and exports relative to GDP gives a rough approximation.

1950s. It reveals that all have become more trade-dependent since the 1960s. Had all other things been equal, this alone would indicate that symptom management policies would have been much more viable in the 1960s than in the 1980s.

The second element of the international economic structure that is critical for understanding structural incentives for international coordination of macroeconomic adjustment policies is the degree of international integration of markets for short-term capital. When short-term capital markets are highly integrated internationally, there is little autonomy in macroeconomic policymaking, even for the largest states. This is because differences in the macroeconomic policies pursued by various countries immediately trigger large flows of capital. Capital flows respond quickly to changes in investors' expectations about interest rates and exchange rates, and these flows have immediate effects on exchange rates.

The effects of monetary and fiscal policies when capital is internationally mobile are much different than the effects when it is not.[20] When capital is highly mobile across national borders, arbitrage between domestic and world capital markets keeps domestic interest rates from diverging widely from international interest rates,[21] and this in turn makes fiscal policy less effective. Fiscal expansion puts upward pressure on domestic interest rates. Capital floods in as international investors take advantage of higher domestic interest rates, causing the domestic currency to appreciate. The international competitive position of domestic producers erodes, exports decline, and imports increase. Not only does the country suffer from a trade deficit, but the harm done to domestic producers can offset the stimulating effect that fiscal expansion was intended to have on output and employment.[22]

When international capital mobility is high, monetary policy is effective in theory but not in practice. Monetary expansion puts downward pressure on domestic interest rates, causing a massive exodus of capital as investors seek higher returns abroad. Capital outflows immediately depreciate the domestic currency, and this shifts demand away from foreign goods (imports) and into domestic goods (import-competing products and exports). Monetary expansion in the context of high capital mobility could therefore stimulate the economy both by reducing interest rates (as in the case of a closed economy) and by depreciating the currency and improving the trade balance. In practice, however, governments are not willing to tolerate the drastic exchange rate fluctuations that accompany monetary policy choices which reflect only

---

20. This section is based on open-economy macroeconomic theory. For a good textbook source, see Francisco L. Rivera-Batiz and Luis Rivera-Batiz, *International Finance and Open Economy Macroeconomics* (New York: Macmillan, 1985).

21. In the context of flexible exchange rates, domestic interest rates equal the international interest rate plus the expected rate of depreciation of the domestic currency.

22. Trade flows adjust more slowly to exchange rate changes than do capital flows. Thus, there is potential for a temporary fiscal stimulus; its length depends on how long it takes goods and services markets to adjust to the instantaneous currency appreciation.

domestic concerns. Expansionary monetary policy can trigger capital flight and a collapse in the value of the currency, both of which could damage a government's domestic standing and undermine its economic policies. Similarly, restrictive monetary policy would push the exchange rate up sharply, thereby damaging the government's standing with exporters and causing a more severe slowdown than intended.[23] The high costs of exchange rate volatility mean that, despite economic theory, international capital mobility does *not* increase the real-world effectiveness of monetary policy.

It was argued above that the trade imbalances generated by macroeconomic policy differences can be managed by intergovernmental lending from surplus to deficit countries. But international capital flows are difficult to manage in this way, for two reasons. First, international capital markets react much more quickly to macroeconomic policy changes than do international trade flows. Capital flows generate deficits or surpluses immediately, while trade balances are not affected until after macroeconomic policies affect domestic demand and prices.[24] Governments have less time to put symptom management into practice when capital is mobile than they have when trade deficits are the main symptom of macroeconomic divergence. Second, the size of capital flows makes them more difficult to manage than trade imbalances. The volume of capital that can flow internationally in response to macroeconomic policies is enormous, and governments are not able to lend to each other on a large enough scale to permit "management" of this symptom of cross-national macroeconomic policy differentials. Coordinated intervention in foreign exchange markets, even when backed by international lending, cannot stabilize exchange rates if investors believe that the currency values sought by central banks are unrealistic,[25] because central bank reserves are far smaller than the volume of foreign exchange trading when capital markets are open. In fact, the *daily* volume of trading on foreign exchange markets typically exceeds the combined foreign reserve holdings of leading central banks.[26]

23. Examples of the effects of expansionary and restrictive monetary policies can be found in the 1980s. France abandoned expansionary monetary policies in 1983 in the face of capital flight (which occurred despite attempts to control capital flows) and severe downward pressure on the franc. The United States relaxed monetary policy in 1985 in part because tight monetary policy, in combination with fiscal expansion, had driven the dollar up to a level that severely eroded the international competitiveness of American industries. After the October 1987 stock market crash, Germany relaxed monetary policy to slow the mark's appreciation against the dollar, which had been weakened by loose monetary policy, and against other European currencies.

24. Ronald I. McKinnon, *An International Standard for Monetary Stabilization* (Washington, D.C.: Institute for International Economics, 1984), pp. 24–25.

25. Examples are legion. In the autumn of 1989, the G-7 attempted to stop the dollar from rising. Its coordinated intervention during a three-week period totaled about $11 billion, but the dollar continued to rise. See *Globe and Mail,* 17 October 1989, pp. B1 and B2.

26. The Bank for International Settlements estimated that the average daily volume of foreign exchange trading in London, New York, and Tokyo in April 1989 totaled $431 billion. See *Globe and Mail,* 14 September 1989, pp. B1 and B4. This estimate includes an unknown amount of purely speculative churning; net flows are undoubtedly less, although certainly substantial, especially when investors believe that a currency is undervalued or overvalued. In contrast, the combined

In the short run, governments can borrow funds on private international capital markets to finance macroeconomic imbalances, but this often requires a reversal of the expansionary monetary policies that generated the outflow in the first place.[27] Deficit countries trying to borrow on international markets soon find that they must raise interest rates, since private investors are not willing to lend indefinitely to governments that do not move quickly to restore balance in their domestic and international accounts.

Consequently, coordination of symptom management policies alone cannot reconcile divergent national macroeconomic policies when capital markets are integrated internationally. Governments that face external imbalances must turn to other types of adjustment policy. Trade and capital controls are not an attractive alternative, since powerful domestic groups oppose controls that would interfere with transnational economic linkages. Nevertheless, the possibility that threatened industries in deficit countries will succeed in their demands for trade protection remains, as demonstrated in the United States in 1985.

These problems with external strategies and symptom management strategies mean that governments experiencing international macroeconomic imbalances face powerful incentives to press foreign countries to alter their internal policies. Deficit countries will try to persuade surplus countries to reflate, and surplus countries will try to persuade deficit countries to deflate. The bargaining asymmetries identified above are still valid, but even large surplus countries can be pressured to reflate in order to keep deficit countries from restricting trade. Merely lending money to deficit countries will not be sufficient to ease their imbalances when capital is internationally mobile.

The existence of incentives for fiscal and monetary policy coordination does not guarantee that governments will coordinate these policies. Other political, economic, and intellectual considerations may well interfere with actual coordination. For example, because of political differences between Congress and the President, the United States did not join in negotiated mutual adjustments of fiscal policy in the 1980s.[28] Macroeconomic coordination may also be blocked by different national views of the desirability of specific policy

---

foreign reserve holdings of the central banks of Britain, the United States, and Japan amounted to only $295 billion in the same month, based on data derived from the International Monetary Fund (IMF), *International Financial Statistics* (Washington, D.C.: IMF, September 1989), pp. 45, 48, and 50. Similar data are not available for the 1960s, but a comparison of indicators for which data are available reveals that the annual volume of international bank loans and bond issues represented only 13 percent of the annual volume of total national reserves of advanced capitalist countries during the 1964–67 period but represented roughly 103 percent during the 1985–87 period. See Webb, "International Coordination of Macroeconomic Adjustment Policies," Table II:3, pp. 64–65.

27. The appeal of this option is also undermined by concerns about indebtedness to foreigners, especially if indebtedness is accompanied by rising inward foreign direct investment, as in the United States in the late 1980s.

28. As discussed below, the United States was uniquely able to force other countries to adjust their policies to compensate for destabilizing American monetary and fiscal policies.

adjustments—differences that may reflect a lack of consensus within the economics profession about the international implications of monetary and fiscal policies,[29] disputes about how much of the burdens of adjustment should be borne by each of the participating countries, and conflicting views about appropriate trade-offs between growth and price stability.

Despite these obstacles, governments have responded to the incentives for macroeconomic policy coordination. Monetary and fiscal policies were subject to negotiated mutual adjustment in the 1980s, even though coordination was not extensive enough to eliminate cross-national policy differentials that generate massive payments imbalances. Incentives for this type of coordination were much less significant in the 1960s, and macroeconomic policy coordination was correspondingly much lower.

Patterns of coordination in the 1960s and the 1980s

This section assesses the historical record of international coordination of macroeconomic adjustment policies. First, it demonstrates that patterns of international coordination did conform in part to the expectations of the model developed above. In the late 1950s and the 1960s, when international trade flows were moderate in volume and international capital flows were relatively minor, macroeconomic policies were made independently and international coordination focused on symptom management policies. In the 1980s, when international trade flows were somewhat larger and capital was highly mobile internationally, international coordination focused on monetary and fiscal policies. Second, the review of these two periods reveals that the overall level of international coordination of macroeconomic adjustment policies was at least as high in the late 1980s as in the 1960s, contrary to the assertions of the hegemonic stability theory.

Policy coordination from 1958 to 1968

During the late 1950s and the 1960s, macroeconomic policies were made independently. The only negotiated mutual adjustment of monetary and fiscal policies occurred in isolated cases of conditional International Monetary Fund (IMF) lending to Britain in 1967 and 1969 and to France in 1958 and 1969.[30] Both of these countries stated their intentions to pursue restrained fiscal and

---

29. Regarding the effects of the lack of consensus among economists, see, for example, Jeffrey A. Frankel, *Obstacles to International Macroeconomic Policy Coordination* (Princeton, N.J.: International Finance Section, Department of Economics, December 1988). It should be stressed, however, that governments did coordinate macroeconomic policies after 1985, despite substantial disagreement about the appropriateness of specific policies.

30. Britain had also borrowed heavily from the IMF in 1956, 1964, and 1965 but was not required to accept substantive policy conditions.

monetary policies in order to reduce their deficits, but only in the case of Britain in 1969 can IMF pressure be credited with causing the borrowing country to alter its policies. IMF involvement did, however, assist domestic leaders who favored restraint in debates with their more expansionist colleagues.[31] The United States, the largest deficit country during the period, borrowed little from the IMF because it wanted to avoid policy conditionality and because it was able to persuade its allies to finance its deficits by other means, as discussed below.

According to some analysts, the macroeconomic policies of leading states were "harmonized" by finance ministers and central bank governors in meetings of the Organization for Economic Cooperation and Development (OECD), the G-10, and the Bank for International Settlements (BIS).[32] But these meetings had little impact on national policies.[33] On the basis of extensive interviews with G-10 officials, Robert Russell concluded that monetary and fiscal policies were characterized primarily "by attempts to intellectually rationalize policies that governments were already intent upon pursuing."[34] The participants avoided making specific policy recommendations because they felt that this was the responsibility of national governments alone.[35]

Alternatively, others have argued that explicit coordination of macroeconomic policies was not necessary in the late 1950s and the 1960s, since the rules of the Bretton Woods regime—a regime that was created by the American hegemon at the end of World War II—ensured that countries would pursue macroeconomic policies which were consistent with international stability. This view was reflected, for example, in a 1988 report of the G-30, which described the Bretton Woods era as "one of significant policy coordination [achieved]

31. For a detailed discussion of these cases, see Webb, "International Coordination of Macroeconomic Adjustment Policies," chap. 6. See also Margaret Garritsen de Vries and J. Keith Horsefield, *The International Monetary Fund, 1945–1965: Twenty Years of International Monetary Cooperation,* vol. 2 (Washington, D.C.: IMF, 1969); Margaret Garritsen de Vries, *The International Monetary Fund, 1966–1971: The System Under Stress* (Washington, D.C.: IMF, 1976); and Susan Strange, *International Monetary Relations,* vol. 2 of Andrew Shonfield, ed., *International Economic Relations of the Western World, 1959–1971* (London: Oxford University Press, 1976).

32. See Robert W. Cox, "Social Forces, States and World Orders: Beyond International Relations Theory," *Millenium* 10 (Summer 1981), pp. 145–46; and Robert O. Keohane and Joseph S. Nye, *Power and Interdependence: World Politics in Transition* (Boston: Little, Brown, 1977), pp. 117–19.

33. In the case of Britain, however, the policy conditions attached to IMF credits in 1967 and 1969 had been worked out in G-10 meetings.

34. Robert W. Russell, "Transgovernmental Interaction in the International Monetary System, 1960–1972," *International Organization* 27 (Autumn 1973), p. 457.

35. For an excellent discussion of the G-10 meetings, see ibid., pp. 431–64. In *International Monetary Relations,* p. 163, Susan Strange points out that central banks from creditor countries were reluctant to press Britain too hard for changes in monetary policies for fear of undermining the principle of central bank policymaking autonomy. Regarding the BIS, see Charles A. Coombs, *The Arena of International Finance* (New York: Wiley, 1976), pp. 28 and 198; and Cooper, *The Economics of Interdependence,* pp. 198–99. According to Cooper, central bankers "avoided candid discussions" of pending policy changes.

through countries adjusting their policies in response to the discipline imposed by the rules."[36]

If this is an accurate description, then governments must have adjusted monetary and fiscal policies to eliminate external payments surpluses or deficits that threatened fixed exchange rates. But careful study of the period indicates that in most cases governments did not do so. In *The Responsiveness of Demand Policies to Balance of Payments,* Michael Michaely identified periods of payments imbalance for the G-10 countries and assessed whether their monetary and fiscal policies shifted as economic theory would prescribe—that is, deficits should be met with more restrictive policies, and surpluses with more expansionary policies. He found that in each of the countries, fiscal policy "was not responsive to the requirements of the balance of payments."[37] Monetary policy was also not generally responsive to the balance of payments, but there were exceptions. Japan and Britain consistently relaxed monetary policy when in surplus and restrained monetary policy when in deficit.[38] Belgium, France, and the Netherlands tightened monetary policy when they were faced with payments deficits; but they did not relax monetary policy during periods of payments surpluses, which included most of the 1960s. Monetary policy in the United States, Germany, and Sweden was "consistently nonresponsive to the needs of the balance-of-payments position."[39]

Furthermore, there was evidence that governments deliberately moved to *prevent* other governments' macroeconomic policy adjustments from having the desired effect on international payments balances. Monetary policy tended to shift in parallel in different countries at any given time (except in the United States, whose policies did not respond to international influences).[40] According to Michaely, this pattern of policies "does not conform with the directives of balance-of-payments adjustment: the latter would require two countries which undergo opposite experiences in their balance of payments to undertake policies in opposite directions, rather than to coordinate their policies so that they will move in parallel with each other."[41] This finding directly contradicts

36. Report of the G-30, cited by Jacques J. Polak in "Comments," in Ralph C. Bryant et al., eds., *Macroeconomic Policies in an Interdependent World* (Washington, D.C.: Brookings Institution, IMF, and Center for Economic Policy Research, 1989), p. 373. Note that the G-30 statement defines coordination in the same manner as Wallich does; see footnote 5, above.

37. See Michael Michaely, *The Responsiveness of Demand Policies to Balance of Payments: Postwar Patterns* (New York: National Bureau of Economic Research, 1971), pp. 30 and 32–33. This finding excludes Canada, which had a floating exchange rate until 1962 and therefore could not logically have been constrained by IMF exchange rules.

38. Ibid., p. 42. There was also limited evidence of such a tendency in the case of Italy.

39. Ibid., pp. 42–43.

40. Ibid., pp. 53–57.

41. Ibid., p. 57. Against Michaely's statement must be set some evidence that on brief occasions in 1960–61, 1963, and 1967, international consultations helped halt interest rate spirals set off by several countries' reciprocal moves to tighten credit and thereby prevent outflows of capital. If this did occur, it is evidence of the incentives to coordinate monetary policy when capital is even slightly mobile internationally. For brief mentions of these episodes, see Robert V. Roosa, *The Dollar and World Liquidity* (New York: Random House, 1967), p. 55; Henry G. Aubrey, *Atlantic Economic*

the argument that macroeconomic policies were coordinated by virtue of countries adhering to the rules of the Bretton Woods regime. Taken as a whole, Michaely's findings indicate that the governments of the largest countries had considerable freedom to ignore the balance-of-payments constraints suggested by economic theory.

In order to assess arguments that explicit coordination of macroeconomic policies was unnecessary in the 1960s because policies were harmonized by means of some other dynamic, it would be useful to compare divergence among monetary and fiscal policies in the 1960s with divergence in the 1980s. Although reliable and accurate data on this issue are difficult to find and the problems are compounded by the fact that data covering the periods must be drawn from several sources, we can turn to two crude measures of the expansiveness of monetary and fiscal policies in the largest advanced capitalist countries: the money supply growth rate (percentage of annual change in M1) and fiscal balance (surplus or deficit as a percentage of national GDP). If the rules of the Bretton Woods system had forced countries to adjust their macroeconomic policies to maintain fixed exchange rates and if the fluctuating exchange rate system of the 1970s and 1980s provided greater autonomy for macroeconomic policymaking, then we ought to see greater cross-national variability in these indicators during the earlier period.

A comparison of Tables 2 and 3, which present the data for the G-5 countries during the 1958–68 period and the 1978–89 period, reveals mixed evidence. With regard to money supply, rates of growth were more divergent in the earlier period, as indicated by the greater standard deviation from the mean G-5 increase in money supply. We should be careful about reading too much into money supply data, given the recognized problems of interpretation. Nevertheless, the data do not support the argument that because governments adhered to the rules of a strong international monetary regime, the explicit coordination of macroeconomic policies was not required in the 1960s. The data are consistent with the argument advanced in this article: the relative insulation of national capital markets in the 1960s permitted different governments to pursue different macroeconomic policies without generating enormous international payments imbalances.

With regard to the fiscal data, Tables 2 and 3 indicate that deficits were substantially larger on average in the 1978–89 period than they had been in the earlier period, and the standard deviation from the mean G-5 deficit was also larger in the 1978–89 period. Again, we should be cautious in interpreting this finding, especially given that the data had to be drawn from a variety of sources. Nevertheless, it does appear that there was less divergence among fiscal policies in the earlier period. As the preceding discussion made clear, this was

Cooperation: The Case of the OECD (New York: Praeger, 1967), pp. 108–9 and 195; Cooper, *The Economics of Interdependence,* pp. 145, 161–62, and 199; and Strange, *International Monetary Relations,* p. 265.

not because governments tailored fiscal policy to the requirements of the balance of payments. Instead, the difference between the two periods appears to be a consequence of the secular trend toward larger fiscal deficits, a trend that has been more pronounced in some countries than in others. As Table 3 shows, U.S. budget deficits have been significantly larger than those of other G-5 countries since the early 1980s. The reasons for this are to be found in domestic political institutions and the unique ability of the United States to avoid international market consequences of domestic policy choices, both of which are discussed in detail in the next section. It is important to note here, however, that the United States was able to persuade Japan and Germany to pursue more expansive fiscal policies in the late 1980s; in the absence of this policy coordination, fiscal policy divergence would have been greater. Finally, it should be noted that the consequences of fiscal policy divergence for international payments imbalances depend on the degree to which fiscal policies were accommodated by monetary policy, a question that cannot be answered with the present data.

If macroeconomic policies were not coordinated in the 1960s, either explicitly or implicitly, then what accounts for the stability of exchange rates and payments balances in the 1960s relative to the 1980s? Two factors are crucial. First, national capital markets were not internationally integrated during this period. Although international trade was substantial and payments imbalances did emerge, the insulation of capital markets limited the volume of the imbalances that could be generated by the pursuit of different monetary and fiscal policies in different countries. Second, there was extensive international coordination focusing on the management of the symptoms of incompatible national macroeconomic policies. Central banks from the G-10 countries coordinated intervention in foreign exchange markets on an ongoing basis to maintain fixed exchange rates. This intervention was underwritten by extensive international coordination of balance-of-payments lending to deficit countries. Central banks offered short-term loans to support currencies under attack in foreign exchange markets, and the IMF provided longer-term credits. The United States was able to finance its own payments deficit by persuading allied countries to hold their growing foreign reserves in dollar-denominated securities instead of converting them into gold or other currencies.[42]

The success of these symptom management policies in preserving national macroeconomic policymaking autonomy at a time when international trade was being liberalized was critically dependent on the relatively small imbalances that had to be financed. For example, a rescue operation mounted in 1964 lent $3 billion to Britain and permitted it to support the fixed parity for sterling in

---

42. An important example of this type of policy coordination was the March 1967 understanding reached by Germany and the United States. In exchange for Germany's agreement not to present its growing dollar holdings for conversion to gold, the United States agreed to continue stationing hundreds of thousands of American troops in Germany. See Strange, *International Monetary Relations*, p. 272; and Block, *The Origins of International Economic Disorder*, p. 184.

TABLE 2. *The G-5 countries: money supply growth rate (percentage of annual change in M1) and fiscal balance (surplus or deficit as a percentage of national GDP), 1958–68*

	1958	1959	1960	1961	1962	1963	1964	1965	1966	1967	1968	1958–68
Money supply												
United States	4.3	0.1	−0.4	2.9	2.1	2.8	4.1	4.3	4.6	3.9	7.0	
Japan	12.8	16.5	19.1	19.0	17.1	26.3	16.8	16.8	16.3	13.4	14.6	
Germany	13.1	11.8	6.8	14.8	6.6	7.4	8.3	8.9	4.5	3.3	7.6	
France	6.4	11.4	13.0	15.5	18.1	16.7	10.3	9.0	8.9	6.2	5.5	
Britain	3.0	4.6	−0.8	3.2	4.4	0.3	5.0	2.7	2.6	3.2	6.0	
G-5 mean	7.9	8.9	7.5	11.1	9.7	10.7	8.9	8.3	7.4	6.0	8.1	8.6
Standard deviation	4.8	6.5	8.6	7.5	7.4	10.7	5.1	5.5	5.5	4.3	3.7	6.3
Fiscal balance												
United States	−1.6	−1.6	0.0	−0.7	−1.3	−0.8	−0.9	−0.2	−0.5	−1.1	−1.8	
Japan	−0.8	−0.1	0.7	1.2	−0.3	−0.8	−0.2	−0.9	−1.6	−1.4	−1.0	
Germany	−0.2	−1.7	−0.6	−1.0	−0.4	−0.8	−0.3	−0.5	−0.5	−1.7	−0.7	
France	−2.8	−2.3	−1.4	−1.4	−1.7	−2.0	−0.3	0.0	−0.4	−1.1	−1.5	
Britain	−0.4	−0.6	−1.2	−0.8	0.3	−0.5	−1.3	−1.7	−1.4	−2.9	−1.7	
G-5 mean	−1.2	−1.3	−0.5	−0.5	−0.7	−1.0	−0.6	−0.7	−0.9	−1.6	−1.3	−0.9
Standard deviation	1.1	0.9	0.9	1.0	0.8	0.6	0.5	0.7	0.6	0.7	0.5	0.8

Sources. For money supply growth rates, Federal Reserve Bank of St. Louis, *International Economic Conditions,* June 1985, as reported in Ronald I. McKinnon, "The Dollar Exchange Rate and International Monetary Cooperation," in R. W. Hafer, ed., *How Open Is the U.S. Economy?* (Lexington, Mass.: D.C. Heath, 1985), pp. 216–17. For central government fiscal surplus and deficit data, IMF, *International Financial Statistics* (Washington D.C.: IMF, various years); and OECD, *Economic Survey: Japan* (Paris: OECD, July 1977), p. 44.

TABLE 3. *The G-5 countries: money supply growth rate (percentage of annual change in M1) and fiscal balance (surplus or deficit as a percentage of national GDP), 1978–89*

	1978	1979	1980	1981	1982	1983	1984	1985	1986	1987	1988	1989	1978–89
Money supply													
United States	8.2	7.7	6.2	7.3	6.6	11.1	7.0	9.0	13.6	11.6	4.9	0.9	
Japan	10.8	9.9	0.8	3.7	7.1	3.0	2.9	4.6	7.4	9.0	10.3	-2.2[a]	
Germany	13.3	7.5	2.4	1.2	3.5	10.4	3.3	4.2	10.0	9.0	10.6	5.3	
France	—	12.9	8.9	11.5	11.8	9.9	10.7	9.0	7.8	4.6	3.2	10.1	
Britain	20.1	11.5	4.5	11.6	14.2	13.0	14.7	16.5	21.1	22.8	14.4	6.0	
G-5 mean	13.1[b]	9.9	4.6	7.1	8.6	9.5	7.7	8.7	12.0	11.4	8.7	4.0	8.8
Standard deviation	5.1[b]	2.4	3.2	4.6	4.3	3.8	5.0	5.0	5.7	6.9	4.6	4.8	4.6
Fiscal balance													
United States	-2.8	-1.5	-2.9	-2.7	-4.1	-6.2	-4.9	-5.4	-5.1	-3.6	-3.0	-2.8	
Japan	-4.9	-5.8	-5.5	-5.3	-5.2	-4.9	-4.1	-3.7	-3.1	-1.9	-1.1	-0.8	
Germany	-2.1	-2.0	-1.8	-2.3	-2.0	-2.0	-1.8	-1.1	-0.9	-1.4	-1.7	-0.4	
France	-1.4	-1.5	0.0	-2.7	-3.1	-3.6	-3.0	-2.7	-3.2	-2.3	-2.0	-1.7	
Britain	-5.2	-5.7	-4.8	-4.9	-3.3	-4.5	-3.2	-3.2	-1.8	-1.1	1.1	1.3	
G-5 mean	-3.3	-3.3	-3.0	-3.6	-3.5	-4.2	-3.4	-3.2	-2.8	-2.1	-1.3	-0.9	-2.9
Standard deviation	1.7	2.2	2.2	1.4	1.2	1.6	1.2	1.6	1.6	1.0	1.5	1.5	1.6

[a]Japan's money supply grew relatively rapidly until the Bank of Japan tightened policy in the autumn of 1989, producing a decline for the year as a whole.

[b]Data for France in 1978 are not available; summary statistics therefore exclude France.

Sources. For money supply growth rates, Federal Reserve Bank of St. Louis, *International Economic Conditions,* July 1989; and *Economist,* "Economic and Financial Indicators," various issues. For central government fiscal surplus and deficit data, IMF, *International Financial Statistics* (Washington, D.C.: IMF, various years); OECD, *Economic Outlook,* no. 47, June 1990, Table 7; and OECD, *National Accounts Statistics, 1976–1988,* vol. 2 (Paris: OECD, 1990), pp. 61 and 69.

the face of what was regarded at the time as a severe balance-of-payments crisis. In contrast, foreign central banks lent $120 billion to the United States in 1987, but this did not prevent the dollar from depreciating by 14 percent (in terms of special drawing rights) over the course of the year.[43]

Payments imbalances were relatively small in the late 1950s and the 1960s because governments continued to rely on border controls to insulate their economies from international market influences. Restrictions on trade were considerable, but since these constituted a serious obstacle to the creation of a liberal international economy, the period was also characterized by extensive international coordination (led by the United States) to relax trade barriers and limit their use as instruments of international macroeconomic adjustment.

In contrast, controls on short-term capital flows were universally used as instruments of macroeconomic adjustment in the 1960s, and policymaking was unilateral. Deficit countries used controls to block capital outflows that would otherwise have led to devaluation or deflation. The United States imposed increasingly stringent controls on capital outflows beginning in 1963. Surplus countries, mainly in continental Western Europe, also relied on capital controls, in this case to block capital inflows that threatened to lead to currency appreciation or domestic inflation.[44]

At the same time, the governments of surplus and deficit countries permitted the Eurodollar market to emerge in the mid-1960s. They did so because it provided private agents and the central banks of surplus countries with the opportunity to hold on to dollars instead of converting them into stronger currencies or into gold. Thus, the Eurodollar market helped finance international payments imbalances, making it easier for deficit and surplus countries to avoid macroeconomic policy adjustments. The permissive attitude adopted by leading governments also reflected the widespread beliefs that national markets could be insulated from Euromarket influences and that the Eurodollar market would therefore have no adverse impact on national macroeconomic conditions and policies.[45] Thus, as Susan Strange noted, "The Eurodollar business began with the approval or at least the silent blessing of the main governments concerned, even though it may prove to have been the most important single development of the century undermining national monetary sovereignty."[46] The Eurodollar market represented the first step toward the capital market integration that so altered the problems of international macroeconomic adjustment in the 1970s and the 1980s.

43. The loan probably did prevent the dollar from falling even further, however. The estimate of the 1987 increase in foreign central bank holdings of U.S. dollars is from I. M. Destler and C. Randall Henning's *Dollar Politics: Exchange Rate Policymaking in the United States* (Washington, D.C.: Institute for International Economics, 1989), p. 61. The decline in the dollar is calculated from the IMF's *International Financial Statistics Yearbook, 1988* (Washington, D.C.: IMF, 1988), p. 717.

44. For a detailed list of capital controls in effect in the late 1960s, see Cooper, *The Economics of Interdependence,* pp. 242–48.

45. See Strange, *International Monetary Relations,* p. 190; and George W. McKenzie, *The Economics of the Euro-Currency System* (London: Macmillan, 1976), pp. 9–10.

46. Strange, *Sterling and British Policy,* p. 209.

Overall, the late 1950s and the 1960s were characterized by extensive international coordination of symptom management policies (foreign exchange market intervention and payments financing) and of trade controls and trade-related exchange controls. But capital control policies, which were crucial to preserving macroeconomic policymaking independence, were not coordinated internationally, and monetary and fiscal policies were made independently.

Policy coordination from 1978 to 1990

Macroeconomic policy coordination occurred on an ad hoc basis in the late 1970s and the 1980s. Enormous international payments imbalances and exchange rate movements were generated by international capital flows during these years—capital flows that responded to international interest rate differentials and expectations about future monetary and fiscal policies.

On numerous occasions, a government suffering from external imbalances called on other governments to adopt macroeconomic policies that would help reduce the imbalances or make it easier for the deficit government to alter its own policies in desired directions. For example, the Carter and Reagan administrations called on foreign governments to cut taxes and increase spending in part because they hoped that stronger foreign demand for American goods would help sustain the American economy and make it easier for them to restrain monetary or fiscal policies without causing a recession in the United States. In the European Community (EC), France and other countries frequently called on Germany to pursue more expansive policies that would permit other European governments to stimulate their own economies without generating capital outflows, trade deficits, and exchange rate depreciation. Conversely, after 1985, Germany and Japan repeatedly called on the United States and other deficit countries to reduce fiscal deficits and tighten credit in order to reduce the payments surpluses that were putting upward pressure on the mark and the yen. International market integration gave governments the bargaining levers they needed to persuade foreign governments to adjust their policies. Threats to impose trade restrictions, block further liberalization, or permit currency markets to fluctuate unchecked were commonly used.

While the governments of most leading countries applied pressure on others, the U.S. government was the most successful in actually winning changes. The size and relative insulation of the American economy put the United States in a strong bargaining position. Many countries—and especially Japan—depend more on exports to the United States than the United States depends on exports to them. The threat of American protectionism has therefore served as a powerful bargaining lever and one that the Reagan and Bush administrations used repeatedly and successfully to press for changes in various foreign governments' macroeconomic policies. Furthermore, because international transactions are less important to the American economy than they are to the economies of most smaller countries, the United States has also been less concerned with exchange rate volatility than other countries. Even West European countries, which are less dependent on trade with the United States than is Japan, have been concerned about dollar volatility because it has made it harder to stabilize exchange rates within the European Monetary System. This asymmetric pattern of concern has enhanced the bargaining power of the American government and helped it pressure Japan and Germany to coordinate their monetary and fiscal policies on U.S. terms.[47]

A brief chronology of international monetary diplomacy from the late 1970s to 1990 illustrates these points. The first clear instance of negotiated mutual adjustment of macroeconomic policies occurred at the Bonn summit meeting of 1978. The contrast between expansionary policies in the United States and more restrictive policies abroad was generating large payments imbalances. The Carter administration called on Japan and Germany to pursue more expansive fiscal policies to sustain their domestic growth and stimulate imports from the United States, thereby also stimulating the American economy and offsetting the deflationary impact of the tighter monetary policy that Carter wanted to introduce. After much debate, the United States persuaded Japan and Germany to reflate in return for an American commitment to restrain monetary growth and decontrol oil prices. The Bonn agreement had an impact on the national policies of all of the leading governments.[48]

From 1981 to 1984, demands for international macroeconomic policy coordination came from the governments of the leading countries that were hurt by the first Reagan administration's tight monetary policy and stimulative fiscal policy. Foreign capital flowed quickly into the United States to take advantage of high interest rates and finance the growing American budget deficit, pushing the dollar up sharply. The willingness of foreign investors to buy American government securities, even after the dollar became overvalued and American interest rates began to fall in 1983–84, made it easier for the Reagan administration to ignore the external ramifications of its macroeconomic policy choices and to reject foreign criticism.

Foreign governments were unable to persuade the U.S. government to coordinate its monetary, fiscal, or exchange rate policies internationally, both because they had no credible bargaining threats and because they could reach no consensus. Expansionist governments in France and Canada called for less restrictive American monetary policy and were willing to tolerate expansive American fiscal policy, while more conservative governments in Britain,

---

47. Regarding Japanese and West European concerns, see, for example, Robert D. Putnam and Nicholas Bayne, *Hanging Together: Cooperation and Conflict in the Seven-Power Summits,* rev. ed. (London: Sage, 1987), pp. 192 and 205; and Yoichi Funabashi, *Managing the Dollar: From the Plaza to the Louvre* (Washington, D.C.: Institute for International Economics, 1988), pp. 4 and 106.

48. As Putnam and Bayne pointed out in an earlier edition of their book (*Hanging Together: The Seven-Power Summits* [London: Heinemann Educational Books, 1984], pp. 78–102), each of the leading governments was internally divided, and domestic advocates of the policy adjustments being demanded by foreign governments were able to use international pressures to strengthen their hand in domestic debates.

Germany, and Japan supported tight monetary policy and deplored lax fiscal policy in the United States.[49]

By 1985, Reagan administration leaders were beginning to understand that their unilateral policies were hurting the United States, and they were also becoming more interested in international policy coordination to correct some of the external problems caused by the policies of the previous four years. The dollar was sharply overvalued, and American manufacturing industries (excluding defense) suffered badly. In Congress, this had generated powerful protectionist pressures that threatened to undermine the liberal international trading system. The United States was also rapidly becoming the world's biggest debtor country because of heavy borrowing from foreigners to finance its budget and trade deficits.

The Reagan administration hoped to correct these problems in part by persuading foreign countries to stimulate domestic demand. Stronger demand abroad would reduce foreign countries' trade surpluses and the American trade deficit and would help correct the overvaluation of the dollar. Japan and Germany initially resisted American demands to reflate, which they feared would lead to renewed inflation. During 1985–86, the Reagan administration backed its demands for foreign reflation by pointing to the danger of congressional protectionism if the American trade balance did not improve and by threatening to let dollar volatility continue unchecked (although by late 1986 the administration was becoming concerned that dollar volatility was scaring foreign lenders and impeding efforts to finance the American budget and trade deficits).[50]

By early 1987, foreign governments were willing to reflate in return for an American agreement to join in coordinated foreign exchange market intervention to stabilize currencies and for an American commitment to reduce the U.S. budget deficit. The key bargain was struck in the Louvre Accord,[51] which arose from meetings of the G-5 and G-7 finance ministers in February 1987. The finance ministers established a system of exchange rate coordination (discussed below), and some participants hoped that the establishment of target ranges for exchange rates would encourage governments to adjust monetary policies to support the group's exchange rate objectives.[52] There were also explicit negotiated mutual adjustments to macroeconomic policies. Germany promised to increase a tax reduction package already planned for 1990

49. For a detailed account of international debates during these years, see Putnam and Bayne, *Hanging Together,* rev. ed.
50. International debates during 1985–87 are chronicled by Funabashi in *Managing the Dollar* and by Putnam and Bayne in *Hanging Together,* rev. ed.
51. For a detailed discussion of the Louvre Accord, see Funabashi, *Managing the Dollar.* My account draws on this source.
52. Interview with a senior official in the foreign ministry of a G-7 country, May 1990. There is some evidence that exchange rate coordination established by the Louvre Accord has had this effect. A recent IMF study argues that the process of economic policy coordination "has enhanced the role of exchange rates as a guide for policy in all of the major industrial countries." See Dallas S. Batten et al., "The Conduct of Monetary Policy in the Major Industrial Countries: Instruments and Operating Procedures," occasional paper no. 70, IMF, Washington, D.C., July 1990, p. 1.

and to move the package ahead to 1988. Japan agreed to pass a supplementary budget in spring 1987 that would stimulate domestic demand and also agreed to cut interest rates. The United States committed itself to reducing its budget deficit through restraints in spending.

Monetary and fiscal policies in the three leading countries reflected the impact of the Louvre bargain over the next three years (1987–89). Japan kept interest rates low and monetary growth rapid in order to stimulate domestic demand and encourage Japanese investors to buy American treasury securities, thereby financing the American budget and trade deficits and preventing a collapse of the dollar.[53] The Japanese government also increased domestic spending, even though this conflicted with the desire of its finance ministry to begin to reduce the enormous government debt that had accumulated since the 1970s.[54] Japanese monetary and fiscal policy adjustments had the intended impact; domestic demand grew strongly, the economy became less export-dependent, and the current account surplus shrank.[55]

German macroeconomic policy also revealed the impact of international policy coordination. The Bundesbank's efforts to support the dollar in 1987 resulted in rapid money supply growth which fed through to higher inflation in 1988 and 1989.[56] Although the Bundesbank briefly raised interest rates contrary to American preferences in September and October of 1987, it lowered the rates in coordination with other G-7 central banks in the wake of the October 1987 stock market crash.[57] On a number of occasions in 1988 and 1989, the Bundesbank resisted raising interest rates to contain inflation in its usual manner because of the protests that would have been forthcoming from other EC countries and the United States.[58] The German government resisted foreign demands for accelerated tax cuts and spending increases, but its fiscal policy was more stimulative than that of the other G-7 countries in the 1986–88 period, according to the OECD's calculations of cyclically adjusted budget balances.[59] Like Japan, Germany continued to run fiscal deficits in the late 1980s despite the government's desire to reduce the national debt.[60]

---

53. See *The New York Times,* 14 January 1988, pp. 1 and 33. See also *Economist,* 19 November 1988, p. 93; 14 January 1989, p. 71; and 1 April 1989, pp. 65–66.

54. See *Economist,* 27 February 1988, p. 63; 24 September 1988, pp. 47–48; and 22 July 1989, p. 67. See also *The New York Times,* 15 January 1988, pp. 25–26.

55. See *Economist,* 2 July 1988, pp. 56 and 58; and 29 October 1988, p. 35. See also *Globe and Mail,* 20 June 1990, p. B6.

56. German money supply targets were overshot in 1986, 1987, and 1988. See *Economist,* 5 August 1989, pp. 15–16.

57. Germany was motivated in large part by the fear that if it kept monetary policy tight at a time when the U.S. Federal Reserve Bank and the Bank of Japan were relaxing monetary policy to prevent the crash from spreading, the mark would soar and the European Monetary System would come under severe pressure. See *The New York Times,* 6 November 1987, pp. 1 and 33.

58. See *Economist,* 13 February 1988, p. 79; and 7 May 1988, pp. 71–72. See also *Globe and Mail,* 3 March 1989, pp. B1 and B8.

59. OECD data were reported in *Economist,* 11 March 1989, p. 67. Table 3 shows that German fiscal deficits increased in 1987 and 1988.

60. *Economist,* 24 September 1988, p. 47.

American macroeconomic policies after 1987 revealed the impact of international policy coordination, although in a somewhat perverse fashion. The Federal Reserve Bank occasionally coordinated interest rate adjustments with foreign central banks. But the fiscal deficit remained large, despite rapid economic growth. Budget battles between the Reagan and Bush administrations and Congress were not directly influenced by foreign diplomatic pressures. In fact, relaxed monetary and fiscal policies abroad, combined with exchange rate coordination and balance-of-payments lending, permitted the United States to continue to run enormous fiscal deficits and to finance them by borrowing from abroad, without triggering a collapse in the value of the dollar.[61]

By 1989, negotiated adjustments in the policies of leading countries had reduced the American trade deficit, and domestic concern about the American budget deficit had risen. Consequently, the U.S. government relaxed pressure on most foreign governments to alter their macroeconomic policies—although it persuaded the Japanese to increase their debt-financed domestic spending during the structural impediments initiative talks in spring 1990.[62] Foreign governments called on the U.S. government to reduce its budget deficit in increasingly critical terms,[63] but to no avail. While the budget deficit did decline in 1987–89 (see Table 3), international diplomatic pressures were far less important than domestic considerations.

Internationally, the clarity of the problems faced in 1985–87 was replaced by greater uncertainty about the threats to international economic stability. Policy coordination in 1987–89 had encouraged the leading countries to adopt measures that would reduce international imbalances,[64] thereby reducing market pressure for new negotiated mutual adjustments of policies. Signs of both renewed inflation and recession were evident in 1989–90, and this led to conflicts within governments about whether interest rates needed to be raised to fight inflation or lowered to avoid recession.[65]

In the spring of 1990, Japan tried to negotiate monetary policy adjustments with other G-7 countries. Faced with a declining yen and the risk that higher

---

61. *Economist*, 30 September 1989, p. 12.

62. See *The New York Times*, 29 June 1990, pp. A1 and D2. See also *Economist*, 30 June 1990, pp. 34–35.

63. Criticism of American policy was severe at the G-7 finance ministers' meetings in May 1989 and September 1990. See *Globe and Mail*, 1 June 1989, p. B4; and 24 September 1990, pp. B1 and B4.

64. As Table 3 shows, monetary and fiscal expansion slowed in the United States in 1988–89. Monetary policy was relaxed in Japan and Germany in 1988 and the first half of 1989, and both countries continued to pursue expansionary fiscal policies.

65. This debate has pitted finance ministries, which are generally more concerned about signs of recession, against central banks, which are generally more concerned with inflationary pressures, in many of the OECD countries. See *Economist*, 12 May 1990, p. 67. For example, in April 1990, the Japanese finance ministry wanted foreign interest rates to fall and thereby reduce pressure on the Japanese central bank to raise its interest rates; however, the Bank of Japan was willing to contemplate raising Japanese interest rates to dampen inflationary pressure at home.

domestic interest rates to support the yen would worsen existing pressure on the stock market and real estate market, Japan's finance minister requested cuts in foreign interest rates to help support the yen. The United States and Germany rejected the Japanese request, ostensibly because they wanted to maintain high interest rates to fight domestic inflation.[66] The episode demonstrated the asymmetry in international policy coordination; American requests for foreign assistance in similar situations had rarely been so completely rejected.[67] When Japan reciprocated by not sending its representative to the next meeting of G-7 finance ministers in May 1990, the press began to speculate about the growing irrelevance of the G-7 attempts at coordination.[68]

Meetings of the G-7 finance ministers in the second half of 1990 and in early 1991 focused on issues related to the war in the Gulf, with the United States seeking contributions from Japan and Germany to finance its war effort. Attempts to coordinate interest rates were less successful. The central banks of the United States and some other countries were moving to lower interest rates to combat inflation, while the Bundesbank was raising interest rates to prevent the German government's deficit spending on unification efforts from fueling inflation.[69] Active macroeconomic policy coordination currently appears to be in abeyance, both because other domestic and international problems have emerged to dominate the agenda and because international payments imbalances are smaller and more manageable now than they were in the 1980s.

As the preceding review indicates, international coordination of macroeconomic policies from 1978 to the present has not been sufficient to eliminate international payments imbalances or stabilize exchange rates. In order to cope with these imbalances and instability, the advanced capitalist countries pursued symptom management policies in the form of coordinated foreign exchange market intervention and balance-of-payments financing, just as they had in the 1960s. They also borrowed heavily from private international capital markets.

Exchange rate coordination was most extensive within the European Monetary System, but exchange rate policies were also coordinated among the G-5 and G-7 countries for most of the period. Coordinated measures to

66. See *The New York Times,* 8 April 1990, p. 10; and *Globe and Mail,* 9 April 1990, pp. B1 and B4.

67. The response of the United States was especially interesting, since the government had recently given many indications that it would prefer lower interest rates but could not make a unilateral move in that direction because of the need to keep its rates competitive with overseas rates in order to attract foreign investment in American government and corporate debt. Meeting the Japanese request might therefore have served the government's domestic interests as well as the interests of Japan.

68. See *Globe and Mail,* 8 May 1990, p. B25.

69. See *Globe and Mail,* 21 January 1991, pp. B1 and B2; 22 January 1991, pp. B1 and B2; and 1 February 1991, p. B7.

support the dollar were agreed upon in 1978–79,[70] but the United States rejected calls to join in international efforts to stabilize currency values during the first four years of the Reagan presidency. In January and September 1985, after members of the Reagan administration recognized that exchange rate volatility and misalignment were hurting even the United States, the G-5 countries agreed on coordinated measures to lower the value of the dollar, particularly against the yen and the mark.[71] Discussions during 1986 were characterized by American efforts to "talk down" the dollar to force Japan and Germany to reflate, but since the Louvre Accord of February 1987, exchange rate coordination has been fairly continuous. The accord included target ranges for each of the three leading currencies. These ranges have been adjusted periodically in response to American demands and in accordance with changing market sentiments.[72] Coordinated foreign exchange market intervention has been frequent even when participating countries disagree over macroeconomic policy preferences. For example, in spring 1990, the G-7 countries coordinated intervention to support the yen at the same time as they rejected Japanese requests to lower interest rates to support the yen; and in early 1991, exchange rate coordination was intensive, despite divergent interest rate policies.[73] Indeed, countries have often favored exchange rate policy coordination as a way to deflect foreign pressure for adjustments in fiscal and interest rate policies.[74]

International coordination of exchange rates since 1985 involved agreements to *adjust* exchange rates to more appropriate levels, not simply to coordinate measures to maintain existing fixed exchange rates. This is in contrast to the 1960s, when countries had been unable to agree on adjustments even when existing levels were clearly inappropriate.[75]

Although exchange rate coordination was much less successful in stabilizing exchange rates in the late 1980s than it had been in the 1960s,[76] it was not less

70. See Richard C. Marston, "Exchange Rate Policy Reconsidered," in Martin Feldstein, ed., *International Economic Cooperation* (Chicago: University of Chicago Press, 1988), pp. 101–3.
71. See ibid., pp. 103–6; Putnam and Bayne, *Hanging Together,* rev. ed., p. 199; and Funabashi, *Managing the Dollar,* chap. 1.
72. For a detailed account of exchange rate coordination from summer 1985 to spring 1987, see Funabashi, *Managing the Dollar.* For a brief account from 1985 through 1989, see Destler and Henning, *Dollar Politics,* chap. 4.
73. See *Globe and Mail,* 10 April 1990, pp. B1 and B10; 1 February 1991, p. B7; 9 February 1991, p. B6; and 13 March 1991, p. B8. See also *Economist,* 10 March 1990, pp. 85–86.
74. Funabashi, *Managing the Dollar,* p. 39.
75. For example, extensive negotiations in 1968–69 failed to produce an agreement to raise the value of the German mark and lower the value of the French franc, despite widespread agreement that such a realignment was desirable. In 1969, France and Germany each unilaterally adjusted their exchange rates. See Strange, *International Monetary Relations,* pp. 325–28; and Coombs, *The Arena of International Finance,* pp. 181–86. IMF par values for leading currencies had initially been chosen unilaterally by each government. The inability to agree to realign currency values against the dollar in 1969–71 caused the United States to adopt the policy of "benign neglect" that eventually brought down the system of fixed exchange rates.
76. The EC was an exception, however, since exchange rate coordination was backed by monetary policy coordination among EC members.

extensive. Because of the growth of international capital flows, it was far more difficult in the later period for central banks to stabilize exchange rates unless monetary policies were also coordinated.

Coordination of balance-of-payments financing—the other type of symptom management policy—was less consistent in the 1980s than it had been in the 1960s, although the volumes involved were much greater. Payments financing in the 1980s was predominantly private, with investors lending money to foreign governments by purchasing their treasury securities and corporate securities. Deficit countries had turned to private international capital markets in the 1970s because of the ready availability of large amounts of credit, free of formal policy conditions,[77] and they continued to do so in the 1980s. Nevertheless, governments did coordinate payments financing in the 1980s when private investors were unwilling to lend as heavily to deficit governments as was necessary to stabilize exchange rates. For example, foreign central banks (led by the Bank of Japan) lent $120 billion to the United States to slow the decline of the dollar in 1987, after foreign private investors lost confidence in the American government's determination to reduce its fiscal deficit.[78] We should also not lose sight of the political considerations underlying large-scale private Japanese lending to the United States, which was strongly encouraged by a Japanese government concerned with maintaining good relations between the two countries.[79]

The period since 1978 has been characterized by a striking unwillingness of governments to use trade and capital controls to limit the external imbalances generated by different macroeconomic policies in different countries, despite the severity of these imbalances. In the 1980s, there were extreme disincentives for states to reintroduce comprehensive trade controls. While selective controls were still imposed to deal with sectoral threats, comprehensive controls would have interfered with the globalized structures of production that dominate the economies of all advanced capitalist countries. Comprehensive trade controls to reduce payments deficits would therefore have been costly to the country imposing them, even in the absence of foreign retaliation, and would have been opposed by the largest domestic industries.

The 1980s also witnessed far fewer attempts by governments to use capital controls to insulate national macroeconomic conditions from international influences. This was because selective capital controls had become much less effective in controlling capital flows, and comprehensive controls would have been extremely costly. During the 1970s, many European countries and Japan

---

77. Benjamin J. Cohen, "Balance-of-Payments Financing: Evolution of a Regime," in Stephen D. Krasner, ed., *International Regimes* (Ithaca, N.Y.: Cornell University Press, 1983), pp. 315–36.

78. Lending by foreign central banks financed the bulk of the U.S. current account deficit of $154 billion in 1987. See Destler and Henning, *Dollar Politics,* p. 61.

79. See Robert Gilpin, *The Political Economy of International Relations* (Princeton, N.J.: Princeton University Press, 1987), pp. 328–40. International policy coordination encouraged private lending to the United States by reducing interest rates in Japan and Germany, thereby making investments in the United States more attractive.

had tried to insulate national macroeconomic conditions from international market pressures by controlling speculative capital flows without interfering with trade and investment-related capital flows. However, investors had always been able to find a way around selective controls.[80] Advances in the technology of information and communications and the development of transnational corporations provided capital-holders with a wide variety of mechanisms for transferring funds across national borders when different macroeconomic policies in different countries made international transfers profitable.

Governments could have blocked these speculative capital flows only by reintroducing comprehensive systems of trade and exchange controls, such as existed before the West European and Japanese currencies were made convertible in the late 1950s and early 1960s. But by the 1970s, trade and investment had become highly dependent on international financial flows. Comprehensive attempts to control capital flows would have cut countries off from all but the simplest types of international commerce. Transnational banks and corporations would have been powerfully opposed to any disruption of capital flows, and the internationalization of markets that had occurred since the 1960s had strengthened the position of these actors in domestic politics.[81]

As selective capital controls became less effective in insulating national macroeconomic policies from international pressures, their costs became more salient. Controls not only impeded the integration of national industries into transnational productive structures but also encouraged investors and borrowers to shun protected financial services industries in favor of more liberal, less regulated foreign and international markets.[82] Consequently, all of the leading advanced capitalist countries eventually liberalized their capital controls. In the late 1970s and the 1980s, Britain, Germany, Japan, and the United States each unilaterally relaxed certain capital controls.[83] In 1983–84, U.S.–Japanese negotiations produced agreements that reduced many obstacles to capital flows in and out of Japan.[84] And in the late 1980s, France and Italy both relaxed controls as part of the EC's plan to move toward a "single European market"

---

80. In 1973, the Bundesbank concluded that recent experience had "made it abundantly clear that even stronger administrative action against capital flows from foreign countries . . . does not suffice when speculative expectations run particularly high." Cited by D. C. Kruse in *Monetary Integration in Western Europe: EMU, EMS, and Beyond* (London: Butterworths, 1980), p. 130.

81. Banks are currently under siege in the United States and Japan because of unwise lending (primarily on real estate) in the boom years of the 1980s. Despite their unpopularity, there has been no serious discussion of preventing them from engaging in international activities that are crucial for their own survival and for the operations of transnational corporations.

82. See Ethan B. Kapstein, "Resolving the Regulator's Dilemma: International Coordination of Banking Regulations," *International Organization* 43 (Spring 1989), pp. 323–47; and Edward J. Kane, "Competitive Financial Reregulation: An International Perspective," in Richard Portes and Alexander K. Swoboda, eds., *Threats to International Financial Stability* (Cambridge: Cambridge University Press, 1987), pp. 111–49.

83. See Bank for International Settlements (BIS), *Recent Innovations in International Banking* (Basel: BIS, 1986), p. 149; and Jeffrey A. Frankel, *The Yen/Dollar Agreement: Liberalizing Japanese Capital Markets* (Washington, D.C.: Institute for International Economics, 1984), pp. 19–20.

84. Frankel, *The Yen/Dollar Agreement.*

TABLE 4. *Changes in the pattern of international coordination of macroeconomic adjustment policies*

Type of policy	Pattern in the 1960s	Pattern in the 1980s
External		
Trade controls	Extensive coordination to limit use of controls.	Comprehensive controls not used; no coordination.
Capital controls	Independent policymaking to restrict flows.	Liberalization; independent and coordinated policymaking.
Exchange rates	Extensive coordination to fix rates; no coordination to adjust rates.	Coordination to stabilize and adjust rates in 1978–79 and after 1984.
Symptom management		
Payments financing	Extensive coordination.	Predominantly unilateral and private financing; coordination when private financing inadequate.
Foreign exchange market intervention	Extensive coordination to maintain fixed rates.	Coordination to stabilize and adjust rates in 1978–79 and after 1984.
Internal		
Monetary and fiscal policies	No coordination, except in Britain in 1969.	Ad hoc coordination in 1978–79 and 1985–89.

by 1992.[85] Thus, international policy coordination encouraged the shift away from capital controls during this period, just as it had facilitated trade liberalization in earlier decades.

Changing patterns of policy coordination

Changes in the pattern of international coordination of macroeconomic adjustment policies between the 1960s and the 1980s (see Table 4) are largely consistent with the explanatory argument developed in an earlier section of this article. In the 1960s, international capital mobility was low, and trade flows were moderate. Under these conditions, the international payments imbalances generated by independently chosen monetary and fiscal policies were small enough to be managed by balance-of-payments financing, coordinated intervention in foreign exchange markets, and controls on capital flows. Fixed exchange rates were maintained because it was possible to do so without eliminating national monetary policymaking autonomy.

85. See *Economist,* 18 March 1989, p. 85; 4 November 1989, p. 100; and 27 January 1990, p. 7.

By the late 1970s, international capital mobility had increased dramatically, and trade flows had become much more substantial. Independently chosen macroeconomic policies generated enormous payments imbalances as capital flowed across national borders in search of higher interest rates and appreciating currencies. Governments continued to try to manage the international symptoms of divergent macroeconomic policies by coordinating intervention in foreign exchange markets[86] (which involved much larger sums now than in the 1960s) and by financing from private international capital markets. However, these measures were not sufficient to eliminate problems of exchange rate volatility and misalignment. Monetary and fiscal policies also had to be coordinated in order to reduce payments imbalances, currency problems, and the resulting protectionist pressures. Thus, whereas international economic diplomacy had focused on symptom management policies in the 1960s, it began to focus on monetary and fiscal policies in the 1980s.

Monetary and fiscal policies have traditionally been considered the sole concern of national governments. They are difficult to coordinate because they are the most important economic policy levers available to governments, and their domestic political ramifications are immense. Governments therefore turn to monetary and fiscal policy coordination only as a last resort, when economic problems cannot be resolved with other policy instruments.

The fact that responsibility for monetary and fiscal policymaking is shared by two or more institutions in most leading countries makes it difficult for the individual governments to pursue consistent policies. This is most apparent in the United States, where the power to make budgets is shared by the legislative and executive branches of government. In the 1980s, the two branches had highly differing political priorities. The conflict produced fiscal "policies" that reflected the preferences of neither branch and also failed to respond to the desires of other governments for policy coordination. However, the American situation is not unique. Virtually all of the advanced capitalist countries experienced large and persistent fiscal deficits even in the boom years of the late 1980s. In the five-year period from 1985 to 1989, central government fiscal deficits as a proportion of GDP averaged 4.0 percent in the United States, 4.5 percent in Canada, 2.1 percent in Japan, 1.1 percent in Germany, 2.4 percent in France, 12.1 percent in Italy, and 0.7 percent in Britain (Britain was the only G-7 country to experience fiscal surpluses in any of these years, with surpluses of 1.1 percent in 1988 and 1.3 percent in 1989).[87] This suggests that different advanced capitalist countries faced similar, perhaps structural, constraints in setting fiscal policy, despite their widely varying government structures.

---

86. The U.S. government in 1981–84 was the significant exception to this pattern.

87. Figures for the G-5 countries were calculated from data shown in Table 3. Figures for Italy and Canada were calculated from data in the OECD's *Economic Outlook*, no. 47, June 1990, Table 7. As argued above, the fiscal deficits of Japan and Germany in 1987–89 resulted in part from American pressure, not simply from internal problems.

More generally, responsibility for monetary policy is usually shared between elected political leaders and central banks with some degree of statutory independence. Independent central banks are typically more concerned about price stability and more willing to tolerate slow growth and high unemployment than are elected political leaders. If a country's government is itself divided over macroeconomic policy, it will hardly be in a position to coordinate policies with foreign governments. Since mid-1989, divisions between central banks and finance ministries have become more prominent as evidence of both renewed inflation and recession has increased, and this has contributed to the inconclusive nature of G-7 discussions.

The domestic political constraints on monetary and fiscal policymaking are greater than those on symptom management policymaking. Governments face few domestic political obstacles to international coordination of balance-of-payments financing and intervention in foreign exchange markets, since neither type of policy has a major direct impact on voters or domestic interest groups. Thus, it is easier for governments to adjust symptom management policies in response to international agreements and international market pressures than it is for them to adjust monetary and fiscal policies in response to external pressures.

Conclusions

This article demonstrates that international coordination of macroeconomic adjustment policies was at least as extensive in the 1980s as it had been in the 1960s. Because of changes in the structure of the international economy, however, there were shifts in the pattern of policy coordination: in the 1980s, payments financing coordination was less extensive, capital control coordination was more extensive, exchange rate coordination was as extensively pursued (except by the United States in 1981–84), and, most important, monetary and fiscal policies became the focus of coordination efforts. The pattern of the 1980s reflects the fact that when international capital mobility is high, the plight of a country facing serious external imbalances can be resolved only by adjustments to monetary and fiscal policies—either those of its own government or those of the governments of other leading countries.

These arguments and conclusions are at odds with those generally offered in the international political economy literature. As mentioned earlier, analysts from a variety of theoretical perspectives have argued that international economic policy coordination declined after the 1960s, and many have linked this phenomenon with a posited decline in American hegemony. While an extended discussion of the merits and flaws of the hegemonic stability theory is beyond the scope of this article, we can turn to two considerations that appear to be important in explaining the discrepancy in conclusions: the uncertainty about how to measure hegemonic decline and the imprecision of measurements of international coordination.

Proponents of the declining American hegemony argument appear to have exaggerated the extent of American decline.[88] By almost any measure, the United States is still the most influential country in the international economic system, and its economy is still the largest by a wide margin. During the 1980s, the United States consistently accounted for 40 percent of the aggregate GDP of the OECD countries; in comparison, Japan's share increased from 13 percent to 15 percent over the decade, and Germany's share was stable at around 8 percent.[89] This 40 percent U.S. share did represent a decline from the 50 percent share in the mid-1960s. But even at its relative smallest, the American economy was still two and a half times the size of the next largest economy, that of Japan. This raises a crucial question: When is a country big enough to be called "hegemonic"?[90] In the absence of strong theoretical reasons for claiming that a country is hegemonic when it accounts for 50 percent of total OECD economic output but not when it accounts for 40 percent, the argument comes dangerously close to tautology.[91]

The record of policy coordination reviewed in this article reveals that even in the late 1980s, the United States dominated international policy coordination, much as it had in the 1960s. International coordination of macroeconomic adjustment policies in both periods was characterized by greater adjustments to foreign government policies than to American government policies, even though the latter were at least as responsible for international payments imbalances. In the 1980s, the United States was uniquely able to evade the costs of imprudent macroeconomic policies and uniquely able to win coordination on its own terms. International policy coordination had little impact on American fiscal policy (except perhaps as foreign reflation made it easier for the United States to avoid restraint) even though American budget deficits

88. This argument is well established in the literature. See Bruce Russett, "The Mysterious Case of Vanishing Hegemony; Or, Is Mark Twain Really Dead?" *International Organization* 39 (Spring 1985), pp. 207–32; Susan Strange, *States and Markets* (London: Pinter, 1988); and Stephen Gill, "American Hegemony: Its Limits and Prospects in the Reagan Era," *Millenium* 15 (Winter 1986), pp. 311–36.

89. See OECD, *National Accounts, 1960–1988*, vol. 1 (Paris: OECD, 1990), p. 145. These shares are calculated using purchasing power parities rather than widely fluctuating and misaligned current exchange rates.

90. As an example of this problem, Britain is generally considered to have been "hegemonic" in the late nineteenth century, even though it was not as large relative to other leading countries as the United States is in the 1990s.

91. According to the vast body of literature based on game theory, hegemony is not necessary for cooperation. See especially Keohane, *After Hegemony;* and Duncan Snidal, "The Limits of Hegemonic Stability Theory," *International Organization* 39 (Autumn 1985), pp. 579–614. Recent work has also begun to emphasize the importance of bipolarity and the East–West conflict as factors encouraging the allied Western governments and Japan to coordinate policies, regardless of the degree of American hegemony. See, for example, Michael C. Webb and Stephen D. Krasner, "Hegemonic Stability Theory: An Empirical Assessment," *Review of International Studies* 15 (April 1989), pp. 183–98; and Joanne Gowa, "Bipolarity, Multipolarity, and Free Trade," *American Political Science Review* 83 (December 1989), pp. 1245–56.

have been the single most important source of international economic imbalance since the early 1980s.[92]

The United States felt less constrained than other countries by external market pressures because until 1987, private foreign investors were willing to lend to the United States in its own currency without demanding an interest rate premium to cover the exchange rate risk. They were willing to do so because of the dollar's status as the leading world currency. The unique ability of the United States to borrow from abroad in its own currency replicated the asymmetry of the 1960s, when France and other countries complained that the dollar's role as an international currency allowed the United States to spend freely abroad.

Foreign private investors who suffered when the dollar fell in 1985–87 stopped lending to the United States in 1987, and since that time the United States has been less insulated from the costs of its budget deficits. Private foreign investors now demand higher interest rates to compensate for the risk that the dollar will continue to depreciate, and American monetary policy is much more severely constrained. Nevertheless, the United States has been able to persuade foreign central banks to lower their interest rates, which encourages foreign private investors to continue lending to the United States, and also to finance American budget deficits indirectly by purchasing dollars in foreign exchange markets.

In accounting for the discrepancy between the findings presented here and those presented elsewhere in the literature, we must turn not only to the question of how to measure a decline in hegemony but also to the question of how to measure a decline in international policy coordination. To assess the latter, we must distinguish between (1) the extent of international coordination, defined as the extent of negotiated mutual adjustment of economic policies; and (2) the degree of stability in the international economy. Stability or instability in the international economy reflects political factors (the nature of government policies and the extent of international coordination) as well as the nature of international economic structures and problems. Analysts who argue that international coordination has fallen may be mistaking stability in the international economy for policy coordination among governments and may have failed to see how changes in the structure of the international economy have made the problem of managing international economic relations more difficult. Increased international economic integration in the late 1970s and the 1980s meant that negotiated mutual adjustment of economic policies had to become more extensive simply to maintain the level of stability achieved in the late 1950s and the 1960s.[93]

---

92. American deficits have been especially destabilizing because they are combined with a low domestic savings rate, which means that they are financed by foreign capital to a greater extent than are the deficits of other advanced capitalist states.

93. Similar arguments have been made by Cooper and others. See Cooper, *The Economics of Interdependence*.

The political economy of financial internationalization in the developing world

Stephan Haggard and Sylvia Maxfield

Developing country governments historically have imposed controls on capital movements, the international activities of domestic financial institutions, and the entry of foreign financial institutions. In the last decade, however, a growing number of developing countries have opened their financial systems by liberalizing capital flows and the rules governing the international operations of financial intermediaries; Table 1 provides a typology of these liberalization efforts. Though the number of works studying the political economy of finance in developing countries is growing, few deal primarily with the issue of the internationalization of financial markets.[1] This article seeks to explain both the general trend toward what we call "financial internationalization" as well as variations in the pace and scope of these reform efforts across countries.[2]

The rush to liberalize capital movements and open domestic financial systems to foreign competition is puzzling on several accounts. A growing economic literature on the sequencing of economic reforms underlines a number of preconditions required to make capital account liberalization an optimal policy. Well-documented cases show the extremely high costs of premature and ill-conceived liberalization efforts. Among these efforts are the Southern Cone experiments in Argentina, Chile, and Uruguay during the late 1970s and, more recently, Mexico.[3] It is revealing that the advanced industrial

We thank Peter Beck, Benjamin Cohen, David Cole, Jeffry Frieden, Robert Kaufman, Andrew MacIntyre, John Odell, Manuel Pastor, Ben Schneider, and Jeffrey Winters for comments on earlier drafts. We also wish to thank the participants in the project on internationalization and domestic politics directed by Robert Keohane and Helen Milner. This article will appear in slightly different form in Keohane and Milner forthcoming.
1. Two exceptions are Maxfield 1990; and Winters 1995. See also Frieden 1991b; Woo 1991, 176–203; and Haggard, Lee, and Maxfield 1993.
2. See the appendix for a discussion of the meaning of "financial internationalization" and coding rules for an index of financial openness.
3. See Edwards 1984; 1995; McKinnon 1991; Bisat, Johnston, and Sundarajan 1992; Corbo and de Melo 1985; and 1987.

International Organization 50, 1, Winter 1996, pp. 35–68
© 1996 by The IO Foundation and the Massachusetts Institute of Technology

TABLE 1. *A typology of financial market internationalization*

Liberalization of	Direction of liberalization	
	Inward	*Outward*
Capital movements	Liberalization of rules governing foreign direct investment, including sectoral restrictions, screening practices, and performance requirements	Deregulation of outward direct and portfolio investment by nationals
	Liberalization of foreign access to domestic equities and real estate	Liberalization of restrictions on repatriation of capital and disinvestment by foreign nationals and firms
	Liberalization of rules governing foreign borrowing by domestic firms and the international operations of domestic banks	Liberalization of restrictions on payments for invisibles, including profits and dividends
	Deregulation of sale and purchase of short-term domestic securities by foreigners	Deregulation of domestic foreign currency accounts, for residents and nonresidents
		Deregulation of sale and purchase of short-term foreign securities by domestic residents
Entry	Liberalize entry of foreign banks, securities firms, and other nonbank financial intermediaries	Permit or encourage domestic banks, securities firms, and nonbank financial institutions to establish foreign branches and networks

Sources. Derived from OECD 1990, 11–12; and IMF 1992, 29–31.

states are only now completing internationalization of their own financial markets.[4]

Even when one can make a strong economic case for the liberalization of capital flows, a number of political questions remain. As with trade liberalization, one of these questions is why sectoral interests favored by controls would concede to a change of policy. Governments, in addition to protected financial sectors, can also have a strong stake in capital controls. Increased financial integration holds governments hostage to foreign exchange and capital markets, forcing greater fiscal and monetary discipline than they might otherwise choose.[5] To the extent that capital account liberalization erodes domestic financial controls, it eliminates a tool of both industrial policy and patronage and reduces the opportunity for governments to finance themselves through the sale of government bonds at lower than world interest rates.[6]

4. See Rosenbluth 1989; Pauly 1988; and Goodman and Pauly 1993.
5. See Frieden 1991a; Kurzer 1991; 1993; Goodman and Pauly 1993; Winters 1994; and Andrews 1994.
6. See Alesina and Tabellini 1989; Giovannini and de Melo 1993; and Roubini and Sala-i-Martin 1992.

Given the common trend in policy across a large number of developing countries, there are good reasons to think that international systemic pressures are at work and that the developing countries' growing integration with the world economy has constrained government choices with respect to international financial policy. These pressures have operated through two distinct mechanisms.

The first mechanism includes the effects of increased trade and financial interdependence on the preferences and capabilities of policy-relevant economic interests. We define interdependence as the ratio of foreign to domestic transactions; it is thus similar to what economists typically call "openness." With respect to trade, it is usually operationalized as exports plus imports as a share of gross national product (GNP). With respect to financial interactions, possible measures include foreign savings as a share of capital formation or foreign borrowing or total foreign debt as a share of GNP. Increasing interdependence increases the weight of domestic actors with foreign ties, expands the array of interests likely to benefit from and demand greater openness of financial markets, and thus tilts the balance of political forces in a more internationalist direction. Interdependence also implies a greater political voice for foreign investors in the domestic policy process. Financial firms from advanced industrial countries have become more active lobbyists for market opening and have enlisted their governments to maintain both multilateral and bilateral pressure for liberalization. Moreover, the growing magnitude and complexity of trade and investment relations make capital controls more difficult to enforce because of the myriad opportunities for evasion and arbitrage.

Changing levels of economic interdependence and corresponding shifts in the configuration of policy-relevant interests have been used to explain capital account opening in developed countries and constitute an important backdrop to recent policy developments in developing countries as well. We argue, however, that the proximate cause for financial market opening in the developing countries is more frequently found in a second source of international pressure: balance-of-payments crises.

At first blush, this argument appears counterintuitive; we might expect, rather, that international shocks would be associated with a movement toward closure. Yet the International Monetary Fund (IMF) reports that from 1985 to 1990—a period of profound balance-of-payments difficulties for much of the Third World—the number of liberalizing measures taken by all developing countries with respect to the capital account not only consistently exceeded the number of tightening measures but also increased dramatically over the period: from twenty-two in 1985 to a peak of sixty-two in 1988 before falling to forty-nine in 1990. The IMF collates all policy changes and categorizes them as either "liberalizing" or "tightening"; totaling these measures thus runs the risk of weighting the significant and the trivial equally. Nonetheless, the results do provide an overall sense of the direction in which countries are moving.[7]

---

7. For the data, see IMF 1992.

The reasons for this tendency lie in the high costs that countries pay for inward-oriented responses to crises under conditions of increased financial market integration. Maintaining or increasing financial openness in the face of crisis signals foreign investors that they will be able to liquidate their investments, indicates government intentions to maintain fiscal and monetary discipline, and thus ultimately increases capital inflows.[8]

In the next two sections of this article, we explore the theoretical arguments linking economic interdependence and balance-of-payments crises to policy reform. In the remainder of the article, we explore the plausibility of these arguments by examining reform efforts in four middle-income countries: Chile, Indonesia, Mexico, and South Korea.

Economic interdependence and political pressures for financial internationalization

In the Hecksher–Ohlin model, liberalization of trade and capital movements are substitutes.[9] Standard welfare analysis can thus be used as a starting point for identifying competing interests in financial internationalization and constructing a political economy of the capital account.

In a closed, labor-abundant developing economy, the rate of return to capital in the domestic market exceeds the rate in the rest of the world. Lifting capital controls leads to a capital inflow from which labor gains. Jeffry Frieden has argued, however, that in a more plausible specific-factors model, the distributional consequences are quite different.[10] Specific factors in capital-poor countries do well, since they can now borrow at lower interest rates, while liquid-asset holders face lower returns. Politically privileged clients may benefit from government control over preferential credit, but as international financial markets expand, the major corporate consumers of financial services will find protected, inefficient domestic financial markets and restricted access to international opportunities increasingly costly.[11]

While identifying a politically important source of support for capital account liberalization, Frieden's spare model misses important features of the politics of finance in developing countries and, as a result, overstates the likely resistance to capital account liberalization. In many developing countries, returns to savers can be lower than world interest rates because financial

8. See Laba and Larrain 1993; Bartolini and Drazen 1994; and Drazen and Grilli 1993.
9. See Hanson 1992, 2; Edwards and van Wijnbergen 1986, 141–48; and Alesina, Grilli, and Milesi-Feretti 1993.
10. Frieden 1991a.
11. See Haggard and Maxfield 1993, 313–16; and Frieden 1991a, 437.

intermediation is taxed through restrictions on deposit rates, inflation, and the lack of opportunities to acquire foreign assets. Though liquid-asset holders have recourse to parallel markets where returns are higher, the informal nature of these markets is associated with corresponding risks. To these considerations must be added the substantial political risk that characterizes financial markets in a number of developing countries. As John Williamson argues, liquid-asset holders in a capital-poor country can profit from liberalization of both inflows and outflows. Local investors gain security, albeit at lower yields, by gaining the freedom to invest abroad; foreign investors gain a greater expected yield for a modest cost in terms of security.[12]

Frieden's analysis also needs to be extended to comprehend the interests of financial intermediaries, both domestic and foreign, since they are likely to have a substantial political voice in the liberalization process. These interests cannot be understood without drawing a distinction between the liberalization of capital flows and the liberalization of exit and entry. Domestic financial intermediaries stand to gain from liberalizing capital inflows and outflows, since such liberalization opens opportunities to intermediate foreign purchases of domestic securities and to manage pent-up domestic demand for foreign assets. Given the structure of the financial system in most developing countries, opening the capital account will also provide arbitrage opportunities, since domestic and international interest rates are unlikely to converge quickly if financial markets are organized as oligopolies.[13] Domestic financial institutions are also likely to be a source of pressure for capital account liberalization as their clients' international operations expand. Frances Rosenbluth, for example, concludes that decontrol in Japan was "propelled by financial institutions, acting in cooperation with the Ministry of Finance and sometimes politicians, to construct a new set of rules they need[ed] to compete in a changing economic environment."[14]

Yet if liberalization of flows is accompanied by liberalization of entry, these gains may accrue to foreign financial intermediaries, which have access to large pools of foreign funds, superior technology, and a sophisticated knowledge of foreign market opportunities. Thus the financial sector may support a liberalization of capital movements but take a protectionist stance with reference to the entry of foreign firms.

The pent-up demand for financial services in protected markets will increase the interest of foreign financial institutions in lowering barriers to entry, however. As the so-called emerging markets have grown, the opportunity costs of being closed out of them have grown correspondingly and foreign firms have become active lobbyists for liberalization. U.S.-based financial firms have been particularly aggressive in securing diplomatic support for their interests. These

12. Williamson 1992.
13. Galbis 1986.
14. Rosenbluth 1989, 5. For a similar argument with respect to German banks, see Goodman and Pauly 1993.

political pressures have played out at a number of different levels, from the formulation of the services agenda at the General Agreement on Tariffs and Trade, to regional negotiations such as the North American Free Trade Agreement (NAFTA), to bilateral consultations, such as those between the United States and Japan, South Korea, and Taiwan.

Increasing international economic integration not only changes the distribution of preferences but also is likely to erode the effectiveness of governments in maintaining controls.[15] Governments have a variety of motives for restricting capital account transactions, including an interest in maintaining policy autonomy, access to low-cost finance, and the ability to distribute rents. Evasion of controls has always existed, but growing interdependence increases both the motivation and opportunity for it. The expansion of the tradable-goods sector increases the opportunities for firms to get around capital controls through under- and overinvoicing, as does the growth of illicit trade. As firms from the developing countries invest more extensively abroad, governments face increasing difficulties in monitoring foreign financial operations and the transactions between headquarters and subsidiaries. The increase in travel and the deepening of telecommunications ties also make it easier for individual citizens to circumvent capital controls, even where controls over the international transactions of financial institutions remain in place.

In sum, increases in international trade and investment ties and the opportunities opened by the deepening of international financial markets should increase interest group pressures for financial internationalization, including from foreign firms, while decreasing the effectiveness of government controls. Yet such broad changes are more useful in explaining general trends than they are in accounting for why specific countries liberalize when they do. Crises play an important role in this regard.

Payments crises and financial internationalization

The traditional wisdom is that payments crises generate pressure (1) for capital controls in order to limit capital flight and (2) for increased trade protection to manage short-term balance-of-payments constraints. A number of countries appear to conform to this pattern; the initial responses of Argentina, Mexico, and Venezuela to the debt crisis of 1982–83 constitute examples.[16] However, as the IMF data cited earlier suggest, this pattern was not a general one in the 1980s and early 1990s. Even in the three countries just mentioned, brief episodes of closure quickly were followed by liberalization efforts.

15. Mathieson and Rojas-Suarez 1993.
16. Reinhart and Smith 1995.

To understand why, consider a simple account of a balance-of-payments crisis.[17] Prior to the crisis, the country is running a current account deficit financed by capital inflows, both public and private. External creditors judge that the growth of external debt is on an unsustainable path, and they are unwilling to continue to provide financing at previous levels. This might occur because domestic macroeconomic policies are unsustainable, because of adverse developments in the world economy, or because of a change in the terms of trade. Though the reduction of external finance might in principle be negotiated and gradual, it is more typically made manifest in speculative attacks on the exchange rate, rapid capital flight, and a sudden collapse in the availability of external lending.

Under what conditions will governments respond to such crises with liberalizing policy changes? Where the dependence on foreign finance has been low, where international liquidity is abundant, or where the government is confident in its ability to generate foreign exchange through exports, the cost of a more closed policy response to crisis is low. However, in most middle-income countries, these conditions have not pertained. Dependence on foreign finance grew rapidly in the 1970s when capital was abundant, but lenders retreated en masse from the developing world in the wake of the debt crisis. Moreover, with the exception of the East Asian newly industrializing countries, the development strategies of most middle-income developing countries have been notoriously weak in generating a level of exports adequate to avoid recurrent balance-of-payments difficulties.

Under these conditions, crises are likely to have an important political consequence: they will strengthen the political position of those sectors that are holders or generators of foreign exchange. These include liquid-asset holders, the export sector, private foreign creditors and investors, foreign financial intermediaries, and multilateral financial institutions. This informal coalition does not need to organize or mobilize politically to press its case, though it typically does. Its power also resides in the highly credible threat of exit or in continued unwillingness to lend or invest. The collective action problems that typically plague decentralized political actors are overcome by the fact that coordinated action is generated spontaneously by private responses to market signals.

The holders and generators of foreign exchange favor capital account liberalization, particularly in the wake of a crisis, because it provides an exit option; an open capital account constitutes protection against future government action. From the government's perspective, capital account liberalization helps resolve both short- and long-term foreign exchange problems by increasing the credibility of the government's economic policy stance in the eyes of creditors and earners of foreign exchange.[18] Liberalizing the capital

17. For two contending economic models of balance-of-payments crises, see Krugman 1979 (which emphasizes changes in the economic fundamentals); and Obstfeld 1986 (which emphasizes the significance of speculative behavior).

18. See Bartolini and Bondar 1992; Perez-Campanero and Leone 1992; and Reinhart and Smith 1995.

account is a form of signaling aimed at inducing the resumption of capital inflows.[19]

Such signaling is not limited to changes in discrete policies, but is likely to extend even to institutional changes that increase the cost of policy reversal. These changes include the delegation of policy authority to independent agencies, typically central banks. An increase in the relative scarcity of foreign exchange can therefore change not only the coalitional balance in the economy as a whole but also the balance of power among government ministries and even decision-making structures.[20]

To summarize, secular changes related to growing international economic integration have increased the incentives for capital account liberalization on the part of both economic interests and the government itself. However, crises are likely to increase substantially the power of those forces that favor liberalization, both within and outside the government. The proximate causal mechanism is politicians' perception that liberalization of the capital account will assure investors and thus ultimately induce capital inflows. By contrast, we would expect the pressures for liberalization to be lowest in countries with a low degree of openness that have avoided crises. Easy access to credit and foreign exchange, whether through borrowing or commodity booms, also permits governments the luxury of maintaining controls and exercising selectivity toward foreign investors and financial firms.

The remainder of this article evaluates this argument through an examination of the history of capital account policy in four countries: Chile, Indonesia, Mexico, and South Korea. Though not a random sample, we chose these four countries without considering the number or magnitude of balance-of-payments crises or significant changes in capital account policy in each. The four are broadly representative of the larger, middle-income developing countries that have become identified as emerging markets.

Financial internationalization in four countries: a comparative overview

Devising measures or proxies for the balance-of-payments position of a country or its international financial policy is not straightforward. Quantitative indicators of balance of payments can be highly misleading; large current account deficits may be voluntarily financed in one country, while small deficits signal a loss of confidence and crisis in another. The annual percentage change in international reserves provides a reasonable first approximation of the balance-of-payments situation. A sharp deterioration in reserves is likely to indicate

---

19. A signaling model of policy reform is developed in Rodrik 1989.
20. See North and Weingast 1989; and Maxfield 1995.

balance-of-payments difficulties. Nonetheless, this measure must be supplemented by a qualitative assessment of the country's ability to manage these constraints: its stock of credibility with creditors and investors, the extent of international liquidity, and the capacity to adjust through an expansion of exports.

Combining both quantitative indicators and qualitative judgments, we find eleven periods during which the countries in our sample faced serious balance-of-payments constraints: Indonesia in 1965–66 (which predates our quantitative series on capital account openness), briefly in 1975, in 1981–82, and again in 1986–88; Mexico in 1976 and more or less continuously from the 1982 debt crisis through the late 1980s; Chile in 1971–75 and again in 1981–82; and South Korea in 1971 and in conjunction with the two oil shocks in 1974 and 1980–82.

The overall policy stance of governments is also difficult to assess; it must be derived from a complex of policy actions in different areas, not all of which necessarily covary. Moreover, liberalization programs typically unfold across a number of years, and thus a policy action taken in a given year may have its origins in an earlier period. Nonetheless, to provide a comparative context for our case studies, we devised a coding scheme on the level of financial policy openness in each country for the 1970–90 period based on information contained in the IMF's annual report on exchange arrangements and restrictions and report the results in Table 2. The measure sums our coding of the rules governing transactions in four areas: the international operations of domestic and foreign commercial banks, payments for financial services and repatriation of capital, portfolio investment and borrowing, and direct investment. The indicator varies from the least open score of 0 (0 in all four policy areas) to 12 (a score of 3 in all four areas). A full explanation of the coding is contained in the appendix.

The data reveal eleven episodes of significant changes in financial market policy, defined as a change in the level of openness. We find evidence of liberalization in eight instances: Indonesia in 1970 and 1987–88; Mexico in 1978, 1983, and 1988; Chile in 1974 and 1976–80; and South Korea in 1990. We find three episodes of a move toward greater closure: Indonesia in 1974, Mexico in 1982, and Chile in 1971.

Of the eight episodes of liberalization, all except one originated in a balance-of-payments crisis. Indonesia's (1971) and Chile's (1974) liberalizations came in the aftermath of crises that toppled governments and led to fundamental policy changes. The balance-of-payments crisis that triggered the 1971 reform occurred in 1965–66 and thus predates the data on capital account openness. The 1976–80 reforms in Chile were at one level a continuation of President Pinochet's initial reform moves but were initiated in the wake of the severe balance-of-payments problems Chile experienced after the military coup in conjunction with the first oil crisis. Mexico's 1978 liberalization came in the aftermath of the 1976 crisis. The 1983 liberalization effort was clearly a

TABLE 2. *Internationalization, crises, and financial policy in Indonesia, Mexico, Chile, and South Korea*

Country	Level of financial openness	Exports + imports/ GNP[a]	Percentage change in reserves[b]
Indonesia			
1970	8	21.7	24.4
1971	9	21.3	15.7
1972	9	30.2	66.7
1973	9	39.7	28.9
1974	8	57.9	46.0
1975	8	42.6	−155.1
1976	8	38.8	70.0
1977	8	38.3	40.3
1978	8	34.8	4.5
1979	8	39.3	35.4
1980	8	47.1	24.7
1981	8	42.5	−7.5
1982	8	41.3	−59.5
1983	8	39.2	15.5
1984	8	37.9	22.1
1985	8	32.2	4.0
1986	8	29.0	−22.8
1987	9	34.6	27.6
1988	10	38.2	−10.8
1989	10	42.7	7.4
1990	10	46.7	19.4
Chile			
1970	4	27.1	15.4
1971	0	20.3	−50.2
1972	0	16.9	−43.0
1973	0	21.5	25.6
1974	5	37.8	−66.2
1975	5	35.8	36.0
1976	7	41.7	624.7
1977	7	36.8	5.3
1978	8	34.9	155.6
1979	8	45.6	77.8
1980	9	41.5	319.1
1981	9	33.9	−60.4
1982	9	26.0	−43.5
1983	9	28.2	12.2
1984	9	33.3	13.1
1985	9	37.2	6.4
1986	9	43.4	−4.0
1987	9	50.7	6.5
1988	9	59.4	26.1
1989	9	63.7	14.8
1990	9	61.0	67.2
Mexico			
1970	6	8.5	13.2
1971	6	8.5	24.5
1972	6	10.3	23.0

TABLE 2. *continued*

Country	Level of financial openness	Exports + imports/ GNP[a]	Percentage change in reserves[b]
1973	6	12.4	15.9
1974	6	13.4	6.3
1975	6	11.4	10.5
1976	6	10.0	−16.4
1977	6	10.1	28.0
1978	7	13.5	10.5
1979	7	17.2	11.1
1980	7	21.4	30.0
1981	7	20.8	27.3
1982	4	17.7	−388.5
1983	7	20.5	78.7
1984	7	25.1	46.2
1985	7	23.7	−48.2
1986	7	14.6	13.5
1987	7	22.3	54.5
1988	8	27.2	−136.1
1989	8	26.0	16.6
1990	8	25.5	35.8
South Korea			
1970	5	32.6	9.4
1971	5	34.2	−39.9
1972	5	37.7	17.1
1973	5	56.3	40.9
1974	5	68.0	−219.2
1975	5	60.3	64.5
1976	5	62.0	60.3
1977	5	62.7	33.6
1978	5	62.8	−7.4
1979	5	61.8	6.6
1980	5	64.2	−1.1
1981	5	66.7	−9.1
1982	5	60.7	4.5
1983	5	60.1	−19.7
1984	5	66.1	14.8
1985	5	64.9	4.0
1986	5	62.6	13.6
1987	5	71.8	7.4
1988	5	74.5	71.0
1989	5	66.3	18.8
1990	6	57.9	−2.8

[a]GNP = gross national product; exports and imports were derived on a customs basis.

[b]Change in reserves is measured as total reserves minus gold, measured as the U.S. dollar value of special drawing rights, reserve position, and foreign exchange.

Sources. Changes in reserves are from International Monetary Fund, *International Financial Statistics,* various issues. Trade shares are from World Bank, *World Tables,* various issues. Levels of financial openness were coded from information contained in International Monetary Fund various years. For a full explanation of coding, see the appendix.

response to crisis, quickly reversing the initial move toward a more closed policy stance in 1982. The 1988 reforms must also be seen as an effort to regain access to international capital markets following five years of financial drought and the mid-decade collapse of oil prices. The change in oil prices also helps explain Indonesia's reforms at the end of the 1980s.

The one exception to the rule is South Korea in 1990, when U.S. pressure appears to play a dominant role. However, our case study shows that this liberalization was the culmination of a decade-long liberalization effort that had its origins in the balance-of-payments problems the country experienced in the early 1980s. Moreover, the very gradualness of the program can itself be explained by South Korea's strong balance-of-payments position throughout the decade.

The reform efforts in our sample may be spurred by crises, but do balance-of-payments difficulties always lead to financial opening? One case can justifiably be removed from consideration. The severe balance-of-payments crisis in Chile in 1981–82 was not followed by a further opening of the capital account, but this was due to the fact that the crises of the early 1970s had already generated a substantial opening; indeed, it is striking that the Chilean government did not retreat from its commitment to an open capital account.

Our expectations with respect to the remainder of the cases depend heavily on the extent to which the government is capable of generating finance through other means. The apparent anomalies—Indonesia in 1975 and 1981–82 and South Korea in 1971, 1974, and 1981–82—are precisely the countries in which either abundant international liquidity and ability to borrow (in the 1970s) or strong export performance (in all four episodes) quickly alleviated short-term balance-of-payments problems. In contrast to the other crisis cases, these developments limited the extent to which government leaders saw the fall in international reserves as requiring increased effort to induce capital inflows through an opening of the capital account; in Indonesia, the oil boom even led to a partial reversal of its open stance toward foreign investors.

Case studies

Indonesia

From independence in 1949 until the second half of the 1960s, Indonesia had a relatively restrictive policy regarding capital account transactions.[21] The government subjected payments for services to licensing and controlled foreign investors' remittances. During the first half of the 1960s, Indonesia suffered recurring balance-of-payments crises, related directly to incoherent monetary and particularly fiscal policies. The response to these was a complex system of

---

21. For overviews of the Indonesian economy during this period, see Palmer 1978; Booth and McCawley 1981; Robison 1986; and Winters 1995.

multiple exchange rates that left the rupiah increasingly overvalued. As inflation accelerated, the financial system, dominated by deposit banks, suffered severe financial disintermediation. The balance-of-payments and financial crises came to a head in 1965, adding to the tensions within President Sukarno's fragile coalition between the Communist party and the military and contributing to the bloody collapse of the regime in the autumn of 1965. As Ingrid Palmer summarized the situation, by December 1965, "the only thing left in the national till were some bureaucratic fingers groping for any remaining dollars."[22]

There can be little doubt that the series of reforms of the late 1960s, which culminated in a commitment to full currency convertibility in 1971, were the response of the new government to the crisis of 1965–66. They grew directly out of the interest in attracting foreign capital, including particularly from the multilateral institutions, and to a lesser extent in maintaining the confidence of domestic holders of liquid assets, particularly Chinese businessmen. As Palmer concludes, "Because of lack of foreign exchange and external creditworthiness . . . the first hurdle that had to be cleared . . . was to regain a measure of credibility in the eyes of foreign governments."[23] Numerous foreign advisers were involved in the design of stabilization policies. But on the issue of establishing a regime that would facilitate capital inflow and halt speculative outflows, their views were in accord with those of the Indonesian technocrats and, more importantly, of the President himself.[24]

The reforms unfolded in stages. In 1966 a debt moratorium was put in place and a stabilization plan was initiated by Suharto's "new order" government with support from the IMF. The year 1966 also saw the first steps in liberalization of foreign exchange markets, devaluation of the rupiah, and a commitment to fully eliminate the multiple exchange-rate system. Important legislation liberalizing foreign direct investment followed in 1967, including increased freedom to remit profits and dividends and to repatriate capital. The ability to attain loans or open accounts denominated in dollars and to convert these into rupiah and back dates to 1968.[25] In the context of other legislation designed to help banks attract and keep deposits, the banks themselves began to offer loans and accounts denominated in dollars. When multiple exchange rates were abolished in April 1970, the government temporarily closed these facilities by decree, but they were restored with a new decree of full currency convertibility in 1971.

The government also sought to encourage the entry of foreign financial intermediaries as a way of attracting foreign capital, even though state banks continued to dominate the financial landscape. It eased restrictions on foreign bank entry, resulting in a major expansion of foreign bank presence in Indonesia between 1968 and 1971. Among the foreign banks represented were

22. Palmer 1978, 7.
23. Ibid., 15.
24. See ibid.; MacIntyre 1993, 135–41; and Cole and Slade 1994.
25. Arndt and Suwidjana 1982.

First National City, Bank of Tokyo, Bank of America, and Chase Manhattan.[26] The government also authorized, for the first time, the operation of nonbank financial institutions both domestic and foreign. Prior restrictions on the transfer of most stocks and shares also were lifted in 1970, allowing shares to be denominated in dollars or rupiah, though the stock exchange remained a sleepy institution until the reforms of the 1980s.

Despite this wave of liberalization and institutional change, important restrictions remained that reflected the interests of the government in maintaining political control over the allocation of credit. Even though foreign banks gained entry into Indonesia in the late 1960s, the government blocked foreign bank branching outside of Djakarta in order to prevent international banks from challenging the relatively uncompetitive state deposit banks operating under government protection throughout the archipelago.[27] In particular, the government was unwilling to allow competition that would threaten the discretionary allocation of credit to rural Indonesia, one instrument for maintaining the patron–client networks that underlay much of Suharto's power.[28]

The international operations of Indonesian banks were also restricted through the 1970s and into the 1980s. In 1985, the growth of international opportunities led local banks to lobby for permission to expand overseas through establishment of more agency and representative offices. They argued that international expansion would foster trade and investment with Indonesia, particularly in nonoil goods.[29] Bank Indonesia rebuffed these demands, in part fearing the possibility that the international expansion of Indonesian banks would lead to demands for reciprocity, which in turn would require lifting restrictions on foreign bank operations in Indonesia.

A third area of continued restriction on international capital movements was the prohibition of foreign participation in the Djakarta Stock Exchange (DSE). Following the liberalization of the early 1970s, foreign banks began to take business from local banks because they could raise funds at relatively low cost outside the Indonesian market.[30] The DSE was promoted throughout the 1970s and 1980s as a way to provide capital to businesses not favored by the foreign banks or by the government-controlled system of subsidized credit distribution.[31]

Not only were these restrictions retained but also new ones emerged in the mid-1970s. The implementation of credit ceilings and interest rate controls in 1973 was initially a stabilization measure designed to control the inflationary

26. See Grenville 1981, 104; and Economist Intelligence Unit, *Quarterly Economic Report*, 1971, no. 2:9.
27. Economist Intelligence Unit, *Quarterly Economic Report for Indonesia,* 1971, no. 1:9.
28. See Winters 1992; and MacIntyre 1993.
29. Economist Intelligence Unit, *Quarterly Economic Report,* 1985, no. 1:12.
30. See Economist Intelligence Unit, *Quarterly Economic Report,* 1973, no. 1:6–7; and Palmer 1978, 43.
31. Economist Intelligence Unit, *Quarterly Economic Report,* 1977, no. 1:6; and 1977, no. 4:6.

pressures associated with rising oil revenues and balance-of-payments sur-pluses.[32] However, the controls also garnered support from interventionists in the government who were responsible for dispensing state largesse to a growing network of corporate clients within both the state-owned and private sectors.

Despite the debt problems faced by the state-owned oil firm Pertamina in 1975, the resurgence of oil revenues and renewed lending permitted a more selective and interventionist stance toward foreign investment; this change in policy accounts for our more restrictive coding beginning in 1974. In contrast to the late 1960s and the 1980s, government leaders did not view the 1975 balance-of-payments crisis as warranting a change in capital account policy. Indonesia quickly rescheduled its debts and became the first country to use the so-called Paris club rescheduling facility. The combination of oil and the availability of capital through Eurodollar markets made it easy for government leaders to avoid liberalizing reforms.

The 1980s ushered in a new period of concern over balance of payments as opportunities for international borrowing disappeared. The year 1983 saw an important deregulation of the domestic financial system, but it was in the second half of the 1980s as world oil prices began to drop that external pressures mounted. There were several episodes of moderate capital flight in 1984 and 1985 followed by two bouts of serious capital flight: one in late 1986 and a second in mid-1987. Capital flight not only triggered exchange-rate adjustments but also led to further financial opening.

A broad package of liberalization measures was announced in October 1988.[33] One of these measures, foreign participation in the DSE, was hotly debated because it implied the possibility of increased foreign ownership of Indonesian companies, already a sensitive issue.[34] The concerns of economic policymakers and the prospects for tremendous gains dominated nationalist sentiment, however, and foreign participation was permitted. In 1989 the DSE began to boom, fueled primarily by overseas demand. In the fourth quarter of 1989, estimates put foreign holdings of total shares listed on the DSE at roughly one-third.[35]

The October 1988 package also affected banking. In addition to domestic reforms, restrictions were eased on the operations of foreign banks in an effort to increase the inflow of foreign funds. The government lifted the prohibition on branching outside Djakarta.[36] Domestic banks, leasing and factoring operations, securities trading firms, insurance companies, and credit and consumer finance companies also were permitted to engage in joint ventures

32. Cole and Slade 1994.
33. For analyses of these reforms, see Winters 1992; McKendrick 1989; MacIntyre 1993: 157–59; and Cole and Slade 1994.
34. Economist Intelligence Unit, *Quarterly Economic Report,* 1985, no. 4:8; and 1987, no. 4:12–13.
35. Economist Intelligence Unit, *Quarterly Economic Report,* 1989, no. 4:10–11.
36. The following draws on Economist Intelligence Unit, *Quarterly Economic Report,* 1988, no. 2:13; 1989, no. 1:9; 1989, no. 2:10; 1989, no. 3:15; and 1989, no. 4:10.

with foreign banks with a minimum domestic ownership of 15 percent. As a result, seven Japanese banks and Credit Lyonnais launched joint venture negotiations with local partners. Lifting these barriers to entry naturally implied further liberalization of capital flows: limits on offshore borrowing by banks and nonbank financial institutions were removed as part of the 1988 bank reform.

The timing of major policy changes in Indonesia suggests that the balance-of-payments position has been a major determinant of capital account politics. The first wave of liberalization occurred in the five years following the combined political and economic crisis of 1965–66 and culminated in a dramatic opening of the capital account in 1971. Indeed, these changes were sustained through 1974, when the government tightened the rules governing capital account transactions, particularly by instituting new restrictions on foreign direct investment. The model of crisis-induced policy change would predict a policy shift in the direction of greater openness at the time of the Pertamina crisis in 1975. This crisis was addressed quickly through devaluation and Paris club debt rescheduling, however; it was seen as a short-term liquidity problem. The need to undertake significant policy reform was quickly mitigated by abundant liquidity in international financial markets and, more importantly, by the massive inflow of oil revenues. A second wave of liberalization, centered primarily on the opening of the financial sector and the lifting of restrictions on foreign investment, did not come until the 1980s, when the country experienced declining oil prices and new balance-of-payments difficulties.

Chile

The first change in Chile's capital account policy, and the most dramatic in our sample, came in the first year of the Salvador Allende government, when capital account restrictions increased sharply. Initially, these changes were related to the political program of the government, which included among other things the nationalization of the copper industry and greater restrictions on multinational corporations. By the end of the Allende administration, however, controls reflected the desperate efforts of the government to conserve foreign exchange in the face of hyperinflation, a complete loss of both external and internal confidence, and severe balance-of-payments difficulties.[37]

The crisis contributed directly to the military coup of 1973. The initial focus of the Augusto Pinochet Ugarte government's financial market policy was on domestic deregulation, which had the effect of creating new private-sector actors.[38] The liberalization of interest rates on short-term transactions provided a boost to the creation of new nonbank financial intermediaries, the *financieras*. *Financieras* mushroomed because the government did not lift

---

37. Griffith-Jones 1981.
38. See Dahse 1979; Arellano 1983:7; Silva 1991; 1993; and Hastings 1993, 210–18.

controls on commercial bank deposits until later in the year, and deregulation was not fully effective until after the banks were privatized in 1975. A second pillar of the new financial regime dates to May 1974, when all but one of the nationalized commercial banks were offered for sale, a measure obviously supported by private-sector organizations. The banks were bought by a small number of entrepreneurs who constituted a new generation of economic groups or *grupos* that combined traditional import-substituting activities with greater participation in the export sector and in finance. The abolition of distinctions among different types of banks (commercial, investment, mortgage) encouraged aggressive entry by the new group-based banks into a variety of financial services. With only minimal regulatory oversight, banks favored lending to related companies within their *grupos,* leading to a sharp increase in the degree of concentration in both the manufacturing and the financial sectors.

However, the government's financial market policy was not limited to the domestic market. As we would expect in the wake of crisis, the liberalization of external controls that did take place centered on courting foreign investors. The government lifted restrictions on capital outflows by foreign investors in 1974, making Chile's investment laws the most liberal in Latin America in that regard, and it encouraged foreign banks to enter Chilean financial markets.

Eduardo Silva provides evidence suggesting that these early domestic reforms strengthened a set of financial players—*financieras,* the new more internationally oriented *grupos,* and foreign banks—at the expense of more traditional import-substituting groups.[39] These new actors stood to gain from greater access to international financial markets because they were more heavily engaged in financial activities and because despite deregulation, domestic interest rates remained extremely high, opening tremendous arbitrage opportunities.[40] Those firms lacking access to credit through their membership in a group were critical of capital controls on the grounds that they contributed to the maintenance of high interest rates. In a curious alignment, critics on the left held similar views, arguing that the gradual pace of capital account liberalization and the continuing use of quantitative controls on borrowing provided rents to those groups in the private sector with preferential access to foreign finance.[41] Silva shows that the portion of the economic team in charge of financial market reforms had strong ties to the internationalized segments of the private sector, including the financial sector.[42] As Daniel Wisecarver concludes, "the capital account was finally opened due to pressures from the financial community."[43]

39. See Silva 1991; and 1993.
40. Vylder 1989, 61.
41. Vergara 1986, 95.
42. Silva 1991, 243–48.
43. Wisecarver 1985, 194.

However, these sectoral pressures overlapped with a balance-of-payments crisis that also had a significant influence on government policy toward the liberalization of controls. In response to the near-hyperinflation of the last months of the Allende regime, and to manage the new inflationary and balance-of-payments pressures generated by the oil crisis and a downturn in copper prices, the new Pinochet government experimented with an orthodox stabilization program in 1974–75. The failure of this orthodox shock approach, reflected in continued triple-digit inflation, resulted in a crucial shift in stabilization policy by a new economic team, the infamous "Chicago boys," toward an emphasis on the exchange rate.

The new team designed stabilization policy to influence expectations about government policy and increase foreign and domestic creditor confidence. The assumption upon which they acted was that an exchange-rate-led stabilization, first through a crawling peg and then through fixing the exchange rate, would serve to integrate domestic and international capital markets and reduce domestic interest rates by reducing the anticipated rate of devaluation. Liberalizing capital inflows was crucial to achieving these technical objectives. But central bank officials also saw an open capital account as providing a check on future fiscal and monetary policy and as a way of signaling government intentions. Though this policy collapsed disastrously in 1982, it is worth quoting Sergio de Castro's conception of the plan: "What these programmed revaluations and devaluations had in common was that they gave a signal to the country since certain objective facts (the substantial drop in the fiscal deficit and the surplus in the balance of payments) had not been assimilated rapidly enough by the public."[44]

In September 1977, commercial banks gained authorization to borrow abroad for the first time, though with various limits in terms of aggregate quantities and term structure and a prohibition on direct arbitrage. After 1977, the central bank made numerous small changes in capital account regulations. Sebastian Edwards and Alejandra Edwards argue that capital could not move completely freely until just prior to the crisis of 1982.[45] Nonetheless, June 1979 marked a substantial change in policy: the limits to external borrowings by banks were increased markedly. The only limit retained was the overall borrowing limit, including both internal and external borrowing, of twenty times capital and reserves. The government eliminated monthly restrictions on capital inflows in April 1980, granted commercial banks permission to lend their own resources abroad in June 1980, and authorized commercial banks to invest in foreign financial assets in September 1980.[46]

The crisis that followed in the wake of this global monetarist experiment has been treated extensively elsewhere and need not be detailed here.[47] Under

44. De Castro's quotation is cited in Douglas 1985, 61.
45. Edwards and Edwards 1987, 55.
46. See Corbo 1983; and French-Davis and Arellano 1981.
47. See Foxley 1983; Corbo 1983; Ramos 1986; and Hastings 1993.

extreme pressure from international creditors, the Chilean government reluctantly assumed the external obligations of private financial creditors and effectively renationalized a number of financial institutions. In the short run, the management of the debt crisis demanded controls on external financial transactions, but these did not last. In the early 1980s a more pragmatic economic team with broader private-sector links came to power. Under this team export performance began to boom and the "Chilean miracle" began. Yet despite the pragmatism of the new team, it remained strongly committed to liberal ideas, and the fundamental posture of the government toward capital account openness remained unchanged.

Chile placed some restrictions on capital account transactions from the 1940s until the 1960s, when there was some liberalization. The election of Allende reversed this trend, ushering in a three-year period of tight controls, which mushroomed as balance-of-payments difficulties mounted. Liberalization came in the wake of a regime change that could itself be traced in no small measure to severe economic crisis. The new military government of General Pinochet undertook a substantial liberalization effort immediately on coming to office and then initiated a second round of economic opening following the balance-of-payments problems of 1974–75. By 1981, the capital account was highly open with regard to both capital flows and entry and exit.

In contrast to Indonesia and Mexico, Chile dismantled domestic financial controls prior to liberalizing international capital movements. As a result, important new domestic financial interests stood to gain from the lifting of foreign controls, thus helping to explain why the profound crisis of the early 1980s did not fundamentally alter the government's commitment to an open capital account.

Mexico

Compared with the other three countries examined here, Mexican commitment to currency convertibility, including freedom for foreign investors to remit profits and capital, is of long standing. We must therefore treat the Mexican case in a somewhat longer historical perspective, beginning with the intractable problems with capital flight and financial instability that accompanied and followed the revolution. In the 1920s, gold, silver pesos, paper pesos, and dollars all circulated within the Mexican financial system. Gold and dollars were the preferred stores of value and, with the aid of Mexican banks, hemorrhaged from the national financial system at any sign of a renewal of political or policy instability.

Convinced that the proximity of the United States made it impossible to arrest capital outflows through legal or administrative actions, the government decided in 1930 that speculative capital flows could be limited only through a government guarantee of convertibility. Mexico was heavily indebted to international (mostly New York) banks in the 1920s and struggled to make the minimal debt-service payments necessary to maintain access to international credit markets. Negotiations with international creditors led to the establishment of a fund that would backstop the transition to convertibility. As Ricardo Torres Gaytan writes, this mechanism "linked foreign debt with the exchange problem. . . . It was a way of arresting lack of confidence . . . and lack of foreign capital."[48]

In response to the severe balance-of-payments crisis of the 1930s, the government considered, and rejected, the implementation of capital controls. The populist economic program of President Cárdenas (1934–40) induced growing dollarization of the financial system, since there was no official prohibition on opening fully convertible dollar-denominated accounts with Mexican banks. Between 1934 and 1937, dollar deposits relative to total demand deposits reached levels not seen again until the 1982 financial crisis. Cárdenas did not seek to limit convertibility; his central bank director argued that exchange controls would hurt international trade and could never be enforced.[49] Throughout the 1960s, no exchange controls were applied to incoming or outgoing capital account transactions by Mexican residents or nonresidents. Nor were payments for invisibles restricted; foreign-investor remittances amounted to close to 10 percent of all foreign-exchange outflows in this period.

Commitment to free currency convertibility did not mean a liberal policy on foreign entry into the domestic financial market or freedom of Mexican financial institutions to operate abroad. From 1924 until 1941 the government allowed branches of foreign banks to conduct banking and credit services in Mexico with permission of the Finance Ministry, though they were prohibited from engaging in bond issues. In 1941 the government further curtailed foreign bank activities. From then until the imposition of yet further restrictions in the 1970s, the combination of operational limitations and Ministry of Finance refusal to grant new entry authorizations significantly reduced the foreign bank presence in Mexico. Legislation enacted in 1973 expressly forbade the establishment of foreign bank branches, and though it permitted the operation of foreign bank representative offices, these were prohibited from engaging in domestic financial intermediation.[50]

This protectionist stance reflected the preferences of Mexican banks; uncompetitive by international standards, they enjoyed a regulatory environment that made their operations highly profitable. However, closure also reflected the motivations of the Mexican government. Protection facilitated efforts to control a portion of domestic bank lending for industrial and agricultural policy reasons. Perhaps more importantly, the Mexican government financed its industrial policy in the 1950s and 1960s, including the

48. Gaytan 1980, 184. See also Diaz 1982.
49. See Maxfield 1990, 72; and Martinez 1980.
50. See Quijano 1985; and Martinez 1991.

expansion of the state-owned enterprise sector, in part through reserve requirements on domestic banks. Banks accepted these reserve requirements in return for a government financial policy regime that compensated them for the costs of high reserve requirements, in part through protection from foreign competition.

Mexico experienced its first balance-of-payments crisis in over two decades in 1976. The sharp decline in international reserves and subsequent devaluation were quickly overtaken by euphoria as oil export revenues and commercial banking lending exploded, but the crisis did provide the occasion for some financial liberalization. Legislation passed in 1977 and implemented in 1978 permitted Mexican banks to open foreign branches, in part to service their increasingly internationalized clientele, in part to tap Eurocurrency markets more effectively.

In 1982, Mexico became the first large Latin American country to experience a debt crisis. In a syndrome that was to become all too common, growing current account deficits were followed by the withdrawal of foreign financial support and massive capital flight. When the government declared dollar-denominated accounts inconvertible, instituted broader exchange controls, and nationalized Mexico's banks in 1982, indignant Mexicans referred to the transformation of Mexdollars into "ex-dollars."[51]

This nationalistic response appears to suggest that crises are just as likely to lead to foreign exchange and capital controls as they are to liberalization. However the controls proved surprisingly short-lived; both domestic politics and foreign pressures played a role. First, the controls were wildly unpopular.[52] The incoming President, Miguel de la Madrid, openly opposed the policy and publicly expressed his interest in removing the controls as rapidly as possible. However, the policy stance of the incoming administration was hardly populist; rather, it marked a sharp shift toward the technocratic end of the Mexican political spectrum.[53] This move to the right was in turn closely tied to external considerations. The IMF expected Mexico to end exchange controls as part of its standby agreement, and the standby agreement was central to the successful renegotiation of Mexico's debt to private international creditors.

The effects of the crisis were not limited to the short-run reversal of controls; rather, the crisis ushered in a period of intense economic reform that accelerated following further balance-of-payments difficulties in 1988. The NAFTA-related reforms have been outlined elsewhere; here it is important to note only that reforms included substantial deregulation of the domestic financial market, reprivatization of the banks that had been nationalized in the wake of the crisis, and the opening of the financial sector to foreign competition.[54] U.S. banks had long sought freer entry into the Mexican market,

---

51. For a nationalist interpretation of the crisis, see Tello 1984.
52. Maxfield 1990, 146–53.
53. Centeno and Maxfield 1990, 57–86.
54. On NAFTA reforms, see Hufbauer and Schott 1993, 61–65; and Maxfield 1993, 253–57.

and the negotiation of NAFTA provided them an entry point. Despite the strong external pressure and the Salinas administration's interest in seeing NAFTA succeed, the newly privatized banks were able to win a gradual phase-in of the entry provisions and certain market-share restrictions. However, the crisis of 1994–95 resulted in an acceleration of the NAFTA liberalization timetable.[55]

How do we explain changes in the Mexican government's commitment to free currency convertibility and capital movements? Certainly, close proximity to the United States limited the potential effectiveness of government currency controls from an early date. However, the government was able to devise a system that maintained convertibility while simultaneously placing limits on the behavior of foreign investors and protecting the domestic financial system. The initial response to the debt crisis was closure, but this policy was reversed in a matter of months, giving way to a renewed commitment to an open capital account. Decline in international reserves in 1988 overlapped with the process of negotiating NAFTA and led to a final step in Mexico's financial internationalization: the beginning of the end of the restrictions on foreign banks. Interestingly, the government's international financial policy was not reversed through the first half of 1995, despite a wrenching domestic adjustment.

South Korea

When South Korea's international financial policy is placed in comparative perspective, two facts are striking. First, when compared with other middle-income developing countries, South Korea has been relatively immune to balance-of-payments trouble. Second, the country exhibits a surprisingly low level of policy openness, particularly given the country's strong export orientation. The crises of 1971 and particularly 1974 prompted debate over domestic financial market reform, but a plan for liberalization of the capital account or greater entry for foreign banks was not advanced until balance-of-payments difficulties began in 1979. The implementation of the plan was prolonged, gradual, and partial. The reasons have to do precisely with South Korea's ability to borrow its way out of the oil crises and its sustained ability to generate exports. These conditions limited the influence of those within the government who favored greater financial internationalization. The shift in policy reflected in our coding for 1990 did not come as a response to balance-of-payments difficulties; rather, strong diplomatic pressure from the United States and ultimately a change of government in 1993 appeared to play the central roles. But as throughout the decade, the South Korean response was cautious and gradual.

---

55. Maxfield in press.

The South Korean government consistently has intervened in financial markets.[56] The motive for this intervention has been related to the conduct of industrial policy. Following the military's seizure of power in 1961, the banking system was nationalized and preferential credit to exporters became a central element of South Korea's export-led growth strategy. In the early 1960s, the government turned to foreign borrowing to finance the import of capital goods, but all foreign borrowing was intermediated by state-owned banks and required government approval and guarantee. With the exception of the few export-processing zones, the regime governing foreign direct investment was surprisingly restrictive, and the rules governing individuals' access to foreign exchange were even more draconian than those facing firms.

The balance-of-payments problems the country faced in 1971 resulted in some important domestic financial reforms, but balance-of-payments equilibrium was quickly restored, and the government initiated no fundamental change in foreign financial policy. Following the oil crisis of 1973–74, the government relied even more heavily on both financial subsidies and foreign borrowing in an effort to engineer a "big push" into heavy and chemical industries; this first crisis pushed South Korea toward greater state intervention. After contentious intrabureaucratic conflicts between those committed to the heavy-industry drive and a growing group of technocrats who opposed its excesses, Park Chung Hee acquiesced to a wide-ranging adjustment plan in early 1979.[57] Among other things, the plan called for liberalizing the financial market.[58] Implementation of the plan was interrupted by the assassination of President Park in 1979 and an economic and political crisis in 1980, but following the seizure of power by Chun Doo-Hwan in May 1980, the technocratic reformers, led by Kim Jae Ik, regained their position and initiated a series of important financial reforms, both domestic and foreign.

In January 1981, the government announced its plan to internationalize South Korea's capital markets by allowing foreigners to invest in domestic stocks indirectly through investment trust funds.[59] One motive for this move was the effort to diversify sources of foreign capital away from bank borrowing. South Korea managed to maintain access to foreign capital through the early 1980s because of its dynamic export performance; in no sense did South Korea experience a crisis comparable to the large Latin American debtors. Nonetheless, the country did run high current account deficits following the second oil shock, banks were more wary of lending to South Korea than they had been in the past, and liberalization was seen as a way of improving access to new sources of foreign financing.

56. For an overview of Korean financial policy, see Cole and Park 1983; Woo 1991; Choi 1993.
57. Haggard et al. 1994, chap. 3.
58. For an overview of the reforms, see Park 1995. On the politics of financial market reform in the 1980s, see Choi 1993; and Rhee 1992.
59. See Euh and Baker 1990, 44–47; Mahler 1988: 10–11; and Park 1995.

The early stages of the program emphasized liberalizing capital inflows, rather than outflows, but the strategy was highly gradual and the complete liberalization of the capital account was not envisioned until the early 1990s. Domestic firms were not allowed to raise funds abroad until the second half of the 1980s. Only fourteen of the largest companies were allowed to borrow directly through the issue of convertible bonds, and then only with Ministry of Finance approval, a pattern that conformed with the government's preferential treatment of the *chaebol*, the large conglomerates.

The government also maintained a highly protectionist stance toward the entry of foreign financial intermediaries, a stance that can be explained in part by the politics of a closed and heavily regulated financial system.[60] Domestic banks were just being privatized, capital markets were relatively undeveloped, and important portions of the economic bureaucracy remained wedded to interest-rate controls. Moreover, the banks were saddled with nonperforming assets, many of them policy loans associated with the heavy-industry drive of the late 1970s.[61] Foreign entry would only compound the adjustment problems in the financial sector, not only among banks but in the heavily protected insurance and securities industries as well.

Despite the internationalization of South Korean industry, the *chaebol* had a number of concerns about both domestic deregulation and internationalization as well. First, though they welcomed the opportunity to enter the financial sector and to gain independent access to foreign financial markets, they remained heavily dependent on preferential finance from state-owned banks. Second, despite efforts to diversify ownership, many of the largest groups remained family-dominated enterprises; this was even more true among smaller and medium-sized firms. These firms feared that foreign entry into the capital markets would dilute control. Finally, the export-dependence of the *chaebol* slowed the rapid opening to external capital movements, because of the fear that capital inflows would put upward pressure on the exchange rate, precisely as had happened in Chile after 1979; this remained an important concern well into the 1990s.[62]

In the absence of pressing balance-of-payments constraints, the government was under little pressure to liberalize. In fact, from 1985 through 1988, South Korea experienced large current account surpluses, peaking at over 8 percent of gross national product in 1987. These surpluses generated pressures that were exactly the opposite of those experienced in the crisis cases. On the one hand, the government relaxed its controls on capital export in 1987 and 1988, encouraged firms to prepay their external debt, and promoted outward foreign investment. On the other hand, the rapid accumulation of surpluses created daunting problems of macroeconomic management and strong incentives to

60. Euh and Baker 1990, 19–43.
61. Choi 1993, 40–54.
62. See, for example, the essays in Dornbusch and Park 1995.

slow down the initial timetable for the liberalization of capital inflows. When the current account turned to deficit in 1989, the government returned to its traditional practice of controlling capital export as well.

The main source of pressure on South Korea came not from the balance of payments, but from the U.S. government. Under the 1988 trade bill, the U.S. Treasury Department was authorized to determine whether countries manipulated their exchange rates to prevent effective adjustment or to gain competitive advantage. The department found that South Korea was manipulating its exchange rate, and in February 1990, Financial Policy Talks were launched. The premise of these talks was that the South Korean currency, the won, had failed to appreciate adequately because the continued use of capital controls limited demand for it.[63] These complaints coincided with an array of complaints from American banks that they experienced discrimination in their South Korean operations and from American securities firms that began to develop an interest in gaining access to the lucrative South Korean market.

After 1988, concessions to the United States were balanced by efforts to maintain policy autonomy and to tailor foreign entry to limit the competitive pressure on domestic financial firms. In March 1990, the Korean government introduced a more flexible exchange-rate system. The problem of foreign banks' access to domestic funds—a recurrent complaint—was addressed by increasing the limit on certificate of deposit issues. In June 1991, the revised Foreign Capital Control Act was a move toward a negative list system approach, under which all transactions not explicitly prohibited would be permitted.

Yet the government counterbalanced such liberalizing moves by its continuing interest in control. The opening of the capital market to direct portfolio investment and foreign entry into the securities business provide clear examples. Though it opened direct purchase of South Korean securities to foreigners in January 1992, it limited foreign ownership of the total shares of a single company to 10 percent and ownership by a single firm to 3 percent. Given that some of the largest firms had been allowed to issue convertible bonds, these limits were quickly reached.[64] At the March 1992 Financial Policy Talks with the United States, the Ministry of Finance presented a document outlining a new blueprint for the "comprehensive" liberalization of the financial sector. The first phase included a variety of small measures, such as a marginal increase in certificate of deposit issuance limits for foreign banks—permitting some bond trading by foreign financial institutions—and an expansion of the daily foreign exchange fluctuation band. But the plan stipulated that future stages of liberalization be contingent on the balance of payments, lower inflation, and a narrowing of domestic and international interest-rate differen-

---

63. Balassa and Williamson 1990.
64. *Business Korea,* February 1992, 27.

tials, conditions the United States argued would occur only if the domestic market were opened.[65]

Similar efforts at balancing foreign and domestic pressures are visible in the controversy over opening the domestic financial sector to foreign entry. When the government announced the criteria for foreign securities firms that would be allowed to enter the domestic market, the considerations included the extent to which the entering firm contributed to the development of the domestic (South Korean) industry, implying that joint ventures would be favored over wholly owned ventures. Moreover, the capital requirements were so high and the exact scope of allowed business so vague that a number of foreign firms refused even to apply. All of the Japanese applicants were excluded on the grounds that South Korean entry into the Tokyo market was closed; yet the interpretation given by international financial analysts was that South Korean firms were fearful of cash-rich Japanese companies and that the list had been tailored to respond to American and British trade pressures.[66]

In the absence of a severe foreign-exchange constraint, South Korean liberalization was extremely gradual. The oil crisis was managed through increased borrowing and aggressive promotion of exports. Portions of the economic bureaucracy saw shortcomings in the control-oriented policy style of the late Park years, but the government was constrained by its close relations with the *chaebol.* The largest firms continued to enjoy access to preferential credit, and the domestic financial sector managed to retain a substantial degree of protection. Moreover, the government maintained the political advantage of being able to use the financial system as an instrument both of macroeconomic management and for allocating resources to favored uses.

Conclusion

Our analysis suggests two sources of external pressure on the financial policies of developing country governments. First, we found evidence that increased interdependence and the opportunities provided by deepening financial market integration led to changes in the domestic "preference map" with respect to issues of financial internationalization. These changes also heightened the interests of foreign actors in gaining market access. These changing configurations of interests provided an important background condition for the liberalization episodes we have traced.

However, we placed particular emphasis on similar consequences wrought by a country's balance-of-payments position. Crises strengthened internationalist forces both within the government and in the economy. Episodes of capital account opening appeared to be motivated by the efforts of political leaders to

---

65. U.S. Treasury Department 1992, 20.
66. *Business Korea,* January 1991, 28–29; and April 1991, 49–50.

assure creditors and investors, both domestic and foreign. By contrast, periods of easy access to finance, commodity booms, or successful export-led growth strategies increase the bargaining power of governments vis-à-vis investors and allow politicians to continue to use controls for political ends.

Despite these findings, it is important to emphasize several empirical and theoretical weaknesses in the approach we have outlined here. First, since the extent of economic openness and the opportunity costs of remaining closed change only gradually, it is difficult to assess *ex ante* when the accumulated weight of sectoral interests will tip in the direction of policy reform. In the absence of crisis, both government and sectoral interests in controls remained strong or "sticky" in all cases.

Two further problems pose more difficult challenges to our hypothesis on the role of crisis and of international factors more generally. First, we found that the motives for government intervention and liberalization are not fully captured by a model of policy in which the international position of different sectors is the driving causal mechanism. Governments had political motives for controls and liberalization that go beyond the factor and sectoral approaches that are at the heart of the Frieden–Rogowski approach.[67] These included both the advantages in terms of seigniorage and government finances and the ability to use the financial system for industrial policy and patronage purposes.

A second problem resides in the fact that "international" variables such as external shocks, the openness of the economy, and the opportunity costs of closure are themselves partly a function of past government policy. When we probe the origins of balance-of-payments crises in these four countries, for example, we find, first, that domestic political factors were deeply implicated in each case and, second, that changes of policy occurred only following changes of government or even regime.

In Mexico, the renewed commitment to free currency convertibility in the 1920s and 1930s followed a history of chaotic financial policies associated with the revolution. Subsequent financial reform did constitute an effort to assuage foreign creditors, but its precise form was tailored to the interests of the new party elite in consolidating its hold on power. Mexican political leaders used financial market policies in ways that were not inconsistent with a sectoral story, but that also reflected much broader political motivations. For example, the government used financial controls to fund *itself,* as well as import-substituting industry and agriculture. The restrictions on foreign investors instituted under President Echeverría in the early 1970s were but one component of a broader political reaction against the conservatism and growing inequality of the stabilizing development period. Conversely, the liberalization of the 1980s marked a reaction against the failures of the Echeverría and José López Portillo years.

---

67. See Frieden 1991a; and Rogowski 1991.

In both Chile and Indonesia, the balance-of-payments problems that provided the context for later capital account liberalization can be traced to a tumultuous history of macroeconomic instability and unsustainable exchange rates under the populist governments of Allende and Sukarno, respectively. The resolution of these balance-of-payments crises was not simply the result of an existing government changing course. Rather, the crises contributed to regime changes that marked fundamental realignments in the economic-cum-political coalitions supporting the government, in leadership, and in the basic institutional arrangements of politics as well. In Chile, Pinochet exploited his power to undertake a dramatic restructuring of the economy on new lines; financial market policy was only one component of a neoliberal strategy aimed at rooting out the conditions that had given rise to Allende in the first place. In Indonesia, by contrast, the government liberalized the capital account but continued to exploit the segmentation of markets and financial controls in order to dispense patronage and secure bases of political support.

Finally, the strong control over both fiscal and monetary policy and the long-standing push to promote exports help explain how South Korea managed to avoid the kind of balance-of-payments difficulties that provoked capital account opening in the other cases. But this growth path, in turn, cannot be understood without reference to the intervention of the military in politics in 1961, an intervention that fundamentally altered the nature of state–society relations in South Korea. As in the other countries, financial controls, both domestic and foreign, were a component of a broader political strategy for maintaining power. These instruments of intervention and political control proved surprisingly resistant to change, despite substantial internationalization.

It is beyond the scope of this article to explore the nature of these domestic factors in detail; we have pursued this line of research elsewhere, and our purpose here was to focus on the important effects of internationalization.[68] It is clear, however, that domestic politics plays a significant role in the way internationalization has shaped decisions concerning the capital account in the cases we have examined, and that these domestic political constraints cannot be wholly reduced to shocks or the interests of social groups.

However, we close by noting that the role of such domestic political variables may well decline in the future. As the integration of financial markets deepens, accelerated by the very policy changes that we have analyzed here, international constraints will play an increasing role in future policy decisions, not only with regard to the capital account but also with reference to economic policy more generally.

---

68. On the nature of these domestic sources, see Maxfield 1990; Haggard and Maxfield 1993; and Haggard and Kaufman 1995, chap. 5.

Appendix

We define financial internationalization to include two broad policy areas: rules governing the capital account; and rules governing the international behavior of financial institutions. With respect to the first, the Organization for Economic Cooperation and Development (OECD) Capital Movements Code directs attention to restrictions on direct investment or disinvestment; buying and selling of securities; operations in real estate; credits directly linked to international trade in goods or services; cross-border financial credits and loans; the accounts of financial institutions; personal capital transfers; physical movements of capital assets; and disposal of funds owned by nonresidents.[69] The OECD does not specifically address the rules governing foreign entry in financial services except as one component of the broader regime governing foreign direct investment. As the IMF notes, however, "trade liberalizations in many service industries, in particular the financial industry, have necessitated accompanying liberalizations of capital account transactions."[70]

The index of the openness of international financial policy is the sum of four separate indexes on particular policy areas. The codings are based on a four-point scale from 0 to 3 points, thus permitting a total range of the index of 0 to 12. The coding rules for the four policy areas are shown in Appendix Table 1.

APPENDIX TABLE 1. *Indexes of international openness*

Score	Criteria
	A. International operations of commercial banks
0	No or minimal international operations by private domestic banks; foreign banks either prohibited from entry or subject to substantial controls on all foreign transactions; most foreign financial transactions managed by government-owned banks
1	All international transactions of domestic banks subject to government approval with limits on terms and on the net foreign currency position of the bank; international operations of foreign banks subject to government approval and limits
2	International transactions of domestic and foreign banks subject to some statutory limits, but with substantial freedom within those limits
3	Substantial freedom for outward and inward transactions by domestic banks; substantial freedom of operation for foreign banks and a generally nondiscriminatory environment
	B. Payments for financial services, including profits and dividends, and repatriation of capital
0	All payments for financial services, including repatriation of profits and dividends, subject to limits and government approval; limits on repatriation of capital

---

69. OECD 1990, 11–12.
70. IMF 1992, 27.

APPENDIX TABLE 1. *continued*

Score	Criteria
	B. Payments for financial services, including profits and dividends, and repatriation of capital continued
1	Limits on payments for financial services and repatriation of capital, but guarantees on the repatriation of profits and dividends
2	Substantial freedom to secure foreign exchange for financial services; guarantees on the repatriation of profits, dividends, and capital
3	Complete freedom to secure foreign exchange for all financial services; guarantees on the repatriation of profits, dividends, and capital
	C. Portfolio investment and private borrowing
0	No inward or outward portfolio investment; all foreign borrowing intermediated by the state
1	No or very limited access by domestic residents to foreign securities; no or limited rights for domestic firms to issue securities abroad; substantial limits on foreign holdings of domestic securities; substantial limits on the foreign operations of domestic securities firms and on the domestic operations of foreign securities firms; strict government controls on all foreign borrowing
2	Mechanisms for domestic residents to purchase securities and for domestic firms to issue securities abroad, though with restrictions; some limits on the operations of both domestic and foreign securities firms, typically with continuing discrimination in favor of domestic firms; freedom to borrow abroad, typically with government approval
3	Substantial freedom for domestic residents to purchase securities, for domestic firms to issue securities abroad, and for foreigners to acquire local securities; generally open and nondiscriminatory regime toward foreign securities firms; substantial freedom to borrow abroad
	D. Foreign direct investment
0	Substantial sectoral restrictions, all investment subject to screening and extensive requirements with regard to trade behavior, employment, domestic equity, domestic content, etc.
1	Sectoral restrictions, but some sectors and/or projects open without, or with only nominal, screening; some requirements with regard to trade behavior, employment, domestic equity, domestic content, etc.
2	Sectoral restrictions, but primarily in communication, energy, utilities, and extractive industries; most remaining areas open without government screening, with nominal screening, or screening only for very large projects; limited requirements with regard to trade behavior, employment, domestic equity, domestic content, etc.
3	Very limited sectoral restrictions, freedom to invest outside of those areas with no or minimal screening; no requirements with regard to trade behavior, employment, domestic equity, domestic content, etc.

Sources. All data are coded from information contained in IMF various years. See also IMF 1989; and 1992.

References

Alesina, Alberto, and Guido Tabellini. 1989. External debt, capital flight, and political risk. *Journal of Development Economics,* 27:199–221.

Alesina, Alberto, Vittorio Grilli, and Gian Maria Milesi-Feretti. 1993. The political economy of capital controls. Working paper no. 4353, National Bureau of Economic Research, Cambridge, Mass.

Andrews, David M. 1994. Capital mobility and state autonomy: Toward a structural theory of international monetary relations. *International Studies Quarterly* 38:193–218.

Arellano, Pablo. 1983. De la liberalización a la intervención: El mercado de capitales en Chile: 1974–83 (From liberalization to intervention: The Chilean capital market: 1974–1988). *Colleción Estudios Cieplan* 11:5–49.

Arndt, H. W., and Njoman Suwidjana. 1982. The Jakarta Dollar Market. *Bulletin of Indonesian Economic Studies* 28:35–65.

Balassa, Bela, and John Williamson. 1990. *Adjusting to success: Balance of payments policy in the East Asian NICs.* Washington D.C.: Institute for International Economics.

Bartolini, Leonardo, and G. Bondar. 1992. An analysis of the process of capital account liberalization in Italy. Working paper no. 92/97, International Monetary Fund, Washington, D.C.

Bartolini, Leonardo, and Allan Drazen. 1994. Capital account liberalization as a signal. International Monetary Fund Research Department, Washington, D.C.

Bisat, Amer, R. Barry Johnston, and V. Sundarajan. 1992. Issues in managing and sequencing financial sector reforms: Lessons from experiences in five developing countries. Working paper 92/82, International Monetary Fund, Washington, D.C.

Booth, Anne, and Peter McCawley, eds. 1981. *The Indonesian economy during the Soeharto era.* New York: Oxford University Press.

Centeno, Miguel Angel, and Sylvia Maxfield. 1990. The marriage of finance and order: Changes in the Mexican political elite. *Journal of Latin American Studies* 24:57–86.

Choi, Byung-sun. 1993. Financial policy and big business in Korea: The perils of financial regulation. In Haggard, Lee, and Maxfield 1993.

Cole, David, and Yung-chul Park. 1983. *Financial development in Korea, 1945–1978.* Cambridge, Mass.: Harvard University Press.

Cole, David, and Betty Slade. 1994. Political economy of Indonesian financial reform. Harvard Institute for International Development, Cambridge, Mass.

Corbo, Vittorio. 1983. Chile: Economic policy and international economic relations since 1970. Working paper no. 86, Instituto de Economía, Pontifica Universidad Católica de Chile, Santiago.

Corbo, Vittorio, and Jaime de Melo. 1985. Liberalization with stabilization in the Southern Cone of Latin America: Overview and summary. *World Development* 13:863–66.

———. 1987. Lessons from the Southern Cone policy reforms. *World Bank Research Observer* 2:111–42.

Dahse, Fernando. 1979. *El mapa de la extrema riqueza* (The map of extreme wealth). Santiago: Editorial Aconagua.

Diaz, Eduardo Turrent. 1982. *Historia del Banco de México* (History of the Bank of Mexico). Vol. 1. Mexico City: Banco de México.

Dornbusch, Rudiger, and Yung-chul Park, eds. 1995. *Financial opening: Policy lessons for Korea.* Seoul: Korea Institute of Finance and International Center for Economic Growth.

Douglas, Hernan Cortes. 1985. Stabilization policies in Chile: Inflation, unemployment, and depression, 1975–1982. In *The National Economic Policies of Chile,* edited by Gary Walton. Greenwich, Conn., JAI Press.

Drazen, Allen, and Vittorio Grilli. 1993. The benefits of crisis for economic reforms. *American Economic Review* 83:598–607.

Edwards, Sebastian. 1984. The order of liberalization of the external sector. *Princeton Essays on International Finance,* no. 156.

———. 1995. Comments on *Developing nations and the politics of global integration,* by Stephen Haggard. Washington, D.C.: Brookings Institution.

Edwards, Sebastian, and Alejandra Cox Edwards. 1987. *Monetarism and liberalization: The Chilean experiment.* Cambridge, Mass.: Ballinger.

Edwards, Sebastian, and Sweder van Wijnbergen. 1986. The welfare effects of trade and capital market liberalization. *International Economic Review* 27:141–48.

Euh, Yoon-dae, and James C. Baker. 1990. *The Korean banking system.* New York: Routledge.

Foxley, Alejandro. 1983. *Latin American experiments in neo-conservative economics.* Berkeley: University of California Press.

French-Davis, Ricardo, and Jose Pablo Arellano. 1981. Apertura financiera externa: La experiencía Chilena en 1973–1980. *Estudios Cieplan* 50:127–51.

Frieden, Jeffry. 1991a. Invested interests: The politics of national economic policies in a world of global finance. *International Organization* 45:425–51.

———. 1991b. *Debt, development, and democracy: Modern political economy and Latin America, 1965–1985.* Princeton, N.J.: Princeton University Press.

Galbis, Vicente. 1986. Financial sector liberalization under oligopolistic conditions and a bank holding company structure. *Savings and Development* 10:117–41.

Gaytan, Ricardo Torres. 1980. *Un siglo de devaluaciones del peso mexicano* (A century of Mexican peso devaluations). Mexico City: Siglo 21.

Giovannini, A., and M. de Melo. 1993. Government revenue from financial repression. *American Economic Review* 83:953–63.

Goodman, John, and Louis Pauly. 1993. The obsolescence of capital controls? Economic management in an age of global markets. *World Politics* 46:50–82.

Grenville, Stephen. 1981. Monetary policy and the formal financial sector. In *The Indonesian economy during the Soeharto era,* edited by A. Booth and P. McCawley. New York: Oxford University Press.

Griffith-Jones, Stephany. 1981. *The role of finance in the transition to socialism.* Totowa, N.Y.: Allanheld, Osman.

Haggard, Stephan, and Robert Kaufman. 1995. *The political economy of democratic transitions.* Princeton, N.J.: Princeton University Press.

Haggard, Stephan, and Sylvia Maxfield. 1993. Political explanations of financial policy in developing countries. In Haggard, Lee, and Maxfield 1993.

Haggard, Stephan, Richard Cooper, Susan Collins, Roh Sung-tae, and Kim Chungsoo. 1994. *Macroeconomic policy and adjustment in Korea, 1970–1990.* Cambridge, Mass.: Harvard University Press.

Haggard, Stephan, Chung Lee, and Sylvia Maxfield, eds. 1993. *The politics of finance in developing countries.* Ithaca, N.Y.: Cornell University Press.

Hanson, James A. 1992. *Opening the capital account: A survey of issues and results.* Washington, D.C.: The World Bank.

Hastings, Laura. 1993. Regulatory revenge: The politics of free market financial reforms in Chile. In Haggard, Lee, and Maxfield 1993.

Hufbauer, Gary Clyde, and Jeffrey J. Schott. 1993. *NAFTA: An assessment.* Washington, D.C.: Institute for International Economics.

International Monetary Fund (IMF). Various years. *Annual report on exchange arrangements and exchange restrictions.* Washington, D.C.: IMF.

———. *Developments in international trade and exchange systems.* 1989. Washington, D.C.: IMF.

———. 1992. *Developments in international exchange and payments systems.* Washington, D.C.: IMF.

Keohane, Robert, and Helen Milner, eds. In press. *Internationalization and domestic politics.* New York: Cambridge University Press.

Krugman, Paul. 1979. A model of balance of payments crises. *Journal of Money, Credit, and Banking* 11:311–25.

Kurzer, Paulette. 1991. Unemployment in open economies: The impact of trade, finance, and European integration. *Comparative Political Studies* 24:3–30.

———. 1993. *Political change and economic integration in Western Europe.* Ithaca, N.Y.: Cornell University Press.

Laba, Raul, and Felipe Larrain. 1993. Can liberalization of capital outflows increase net capital inflows? Economics Department, Pontifica Universidad Catolica de Chile, Santiago.

MacIntyre, Andrew. 1993. The politics of finance in Indonesia. In Haggard, Lee, and Maxfield 1993.

Mahler, Walter. 1988. The allocation of the windfall from internationalization of the Korea capital market. Working paper no. 8813, Korea Development Institute, Seoul.

Martinez, Francisco Borja. 1991. *El nuevo sistema financiero mexicano* (The new system of Mexican finance). Mexico City: Fondo de Cultural Economica.

Martinez, Guillermo Ortiz. 1980. La dolarizacion en Mexico: Causas y consecuencias (Dollarization in Mexico: Causes and consequences). Serie de documentos no. 40, Banco de Mexico.

Mathieson, Donald, and Liliana Rojas-Suarez. 1993. Liberalization of the capital account: Experiences and issues. Occasional paper no. 103, International Monetary Fund, Washington, D.C.

Maxfield, Sylvia. 1990. *Governing capital.* Ithaca, N.Y.: Cornell University Press.

———. 1993. The politics of Mexican financial policy. In Haggard, Lee, and Maxfield 1993.

———. 1995. The politics of central banking in developing countries. Department of Political Science, Yale University, New Haven, Conn.

———. In press. Mexican financial liberalization. In *Letting capital loose,* edited by Michael Louriaux. Ithaca, N.Y.: Cornell University Press.

McKendrick, David. 1989. Acquiring technological capabilities: Aircraft and commercial banking in Indonesia. Ph.D. diss. School of Business Administration, University of California, Berkeley.

McKinnon, Ronald. 1991. *The order of economic liberalization: Financial control in the transition to a market economy.* Baltimore, Md.: Johns Hopkins University Press.

North, Douglass, and Barry Weingast. 1989. The evolution of institutions governing public choice in seventeenth century England," *Journal of Economic History* 49:803–32.

Obstfeld, Maurice. 1986. Rational and self-fulfilling balance of payments crises. *American Economic Review* 76:72–81.

Organization for Economic Cooperation and Development (OECD). 1990. *Liberalisation of capital movements and financial services.* Paris: OECD.

Palmer, Ingrid. 1978. *The Indonesian economy since 1965.* London: Frank Cass and Company.

Park, Daekeun. 1995. Financial opening and capital inflow: The Korean experience and policy issues. In *Financial opening: Policy lessons for Korea,* edited by Rudiger Dornbusch and Yung Chul Park. Seoul: Korean Institute of Finance.

Pauley, Louis W. 1988. *Opening financial markets: Banking politics on the Pacific Rim.* Ithaca, N.Y.: Cornell University Press.

Perez-Campanero, J., and A. M. Leone. 1992. Liberalization and financial crisis in Uruguay, 1974–87. In *Banking crisis: Cases and issues,* edited by V. Sundaragjan and T. Balin. Washington, D.C.: International Monetary Fund.

Quijano, Jose Manuel. 1985. Finanzas Latinoamericanas y banca extranjera (Latin American finances and foreign banks). In *Finanzas, desarollo economica, y penetracion extranjera* (Finances, economic development, and foreign penetration), edited by J. Quijano, H. Sanchez, and F. Antia. Puebla, Mexico: Universidad Autonoma de Puebla.

Ramos, Joseph. 1986. *Neoconservative economics in the Southern Cone of Latin America.* Baltimore, Md.: Johns Hopkins University Press.

Reinhart, Carmen M., and R. Todd Smith. 1995. Capital controls: concepts and experiences. Washington, D.C.: International Monetary Fund. Mimeographed.

Rhee, Jong Chan. 1992. The limits of financial liberalization under an authoritarian regime: The political process in South Korea. Paper presented at the annual meeting of the American Political Science Association, 3–6 September, Chicago.

Robison, Richard. 1986. *Indonesia: The rise of capital.* Sydney: Allen and Unwin.

Rodrik, Dani. 1989. Promises, promises: Credible policy reform via signaling. *Economic Journal* 99:756–72.

Rogowski, Ronald. 1991. *Commerce and coalitions.* Princeton, N.J.: Princeton University Press.

Rosenbluth, Frances McCall. 1989. *Financial politics in contemporary Japan.* Ithaca, N.Y.: Cornell University Press.

Roubini, Nouriel, and Xavier Sala-i-Martin. 1992. Financial repression and economic growth. *Journal of Development Economics* 39:5–31.

Silva, Eduardo. 1991. Capitalist coalitions and economic policymaking in authoritarian Chile, 1973–1988. Ph.D. diss., Department of Political Science, University of California, San Diego.

———. 1993. Capitalist coalitions, the state, and neoliberal economic restructuring: Chile, 1973–88. *World Politics* 45:501–25.

Tello, Carlos. 1984. *La nacionalizacion de la banca* (Nationalization of the banks). Mexico City: Siglo 21.

U.S. Treasury Department. 1992. *Report to the Congress on international economic and exchange rate policy.* Washington, D.C.: Government Printing Office.

Vergara, Pilar. 1986. Changes in the economic function of the Chilean state under the military regime. In *Military rule in Chile: Dictatorships and oppositions,* edited by J. Samuel Velenzuela and Arturo Valenzuela. Baltimore, Md.: Johns Hopkins University Press.

de Vylder, Stefan. 1989. Chile, 1973–1987: Los vaivenes de un modelo (Chile, 1973–1987: The rise and fall of a model). In *Economía y política durante el gobierno militar en Chile, 1973–1987* (Economics and politics during the military government in Chile, 1973–1987), edited by Roberto Garcia. Mexico City: Fondo de Cultura Económica.

Williamson, John. 1992. A cost-benefit analysis of capital account liberalization. In *Towards capital account convertibility,* edited by Bernhard Fischer and Helmut Reisen. Development Centre Policy Brief no. 4. Paris: Organization for Economic Cooperation and Development.

Winters, Jeffrey A. 1992. Banking reform in Indonesia: External linkages and created crises. Paper presented for the annual meetings of the American Political Science Association, 3–6 September, Chicago.

———. 1994. Power and the control of capital. *World Politics* 46:419–52.

———. 1995. *Power in motion: Capital mobility and the Indonesian state.* Ithaca, N.Y.: Cornell University Press.

Wisecarver, Daniel L. 1985. Economic regulation and deregulation in Chile." In *The national economic policies of Chile,* edited by Gary Walton. Greenwich, Conn.: JAI Press.

Woo, Jung-en. 1991. *Race to the swift: State and finance in Korean industrialization.* New York: Columbia University Press.

IV.
Emerging Issues

A s an academic specialty rooted in the practicalities of the real world, where change is forever occurring, the field of international political economy is persistently under challenge to revisit assumptions, rethink accepted concepts, or revise its analytical focus. Older policy questions may reappear in unfamiliar guise, demanding fresh answers; new problems may materialize unexpectedly, clamoring for attention. Many issues become topics of major political interest and debate on the global stage. The imperative for scholars is not only to try, where appropriate, to offer practical illumination and policy guidance but also to promote a basic understanding of how such developments may be effectively integrated into the larger corpus of international political economy theory.

While resisting the temptation to pursue every passing fad, International Organization has always understood the need to stay abreast of salient events and trends: to relate specific new developments to more general theoretical questions in ways that provide useful analytical insight for both academic scholarship and policy practice. Toward that end, the journal has regularly offered a forum for serious scrutiny of specialized or emerging issues in the world economy.

One example of such an issue is the problem of world commodity trade, a topic of perennial interest to the many developing nations that depend on sales of primary products—foodstuffs, agricultural raw materials, minerals, or fuels—for the bulk of their export revenues. Key questions repeatedly reassert themselves as new variations on old themes. Should or how may commodity trade be regulated? Who are the key actors in international negotiations to stabilize prices or to raise producer revenues? What is the role of multilateral institutions? How do commodity issues relate to matters of international security, national power, or domestic politics? All of these issues have been addressed over the years in the pages of International Organization, especially including early contributions by Vincent A. Mahler, John Ravenhill, Robert L. Rothstein, and Robert H. Bates and Da-hsiang Donald Lien.[1]

More recent is the essay by Mark W. Zacher (Chapter 10) reevaluating arrangements governing commodity prices and earnings in light of a prominent school of international relations theory, structural realism. As Zacher points out, much diplo-

---

1. See Mahler 1984; Ravenhill 1984; Rothstein 1984; and Bates and Lien 1985.

matic effort has been expended since World War II to negotiate norms and decision-making procedures for regulating trade in primary products—in effect, an international commodity trade regime—focusing, in particular, on such issues as preconditions for and goals of producer–consumer agreements, the legitimacy of producer cartels, and the possibility of compensatory financing schemes for assisting producer states with shortfalls in export revenues. Results, however, have been mixed, with only limited consensus on most major questions. For Zacher, the relatively weak regime for commodity trade largely confirms the premises and predictions of structuralist realist theory. Agreement has proved elusive both because important economic gains and losses have been at stake and because no hegemonic power or coalition of strong states has been available and willing to sustain effective collaborative arrangements. Ultimately, underlying patterns of interest and power have been the key determinants of outcomes.

Another critical emerging issue is the problem of the global environment, from management of scarce resources and protection of endangered species to the challenges of air and water pollution—all sources of growing concern for state and societal actors alike. Here, too, questions abound concerning both the process and outcome of negotiations: how to explain the behavior of key parties and what lessons might be learned for the future. From early articles on the exploitation of seabed minerals[2] to later analyses of oceanic and atmospheric degradation[3] and whaling[4], International Organization has long encouraged serious study of the political economy of environmental regulation.

In a seminal contribution, Oran Young (Chapter 11) asks why formal arrangements to cope with cross-border environmental problems like these are so much more difficult to attain in some issue areas than in others. The answer, he suggests, can be found in what he describes as an institutional bargaining model of regime formation, emphasizing the significance of such key matters as unanimity rules, the "veil" of uncertainty, transnational alliances, and shifting involvements. He places particular emphasis on the need for active and effective leadership to help invent options, fashion deals, and broker interests. Without entrepreneurial policy initiative, Young contends, institutional bargaining on environmental issues will almost certainly fail. Young's essay demonstrates well how much fresh understanding can be gained from systematic analysis relating specific historical events, such as the outcome of negotiations to protect the ozone layer or marine wildlife, to broader questions and theories of international political economy.

A third critical issue is economic regionalism, an old question that keeps reemerging in new and challenging manifestations. What motivates states to band together to promote mutual interests? What accounts for their success or failure? To what extent are regional initiatives compatible with broader global regimes and institutions? All manner of regional trade or monetary agreements have been addressed in the pages

---

2. See Friedheim and Durch 1977; and Hardy 1977.
3. Haas 1989 and 1992.
4. Peterson 1992.

of International Organization, *including cooperative projects in Latin America,[5] the Caribbean,[6] Southern Africa,[7] and Eastern Europe.[8] Not surprisingly, the European Union—born as the Common Market in the 1950s and later known as the European Community—has been of widest interest. Key contributions in this area in recent years include essays by Andrew M. Moravcsik, Geoffrey Garrett, and Wayne Sandholtz.[9]*

Most recently, Brian T. Hanson (Chapter 12) has assessed the external trade policy of the European Union in the 1990s. Many observers had feared that Europe's persistently low growth and high unemployment over the last decade might trigger a new wave of barriers to imports from the outside world—predicting, in effect, the emergence of an alarmingly mercantilist "fortress Europe." Yet in reality the European Union has remained generally committed to liberal trade, successfully resisting most protectionist pressures. What accounts for the apparent bias toward liberalization rather than restriction in EU behavior? Much of the explanation, Hanson argues, can be found in the integration process itself, which has systematically undermined the ability of individual members to replace national policy tools with protectionist measures at the EU level. The explanation would appear to have direct relevance to the analysis of the foreign trade policies of other regional blocs as well.

References

Anglin, Douglas G. 1983. Economic Liberation and Regional Cooperation in Southern Africa: SADCC and PTA. *International Organization* 37 (4):681–712.

Axline, W. Andrew. 1978. Integration and Development in the Commonwealth Caribbean: The Politics of Regional Negotiations. *International Organization* 32 (4):953–73.

Bates, Robert H., and Da-Hsiang Donald Lien. 1985. On the Operations of the International Coffee Agreement. *International Organization* 39 (3):553–60.

Bond, Robert D. 1978. Regionalism in Latin America: Prospects for the Latin American Economic System (SELA). *International Organization* 32 (2):401–24.

Comisso, Ellen. 1986. Introduction: State Structures, Political Processes, and Collective Choice in CMEA States. *International Organization* 40 (2):195–238.

Ferris, Elizabeth G. 1979. National Political Support for Regional Integration: The Andean Pact. *International Organization* 33 (1):83–104.

Friedheim, Robert L., and William J. Durch. 1977. The International Seabed Resources Agency Negotiations and the New International Economic Order. *International Organization* 31 (2):343–84.

Garrett, Geoffrey. 1992. International Cooperation and Institutional Choice: The European Community's Internal Market. *International Organization* 46 (2):533–60.

Haas, Peter M. 1989. Do Regimes Matter? Epistemic Communities and Mediterranean Pollution Control. *International Organization* 43 (3):377–403.

———. 1992. Banning Chlorofluorocarbons: Epistemic Community Efforts to Protect Stratospheric Ozone. *International Organization* 46 (1):187–224.

5. See Bond 1978; and Ferris 1979.
6. Axline 1978.
7. Anglin 1983.
8. See Comisso 1986; and Marrese 1986.
9. See Moravcsik 1991; Garrett 1992; and Sandholtz 1993.

Hardy, Michael. 1977. The Implications of Alternative Solutions for Regulating the Exploitation of Seabed Minerals. *International Organization* 31 (2):313–42.

Mahler, Vincent A. 1984. The Political Economy of North–South Commodity Bargaining: The Case of the International Sugar Agreement. *International Organization* 38 (4):709–31.

Marrese, Michael. 1986. CMEA: Effective but Cumbersome Political Economy. *International Organization* 40 (2):287–327.

Moravcsik, Andrew M. 1991. Negotiating the Single European Act: National Interests and Conventional Statecraft in the European Community. *International Organization* 45 (1):19–56.

Peterson, M. J. 1992. Whalers, Cetologists, Environmentalists, and the International Management of Whaling. *International Organization* 46 (1):147–86.

Ravenhill, John. 1984. What Is to Be Done for Third World Commodity Exporters? An Evaluation of the STABEX Scheme. *International Organization* 38 (3):537–74.

Rothstein, Robert L. 1984. Consensual Knowledge and International Collaboration: Some Lessons from the Commodity Negotiations. *International Organization* 38 (4):733–62.

Sandholtz, Wayne. Choosing Union: Monetary Politics and Maastricht. *International Organization* 47 (1):1–40.

Trade gaps, analytical gaps: regime analysis and international commodity trade regulation
Mark W. Zacher

During the past decade the literature on international regimes has grown significantly.[1] Its basic concerns, namely, the description and explanation of international collaborative arrangements, are not new to the study of international relations. What is new is that this literature has sought to conceptualize collaboration more systematically and to link its explanation more carefully to the central theoretical concerns in international relations than have past writings on the topic. I shall first elaborate on an oft-cited definition of regimes and describe the regime pertaining to international commodity prices and earnings. Then I shall set forth hypotheses concerning the strength and nature of international regimes that flow from the dominant school of international relations theory, namely, structural realism, and examine the extent to which developments in the international commodity trade regime tend to support or suggest modifications in those hypotheses.

I thank the following for their comments: Vinod Aggarwal, Alan Cafruny, Jock Finlayson, Martin Griffiths, Ernst Haas, David Haglund, Kal Holsti, James Keeley, Stephen Krasner, John Ruggie, and Michael Webb. I also thank Emily Wheeler for her editorial assistance. Support for the research came from the Donner Canadian Foundation and the Social Sciences and Humanities Research Council of Canada. A previous version of this article was delivered to the annual meeting of the International Studies Association in March 1986.
    1. Some of the major works are: Ernst B. Haas and John Gerard Ruggie, eds., *"International Responses to Technology: Regimes, Institutions and Technocrats,"* special issue of *International Organization* 29 (Summer 1975); Robert O. Keohane and Joseph S. Nye, *Power and Interdependence: World Politics in Transition* (Boston: Little Brown, 1977); Stephen D. Krasner, ed., *International Regimes* (Ithaca: Cornell University Press, 1983); Robert O. Keohane, *After Hegemony: Cooperation and Discord in the World Political Economy* (Princeton: Princeton University Press, 1984); and Vinod Aggarwal, *Liberal Protectionism: The International Politics of Organized Textile Trade* (Berkeley: University of California Press, 1985). See also Ernst B. Haas, "Why Collaborate? Issue-Linkage and International Regimes," *World Politics* 32 (April 1980), pp. 357–405; and Oran R. Young, "International Regimes: Problems of Concept Formation," *World Politics* 32 (April 1980), 331–56.

International Organization 41, 2, Spring 1987, pp. 173–202

The concept of international regimes

Perhaps the best place to begin an analysis of the concept of regimes is with a definition advanced by contributors to *International Regimes*, edited by Stephen Krasner:

> Regimes can be defined as sets of implicit or explicit principles, norms, rules and decision-making procedures around which actors' expectations converge in a given area of international relations. Principles are beliefs of fact, causation, and rectitude. Norms are standards of behavior defined in terms of rights and obligations. Rules are specific prescriptions or proscriptions for action. Decision-making procedures are prevailing practices for making and implementing collective choice.[2]

Five issues relating to this definition merit attention: the problem of identifying regime injunctions in an issue-area; the presence of both regime and nonregime injunctions in the issue-area; the interrelationships among principles, norms, rules, and decision-making procedures; the meaning of regime "strength"; and the meaning of the "nature" of a regime.

Relevant to the problem of identifying regime injunctions is Krasner's comment that "[p]atterned behavior accompanied by shared expectations is likely to become infused with normative significance. . . ."[3] Building on this evaluation I would suggest that a stable pattern of collective behavior, coupled with statements by at least the most powerful actors in a system that they support certain rights and obligations, provide strong evidence for the existence of regime injunctions. Of course, international treaties and explicit statements of support by large numbers of countries would be even better indications of regime prescriptions and proscriptions, but these are not found in all international issue-areas where states accept behavioral guidelines.

Whether it possible to say that certain injunctions are accepted when periodic aberrations in states' compliance occur is a related question. Occasional noncompliance need not mean that a regime no longer exists if the incidences are minor, do not last for long, and are not supported by important states. But occurrences of major or long-term noncompliance, particularly involving participation of or support by major actors in the system, bring into question the efficacy of regime injunctions. We must doubt the effectiveness of behavioral guidelines if glaring violations are allowed to persist or if states tend to violate norms and rules on those few occasions when they would benefit from doing so. This view of the preconditions for regime injunction reflects that of international legal scholars on the preconditions for the existence of international customary law.[4]

---

2. Stephen D. Krasner, "Structural Causes and Regime Consequences: Regimes and Intervening Variables," in Krasner, ed., *International Regimes*, p. 2.
3. Ibid., p. 18.
4. Michael Akehurst, "Custom as a Source of International Law," *British Yearbook of International Law* (1974–75), pp. 20–31 and 53.

The second important issue related to the definitional analysis of regimes inheres in the possibility that some of the injunctions which guide states' behavior in an issue-area may not be part of a regime. The principle of self-help and more specific injunctions that are mere reflections of it do not, by definition, constrain state behavior and therefore should not be viewed as constituent elements of a regime. The principle of self-help, which both Kenneth Waltz and Hedley Bull regard as the central behavioral guideline in a nonhierarchical system, suggests that states should remain free to pursue their interests unfettered by any community injunctions or commitments to other states.[5] Given that the scholarly interest in regimes is motivated primarily by a desire to understand the extent to which mutually accepted constraints affect states' behavior, it seems logical to conceive of regimes as being composed of those principles, norms, rules, and decision-making procedures that do not entirely reflect the principle of self-help. It is important, however, to admit that the principle of self-help is an omnipresent influence in all international issue-areas since the international system is not hierarchically organized. As Waltz has commented: "Hierarchic elements within international structures limit and restrain the exercise of sovereignty but only in ways strongly conditioned by the anarchy of the larger system."[6]

Having established both that a regime is only comprised of injunctions *not* completely reflecting the principle of self-help and that this principle has an impact in almost all international issue-areas, let us now address our third substantive issue relevant to the definition of regimes: the nature of principles, norms, rules, and decision-making procedures. Principles are general guidelines that concern how states should behave in international issue-areas. Often they have conflicting implications for the design of more specific injunctions. According to the previously cited definition, principles are "beliefs." Also, individual states often attach different priorities to them.

In general, principles are derived from broader regimes of which they are a part. To use Vinod Aggarwal's terminology, specific regimes are "nested" in more general regimes, and the principles (or the "meta-regime") of the former are drawn from the principles of the latter.[7] For example, the major principles in the international issue-area of commodity trade, which are drawn from the broader international trade regime, are self-help (a non-regime prescription) and the desirability both of free markets and of regulating trade relations to promote economic growth in developing countries (both regime injunctions). The conflicts between these principles and their

---

5. Kenneth N. Waltz, *Theory of International Politics* (Reading, Mass.: Addison-Wesley, 1979) pp. 7 and 111; Hedley Bull, *The Anarchical Society: A Study in World Politics* (New York: Columbia University Press, 1977), p. 25.

6. Waltz, *Theory of International Politics*, p. 116.

7. Aggarwal, *Liberal Protectionism*, pp. 18–20 and 37. Aggarwal views both principles and norms as being part of meta-regimes. I view only the principles as being derived from more general regimes. Norms are the most general injunctions of the regime since, in the words of the *International Regimes* definition, they are "rights and obligations."

varied attractiveness to states are obvious. Because states usually differ on the importance they assign to principles in designing rights and obligations, principles should not be regarded as injunctions that states feel obligated to follow in the same sense that they feel committed to norms, rules, and decision-making procedures. Principles are guildelines that states think should have "some role" in shaping specific prescriptions and proscriptions.

Norms, rules, and decision-making procedures are the most important behavioral guidelines in an issue-area because they are products of political bargaining. Norms are the most general prescriptions and proscriptions. They relate to both substantive and procedural issues. Rules and decision-making procedures are designed to reflect or implement the norms. Norms, rules, and decision-making procedures in an issue-area may be mere reflections of the principle of self-help and thus not part of the regime. Alternatively, they can represent trade-offs between self-help and "regime principles," or else be faithful reflections of regime principles.[8]

The above point that international regulatory systems reflect trade-offs among a variety of principles often at polar extremes from one another is true of domestic legal systems as well. The well-known jurisprudential expert Paul Freund has noted that legal systems are and should be based on a variety of principles:

> Doctrinaire thinking in constitutional law is a poor example of the role the law can play in the resolution of tensions, domestic and international. Precisely in a time of warring ideologies there is an opportunity that ought to be embraced for the law to demonstrate its search for underlying points of agreement and to work out accommodations that will be tolerable because they recognize a core of validity in more than one position of the combatants.[9]

He also wrote that "single-minded decisions suffer from a loss of insights that the cross-lights of competing principles would offer."[10] In outlining the character of a regime, it is useful to describe the general principles that are relevant to states' bargaining in an issue-area and to evaluate their relative influence over the formation of specific injunctions. But the most general

8. This discussion represents a modification of the definitions in: Jock A. Finlayson and Mark W. Zacher, "The GATT and the Regulation of Trade Barriers: Regime Dynamics and Functions," in Krasner, ed., *International Regimes*, pp. 276–77 and passim. The injunctions that are labeled "norms" in that article are now conceived of as "principles," since states differ as to the importance that should be assigned to them. Also, what are labeled "sovereignty norms" and "interdependence norms" are now defined as "nonregime principles" and "regime principles." Keohane has noted the problem of categorizing injunctions and suggests that regimes should be viewed as "injunctions of greater and lesser specificity" (*After Hegemony*, p. 59).

9. Paul Freund, "Constitutional Dilemmas," *Boston University Law Review* 45 (Winter 1965), p. 23.

10. Ibid., p. 22. Freund also comments on the polarity of principles and the desirability of integrating them into a system of laws in "Thomas Reed Powell," *Harvard Law Review* 69 (1965), pp. 800–803.

injunctions that constitute the core of a regime are the norms because, unlike principles, they are products of explicit or implicit political bargaining and do not conflict with each other. States may, in fact, feel an even greater sense of obligation to comply with norms than with the more specific rules and decision-making procedures because norms capture the underlying purposes of the collective arrangements. Violations of rules are sometimes excused precisely because they may be perceived as consistent with the norms in some situations.

The fourth important point to note is that if a regime is composed of injunctions limiting the ability of states to resort to self-help, then the *strength* of a regime should be determined by the extent to which the package of injunctions constrains states' behavior.[11] Indicators of the extent to which a regime's *substantive* dimension constrains states' behavior are: the scope of the injunctions (or how many aspects of the issue-area they cover), the specificity of the injunctions, their legal weight, their legitimacy, the extent of states' compliance with them, and the magnitude of financial transfers to jointly funded programs. The choice of external criteria for assessing strength is not easy given that some evaluations of constraints are inevitably subjective. However, certain criteria appear reasonable. The constraints on self-help in the *procedural* or decision-making dimension of a regime are determined by the legal weight of decisions by relevant international organizations and the ability of individual or small groups of states to block such decisions. Obviously, if states accept organizational decisions as legally binding and they cannot block decisions on their own or in concert with a small number of other countries, then the ability of states to pursue their interests unfettered by community constraints has been limited.[12]

One aspect of a regime's strength which deserves some comment is its legitimacy, or the degree to which states support the injunctions because they see them as desirable—regardless of the threats of sanctions by or the bargaining leverage of other countries.[13] An indicator of legitimacy is the extent to which states have agreed on the priority assigned to various principles in the formulation of norms, rules, and decision-making procedures.

---

11. This reflects Aggarwal's definition: " 'Strength' refers to the stringency with which rules regulate the behavior of countries" (*Liberal Protectionism*, p. 20). To "rules" I would add "norms" and "decision-making procedures." What Aggarwal refers to as "norms," I would generally include under "principles."

12. Overall, this conception of strength is mirrored by Hedley Bull's discussion of the relative prominence of the principles of "self-help" and "order" in an international system. However, a problem with this approach is that agreements on certain norms and rules are not in large part a product of attachment to "order" but of agreement on the way interstate relations should be regulated in accordance with certain principles. See Bull, *The Anarchical Society*, chaps. 1–2.

13. Oran Young has made a distinction between "negotiated" and "imposed" regimes which accords with the distinction between regimes possessing and lacking legitimacy. See Young, "Regime Dynamics: The Rise and Fall of Interntional Regimes," in Krasner, ed., *International Regimes*, p. 98–101.

Legitimacy effects the long-term durability of a regime if power relations change. John Ruggie has written that "[n]o order of relations can long endure unless it enjoys some legitimacy or, at minimum, acquiescence."[14] Acquiescence is always necessary. On the other hand, legitimacy is particularly crucial if those states preferring another order of relations gain sufficient bargaining power to undermine an existing one.

Finally, the *nature* of a regime is defined by the prominence or weight given to various principles that shape a regime's norms, rules, and decision-making procedures. This definition is comparable to Aggarwal's, namely, nature "refers to the objects promoted by regime rules and procedures."[15] As noted above, states almost always differ in their support for certain principles. The preferences of the most powerful states, if they share a common perspective, tend to determine the priority accorded certain principles—and hence the nature of the regime. In negotiating regime prescriptions for the international commodity trade issue-area, the central tension has been between those favoring free markets and those supporting interventions to assist developing producers.

The international commodity trade regime

The international regulation of the prices of and earnings from commodity exports has been discussed frequently and at great length in the postwar period. In large part the negotiations have pitted developing producing states against developed consuming states. Their debates have been central to what has been called the "North-South dialogue." The importance of the commodity negotiations to this dialogue is hardly surprising, given that 80 percent of the export earnings of developing countries comes from commodity exports—and 60 percent of all export earnings if petroleum is excluded.[16] Third World producers hold that the prevailing system of commodity trade is responsible for severe price instability, declines in real prices, and, of course, declines in export earnings, which result from instability and declines in real prices. To rectify these problems they have frequently supported several types of intergovernmental arrangements: producer-consumer international commodity agreements (ICAs), which control prices through export quotas, buffer stocks, and multilateral contracts; producers' cartels; and compensatory financing schemes that provide funds to states

14. John Gerard Ruggie, "Another Round, Another Requiem? Prospects for the Global Negotiations," in Jagdish N. Bhagwati and Ruggie, eds., *Power, Passions and Purpose: Prospects for North-South Negotiations* (Cambridge: MIT Press, 1984), p. 40.

15. Aggarwal, *Liberal Protectionism*, p. 21. Oran Young uses the term "direction" rather than "nature" in "International Regimes: Problems of Concept Formation," p. 342.

16. Rachel McCulloch and Jose Pinera, "Alternative Commodity Trade Regimes," in Ruth W. Arad et al., *Sharing Global Resources* (New York: McGraw-Hill, 1979), pp. 107–8.

with declining commodity export earnings. Occasionally Third World producers call on developed states not to subsidize their own producers, but since they are reluctant to accept comparable responsibilities, they tend not to press the point.[17]

In the immediate aftermath of World War II major diplomatic efforts were made to develop norms and decision-making procedures for regulating international commodity trade as part of the deliberations to formulate a charter for the International Trade Organization, or ITO (the Havana Charter of 1948). The charter's chapter on ICAs largely reflected the preferences of the Western developed countries, since the latter possessed overwhelming power in the international economic system and since the developing countries only became involved in the final stages of the negotiations.[18] When the Havana Charter failed to obtain adequate support to enter into force, responsibility for promoting international commodity negotiations devolved upon the United Nations and the Food and Agriculture Organization (FAO). The UN Economic and Social Council had passed a resolution in 1947 supporting the provisions of the draft ITO Chapter relating to commodity trade, and the provisions became the framework for subsequent UN activities in this area.[19] Many developing countries objected to the framework of the Havana Charter which limited producer-consumer regulatory agreements solely to very unstable markets, restricted the ICAs to the promotion of price stabilization, and implicitly outlawed producers' cartels. But their efforts to persuade the industrialized nations to alter the normative guidelines proved unsuccessful.[20]

During the 1950s and early 1960s the developing states did create ICAs for tin, sugar, and coffee, although they did not gain acceptance for a number of provisions they favored. They were also able in 1963 to gain the backing of the industrialized nations for the creation of the Compensatory Financing Facility (CFF) within the International Monetary Fund (IMF). The CFF provides low-interest loans to countries experiencing balance-of-payments deficits because of declines in export earnings. It was created particularly to address the problems faced periodically by commodity exporters from developing countries in declining or weak markets.[21] It is also of interest that in

17. Evaluations of alternative regulatory approaches are in ibid.; Christopher P. Brown, *The Political and Social Economy of Commodity Control* (New York: Praeger, 1980); Jere R. Behrman, *Development, the International Economic Order, and Commodity Agreements* (Reading, Mass.: Addison-Wesley, 1978); Gerard Adams and Sonia Klein, eds., *Stabilizing World Commodity Markets: Analyses, Practice and Policy* (Lexington, Mass.: Lexington Books, 1979).

18. Clair Wilcox, *A Charter for World Trade* (New York: Macmillan, 1949), chap. 11; and William A. Brown, *The United States and the Restoration of World Trade* (Washington, D.C.: Brookings, 1950), pp. 119–25 and 217–22. The submissions to and debates in the committee dealing with commodity trade issues are in the UN document series E/CONF.2/C.5(1948).

19. ECOSOC Resolution 39(IV)(1947).

20. See note 18.

21. Louis M. Goreux, *Compensatory Financing Facility* (Washington, D.C.: IMF, 1980).

this immediate postwar period one ICA was created for a commodity market where the developed countries were the major exporters: the International Wheat Agreement. Unlike the other ICAs, which used export quotas and/or buffer stocks to control price movements, the International Wheat Agreement utilized multilateral contracts during its lifespan from 1949 through the late 1960s.[22]

In 1964 primary responsibility for international commodity trade issues passed from the UN to the newly created United Nations Conference on Trade and Diplomacy (UNCTAD). At its founding conference as well as at meetings of various UNCTAD bodies in subsequent years, the developing countries (organized into the Group of 77) sought to reformulate the guidelines for regulating international commodity markets and to formulate new ICAs.[23] Their efforts to formulate new general guidelines met with little success, and by the early 1970s they had succeeded in promoting the creation of only one more ICA (that for cocoa), despite deliberations in both UNCTAD and the FAO on a variety of commodities.

The environment for international commodity trade negotiations changed dramatically in 1973–74 with the success of the oil producers' cartel, OPEC (Organization of Petroleum Exporting Countries). Existing producers' organizations became more assertive, and new bodies were formed to try to emulate OPEC's success.[24] The Group of 77 secured the passage of resolutions in the UN, over the objections of most developed countries, which articulated their preferred normative guidelines for international commodity markets (especially the Declaration and Program of Action for a New International Economic Order and the Charter of Economic Rights and Duties of States).[25] In addition, within UNCTAD they began to develop the Integrated Program for Commodities (IPC). Under this program, which was accepted at the 1976 UNCTAD conference, negotiations to create ICAs for eighteen commodities and a fund to finance the buffer stocks of ICAs (the proposed Common Fund) were launched.[26]

Over the next five years only one new ICA was created (that for natural

22. The history of the International Wheat Agreements is summarized in UN Doc. TD/B.C.1/258 (1985). See also John McLin, "Surrogate International Organization and the Case of World Food Security, 1949–1969," *International Organization* 33 (Winter 1979), pp. 35–56.

23. The debates at UNCTAD I are in the UN document series E/CONF.46/C.1(1964). Subsequently debates were in the Committee on Commodities and are summarized in the UN document series TD/B/C.1. See also Branislav Gosovic, *UNCTAD: Conflict and Compromise* (Leiden: A. W. Sijthoff, 1972).

24. Brown, *The Political and Social Economy of Commodity Control,* chap. 2; H. Hveem, *The Political Economy of Third World Producer Associations* (New York: Columbia University Press, 1978); Zuhayr Mikdashi, *The International Politics of Natural Resources* (Ithaca: Cornell University Press, 1976).

25. General Assembly Resolutions 3201 and 3202 (S-VI) and 3281 (XXIX) (1974).

26. UNCTAD Resolution 93(IV)(1976). For analyses of the development of the IPC, see Brown, *The Political and Social Economy of Commodity Control*; and Robert L. Rothstein, *Global Bargaining: UNCTAD and the Quest for a New International Economic Order* (Princeton: Princeton University Press, 1979).

rubber). Moreover, the agreement establishing the Common Fund for commodities, adopted in 1980, did little to transfer resources to Third World producers. It now appears that the treaty will not enter into force because of the reluctance of the United States and the Soviet Union to ratify it.[27] Disappointment with the results of the IPC negotiations led the Group of 77 to turn its attention to the development of new and more ambitious compensatory financing schemes in the late 1970s and early 1980s, but with little success.[28] The recession and depressed commodity markets of the 1980s have created a pervasive pessimism about reforming the international commodity trade order. In fact, the negotiations to renew one of the five ICAs (that for sugar) collapsed in 1984. Finally, the International Tin Agreement has been inoperative since a serious crisis in late 1985 and will almost certainly not be renewed before its formal expiration in June 1987.

Over the past four decades a limited number of substantive and procedural issues have been at the heart of negotiations relating to the regulation of international commodity markets. The three major substantive issues are: the preconditions for and goals of producer-consumer ICAs; the legitimacy of producers' cartels; and compensatory financing schemes for assisting producing states with shortfalls in export earnings. An issue that global bodies have discussed with less frequency has been state assistance to domestic producers which alters trade patterns. The three key procedural issues are: the procedures for creating ICAs; the distribution of voting power in organizations operating ICAs or dispensing funds to producers; and the requirements for passage of binding decisions by the latter bodies. I shall treat the development of regulatory arrangements pertaining to each of these issues in turn and then evaluate the strength and nature of the regime.

Substantive dimension of the regime

International commodity agreements. The central issue in negotiations about the regulation of commodity markets has been the creation of producer-consumer ICAs—and more particularly, the conditions that justify their formation and the goals that they pursue. As noted above, the negotiations to formulate a charter for the ITO saw the developed countries, especially the United States, argue against any intergovenmental intervention in competitive markets, save in those occasional situations of severe price instability. The developed countries also asserted that ICAs should confine themselves to encouraging price stability rather than seeking to raise market

---

27. UN Doc. TD/IPC/CF/CONF/24(1980); Paul D. Reynolds, *International Commodity Agreements and the Common Fund: A Legal and Financial Analysis* (New York: Praeger, 1978).

28. The decision that launched the negotiations on a new scheme is in UNCTAD Resolution 124(V)(1979). The key secretariat studies and proposals are in UN Docs. TD/B/C.1/214(1980), 221 and 222(1981), and 234(1982).

trends. The developing producing states, largely from Latin America, took the contrary position, arguing that ICAs should be created for raw materials whose producers were not earning adequate incomes and that in many cases they should try to shore up market price trends.[29]

Chapter 6 of the ITO Charter largely reflected the preferences of the industrialized nations, because the developing producers did not possess adequate leverage to extract important concessions from them. Commodity price-control schemes were only to be established when there was "a burdensome surplus" and "widespread unemployment or under-employment" that "would not be corrected by normal market forces in time to prevent widespread and undue hardship to workers" (Art. 62). Also, a variety of provisions indicated that ICAs should confine themselves to encouraging price stability.[30]

Over the years this framework has changed little, despite regular attempts by Third World producers or the Group of 77 to alter it. The Western nations have supported ICAs solely in very unstable markets, and even in such circumstances they have not assumed an obligation to create them. The prevailing orientation of the ICAs toward price objectives has favored stabilizing a given market trend although some modest buoying of that trend is permissible. All of the five commodities for which ICAs were formed—tin and sugar (1953), coffee (1962), cocoa (1972), and natural rubber (1979)—had particularly unstable markets in the years prior to their creation. For the most part the markets demonstrated instability even after passage of the ICAs.[31] However, ICAs have been rejected for such commodities as copper, jute, and hard fibers whose prices have been quite unstable. Moreover, attempts to renegotiate the International Sugar Agreement in the very depressed market of the 1980s did not come to fruition. The major industrialized powers have rejected out of hand proposals of ICAs for those commodities with declining real prices but relatively stable price trends, such as iron ore, manganese ore, and bananas.[32]

The ICAs for tin, coffee, and sugar have buoyed the price trends of these commodities during certain periods. Western industrialized countries have backed these ICAs largely because it is in their self-interest to assist certain producing states. However, their receptivity to using ICAs for transferring resources to the latter has been attenuating since the late 1970s, as is indi-

29. See note 18.

30. Articles 57 and 63. The text of the charter is in Wilcox, *A Charter for World Trade*, pp. 227–327.

31. For analyses of the ICAs, see Jock A. Finlayson and Mark W. Zacher, *The Politics of International Commodity Trade Regulation: Developing Countries and Regime Reform* (New York: Columbia University Press, forthcoming), chaps. 3 and 4.

32. Ibid., chap. 5; and Jock A. Finlayson and Mark W. Zacher, "The Third World and the Management of International Commodity Trade: Accord and Discord," in W. Ladd Hollist and F. LaMond Tullis, eds., *An International Political Economy* (Boulder: Westview, 1985), pp. 199–222.

cated by the exclusion of export quotas from the 1979 natural rubber agreement and the 1980 and 1986 cocoa agreements, and by the European Community's (EC's) insistence of stocking (as opposed to export quotas) in the abortive 1983–84 sugar negotiations. Another indication of their reservations concerning price regulatory schemes is the failure of the late 1970s UNCTAD negotiations to create ICAs for most of the commodities included in the IPC.[33]

One minor concession the developed consuming nations did make to Third World producers was to share the costs of buffer stocks used in some ICAs between the two groups. However, they rejected the Group of 77's proposal of a "source model" for the Common Fund, which would have meant that a disproportionate share of expenses for buffer stocks would have been placed on the developed world. It would also have facilitated the creation of market-control schemes and the buoying of market price trends by ICAs, both things that the Western countries opposed. The acceptance of a "pool model" for the Common Fund in 1980 means that the new organization (if it ever comes into existence) will have minimal effect on market regulation. Under the pool model almost all funding is provided by international commodity organizations administering ICAs (rather than directly by states). Hence, equal amounts are contributed by producers and consumers since the individual ICAs all prescribe equal cost sharing.[34]

Over the past four decades the outlook on producer-consumer regulation of international commodity markets has apparently changed very little. ICAs are still viewed by the developed world as exceptional responses to problems that developing producing states face as a result of serious price instability. The industrialized nations have also refrained from committing themselves to support ICAs under specific market conditions.

Cartels. At the time of the Havana Charter negotiations in the late 1940s, most developed nations, particularly the United States, disapproved of the formation of producers' cartels. They were seen to undermine economic efficiency and to impose serious economic burdens on developed states. Although unable to secure explicit provisions in the charter forbidding cartels, the developed states did regard the charter's legitimization of agreements only between producers and consumers or of ICAs as implicitly banning producers' attempts to manipulate prices. The industrialized nations would subsequently rebuff Third World attempts to secure their approval of collaboration among producers, most notably at the 1964 UNCTAD conference, the 1974 Sixth Special Session of the United Nations General Assembly, and the deliberations on the Charter of Economic Rights

---

33. Ibid.; and Brown, *The Political and Social Economy of Commodity Control,* chap. 6.
34. See note 27; and Finlayson and Zacher, *The Politics of International Commodity Trade Regulation,* chap. 2.

and Duties of States in 1974.[35] However, their own inconsistent policies toward specific cartels as well as the creation and occasional success of some interventions by producers in markets during recent decades belie the existence of a meaningful norm circumscribing the creation of such endeavors.

In the early 1950s tea producers operated a cartel for several years, unopposed by the developed nations.[36] Then, in the late 1950s and early 1960s, the Western countries, particularly the United States, actually encouraged the creation of a coffee producers' cartel.[37] Moreover, a number of important Western states were instrumental in the creation of a uranium cartel in the early 1970s.[38] There have also been numerous attempts by producers in developing states to operate cartels since the 1950s, but only one, OPEC, seemed to be a major success—at least until recently.[39] The developed nations may oppose cartels and may be able to thwart their success most of the time, but it would be inappropriate to suggest that an effective normative constraint against their operation exists. In fact, important Western states have been inconsistent in their policies toward cartels and in their ability to terminate cartels when they favor that outcome.

Compensatory financing. Beginning in the 1950s Third World producers argued that because sudden declines in world commodity prices had disastrous effects on their economic development, the developed consuming nations should compensate them for shortfalls in their export earnings. The developed states initially rebuffed their claim, arguing that all countries suffered from falls in prices of their exports and benefited by periodic rises. Just as it did not make sense to require paybacks by producers to consumers when prices were high, it did not make sense to demand transfers in the other direction when the market was depressed. However, after several years of discussions the industrialized nations conceded that some financial assistance to states that had suffered balance-of-payments deficits as a result of declines in export earnings (especially from commodity sales) was justifiable. Both sides thus agreed in 1963 that the CFF would be created within the IMF and that it would offer loans at regular IMF rates, which are below commercial market rates. The only way that CFF loans differ from loans from other IMF "facilities" is that the "conditions" required of the borrowing state are not quite as stringent. Since the mid-1960s the funds available

---

35. General Assembly Resolutions 3201 and 3202(S-VI)(1974) and 3281(XXXIX)(1974).

36. Liaquat Ali, "The Regulation of Trade in Tea," *Journal of World Trade Law* 4 (July–August 1970), pp. 570–72.

37. S. Bart Fisher, *The International Coffee Agreement: A Study in Diplomacy* (New York: Praeger, 1971), pp. 19–30.

38. Larry R. Stewart, "Canada's Role in the Uranium Cartel," *International Organization* 35 (Autumn 1981), pp. 657–90.

39. See note 24.

through the CFF have increased significantly, and there was, at least until the early 1980s, some marginal relaxation in the original conditions policy.[40]

An important departure from the CFF model was the creation of the STABEX scheme linking the EC and a large number of African, Caribbean, and Pacific (ACP) countries in 1975. It provided for grants or no-interest loans from the EC to ACP states experiencing shortfalls in export earnings. The EC set aside a maximum yearly amount for the program, but it has not been adequate to cover all the shortfalls.[41] In the late 1970s the Group of 77 began to push for the creation of a new compensatory financing scheme along the lines of STABEX, but most Western countries refused to alter their traditional stance on the matter.[42]

At the global level (or quasi-global level, since most communist states do not participate in such arrangements), the developing countries have made little progress in persuading the industrialized nations to assist them when they face shortfalls in commodity export earnings. At most, low-interest loans have been offered in situations in which the shortfalls lead to balance-of-payments deficits. This policy flows from a reluctance to interfere dramatically with international market mechanisms for the purpose of promoting economic welfare in the developing world. If for political reasons the developed nations judge that it is desirable to transfer resources to developing countries, they usually favor methods that do not seriously compromise the system of market rewards and that allow them to select which countries will receive aid.

Assistance to domestic producers. An issue often raised but seldom analyzed in depth in international deliberations on commodity markets is whether states should be free to assist their own producers regardless of the impact of such assistance on international markets. Most states have simply regarded their freedom to do what they want in this area as a nonnegotiable right. Indicative of this attitude is the inclusion of a provision in the General Agreement on Tariffs and Trade (GATT) permitting subsidies for commodity

40. Goreux, *Compensatory Financing Facility*. The international discussions concerning the creation of the CFF are described in J. Keith Horsefield, *The International Monetary Fund, 1945–1965*, vol. 1 (Washington, D.C.: IMF, 1969), pp. 531–36; and vol. 3, pp. 442–57; and Margaret G. de Vries and J. Keith Horsefield et al., *The International Monetary Fund, 1945–1965*, vol. 2 (Washington, D.C.: IMF, 1969), pp. 416–24.

41. Analyses of STABEX and MINEX are in John Ravenhill, "What Is to Be Done for Third World Commodity Exporters? An Evaluation of the STABEX Scheme," *International Organization* 38 (Summer 1984), pp. 544–46; Goreux, *Compensatory Financing Facility*, pp. 80–84; Reynolds, *International Commodity Agreements and the Common Fund*, pp. 165–69; J.D.A. Cuddy, "Compensatory Financing in the North-South Dialogue: The IMF and STABEX (EEC) Schemes," *Journal of the World Trade Law* 13 (January–February 1979), pp. 66–76; Sidney Dell, "Fifth Credit Tranche," *World Development* 13 (1985), pp. 245–49; and UN Doc. TD/B/C.1/222(1981).

42. See note 28; and Finlayson and Zacher, *The Politics of International Commodity Trade Regulation*, chap. 2.

producers (Art. 16).[43] Subsidies, including government-ensured prices, are especially prevalent in agricultural sectors, and in some cases (such as sugar), they distort the economics of comparative advantage to such an extent that they profoundly influence patterns of world production and trade.

In analyzing what they label the "international food regime," Raymond Hopkins and Donald Puchala have noted the centrality of two principles, "respect for a free international market" and "national sovereignty." They write that "the principle of national sovereignty proscribed external interference or penetration into matters defined as 'domestic affairs'."[44] Ruggie has observed that most postwar international economic regimes have balanced the promotion of free markets with the bestowal of significant domestic autonomy on states, a balance he has called "embedded liberalism." "Within this framework . . . multilateralism and domestic stability are linked to and conditioned by one another. Thus, movement toward greater openness in the international economy is . . . coupled with measures designed to cushion the domestic economy from external disturbances."[45]

Procedural dimension of the regime

The creation and operation of an international regime, especially one as multifaceted as that in the commodity trade issue-area, involve a large number of procedural or decision-making issues. However, only four matters are truly central to the procedural dimension: the obligation of states to accept international treaties or organizational decisions; requirements for the entry into force of agreements; the distribution of votes in international bodies administering agreements and providing financial assistance; and requirements for the passage of binding decisions. There has not been as much controversy about these questions as there was over a number of the substantive issues discussed above. In fact, the central procedural guidelines were established in the immediate postwar years.

Obligation to accept treaties and organizational decisions. It is a truism of the international system that conferences convened to formulate treaties and international organizations cannot make legally binding decisions through their standard two-thirds majority voting system. The developing countries have tried, on occasion, particularly at the time of UNCTAD's creation in

43. John H. Jackson, *World Trade and the Law of the GATT* (Indianapolis: Bobbs-Merrill, 1969), pp. 392–96. Article 16(3) does stipulate that subsidies for primary products should not result in the exporting countries "having more than an equitable share of world export trade." However, this does not have a constraining effect.

44. Donald J. Puchala and Raymond F. Hopkins, "International Regimes: Lessons from Inductive Analyses," in Krasner, ed., *International Regimes*, p. 81.

45. John Gerard Ruggie, "International Regimes, Transactions and Change: Embedded Liberalism in the Postwar Economic Order," in Krasner, ed., *International Regimes*, p. 221.

1964, to secure recognition for the legal authority of UN bodies whose membership includes most states in the world, but they have never succeeded.[46] In fact, if the Western countries had ever indicated any real willingness to accede to this demand, many Third World countries would soon have retracted support for the idea since they would have feared the imposition of agreements upon themselves.

Requirements for the entry into force of ICAs. The Havana Charter did not speak directly to this issue, but it did do so implicitly when it prescribed that votes in international commodity organizations created to administer ICAs be divided equally between producers and consumers.[47] From the time of the creation of the first ICAs for wheat in 1949 and for tin and sugar in 1953, it has been recognized that such accords should be ratified by those importing and exporting states that acounted for significant shares of the market before the ICAs entered into force. Governments recognize that the absence of major participants in the market would both weaken the efficacy of the agreements and impose significant costs on those states that had ratified them. Most ICAs have required states accounting for about two-thirds of both imports and exports to ratify the agreement before it enters into force. And there has been little controversy about this matter.[48]

Distribution of votes. Organizations administering ICAs (e.g., the International Coffee Organization) as well as those dispensing funds to producing states (e.g., the IMF) make legally binding decisions with important effects on the welfare of countries. Therefore, those countries whose support and contributions are necessary for the successful operation of the ICAs and financial organizations want to have significant influence in their decision-making. Most states recognize that the backing of the most powerful countries is necessary for organizational effectiveness and consequently give them a disproportionate share of the votes.

The Havana Charter stipulated that votes in organizations administering ICAs should be evenly divided between exporters and importers. Conferences responsible for creating ICAs have distributed votes within each group largely according to shares of global exports and imports.[49] In fund-

---

46. Diego Cordovez, "The Making of UNCTAD," *Journal of World Trade Law* 1 (May–June 1967), pp. 243–79; Gosovic, *UNCTAD*.

47. Articles 63–64 of ITO Charter.

48. The most recent agreements for the five commodities have quite similar provisions, and they have not changed too much over the years. The basic guideline is that countries accounting for 65–80% of both exports and imports must ratify an agreement before it enters into force, but the precise ways in which this requirement is spelled out varies. Sometimes export and import figures are used, and in other cases export quotas, number of votes, and production/consumption figures are used. See UN Docs. TD/SUGAR/9/10(1977), Art. 75; TD/RUBBER/15/Rev.1(1979), Art. 61; TD/COCOA/6/7(1980), Art. 66; and TD/TIN/6/4/14(1981), Art. 55; also, International Coffee Organization, "International Coffee Agreement 1983," Art. 61.

49. Articles 63–64 of ITO Charter.

dispensing organizations the providers of financial resources have been able to claim pride of place. In the IMF, for instance, voting power is correlated largely with financial subscriptions; the Western countries have over 60 percent of the votes.[50] The Common Fund (which may not come into existence) also allocates an important share of votes to the developed countries, though not in the same proportion as in the IMF. (The Western states will receive 42 percent of the votes; the Soviet bloc states, 8 percent.)[51] The significance of these provisions, which raise power above democracy as the central principle, is even greater when they are examined in the light of the requirements for the passage of resolutions.

Requirements for the passage of binding decisions. Organizations operating ICAs as well as those dispensing financial assistance give a veto power to states whose cooperation is essential for their functioning or effectiveness. The former organizations do this by requiring important decisions to have two-thirds of the votes from both the consuming and the producing members.[52] This was not required by the Havana Charter, but it soon became the practice. In the financing organizations it is accomplished by requiring voting majorities between 60 and 85 percent, meaning that the major funders must give their approval for resolutions to be passed.[53] Although the developed capitalist countries have a lower percentage of the total votes in the Common Fund than they do in the IMF, they still possess enough votes to veto decisions. The states that provide the largest sums to the purse obviously demand the right to determine when the purse strings should remain drawn.

Strength of the regime

What does a very strong regime look like? Clearly, the substantive dimension of such a regime in the international commodity trade issue-area would

---

50. A. W. Hooke, *The International Monetary Fund: Its Evolution, Organization and Activities* (Washington, D.C.: IMF, 1981), pp. 17–18. Also see Stephen Zamora, "Voting in International Economic Organizations," *American Journal of International Law* 74 (1980), pp. 566–608.

51. UN Doc. TD/IPC/CF/CONF/24(1980), Articles 11-14, 35, and 51.

52. The voting rules of ICAs are now almost identical, although they did vary a bit more in the past. Each ICA distributes 5–15% of the 1,000 votes of the exporter and importer groupings equally among the members. The remaining votes are distributed according to shares of global exports and imports, but the methods of doing this vary. Each agreement also indicates that decisions are made by a simple distributed majority unless stipulated that a two-thirds distributed majority voting rule should apply. The texts of the ICAs specify that all of the important issues should be decided by the latter method. See UN Docs, TD/SUGAR/9/10(1977), Arts. 2(7-8), 11 and 13; TD/RUBBER/15/Rev.1(1979), Arts. 2(8 and 10), 15 and 18; TD/COCOA/6/7(1980), Arts. 2(n and o), 10 and 12; and TD/TIN/6/14(1981), Arts. 2, 14, and 15. Also, International Coffee Organization, "International Coffee Agreement 1983," Arts. 3(9-10), 13, and 15.

53. See notes 50 and 51.

have straightforward prescriptions and proscriptions concerning both the conditions under which producer-consumer and producer regulatory arrangements and assistance to domestic producers are legitimate and illegitimate, and the goals that the commodity organizations should pursue. National policies and intergovernmental arrangements would comply with these injunctions. Moreover, guidelines and programs for compensatory financing would be highly developed. It is important to stress that two hypothetical regimes could each be very strong but could nevertheless have quite different characteristics, if the principles on which they were based varied significantly. Procedurally, a strong regime would allow the majority of states to legislate agreements for all. The central decision-making bodies would not necessarily lack an element of weighted voting, but they would not allow one state or a very small group of states to block organizational decisions. A reasonable majority of the members would be able to pass authoritative decisions.

The substantive dimension of the commodity trade regime is obviously not very strong, although there are some elements of modest strength. The regime lacks significant restraints with regard to cartels and government assistance to domestic producers. The implicit norm for compensatory financing is that only producers whose export-earnings shortfalls lead to balance-of-payments deficits are eligible for low-interest loans. Such a policy surely indicates a weak financial commitment by the international community, particularly the wealthy industrialized nations, and is tantamount to their saying to Third World producers: Your shortfalls in commodity export earnings do not bother us so long as they do not threaten your ability to pay for the goods you purchase from us.

The strongest area of the regime relates to ICAs. States have backed two central normative guidelines of the Havana Charter: ICAs are legitimate solely in very unstable markets; and ICAs should not try to raise prices very far above the market trend. The six ICAs for wheat, tin, sugar, coffee, cocoa, and natural rubber have met these criteria. However, there are signs of weakness in the regulatory system relating to producer-consumer accords. The norms have been read as indicating what could be done, not what had to be done, and the conditions justifying the creation of ICAs and the price objectives they should follow are only vaguely understood. Given the myriad negotiations on general commodity trade problems and specific commodity markets, we might have expected more significant constraints on government and private actors in markets.

The decision-making or procedural arrangements in the international commodity trade regime are also not particularly strong, but certain elements do modify the traditional legal order whereby states did not derogate any authority to international conferences or organizations where they did not possess a veto power over all decisions. This order was based on the traditional understanding of the principle of sovereign equality.[54] ICAs, which are treaties, can be formulated by two-thirds of the states at a conference. However, no state can be forced to join an ICA, and a small group of states accounting for a modest share of world exports or imports of a particular commodity can block the entry-into-force of an agreement. On the other hand, the articles of ICAs usually do allow a treaty to enter into force over the opposition of one or even a couple of important recalcitrant states. International commodity and financial organizations are given the authority to pass legally binding decisions, but their constitutions do give a veto power to a small number of important actors or a large number of minor ones. In the politics of negotiating international regimes there is a trade-off between securing binding decision-making powers for organizations and accepting the right of a few key actors to block decisions. In one sense, the greatest weakness in the procedural side of the regime is not that major importers and exporters have so much power in ICAs but that there are so few ICAs. Most markets do not have regulatory bodies, such as those that still exist for coffee, cocoa, and natural rubber—and formerly existed for wheat, sugar, and tin. The nature of the decision-making arrangements for ICAs is not nearly as important a sign of regime weakness as is the limitation of ICAs to such a small number of commodities.

The international commodity trade issue-area has not proven very susceptible to global regulation. Constraints have been limited largely to some general guidelines for the creation of ICAs and to specific rules for the six commodity markets for which ICAs have existed for varying periods of time. At the present time, consensus even in these areas seems to be eroding with the failure to renew the sugar agreement and the de facto demise of the tin accord. As I shall elaborate in the final section of this article, it is not easy to secure agreement on rules of the game in economic areas where important gains and losses are at stake.

Nature of the regime

The central issue in evaluating the nature of the international commodity trade regime is the extent to which regime norms and rules (which only concern ICAs and compensatory financing) reflect the broader free market and development principles or, to use Krasner's terminology, the "market-oriented" and "authoritative" principles.[55] The norms relating to the cre-

---

54. The traditional legal order with its unanimity rule, based on an interpretation of the principle of sovereign equality, is discussed in Zamora, "Voting in International Economic Organizations"; and Inis L. Claude, *Swords into Plowshares: The Problems and Progress of International Organization*, 3d ed. (New York: Random House, 1964) pp. 111–31.

55. Stephen Krasner has posited that the basic conflict between North and South is between the "market-oriented" principles and "authoritative" principle. I use the term "development" instead of "authoritative" because the developing countries were not merely trying to gain

ation and character of ICAs and compensatory financing, as well as the rules of specific ICAs and the CFF provide only weak support for the principle of economic redistribution.

For the most part the industrialized countries have acceded to intergovernmental regulations and programs that derogate the free market principle solely in order to alleviate some of the worse side-effects of its application (i.e., periodic dramatic falls in prices and export earnings for poor producing states). Also, the resource transfers have not been large. They have supported modest financial transfers to prevent producers in developed countries from becoming alienated from liberal international economic systems and the North generally. Their goal has been to preserve to the greatest extent possible the international economic status quo, not to reform it fundamentally or to bring about large-scale economic redistribution in favor of the developing world. The situation is not atypical of other international postwar economic regimes. "There is no sign that the liberalization-stabilization nexus of principles has yielded in any instance to redistributive concerns, either in response to warnings of the perils that lie ahead, or to the prospects of mutual gains that could be reaped. Instead, what we see is that the existing set of principles govern the adaptive redeployment of regime rules and, in a more limited fashion, regime norms so as to accommodate new situations."[56] This analysis may somewhat underestimate the degree to which development concerns have been prevalent among Western states, but Third World development does not seem to be high on the list of general objectives of the industrialized world.

The nature of the procedural side of the regime (that is, provisions that diverge from the requirement of unanimity) relates to the relative prominence of the principles of democracy and power in the design of decision-making arrangements. The democracy principle is that a majority of states should be able to pass and block binding decisions; the power principle is that those states with the most resources or most prominent positions in the issue-area should have comparable roles.[57] With regard to the creation of an ICA, the support of two-thirds of the countries attending a commodity con-

---

acceptance of intergovernmental control of economic relations; they were seeking intergovernmental controls that would transfer resources to them and hence promote their development. See Krasner, *Structural Conflict: The Third World against Global Liberalism* (Berkeley: University of California Press, 1985), pp. 5, 66, 290, 311–12, and passim.

56. John Gerard Ruggie, "Political Structure and Change in the International Economic Order: The North-South Dimension," in Ruggie, ed., *The Antinomies of Interdependence: National Welfare and the International Division of Labor* (New York: Columbia University Press, 1983), p. 464.

57. Claude and Zamora (the latter using the terminology of the former) identify three principles and voting norms: equalitarianism (unanimity), majoritarianism (majority rule) and elitism (weighted voting). For our purposes equalitarianism (unanimity) is relevant to an analysis of regime *strength*—not the *nature* of a regime. There is no regime with regard to the procedural dimension of an issue-area if all decisions require unanimity. I prefer the terms "democracy" and "power" instead of "majoritarianism" and "elitism." Zamora, "Voting in International Economic Organizations"; and Claude, *Swords into Plowshares*, pp. 111–31.

ference is adequate to create a treaty. But the provisions for its entry-into-force require the consent of those countries accounting for high percentages of both exports and imports—and they pay little attention to the number of states ratifying the agreement. In the case of organizations administering ICAs and dispensing financial assistance, the same system holds: generally, a majority of the member states must back a resolution for it to be passed, but most of the major exporters and importers (or largest donors) must also support it. The key to the system is that those countries having large roles in the issue-areas or providing most of the resources possess a veto. In other words, the principle of power has sway over that of democracy.

Structural realist theory and the international commodity trade regime

In recent years a number of authors have analyzed realist perspectives on international regimes.[58] In this section I shall examine the hypotheses of structural realist theory concerning international regimes and analyze their ability to explain developments in international commodity trade regulation. More generally, the section seeks to develop and refine our understanding of the political dynamics of international collaboration.

At the heart of structural realism are a number of assumptions: states are the major actors in the international system; states are egoistic and compete for a variety of values; states are only bound by prescriptions and proscriptions they have accepted; and their preeminent interest is security (or independence from external control). Structural realist theorists do not generally stress the traditional realist maxim that in order to attain security and other values states must always seek to maximize their power or their ability to influence the behavior of other states. The international environment affects states' efforts to acquire power. Structural realists also recognize that states are interested in maximizing their economic welfare. However, they say that when security and economic welfare conflict, the former will have precedence.

From these assumptions flow a number of hypotheses regarding the strength and nature of international regimes, the most important of which are listed below. Arguably, the more relevant concern strength.

1. Strength is decidedly greater in economic issue-areas than in issue-areas involving military security.[59]

---

58. Some of the key works are Robert O. Keohane and Joseph S. Nye, *Power and Interdependence: World Politics in Transition* (Boston: Little Brown, 1977); Krasner, ed., *International Regimes,* especially the articles by Krasner; Krasner, *Structural Conflict: Third World against Global Liberalism*; Keohane, *After Hegemony*; Aggarwal, *Liberal Protectionism*.

59. Robert Jervis, "Cooperation under the Security Dilemma," *World Politics* 30 (1978), pp. 167–214; Charles Lipson, "International Cooperation in Economic and Security Matters," *World Politics* 37 (October 1984), pp. 1–23.

2. Strength is negatively correlated with the extent to which the issues concern the autonomous control of governments over their own societies. This is a logical outgrowth of the preeminence of security among state objectives.[60]

3. If the issue-area is fundamentally economic in character, strength is negatively correlated with the extent to which the issues concern the central terms of competition. Obviously states will find it more difficult to agree on guidelines that seriously influence the relative magnitude of their gains.

4. Strength is negatively correlated with the degree of "publicness" of the goods being regulated. In a nonhierarchical political system, there is suboptimal production of public goods because of the problem of free-riding. Publicness refers to the inability of producers of a good available to all to exclude states that refuse to contribute to its cost from consuming it.[61]

5. A strong regime is likely to emerge when there is a hegemonic power. A hegemonic state has the resources and sense of security to support and secure acceptance of collaborative arrangements.[62]

6. A strong regime is likely when there is a coalition of (or mutuality of interests among) the most powerful states involved in an issue-area.[63]

7. Strength is not influenced by the institutional and substantive dimensions of a prevailing regime. Regimes reflect the prevailing patterns of interest and power in the issue-area, and they change as these patterns change.[64]

60. In *Structural Conflict* (especially chaps. 1 and 12), Krasner notes that realists believe that the central goals of states are "power" and "control." By control he means the ability of states to govern their societies free from constraints imposed by foreign actors.

61. Structural realist theorists have not tended to focus on this hypothesis, but it does flow from their assumptions. Studies that apply public goods theory to international collaboration are John G. Ruggie, "Collective Goods and Future International Collaboration," *American Political Science Review* 66 (September 1972), pp. 874–93; Bruce Russett and John Sullivan, "Collective Goods and International Organization," *International Organization* 25 (Autumn 1971), pp. 845–65; Duncan Snidal, "Public Goods, Property Rights and Political Organization," *International Studies Quarterly* 23 (December 1979), pp. 532–66.

62. Keohane, *After Hegemony,* chaps. 3 and 8–10; Aggarwal, *Liberal Protectionism*; Charles Kindleberger, "Dominance and Leadership in the International Economy," *International Studies Quarterly* 25 (June 1981), pp. 242–54; Bruce Russett, "The Mysterious Case of Vanishing Hegemony; or Is Mark Twain Really Dead?", *International Organization* 39 (Spring 1985), pp. 207–32; and Duncan Snidal, "The Limits of Hegemonic Stability Theory," *International Organization* 39 (Autumn 1985), pp. 579–614; Timothy McKeown, "Hegemonic Stability Theory and 19th-Century Tariffs in Europe," *International Organization* 37 (Winter 1983), pp. 73–94; and Peter Cowhey and E. Long, "Testing Theories of Regime Change: Hegemonic Decline or Surplus Capacity," *International Organization* 37 (Spring 1983), pp. 457–83.

63. Most of the literature on hegemonic stability cited in note 62 touches on this issue. See esp. the articles by Keohane and McKeown.

64. Keohane, *After Hegemony,* esp. chaps. 1, 4–7, and 11; Nye and Keohane, *Power and Interdependence,* esp. chap. 3; Krasner, ed., *International Regimes,* esp. articles by Krasner and Keohane; Oran R. Young, *Compliance and Public Authority: A Theory with International Applications* (Baltimore: Johns Hopkins University Press, 1979).

The hypotheses relating to the *nature* of a regime are few and parallel those directly above.

1. The nature of a regime, or the extent to which various principles shape the norms, rules, and decision-making procedures, reflects the preferences of the hegemonic actor.
2. The nature of a regime reflects the preferences of a coalition of the most powerful states in the issue-area.
3. The nature of a regime is not influenced by the prevailing regime in the issue-area.

In this section, I shall apply the above hypotheses to an analysis of the international commodity trade regime, mindful that the "test," because it depends on only one case study, cannot be regarded as a thorough examination of their validity.

Strength of the commodity trade regime

Economic/security character of the issue-area. The economic as opposed to the security character of the issue-area did facilitate the development of some moderately important regulatory arrangements regarding the six ICAs and the CFF. It is easier to monitor state behavior in this area than in the military security sphere, and the costs of defection or noncompliance are not especially serious. In fact, periodic noncompliance with the rules of ICAs did not become highly politicized, and such incidences were fairly common. Violations of the export quota provisions of the coffee and sugar accords occurred regularly, and the same could be said about the tin agreement if one includes lax government policies toward smuggling.[65]

Implications for government control of society. The reluctance of states to accept constraints on their domestic policies was the central factor preventing acceptance of any obligations to provide subsidies to national producers—assistance that often had important effects on trade patterns. States' reluctance to accept restrictions has, in fact, been strengthened in recent decades as governments have assumed greater responsibility for ensuring their citizens' economic welfare. However, it is important to point out that export quota provisions in the tin, sugar, and coffee ICAs did indirectly require some constraints on production. But how governments handled these problems was up to them. They had a great deal of latitude with respect to matters such as storage of commodities, assistance to miners and farmers, tax policies, and the prices at which the commodities were purchased from producers. Overall, one can conclude that states will accept

---

65. Finlayson and Zacher, *The Politics of International Commodity Trade Regulation*, chaps. 3 and 4; Fisher, *The International Coffee Agreement*; S. Bart Fisher, "Enforcing Export Commodity Agreements: The Case of Coffee," *Harvard International Law Journal* 12 (1971).

regulations that require adjustments in domestic policies as long as they have significant latitude in the ways that they meet certain objectives.

Salience to central terms of competition. In international economic relations, specific issues in a general issue-area can be divided into several categories. Certain matters concern the facilitation or acceptability of particular exchanges. These include methods for conducting financial transactions, labeling standards, certain technical standards, liability and compensation for damages, and the control of negative externalities (e.g., safety and pollution). Such matters generally have only marginal impacts on the terms of competition or the advantages of national industries in selling and purchasing goods. On the other hand, issues such as prices, earnings, and market shares are central to competition for profits and relative economic gains. Realist theory implies that these latter issues are much less susceptible to international controls since certain rules tend to impose varied and significant gains and losses on states.

This perspective definitely appears to have considerable validity when applied to those international commodity trade issues included here. Producer-consumer agreements or ICAs have been so few in number and have been designed to have modest impacts on markets precisely because any system of rules imposes gains and losses of varying magnitude on different states. The implications often vary as much among producers as between producers and consumers. For the same reason there has not been a meaningful consensus on producers' cartels: they benefit certain countries to the detriment of others. In very few commodity markets is it possible to design agreements that everyone sees as beneficial. When accords do result, it is generally because one group of states has political concerns or concerns outside the issue-area which lead them to accept some economic sacrifices or resource transfers. The creation of the five ICAs for commodities that were largely exported by Third World states was definitely attributable to the politico-security concerns of the developed consuming nations.

Publicness of a good. A final hypothesis relating to characteristics of an issue-area is: the greater the publicness of a good (more particularly, the greater the inability to exclude actors who do not contribute to a good available to all states), the weaker the regime is likely to be. The main ''good'' that is produced by ICAs is a more stable and/or higher price trend. This good does not display a high degree of publicness because states can be excluded from benefiting from it. ICAs that rely on export quotas can prevent producers that do not join from benefiting from a higher price by stipulations that consuming states bar or limit imports from these producers. Also, if producing states exceed a quota, their future quotas can be reduced. Even in an ICA that relies solely on a buffer stock, consuming states can restrict the imports of nonmembers, although generally this does not occur. The ICAs that have relied on export quotas (tin, coffee, sugar, and the early cocoa agreements) have had provisions of varied stringency that restricted imports from nonmembers and members who violated the rules. Without the inclusion of such provisions, the conclusion and operation of the accords would have been very difficult.[66]

Existence of a hegemonic state. A central theme in the writings of some realist scholars is that strong regimes will emerge when there is a hegemonic state, but are very unlikely to develop when there is not. The range of rationales for this hypothesis includes the hegemon's ability to afford to pay for public goods, the positive and negative sanctioning power at its disposal, its ability to cooperate without worrying about implications for its security, and its ability to provide security to others. In the international commodity trade issue-area, the evidence in support of this hypothesis is mixed. In the negotiations to formulate the Havana Charter, the United States did seek acceptance of norms and rules with regard to producer-consumer ICAs and producers' cartels, but it did not favor constraints on governments' assistance to domestic producers capable of distorting trade patterns. Hence it did not back strong regulatory arrangements with regard to all aspects of the issue-area. In the end the Havana Charter did largely reflect American preferences, although the United States was unable to secure an explicit prohibition of cartels.

When the Havana Charter was not accepted by the United States and most other states, the task of promoting its provisions relevant to commodity trade fell to the UN, commodity conferences and organizations, and states acting on their own. In international meetings the United States played an important role by promoting the guidelines relating to international commodity organizations: ICAs were to be created only for a few commodities whose markets were very unstable and were to be largely oriented toward the promotion of price stability. However, the views of the United States on these matters were not very different from those of the other developed consuming states. Hegemonic status in the global system does not seem to have been a prerequisite for support for these guidelines.

The United States continued to oppose producers' cartels in principle, but on several occasions it overlooked or actually supported some forms of collaboration among producers which resembled cartels. It did not, for instance, try to undermine a tea producers' cartel in the early 1950s; and in the late 1950s it actively supported attempts by coffee producers to raise prices through export quotas. Such actions were, however, followed by U.S. resistance to attempts by cocoa and sugar producers to operate cartels in the 1960s.

---

66. The ICAs for sugar, coffee, and cocoa had restrictions on imports from nonmembers. See UN Docs. TD/SUGAR/9/10(1977), Art. 57; and TD/COCOA.6/7(1980), Art. 51. Also, International Coffee Organization, "International Coffee Agreement 1983," Art. 45.

In the 1970s there were, of course, a number of attempts by Third World producers to operate cartels although only that of the oil producers achieved a significant measure of success. Also, a number of developed countries supported a uranium producers' cartel. Although the United States was not among its members, American authorities were certainly aware of its operation; and they did nothing to terminate it. Overall, since the 1940s U.S. opposition to regulation of certain matters (aid to domestic producers), its inconsistency on cartels, the success of some cartels, and the importance of collaboration among the major industrialized nations for certain regime injunctions have cast serious doubt on the thesis of hegemonic stability.

In the case of an individual commodity market, a hegemon may be either a large exporter or a large importer, depending on the elasticities of supply and demand. If supply (including substitutes) does not expand and demand does not fall as the price rises, then market power lies with a dominant producer. On the other hand, if this is not the case, bargaining power lies on the consumer side. In almost all commodity markets (oil for a long while being the exception) power lies with the buyer or is monopsonistic.[67] It is, however, also usually the case that a single state or actor does not have a dominant share of global imports (close to 50 percent). Imports are usually divided among the United States, Japan, and members of the EC (who coordinate their policies to a certain extent in this area).

In a few markets there has been an occasional hegemon (generally the United States). In recent decades members of the EC have accounted for half or more of global imports of certain commodities, but their policies in these markets are insufficiently coordinated to call the EC a hegemon. During the early coffee agreements, the United States, with more than 40 percent of global imports, occupied such a role for that commodity. Its role enabled it to exert a tremendous effect on the conclusion of and compliance with the International Coffee Agreement, but on its own it could not dictate the creation of and maintain a strong regime. An importer has to control a tremendous share of a market in order to be able to control the fate of a regime. Moreover, dominant importers have not always wanted strong regulatory arrangements. This was the case at different periods for the United States in the bauxite and banana markets and for Britain in the tea market. The overall impact of a dominant importer is not at all clear.

Another aspect of power structure is of relevance here—the presence of one or two dominant exporters.[68] It is clear that dominant exporters do not always favor price control schemes: examples are Morocco in the phosphate

67. F. M. Sherer, *Industrial Market Structure and Economic Performance* (Chicago: Rand-McNally, 1980), chaps. 6 and 7; Paul Streeton, "The Dynamics of the New Poor Power," *Resources Policy* 2 (June 1976), pp. 73–86; Walter C. Labys, *Market Structure, Bargaining Power, and Resource Price Formation* (Lexington, Mass.: Lexington Books, 1980).
68. Data on market shares are in the World Bank's annual publication *Commodity Trade and Price Trends*. Analysis of the roles of exporting countries in bargaining on ICAs is in Finlayson and Zacher, *The Politics of International Commodity Trade Regulation*.

rock market and Brazil in the hard fiber market. Moreover, even if producing states with large shares of global exports back an agreement, other producers may not necessarily support it. A good example is the inability of India and Sri Lanka, the largest tea exporters, to secure the backing of Kenya for a tea agreement. On the other hand, the existence of one or two dominant exporters sympathetic to a price-control scheme can have a very positive effect. The support of Brazil and to a lesser extent Colombia has been crucial to the viability of the coffee agreement. The same is true for Malaysia and the tin and natural rubber accords, and for Cuba and the early sugar agreements.[69] Structure can influence the development of strong regimes but only when the major actors back price-control schemes. This backing cannot be inferred from the structure.

Supporting coalition of major states. The hypothesis that the support of a group of the most powerful states can sustain strong international regimes is not central to the writings of some structural realists. (In fact, some might regard such coalitions as quite unlikely.) But such a hypothesis does appear in the writings of a number of authors writing in the realist tradition and is consistent with structural realist assumptions.[70] In the international commodity trade issue-area, the major developed capitalist states, whose interests and policies have been largely congruent, have formed such a coalition. Their monopsonistic power and financial resources have given them considerable say in whether or not there should be a strong regime. In fact, they have generally not favored stringent constraints on state behavior. They have opposed restrictions on subsidization of their own producers and on support for certain intergovernmental cartels or collusive practices among firms. They have also wanted some choice as to when ICAs should be created and what their pricing policy should be. In addition, they have not been inclined to devote large sums to ensuring that producers receive stable levels of earnings. Insofar as there have been any significant regime injunctions (the norms and rules relating to ICAs and the CFF), they have resulted from the common interests and leverage of the developed capitalist states. But such an evaluation of their influence is quite different from a finding that a dominant coalition favors strong regime injunctions for all aspects of an issue-area.

Existing international regimes. An important issue in the literature on international regimes is whether the substantive and procedural dimensions of prevailing regimes influence their evolution.[71] The postwar commodity

---

69. Finlayson and Zacher, *The Politics of International Commodity Trade Regulation*, especially chaps. 3–5.

70. See note 64.

71. Keohane, *After Hegemony*, chaps. 1 and 4–7; and Robert O. Keohane, "The Demand for International Regimes," in Krasner, ed., *International Regimes*, pp. 141–72.

regime's greatest influence on the development of specific accords was exerted through the institutions that were created to discuss international commodity problems and consider the appropriateness of agreements. The organizations "provide[d] forums for meetings and secretariats that . . . act[ed] as catalysts for agreement."[72] It is unlikely that many of the ICAs and other types of commodity accords (e.g., the CFF and the Common Fund) would have been created and maintained had it not been for the existence of a number of UN and UNCTAD bodies, the FAO, the international commodity organizations, and the IMF. They gave states an opportunity to deliberate on the need for intergovernmental agreements, generated studies pertinent to these problems, and to some extent fostered feelings of camaraderie and common knowledge among governmental representatives. This latter phenomenon was particularly prevalent in such commodity organizations as the International Coffee Organization and the International Tin Council, as well as in the IMF.

Central to the generation of information and the development of decision-making networks were the international secretariats of the various bodies. Often they linked their own success and legitimacy to the conclusion of agreements. They usually identified themselves with the interests of the developing countries whom the accords would largely assist. In no institution was this more true than UNCTAD. Its secretariat was instrumental in the conclusion of the 1968 sugar and the 1972 cocoa agreements, and it had a major influence on the launching of the Integrated Program for Commodities which led to the International Natural Rubber Agreement and the Common Fund accord.[73]

Commodity organizations also strengthen regimes by promoting compliance with the agreements for which they are responsible. The organizations collect information on trade patterns, and states' compliance with rules is subject to scrutiny and criticism. Such information gathering and diplomatic scrutiny, as Oran Young has noted, tend to spawn a "compliance culture," although he also remarks that one should not overstate the impact of such a culture.[74] Neither should the influence of organizational monitoring be exaggerated, since many parties would comply even without organizational reviews and some members violate organizational injunctions despite the likelihood of detection. However, in the case of ICAs with provisions for quotas on exports, there would be more cases of noncompliance without the organizations' monitoring activities or the sanctions they have at their dis-

---

72. Keohane, *After Hegemony*, p. 89.

73. An excellent study on the development of the IPC and the role of the secretariat is Rothstein, *Global Bargaining*. Also, see Finlayson and Zacher, *The Politics of International Commodity Trade Regulation*; and Brown, *The Political and Social Economy of Commodity Control.*

74. Oran R. Young, "International Resource Regimes," in Clifford S. Russell, ed., *Collective Decision Making: Applications from Public Choice Theory* (Baltimore: Johns Hopkins University Press, 1979), pp. 241–82; and Young, *Compliance and Public Authority.*

posal. It is important to note that the pressure exerted by these organizations is also directed at importing governments, which often have incentives to allow cheaper illegal shipments into their countries. In the case of the International Coffee Agreement, the United States has on a number of occasions used the findings of the International Coffee Organization to put pressure on other importers to respect the rules.

General regime injunctions are also viewed as facilitating new accords and shaping their character.[75] The norms and rules related to the procedural dimension of ICAs in the Havana Charter and their subsequent inclusion in the 1949 wheat and 1953 tin and sugar agreements helped to eliminate wrangling over these aspects of ICAs. Major producing and consuming states both viewed the decision-making model set forth in the Havana Charter and the early ICAs in a generally favorable light. Knowledge of the regime's substantive guidelines did not significantly expedite negotiations because developing states generally preferred alternatives that gave greater weight to the development of economic redistribution principle. In particular negotiating contexts, they frequently hoped that the developed importing countries could be persuaded to utilize ICAs or compensatory financing schemes as major resource-transfer mechanisms. Negotiations over price ranges and rules governing export quotas and buffer stocks usually turned on the question of whether or not the ICAs should raise market price trends. When regime injunctions are "imposed" and the dominated group perceives that some changes are possibly occurring in the dominant group's interests and bargaining leverage, challenges to the existing order of relations are bound to occur.

Nature of the commodity trade regime

Hegemony and coalition of the major powers. In the first two decades after the war the international commodity trade regime certainly reflected the basic preferences of the hegemonic actor. It reflected the free market principle in certain areas and the self-help principle in others, and in both gave only marginal weight to the development interests of Third World states. However, with the attentuation of the role of the United States in global politics, the regime did not change in any important ways. What shaped the regime and influenced its stability were the commonality of interests and backing of the developed capitalist countries, particularly the five or so key ones. Their monopsonistic power was so great in almost all commodity markets that they could establish the guidelines for any producer-consumer agreements. In the case of compensatory financing, their provision of the bulk of the financial resources obviously gave them the needed leverage to shape the norms and rules. Since the Third World producing

---

75. Keohane, *After Hegemony*, p. 89.

states were in a position of having to ask for arrangements that transferred resources from the developed countries to themselves, the Western countries were in a position of saying how far they were willing to go. The proposition that in nonhierarchical systems regimes are "shaped largely by their most powerful members" holds in this issue-area.[76]

Existing international regime. An existing international regime can shape its own development as a result of states' attachment to traditional ways of doing things and the power or leverage that decision-making structures bestow on certain countries (generally the large number of weaker states). It is, however, difficult to posit that the international commodity trade regime had important effects on states' conceptions of their interests or of those policies that would best realize their interests. This is especially the case with respect to the norms. With regard to the use of particular regulatory instrumentalities in ICAs and the rules governing them, states often did exhibit a proclivity to go along with the "tried and tested." Significant continuities in the characteristics of ICAs over time illustrate this tendency. However, at the same time, conferences convened to renegotiate ICAs almost always became settings for debates on the suitability of past provisions followed by some changes in previous regulatory arrangements. As in the cocoa and sugar deliberations in the 1980s, very marked departures in the approaches of states toward market control sometimes occur.[77] Custom and habit had marginal impacts on the nature of the regime. Custom and habit may have greater impacts when regimes are more highly formalized and when they have existed for longer periods of time.

Since the 1960s decision-making in international organizations has changed considerably because of the emergence of a Third World voting majority. It is often argued that international organizations created to oversee, implement, and revise existing regimes provide the developing countries with leverage to alter these regimes, because of their "democratic" orientation and the opportunities for rhetorical and voting pressure they afford.[78] There is some truth to this assertion in the international commodity trade issue-area, but the influence accorded to developing countries has been modest. Third World states have failed to secure important changes in regime norms despite innumerable attempts to do so. As the late economist Harry Johnson once noted: " 'the process of confrontation of the two groups at time-consuming monster meetings has lost its moral shock-power

76. Ibid., p. 63.

77. Finlayson and Zacher, *The Politics of International Commodity Trade Regulation*, chap. 4.

78. Roger D. Hansen, *Beyond the North-South Stalemate* (New York: McGraw-Hill, 1979), pp. 38–39; Keohane and Nye, *Power and Interdependence*, pp. 36 and 54–58; and Stephen D. Krasner, "North-South Economic Relations: The Quests for Economic Well-Being and Political Autonomy," in Kenneth A. Oye, Robert J. Lieber, and Donald Rothschild, eds., *Eagle Entangled: U.S. Foreign Policy in a Complex World* (New York: Longman, 1979), p. 129.

and . . . its expense, inefficiency and irrelevance to the solution of the concrete issues are not justified by the possibilities of its forcing progress.' ''[79] Johnson's harsh appraisal was partly due to his substantive disagreements with what the Group of 77 was advocating, but his point still has merit. Fundamental regime changes require redefinitions of interests within important coalitions, or shifts in structural power relations within an issue-area or within other issue-areas which can be linked to the questions under discussion. Such redefinitions or shifts have not occurred in the commodity issue-area, and thus only minor changes have resulted. If anything, the development principle has attenuated somewhat in the commodity issue-area since the late 1970s, despite a plethora of diplomatic meetings and conferences.

An analysis of the international commodity trade regime suggests certain modifications in the structural realist hypotheses concerning the strength and nature of international regimes, but they are not major. Structural realism appears to have serious weaknesses only if the presence of a hegemon is viewed as producing strong regimes and if a coalition of major states is judged to be improbable—and inadequate to sustain important collaborative arrangements. I do not think that these projections flow from the theory's assumptions.

A global hegemonic state does not necessarily favor strong constraints with regard to all issues, and it cannot secure agreement on all matters. Its backing for accords is very important, but of greater salience is the support of a coalition of the most powerful countries. Dominant exporters or importers in particular markets do not seem necessarily to favor strong regulatory arrangements. Sometimes they favor intergovernmental regimes and sometimes they do not. Also, although their support is always very influential, it is never sufficient for a successful regime.

Prevailing international regimes do influence their own future development, but in the case of the commodity trade regime such influence is felt largely through the regime's decision-making structures—not its substantive provisions. Institutions provide regular opportunities for states to deliberate on possible accords, and they create greater transparency and hence ability to project the effects of various proposals. They encourage mediation by secretariats and participating states, and they provide opportunities for monitoring compliance with agreements. These impacts should not be underestimated. However, ultimately underlying patterns of interests and power are the key determinants of the strength and nature of regimes. Institutions can only facilitate the creation and maintenance of such collaborative arrangements within the context of these realities.

---

79. Quoted in J.E.S. Fawcett, "UNCTAD IV: Another Bill of Rights," *World Today* 32 (1976), p. 158.

The politics of international regime formation: managing natural resources and the environment
Oran R. Young

Why do actors in international society succeed in forming institutional arrangements or regimes to cope with some transboundary problems but fail to do so in connection with other, seemingly similar, problems? In this article, I employ a threefold strategy to make progress toward answering this question. The first section prepares the ground by identifying and critiquing the principal models or streams of analysis embedded in the existing literature on regime formation; the second section articulates an alternative model, called institutional bargaining. The third section employs this alternative model to derive some hypotheses about the determinants of success in institutional bargaining and uses these hypotheses, in a preliminary way, to illuminate the process of regime formation in international society.

To provide a ready source of cases with which to illustrate hypotheses about regime formation as well as to lend empirical content to my argument, I draw repeatedly on evidence pertaining to institutional arrangements for natural resources and the environment.[1] I therefore proceed by asking several questions: Why is an international regime emerging now to deal with the depletion of stratospheric ozone but not with the greenhouse effect or the problem of biological diversity? Why are relatively complex international arrangements being put into place for early notification and emergency relief in connection with radioactive fallout resulting from nuclear accidents, while efforts to devise arrangements covering the transboundary aspects of acid precipitation have met with greater resistance and produced different results

This article is a revised version of a paper presented at the 1988 convention of the International Studies Association. I am grateful to those who attended this presentation and offered helpful suggestions for revisions. I also thank Stephen D. Krasner, Olav Schramm Stokke, and several anonymous reviewers for their constructive criticisms.
1. Regimes for natural resources and the environment presumably do not differ from other international regimes in any fundamental way, so their use as evidence entails no loss of generality in the analysis that follows.

International Organization 43, 3, Summer 1989, pp. 349–75

in Europe and North America? Why is there a robust international regime for polar bears but not for other marine mammals such as walruses, sea lions, and sea otters? Why do we have a comprehensive regime for Antarctica but not for the Arctic? For ease of reference, Table 1 lists the issue-areas and specific institutional arrangements referred to in the text of this article.[2]

Existing models: a critique

Two streams of analysis dominate the study of regime formation in international society. Those trained to look at the world through the prism of mainstream utilitarian models focus on the behavior of rational utility maximizers and typically assume that actors of this type will reach agreement on the content of mutually beneficial institutional arrangements, including international regimes, whenever a distinct contract zone or zone of agreement exists.[3] Working with models emanating from game theory or microeconomics, the utilitarians seek to predict (or prescribe) the locus of final settlements as well as the trajectories of sequences of offers and counteroffers leading to these settlements.[4] Because they generally regard the process of institution-building as unproductive, these analysts expect rational actors to realize feasible joint gains while simultaneously devising procedures to keep the attendant transaction costs under control.[5]

Political scientists and others trained to look to the distribution of power in society as the key to understanding collective outcomes, by contrast, regularly assume that institutional arrangements, such as international regimes, reflect the configuraton of power in the relevant social system; specific arrangements come into existence when those possessing sufficient power take the necessary steps to create them.[6] These realists (or neorealists) have

2. For descriptive accounts of a number of these institutional arrangements, see, for example, Seyom Brown et al., *Regimes for the Ocean, Outer Space, and Weather* (Washington, D.C.: Brookings Institution, 1977); Lynton Keith Caldwell, *International Environmental Policy* (Durham, N.C.: Duke University Press, 1984); Simon Lyster, *International Wildlife Law* (Cambridge: Grotius Publications, 1985); Marvin S. Soroos, *Beyond Sovereignty: The Challenge of Global Policy* (Columbia: University of South Carolina Press, 1986); and World Commission on Environment and Development, *Our Common Future* (New York: Oxford University Press, 1987).

3. For a sophisticated exposition of the concept of a contract zone or zone of agreement, see Howard Raiffa, *The Art and Science of Negotiation* (Cambridge, Mass.: Harvard University Press, 1982).

4. For a survey of the principal models, see Oran R. Young, ed., *Bargaining: Formal Theories of Negotiation* (Urbana: University of Illinois Press, 1975).

5. For a forceful expression of this point of view, see Gordon Tullock, *Private Wants, Public Means: An Economic Analysis of the Desirable Scope of Government* (New York: Basic Books, 1970), chap. 3.

6. See Susan Strange, "*Cave! hic dragones:* A Critique of Regime Analysis," in Stephen D. Krasner, ed., *International Regimes* (Ithaca, N.Y.: Cornell University Press, 1983), pp. 337–54; Stephen D. Krasner, *Structural Conflict: The Third World Against Global Liberalism* (Berkeley: University of California Press, 1985); and Robert Gilpin, *The Political Economy of International Relations* (Princeton, N.J.: Princeton University Press, 1987).

TABLE 1. *International regimes for natural resources and the environment*

Issue-area	Regime
Wildlife (whales, northern fur seals, polar bears)	International Convention for Regulation of Whaling, 1946; Interim Convention on the Conservation of North Pacific Fur Seals, 1957 and subsequent protocols[a]; and Agreement on the Conservation of Polar Bears, 1973.
Marine life	Convention on the Conservation of Antarctic Marine Living Resources, 1980.
Wild fauna and flora	Convention on International Trade in Endangered Species of Wild Fauna and Flora, 1973.
Deep seabed minerals	Regime for the Area (the deep seabed) under Part XI of the United Nations Convention on the Law of the Sea, 1982.
Electromagnetic spectrum (broadcast frequencies, orbital slots)	Regime devised by the World Administrative Radio Conference (WARC) under the International Telecommunications Convention, 1982.
Regional pollution	Convention for the Protection of the Mediterranean Sea Against Pollution, 1976 and subsequent protocols.
Radioactive fallout	Convention on Early Notification of a Nuclear Accident, 1986; and Convention on Assistance in the Case of a Nuclear Accident or Radiological Emergency, 1986.
Stratospheric ozone	Convention for the Protection of the Ozone Layer, 1985 and the 1987 protocol.
Polar regions Antarctica	Antarctic Treaty, 1959; Convention on the Conservation of Antarctic Marine Living Resources, 1980; and Antarctic Minerals Convention, 1988.
The Arctic	No comprehensive regime for the Arctic in place at this time.
Acid precipitation Europe	Convention on Long-Range Transboundary Air Pollution, 1979 and subsequent protocols.
Other areas	No analogous regime in place for North America or the world as a whole.
Biological diversity	No international regime in place at this time.
Global climate change (greenhouse effect)	No international regime in place at this time.

[a]The fur seal regime was established initially in 1911 under the terms of the Treaty for the Preservation and Protection of Fur Seals.

come to stress the role of preponderant actors or, in the current vocabulary of international relations, hegemons in the process of regime formation. Some even assert that the presence of a hegemon is a necessary condition for the emergence of institutional arrangements at the international level.[7]

Not only do these streams of analysis license disparate explanations of regime formation in international society, but advocates of each perspective also tend to treat the very factor singled out by the other as an impediment to the promotion of social welfare. The utilitarians ordinarily react negatively to extreme concentrations of power on the grounds that such conditions result in monopoly (or monopsony), which in turn leads to misallocations of resources and reduces social welfare.[8] Conversely, the power theorists typically view the dispersal of power or the presence of numerous parties possessing roughly equal bargaining strength as a problem, basing their view on the theory that such conditions raise transaction costs, sometimes to the point where they prevent the emergence of agreement on institutional arrangements altogether.[9] Under the circumstances, the two groups differ in their prescriptions for achieving success in efforts to form international regimes as well as in the predictions they offer regarding probable outcomes in the realm of regime formation. Whereas the realists recommend concentration of power in the hands of a preponderant actor as a recipe for success, the utilitarians prescribe the dispersal of power among a sizable number of rational utility maximizers.

How can we come to terms with these conflicting perspectives on institution-building in the interests of formulating a satisfactory account of regime formation in international society? In this section, I argue that the models of both the power theorists and the mainstream utilitarians are seriously flawed when it comes to accounting for the actual record of success and failure in efforts to form international regimes. From this, I conclude that we need to develop a more realistic model of the interactions involved in regime formation to guide our thinking in this realm.

Realist or neorealist models

Mesmerized by the role of Great Britain in creating regimes for international commerce and the oceans during the nineteenth century and the role of the United States in establishing monetary and trade regimes in the after-

---

7. See Robert O. Keohane, "The Theory of Hegemonic Stability and Changes in International Economic Systems, 1967–1977," ACIS working paper no. 22, Center for International and Strategic Affairs, University of California, Los Angeles, 1980.

8. For a standard exposition of the importance of competition in systems of social exchange, see Robert H. Haveman and Kenyon A. Knopf, *The Market System*, 3d ed. (Santa Barbara, Calif.: John Wiley, 1979).

9. For an account stressing the role of transaction costs in connection with international institutions, see Todd Sandler and Jon Cauley, "The Design of Supranational Structures: An Economic Perspective," *International Studies Quarterly* 21 (June 1977), pp. 251–76.

math of World War II, many students of international relations are currently preoccupied with the place of preponderant actors or hegemons in international society.[10] There is much talk, for instance, about the sources of hegemonic power and the factors governing the rise and fall of dominant states,[11] and a lively debate has sprung up concerning the viability of existing international institutions in the wake of the presumed decline of American dominance in international affairs.[12] Given the existence of this intellectual climate, it is not hard to understand why students of international relations are attracted to the view that the presence of a hegemon constitutes a critical, perhaps necessary, condition for regime formation at the international level.

Yet it is easy to demonstrate that arguments relying so heavily on the role of preponderant actors in the formation of international regimes cannot withstand the test of empirical application. Consider, in this connection, just a few significant examples. The regime for northern fur seals, established initially in 1911 and long regarded as a model for international conservation efforts, involved a mutually beneficial deal among four major powers: the United States, Japan, Russia, and Great Britain (acting on behalf of Canada).[13] The more recent complex of arrangements for Antarctica and the Southern Ocean encompasses not only the two superpowers but also a number of other important powers working together as members of the Antarctic club.[14] The pollution control regime for the Mediterranean Basin, by contrast, does not include either of the superpowers. It does encompass among its members, however, a number of important states that span the Arab–Israeli conflict and the Greek–Turkish conflict as well as the East–West conflict.[15] What is more, in my sample of institutional arrangements, the drive to form several of the regimes was spearheaded by intergovernmental organizations or by international nongovernmental organizations, so that states did not even take the lead in the relevant processes of regime formation. There is general agreement, for example, that the International Union for the Con-

---

10. Although he may have come to regret it, it seems clear that Kindleberger's analysis of international economic relations in the 1930s played an important part in the development of this set of intellectual concerns. See Charles P. Kindleberger, *The World in Depression, 1929–1939* (Berkeley: University of California Press, 1973).

11. For an account that has received much popular acclaim, see Paul Kennedy, *The Rise and Fall of the Great Powers* (New York: Random House, 1987).

12. See Robert O. Keohane, *After Hegemony: Cooperation and Discord in the World Political Economy* (Princeton, N.J.: Princeton University Press, 1984). For a forceful presentation of the view that the dominance of the United States in international affairs persists, see Susan Strange, "The Persistent Myth of Lost Hegemony," *International Organization* 41 (Autumn 1987), pp. 551–74.

13. See Lyster, *International Wildlife Law*, chap. 3; and Oran R. Young, *Natural Resources and the State* (Berkeley: University of California Press, 1981), chap. 3.

14. Gillian D. Triggs, ed., *The Antarctic Treaty Regime: Law, Environment and Resources* (Cambridge: Cambridge University Press, 1987).

15. Peter M. Haas, "Do Regimes Matter? A Study of Evolving Pollution Control Policies for the Mediterranean Sea," paper presented at the annual convention of the International Studies Association, April 1987.

servation of Nature and Natural Resources (IUCN) was the motivating force in establishing the regime regulating trade in endangered species of fauna and flora spelled out in the provisions of the Convention on International Trade in Endangered Species.[16] And there is no escaping the central role that the United Nations Environment Programme (UNEP) played in the negotiating process that resulted in the 1985 convention and the 1987 protocol on ozone depletion.[17]

From the perspective of those desiring to promote international cooperation through regime formation, this is just as well, since as many observers are coming to realize, hegemony is an extreme case in international society. This is not to deny, of course, the existence of striking asymmetries among parties interested in a given issue-area both with respect to the intensity of their interest in the problem and with respect to usable bargaining strength at their disposal. Nonetheless, there are several interlocking reasons why true hegemony is the exception rather than the rule in international society.[18] There is, to begin with, the well-known fact that power in the sense of control over resources or tangible capabilities is often difficult to translate into power in the sense of the ability to determine collective outcomes.[19] Situations in which other states coalesce in opposition to a state that appears to have hegemonic pretensions are routine in international society.[20] It will come as no surprise, therefore, that even acknowledged great powers are apt to find the opportunity costs of exercizing power high in specific situations. Given the fact that great powers always strive to participate actively in a number of issue-areas or arenas simultaneously, moreover, the prospect of high opportunity costs is sufficient to induce such powers to negotiate rather than impose the terms of international regimes relating to most specific activities.[21]

What is more, contemporary international society features many situations in which a number of states possess blocking power or the capacity to veto institutional arrangements they dislike, even if they cannot impose their own

16. See Lyster, *International Wildlife Law*, chap. 12; and Laura H. Kosloff and Mark C. Trexler, "The Convention on International Trade in Endangered Species: No Carrot, But Where's the Stick?" *Environmental Law Reporter* 17 (July 1987), pp. 10222–36.

17. Philip Shabecoff, "Ozone Agreement Is Hailed as a First Step in Cooperation," *The New York Times*, 5 May 1987, pp. C1 and C7.

18. See also Duncan Snidal, "The Limits of Hegemonic Stability Theory," *International Organization* 39 (Autumn 1985), pp. 579–614.

19. Jeffrey Hart, "Three Approaches to the Measurement of Power in International Relations," *International Organization* 30 (Spring 1976), pp. 299–305.

20. Zeev Maoz and Dan S. Felsenthal, "Self-Binding Commitments, the Inducement of Trust, Social Choice, and the Theory of International Cooperation," *International Studies Quarterly* 31 (June 1987), pp. 177–200.

21. The growth of international interdependencies in the modern era reinforces the argument of this paragraph, since this growth drives up the opportunity costs associated with all efforts to exercise power. See Oran R. Young, "Interdependencies in World Politics," *International Journal* 24 (Autumn 1969), pp. 726–50.

preferences on others.[22] Consider, in this connection, problems such as the control of radioactive fallout crossing national boundaries or the regulation of the emission of greenhouse gases giving rise to the global warming trend that is widely expected to become pronounced during the foreseeable future.[23] In such cases, it is hard to see how any international regime could be effective if it failed to satisfy the concerns of all the industrialized members of international society. For all practical purposes, then, the great powers today routinely find themselves in situations in which they must negotiate the terms of international regimes covering specific issue-areas, whether they like it or not.

All of this puts a premium on a form of leadership that differs from the kind of unilateralism or imposition we ordinarily associate with the actions of a hegemon. Contrary to Charles Kindleberger's argument that "a hegemon presumably wants to do it in his own behalf" and that "a leader, one who is responsible or responds to need, who is answerable or answers to the demands of others, is forced to 'do it' by ethical training and by the circumstances of position,"[24] leadership is not simply a matter of motivation. Nor is leadership merely a form of benevolent behavior exhibited by the principal members of privileged groups who act in such a way as to supply public goods to others regardless of their unwillingness to contribute toward the supply of such goods.[25] Rather, leadership in connection with the formation of international regimes is a matter of entrepreneurship; it involves a combination of imagination in inventing institutional options and skill in brokering the interests of numerous actors to line up support for such options.[26] A leader in this context is an actor who, desiring to see a regime emerge and realizing that imposition is not feasible, undertakes to craft attractive institutional arrangements and to persuade others to come on board as supporters of such arrangements. When commentators say that UNEP played a leadership role in the development of the Mediterranean Action Plan in the 1970s, they surely have this entrepreneurial conception of leadership in mind. And much the same is true when states become leaders in institution-building, as the United States did in gaining agreement on the 1987 Montreal protocol to the convention on ozone depletion.

22. For an extensive analysis of blocking as well as winning coalitions, see William H. Riker, *A Theory of Political Coalitions* (New Haven, Conn.: Yale University Press, 1962).

23. James G. Titus, ed., *Effects of Changes in Stratospheric Ozone and Global Climate,* vol. 1 (Washington, D.C.: U.S. Environmental Protection Agency and U.N. Environmental Programme, 1986).

24. Charles P. Kindleberger, "Hierarchy Versus Inertial Cooperation," *International Organization* 40 (Autumn 1986), pp. 845–46.

25. On privileged groups, see Mancur Olson, Jr., *The Logic of Collective Action* (Cambridge, Mass.: Harvard University Press, 1965), chap. 1.

26. For a discussion of political leadership as a form of entrepreneurship, see Norman Frohlich, Joe A. Oppenheimer, and Oran R. Young, *Political Leadership and Collective Goods* (Princeton, N.J.: Princeton University Press, 1971).

Utilitarian models

For their part, the mainstream utilitarians exhibit an unjustified faith in the ability of rational utility maximizers to realize feasible joint gains. As all well-trained students of international affairs now realize, even rational actors regularly experience difficulties in cooperating, with the result that suboptimal (sometimes drastically suboptimal) outcomes are a common occurrence.[27] More than anything else, this realization is what has provided the impetus for the remarkable rise of the field of public choice in recent years and made a growth industry of the analysis of institutional arrangements designed to overcome or alleviate collective-action problems.[28]

Even when there is general agreement on the existence and the dimensions of a zone of agreement, those negotiating the terms of institutional arrangements often encounter severe obstacles in their efforts to work out the details of mutually acceptable regimes: (1) Difficulties frequently ensue from widespread resort to strategic behavior or committal tactics on the part of those wanting the outcomes to favor their interests to the maximum degree possible.[29] The behavior of the American negotiators that resulted in the refusal of the United States to accept the regime for deep seabed mining set forth in Part XI of the 1982 United Nations Convention on the Law of the Sea is a case in point.[30] (2) Intra-party bargaining that pits powerful forces against each other within one or more of the states negotiating the provisions of an international regime can make it difficult to reach agreement at the international level.[31] Such internal problems undoubtedly played a role in the decision of the United States to abandon the fur seal regime in the 1980s, and they would surely afflict the negotiating posture of a number of the participants in any serious effort to devise a regime to regulate global climate change at the present time. (3) There are commonly problems attributable to linkages among issue-areas in international society. Thus, parties are frequently loath to make concessions regarding specific issues more out of a concern for how this might affect their negotiating postures in other issue-areas than out of any commitment to the particular issue at hand.[32] Certainly,

27. See Russell Hardin, *Collective Action* (Baltimore. Md.: Johns Hopkins University Press, 1982); and Kenneth A. Oye, ed., *Cooperation Under Anarchy* (Princeton, N.J.: Princeton University Press, 1986).

28. For a seminal example, see James M. Buchanan and Gordon Tullock, *The Calculus of Consent* (Ann Arbor: University of Michigan Press, 1962). For a variety of perspectives on the use of public choice theory to examine institutional arrangements, see Clifford S. Russell, ed., *Collective Decision Making: Applications from Public Choice Theory* (Baltimore. Md.: Johns Hopkins University Press, 1979).

29. Thomas C. Schelling, *The Strategy of Conflict* (Cambridge, Mass.: Harvard University Press, 1960).

30. James L. Malone, "Who Needs the Sea Treaty?" *Foreign Policy* 54 (Spring 1984), pp. 27–43.

31. Robert D. Putnam, "Diplomacy and Domestic Politics: The Logic of Two-Level Games," *International Organization* 42 (Summer 1988), pp. 427–60.

32. For a more general account, see James K. Sebenius, "Negotiation Arithmetic: Adding and Subtracting Issues and Parties," *International Organization* 37 (Spring 1983), pp. 281–316.

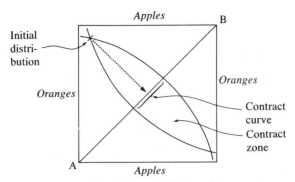

FIGURE 1. *Edgeworth box diagram*

the reluctance of the United States and some other industrialized states to go very far toward meeting the "common heritage of mankind" arguments of the developing states in the context of the law of the sea negotiations was based in considerable measure on a concern that this would simply reinforce the demands of the developing states in negotiations regarding satellite broadcasting, Antarctica, and, ultimately, an array of issues grouped under the heading of the New International Economic Order (NIEO).[33] (4) Negotiators also regularly encounter difficulties in settling on the terms of international regimes because some of the participants do not trust others to comply with the terms of the resultant arrangements rather than because they are unhappy with the substantive provisions of the arrangements themselves.[34] In some cases, this is essentially a problem of verification, as in pollution control measures relating to non-point source pollutants or in efforts to control the illegal trade in endangered species.[35] In other cases, it is more a matter of devising appropriate incentives or sanctions, as in arrangements aimed at avoiding the destruction of habitat necessary for the maintenance of biological diversity. But in either situation, it is not hard to understand the reluctance of states to subscribe to international regimes that seem likely to end up as dead letters as a consequence of widespread noncompliance with their substantive provisions.[36]

More profoundly, mainstream utilitarian accounts of international regime foundation rest on an inappropriate, albeit well-specified and analytically appealing, model of bargaining. All this work takes as its point of departure either an Edgeworth box diagram with its depiction of a well-defined contract curve (see Figure 1) or a game-theoretic formulation with its identification

33. For a straightforward introduction to the components of the NIEO, see Soroos, *Beyond Sovereignty,* chap. 6.

34. For an analysis of this issue, treated as the problem of cheating, see Schelling, *The Strategy of Conflict.*

35. On the illegal trade in endangered species, see Kosloff and Trexler, "The Convention on International Trade in Endangered Species."

36. For a broader analysis of compliance problems, see Roger Fisher, *Improving Compliance with International Law* (Charlottesville: University Press of Virginia, 1981).

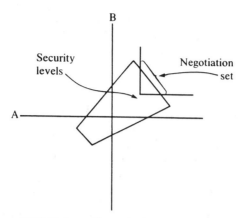

FIGURE 2. *Negotiation set*

of a well-defined negotiation set (see Figure 2).[37] Both of these analytic devices abstract away a great many considerations that are major preoccupations of negotiators under real-world circumstances.[38] They assume, for instance, that the identity of the participants is known at the outset and fixed during the course of negotiations, that the alternatives or strategies available to the parties are fully specified, that the outcome associated with every feasible combination of choices on the part of the participants is known, and that the preference orderings of the parties over these outcomes are identifiable (at least in ordinal terms) and not subject to change. It is, in fact, the introduction of these assumptions that makes it possible to specify the parameters of the utility possibility set in an Edgeworth box or the payoff space in a game-theoretic analysis. And it is a short step from this point to the preoccupation with defining solution concepts that characterizes game-theoretic analyses of bargaining and the concern with "the process of concession" that dominates economic models of bargaining.[39]

As appealing as the resultant constructs may be in analytic terms, they are of limited value in helping us comprehend the politics of international regime formation. The identity of the relevant participants in these negotiations is seldom cast in concrete. As recent experience in both the Arctic and the Antarctic suggests, the scope of the membership in international regimes can become an important focus of bargaining in its own right. It will come as no surprise, then, that efforts to spell out menus of alternatives or

37. See Young, *Bargaining*. Part I of this book deals with game-theoretic models of bargaining based on the concept of the negotiation set. Part II turns to economic models of bargaining stemming from the Edgeworth box construct.

38. Young, *Bargaining*, pp. 391–408.

39. See R. Duncan Luce and Howard Raiffa. *Games and Decisions* (New York: John Wiley, 1957); and John G. Cross, *The Economics of Bargaining* (New York: Basic Books, 1969). The quotation is from Cross, p. 8.

strategy sets in advance of these negotiations are generally doomed to failure. No doubt, there is some heuristic value in analyzing the extent to which specific collective-action problems in international society resemble prisoner's dilemma, chicken, stag hunt, or other analytic models.[40] But mapping the contours of real-world collective-action problems in terms of such analytic models is seldom a feasible proposition,[41] and our ability to foresee the consequences, unfolding over time, which result from the choice of specific options is particularly limited in connection with ongoing arrangements such as international regimes. Those who approach these matters in contractarian terms have pointed out that this may well be a good thing, since it serves to dilute the relevance of particularistic interests in the responses of individual parties to proposed institutional arrangements at the international level.[42] Even so, it is important to note that this fact typically rules out the specification of a well-defined contract curve or negotiation set in connection with negotiations focusing on the formation of international regimes.

An alternative model: institutional bargaining

The principal conclusion to be drawn from the preceding discussion is that we must develop an alternative model of regime formation in order to come up with a satisfactory answer to the question posed at the beginning of this article. In my judgment, this model should retain an emphasis on negotiations among self-interested parties as a means of dealing with collective-action problems. But it should, at the same time, depart in several fundamental ways from the mainstream utilitarian accounts of the bargaining process. In this section, I spell out the defining characteristics of such a model, which I call institutional bargaining, and draw on the cases referred to in Table 1 to illustrate the major features of this model under real-world conditions. This sets the stage for the next section of the article, which begins the process of deriving hypotheses from the model of institutional bargaining that can help us understand why efforts to form international regimes are successful in some cases but not in others.

40. See Duncan Snidal, "Coordination Versus Prisoner's Dilemma: Implications for International Cooperation and Regimes," *American Political Science Review* 79 (December 1985), pp. 923–42; and Kenneth A. Oye, "Explaining Cooperation Under Anarchy," in Oye, *Cooperation Under Anarchy,* pp. 1–24.

41. Anatol Rapoport, *Two-Person Game Theory: The Essential Ideas* (Ann Arbor: University of Michigan Press, 1966), chap. 12.

42. For a general discussion of this point, see Geoffrey Brennan and James M. Buchanan, *The Reason of Rules: Constitutional Political Economy* (Cambridge: Cambridge University Press, 1985), chap. 2.

Multiple actors and unanimity rules

While there may be disagreement (and sometimes even hard bargaining) regarding the identity of the parties that are or should be included in specific cases, efforts to devise international regimes generally involve a number of autonomous participants. This may mean a handful, such as the four states that negotiated the fur seal regime, or a modest number, such as the sixteen parties to the regime for Antarctic marine living resources or the twenty-three parties to the 1987 protocol to the ozone depletion convention. In extreme cases, it may involve over 150 states, as in the efforts to work out a deep seabed mining regime in the context of the law of the sea negotiations. And though it would certainly be helpful in analytic terms, it is seldom feasible to collapse the resultant negotiations into two-sided bargaining processes by grouping the players into two coalitions or blocs. This means that analytic constructs closely tied to a two-party view of the world, like the Edgeworth box, cannot carry us far in coming to terms with the politics of international regime formation.[43]

Equally important, the multilateral interactions involved in regime formation do not lend themselves well to treatment in terms of the usual analytic responses to n-party situations, which center on the identification of sets of winning coalitions coupled with efforts to single out those coalitions that are most likely to form.[44] Unlike the situation prevailing in most municipal legislatures, efforts to form international regimes generally focus on the specification of arrangements that all those engaged in the negotiations can accept. This is tantamount to saying that institutional bargaining in international society operates on the basis of a unanimity rule in contrast to a majority rule or some other decision rule justifying a focus on the development of winning coalitions.[45] No doubt, those negotiating the terms of international regimes may seek to exclude parties deemed likely to object to any reasonable institutional arrangements or threaten to go forward with particular arrangements regardless of the opposition of one or more parties. Such concerns may account, for example, for the resistance that members of the Antarctic club have displayed toward proposals to shift negotiations regarding Antarctica into the arena of the United Nations, and they may well underlie some of the problems that have arisen in efforts to devise workable regimes for deep seabed mining or the use of the electromagnetic spectrum.[46]

43. In principle, we can think of an Edgeworth box in n-space. But such a construct would not be analytically tractable.

44. For a classic account of the principal constructs of n-person game theory, see Luce and Raiffa, *Games and Decisions.*

45. Of course, this does not rule out an array of devices, threats, promises, or side payments that are aimed at inducing parties to accept particular institutional arrangements. For an account that emphasizes the attractions of the unanimity rule, see Buchanan and Tullock, *The Calculus of Consent.*

46. On the case of Antarctica, see Lee Kimball, "Antarctica: Testing the Great Experiment," *Environment* 27 (September 1985), pp. 14–17 and 26–30.

Yet once the membership of the relevant group is set, negotiations regarding international regimes generally revolve around efforts to come up with arrangements that all participants in these negotiations can accept.

Integrative bargaining

One thing that saves the resultant negotiations from certain failure is that regime formation in international society typically centers on integrative (or productive) bargaining in contrast to distributive (or positional) bargaining.[47] As Richard Walton and Robert McKersie observed in their early and influential discussion of integrative bargaining, the key to this distinction lies in the presence or absence of a fixed, unchanging, and generally acknowledged contract curve or negotiation set.[48] Negotiators who know the locus of a contract curve or the shape of a welfare frontier to begin with will naturally be motivated primarily by a desire to achieve an outcome on this curve or frontier that is as favorable to their own interests as possible. They will, therefore, immediately turn to calculations regarding various types of strategic behavior or committal tactics that may help them achieve their distributive goals.[49]

Negotiators who do not start with a common understanding regarding the contours of the contract curve or the locus of the negotiation set, by contrast, have compelling incentives to engage in exploratory interactions to identify opportunities for devising mutually beneficial deals. Such negotiators may never discover the actual shape of the contract curve or locus of the negotiation set, and they may consequently end up with arrangements that are Pareto-inferior in the sense that they leave feasible joint gains on the table.[50] At the same time, however, they are less likely to engage in negotiations that bog down into protracted stalemates brought about by efforts to improve the outcome for one party or another through initiatives involving strategic behavior and committal tactics.

The veil of uncertainty

Another factor that serves to mitigate the threat of stalemate in interactions governed by unanimity rules is what James Buchanan has described as the veil of uncertainty. It is not that those negotiating the terms of international

---

47. The term "productive bargaining" is from Cross, *The Economics of Bargaining*. The term "positional bargaining" is from Roger Fisher and William Ury, *Getting to Yes* (Harmondsworth, U.K.: Penguin, 1981).

48. Richard Walton and Robert B. McKersie, *A Behavioral Theory of Negotiations* (New York: McGraw-Hill, 1965), chaps. 2–5.

49. For a classic account of such tactics, see Schelling, *The Strategy of Conflict*.

50. The result is a kind of collective analog to Simon's notion of "satisficing" with regard to individual decision making. See James G. March and Herbert A. Simon, *Organizations* (New York: John Wiley, 1958), especially chap. 3.3.

regimes ordinarily lack information about their own roles in society, as John Rawls supposes in his concept of the veil of ignorance constraining the behavior of those negotiating social contracts under conditions approximating what he calls the original position.[51] The point is, rather, that institutional arrangements, unlike specific or self-contained choices, typically apply across a wide range of contexts and over a more or less extended period of time. And, to use the formulation of Geoffrey Brennan and James Buchanan, "As both the generality and the permanence of rules are increased, the individual who faces choice alternatives becomes more uncertain about the effects of alternatives on his own position."[52] This uncertainty actually facilitates efforts to reach agreement on the substantive provisions of international regimes. As Brennan and Buchanan observe, in a discussion directed toward municipal institutions, "to the extent that a person faced with constitutional choice remains uncertain as to what his position will be under separate choice options, he will tend to agree on arrangements that might be called 'fair' in the sense that patterns of outcomes generated under such arrangements will be broadly acceptable, regardless of where the participant might be located in such outcomes."[53]

Surely, this observation applies with equal force to the behavior of collective entities, such as nation-states, that dominate negotiations regarding the content of international regimes. This line of analysis undoubtedly helps to account for the fact that collections of actors have reached agreement regarding the provisions of arrangements governing whaling, the pollution of the Mediterranean Basin, and some of the problems associated with the transboundary flow of radioactive fallout. It also helps us understand the difficulties that plague efforts to devise mutually acceptable arrangements dealing with acid precipitation, biological diversity, or the global warming trend. To put it simply, the key players find it easier to see through the veil of uncertainty in these cases than in a number of other areas referred to in this discussion.

Problems and approaches

Faced with negotiations characterized by integrative bargaining under a veil of uncertainty, the parties endeavoring to form international regimes seldom, if ever, make a sustained effort to perfect their information regarding the full range of outcomes and the dimensions of contract zones before getting down to serious bargaining. Instead, they typically zero in on a few key problems, articulate several approaches to the treatment of these problems, and seek to reconcile differences among these approaches in the course

---

51. John Rawls, *A Theory of Justice* (Cambridge, Mass.: Harvard University Press, 1971), especially pp. 136–42.
52. Brennan and Buchanan, *The Reason of Rules*, pp. 29–30.
53. Ibid., p. 30.

of their negotiations. In the case of deep seabed mining, for instance, the problems included matters such as the role of the Enterprise in the conduct of mining operations, production controls in the hands of the International Seabed Authority, and technology transfer.[54] Those negotiating the regime for Antarctic marine living resources focused on the problem of whether to adopt a whole ecosystems approach, as advocated by the United States, or some approach emphasizing the pursuit of maximum sustainable yield on a species-by-species basis, as advocated by a number of other participants.[55] Similarly, the negotiations leading to the 1987 protocol on the protection of the ozone layer centered, for a time, on the relative merits of emphasizing a comprehensive ban on aerosols or of mandating an across-the-board cut in the production of chlorofluorocarbons (CFCs).[56]

There is no guarantee, of course, that the parties can reconcile divergent approaches to such problems, although it helps to be dealing with several differentiable concerns so that it becomes possible to devise trades among those who feel more or less intensely about individual problems and approaches. But when it does prove feasible to make progress in reconciling divergent approaches to relatively well-defined problems, the parties typically begin to formulate a negotiating text and to use this device to structure their ongoing efforts to develop the deals required to reach agreement on the terms of a regime.[57] Such a text can serve both to organize the negotiations involved in regime formation, as in the case of the various negotiating texts used in the law of the sea negotiations, and to provide a basis to guide the expansion or extension of a regime over time, as in the cases of the negotiation of several subsequent protocols to the 1976 convention on pollution control in the Mediterranean Basin and of the 1987 protocol to the 1985 convention on ozone depletion.[58]

Transnational alliances

As many observers have pointed out, negotiations pertaining to the formation of international regimes commonly involve extensive intra-party bargaining, which is apt to occur simultaneously with the relevant inter-party bargaining.[59] There is nothing surprising about this when we stop to consider that states are complex collective entities encompassing numerous groups

---

54. For a straightforward descriptive account, see Soroos, *Beyond Sovereignty,* chap. 8.
55. Lyster, *International Wildlife Law,* chap. 9.
56. For helpful background on this case, see Allan S. Miller and Irving M. Mintzer, "The Sky Is the Limit: Strategies for Protecting the Ozone Layer," *Research Report,* no. 3 (Washington, D.C.: World Resources Institute, 1986).
57. For a helpful account rooted in an analysis of the law of the sea negotiations, see Robert L. Friedheim, *Negotiating the Ocean Regime,* work in progress.
58. For additional comments on the role of negotiating texts, see Raiffa, *The Art and Science of Negotiation.*
59. Putnam, "Diplomacy and Domestic Politics."

whose interests often differ widely with respect to any given issue-area. The about-face of the United States regarding the law of the sea convention, for example, is surely attributable more to the advent of an administration more attuned to the concerns of big business than its predecessor than to any objective change in the national interests of the United States. Internal splits between industrialists and environmentalists are common in connection with most pollution control arrangements. And a number of members of the European Community experienced relatively sharp internal conflicts regarding the positions they took in negotiating a regime to protect stratospheric ozone.

What is interesting in connection with this discussion of institutional bargaining, however, is the potential that situations of this kind generate for the development of transnational alliances among interest groups supporting the formation of specific international regimes. An extensive network of scientific supporters located in all the Mediterranean Basin states has played an important role in bringing pressure to bear on hesitant governments to become supporters of the pollution control regime for the Mediterranean.[60] The transnational environmental community played a central, perhaps dominant, role in pushing through the regime governing international trade in endangered species. And the transnational scientific and environmental communities have often joined forces in their efforts to develop and defend effective regimes for Antarctica.[61] In some cases, these efforts are facilitated by organizations that serve to aggregate and articulate the concerns of transnational interest groups regarding international regimes. For example, the IUCN clearly played a critical role in devising the regime governing trade in endangered species.[62] The Scientific Committee on Antarctic Research (SCAR), together with its parent organization, the International Council of Scientific Unions, has certainly been instrumental in the development of regimes relating to Antarctica.[63] And it is intriguing to consider the remarkable role of UNEP in the negotiations leading to the 1985 convention and the 1987 protocol regarding the protection of stratospheric ozone. None of this is to suggest that states no longer dominate bargaining in international society; far from it. But it would be a serious mistake to overlook the role of transnational alliances among influential interest groups in developing and maintaining regimes at the international level.[64]

60. Haas, "Do Regimes Matter?"

61. This has resulted, among other things, in the development of the Antarctic and Southern Ocean Coalition, a nongovernmental organization that has been able to exercise considerable influence on negotiations relating to Antarctica.

62. Kosloff and Trexler, "The Convention on International Trade in Endangered Species."

63. Polar Research Board, *Antarctic Treaty System: An Assessment* (Washington, D.C.: National Academy Press, 1986).

64. The recent work of Peter Haas and his colleagues on the role of epistemic communities in regime formation is suggestive in this context.

Shifting involvements

While the vision of negotiation incorporated in the mainstream utilitarian models emphasizes self-contained interactions, institutional bargaining of the type involved in the formation of international regimes almost always features a rich array of linkages to other events occurring in the socioeconomic or political environment.[65] Sometimes this poses more or less serious problems for those engaged in institutional bargaining at the international level.[66] Parties may deliberately drag their feet in hopes that their bargaining strength will increase with the passage of time. Individual participants may deliberately complicate the negotiations by linking several issues in such a way as to necessitate the development of complex bargains over an array of problems. Players may become so preoccupied with domestic matters, such as protracted election campaigns or serious civil strife, that they are not in a position to pursue institutional bargaining at the international level vigorously. Or they may simply choose to emphasize other issue-areas for the time being in recognition of their limited capacity to engage in international negotiations. An examination of the history of efforts to form regimes governing deep seabed mining, satellite broadcasting, and the trade in endangered species offers a rich array of examples of such problems.

In some cases, however, linkages of this type work in favor of efforts to form international regimes. Those concerned about possible erosions of bargaining strength in the future may be willing to make significant concessions to reach agreement quickly on the terms of specific regimes. Linking together disparate issues sometimes opens up possibilities for mutually acceptable arrangements by creating opportunities for the international equivalent of logrolling and the formulation of package deals.[67] Those possessing insufficient capacity to handle numerous issues simultaneously may be willing to leave much of the negotiating about the terms of certain regimes to nongovernmental actors who are part of a transnational network and who have developed a considerable ability to work together in the course of prior interactions. The package deals incorporated in the 1982 law of the sea convention and the role of nongovernmental experts in devising the regimes covering polar bears and trade in endangered species certainly illustrate these possibilities. The conclusion to be drawn from this discussion, therefore, is not that these linkages necessarily make it difficult to form international regimes but, rather, that those involved in processes of regime formation must remain alert at all times to connections of this sort. That is, the natural tendency to become preoccupied with the technical aspects of the specific

---

65. See also Fred Charles Ikle, *How Nations Negotiate* (New York: Harper & Row, 1964).
66. For an accessible account of a number of these problems as well as techniques for coping with them, see I. William Zartman and Maureen R. Berman, *The Practical Negotiator* (New Haven, Conn.: Yale University Press, 1982).
67. Sebenius, "Negotiation Arithmetic."

subject at hand can easily lead to failure in negotiating processes relating to regime formation which are highly sensitive to occurrences in the broader socioeconomic or political environment.

Determinants of success: hypotheses about international regime formation

The record clearly shows that institutional bargaining results in the formation of new international regimes under some conditions. Consider, just to name some recent examples, the development of institutional arrangements pertaining to transboundary radioactive fallout, stratospheric ozone, and Antarctic minerals. Yet success is far from ensured in such endeavors. Like self-interested actors in all social arenas, those attempting to work out the terms of international regimes are often stymied by bargaining impediments that prolong negotiations over institutional arrangements and can easily result in deadlocks. It is not surprising, for instance, that the negotiations over a regime for deep seabed mining took so long and had such an ambiguous outcome. Nor is it hard to understand why interested parties have so far failed to devise workable arrangements to protect the biological diversity of the earth's ecosphere or to cope with the global climate change expected to result from the emission of greenhouse gases.[68]

The next task, then, is to make use of the model of institutional bargaining to pinpoint the determinants of success and failure in efforts to form institutional arrangements in international society. In this section, I initiate this process by deriving some hypotheses about factors governing the likelihood of success in efforts to form international regimes and applying these hypotheses, in a preliminary way, to the set of cases under consideration throughout this article. Needless to say, this initial analysis is not sufficient to constitute a rigorous test of any of the hypotheses. Even so, it should suffice to trigger a line of analysis that could well result in the formulation of a fully satisfactory answer to the question with which this article began.

1. Institutional bargaining can succeed only when the issues at stake lend themselves to contractarian interactions.

Those engaged in efforts to form international regimes experience incentives to approach this process as a problem-solving exercise aimed at reaching agreement on the terms of a social contract when the absence of a fully specified zone of agreement encourages integrative bargaining and the pres-

---

68. For a variety of perspectives on global climate change, see the essays in Titus, *Effects of Changes in Stratospheric Ozone and Global Climate;* and Irving M. Mintzer, "A Matter of Degrees: The Potential for Controlling the Greenhouse Effect," *Research Report,* no. 5 (Washington, D.C.: World Resources Institute, 1987).

ence of imperfect information ensures that a veil of uncertainty prevails. In situations governed by unanimity rules, a contractarian environment of this sort is necessary to avoid the positional deadlocks that commonly arise in connection with distributive bargaining. It is therefore critical to observe that collective-action problems in international society of the sort engendering an interest in devising arrangements to institutionalize cooperation vary in the degree to which they lend themselves to treatment in contractarian terms. And it is worth noting that those involved in efforts to form international regimes often differ markedly in terms of the skill they display in presenting problems of regime formation in contractarian terms.

To see the relevance of this factor to the success of institutional bargaining, consider, to begin with, some extreme cases. It is exceedingly difficult, for instance, to portray the problem of controlling acid precipitation in North America in contractarian terms both because the producers of the relevant emissions and the victims of acid deposition are so clearly identified at the outset and because there is not much overlap in the membership of the two groups.[69] The problem of controlling transboundary radioactive fallout resulting from nuclear accidents, by contrast, is comparatively easy to treat in contractarian terms.[70] Although a good deal is known about the dangers of radioactive fallout, individual members of international society ordinarily cannot know in advance whether they will occupy the role of site of an accident, victim state, or unharmed bystander with respect to specific accidents. This is exactly the sort of situation that gives rise to incentives to consider the common good in devising institutional arrangements.

Although they are less extreme, other cases add to our understanding of the importance of this proposition about the significance of contractarianism. There are important differences, for example, between the problems of ozone depletion and global climate change that affect the extent to which they lend themselves to formulation in contractarian terms. While the impact may vary somewhat on the basis of latitude, human populations in every part of the world will be harmed if the depletion of stratospheric ozone continues at its present rate.[71] In the case of global warming, on the other hand, there will almost certainly be winners and losers who are comparatively easy to differentiate.[72] Significant increases in sea level will cause severe damage to certain low-lying coastal areas (for example, one-half to two-thirds of Bangladesh could easily be inundated) while bestowing benefits on other regions.

69. The fact that some countries, such as the Federal Republic of Germany, are both major producers of acid precipitation and important victims of this form of pollution makes the problem of devising a regime to control acid precipitation more tractable in Europe than it is in North America.
70. Oran R. Young, *International Cooperation: Building Regimes for Natural Resources and the Environment* (Ithaca, N.Y.: Cornell University Press, 1989), chap. 6.
71. See also the projections in Miller and Mintzer, "The Sky Is the Limit."
72. For some interesting projections regarding this point, see E. F. Roots, "The Cost of Inaction: An Example from Climate Change Studies," unpublished paper, 1988.

Global warming is expected to make some areas increasingly hospitable to large-scale agriculture even as other areas lose their current role in agricultural production. And the impact of these differences on processes of regime formation is heightened by the fact that the sources of greenhouse gas emissions are numerous and widely dispersed, whereas the producers of CFCs are few in number and located in a relatively small number of states. Under the circumstances, it is no cause for surprise that the foundations for an international regime designed to protect the ozone layer are now in place, whereas a regime to deal with global climate change is not yet in sight.

2. The availability of arrangements that all participants can accept as equitable (rather than efficient) is necessary for institutional bargaining to succeed.

Economists and others who approach the issue of regime formation as a problem in comparative statics generally place primary emphasis on the achievement of allocative efficiency in discussing the formation of new institutions as well as in evaluating the performance of existing arrangements.[73] Such analysts are apt to be highly critical of arrangements that encourage misallocations of scarce resources or that seem likely to produce outcomes lying inside the relevant welfare frontier. To be more concrete, they find much to criticize in arrangements allocating some of the choicest deep seabed mining sites to the Enterprise, imposing across-the-board percentage cuts on the production of CFCs by current producers, or reserving at least one orbital slot for each state that may become interested in satellite broadcasting.[74]

Yet those who negotiate the terms of international regimes seldom focus on these questions of allocative efficiency. In a negotiating environment featuring the rule of unanimity, they must occupy themselves, for the most part, with considerations of equity on the understanding that institutional bargaining in international society can succeed only when all of the major parties and interest groups come away with a sense that their primary concerns have been treated fairly. Allocative efficiency is an abstract concept. No one can determine whether the outcomes flowing from a given regime are in fact efficient until much later. And even then, economists often dis-

---

73. For a helpful introduction to the principal approaches to the concept of efficiency, see Robert Dorfman and Nancy S. Dorfman, eds., *The Economics of the Environment*, 2d ed. (New York: Norton, 1977), pp. 1–37. For an explicit assertion regarding the appropriateness of emphasizing efficiency in this context, see Ross D. Eckert, "Exploitation of Deep Ocean Minerals: Regulatory Mechanisms and United States Policy," *Journal of Law and Economics* 17 (April 1974), pp. 143–77.

74. See Daniel J. Dudek, "Chlorofluorocarbon Policy: Choice and Consequences," a paper distributed by the Environmental Defense Fund, April 1987; and Gregory C. Staple, "The New World Satellite Order: A Report from Geneva," *American Journal of International Law* 80 (July 1986), pp. 699–720.

agree vigorously in their assessments of the efficiency of observable outcomes. Equity, by contrast, is an immediate concern that evokes strong feelings on all sides. To return to the previous examples, no reasonable observer could have expected the less developed countries participating in the law of the sea negotiations to accept an arrangement that explicitly excluded the Enterprise from mining operations, thereby ensuring that a few highly industrialized states would dominate this commercial activity. There is a sense of fairness that everyone can relate to in across-the-board percentage cuts which is hard to match in more complex arrangements featuring charges or transferable production permits.[75] And it is surely easy to understand why the less developed countries regard as unjust any system that features the allocation of orbital slots on a first come, first served basis. While it is important to recognize that there are no objective standards of equity which can be applied to human affairs, it is also worth noting that identifiable community standards regarding equity do exist in specific social settings. And there is much to be said for the proposition that satisfying these standards is a necessary condition for international regime formation, whatever outside observers may think of the long-term consequences of the resultant arrangements with respect to allocative efficiency.

3. The existence of salient solutions (or focal points describable in simple terms) increases the probability of success in institutional bargaining.

Those endeavoring to craft statutes in municipal legislatures sometimes proceed, for tactical reasons, to construct formulas that are so complex or obscure that interest groups actually or potentially opposed to the relevant provisions have difficulty comprehending what is being put to a vote. No doubt, such tactics can prove useful in the efforts to form winning coalitions that dominate legislative bargaining. For the most part, by contrast, salience based on simplicity and clarity contributes to success in institutional bargaining involving numerous parties operating under unanimity rules.[76] The idea of a simple ban or prohibition on pelagic sealing, for example, was a key factor in the success of the negotiations that produced the original regime for the conservation of northern fur seals in 1911. In more contemporary terms, the salience of the formula of across-the-board percentage cuts in the production and consumption of CFCs certainly played a role in the successful effort to reach agreement on the 1987 protocol regarding ozone depletion. And the fact that early warning procedures are markedly simpler than provisions covering compensation for damages surely has much to do with the

75. On the distinctions among these policy instruments, see Dudek, "Chlorofluorocarbon Policy."

76. For a seminal account of the role of salience in facilitating the convergence of expectations in such settings, see Schelling, *The Strategy of Conflict.*

ease of achieving agreement on the early notification convention of 1986 as well as with the failure to incorporate compensation provisions into the two 1986 conventions relating to nuclear accidents.[77]

Conversely, it is hard to avoid the conclusion that the complexity of arrangements encompassing permits or licenses, production controls, technology transfers, the role of the Enterprise, and so forth bedeviled the effort to negotiate a regime for the deep seabed (known as the Area) in the law of the sea negotiations and played a significant role in accounting for the ambiguity of the final outcome. And similar problems might well plague efforts to come to terms on the provisions of a regime relating to global climate change. The power of salience can become a serious constraint on efforts to devise appropriate institutional arrangements. It constitutes a barrier to the introduction of some clever and attractive devices that students of institutional design have come up with to handle collective-action problems.[78] But this in no way detracts from the role of salience as a determinant of success in the formation of regimes in international society.

4. The probability of success in institutional bargaining rises when clear-cut and effective compliance mechanisms are available.

It is common knowledge among those who study collective-action problems that negotiators can fail to reach agreement on arrangements capable of yielding benefits for all parties concerned because they do not trust each other to comply with the terms of the arrangements once they are established.[79] This places a premium on the development of requirements that are easy to verify, as in the case of cuts in the production of CFCs by a small number of clearly identified producers.[80] It also accounts for the attractions of arrangements that are comparatively easy to police, such as the licensing system for deep seabed mining contemplated under the regime for the Area. Presumably, some such reasoning played a role, as well, in the decision to orient the regime for endangered species toward the regulation of international trade in contrast to the control of habitat destruction within individual nations. While trade restrictions are hard enough to verify and

---

77. For an excellent account of the prior legal developments leading to these conventions, see Phillippe J. Sands, "The Chernobyl Accident and Public International Law," paper prepared for a conference on global disasters and international communications flows, Washington, D.C., October 1986.

78. For a discussion of some of these devices in connection with the problem of ozone depletion, see Dudek, "Chlorofluorocarbon Policy."

79. See also Schelling, *The Strategy of Conflict;* and Robert Axelrod, *The Evolution of Cooperation* (New York: Basic Books, 1984).

80. Konrad von Moltke, "Memorandum on International Chlorofluorocarbon Controls and Free Trade," a paper distributed by the Institute for European Environmental Policy, 1987.

police, it is not easy even to imagine how to implement a regime requiring the individual members to take effective steps to control the forces causing habitat destruction within their jurisdictions. Similar problems would undoubtedly afflict any effort to devise a workable regime to protect biological diversity.

At the same time, the lack of well-entrenched and properly financed supranational organizations in international society ensures that international regimes must rely heavily on the ability and willingness of individual members to elicit compliance with key provisions within their own jurisdictions.[81] A problem that has dogged the regime for endangered species, for example, is the sheer inability of many states to control the activities of poachers and others involved in the illegal trade in furs, skins, and animal parts within their jurisdictions.[82] Contrast this with the case of the fur seal regime, under which any harvest of seals was either closely regulated or actually carried out by state agencies, thereby enabling municipal governments to exercise effective control over the relevant activities whenever they chose to do so.[83] Under the circumstances, it is easy enough to understand why regime formation in international society is most apt to succeed when the participants can rely on relatively simple, nonintrusive compliance mechanisms that municipal governments can operate without undue effort or the need to expend scarce political resources. The 1987 protocol on ozone depletion, which has a remarkably straightforward formula coupled with explicit delegation of implementation to individual participants, offers a clear illustration of this proposition.

*5. For the most part, exogenous shocks or crises increase
the probability of success in efforts to negotiate the terms of
international regimes.*

Even in negotiations that allow considerable scope for integrative bargaining under a veil of uncertainty, institutional bargaining exhibits a natural tendency to bog down into a kind of sparring match in which participants jockey for positional advantages and lose track of their common interest in solving the relevant collective-action problems. All too often, the net result is a failure to reach agreement regarding feasible arrangements that would prove mutually beneficial. Given this background, it will come as no surprise that exogenous shocks or crises frequently play a significant role in breaking these logjams and propelling the parties toward agreement on the terms of

---

81. For a more general discussion of compliance in decentralized social settings, see Oran R. Young, *Compliance and Public Authority, A Theory with International Applications* (Baltimore, Md.: Johns Hopkins University Press, 1979).
82. Kosloff and Trexler, "The Convention on International Trade in Endangered Species."
83. Young, *Natural Resources and the State*, chap. 3.

institutional arrangements. The precipitous decline in the northern fur seal population in the early years of this century and the extraordinary drop in blue whale stocks in the 1930s clearly played major roles in inducing the relevant parties to drop their bargaining ploys in the interests of reaching agreement on the provisions of regulatory regimes before it was too late.[84] It is hard to overstate the shock value of the 1986 Chernobyl accident in motivating the parties to come to terms on at least some of the provisions of a regime for nuclear accidents within six months of this dramatic event.[85] And the 1985 discovery and subsequent publicization of an ozone "hole" over Antarctica emerged clearly as a driving force behind the efforts which produced the 1987 protocol on stratospheric ozone and which may well lead to additional regulatory arrangements in the near future, despite the fact that ozone depletion over Antarctica is not an immediate threat to major centers of human population.[86]

Compare these cases with the problem of global climate change. There is a good case to be made for the proposition that the disruptive impacts of nuclear accidents and ozone depletion are likely to pale by comparison with the consequences of the global warming trend over the next century.[87] To date, however, we have not experienced an exogenous shock or crisis in this realm that can compare with the Chernobyl accident or the ozone hole in capturing and galvanizing the attention of policymakers and broader publics alike. Talk of a creeping crisis with regard to global warming simply cannot produce the impact of the exogenous shocks mentioned previously as a force in breaking the logjams that commonly arise in institutional bargaining. This is no doubt frustrating to those working on a number of important collective-action problems. It is hard to contrive credible crises, and there is no reason to suppose that the occurrence of exogenous shocks will correlate well with the ultimate importance of the problems at hand. But none of this can detract from the role of exogenous shocks or crises as a determinant of success in efforts to build regimes in international society.[88]

---

84. On the case of the blue whale, see George L. Small, *The Blue Whale* (New York: Columbia University Press, 1971).

85. Stuart Diamond, "Chernobyl Causing Big Revisions in Global Nuclear Power Policies," *The New York Times*, 27 October 1986, pp. A1 and A10.

86. Shabecoff, "Ozone Agreement Is Hailed as a First Step in Cooperation."

87. In November 1988, for example, a broad coalition of American environmental groups designated the global warming trend as the most serious environmental threat of the foreseeable future.

88. Note that the effects of exogenous shocks or crises on the maintenance of existing regimes may differ from those on the formation of regimes. It is widely believed, for example, that the refusal of the United States to ratify a 1984 protocol extending the life of the fur seal regime was the result of a sharp decline in the northern fur seal population during the 1980s and the belief of many American advocates of animal rights that the regime was inadequate to cope with this problem.

6. Institutional bargaining is likely to succeed when effective leadership emerges; it will fail in the absence of such leadership.

We come back, in the end, to the role of leadership in determining outcomes arising from institutional bargaining in international society. It is no exaggeration to say that efforts to negotiate the terms of international regimes are apt to succeed when one or more effective leaders emerge. In the absence of such leadership, they will fail. Those engaged in institutional bargaining must strive to invent options capable of solving major problems in a straightforward fashion and to fashion deals that are acceptable to all. To the extent that the participants have incentives to engage in integrative bargaining and to the extent that a veil of uncertainty prevails and linkages among problems allow for logrolling, the task of those negotiating the terms of international regimes will be made easier. But such considerations cannot eliminate the crucial role of entrepreneurship at the international level.

Entrepreneurial leaders in institutional bargaining are neither hegemons who can impose their will on others nor ethically motivated actors who seek to fashion workable institutional arrangements as a contribution to the common good or the supply of public goods in international society. Rather, international entrepreneurs are actors who are skilled in inventing new institutional arrangements and brokering the overlapping interests of parties concerned with a particular issue-area.[89] Such actors are surely self-interested in the sense that they seek gains for themselves either in the form of advantageous institutional arrangements if they are states or in the form of enhanced reputations or rewards if they are individuals. But this in no way detracts from the role that such entrepreneurial actors play. There is, in fact, much that is reassuring in the observation that leaders are motivated to engage in entrepreneurial activities out of a durable sense of self-interest rather than more fleeting considerations of ethical behavior or altruism.[90]

The preceding discussion suggests, as well, that nongovernmental organizations or even individuals can become leaders in efforts to form international regimes. The role of the Comité Spécial de l'Année Geophysique Internationale in establishing SCAR in 1958 and, through SCAR, in forming the regime for Antarctica in 1959 is comparatively well known. But the role of IUCN in promoting the regimes governing trade in endangered species and conservation of polar bears as well as the role of UNEP in creating the regime for controlling pollution in the Mediterranean Basin are also striking examples of success in international entrepreneurship. And the remarkable role of Mustafa Tolba, UNEP's executive director, in shepherding the ne-

---

89. Frohlich, Oppenheimer, and Young, *Political Leadership and Collective Goods.*
90. For a somewhat similar account, see Anthony Downs, *An Economy Theory of Democracy* (New York: Harper & Row, 1957), chap. 15.

gotiations regarding the protection of stratospheric ozone to a successful conclusion is worthy of much more systematic examination.[91] None of this means, of course, that states cannot assume leadership roles in negotiating international regimes; far from it. The activities of the United States in connection with the 1987 protocol on ozone, of France in the case of Mediterranean pollution control, and of several developing countries in the context of deep seabed mining stand out, to name just a few examples.

Neither the mainstream utilitarians nor the power theorists work with constructs capable of offering significant analytic leverage on the type of entrepreneurial leadership under consideration here. Yet there is ample evidence to demonstrate convincingly that such entrepreneurial activities are necessary for success in regime formation at the international level. It follows, therefore, that an enhanced effort to understand entrepreneurial leadership must loom large in any research program directed toward the study of institutional bargaining in international society.

Conclusion

The analytic perspectives currently dominating the study of regime formation in international society not only clash with one another but are also incapable of capturing some of the essential features of the processes involved in the formation of international regimes. The mainstream utilitarians fail to attach sufficient weight to an array of factors that can block the efforts of rational utility maximizers to realize feasible joint gains. Moreover, they base their accounts of regime formation on models of bargaining that are fundamentally inappropriate, even though they are well specified and appealing for their analytic tractability. For their part, the power theorists overemphasize the role of preponderant actors or hegemons in the formation of institutional arrangements at the international level. As it turns out, this is just as well, since true hegemons are the exception rather than the rule in international society.

What is required to provide fully satisfactory answers to questions about regime formation is a model of institutional bargaining that takes into account the essential features of international society, including several that distinguish this social setting from the situations that prevail in domestic societies. The central section of this article, which sketches the defining characteristics of such a model of institutional bargaining, emphasizes the significance of unanimity rules, integrative bargaining, the veil of uncertainty, problem-solving activities, transnational alliances, and shifting involvements.

---

91. Similar comments are probably in order regarding the role of Hans Blix, the executive director of the International Atomic Energy Agency, in promoting the 1986 conventions relating to nuclear accidents.

Institutional bargaining does yield successful outcomes in some efforts to reach agreement on the terms of international regimes. But it certainly offers no guarantee of success in this realm. On the contrary, ventures in institutional bargaining that fail to result in the formation of new international regimes are just as common as those that do succeed. Accordingly, the third section of the article initiates a process of deriving hypotheses about the determinants of success in institutional bargaining in international society. It points both to the role of structural considerations, such as the extent to which collective-action problems lend themselves to contractarian formulations, and to process considerations, such as the degree to which the parties can devise arrangements that meet the principal equity demands of all participants. Because the perspectives of the power theorists and the mainstream utilitarians have dominated prior thinking in this realm, our understanding of institutional bargaining in international society currently leaves much to be desired. To the extent that the argument set forth in this article is convincing, then, it should be apparent that we need to devote much more attention in the future to exploring the nature of institutional bargaining.

What happened to fortress europe?: external trade policy liberalization in the european union

Brian T. Hanson

One of the most striking features of the international economy since the mid-1980s has been the proliferation and intensification of regional trading arrangements around the world. Among the most prominent developments, the European Union (EU) implemented a program to create the world's largest single market, embarked on creating a common currency, added five new member states, and is contemplating the further addition of ten or more countries.[1] The United States, Canada, and Mexico launched the North American Free Trade Agreement and have announced their intention to expand the arrangement widely in Latin America to create a Free Trade Area of the Americas. In Asia, the rapid growth of regional trade and investment flows has piqued interest in the creation of formal regional trade arrangements. The most ambitious plan has been the declaration of the Asia-Pacific Economic Cooperation group to create a regional free trade area by 2020.

This eruption of regional economic initiatives has aroused deep concerns about their impact on the international economy. Many fear that decades of progress toward increased international trade liberalization reached though the rule-based multilateral system of the General Agreements on Tariffs and Trade (GATT) and the World Trade Organization (WTO) will be destroyed as Europe, North America, and Asia become "fortresses" in which some trading partners obtain refuge, while others

For their thoughtful comments on earlier drafts, I would like to thank Karen Alter, Phineas Baxandall, Suzanne Berger, James Caporaso, Cliff Bob, Brian Burgoon, Mark Duckenfield, Jeffry Frieden, Eugene Gholz, Peter Gourevitch, Peter Hall, Torben Iversen, David Lake, Richard Locke, Sophie Meunier, Andy Moravcsik, Ken Oye, Paul Pierson, Dick Samuels, Alberta Sbragia, Nick Ziegler, and three anonymous reviewers. Research for this article was supported by the Program for the Study of Germany and Europe, Center for European Studies, Harvard University, and by the Bundeskanzler Scholarship Program of the Alexander von Humboldt Stiftung.

1. In order to minimize confusion, the designation *European Union (EU)* will be used throughout this article as a simplification. It should be noted, however, that trade policy falls under the first pillar of the European Union, which continues to be named the European Community. Further, references in the text to "EU states" are meant to apply only to the states in the European Community or European Union at the time referred to by the statement.

International Organization 52, 1, Winter 1998, pp. 55–85

are excluded by trade barriers.[2] In 1996 Director-General Renato Ruggiero of the WTO warned, "[Regional economic initiatives risk] a division of the trading world into two or three intercontinental preferential areas, each with its own rules and with free trade inside the area, but with external barriers existing among the blocs."[3]

In this context, assessing the direction of external trade policy in Europe is especially important. Regional integration has proceeded further in Europe than anywhere else in the world. Moreover, numerous alarming predictions have been made about the course of European trade policy during the last decade, and the European Union is seen as the region most likely to adopt a "fortress" trade policy.[4] Some analysts have warned that with the completion of the single market, the EU would open trade internally, while building a wall against goods from outside. Concerns about Europe closing its markets intensified with the souring of European economies in the 1990s, accompanied by record levels of unemployment in many member states. Conventional wisdom and many prominent theories hold that during economic hardship protectionism tends to increase. Indeed, in the 1970s and 1980s recession and unemployment in Europe sparked sharp increases in trade protection.

What is most remarkable about European trade policy in the 1990s is that, despite ominous warnings and theoretical expectations, fortress Europe has not been built. To the contrary, this article shows that since the late 1980s not only have few new trade barriers been erected, but external trade policy in Europe has been significantly liberalized in recent years, even in politically and economically sensitive sectors. This marks a significant departure from the past and occurred at a time when liberalization was least expected. How can European external trade policy liberalization during hard times be explained? What might it tell us about the implication of regional trade blocs for the global economy?

I argue that European integration has played a considerable role in the liberalization of European external trade policy by changing the institutional context in which trade policy is made, creating a systematic bias toward liberalization over increased protection. Although the EU has formally had jurisdiction over trade policy since 1969, in practice member states used national policy measures to protect sensitive sectors in the 1970s and early 1980s. The completion of the internal market, however, greatly undermined the ability of member states to use national policy tools, and EU voting rules make it very difficult to replace national policies with protectionist measures at the EU level. Thus, contrary to those who expected integration to lead to a fortress Europe, regional integration in Europe has led to trade policy liberalization. The specific details of my explanation apply primarily to the EU. However, the analysis of how integration can affect national policy tools and how policymaking rules at the supranational level create policy biases suggests a research strategy for examining variation across regional trade blocs.

2. For example, see Thurow 1992; Bhagwati 1991, 58–79; and Stoeckel, Pearce, and Banks 1990.
3. Ruggiero 1996.
4. See Thurow 1992; Stoeckel, Pearce, and Banks 1990; and Wolf 1994.

The first section of the article presents evidence of the recent trend toward liberalization of trade policy in Europe. The second section probes the trade policy literature for possible explanations of the pattern of liberalization and suggests that existing theories do not account well for recent policy outcomes in Europe. The third section presents an alternative explanation for how the combination of the completion of the single market and EU decision-making rules has undermined the effectiveness of national trade restrictions and led to a systematic pattern of external trade policy liberalization. The fourth section briefly applies this explanation to the critical case of the motor vehicle sector. The conclusion discusses the implications of this analysis for European trade policy and for understanding the politics underpinning the increased openness of the international economy.

The Puzzle of Liberalizing External Trade Policy in Europe

There are several reasons why one would have expected levels of protection in the EU to have increased significantly in the 1990s. First, analysts widely predicted that the completion of the internal market in the EU would lead to the creation of a "fortress Europe." Some analysts argued that in order to make internal free trade politically sustainable, EU member states would offset new competition from other member states by imposing restrictions on imports from third countries—in effect, by replacing goods that were currently imported with goods supplied from within the EU.[5] Other analysts contended that EU voting rules requiring the support of super majorities or unanimity on most trade issues would promote logrolling and produce trade policies catering to the most protectionist member states. According to this view, states would simply veto any legislation that would not provide sufficient protection for their producers.[6] Still others contended that the EU might block imports in an attempt to create "EU Champions" capable of competing on world markets.[7] These predictions have not disappeared, and analysts continue to warn that the EU is inherently inclined to increasing levels of external protection.[8]

Fears that Europe would become more protectionist have also been fueled by severe recession and record levels of unemployment in Europe during the 1990s. According to several well-accepted theories, economic downturns and high levels of unemployment tend to trigger protectionist trade policy responses. Firms and workers are more likely to demand protection under these circumstances, and politicians are more likely to grant it.[9]

5. See Sapir 1990, 205–206; Conybeare 1993; and Thurow 1992, 68.
6. See Patterson 1983; Conybeare 1993, 145–49; and Jackson 1995, 343.
7. Koopmann and Scharrer 1989, especially 212–13.
8. For example, Wolf 1995.
9. In times of high domestic demand and economic growth, it is relatively easy for the domestic economy to absorb imports without imposing severe adjustment costs on domestic firms and workers. During periods of recession, however, increasing imports threaten to reduce profits, idle existing productive facilities, and cause worker layoffs. Furthermore, widespread unemployment increases the costs to workers of adjusting to rising levels of imports. Workers who are displaced by imports will find it progres-

During the serious recessions of the 1970s and 1980s, which were characterized by stagnating or declining levels of output and rising levels of unemployment, trade policy in Europe followed exactly this pattern. By 1980 European unemployment rates had climbed to 6 percent in France, 7 percent in Italy and Great Britain, and 3 percent in West Germany and were decried as intolerable.[10] At the time most Europeans saw rising unemployment as the direct result of growing imports, particularly from Japan and the newly industrializing countries.[11] Greater opening of their economies to non-European competitors, it was widely feared, would fuel even higher levels of mass unemployment and pose a direct threat to the social and political peace that the postwar welfare state had achieved.[12] Given this situation, many concluded that increased protectionism was necessary, and numerous economic theories were advanced, particularly in Great Britain, France, and Germany, advocating higher trade barriers.[13]

Policy reflected this analysis, and national nontariff barriers soared across the EU from the mid-1970s to the early 1980s.[14] The number of known voluntary restraint agreements increased five-fold from 1970 to 1980.[15] The sectors most effected were electronics, motor vehicles, steel, and agriculture. The number of import surveillance and monitoring measures jumped from seven in 1971 to ninety-seven by 1985.[16] The number of antidumping measures in force in the EU shot up from 5 in 1973 to 187 by 1984.[17] In the textile and apparel sector, quotas were dramatically tightened with the implementation of the first set of bilateral agreements under the 1973 Multi-fiber Arrangement (MFA), which extended the trade regime from cotton to also include woolen goods and all synthetic fibers. The MFA was further tightened with its renewals in 1978 and 1982.[18] Even relatively free-trade-oriented countries, such as West Germany, negotiated new trade restrictions for sensitive sectors, such as automobiles, consumer electronics, and textiles and apparel. At the EU level, manifestations of an increasingly restrictive trade policy included the unwillingness of the European Economic Community to make substantial new concessions under the renewed Lomé Convention and the retention of tight safeguards under the Generalized System of

---

sively more difficult to obtain alternative employment, and when they do, their wages are likely to be lower. Together, recession and high levels of unemployment result in increasing demands to restrict the flow of imports. For elaboration of these arguments, see Magee and Young 1987; Takacs 1981; Bergsten and Cline 1983; McKeown 1984; Cassing, McKeown, and Ochs 1986; and Mansfield and Busch 1995. Politicians seeking to enhance their electoral fortunes have incentives to provide protectionist policies during periods of high unemployment, because such measures are likely to be popular and may blunt the short-term effects of macroeconomic pressures. See Lewis-Beck 1988; Kiewiet 1983; Kinder and Kiewiet 1979; and Kramer 1971.

10. Lewis-Beck 1988, 3.
11. Hine 1985, 8–9.
12. See Hager 1982; Keohane 1984, 34–35; and Gilpin 1987, 373–74.
13. Kahler 1985.
14. Grilli 1988.
15. This number excludes new restraint agreements for the textile and apparel sector, which fall under the Multi-fiber Arrangement. Grilli 1991.
16. Ibid., 153.
17. See GATT 1991, 114; and Grilli 1991, 158.
18. See Aggarwal 1985; and Cline 1987.

Preferences. Recession also contributed to the slow progress and meager results of the multilateral Tokyo Round of GATT.[19]

Given this history, one would have expected a surge of protectionism during the 1990s recession, when many European countries faced even greater economic hardships than they had in the 1970s and 1980s. The economic downturn of the 1990s has been the largest recession since World War II for many EU states, and levels of unemployment have grown precipitously, setting new records in many countries. In the three years from 1991 to 1994, six million jobs were lost EU-wide, and the average unemployment rate reached 11 percent. Moreover, the number of people employed in the EU declined by 4 percent in this period—a decline twice as large as in any comparable period since World War II—and has been felt throughout the EU. From 1991 to 1994, Italy suffered a decline in employment of over 1.7 million. The United Kingdom lost almost nine hundred thousand jobs, following a decrease of almost the same size in 1990. Spain lost over eight hundred thousand jobs, the former West Germany lost almost six hundred thousand jobs, and the former East Germany lost more than a million jobs during these three years.[20] Given the massive increase in unemployment combined with rising import competition, many feared increased protection would follow. At a minimum, these countries were expected to retain the level of protection already in place.

Surprisingly, despite severe economic distress, a history of protectionism during hard times, and predictions of a "fortress Europe," external trade barriers have not increased during the 1990s. To the contrary, an overview of trade policy developments during this period reveals a remarkable pattern of trade policy liberalization that extends across sectors and across types of trade policy instruments. Since 1990, individual EU member states have unilaterally abolished over sixty-three hundred quantitative restrictions against imports from third countries.[21] The number of surveillance measures (designed to signal to exporting countries that their activities are being monitored and more restrictive measures are under consideration) has also decreased significantly, even in the most sensitive sectors. In 1992, for example, the EU discontinued import surveillance for certain machine tools and electrical and electronic products from Japan that had been introduced in 1983 and extended annually ever since.[22] And although the use of antidumping measures has not declined significantly, it has also not increased. From 1990 to 1995, the number of antidumping measures in force has remained about 150, with that number declining somewhat

---

19. For further description of the trade policies of European states during the 1970s and 1980s, see Hayes 1993; Pearce, Sutton, and Batchelor 1985; and Hine 1985.

20. See European Commission 1995a; and World Trade Organization 1995, 57–58.

21. Only a very few of these national restrictions have been replaced with EU-level trade restrictions. The four product areas where major new EU quotas have replaced national restrictions are auto imports from Japan, bananas, canned tuna, and canned sardines. In addition, EU measures have replaced national restrictions on a few consumer products from China (working gloves, six types of footwear, tableware of porcelain or ceramic, glassware, car-radios, and three types of toys) and iron and certain steel categories from Mongolia, Vietnam, and some members of the Commonwealth of Independent States. World Trade Organization 1995, 57–60.

22. GATT 1993.

for the years 1992–93.[23] Regarding subsidies, new common guidelines clarified or tightened rules for state aid, especially in traditional manufacturing industries facing tough import competition, such as textiles and clothing, motor vehicles, shipbuilding, steel, and other base metals, and industrial subsidies on the whole have declined during this period.[24]

The EU has also provided increased market access for imports from non-EU countries through both multilateral and bilateral trade agreements negotiated during the recession of the 1990s. In the Uruguay Round of the GATT talks, the EU agreed to deep tariff cuts, reducing its tariffs on manufactured goods by an average of 38 percent. In addition, tariffs were eliminated for many product categories, including construction equipment, agricultural equipment, medical equipment, pharmaceuticals, most steel categories, paper products, and furniture.[25]

Since 1990 the EU has signed twenty-six bilateral free-trade-area agreements to increase EU market access for non-EU countries.[26] Among the most prominent are the so-called Europe Agreements. These bilateral preferential trade agreements between the EU and six central European countries (Bulgaria, the Czech Republic, Hungary, Poland, Romania, and the Slovak Republic) were concluded between 1991 and 1993 and allow most industrial products originating in these countries to enter the EU market free of tariffs and quantitative restrictions.[27] Increased market access was even granted in the most sensitive sectors, such as textiles, apparel, and steel. Bilateral free-trade agreements were also signed with Estonia, Latvia, and Lithuania in 1994, which removed EU tariffs and quantitative restrictions on their imports. A free-trade agreement negotiated with Turkey in 1995 allowing the free movement of industrial goods beginning in January 1996 is notable for its potential threat to EU textile and apparel producers.[28] Of the other free-trade agreements negotiated by the EU, some of the most important are with Switzerland, Norway, Israel, and Slovenia.[29]

In sum, European trade policy has liberalized significantly in recent years. Despite severe recession, extraordinarily high rates of unemployment, and predictions of fortress Europe, levels of external protection have not increased in the way they did during the periods of economic hardship in the 1970s and 1980s. This is not to say that the EU has suddenly abandoned all forms of protection in all industries. Rather, recent EU trade policy has been marked by two characteristics: the erection of very few new protectionist trade barriers and a significant reduction in levels of protection

23. European Commission 1995b.
24. See GATT 1993; Adams 1995, 107–108; and Dylla 1997.
25. World Trade Organization 1995, 51–52.
26. *The Financial Times*, 16 February 1996, 6.
27. The Europe agreements for Hungary and Poland entered into force on 1 February 1994, and those for Bulgaria, the Czech Republic, Romania, and the Slovak Republic on 1 February 1995. For additional details of the Europe Agreements, including implementation periods and safeguard provisions, see GATT 1993, Chapter II(5)(iii). At the worst point of the recession, in June 1993, the EU even agreed to accelerate the tariff liberalization schedule for these agreements and agreed to lift almost all tariffs and quantitative restrictions on industrial imports from these central European countries. World Trade Organization 1995.
28. Ibid., 21–23.
29. *The Financial Times*, 16 February 1996, 6.

for many industries. In other words, industries that demanded and received increased trade barriers during periods of economic hardship in the past now face similar economic challenges but can no longer obtain the same levels of trade protection. How can this change in trade policy outcomes be explained? Why has external trade policy in Europe liberalized despite inauspicious economic conditions?

Alternative Explanations of Trade Liberalization

Broadly speaking, the existing trade policy literature lays out two types of approaches to explain trade policy liberalization. One approach emphasizes interest group politics among societal actors, whereas a second approach emphasizes the autonomous role of state actors in shaping trade policy. Liberalization is then explained by changes in the preferences of either societal or state actors.

The societal approach offers three prominent explanations for trade liberalization, each of which provides a different argument for how increased international economic integration should induce changes in the character of societal demands for protection.[30] The first explanation, *sectoral attrition,* contends that liberalization occurs when increased international competition erodes the size of uncompetitive sectors to the point that they are no longer economically or politically important enough to retain their level of protection. The second explanation, *sectoral internationalization,* argues that liberalization occurs within a sector when the increasing dependence on the global economy drives the preponderance of firms within that sector to switch their trade policy preference from protectionism to free trade. The third explanation, *societal counter mobilization*, argues that as international trade flows increase, the political power of groups benefiting from economic openness increases, as do the incentives for these groups to mobilize against those demanding trade protection.

The most prominent state-centered explanation contends that rather than shifts in interest group politics, liberalization is primarily driven by changes in the beliefs of national policymakers. Policymakers reject the notion that trade protection is beneficial in times of economic hardship and adopt the belief that liberalization will provide greater economic benefits. How well can these explanations account for the recent pattern of external trade policy liberalization in Europe?

The Attrition of Uncompetitive Sectors

The first possible explanation for trade liberalization, sectoral attrition, is that all of the uncompetitive sectors that had received protection in the past have either disappeared or lost political influence by the 1990s. In this view, levels of trade protection are seen primarily as functions of the political strength of the interest groups demanding protection. Liberalization comes about as exposure to international competition

---

30. By increased international economic integration or globalization, I am referring to increased flows of international trade of goods and services, and foreign direct investment.

wears down uncompetitive sectors, causing them to shed so many workers and to become so unimportant economically that their demands for protection can be safely ignored by politicians. Politicians are no longer able to preserve large numbers of domestic jobs by providing protection to these sectors, and the electoral cost of liberalizing these sectors has become very low. The French shipbuilding industry might be offered by proponents of this view as an illustrative example in Europe. Once an important industry in the French economy that received increasing levels of protection in the 1970s, shipbuilding today has dwindled to almost nothing, and trade policy toward the sector has been greatly liberalized.

Although some sectors in some EU countries have been devastated by international competition, as a general explanation for trade policy liberalization in Europe, this explanation has three significant problems. First, the pattern of external trade policy liberalization has not been limited to small insignificant sectors. Rather, substantial liberalization has occurred in some of Europe's most important industries, such as motor vehicles, and textiles and apparel.[31]

Second, this explanation implies that intense international competition is currently a problem only for small and politically impotent industries. If large and politically important sectors were threatened by foreign competition, they still would be expected to demand and obtain protection. In fact, many of the sectors most central to European economies are being hard hit by import competition. Seven out of the eight largest EU industrial sectors, in terms of employment, have faced sharp increases in import penetration or significant declines in export dependence in recent years or both.[32] As Table 1 demonstrates, a number of important sectors that still employ large numbers of workers or are important to EU economic performance are struggling to compete domestically and internationally.[33]

Third, the attrition explanation has difficulty accounting for the timing of the current liberalization in Europe. To the extent that economic sectors have shrunk or lost employment, they have done so at different rates over the last couple of decades. Why is trade liberalization occurring now, and why has it occurred simultaneously across so many different sectors in so many different countries?

Sectoral Internationalization and Changing Firm Preferences

The second societal explanation, sectoral internationalization, sees trade policy liberalization as the consequence of an increase in the international sales and investments of firms in a given sector.[34] This view assumes that trade policy is primarily determined by the preferences of the firms within a given sector. Liberalization is ex-

---

31. World Trade Organization 1995, especially 99–107.

32. These sectors include textiles and apparel; electrical engineering; food, drink, and tobacco; mechanical engineering; metal products; motor vehicles and parts; chemicals and synthetic fibers; and rubber and plastics. European Commission 1994.

33. Because these industries tend to be concentrated in a limited number of member states, the proportion of overall employment and economic activity represented by a state in which one of these industries is located is likely to be even greater than the aggregate numbers imply.

34. Milner 1988.

TABLE 1. *Industry performance data in the EU*

Industry	EU employees, 1992	EU production, 1992 (in millions of ECU)	Import penetration, 1992[a]	Change in import penetration, 1986–92	Export dependence, 1992[b]	Change in export dependence, 1986–92
Textiles and clothing	2,730,000	188,000	20.9%	59.0%	15.5%	16.0%
Electrical engineering	1,489,000	171,168	29.2%	20.6%	18.8%	1.6%
Metal products	2,129,174	181,211	5.3%	35.9%	7.7%	18.0%
Motor vehicles and parts	1,820,774	265,643	9.0%	4.6%	11.6%	−65.5%
Chemicals and synthetic fibers	1,714,338	295,794	13.0%	16.1%	16.9%	−2.3%
Telecommunications equipment	880,785	25,378	13.5%	12.7%	20.3%	−17.1%
Consumer electronics	338,000	39,684	40.1%	27.7%	22.4%	28.0%
Computer and office equipment	251,100	46,259	40.3%	24.0%	21.6%	0.1%

Source: Eurostat, with calculations by the author.
[a]Extra-EU imports as percentage of apparent consumption.
[b]Extra-EU exports as percentage of production.

pected when the balance of firm policy preferences in a given sector changes from protection to free trade.

In her widely cited study, Helen Milner argues that a firm's trade policy preference is determined by its degree of export dependence and multinationality, measured in terms of direct foreign investment, profitability of foreign operations, and intrafirm trade.[35] The more export dependent and multinational the firm, the more it is expected to oppose protection and promote liberalization. For firms with international ties of this nature, the expected costs of protecting the domestic market are greater than the benefits of protection, because protection could trigger foreign retaliation that might threaten the firm's exports and could increase relative production costs by imposing tariffs or restrictions on imported inputs. Under these conditions, even when a firm with extensive international ties comes under intense pressure from import competition, it is expected to favor free-trade policies for itself and for its industry as a whole. Liberalization, according to this view, should proceed sector by sector, following patterns of increased internationalization of firms within each sector.

Although it is true that many European firms have increased sales and investment in foreign countries, this explanation runs into many difficulties when trying to account for the recent pattern of trade liberalization. The first problem is that it fundamentally mispredicts the general direction of European trade policy in the 1990s. Instead of expecting liberalization of trade policy in Europe, it seems to predict that

35. Ibid., especially 18–44.

the completion of the internal market in the EU would have significantly *increased* protectionist demands by European firms. With the completion of the internal market, trade barriers between European countries are to be eliminated, and the only remaining trade protections are against non-EU countries. Since trade barriers at the EU level do not affect trade within the EU, sales, production, and earnings from the firm's operations in other EU states should no longer be considered "international" for purposes of predicting a firm's trade policy preference. Companies whose "international" activities are largely limited to the EU would seem to lose their incentive to press for trade policy liberalization. Indeed, given that intra-EU trade represents 50–70 percent of total trade for individual EU member countries, one might reasonably expect that the completion of the internal market would significantly *increase* the proportion of firms that could be considered highly domestically oriented and likely to demand protectionist trade policies.[36] This is precisely the logic that led many people to erroneously predict the emergence of a fortress Europe.

This explanation also has difficulty accounting for the general pattern of European trade policy liberalization in four additional ways. First, significant trade liberalization has occurred in sectors that have not experienced increases in export dependence or multinational investment. In the automobile sector, for example, liberalization has occurred despite a 65 percent drop in export dependence.[37] Second, with its emphasis on linking producer demands to policy outcomes, this explanation cannot help us understand why some of the most significant liberalization has occurred in sectors where the vast majority of firms continue to want protection, for example, motor vehicles and textiles. As I demonstrate later, liberalization in the automobile sector occurred even though there was no change in the trade policy preferences of auto producers toward liberalization. Third, this explanation does not seem to account well for enduring calls for protection by industries that have significantly increased their degree of international activity. The data in Table 1, for example, suggest that protectionist demands should have decreased in the consumer electronics and metal products sectors; yet in both cases demand for trade barriers has remained strong.[38] Finally, given different rates of internationalization of firms in different industries, it is not clear why such a pronounced pattern of liberalization should occur across so many sectors at the same time.

Societal Counter Mobilization for Liberalization

The third type of explanation, societal counter mobilization, encompasses several specific theories, all of which emphasize the role of cross-sectoral or cross-class pressures in the liberalization of trade policy. In simplified terms proponents of these theories argue that increasing international flows of goods, services, and capital change

36. World Trade Organization 1995, 5.
37. See Table 1. Because the data in Table 1 are aggregate data for the entire sector and not firm level data, they may not reflect variations between firms. Even so, they do provide an overview of the aggregate position of all firms in a given sector.
38. See Flamm 1990; and Koopman and Scharrer 1989.

the economic opportunities and constraints facing societal actors and therefore their preferences over what trade policy best serves their interests.[39] Those sectoral or class-based interest groups that benefit from increased liberalization mobilize to promote trade policy liberalization and to oppose the demands of groups seeking protectionist policies. Employing a pluralist logic, proponents of this view expect that as the proportion of groups in society with an interest in free trade grows, they will become politically more powerful and able to outweigh protectionist interests in the political process.

The groups expected to support or oppose protection varies by author. Some predict that those sectors with high levels of asset specificity (meaning employing labor skills or capital that cannot be easily redeployed to other economic uses) will seek protection, whereas industries with more mobile assets will fight protection.[40] Others predict that groups benefiting from imports (that is, producers using imported inputs, retailers, and consumers) will lobby for openness against nationally oriented firms' demands for protection.[41] Others see demand for or against protection breaking down along factor lines (that is, labor, capital, and land), with abundant factors clamoring for openness and scarce factors demanding protection.[42] Thus, in Europe capital would be expected to support liberalization, and labor would be expected to support protection.

It is certainly true that some societal actors benefit from liberalization and could be expected to favor the liberalization of trade policy. However, in the case of recent European trade policy a key question for these explanations is whether a sufficiently large coalition of political supporters has developed to account for the wide-ranging liberalization of some of the largest economic sectors in Europe. If trade policy liberalization is the product of contesting societal interest groups, one would expect that it would take a large and powerful coalition to roll back protection held by such important economic sectors as automobiles. This explanation is convincing to the extent one can demonstrate the existence of such a set of societal interests and show that their policy preferences were decisive in determining trade policy outcomes. After consulting secondary literature, however, and conducting interviews with government officials, industry representatives, and labor unions in France, Germany, Great Britain, and Brussels, I have not found much evidence that a counter mobilization of societal groups has been responsible for the pattern of trade policy liberalization in European countries. Moreover, societal interests rarely seem to divide along the class or sectoral lines predicted by many of these counter-mobilization explanations.

The Changing Beliefs of Policymakers

Whereas the three preceding explanations of trade policy liberalization emphasize the preferences of societal actors, the explanation discussed in this section sees states

39. For a fuller discussion of these arguments, see Milner and Keohane 1996.
40. Frieden and Rogowski 1996.
41. See Destler and Odell 1987; and Frieden and Rogowski 1996.
42. See Midford 1993; Rogowski 1989; and Frieden and Rogowski 1996.

as having some degree of autonomy from these interests and policy as being shaped by the ideas and beliefs of policymakers. Judith Goldstein argues that in most cases policymakers have incomplete information about their environment and thus must rely on causal models in making policy choices.[43] Ideas, defined as shared beliefs about causal connections between interests and policies, act like road maps linking policies to a constellation of interests by showing actors how to maximize their interests. For example, policymakers may know that they want to promote the competitiveness of their domestic firms, but their understanding of what policies will be most beneficial for improving the competitiveness of their firms may vary. Some policymakers may believe that competition brought about by freer trade is the best spur to improve firm performance, whereas others may think that protection, which provides an opportunity for firms to restructure, is the best policy.

Applied to recent European trade policy, an argument along these lines would be that in the 1970s and 1980s European countries used protectionist measures to combat pressure from imports in order to allow domestic firms to become more competitive and to protect domestic jobs. This policy failed and was discredited when protected industries did not become internationally competitive and levels of unemployment remained high. By the late 1980s or early 1990s, European policymakers abandoned their belief in the virtues of protectionism and searched for alternative causal ideas. They adopted the neoliberal economic belief that exposing domestic firms to international competition is more effective than protection for improving the competitiveness of domestic producers and promoting economic prosperity for the society.

Over the last decade or so, neoliberal economic ideas and policies have been on the rise in Europe; however, evidence suggests that there may not be consensus around the idea of liberal trade policy in all member states. France, for example, has a long tradition of ideological support for protectionist policies, and it is not clear that French political leaders, the French public, or French economists have completely abandoned their ideas about the virtues of protection, especially against non-EU producers. Indeed, at the height of the French recession in the summer of 1993, both President François Mitterrand and Prime Minister Édouard Balladur advocated that the EU abandon free trade in favor of a European preference system.[44] This plan proposed to discriminate between the imports of countries based on their level of social standards, allowing those countries with labor, social, and environmental regulations closest to those in Europe to have the least restricted access, whereas countries with lower social and environmental standards would have substantially less access to the European market. The French public also supports protectionist policies, as reflected in a 1993 public opinion poll in which 67 percent of the respondents agreed that the importation of non-European products into the EU and into France should be limited.[45] Even among professional economists in France there is no con-

43. Goldstein 1993.
44. Berger 1995, 203–205.
45. *Le Parisien*, 22 June 1993, 2–3, as cited in ibid., 196.

sensus against protectionist trade policy. In a survey published in 1984 only 27 percent of French economists said they generally believed that protection reduces the economic welfare of a country.[46] Although France is only one country in the EU, it is particularly important because of its size, its central role in EU politics, and because it has been one of the countries whose key industries have been the most affected by trade liberalization in Europe. If beliefs about trade policy have been slow to change in France, it is likely that they have also been slow to change in other EU countries that have significant postwar traditions of protectionism.

I have reviewed the most prominent theories for the resilience or expansion of liberal trade policy during times of economic hardship. None accounts very well for recent patterns of external trade liberalization and resistance to new protectionist measures. How then can trade policy in Europe be explained?

The Politics of Trade Liberalization in Europe

In contrast to explanations of European trade policy that focus on changes in the preferences of domestic political actors, I argue that much of the timing and scope of trade policy liberalization and the general resistance to new protectionist measures in Europe can best be understood as an unintended consequence of European integration. The completion of the single market initiated a two-step process that both liberalized existing trade policies and systematically disadvantaged interests seeking new trade protection. First, the completion of the internal market induced the liberalization of protected markets by severely eroding the effectiveness of national trade measures. Second, restoring protection lost at the national level required the establishment of new trade policy measures at the EU level, which was made difficult because of institutional arrangements that significantly advantaged those states wanting to block the expansion of EU protection. The result has been that industries have lost protection at the national level and have been unable to reestablish it at the EU level. Furthermore, other attempts to create new protectionist measures also have been made vastly more difficult due to the same institutional impediments.[47]

Completing the Internal Market: Changing the Political Context
of Trade Policymaking

The implementation of the Single European Act (SEA) created a widespread, de facto liberalization of trade policy in EU member states by undermining the effectiveness of national trade barriers. Before the SEA, member states could limit imports by a variety of national regulations—bilateral import quotas and voluntary export

---

46. This compares to 79 percent of American economists who responded that protection reduces national welfare. See Frey, Pommerehne, Schneider, and Gilbert 1984.

47. For an innovative view of the ways in which European integration has affected the bargaining strength of the EU in international trade negotiations, see Meunier forthcoming.

restraint agreements with non-EU states, and health, safety, and technical standards.[48] With the completion of the single market, states lost the tools they needed to maintain effective national trade barriers even against non-EU imports.

In order for these national trade barriers to be effective EU states must be able both to shut out direct imports and to block the transshipment of non-EU imports through other EU countries. If free trade is allowed between countries of customs unions or free-trade areas, national trade barriers can be circumvented by importing a non-EU-produced good first into another EU member state with lower trade barriers and then shipping it freely from there into the member state with higher levels of protection. One way member states blocked indirect imports was through Article 115 of the Treaty of Rome. Under Article 115 member states could request European Commission approval to block indirect imports to preserve preexisting national import restrictions, and, as Table 2 shows, Article 115 exemptions were widely used.[49] States also employed a wide range of national policy measures to block indirect imports, including national border controls, customs procedures, and nontariff barriers such as health, safety, and technical standards.

One of the primary goals of the SEA was to eliminate exactly these types of barriers to trade between member states in order to create a single market, which was defined as "an area without internal frontiers in which the free movement of goods, persons, services, and capital is ensured."[50] From 31 December 1992 all national border controls between member states were to be made illegal.[51] This meant that states could no longer use Article 115. The Commission ruled out the possibility of revitalizing Article 115 authorizations on the grounds that with the disappearance of internal border controls, as demanded by the internal market, the legal grounds for Article 115 no longer existed.[52] As shown in Table 2, Article 115 authorizations came to an end in 1993.

The program to complete the single market also eliminated national nontariff barriers between EU states. The EU launched an ambitious program of both harmoniza-

48. Despite the commitment made in the 1957 Treaty of Rome to pursue a unified common commercial policy, in practice member states had retained a large measure of national autonomy over their external trade policies. Even after 1968, when the EU adopted a single set of external tariff rates, individual countries retained control over a myriad of nontariff barriers, which they imposed more or less at will. The surge of import protection in Europe during the 1970s and 1980s is mostly accounted for by increases in these national trade barriers. Although the majority of restrictions were imposed by Italy, France, Great Britain, Greece, and the Irish Republic, at some point during the 1970s and 1980s all EU states resorted to such national measures. For discussions of trade restrictions before the SEA, see Koopmann 1989; Sapir 1990; Koopman and Scharrer 1989; European Commission 1992; World Trade Organization 1995; Hayes 1993; and Hine 1985.

49. The Commission considered that Article 115 could only be used to defend commercial policy measures taken in accordance with the Treaty of Rome (meaning formal quotas) and not to defend voluntary restraint agreements or other such informal arrangements. The duration of Article 115 restrictions varied between two months and one year, depending on the Commission's decision. GATT 1993.

50. Article 8a of the SEA.

51. European Commission 1992.

52. Interestingly, the Maastricht Treaty on European Union, signed in February 1992, modifies rather than discards Article 115. The new language continues the provision for restraint of imports of particular items into individual member countries "to ensure that the execution of measures of commercial policy taken in accordance with the Treaty by any Member State is not obstructed by deflection of trade, or where differences between such measures lead to economic difficulties in one or more Member States." GATT 1993; and interviews by the author of EU Commission officials, May 1994.

TABLE 2. *Article 115 measures approved by year*

Year	Measures approved	Year	Measures approved
1976	74	1985	176
1977	79	1986	141
1978	197	1987	157
1979	260	1988	128
1980	222	1989	119
1981	166	1990	79
1982	174	1991	48
1983	188	1992	8
1984	165	1993	0

Source: Official Journal of the European Communities, various issues.

tion and mutual recognition of product standards. A key component of this effort was the nearly three hundred pieces of EU legislation to eliminate national trade barriers.[53] Where there was not harmonization of national regulations through common EU legislation, the principle of mutual recognition applied.[54] In other words, goods meeting the standards of one EU state are now entitled to be imported without discrimination into any other member state. Although national derogations from harmonized policies are still possible on the grounds of "major needs," the Commission has emphasized that any such exemptions will be of exceptional character.[55] As health, safety, and technical standards have been either harmonized or mutually recognized, states have lost their ability to use such standards to keep indirect imports out of their markets.

Implementing the SEA meant the de facto liberalization of the *external* trade policies of EU states. *Because the national trade measures of any given state could be circumvented, individual member states found that the external trade policy status quo had changed from protection through national policy to liberalization through transshipment.* New protectionist measures were required at the EU level, even just to retain the levels of protection previously provided nationally.

EU Decision-Making Rules: A Liberal Bias

When states looked to the EU level to replace eroded national protections, they found that EU decision-making rules and procedures systematically disadvantaged those

53. According to the Commission, this program has been remarkably successful, with some 95 percent of the policy measures adopted into EU legislation by the end of 1993. Of the 219 policy measures that also needed to be formally adopted in the member states by April 1995, about 90 percent had become national law in at least ten member states. World Trade Organization 1995, 16.

54. Although the principle of mutual recognition was implied by the European Court of Justice's *Cassis de Dijon* decision in 1979, the decision on its own did not lead to de facto mutual recognition, as shown by Alter and Meunier-Aitsahalia 1994.

55. So far it appears that only one case has been approved by the Commission, German restrictions on sales of PCBs. World Trade Organization 1995, 14.

seeking to replace national trade barriers with equally effective EU measures. New trade measures, like most other policy areas, require the approval of the Council of Ministers, which is composed of representatives from each member state. Formal voting rules for most trade measures require the support of a qualified majority of member states for passage. Thus the dissent of a small coalition of states can prevent the passage of a new external trade measure.[56]

Given the decision-making rules of the EU, the states seeking the most liberal trade policy are in a very strong bargaining position, and trade policy outcomes tend to reflect their preferences. The bargaining strength of states favoring more liberal policies is based on their ability to credibly threaten to veto any proposed trade measure more restrictive than those they favor. For states confronting a situation of national trade measures made obsolete through the completion of the single market, almost any agreement is better than the liberalization of its domestic market by the unregulated flow of indirect imports into their markets. Thus liberal states have little incentive to agree to greater levels of protection than they favor, and states seeking protection have little leverage to obtain more than they are offered. Trade policy outcomes, under these conditions, tend to reflect the policy preferences of the producing state favoring the most liberal policy, and EU trade policy is likely to be *more* liberal than a simple summing up of all the national trade policies in effect before the implementation of the SEA.

From this logic one might expect that EU trade policy for a given sector would be largely determined by the preferences of states with no production in a given industry. Such countries would be expected to favor complete free trade, because liberalization of the sector would provide its consumers with cheaper products and have no negative impact on its industries or employment level. In practice, however, intra-EU negotiations over important trade policy matters are largely left to the states with significant production in a given sector, and smaller states without significant production typically do not get involved in negotiations over trade policy for that industry.[57] This means that the states in the strongest bargaining position are those preferring the most liberal trade policy for an industry in which it has significant production.[58]

This explanation provides an account not only for liberalization of trade policy, but also for the resistance to new protectionist measures in Europe. In the 1970s and 1980s new trade protections usually took the form of national policy measures, but completing the single market has undermined this strategy as a viable option. Now, new trade protections must be agreed to at the EU level, which is difficult because they can be easily vetoed by a small coalition of states.

This is not to say that protectionist policies will never be made at the EU level, or that states will never be able to replace national protection with equally protective EU measures. Rather, my argument is that policy outcomes will largely reflect the distribution of trade policy preferences of member states and their relative bargain-

56. In practice, some aspects of trade policy require unanimity for action. Meunier forthcoming.
57. Interviews by the author with various officials at the European Commission, June 1994.
58. In many cases, this state is Germany.

ing strength based on the status quo trade policy. If all states with significant production in an industry prefer retaining or increasing levels of protection, new protectionist policies will likely be adopted at the EU level. This scenario, however, is understandably rare, because small minorities can so easily block the establishment of new trade restrictions.

Within the EU framework, societal groups and states preferring protectionist barriers higher than they are able to obtain through the EU have very little recourse. Even if they would like to, national governments within the EU are not able to reconstitute national trade restrictions without blocking indirect imports from other EU states. To do so would require violating their treaty commitments to allow the free flow of goods within the internal market, and these obligations can be enforced by injured parties through the European Court of Justice. Absent the ability to negotiate a change of policy in the EU, states would have either to leave the European Union or obtain an agreement to change the fundamental character of the EU in order to be able to provide higher levels of protection. These alternatives seem quite extreme and would likely be unappealing for states, because the economic and political costs of abandoning the EU would be large.

In sum, implementing the SEA has produced a systematic liberalization of external trade policy in Europe. Liberalization has occurred as national trade protection has been undermined by the threat of indirect imports, and states have not been able to reestablish protection at the EU level because of decision-making rules biased against them. This explanation would expect a sweeping liberalization of trade policy in the EU in the aftermath of the SEA, which would occur in sectors protected by national trade policy measures. The extent of liberalization would be expected to largely reflect the preferences of the most liberal producing state in the sector. In addition, the explanation would expect that erecting new trade barriers of any kind would be difficult without great consensus among member states.

The Question of Foresight: Was the SEA Intended to Liberalize External Trade Policy?

If completing the internal market made it more difficult to protect against third-country imports, one must wonder whether this was not the intent all along. Were states looking to tie their hands so as to be better able to deflect protectionist demands? Were multinationally oriented firms trying to create an inherent bargaining advantage for themselves? Was the Commission acting to shape an outcome it desired?

Both economic theory and historical precedent are clear that internal liberalization within a trade bloc does not necessarily lead to external trade policy liberalization. Economic theory on customs unions shows that there is no necessary economic link between internal and external trade policies; it is possible to liberalize the internal market in combination with external protectionism.[59] Looking back in history, inter-

---

59. The classic statement is Viner 1950.

nal trade liberalization frequently does not lead to external trade liberalization. For example, the previous wave of regional trade blocs in the 1960s consisted mostly of arrangements that combined internal free trade with external protection.[60]

In the case of Europe, most evidence indicates that neither governments, business, nor the Commission foresaw that completing the internal market would result in a significant liberalization of external trade policy. There is a strong consensus in the literature that negotiations on the SEA focused intensely on the implications of completing the single market on *internal* trade barriers and virtually ignored consideration of *external* trade barriers.[61] This view is supported by the documents and agreements that guided the project. The Cockfield White Paper of 1985, which launched the single market project, lacked any serious consideration of the external trade aspects of the internal market. The only sentence about the subject is, if anything, somewhat threatening: "The commercial identity of the Community must be consolidated so that our trading partners will not be given the benefit of a wider market without themselves making similar concessions."[62] Moreover, the actual text of the SEA is nearly silent on the issue of external trade for the EU.[63]

Turning attention to specific actors, little evidence suggests that national policymakers recognized that completing the single market would lead to external liberalization in the ways described in the last section of this article. Indeed, in some respects the idea of liberalizing external trade policy goes against the purposes articulated for creating the single market. Driven by concerns over Europe's slumping international competitiveness, the single market was intended to create greater economies of scale for EU firms and promote closer collaboration among EU producers in order to benefit European producers.[64] The idea was not to create greater market access for the benefit of foreign competitors, such as the Japanese. Indeed, some member states argued for a policy of internal market liberalization combined with external protection in order to permit certain sectors of European industry to become internationally competitive. In a memorandum circulated during the negotiations over the single market, the French government advocated eliminating internal barriers to trade and raising external barriers so European producers could "reconquer" the European market and strengthen international competitiveness of European producers.[65] The French did not hold this view alone. Many saw external protection as an important element in capturing the benefits of the single market for European firms. The articulation of these positions was one of the main sources of widespread fear of a coming fortress Europe.

---

60. Examples include the Andean Pact, the Central American Common Market, and the Caribbean Common Market.

61. See, for example, Redmond 1992. Notably, in the literature analyzing the motives and goals of actors involved in the negotiation of the SEA, external trade policy goals are not discussed. See Cameron 1992; Cowles 1994; Moravcsik 1991; Sandholtz and Zysman 1989; and Tsoukalis 1993.

62. European Commission 1985, 8.

63. The main exception being that it requires European parliamentary approval for EU external trade agreements.

64. See Milward 1992, 430–40; Sandholtz and Zysman 1989; and Tsoukalis 1993, 301.

65. Pearce, Sutton, and Batchelor 1985, especially 68–73; and Tsoukalis 1993, 300–302.

Those opposed to French calls for new external protection did not trumpet the virtues of liberalizing external trade policy, but rather argued for maintaining the status quo. At the time of the SEA negotiations, close observers predicted that if fortress Europe was not realized, "For the foreseeable future the present tendencies of European trade policy are likely to persist. Even if the European economies revive, and there is no upsurge in protectionism elsewhere in the world, lack of international competitiveness will continue to generate pressure to protect some sectors in some or all member states. The inclination of governments to yield to these pressures will probably not change much."[66]

Little evidence suggests that large multinational corporations advocated completing the internal market in order to achieve liberalization of external trade policy. To the contrary, in 1985 the European Round Table of Industrialists (ERT) put forward a proposal for completing the single market in which external trade *protection* was a key component.[67] In addition, position papers by the ERT show that to many of Europe's largest firms the single market program primarily meant a bounty of trans-European infrastructure projects such as new railroad lines.[68] Little evidence indicates that promoting external trade liberalization was a goal of the multinational businesses supporting the completion of the single market.[69] Rather, many large multinational firms advocating completion of the single market were also advocating protection. Philips, for example, made this case to the National Economic Development Office in London.[70] Furthermore, many of the firms active in business groups advocating the completion of the single market, such as Renault, have subsequently found themselves fighting to prevent the resulting liberalization of external trade policy in their sector. The linkage between the internal market and external trade policy seems to have been a surprise.

Finally, little evidence demonstrates that the Commission was able to intentionally shape the SEA to promote external trade openness. As mentioned earlier, Lord Cockfield's White Paper did not indicate that the Commission intended to promote external liberalization through the SEA. After the passage of the SEA, statements from the Commission responding to concerns about the emergence of a fortress Europe disturbed as much as they pacified. A 1988 Commission document, "Europe 1992: Europe World Partner," which sought to clarify the position of the EU on the impact of the SEA on its external relations, talks of "vigilantly" applying trade policy measures, and following a trade policy of reciprocity that seems at times menacing.[71] In addition, some of the early proposals made by the Commission seemed blatantly protectionist. The most obvious example is the first draft of the Second Banking Directive, which restricted bank access to the European market to those banks whose

66. Pearce, Sutton, and Batchelor 1985, 87.
67. Mayes 1993, 8–9.
68. European Round Table of Industrialists 1984.
69. For a detailed discussion of the role of European business in the negotiation of the SEA, see Cowles 1994.
70. Mayes 1993, 9.
71. For a fuller discussion, see Redmond 1992.

home countries provided reciprocal benefits to European banks. This would have required the United States to provide more favorable benefits to European banks than to U.S. banks![72] Protectionist threats continued to be issued from the Commission as well. Jacques Delors, president of the Commission, declared, "The single market will be open, but it will not be given away."[73] Commissioner Willy De Clerq, who was in charge of external trade policy for the EU, declared, "We are not building a single market in order to turn it over to hungry foreigners."[74] As late as 1988 he was arguing for a quota limiting the Japanese to importing only two cars into Europe for every one European car imported into Japan. Given the huge trade imbalance in automobiles at the time, and the fact that Europe tends to sell much higher priced cars in Japan, this would have been an extremely restrictive trade measure.

There is little evidence that the external trade policy consequences of implementing the SEA were understood at the time of its negotiation. The key actors, national government, business interests, and the Commission, were focused overwhelmingly on the internal aspects of creating a common market. To the extent external trade was even considered, many of these actors believed that internal market opening should be combined with external protection. Rather than being the product of intentional maneuvering for advantage, the external trade consequences of the SEA provide striking evidence of how decisions taken at one time can have profound effects on future events by shifting the institutional rules under which policy is made. Current external trade policy in Europe cannot be derived from the aspirations of those who created the SEA.[75]

The Motor Vehicle Case

Recent trade liberalization in the European motor vehicle industry illustrates the argument developed in this article. In this section, I show that the institutional argument about the effects of implementing the SEA provides a more compelling explanation of trade policy developments in this sector than explanations based on changing societal or state preferences. This application can hardly be considered a full test of my explanation, but in many ways the motor vehicle sector is a critical case. It is one of the largest industries in Europe, has faced tremendous import pressures and declining levels of international competitiveness, and has been protected under similar circumstances in the 1970s and 1980s. If any industry should have been able to retain its protection, it was the motor vehicle sector.

The automobile industry has traditionally been successful in winning protection. When facing economic hardship in the 1970s and 1980s, every state with significant motor vehicle production provided vigorous protection for its industry, usually in the

---

72. Mayes 1993.
73. Wolf 1994, 48.
74. Winters 1993, 207.
75. For a more general discussion of this phenomenon in the context of European integration, see Pierson 1996.

form of national quotas and voluntary export restraints (VERs) against Japanese auto imports. Great Britain imposed a limit on Japanese imports of 10–11 percent in 1975, and two years later France restricted Japanese imports to 3 percent of market share. Italy, Spain, and Portugal had even tighter restrictions in place: Italy kept Japanese market share to 0.14 percent; Spain limited imports to one thousand cars and two hundred commercial vehicles; and Portugal allowed in only twenty thousand passenger cars. Even the relatively free-trade-oriented Germans negotiated a 10 percent cap on Japanese imports during the early 1980s.[76]

Furthermore, the automobile industry came under increased pressure from foreign competition in the late 1980s. Export sales fell a staggering 65.5 percent relative to total EU production from 1986 to 1992.[77] In 1990, a global study of automobile industry performance found that European companies, both volume producers and the specialist producers, had significantly lower levels of productivity and product quality than either Japanese or even the struggling American producers.[78] Given the uncompetitive state of European producers, there were widespread fears in Europe that trade policy liberalization would lead to potentially huge market share losses, especially to Japanese producers.[79]

The auto industry has been so successful in obtaining protection because it is one of the largest employers in several large member states and is seen as critical to future economic prosperity. Both these conditions continue to hold in the 1990s. In 1992 the industry directly employed over 1.8 million people in the EU as a whole.[80] Adding in the industry's suppliers, total employment has been estimated to be 4.5 million workers or about 15 percent of EU industrial employment.[81] One 1991 study concludes that one in every ten jobs in the EU is either directly or indirectly dependent on the automotive sector.[82] In addition the sector is often viewed as a creator of demand in the rest of the economy because of its high wage jobs and consumption of high value-added production inputs.[83] Liberalizing this sector in the midst of a recession seemed unlikely because it could be expected to exacerbate the intensity of the economic downturn and worsen unemployment. Moreover, because the industry is highly concentrated, it should also have been able to organize itself relatively easily for political action to assure continued protection.[84]

Finally, one would have expected trade liberalization of autos to be rejected outright by France and Italy because of the particularly severe impact it would have on their producers. French and Italian automakers rely extremely heavily on sales in

---

76. See Mason 1994; and Hayes 1993. During the recession of 1981, states with smaller levels of car production, including the Netherlands, Belgium, and Sweden, also obtained promises by Japan to limit imports in their markets to 10 percent. Womack and Jones 1994.
77. See Table 1.
78. Womack, Jones, and Roos 1990.
79. See Stephen 1996; and Mason 1994.
80. Direct employment levels in the four largest EU economies in 1992 were 794,100 in Germany, 343,000 in France, 257,600 in Great Britain, and 203,700 in Italy (Eurostat).
81. Vigier 1992.
82. European Commission 1991, 13–18.
83. Holmes and Smith 1995, 128.
84. Olson 1971.

some of the most protected markets in Europe. Two-thirds of Fiat's West European car sales are in Italy alone, and the two French producer groups control 60 percent of the French motor vehicle market and over 30 percent of the Spanish market.[85] Liberalization would hit these firms especially hard as more efficient foreign competitors rushed into these markets. France and Italy would have been predicted to be adamantly opposed to the liberalization of this sector because the adjustment costs would fall particularly hard on their domestic producers. In short, the motor vehicle sector is the type of industry that would have been most likely to have maintained or increased its level of protection during the recent recession. Yet in this period external trade barriers were liberalized to a surprising extent.

In July 1991 the Commission and the Japanese Ministry of International Trade announced an agreement to replace the bilateral VERs between individual member states and Japan with an EU-wide agreement. Although the agreement still provides protection to the five "restricted" markets, and it is possible that the full liberalization date may be renegotiated and delayed, the agreement is still significantly more liberal than the bilateral agreements it replaces. Compared with the national trade restrictions previously in place, the 1991 agreement with Japan liberalizes motor vehicle imports in two important ways.

First, the agreement commits the EU to the "progressive and full liberalization" of the importation of Japanese motor vehicles (cars, off-road vehicles, and light commercial vehicles) by the beginning of 2000. This commitment is far more liberal than the national VERs it replaced, which had no fixed end date and could have been continued indefinitely. Second, even in the interim period, before the full liberalization of the EU market (1993–99), import quotas for Japanese cars were substantially increased for those EU states that had national import quotas. By 1999 the estimated Japanese export levels to the five "restricted" markets are France, 150,000 (5.3 percent of market); Italy, 138,000 (5.3 percent of market); Spain, 79,000 (5.4 percent of market); Portugal, 23,000 (8.4 percent of market); and the United Kingdom, 190,000 (7 percent of market). The share of the remaining EU markets allotted to exports from Japan would be 12.5 percent.[86] This represents an almost fourfold increase in the number of Japanese cars allowed into Italy and a near doubling of the quota for France. After this agreement took effect market shares of Japanese cars shot up in previously restricted member states.[87] This liberalizing outcome is even more surprising because it does not appear that Japan offered any significant concessions to obtain increased market access to the EU or specific member states. How can one explain the content and timing of this liberalizing trade agreement? Why did the states with the most to lose, such as France and Italy, agree to these terms?

Neither the theories based on societal preferences nor those based on state preferences seem to be able to account for this trade policy liberalization. The sector attrition explanation, that the auto sector was liberalized because it had atrophied to the

---

85. Holmes and Smith 1995, 127.
86. GATT 1993, 170.
87. World Trade Organization 1995, 104–105.

point that it had become politically and economically marginal, is easily refuted. Given the sector's level of employment and its importance for national economic performance in many states, it is hard to argue that the motor vehicle sector has lost its political significance. To the contrary, trade liberalization in this sector during a recession would be predicted to be very difficult and would likely add to the already massive levels of unemployment.

The sectoral internationalization explanation would expect liberalization to result from the changing balance of firm trade preferences within the auto sector, with firms having changed from desiring protection to supporting free trade as they become more export dependent and more multinational. However, no firm within the motor vehicle sector changed its trade policy preference toward liberalization leading up to or during this period. Indeed, with external export dependence of the sector plummeting 65.5 percent between 1986 and 1992, this theory would have predicted an *increase* in protectionist sentiments within the sector. And, in fact, the large majority of auto producers became increasingly concerned about Japanese auto imports during this period.[88]

The liberalization of the auto industry is particularly confounding for this explanation, because, within the sector, interests favoring liberalization seem to have been hopelessly outnumbered in all the states with national protectionist measures in force at the time and in the EU as a whole. The only car makers supporting liberalization were Daimler-Benz, BMW, and Porsche, and the only major motor-vehicle-producing country supporting increasing liberalization was Germany, reflecting the interests of their luxury car manufacturers over the protectionist sentiments of the volume producers in the country, including German-owned Volkswagen, and U.S.-owned Ford and Opel (General Motors).[89] The other European automobile producers and four of the other vehicle producing states—France, Italy, Spain, and Portugal— actively pressed for strong controls over Japanese vehicle exports to the EU after 1992, reflecting the positions of their producers who felt very threatened by Japanese competition. Even Great Britain quietly signaled its willingness to support continued import controls on Japanese autos and concentrated on its demands for complete freedom of Japanese transplants to produce and ship their goods throughout the EU. The six EU states without significant domestic auto industries—Belgium, Denmark, Greece, Ireland, Luxembourg, and the Netherlands—remained largely silent during the formulation of this policy.[90] In sum, the trade liberalization of the auto industry cannot be explained by a change in the balance of auto firm preferences.

The societal counter-mobilization explanation would expect that liberalization would stem from antiprotection firms, sectors, or factors (that is, capital) mobilizing against protection for the automobile sector. The negotiations over the content of this

---

88. Mason 1994, 439–50.
89. Even the support of German producers for liberalizing the EU market waned with the arrival of the Lexus, which proved a potent competitor for German luxury car producers. Interview by the author at the Association of the German Automobile Industry (VDA), 4 December 1996.
90. For more detail on the positions taken by automobile producers and national governments, see Camerra-Rowe 1993; Mason 1994; and Stephen 1996.

deal were limited to the automobile producers, and I have not come across evidence of other societal interests either initiating a movement against motor vehicle protection or lobbying to influence the outcome of these negotiations. In interviews with national government officials, European auto producers, EU officials, and trade unions the notion that protection in the automobile sector was sacrificed to satisfy other groups in society was dismissed. Furthermore, one would be hard pressed to predict the content of the auto agreement with Japan based on the structure of societal demands within member states or the summing of the policy preferences of EU states.

The ideation explanation, that liberalization followed a shift in the beliefs of policymakers, also seems problematic. There is evidence that the political elites of important member states had not given up their beliefs in the benefits of external protection. For example, trade liberalization for the auto industry was opposed by the French government from the inception of the negotiations with Japan.[91] The French prime minister went so far as to actively encourage the mobilization of French producers to fight for the maintenance of strong protection against Japanese imports, and the French government continued to strongly oppose the auto agreement when it was finalized.[92] Although in the end French president Mitterrand had little choice but to consent to the agreement, he had deep concerns about its effect on the French automobile industry.[93] French political elites strongly resisted, rather than favored, liberalization of auto industry trade policy. Yet, despite the objections of national leaders, the French market was among the most significantly affected by the agreement with Japan. Rather than reflecting the preferences of state actors, the terms of the auto agreement with Japan were also clearly opposed by Italian, Spanish, and Portuguese political leaders.

I argue that understanding liberalization of the auto sector as the consequence of implementing the SEA better accounts for both the timing and the content of the auto agreement with Japan than any of these other explanations. The effectiveness of nationally imposed trade restrictions on Japanese auto imports relied on a variety of administrative measures, such as explicit border controls and car registration procedures based on discriminatory technical standards.[94] These measures allowed protectionist member states to block the importation of cars from both member and nonmember states, thus preventing the circumvention of national trade barriers by transhipment. With the completion of the internal market, however, explicit border measures were outlawed, and technical requirements were harmonized, so that auto producers only needed to meet one set of standards to sell their vehicles anywhere in the EU. This meant that national VERs and quotas with Japan could be circumvented by indirect imports through other more liberal member states.

Furthermore, Japanese auto producers responded to plans for completing the single market with a strategy of establishing transplant production capability within the EU,

91. Gandillot 1992.
92. See Stephen 1996, 243; and Gandillot 1992.
93. Gandillot 1992.
94. Mattoo and Mavroidis 1995.

especially in Great Britain, and then exporting freely throughout the EU. Producers and governments of member states with protected markets grew increasingly alarmed by the possibility of Japanese transplant production being imported into their markets without restraint.[95] The extent of the concern was demonstrated in 1988 when French authorities threatened to block imports of Nissan Bluebirds assembled and partially manufactured in Great Britain.[96] This episode underscored the difficulty faced by countries trying to maintain national trade barriers in the context of the single market. Blocking the importation of cars made in Britain, even if they were the products of Japanese transplant factories, was not sustainable within a single market. It would have been a clear violation of the free movement of goods and would have led to a case in front of the European Court of Justice. Reestablishing protection from Japanese auto imports could not be accomplished through national policy but required the negotiation of an EU-wide auto agreement with Japan.[97] Negotiations began in early 1988 and were finalized before the deadline for completing the internal market. Without the launch of the single market program, it is unlikely that an initiative would have emerged to liberalize quota levels for Japanese imports in the early 1990s.

The content of the agreement seems to reflect the relative bargaining strength of the producing state favoring the most liberal policy outcome, Germany. Germany was the only major producing country favoring easier EU market access for Japanese vehicle imports. The five other major auto-producing states—France, Italy, Spain, Portugal, and even Great Britain—favored a more protectionist policy. The German government, however, wanted to maintain some level of protection for the industry. Volkswagen was struggling against Japanese imports; and the growing success of Japanese luxury car lines, such as Acura, Infiniti, and Lexus, were posing an increasing challenge for German high-end producers. The content of the final deal matched closely the preferences of the German government.[98] Apparently, Germany was able to convince other auto-producing countries to consent to a significantly more liberal agreement than they wanted because the German position at least offered more protection to these countries than if no agreement were reached. As a result, countries with strong traditions of protection for their automobile industries agreed to a greater degree of market opening than one would have expected.

On a final note, the EU-based explanation suggests that even if this auto agreement with Japan is renegotiated and extended before full liberalization of the EU market occurs, the renegotiation will take place in a context that once again favors the producer states preferring the most liberal trade policy. Because full liberalization on 1 January 2000 has become the new status quo policy, states seeking an extension of protection will once again be vulnerable to the veto threat of more liberal states.

95. Interviews by the author at European Commission, May 1994.
96. Mason 1994, 438.
97. Many believe that the Japanese auto agreement also placed limits on Japanese production at transplant factories within the EU. For example, see Mason 1994.
98. Interviews by the author at the Association of the German Automobile Industry (Verband der Automobilindustrie) and with German auto producers, November 1996.

This case study provides support for the EU-based explanation of trade liberalization in Europe during the recession of the 1990s. Moreover, it raises questions about the ability of existing trade literature to explain external liberalization in Europe. Neither changes in societal demand for protection nor changes in policymakers' beliefs account very well for the liberalization of the automobile industry. One case study, of course, is not a rigorous test of the alternative hypotheses presented in the article. However, this case study does establish the plausibility of the explanation based on the completion of the single market for the type of liberal trade policy outcomes observed.

There are many other sectors for which new trade policy measures have been negotiated during the recession of the 1990s. The fact that over sixty-three hundred national quantitative restrictions have been discarded by member states since 1990 gives one a sense of how widespread the changes in European trade policy may be if the single market-based hypothesis I have presented is correct. Other prominent industrial sectors in which new trade measures have been negotiated in the 1990s include textiles, apparel, consumer electronics, semiconductors, computer and office equipment, machine tools, chemicals, instrument engineering, and pharmaceuticals.

Conclusion

As regional integration has advanced in the world, so have fears that this process will lead to a world divided into closed regional trading blocs in competition with each other. Among those who worry about such a possibility, the EU is usually seen as the most likely domino to fall. If the EU were to turn significantly more protectionist, the negative effect on the world economy would be serious and the danger to the liberal international trading order substantial. EU imports account for about 20 percent of the total exports of the rest of world, and its internal market is the largest in the world.[99] About 27 percent of total U.S. exports and 21 percent of all Japanese exports are sold within the EU.[100] The United States would be especially vulnerable to further protection of "strategic" industries, because almost one-half of its exports to Europe are high-technology goods.[101] One study estimates that "fortress Europe" could result in an annual loss in gross domestic product of $64 billion in North America and $214 billion worldwide.[102] A move toward increased protectionism by the EU would also have wider effects, because the EU influences the international trading system not only through its own actions, but also through the pressures that it exerts on the policies of other countries and its important role in influencing the rules governing international trade through such bodies as the WTO.

---

99. Hayes 1993.
100. Based on 1991 data. GATT 1993.
101. Conybeare 1993.
102. Stoeckel, Pearce, and Banks 1990.

There were many reasons to expect that the EU would have increased external trade barriers during the 1990s: Europe has experienced a severe economic downturn and record levels of unemployment; EU states have a history of providing protection in periods of economic hardship; and the completion of the single market brought forth predictions of an impending fortress Europe. During this period, however, as I demonstrate, there has been a remarkably strong resistance to new protectionism and a liberalization of trade policy in politically and economically sensitive sectors. I have suggested that the trade policy literature has had difficulty accounting for these developments in European trade policy. Increasing openness and resistance to new protection does not seem to be a reflection of the changing interests of producer groups or the product of fundamental shifts in the trade policy beliefs of national leaders in the ways expected by the literature. Rather, I have made an institutional argument that trade policy liberalization is largely the result of changes in the institutional context of trade policymaking brought about by developments in European integration, namely the completion of the single market.

One of the most striking features of this explanation is that as a result of European integration well-established national policymaking processes have been deeply disrupted. Increased European integration has meant that trade policy outcomes have become divorced from their relationship to underlying preferences of state and societal actors for some large and important member states. The demands of politically important societal interests—namely, domestic producers and organized labor in uncompetitive industries, and the unemployed—have been quashed, and politicians have been blocked from political programs they would otherwise have pursued. A number of questions about the domestic politics within member states are raised by this finding. Can liberalization achieved in this manner be sustained? How long can politicians blame the EU for forcing external trade liberalization? Why have groups that were once so effective in demanding and obtaining protection not found an avenue for restoring the policies they prefer? To what extent have the strategies of domestic groups changed in the face of EU constraints on trade policy? Have state actors tried to reshape the types of demands groups make, the composition of trade policy coalitions, or the manner in which societal interests are aggregated?

The analysis in this article represents an important step in building our understanding of the politics of trade liberalization. It raises serious questions about the explanations offered by current trade policy literature and identifies a set of important mechanisms through which European integration has imposed a powerful constraint on national trade policies. In the end, this explanation must be only partial. The next step requires additional research and further case studies to fill out our understanding of the politics of trade policy liberalization in Europe by developing a better understanding of the nature and extent of societal and state support for sustaining increased liberalization. In the process, we are likely to acquire a better understanding of the forces driving the increased openness of the international economy, not only in Europe, but in other parts of the world as well.

References

Adams, William James. 1995. France and Global Competition. In *Remaking the Hexagon: The New France in the New Europe*, edited by Gregory Flynn, 87–115. Boulder, Colo.: Westview Press.

Aggarwal, Vinod K. 1985. *Liberal Protectionism: The International Politics of Organized Textile Trade*. Berkeley: University of California Press.

Alter, Karen J., and Sophie Meunier-Aitsahalia. 1994. Judicial Politics in the European Community: European Integration and the Pathbreaking *Cassis de Dijon* Decision. *Comparative Political Studies* 24 (4):535–61.

Berger, Suzanne. 1995. Trade and Identity: The Coming Protectionism? In *Remaking the Hexagon: The New France in the New Europe*, edited by Gregory Flynn, 195–210. Boulder, Colo.: Westview Press.

Bergsten, C. Fred, and William R. Cline. 1983. Trade Policy in the 1980s: An Overview. In *Trade Policy in the 1980s*, edited by William R. Cline, 59–98. Washington, D.C.: Institute for International Economics.

Bhagwati, Jagdish. 1991. *The World Trading System at Risk*. New York: Harvester Wheatsheaf.

Cameron, David R. 1992. The 1992 Initiative: Causes and Consequences. In *Euro-politics: Institutions and Policy Making in the "New" European Community*, edited by Alberta Sbragia, 23–74. Washington, D.C.: Brookings Institution.

Camerra-Rowe, Pamela. 1993. *The Political Response of Firms to the 1992 Single Market Program: The Case of the German Automobile Industry*. Program for the Study of Germany and Europe Working Paper. Cambridge, Mass.: Harvard University Center for European Studies.

Cassing, James, Timothy J. McKeown, and Jack Ochs. 1986. The Political Economy of the Tariff Cycle. *American Political Science Review* 80 (3):843–62.

Cline, William R. 1987. *The Future of World Trade in Textiles and Apparel*. Washington, D.C.: Institute for International Economics.

Conybeare, John A. C. 1993. 1992, the Community, and the World: Free Trade or Fortress Europe? In *The 1992 Project and the Future of Integration in Europe*, edited by Dale L. Smith and James Lee Ray, 143–63. Armonk, N.Y.: M. E. Sharpe.

Cowles, Maria Green. 1994. The Politics of Big Business in the European Community: Setting the Agenda for a New Europe. Ph.D. diss., The American University.

Destler, I. M., and John S. Odell. 1987. *Anti-Protection: Changing Forces in U.S. Trade Politics*. Washington, D.C.: Institute for International Economics.

Dylla, Bronwyn. 1997. Assisting National Industries in the European Union: How Partisanship Influences State Aid Expenditure. Paper presented at the 93rd Annual Meeting of the American Political Science Association, 28–31 August, Washington, D.C.

European Commission. 1985. Completing the Internal Market. White Paper from the Commission to the European Council. Luxembourg: Office for Official Publications of the European Communities.

———. 1991. *Panorama of EC Industry 1991–1992*. Luxembourg: Office for Official Publications of the European Communities.

———. 1992. Abolition of Border Controls. Commission Communication to the Council and to Parliament. Luxembourg: Office for Official Publications of the European Communities.

———. 1994. *Panorama of EU industry '94*. Luxembourg: Office for Official Publications of the European Communities.

———. 1995a. Employment in Europe. Luxembourg: Office for Official Publications of the European Communities.

———. 1995b. Thirteenth Annual Report from the Commission to the European Parliament on the Community's Anti-Dumping and Anti-Subsidy Activities (1994). Luxembourg: Office for Official Publications of the European Communities.

European Round Table of Industrialists. 1984. Missing Links: Upgrading Europe's Transborder Ground Transportation Infrastructure. Brussels: European Round Table of Industrialists.

Flamm, Kenneth. 1990. Semiconductors. In *Europe 1992*, edited by Gary Clyde Hufbauer, 225–92. Washington, D.C.: Brookings Institution.

Frey, Bruno S., Werner W. Pommerehne, Friedrich Schneider, and Guy Gilbert. 1984. Consensus and Dissension Among Economists: An Empirical Inquiry. *American Economic Review* 74:986–94.

Frieden, Jeffry, and Ronald Rogowski. 1996. The Impact of the International Economy on National Policies: An Analytical Overview. In *Internationalization and Domestic Politics*, edited by Robert Keohane and Helen Milner, 25–47. New York: Cambridge University Press.

Gandillot, Thierry. 1992. *La dernière bataille de l'automobile européene*. Paris: Fayard.

GATT. 1991. *Trade Policy Review: The European Communities 1991*. Vol. 1. Geneva: General Agreements on Tariffs and Trade.

———. 1993. *Trade Policy Review: European Communities*. Vol. 1. Geneva: General Agreement on Tariffs and Trade.

Gilpin, Robert. 1987. *The Political Economy of International Relations*. Princeton, N.J.: Princeton University Press.

Goldstein, Judith. 1993. *Ideas, Interests, and American Trade Policy*. Ithaca, N.Y.: Cornell University Press.

Grilli, Enzo. 1988. Macro-Economic Determinants of Trade Protection. *The World Economy* 11:313–326.

———. 1991. Contemporary Protectionism in an Unstable World Economy. In *Protectionism and International Banking*, edited by Gerhard Fels and George Sutija, 144–72. London: Macmillian.

Hager, Wolfgang. 1982. Protectionism and Autonomy: How to Preserve Free Trade in Europe. *International Affairs* 58:413–28.

Hayes, J. P. 1993. *Making Trade Policy in the European Community*. New York: St. Martin's Press.

Hine, R. C. 1985. *The Political Economy of European Trade: An Introduction to the Trade Policies of the EEC*. New York: St. Martin's Press.

Holmes, Peter, and Alasdair Smith. 1995. Automobile Industry. In *European Policies on Competition, Trade, and Industry: Conflict and Complementarities*, edited by Pierre Buigues, Alexis Jacquemin, and André Sapir, 125–59. Brookfield, Vt.: Edward Elgar Publishing Company.

Jackson, John H. 1995. The European Community and World Trade: The Commercial Policy Dimension. In *Singular Europe: Economy and the Polity of the European Community After 1992*, edited by Will James Adams, 321–45. Ann Arbor: University of Michigan Press.

Kahler, Miles. 1985. European Protectionism in Theory and Practice. *World Politics* 37:475–502.

Keohane, Robert. 1984. The World Economy and the Crisis of Embedded Liberalism. In *Order and Conflict in Contemporary Capitalism: Studies in the Political Economy of Western European Nations*, edited by John Goldthorpe, 15–38. Oxford: Clarendon Press.

Kiewiet, D. Roderick. 1983. *Macroeconomics and Micropolitics: The Electoral Effects of Economic Issues*. New Haven, Conn.: Yale University Press.

Kinder, Donald R., and D. Roderick Kiewiet. 1979. Economic Discontent and Political Behavior: The Role of Personal Grievances and Collective Economic Judgments in Congressional Voting. *American Journal of Political Science* 23:493–527.

Koopmann, Georg. 1989. Handelspolitik der EG im Zeichen des Binnenmarktes. *Wirtschaftsdienst* 69 (8):405–12.

Koopmann, Georg, and Hans-Eckart Scharrer. 1989. EC Trade Policy Beyond 1992. *Intereconomics* (September–October):207–15.

Kramer, Gerald H. 1971. Short-Term Fluctuations in U.S. Voting Behavior, 1896–1964. *American Political Science Review* 65:131–43.

Lewis-Beck, Michael S. 1988. *Economics and Elections: The Major Western Democracies*. Ann Arbor: University of Michigan Press.

Magee, Stephen P., and Leslie Young. 1987. Endogenous Protection in the United States, 1900–1984. In *U.S. Trade Policies in a Changing World Economy*, edited by Robert M. Stern, 145–89. Cambridge, Mass.: MIT Press.

Mansfield, Edward D., and Marc L. Busch. 1995. The Political Economy of Nontariff Barriers: A Cross-National Analysis. *International Organization* 49:723–49.

Mason, Mark. 1994. Elements of Consensus: Europe's Response to the Japanese Automotive Challenge. *Journal of Common Market Studies* 32:433–53.

Mattoo, Aaditya, and Petros C. Mavroidis. 1995. The EC-Japan Consensus on Cars: Interaction Between Trade and Competition Policy. *The World Economy* 18:345–65.

Mayes, David. 1993. The Vision of Europe. In *Public Interest and Market Pressures*, edited by David Mayes, 1–23. New York: St. Martin's Press.

McKeown, Timothy. 1984. Firms and Tariff Regime Change. *World Politics* 36:215–33.

Meunier, Sophie. Forthcoming. Divided but United: European Trade Integration and EC–US Agricultural Negotiations in the Uruguay Round. In *The European Union in the World Community*, edited by Carolyn Rhodes. Boulder, Colo.: Lynne Reinner.

Midford, Paul. 1993. International Trade and Domestic Politics: Improving on Rogowski's Model of Political Alignments. *International Organization* 47:535–64.

Milner, Helen. 1988. *Resisting Protection: Global Industries and the Politics of International Trade*. Princeton, N.J.: Princeton University Press.

Milner, Helen, and Robert Keohane. 1996. Internationalization and Domestic Politics: An Introduction. In *Internationalization and Domestic Politics*, edited by Robert Keohane and Helen Milner, 3–24. New York: Cambridge University Press.

Milward, Alan. 1992. *The European Rescue of the Nation-State*. Berkeley: University of California Press.

Moravcsik, Andrew. 1991. Negotiating the Single European Act: National Interests and Conventional Statecraft in the European Community. *International Organization* 45:19–56.

Olson, Mancur. 1971. *The Logic of Collective Action: Public Goods and the Theory of Groups*. Cambridge, Mass.: Harvard University Press.

Patterson, Gardner. 1983. The European Community as a Threat to the System. In *Trade Policy in the 1980s*, edited by William R. Cline, 223–42. Washington, D.C.: Institute for International Economics.

Pearce, Joan, and John Sutton, with Roy Batchelor. 1985. *Protection and Industrial Policy in Europe*. Boston: Routledge & Kegan Paul.

Pierson, Paul. 1996. The Path to European Integration: A Historical Institutionalist Analysis. *Comparative Political Studies* 29:123–63.

Redmond, John, ed. 1992. *The External Relations of the European Community: The International Response to 1992*. New York: St. Martin's Press.

Rogowski, Ronald. 1989. *Commerce and Coalitions: How Trade Affects Domestic Political Alignments*. Princeton, N.J.: Princeton University Press.

Ruggiero, Renato. 1996. Implications for Trade in a Borderless World. Speech given to the World Trade Congress, 24 April, Singapore.

Sandholtz, Wayne, and John Zysman. 1989. 1992: Recasting the European Bargain. *World Politics* 42:95–128.

Sapir, André. 1990. Does 1992 Come Before or After 1990? On Regional Versus Multilateral Integration. In *The Political Economy of International Trade*, edited by Ronald W. Jones and Anne O. Krueger, 197–222. Cambridge, Mass.: Basil Blackwell.

Stephen, Roland. 1996. Integrating Europe: Interests, Institutions, and the Liberalization of the European Automobile Industry. Ph.D. diss., UCLA.

Stoeckel, Andrew, David Pearce, and Gary Banks. 1990. *Western Trade Blocs: Game, Set, or Match for Asia-Pacific and the World Economy*. Canberra, Australia: Centre for International Economics.

Takacs, Wendy E. 1981. Pressures for Protectionism: An Empirical Analysis. *Economic Inquiry* 19:687–93.

Thurow, Lester. 1992. *Head to Head: The Coming Battle Among Japan, Europe, and America*. New York: William Morrow.

Tsoukalis, Loukas. 1993. *The New European Economy: The Politics and Economics of Integration*. New York: Oxford University Press.

Vigier, Pierre. 1992. La politique communautaire de l'automobile. Parts 1 and 2. *Revue du Marché Unique Européen* 2:73–112, and 3:73–126.

Viner, Jacob. 1950. *The Customs Union Issue*. New York: Carnegie Endowment for International Peace.

Winters, L. Alan. 1993. The European Community: A Case of Successful Integration? In *New Dimensions in Regional Integration*, edited by Jaime de Melo and Arvind Panagariya, 202–28. New York: Cambridge University Press.

Wolf, Martin. 1994. *The Resistible Appeal of Fortress Europe*. Washington, D.C.: American Enterprise Institute for Public Policy Research.

———. 1995. Cooperation or Conflict? The European Union in a Liberal Global Economy. *International Affairs* 71:327–37.

Womack, James P., and Daniel T. Jones. 1994. European Automotive Policy: Past, Present, and Future. In *Europe and the United States: Competition and Cooperation in the 1990s*, edited by Glennon Harrison, 193–213. Armonk, N.Y.: M. E. Sharpe.

Womack, James P., Daniel T. Jones, and Daniel Roos. 1990. *The Machine That Changed the World*. New York: Rawson Associates/Macmillan.

World Trade Organization. 1995. *Trade Policy Review: European Union 1995*. Vol. 1. Geneva: World Trade Organization.